John Willis
Theatre World
1983-1984 SEASON

VOLUME 40

CROWN PUBLISHERS, INC.

ONE PARK AVENUE • NEW YORK, NEW YORK 10016

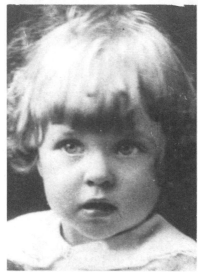

TO
DOROTHY LOUDON

whose presence on stage makes theatre-going a pleasure, and whose many honors attest to her delightfully unique talents.

CONTENTS

EDITOR: JOHN WILLIS

Assistants: Terence Burk, Stanley Reeves, John Sala, Tiko Vargas
Staff Photographers: Bert Andrews, J. M. Viade, Van Williams
Designer: Peggy Goddard

Page opposite: (clockwise from top left) Dorothy Loudon as a child; Louise Quick, Dorothy Loudon, David Cassidy in "Fig Leaves Are Falling"; "The Women"; with George Hearn in "Sweeney Todd"; "Noises Off"; with orphans in "Annie" (Tony-winning role); with Katharine Hepburn in "West Side Waltz"; with Vincent Gardenia in "Ballroom"
Friedman-Abeles, Martha Swope, Van Williams Photos

GLENN CLOSE and JEREMY IRONS in "THE REAL THING"
Martha Swope Photo

1984 "Tony" Awards for Best Play, Outstanding Actress and Actor
(see page 26)

THE SEASON IN REVIEW
(June 1, 1983–May 31, 1984)

It is disheartening to report that the number of new plays produced this season is the smallest in recorded Broadway history. Of the 36 productions during the year, there were 20 plays: 5 were new American plays, 6 were English imports, and 4 were Off-Broadway transplants. Of the 15 musicals, 4 were revivals, and only 5 of the new ones ran for more than 100 performances. The season was only occasionally exciting and rewarding. However, the total boxoffice intake showed an increase over the 1982–83 season, making it the highest grossing season in Broadway history, in spite of the fact that attendance decreased over five percent. The increase in ticket prices was responsible for this record. The average price for tickets rose from $24 to $28, and the highest priced ducats were $47.50. The astronomical rise in production costs (especially for tv advertising) were partially responsible for the increased price of admissions. The top money earners were all musicals, 5 from previous seasons and the new "La Cage aux Folles." Seemingly the audience for drama has diminished. The only successful American play was David Mamet's Pulitzer-Prize-winning "Glengarry Glen Ross" that was transferred from Chicago's Goodman Theatre. One of the best farces in many years was "Noises Off," imported from London, and the entire cast headed by star Dorothy Loudon, gave one of the best ensemble performances of this year or any year in memory. One of the most memorable nights in the theatre took place on Thursday, Sept. 29, 1983 when "A Chorus Line" played its 3389th performance to become the longest running production in Broadway's history.

As too often happens, the predicted "Tony" nominees did not appear on the ballot, provoking the usual controversy. After the tabulation of ballots, the winners were announced on Sunday, June 3, 1984 in the Gershwin Theatre when the American Theatre Wing presented its 38th annual Antoinette Perry Awards ceremony. "The Real Thing," a British comedy-drama by Tom Stoppard, received 5 Tonys, including Best Play, Outstanding Actor and Actress (Jeremy Irons and Glenn Close respectively), and Outstanding Featured Actress (Christine Baranski). Joe Mantegna of "Glengarry Glen Ross" received the Tony for Outstanding Featured Actor in a Play. The musical "La Cage aux Folles" was honored with 6 Tonys, including Best Musical and Outstanding Actor in a Musical (George Hearn). Outstanding Actress in a Musical was Chita Rivera in "The Rink." Outstanding Featured Actress and Actor in a Musical were Lila Kedrova of "Zorba" and Hinton Battle of "The Tap Dance Kid." The Tony for Outstanding Reproduction was awarded "Death of a Salesman" by Arthur Miller, starring Dustin Hoffman. The tv presentations were again produced by Alexander H. Cohen, and were a salute to musical theatre writers John Kander and Fred Ebb, Stephen Sondheim, and Jerry Herman. Enlargements of Al Hirschfeld's line drawings of theatrical personalities were used as a curtain and as set pieces. Mr. Hirschfeld was presented the first Brooks Atkinson Award for a lifetime achievement related to the theatre. A well-deserved Special Tony was presented to Michael Bennett for his memorable staging of the record-breaking "A Chorus Line" performance, a glittering gala with 332 performers on stage for the finale, a sentimental once-in-a-lifetime experience for those privileged to be in attendance. The New York Drama Critics Circle cited "The Real Thing" as Best Play, "Glengarry Glen Ross" as Best American Play, and "Sunday in the Park with George" by Stephen Sondheim and James Lapine as Best Musical.

In addition to the above mentioned, outstanding Broadway performers were Martine Allard, Gene Barry, Kate Burton, Laura Dean, Sandy Duncan, Peter Gallagher, Victor Garber, Stephen Geoffreys, Todd Graff, Rosemary Harris, Rex Harrison, John Heard, Jo Henderson, Rhetta Hughes, Dana Ivey, J. J. Johnston, Ben Kingsley, Bonnie Koloc, Angela Lansbury, Peggy Lee, Calvin Levels, Shirley MacLaine, John Malkovich, Ian McKellen, Liza Minnelli, Donald Moffat, Ron Moody, Kate Nelligan, Cynthia Nixon, Carroll O'Connor, Al Pacino, Mandy Patinkin, Bernadette Peters, Anthony Quinn, Alyson Reed, Alfonso Ribeiro, Marilyn Rockafellow, John Shea, Rex Smith, Linda Thorson, Peter Ustinov, Christopher Walken, the chorus of "The Rink" and the cast of "Glengarry Glen Ross."

As has been customary for the past few years, Off Broadway presented the most adventurous productions, full of quality performances and performers. Among the musicals were "A. . . . My Name Is Alice," "Blue Plate Special," "Brownstone," "The Cradle Will Rock," "Do Lord Remember Me," "Elizabeth and Essex," "Gospel at Colonus," "Love," "Mighty Fine Music," "Nite Club Confidential," "Pacific Overtures," "Taking My Turn," "Tallulah" and "Up from Paradise." Best of the plays includes "Ah, Wilderness!," "And a Nightingale Sang," "Baby with the Bathwater," "Balm in Gilead," "Cinders," "Children," "Fen," "Found a Peanut," "Full Hookup," "The Golden Age," "Isn't It Romantic," "Jeeves Takes Charge," "The Killing of Sister George," "Last of the Knucklemen," "Levitations," "Laughing Stock," "The Miss Firecracker Contest," "Nest of the Wood Grouse," "Old Times," "On Approval," "Other Places," "Orgasmo Adulto," "The Philanthropist," "Painting Churches," "A Private View," "Rockaby," "Secret Honor," "Serenading Louie," "Sound and Beauty," "Split Second," "Spookhouse," "To Gillian on Her 37th Birthday," "Weekend Near Madison" and the South African import "Woza Albert."

Off-Broadway performances worthy of note were Ernest Abuba, Loni Ackerman, Jane Alexander, Joan Allen, Kaye Ballard, Lisa Banes, Kathy Bates, Eric Bogosian, Philip Bosco, Scott Burkholder, Ellen Burstyn, Joanne Camp, Mark Capri, Timothy Carhart, Len Cariou, Stockard Channing, Tandy Cronyn, Lindsay Crouse, Gretchen Cryer, Edward Duke, Cara Duff-MacCormick, Giancarlo Esposito, Pauline Flanagan, Robert Foxworth, Helen Gallagher, Daniel Gerroll, Dody Goodman, Joanna Gleason, Tammy Grimes, Philip Baker Hall, Glenne Headley, Anthony Heald, Anthony Hopkins, Katharine Houghton, Robin Howard, Holly Hunter, Judith Ivey, Robert Joy, Judy Kaye, Stephen Keep, Laurie Kennedy, Christine Lahti, Delphi Lawrence, John Lone, Peter MacNicol, Dinah Manoff, Marsha Mason, E. G. Marshall, David McCallum, Elizabeth McGovern, Anne Meara, Laurie Metcalf, Joe Morton, Craig T. Nelson, Michael O'Keefe, Estelle Parsons, Anne Pitoniak, Alice Playten, Lonny Price, Dennis Quaid, Ann Reinking, Marian Seldes, Carole-Ann Scott, Victor Slezak, Frances Sternhagen, Sada Thompson, Anne Twomey, Eli Wallach, Douglass Watson, James Ray Weeks, Peter Weller, Billie Whitelaw, Dianne Wiest, Charlaine Woodard, Irene Worth, and the cast of "Taking My Turn."

Random Notes: New contracts (between AEA and the League of NY Theatres) for actors on Broadway and in touring companies raised minimum and living expenses. . . . Sunday, Jan. 15, 1984 at the Palace Theatre, the Songwriters Guild held a celebration of American Songwriters with 30 to 40 singing or playing their own songs. . . . The prize-winning " 'night, Mother" moved off Broadway unsuccessfully . . . The Public Theater hosted the annual Young Playwrights (18 and younger) Festival with 5 plays. . . . The second annual "Waitin' in the Wings" (the night the understudies take center stage) opened the new Manhattan Performing Center on Sunday, Jan. 13, 1984. . . . The Vivian Beaumont Theatre, after a five year hiatus, re-opened successfully, proving that it is functional. . . . Resurgent talk of a national theatre: Actors Equity announced an outline for such a nationwide project, as did Roger L. Stevens for Kennedy Center, and Joseph Papp for Broadway. . . . Second Stage finally moved into a permanent home and named its theatre for two deceased actors, Walter McGinn and John Cazale. . . . The Alvin Theatre became the Neil Simon Theatre on June 29, 1983, the Little Theatre became the Helen Hayes on July 22, 1983, the Lion became the Judith Anderson Theatre on June 11, 1984. . . . The estate of Tennessee Williams blocked the re-naming of the Playhouse for him. . . . The National Endowment for the Arts announced that "the theatre's artistic vitality is showing signs of erosion due to economic and institutional pressures, forcing 20 regional theatres to close". . . . On Wednesday, Feb. 15, 1984 the lights on Broadway were dimmed for a minute to honor the incomparable musical star Ethel Merman who had died.

5

BROADWAY PRODUCTIONS

(June 1, 1983 through May 31, 1984)

5–6–7–8. . . . DANCE!

(RADIO CITY MUSIC HALL) Written by Bruce Vilanch; Original Songs, David Zippel & Wally Harper; Directed and Choreographed by Ron Field; Associate Director, David Rubinstein; Associate Choreographer, Marianne Selbert; Musical Director, Thomas Helm; Scenery, Tom H. John; Costumes, Lindsay W. Davis; Lighting, Richard Nelson; Film Sequences, Christopher Dixon; Musical Supervisor, Wally Harper; Orchestrations, Bill Byers; Dance Arrangements, Mark Hummel & Donald York; Production Coordinator, Stephen Nisbet; Stage Managers, Raymond Chandler, Howard Kolins, Jon Morton, Nelson Wilson; Director Rockettes, Violet Holmes; Props, Joseph Bivone, Thomas Coughlin; Wardrobe, Barbara Van Zandt, Donna Peterson; Hairstyling, James Amaral, James Perez; Presented by Radio City Music Hall Productions (Bernard Gersten, Executive Producer); General Managers, James A. McManus, Patricia M. Morinelli; Press, Gloria M. Ciaccio, Neil S. Friedman. Opened Wednesday, June 15, 1983 and closed September 5, 1983 after 149 performances.

CAST

Sandy Duncan, Don Correia, Bill Irwin, Armelia McQueen, Ken Sacha, Marge Champion, The Rockettes
SINGERS: Freida A. Williams, Holly Lipton Nash, Lois Sage, Roger Berdahl, Michael Halpern, Wayne Mattson, Wes Skelley, Paul Solen
DANCERS: Robin Alpert, Christine Colby, Carol Estey, Edyie Fleming, Blanche, Sonya Hensley, Jodi Moccia, Gayle Samuels, Gregory Brock, Ciscoe Bruton II, Daniel Esteras, Douglas Graham, Michael Lafferty, Dan McCoy, Rodney Pridgen, Adrian Rosario
MUSICAL NUMBERS: 5–6–7–8 . . . Dance!, Life Is a Dance, Dance, It's Better with a Band, I've Got Your Number, You Mustn't Kick It Around, It Only Happens When I Dance with You, Singers Protest, One Step, It Had to Be You, Bad Habits, It's Not What You Weigh, Sing Sing Sing, Make Way for Tomorrow, Cheek to Cheek, I Go to Rio!, I'm Flying, She Just Loves Las Vegas, Dance with Me, Neverland, Tea for Two, I Love to Dance, Tres Moutarde, La Cumparcita, The Continental, Our Love Is Here to Stay, Where Did You Learn to Dance, Broadway Rhythm, Body Language.

George A. LeMoine Photo

Sandy Duncan (center), Don Correia (right)
Top Right: Armelia McQueen

THE GUYS IN THE TRUCK

(NEW APOLLO THEATRE) By Howard Reifsnyder; Director, David Black; Scenery and Costumes, John Falabella; Lighting, John Gleason; Sound, T. Richard Fitzgerald; Presented by James Conley; Associate Producer, Paul Levine; General Management, Theatre Now, Inc.; Stage Managers, Frank Marino, John Actman; Production Supervisor, Jeremiah Harris; Props, Laura Koch; Wardrobe, Kathleen Gallagher; Casting, Laura Gleason; Press, Jacqueline Burnham, Edward Callaghan, Jay Schwartz, Lynda Kinney, Jeanne Browne, Efren Vaca. Opened Sunday, June 19, 1983.*

CAST

Al Klein	Harris Laskawy†
Louie DeFalco	Lawrence Guardino
Charlie Johnson	Geoffrey C. Ewing
Doug Frischetti	Mike Starr
Harvey Olmstead	James Gleason
Les Hammond	Robert Trumbull
Nick Caruso	Lloyd Battista
Billie Fenstermacher	Bobbi Jo Lathan
Hugo Broonzy	Gary Klar

A comedy in 2 acts and 5 scenes. The action takes place at the present time in a television remote control truck parked under Cleveland Municipal Stadium.

*Closed June 19, 1983 after one performance and 22 previews.
†Played in previews by Elliott Gould

Carol Rosegg Photos

James Gleason, Harris Laskawy
Top Right: Harris Laskawy

Angela Lansbury, Anne Francine

MAME

(GERSHWIN THEATRE) Book by Jerome Lawrence & Robert E. Lee; Based on book "Auntie Mame" by Patrick Dennis, and the play by Lawrence and Lee; Music and Lyrics, Jerry Herman; Director, John Bowab; Production Supervisor, Jerry Herman; Scenery, Peter Wolf; Based on original design by William and Jean Eckart; Lighting, Thomas Skelton; Sound, Christine Voellinger; Hairstylist, Hiram Ortiz; Costumes, Robert Mackintosh; Furs by Maximilian; Musical Director, Jim Coleman; Choreography re-created by Diana Baffa-Brill; Based on original by Onna White; Casting, Mark Reiner; Orchestrations, Philip J. Lang; Vocal Arrangements, Donald Pippin; Executive Producer, Michael Lynne; Associate Producer, Manny Kladitis; Presented by the Mitch Leigh Company; General Management, Niko Entertainment, Ltd.; Production Manager, Frank Hartenstein; Associate Conductor, Phil Hall; Wardrobe, Barrett Hong, Barbara Hladsky; Props, Sam Bagarella, John Godsey; Assistant Company Manager, Burton Greenhouse; Stage Managers, Paul Phillips, Peter J. Taylor; Press, John A. Prescott. Opened Sunday, July 24, 1983.*

CAST

Patrick Dennis (age 10)	Roshi Handwerger
Agnes Gooch	Jane Connell
Vera Charles	Anne Francine
Mame Dennis	Angela Lansbury
Ralph Devine	Jacob Mark Hopkin
Bishop	Merwin Foard
M. Lindsay Woolsey	Donald Torres
Ito	Sab Shimono
Doorman	Brian McAnally
Elevator Boy	Marshall Hagins
Messenger	David Miles
Dwight Babcock	Willard Waterman
Bubbles the Clown/Gregor	Ken Henley
Dance Teacher/Mrs. Upson	Louise Kirtland
Bird Dancers	Suzanne Ishee, Patrick Sean Murphy
Leading Man/Uncle Jeff	Kenneth Kantor
Stage Manager	Richard Poole
Mme. Branislowski/Mother Burnside	Fran Stevens
Beauregard Jackson Pickett Burnside	Scot Stewart
Cousin Fan	Carol Lurie
Sally Cato	Barbara Lang
Patrick Dennis (age 19–29)	Byron Nease
Junior Babcock	Patrick Sean Murphy
Mr. Upson	John C. Becher
Gloria Upson	Michaela Hughes
Pegeen Ryan	Ellyn Arons
Peter Dennis	Daniel Mahon

MAME'S FRIENDS: Ellyn Arons, Alyson Bristol, Merwin Foard, Marshall Hagins, Ken Henley, Jacob Mark Hopkin, Michaela Hughes, Suzanne Ishee, Kenneth Kantor, Harry Kingsley, Melinda Koblick, David Loring, Carol Lurie, Brian McNally, David Miles, Patrick Sean Murphy, Viewma Negromonte, Michele Pigliavento, Cissy Rebich, Richard Poole, Joseph Rich, Mollie Smith.

UNDERSTUDIES: Daniel Mahon (Patrick), Cissy Rebich (Agnes), Barbara Lang (Vera), Kenneth Kantor (Woolsey/Ito/Babcock/Upson), Louise Kirtland (Mme. Branislowski/Mother Burnside), Donald Torres (Beauregard), Carol Lurie (Sally), Merwin Foard (Patrick 19–29), Fran Stevens (Mrs. Upson), Roshi Handwerger (Peter), Ken Henley (Ito)

MUSICAL NUMBERS: St. Bridget, It's Today, Open a New Window, The Man in the Moon, My Best Girl, We Need a Little Christmas, The Fox Hunt, Mame, Bosom Buddies, Gooch's Song, That's How Young I Feel, If He Walked into My Life

A musical in 2 acts and 16 scenes. The action takes place in Mame's Beekman Place apartment and various locales in which she becomes involved from 1928 to 1946.

*Closed Aug. 28, 1983 after 41 performances and 7 previews. Original production opened at the Winter Garden on May 24, 1966 and ran for 1508 performances. In the cast were Angela Lansbury, Beatrice Arthur, Charles Braswell, Jerry Lanning.

Kenn Duncan Photos

Top Left: Angela Lansbury, Roshi Handwerger
Below: Byron Nease, Angela Lansbury, Jane Connell

THE CORN IS GREEN

(LUNT-FONTANNE THEATRE) By Emlyn Williams; Director, Vivian Matalon; Scenery, William Ritman; Costumes, Theoni V. Aldredge; Lighting, Richard Nelson; Sound, Jack Mann; Casting, Hughes/Moss; Hairstylist, Paul Huntly; General Management, Alexander Morr; Presented by The Elizabeth Group (Zev Bufman/Elizabeth Taylor); Company Manager, G. Warren McClane; Stage Managers, Charles Blackwell, Henry Velez, Connie Roderick; Props, George Green, Robert Bostwick; Wardrobe, Patricia Britton; Musical Supervision, Don Jones; Wigs, Andre Douglas; Press, Fred Nathan, Charles Cinnamon, Eileen McMahon, Anne Abrams, Bert Fink. Opened Monday, August 22, 1983.*

CAST

John Goronwy Jones	Frank Hamilton
Miss Ronberry	Elizabeth Seal
Idwal Morris	Neal Joes
Sarah Pugh	Myvanwy Jenn
A Groom	Michael Rothhaar
The Squire	Gil Rogers
Mrs. Watty	Marge Redmond
Bessie Watty	Mia Dillon
Miss Moffat	Cicely Tyson†
Robbart Robbatch	Ciaran O'Reilly
Morgan Evans	Peter Gallagher
Glyn Thomas	Michael Nostrand
John Owen	Robert McNeil
Will Hughes	Loris Sallahian
Old Tom	John Eames
A Mother	Kristin Linklater
Knox	Donald Buka
Dix	Michael Rothhaar
Myfanwy	Connie Roderick
Ash Grove Quartet	Myvanwy Jenn, Neal Jones, Kristin Linklater, Robert McNeill

WELSH CHORUS: Donald Buka, John Eames, Myvanwy Jenn, Neal Jones, Kristin Linklater, Robert McNeill, Michael Nostrand, Ciaran O'Reilly, Connie Roderick, Michael Rothhaar, Loris Sallahiar
UNDERSTUDIES: Connie Roderick (Bessie/Owen/Glyn), Myvanwy Jenn (Miss Ronberry/Mrs. Watty), John Eames (John Goronwy Jones), Kristin Linklater (Sarah), Donald Buka (Old Tom/Squire), Michael Rothhaar (Robert/Idwal/Will), Kristin Linklater (standby for Miss Moffat), Neal Jones (standby for Morgan)

A play in 3 acts and 5 scenes. The action takes place in the living room of a house in Glansarno, a small village in a remote Welsh countryside during the latter part of the last century and covers a period of three years.

*Closed Sept. 18, 1983 after 32 performances and 21 previews.
†Succeeded by Kristin Linklater for last four performances.

Martha Swope Photos

Top Right: Peter Gallagher, Cicely Tyson

Peter Gallagher, Mia Dillon

Cicely Tyson (c) and company

LA CAGE AUX FOLLES

(PALACE THEATRE) Music and Lyrics, Jerry Herman; Book, Harvey Fierstein; Based on play of same title by Jean Poiret; Director, Arthur Laurents; Choreography, Scott Salmon; Settings, David Mitchell; Costumes, Theoni V. Aldredge; Lighting, Jules Fisher; Sound, Peter J. Fitzgerald; Hairstylist, Ted Azar; Musical Direction-Vocal Arrangements, Donald Pippin; Orchestrations, Jim Tyler; Dance Music Arrangements, G. Harrell; Assistant Choreographer, Richard Balestrino; Casting, Pulvino & Howard; Produced in association with Jonathan Farkas, John Pomerantz, Martin Heinfling; Presented by Allan Carr, Kenneth D. Greenblatt, Marvin A. Krauss, Stewart F. Lane, James M. Nederlander, Martin Richards; Executive Producers, Barry Brown, Fritz Holt; Original cast album on RCA Records and Tapes; General Management, Marvin A. Krauss, Gary Gunas, Steven C. Callahan; Stage Managers, James Pentecost, David Caine, Robert Schear; Props, Charles Zuckerman, Jack Cennamo, Alan Steiner; Assistant Conductor, Rudolph Bennett; Wardrobe, Gayle Patton, Irene Bunis; Associate Lighting Designer, Dawn Chiang; Press, Shirley Herz, Sam Rudy, Peter Cromarty. Opened Sunday, August 21, 1983.*

CAST

Georges	Gene Barry [1]
Les Cagelles:	
Chantal	David Cahn
Monique	Dennis Callahan
Dermah	Frank DiPasquale
Nicole	John Dolf
Hanna	David Engel
Mercedes	David Evans
Bitelle	Linda Haberman
Lo Singh	Eric Lamp
Odette	Dan O'Grady
Angelique	Deborah Phelan
Phaedra	David Scala
Clo-Clo	Sam Singhaus
Francis	Brian Kelly
Jacob	William Thomas, Jr.
Albin	George Hearn [2]
Jean-Michel	John Weiner
Anne	Leslie Stevens
Jacqueline	Elizabeth Parrish
Renaud	Walter Charles [3]
St. Tropez Townspeople	
Mme. Renaud	Sydney Anderson
Paulette	Betsy Craig
Hercule	Jack Neubeck
Etienne	Jay Pierce
Babette	Marie Santell
Colette	Jennifer Smith
Tabarro	Mark Waldrop
Pepe	Ken Ward [4]
Edouard Dindon	Jay Garner
Marie Dindon	Merle Louise
Swing Performers	Robert Bruback [5], Drew Geraci, Jan Leigh Herndon, Leslie Simons

UNDERSTUDIES: Walter Charles (Albin/Dindon), Ken Ward (Jacob), Drew Geraci (Jean-Michel/Hercule/Tabarro/Chantal/Hanna/Mercedes/Dermah), Jan Leigh Herndon (Anne/Mme. Renaud/Paulette/Babette/Colette/Angelique), Betsy Craig (Mme. Dindon), Sydney Anderson (Jacqueline), Robert Brubach (Francis/Etienne/Photographer/Pepe/Phaedra), Jack Neubeck (M. Renaud), Jamie Ross (Standby for Georges)

MUSICAL NUMBERS: We Are What We Are, A Little More Mascara, With Anne on My Arm, The Promenade, Song on the Sand, La Cage aux Folles, I Am What I Am, Masculinity, Look Over There, Cocktail Counterpoint, The Best of Times, Grand Finale

A musical in 2 acts. The action takes place in summer in St. Tropez, France, at the present time.

*Still playing May 31, 1984. Winner of 1984 "Tonys" for Best Musical, Best Musical Book, Best Musical Score, Outstanding Actor in a Musical (George Hearn), Outstanding Direction of a Musical, Outstanding Costumes.
[†]Succeeded by: 1.Jamie Ross during vacation, 2. Walter Charles during illness, 3. Jack Davison, 4. Thom Sesma, 5. David Klatt

Martha Swope, Kenn Duncan Photos

Top Left: Gene Barry, George Hearn

Les Cagelles

William Thomas, Jr., Gene Barry, John Weiner
Above: Les Cagelles

(L) Gene Barry, George Hearn Top: Jay Garner,
Merle Louise, Hearn, Barry

11

BEN KINGSLEY AS EDMUND KEAN

(BROOKS ATKINSON THEATRE) By Raymund Fitzsimons; Director, Alison Sutcliffe; Lighting, John Watt; Designed by Martin Tilley; Choreography, Cleone Rive; Coordinating Producer, Roy Somlyo; Presented by Alexander H. Cohen & Hildy Parks in association with Duncan C. Weldon, Paul Gregg, Lionel Becker, Peter Wilson; Stage Managers, Alan Hall, Jodi Moss, Ruth E. Rinklin; Wardrobe, Elonzo Dann; Assistant Director, Carol Thorpe; Press, Sid Garfield, Merle Debuskey, David Roggensack. Opened Tuesday, September 27, 1983.*

CAST

BEN KINGSLEY
as Edmund Kean

Presented in two parts.
*Closed Oct. 29, 1983 after 29 performances and 6 previews.

Martha Swope Photos

Right: Ben Kingsley

Ben Kingsley

ZORBA

(BROADWAY THEATRE) Book, Joseph Stein; Based on novel by Nikos Kazantzakis; Music, John Kander; Lyrics, Fred Ebb; Director, Michael Cacoyannis; Choreography, Graciela Daniele; Scenery, David Chapman; Costumes, Hal George; Lighting, Marc B. Weiss; Sound, T. Richard Fitzgerald; Hairstylist, Steve Atha; Casting, Howard Feuer & Jeremy Ritzer; Musical Supervisor, Paul Gemignani; Musical Director, Randolph Mauldin; Orchestrations, Don Walker; Dance Arrangements, Thomas Fay; Associate Producer, Alecia Parker; Presented by Barry and Fran Weissler, Kenneth-John Productions. Cast album on RCA Records and Tapes; General Manager, National Artists Management Co.; Company Manager, Robert H. Wallner; Stage Managers, Peter Lawrence, Jim Woolley, James Lockhart; Props, George A. Wagner, Jr., John Lofgren; Wardrobe, Frank Green, Kathleen Melcher; Press, Fred Nathan, Anne Abrams, Leslie Anderson, Bert Fink. Opened Sunday October 16, 1983.*

CAST

The Woman	Debbie Shapiro †1
Konstandi/Turkish Dancer/Russian Admiral	Frank DeSal
Thanassai/French Admiral/Monk	John Mineo
Constable	Raphael LaManna
Athena/Crow	Suzanne Costallos
Niko	Robert Westenberg †2
Zorba	Anthony Quinn
Despo/Crow	Panchali Null
Marika/Crow	Angelina Fiordellisi
Katina	Susan Terry
Vassilakas	Chip Cornelius
Marinakos/Monk	Peter Marinos
Mimiko	Aurelio Padron
Katapolis/Monk	Peter Kevoian
Yorgo/Italian Admiral	Richard Warren Pugh
Sophia/Crow	Pamela Trevisani
Mavrodani	Charles Karel
Pavli	Thomas David Scalise
Manolakas	Michael Dantuono
The Widow	Taro Meyer
Priest/English Admiral	Paul Straney
Madame Hortense	Lila Kedrova †3
Marsalias/Monk	Rob Marshall
Anagnosti	Tim Flavin †4
Maria/Cafe Whore	Karen Giombetti

STANDBYS & UNDERSTUDIES: Charles Karel/James Lockhart (Zorba), Suzanne Costallos (Hortense), Angelina Fiordellisi (The Woman), Michael Dantuono (Niko), Susan Terry (The Widow), James Lockhart (Mavrodani), John Mineo (Mimiko), Chip Cornelius (Manolakas), Jim Litten/Danielle R. Striker (Swings), Jim Litten (Dance Captain)

MUSICAL NUMBERS: Life Is, The First Time, The Top of the Hill, No Boom Boom, Vive La Difference, Mine Song, The Butterfly, Goodbye Canavaro, Grandpapa, Only Love, The Bend of the Road, Yassou, Woman, Why Can't I Speak, That's a Beginning, Easter Dance, Miner's Dance, The Crow, Happy Birthday, I Am Free

A musical in 2 acts and 15 scenes. The action takes place in Greece.

*Closed Sept. 2, 1984 after 362 performances and 14 previews. Miss Kedrova received a 1984 "Tony" for Outstanding Supporting Actress in a Musical
†Succeeded by: 1. Angelina Fiordellisi during illness, 2. Jeff McCarthy, 3. Vivian Blaine during vacation, 4. Jim Litten

Martha Swope Photos

Taro Meyer (top center) and chorus
Top Right: Anthony Quinn, Robert Westenberg

Lila Kedrova, Anthony Quinn
Above: Debbie Shapiro

13

AMERICAN BUFFALO

(BOOTH THEATRE) By David Mamet; Director, Arvin Brown; Setting, Marjorie Bradley Kellogg; Costumes, Bill Walker; Lighting, Ronald Wallace; General Manager, Leonard A. Mulhern; Company Manager, Paul Matwiow; Casting, Marjorie Martin; Wardrobe, Barbara Hladsky; Stage Manager, Wally Peterson; Press, Jeffrey Richards, C. George Willard, Robert Ganshaw, Eileen McMahon, Ben Morse, Richard Dahl, Mary Ann Rubino, Anne Katz; The Long Wharf Theatre Production presented by Elliott Martin and Arnold Bernhard. Opened Thursday, October 27, 1983.*

CAST

Donny Dubrow .... J. J. Johnston
Bobby .... James Hayden †
Walter Cole (Teacher) .... Al Pacino

UNDERSTUDIES: John Shepard for James Hayden, Ralph Monaco for Mr. Johnston

A drama in two acts. The action takes place at the present time in Don's Resale Shop in Chicago on a Friday.

*Closed Feb. 27, 1984 after 104 performances and 21 previews.
†Succeeded by John Shepard, Bruce MacVittie

Peter Cunningham, Stephanie Saia Photos

J. J. Johnston, Al Pacino, James Hayden
Top Left: Al Pacino, J. J. Johnston

BROTHERS

(THE MUSIC BOX) By George Sibbald; Director, Carroll O'Connor; Scenery, Thomas A. Walsh; Costumes, Merrily Murray-Walsh; Lighting, Craig Miller; Casting, Julie Hughes/Barry Moss; General Management, Joseph P. Harris, Peter T. Kulok, Steven E. Goldstein; Company Manager, Steven H. David; Stage Managers, Bethe Ward, Hugh O'Connor; Props, Joseph Harris, Jr., Clyde Churchill, Jr.; Wardrobe, Anthony Karniewich; Presented by Noel Pearson in association with Orion Television Inc. and Carnan Productions; Press, Seymour Krawitz, Patricia Krawitz, Robert Larkin. Opened Wednesday, November 9, 1983.*

CAST

Tommy .... Dennis Christopher
Earl .... Gary Klar
Jim .... Carroll O'Connor
James .... Pat McNamara
Harry .... Frank Converse

UNDERSTUDIES: Joseph McCaren (Tommy/Harry), Richard Greene (Earl/James)

A drama in two acts. The action takes place in the backyard of a house in a solid working-class neighborhood in an eastern seaport city on a warm evening in late summer of the present time.

*Closed Wednesday, Nov. 9, 1983 after one performance and seven previews.

Martha Swope Photos

**Top Left: Carroll O'Connor, Dennis Christopher,
Gary Klar Right: Carroll O'Connor, Frank Converse**

Frank Converse, Gary Klar, Dennis Christopher,
Pat McNamara, Carroll O'Connor (front)

AMEN CORNER

(NEDERLANDER THEATRE) Book, Philip Rose, Peter Udell; Based on play of same title by James Baldwin; Music, Garry Sherman; Lyrics, Peter Udell; Director-Associate Producer, Philip Rose; Choreography, Al Perryman; Scenery, Karl Egsti; Costumes, Felix E. Cochren; Lighting, Shirley Prendergast; Orchestrations, Garry Sherman, Dunn Pearson; Vocal Arrangements, Garry Sherman; Dance Arrangements, Dunn Pearson, George Butcher; Musical Director, Margaret Harris; Sound, Peter J. Fitzgerald; Assistant Musical Director, Joseph Joubert; General Manager, Theatre Now (William Court Cohen, Edward H. Davis, Norman E. Rothstein, Ralph Roseman, Charlotte Wilcox); Company Manager, Helen V. Meier; Stage Managers, Mortimer Halpern, Dwight R. B. Cook, Sherry Lambert; Props, Peter Gardner, Ronald Weigel; Wardrobe, Kathleen Gallagher; Original cast album on CBS Records; Presented by Prudhomme Productions, Edward Mann, Judith Henry, Joel Goldstein, Gil Gerard; Press, Fred Nathan, Anne Abrams, Leslie Anderson, Bert Fink. Opened Thursday, November 10, 1983.*

CAST

Margaret Alexander	Rhetta Hughes
Sister Moore	Jean Cheek
Odessa	Ruth Brown
David	Keith Lorenzo Amos
Sister Boxer	Helena-Joyce Wright
Brother Boxer	Chuck Cooper
Luke	Roger Robinson

MEMBERS OF THE CONGREGATION: Loretta Abbott, Leslie Dockery, Cheryl Freeman, Gene Lewis, Denise Morgan, Lewis Robinson, Renee Rose, Vanessa Shaw, Jeffery V. Thompson.
DANCERS: Loretta Abbott (Captain), Leslie Dockery, Renee Rose, Swings: Venida Evans, Leonard Piggee

UNDERSTUDIES: Denise Morgan (Margaret), Venida Evans (Odessa), Vanessa Shaw (Sister Moore), Cheryl Freeman (Sister Boxer), Jeffery V. Thompson (Brother Boxer), Lewis Robinson (David), Gene Lewis (Luke)
MUSICAL NUMBERS: Amen Corner, That Woman Can't Play No Piano, In the Real World, You Ain't Gonna Pick Up Where You Left Off, We Got a Good Thing Goin', In His Own Good Time, Somewhere Close By, Leanin' on the Lord, I'm Already Gone, Love Dies Hard, Rise Up and Stand Again

A musical in 2 acts and 6 scenes. The action takes place in a sanctified storefront church in Harlem and in the adjoining apartment early in the 1960's.

*Closed Dec. 4, 1983 after 83 performances and 29 previews.

Martha Swope Photos

Rhetta Hughes and Company Top Right: Rhetta Hughes, Ruth Brown
Below: Roger Robinson, Rhetta Hughes

LA TRAGEDIE DE CARMEN

(VIVIAN BEAUMONT THEATER) Adapted from Georges Bizet's opera by Marius Constant, Jean-Claude Carriere and Peter Brook; English Lyrics, Sheldon Harnick; Director, Peter Brook; Musical Director, Marius Constant; Scenery, Jean-Guy Lecat; Costumes, Chloe Obolensky; Conductors, Randall Behr, Roger Cantrell; Artistic Adviser, Bernard Lefort; Associate Director, Maurice Benichou; Presented by Alexander H. Cohen and Hildy Parks in association with James Nederlander, Jr. and Arthur Rubin; Co-Producer, Roy A. Somlyo; Company Manager, Jodi Moss; Stage Managers, Robert L. Borod, Christopher A. Cohen; Production Associate, Seymour Herscher; Wardrobe, Elonzo Dann; Press, Merle Debuskey, David Roggensack, Sid Garfield. Opened Thursday, November 17, 1983.*

COMPANY

Ann-Christine Biel	James Hoback
Evan Bortnick	Agnes Host
Cynthia Clarey	Andreas Katsulas
Laurence Dale	Ronald Madden
Helene Delavault	Alain Maratrat
Jean-Paul Denizon	Beverly Morgan
Veronique Dietschy	Peter Puzzo
Carl Johan Falkman	John Rath
Jake Gardner	Eva Saurova
Emily Golden	Patricia Schuman
Howard Hensel	Tapa Sudana

An 80-minute adaptation of the opera presented without intermission and alternating casts singing in French. Toward the end of the run, an English version was added in repertory.

*Closed Apr. 28, 1984 after 187 performances and 29 previews. It received a Special 1984 "Tony" Award.

Martha Swope Photos

Right: John Rath, Eva Saurova

Clockwise: Emily Golden (seated), Eva Saurova, Helene Delavault, Cynthia Clarey, Patricia Schuman

Peter Puzzo, Patricia Schuman

17

MARILYN: AN AMERICAN FABLE

(MINSKOFF THEATRE) Libretto, Patricia Michaels; Music and Lyrics, Jeanne Napoli, Doug Frank, Gary Portnoy, Beth Lawrence, Norman Thalheimer; Direction and Choreography, Kenny Ortega; Scenery, Tom H. John; Costumes, Joseph G. Aulisi; Lighting, Marcia Madeira; Sound, T. Richard Fitzgerald; Musical Supervision, Direction, Vocal and Orchestral Arrangements, Steven Margoshes; Orchestrations, Bill Brohn; Dance Arrangements and Additional Orchestrations, Donald Johnston; Additional Dance Arrangements, Ronald Melrose; Casting, Julie Hughes & Barry Moss; Consultant Producer, Janet Robinson; Music Consultants, Fred Bestall, Lance Reynolds; Assistant Director, Greg Smith; Assistant Choreographer, Veda Jackson; Hairstylist, Phyllis Della; Associate Producers, Peter Duke, Paul Faske, France Weiner; Presented by Malcolm Cooke, William May, Dolores Quinton, James Kabler, Joseph DioGuardi, John Ricciardelli, Arnold Bruck, Tom Kaye, Leo Rosenthal, Harper Sibley, June Curtis, Renee Blau in association with Jerome Minskoff; General Management, Joseph P. Harris, Peter T. Kulok, Steven E. Goldstein; Company Manager, Jean Rocco; Stage Managers, Steve Zweigbaum, Arturo E. Porazzi, Sherry Cohen; Props, Paul Biega, Fred Becker; Wardrobe, Joseph Busheme; Assistant Conductor, Donald Rebic; Press, Shirley Herz, Sam Rudy, Peter Cromarty. Opened Sunday, November 20, 1983.*

CAST

Young Norma Jean	Kristi Coombs
Destiny	Peggie Blue, Michael Kubala, T. A. Stephens
Norma Jean/Marilyn Monroe	Alyson Reed
Jim Dougherty	George Dvorsky
Pat	Debi Monahan
Factory Girls	Melissa Bailey, Deborah Dotson, Jodi Marzorati, Mary Testa, Dooba Wilkins
Photographer	James Haskins
Servicemen	Gary-Michael Davies, Mark Ziebell
Agent	Mitchell Greenberg
Studio Head	Alan North
Director	Gary-Michael Davies
Assistant Director	Ty Crowley
Camera Man	Ed Forsyth
Hairdresser	Deborah Dotson
Hedda	Mary Testa
Designer	Michael Rivera
Louella	Melissa Bailey
Joe DiMaggio	Scott Bakula
Sis	Lise Lang
Tommy	Willy Falk
Coach/Companion	Dooba Wilkins
Arthur Miller	Will Gerard
Strasberg	Steve Schocket
Acting Coach	Ty Crowley

ENSEMBLE: Melissa Bailey, Eileen Casey, Andrew Charles, Kevin Cort, Ty Crowley, Gary-Michael Davies, Deborah Dotson, Mark Esposito, Ed Forsyth, Marcial Gonzalez, Christine Gradi, Marguerite Lowell, Jodi Marzorati, Debi Monahan, Michael Rivera, Steve Schocket, Mary Testa, Dooba Wilkins, Mark Ziebell, Swings: Ivson Polk (Captain), Maryellen Scilla

UNDERSTUDIES: Deborah Dotson/Michael Rivera/Mark Ziebell (Destiny), Sarah Litzsinger (Young Norma Jean), Marguerite Lowell (Norma Jean/Marilyn), James Haskins (Dougherty), Andrew Charles (Photographer), Steve Schocket (Agent/Studio Head), Christine Gradl (Sis), Mark Ziebell (Tommy), Gary-Michael Davies (DiMaggio), Mitchell Greenberg (Arthur Miller)

MUSICAL NUMBERS A Single Dream, Jimmy Jimmy, Church Doors, Swing Shift, The Golden Dream, When You Run the Show, Gossip, Cold Hard Cash, I'm a Fan, Finally, It's a Premiere Night, We'll Help You Through the Night, Run Between the Raindrops, You Are So Beyond, Cultural Pursuits, Don't Hang Up the Telephone, All Roads Lead to Hollywood, My Heart's an Open Door, Miss Bubbles, The Best of Me, We Are the Ones.

A musical in 2 acts and 16 scenes. The action takes place from 1934 to 1962 in Hollywood and New York City.

*Closed Dec. 3, 1983 after 16 performances and 35 previews.

Martha Swope Photos

Top Left: Alyson Reed (c) and chorus

Alyson Reed, Scott Bakula

DOONESBURY

(BILTMORE THEATRE) Book and Lyrics, Garry Trudeau; Based on "Doonesbury" comic strip by Garry Trudeau. Music, Elizabeth Swados; Director Jacques Levy; Choreography, Margo Sappington; Scenery, Peter Larkin; Costumes, Patricia McGourty; Lighting, Beverly Emmons; Sound, Tom Morse; Orchestrations, Elizabeth Swados; Arrangement and Muscial Direction, Jeff Waxman; Casting, Juliet Taylor; General Management, James Walsh; Company Manager, Susan Bell; Stage Managers, Warren Crane, Deborah Clelland, Scott Evans; Props, Robert Saltzman; Wardrobe, Mary P. Eno; Puppets, Edward G. Christie; Presented by James Walsh in association with Universal Pictures; Press, Jeffrey Richards, C. George Willard, Eileen McMahon, Ben Morse, Robert Ganshaw, Richard Dahl, Mary Ann Rubino, Susan Wasson. Opened Monday, November 21, 1983.*

CAST

Roland	Reathel Bean
Mike Doonesbury	Ralph Bruneau
Mark	Mark Linn-Baker
B. D.	Keith Szarabajka
Boopsie	Laura Dean
Zonker	Albert Macklin
Duke	Gary Beach
Honey	Lauren Tom
J. J.	Kate Burton
Joanie	Barbara Andres
Provost	Peter Shawn

UNDERSTUDIES: Max Cantor (Mike/Mark/B.D.), Peter Shawn (Roland), Scott Evans (Zonker), Eve Bennett-Gordon (J.J./Boopsie), Deborah Darr (Joanie), Janet Wong (Honey)

MUSICAL NUMBERS: Graduation, Just One Night, I Came to Tan, Guilty, I Can Have It All, Baby Boom Boogie Boy, Another Memorable Meal, Just a House, Complicated Man, Real Estate, Mother, It's the Right Time to Be Rich, Muffy and the Topsiders

A musical in 2 acts and 11 scenes. The action takes place in late spring of the present time in Walden, an off-off-campus house.

*Closed Feb. 19, 1984 after 104 performances and 21 previews.

Martha Swope Photos

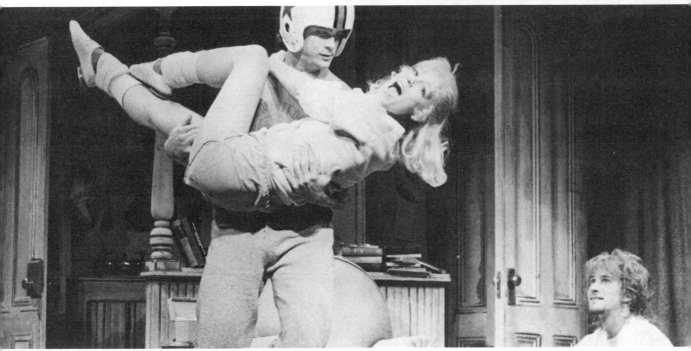

Keith Szarabajka, Laura Dean, Albert Macklin
Top: Entire Cast

THE GLASS MENAGERIE

(EUGENE O'NEILL THEATRE) By Tennessee Williams; Director, John Dexter; Setting, Ming Cho Lee; Costumes, Patricia Zipprodt; Lighting, Andy Phillips; Sound Otts Munderloh; Music Paul Bowles; General Management, McCann & Nugent; Production Coordinator, Mary Nealon; Company Manager, Susan Gustafson; Props, Mel Saltzman; Wardrobe, Rosalie Lahm; Hairstylist, Ray Iagnocco; Presented by Elizabeth I. McCann, Nelle Nugent, Maurice Rosenfield, Ray Larsen; Press, Solters/Roskin/Friedman, Joshua Ellis, Louise Ment, Cindy Valk. Opened Thursday, December 1, 1983.*

CAST

The Mother ....Jessica Tandy
Her Son ....Bruce Davison
Her Daughter ....Amanda Plummer
The Gentleman Caller ....John Heard

STANDBYS: Mary Doyle (Mother), Kymberly Dakin (Daughter), Alfred Karl (Son), Bennett Liss (Gentleman Caller)

A drama in two acts. The action takes place in an alley in St. Louis, Missouri, in the past.

*Closed Feb. 19, 1984 after 92 performances and 8 previews. Original production opened March 31, 1945 at The Playhouse and played 563 performances. In the cast were Laurette Taylor, Eddie Dowling, Julie Haydon and Anthony Ross.

Ken Howard Photos

**Top: Bruce Davison, Jessica Tandy,
Amanda Plummer, John Heard**

Jessica Tandy, Bruce Davison

20

BABY

(ETHEL BARRYMORE THEATRE) Book, Sybille Pearson; Music, David Shire; Lyrics, Richard Maltby, Jr.; Based on story developed by Susan Yankowitz; Director, Richard Maltby, Jr.; Musical Staging, Wayne Cilento; Scenery, John Lee Beatty; Costumes, Jennifer von Mayrhauser; Lighting, Pat Collins; Film Design, John Pieplow; Film Sequences, Lennart Nilsson, Bo G. Erikson, Carl O. Lofman, Swedish Television; Orchestrations, Jonathan Tunick; Music Direction, Peter Howard; Sound, Jack Mann; Sound Textures/Electronic Programming, Dan Wyman; Casting, Johnson-Liff Associates; General Management, Fremont Associates/Barbara Darwall; Associate Producers, Ronald Licht, Robert A. Stewart, J. C. Associates, Elaine Yaker, Karen Howard, Lillian Steinberg; Presented by James B. Freydberg and Ivan Bloch, Kenneth-John Productions, Suzanne J. Schwartz in association with Manuscript Productions; Stage Managers, Peter B. Mumford, Gary M. Zabinski, Dana Sherman; Production Supervisor, Arthur Siccardi; Props, Val Medina, Ralph Bloom III; Wardrobe, Lancey Saunders Clough; Hairstylist, Esther Teller; Press, Judy Jacksina, Glenna Freedman, Susan Chicoine, Marcy Granata, Marc P. Thibodeau, Kevin Boyle. Opened Sunday, December 4, 1983.*

CAST

Lizzie Fields	Liz Callaway
Danny Hooper	Todd Graff †1
Arlene MacNally	Beth Fowler
Alan MacNally	James Congdon
Pam Sakarian	Catherine Cox
Nick Sakarian	Martin Vidnovic
Nurse	Barbara Gilbert
Doctor	John Jellison †2
Mr. Weiss	Philip Hoffman
Dean Webber/Mr. Hart	Dennis Warning
Intern	Lon Hoyt †3
First/Fifth Woman	Judith Thiergaard †4
Second Woman	Lisa Robinson †5
Third Woman	Kirsti Carnahan
Fourth Woman	Barbara Gilbert
Sixth Woman	Kim Criswell †6

TOWNSPEOPLE: Kirsti Carnahan, Kim Criswell, Barbara Gilbert, Philip Hoffman, Lon Hoyt, John Jellison, Lisa Robinson, Judith Thiergaard, Dennis Warning
STANDBYS & UNDERSTUDIES: Kirsti Carnahan (Lizzie), Lon Hoyt (Danny), Judith Thiergaaad (Arlene), John Jellison (Alan), Lisa Robinson (Pam), Philip Hoffman (Nick), Michael Waldron (Doctor), Swings: Judith Bliss, Michael Waldron
MUSICAL NUMBERS: We Start Today, What Could Be Better?, The Plaza Song, Baby Baby Baby, I Want It All, At Night She Comes Home to Me, Fatherhood Blues, Romance, I Chose Right, The Story Goes On, The Ladies Singin' Their Song, Easier to Love, Two People in Love, With You, And What If We Had Loved Like That

A musical in 2 acts and 24 scenes. The action takes place at the present time from March through November.

*Closed July 1, 1984 after 241 performances and 35 previews.
†Succeeded by: 1. Lon Hoyt, 2. Joe Warfield, 3. Michael Brian, 4. Alaina Warren Zachary, 5. Susan Goodman

Martha Swope, Marc Raboy Photos

Martin Vidnovic, Catherine Cox, John Jellison
Top Right: Martin Vidnovic, Catherine Cox

Todd Graff, Liz Callaway
Above: James Congdon, Beth Fowler

HEARTBREAK HOUSE

(CIRCLE IN THE SQUARE) By George Bernard Shaw; Director, Anthony Page; Scenery, Marjorie Bradley Kellogg; Costumes, Jane Greenwood; Lighting, Paul Gallo; Wigs, Paul Huntley; Fight Staging, B. H. Barry; Company Manager, William Conn; Stage Managers, Michael F. Ritchie, Ted William Sowa; Casting, Pulvino/ Howard; Props, Frank Hauser; Presented by Circle in the Square (Artistic Director, Theodore Mann; Managing Director, Paul Libin); Press, Merle Debuskey, David Roggensack. Opened Wednesday, December 7, 1983.*

CAST

Ellie Dunn ....Amy Irving
Nurse Guiness .... Jan Miner
Captain Shotover ....Rex Harrison
Ariadne Utterwod .... Dana Ivey
Hesione Hushabye .... Rosemary Harris
Mazzini Dunn .... William Prince
Hector Hushabye .... Stephen McHattie
Boss Mangan .... Philip Bosco
Randall Utterword ....Bill Moor

A comedy in three acts. The action takes place in 1914 in the house of Captain Shotover situated in the hilly country on the north edge of Sussex, England.

*Closed Feb. 4, 1984 after 65 performances and 21 previews. First produced in NYC at the Garrick Theatre, Nov. 10, 1920 and played 125 performances. In the cast were Albert Perry, Helen Westley, Lucille Watson, Effie Shannon and Dudley Digges.

Martha Swope Photos

Left: Rex Harrison

Rex Harrison, Amy Irving

Dana Ivey

NOISES OFF

(BROOKS ATKINSON THEATRE) By Michael Frayn; Director, Michael Blakemore; Settings and Costumes, Michael Annals; Lighting, Martin Aronstein; Casting, Howard Feuer/Jeremy Ritzer; General Management, Joseph P. Harris, Peter T. Kulok, Steven E. Goldstein; Stage Managers, Susie Cordon, Laura deBuys, Patrick Clear; Props, Paul Biega, Tommy Ciaccio; Wardrobe, Karen Lloyd; Stunt Coordinator, B. H. Barry; Presented by James Nederlander, Robert Fryer, Jerome Minskoff, The Kennedy Center, Michael Codron, In association with Jonathan Farkas, MTM Enterprises; Press, Fred Nathan, Anne Abrams, Leslie Anderson, Ted Killmer, Bert Fink. Opened Sunday, December 11, 1983.*

CAST

Dotty Otley	Dorothy Loudon
Lloyd Dallas	Brian Murray
Garry Lejeune	Victor Garber †
Brooke Ashton	Deborah Rush
Poppy Norton-Taylor	Amy Wright
Frederick Fellowes	Paxton Whitehead
Belinda Blair	Linda Thorson
Tim Allgood	Jim Piddock
Selsdon Mowbray	Douglas Seale

STANDBYS: Patricia Kilgarriff (Dottie/Belinda), Elizabeth Austin (Brooke/Poppy), Herb Foster (Selsdon), Rudolph Willrich (Lloyd/Frederick), Patrick Clear (Garry/Tim)

A comedy in three acts. The action takes place at the present time on stage in the Grand Theatre, Weston-Super-Mare, Monday, January 14; Theatre Royal, Goole, Wednesday Matinee, February 13; Municipal Theatre, Stockton-On-Tees, Saturday, March 8.

*Still playing May 31, 1984
†Succeeded during illness by Patrick Clear

Martha Swope Photos

**Top: Dorothy Loudon, Victor Garber,
Deborah Rush, Linda Thorson, Brian Murray**

**Paxton Whitehead, Dorothy Loudon, Brian Murray,
Linda Thorson (top), Victor Garber**

23

PEG

(LUNT-FONTANNE THEATRE) Story and New Lyrics, Peggy Lee; New Music, Paul Horner; Director, Robert Drivas; Creative Consultant, Cy Coleman; Musical Director, Larry Fallon; Vocal Arrangements, Ray Charles; General Management, Theatre Now, Inc.; Scenery, Tom H. John; Costumes, Florence Klotz; Lighting, Thomas Skelton; Hairstylist/Makeup, Vincent Roppatte; Sound Consultant, Phil Ramone; Sound Design, Jan Nebozenko; Orchestrations, Artie Butler, Larry Fallon, Dominic Frentiere, Bill Holman, Gordon Jenkins, Philip J. Lang, Johnny Mandel, Billy May, Leon Pendarvis, Don Sebesky, Larry Wilcox, Tore Zito; Company Manager, Michael Lonergan; Stage Managers, Larry Forde, Mark Rubinsky; Props, Abe Einhorn; Assistant Director, Martin Jackman; Wardrobe, Peter FitzGerald; Presented by Zev Bufman, Marge and Irv Cowan, Georgia Frontiere; Press, David Powers. Opened Wednesday, December 14, 1983.*

CAST

PEGGY LEE

ACT I: Fever, Soul, Daddy Was a Railroad Man, Mama, That Old Piano, One Beating a Day, That's How I Learned to Sing the Blues, Goody Goody, Sometimes You're Up, He'll Make Me Believe That He's Mine, Why Don't You Do Right
ACT II: Overture, I Love Being Here with You, The Other Part of Me, I Don't Know Enough about You, Angels on Your Pillow, It's a Good Day, Manana, What Did Dey Do to My Goil?, Stay Away from Louisville Lou, No More Rainbows, Flowers and Flowers, Lover, Big Spender, I'm a Woman, Is That All There Is?, There Is More, Bows and Exit Music

A musical autobiography in two acts about and performed by Peggy Lee.

*Closed Dec. 17, 1983 after 5 performances and 13 previews.

Martha Swope Photos

Peggy Lee

Peggy Lee (also top)

24

THE TAP DANCE KID

(BROADHURST THEATRE) Moved March 27, 1984 to the Minskoff Theatre; Book, Charles Blackwell; Music, Henry Krieger; Lyrics, Robert Lorick; Based on novel "Nobody's Family Is Going to Change" by Louise Fitzhugh; Director, Vivian Matalon; Dances and Musical Staging, Danny Daniels; Musical Supervision/Orchestra and Vocal Arrangements, Harold Wheeler; Scenery, Michael Hotopp and Paul dePass; Costumes, William Ivey Long; Lighting, Richard Nelson; Musical and Vocal Direction, Don Jones; Dance Music Arrangements, Peter Howard; Sound, Jack Mann; Assistant Choreographer, D. J. Giagni; Scenic Photography, Mark Feldstein; Wigs, Paul Huntley; Presented by Stanley White, Evelyn Barron, Harvey J. Klaris, Michel Stuart; Associate Producers, Mark Beigelman, Richard Chwatt; Produced in association with Michel Kleinman Productions; General Management, Theatre Now, Inc. (William C. Cohen, Edward H. Davis, Norman E. Rothstein, Ralph Roseman, Charlotte Wilcox); Company Manager, Mark A. Schweppe; Stage Managers, Joe Lorden, Jack Gianino, Ed Fitzgerald; Props, Liam Herbert, Walter Wood; Wardrobe, Kathleen Gallagher, Randy Beth; Hairstylists, Andrew Reese, James Jeppi; Assistant Conductor, Jerry Sternbach; Production Associates, Roberta Haze, Sally Fisher; Press, Judy Jacksina, Glenna Freedman, Susan Chicoine, Marcy Granata, Marc P. Thibodeau, Kevin Boyle. Opened Wednesday, December 21, 1983.*

CAST

Willie	Alfonso Ribeiro †1
Ginnie	Hattie Winston †2
Dulcie	Barbara Montgomery
Emma	Martine Allard
William	Samuel E. Wright
Dipsey	Hinton Battle
Mona	Karen Paskow
Carole	Jackie Lowe
Daddy Bates	Alan Weeks
Winslow	Michael Blevins

LITTLE RIO DANCERS & NEW YORKERS: Leah Bass (Captain), Kevin Berdini, Michael Blevins, Karen Curlee, Suzzanne Douglas, Rick Emery, Karen E. Fraction, D. J. Giagni, J. J. Jepson, Karen Paskow, Rodney Alan McGuire, Jackie Patterson, Mayme Paul, Jamie M. Pisano, Ken Prescott, Oliver Woodall, James Young, Swings: Lloyd Culbreath, Linda Von Germer.
STANDBYS AND UNDERSTUDIES: Jackie Patterson (Dipsey/Daddy Bates), Suzzanne Douglas (Ginnie), Tracey Mitchem (Emma), David Calloway/Jimmy Tate (Willie), Leah Bass (Carole/Dulcie), D. J. Giagni (Winslow), Jamie M. Pasano (Mona), Donny Burks (William)
MUSICAL NUMBERS: Another Day, Four Strikes Against Me, Class Act, They Never Hear What I Say, Dancing Is Everything, Crosstown, Fabulous Feet, I Could Get Used to Him, Man in the Moon, Like Him, Someday, My Luck Is Changing, I Remember How It Was, Lullabye Tap Tap, Dance If It Makes You Happy, William's Song

A musical in 2 acts and 15 scenes. The action takes place at the present time in NYC's Manhattan and Roosevelt Island.

*Still playing May 31, 1984. Winner of 1984 "Tonys" for Outstanding Featured Actor in a Musical (Hinton Battle), and Outstanding Choreography.
†Succeeded by: 1. Jimmy Tate, 2. Gail Nelson

Kenn Duncan, Marc Raboy Photos

Alfonso Ribeiro, Hinton Battle and chorus
Top Right: Alan Weeks, Hinton Battle

Hinton Battle Above: Alfonso Ribeiro,
Martine Allard

25

THE REAL THING

(PLYMOUTH THEATRE) By Tom Stoppard; Director, Mike Nichols; Scenery, Tony Walton; Costumes, Anthea Sylbert; Lighting, Tharon Musser; Sound, Otts Munderloh; Production Supervisor, Martin Herzer; General Manager, Jose Vega; Hairstylist, Richard Stein;' Casting, Mary Goldberg-David Rubin; Wigs, Paul Huntley; Makeup, J. Roy Helland; Props, Jan Marasek, Earl Kirby; Assistant Company Manager, Leslie Butler; Stage Managers, Alan Hall, Jane E. Cooper; Wardrobe, Penny Davis; Presented by Emanuel Azenberg, The Shubert Organization, Icarus Production, Byron Goldman, Ivan Bloch, Roger Berlind, Michael Codron; Press, Bill Evans, Sandra Manley. Opened Thursday, January 5, 1984.*

CAST

Max	Kenneth Welsh †1
Charlotte	Christine Baranski †2
Henry	Jeremy Irons †3
Annie	Glenn Close †4
Billy	Peter Gallagher †5
Debbie	Cynthia Nixon †6
Brodie	Vyto Ruginis

STANDBYS: Edmond Genest (Henry/Max), Leslie Lyles (Annie/Charlotte), Yeardley Smith (Debbie), Todd Waring (Billy/Brodie)

A comedy in two acts. The action takes place at the present time. Two years elapse between Acts I and II.

*Still playing May 31, 1984. Recipient of 1984 "Tonys" for Best Play, Outstanding Actor in a Play (Jeremy Irons), Outstanding Actress in a Play (Glenn Close), Outstanding Featured Actress in a Play (Christine Baranski), Outstanding Direction of a Play. The NY Drama Critics Circle also cited this play as the best new play of the season, as did the Drama Desk.

†Succeeded by: 1. Simon Jones, 2. Sara Botsford, 3. John Vickery, 4. Caroline Lagerfelt, 5. Todd Waring, 6. Yeardley Smith, Cynthia Nixon

Martha Swope Photos

**Left: Christine Baranski,
Jeremy Irons, Cynthia Nixon**

Jeremy Irons, Glenn Close

Glenn Close, Peter Gallagher

IAN McKELLEN ACTING SHAKESPEARE

(RITZ THEATRE) Presented by Arthur Cantor, Bonnie Nelson Schwartz, Rebecca Kuehn; Associate Producer, Harvey Elliott; General/Company Manager, Harvey Elliott; Stage Manager, Mitchell Erickson; Lighting, Charles Bugbee; Press, Arthur Cantor Associates. Opened Thursday, January 19, 1984.*

PROGRAM

PART I: Jacques from "As You Like It," King Henry V, Polonius/Hamlet/First Player from "Hamlet," Bully Bottom from "A Midsummer Night's Dream," Chorus from "Henry V," Duke of Gloucester from "Henry VI Part 3," Prince Hal/Sir John Falstaff from "Henry IV Part 1," Mrs. Quickly from "Henry V," Sonnet XX, Romeo and Juliet
PART II: "The Tragedy of King Richard II," Samuel Pepys, David Garrick, Bernard Shaw, MacBeth, Prospero from "The Tempest"

*Closed Feb. 19, 1984 after limited engagement of 37 performances and 3 previews.

Lance Moore Photos

Ian McKellen

27

OPEN ADMISSIONS

(THE MUSIC BOX) By Shirley Lauro; Director, Elinor Renfield; Scenery, David Gropman; Costumes, Ann Roth, Gary Jones; Lighting, Tharon Musser; Sound, Chuck London Media/Stewart Werner; General Management, The Kingwill Office; Casting, Meg Simon/Fran Kumin; Associate Producer, Bonnie Champion; Presented by Stevie Phillips in association with Universal Pictures; Props, Val Medina; Wardrobe, John Allen; Stage Managers, Paul Phillips, Michael J. Frank; Press, Shirley Herz, Sam Rudy, Peter Cromarty, Pete Sanders, Larry Reitzer. Opened Sunday, January 29, 1984.*

CAST

Calvin Jefferson	Calvin Levels
Salina Jones, his sister	Nan-Lynn Nelson
Georgia Jones, her daughter	Pam Potillo
Ginny Carlsen	Marilyn Rockafellow
Peter Carlsen, her husband	Kevin Tighe
Cathy Carlsen, her daughter	Maura Erin Sullivan
Professor Clare Block	Sloane Shelton
Kitty Shim	Una Kim
Nick Rizzoli	Vincent D'Onofrio
Juan Rivera	Evan Miranda
Mrs. Brewster	C. C. H. Pounder

STANDBYS & UNDERSTUDIES: Joy Franz (Ginny), Faith Geer (Prof. Block/Mrs. Brewster), Richard Fitzpatrick (Peter), June Angela (Kitty), Tahra Takeesha Brown (Georgia), Al Ferrer (Nick/Juan), C. C. H. Pounder (Salina), Jessica Rubinstein (Cathy)

A drama in two acts. The action takes place at the present time, one day in January, in and near Calvin's and Ginny's Manhattan apartments, and in a public college in New York City.

*Closed Feb. 12, 1984 after 17 performances and 7 previews.

Martha Swope Photos

Calvin Levels, Marilyn Rockafellow
Top: Calvin Levels, Nan-Lynn Nelson, Pamela Potillo

THE RINK

(MARTIN BECK THEATRE) Book, Terrence McNally; Music, John Kander; Lyrics, Fred Ebb; Director, A. J. Antoon; Choreography, Graciela Daniele; Scenery, Peter Larkin; Costumes, Theoni V. Aldredge; Lighting, Marc B. Weiss; Sound, Otts Munderloh; Hairstylist/Makeup, J. Roy Helland; Musical Director, Paul Gemignani; Dance Arrangements, Tom Fay; Orchestrations, Michael Gibson; Assistant Choreographer, Tina Paul; Associate Producer, Tina Chen; General Management, Marvin A. Krauss; Casting, Johnson-Liff; Executive Producer, Robin Ullman; Produced in association with Jujamcyn Theatres Corp.; Presented by Jules Fisher, Roger Berlind, Joan Cullman, Milbro Productions, Kenneth-John Productions in association with Jonathan Farkas; Company Manager, Sue Frost; Props, Charles Zuckerman, Paul C. Taylor; Wardrobe, Stephanie Edwards; Press, Merle Debuskey, William Schelble. Opened Thursday, February 9, 1984.*

CAST

Angel	Liza Minelli †
Little Girl	Kim Hauser
Anna	Chita Rivera
Lino/Lenny/Punk/Uncle Fausto	Jason Alexander
Buddy/Hiram/Mrs. Jackson/Charlie/ Suitor/Junior Miller	Mel Johnson, Jr.
Guy/Dino/Father Rocco/Debbie Duberman	Scott Holmes
Lucky/Sugar/Punk/Arnie/Suitor/Bobby Perillo/Danny	Scott Ellis
Tony/Tom/Punk/Suitor/Peter Reilly	Frank Mastrocola
Ben/Dino's Father/Mrs. Silverman/ Sister Philomena	Ronn Carroll

STANDBYS & UNDERSTUDIES: Patti Karr (Anna), Lenora Nemetz/Mary Testa (Angel), Rob Marshall (Lino/Lucky/Tony), Frank Mastrocola (Guy), Jim Tushar (Ben/Buddy), Kim Parks (Little Girl)

MUSICAL NUMBERS: Colored Lights, Chief Cook and Bottle Washer, Don't Ah Ma Me, Blue Crystal, Under the Roller Coaster, Not Enough Magic, We Can Make It, After All These Years, Angel's Rink and Social Center, What Happened to the Old Days?, The Apple Doesn't Fall, Marry Me, Mrs. A, The Rink, Wallflower, All the Children in a Row

A musical in two acts. The action takes place in a roller rink somewhere on the Eastern seaboard during the 1970's.

*Closed Aug. 4, 1984 after 204 performances and 29 previews. Chita Rivera received a 1984 "Tony" for Best Actress in a Musical.
†Succeeded by Mary Testa, Stockard Channing

Ken Howard Photos

Top Right: Chita Rivera

Chita Rivera, Liza Minnelli .

Jason Alexander, Scott Holmes,
Mel Johnson, Jr., Chita Rivera, Ronn Carroll,
Scott Ellis, Frank Mastrocola

AWAKE AND SING!

(CIRCLE IN THE SQUARE THEATRE) By Clifford Odets; Director, Theodore Mann; Scenery, John Conklin; Costumes, Jennifer von Mayrhauser; Lighting, Richard Nelson; Company Manager, William Conn; Casting, Hughes/Moss; Props, Frank Hauser; Wardrobe, Claire Libin; Hairstylist, David Lawrence; Stage Managers, Michael F. Ritchie, Ted William Sowa; Press, Merle Debuskey, David Roggensack. Opened Thursday, March 8, 1984.*

CAST

Ralph Berger	Thomas G. Waites
Myron Berger	Dick Latessa
Hennie Berger	Frances McDormand
Jacob	Paul Sparer
Bessie Berger	Nancy Marchand
Schlosser	Luke Sickle
Moe Axelrod	Harry Hamlin
Uncle Morty	Michael Lombard
Sam Feinschreiber	Benjamin Hendrickson

STANDBYS & UNDERSTUDIES: Phyllis Newman (Bessie), Roger Serbagi (Uncle Morty/Jacob/Myron/Schlosser), Jacob Harran (Ralph/Moe/Sam), Kathryn C. Sparer (Hennie)

A drama in 2 acts and 4 scenes. The action takes place in 1933 in an apartment in The Bronx.

*Closed April 29, 1984 after 61 performances and 23 previews. First produced Feb. 19, 1935 at the Belasco Theatre for 209 performances. The cast included Stella Adler, Morris Carnovsky, Phoebe Brand, Jules (John) Garfield, Luther Adler, Sanford Meisner

Martha Swope Photos

Dick Latessa, Harry Hamlin, Frances McDormand, Benjamin Hendrickson, Paul Sparer, Thomas G. Waites, Nancy Marchand, Luke Sickle, Michael Lombard
Top Left: Nancy Marchand, Harry Hamlin

GLENGARRY GLEN ROSS

(JOHN GOLDEN THEATRE) By David Mamet; Director, Gregory Mosher; Scenery, Michael Merritt; Costumes, Nan Cibula; Lighting, Kevin Rigdon; General Management, Joseph P. Harris, Peter T. Kulok, Steven E. Goldstein; Company Manager, Mitzi C. Harder; Props, Paul Biega; Wardrobe, Anthony Karniewich; Stage Managers, Joseph Drummond, James Dawson, Daniel Miller Morris; Presented by Elliot Martin, Arnold Bernhard, The Shubert Organization, The Goodman Theatre; Press, Jeffrey Richards, C. George Willard, Robert Ganshaw, Eileen McMahon, Ben Morse, Richard Dahl. Opened Sunday, March 25, 1984.*

CAST

Shelly Levene	Robert Prosky†
John Williamson	J. T. Walsh
Dave Moss	James Tolkan
George Aaronow	Mike Nussbaum
Richard Roma	Joe Mantegna
James Lingk	Lane Smith
Baylen	Jack Wallace

STANDBYS: Alfred Karl (Baylen/Moss/Roma), Chuck Stransky (Lingk/Moss/Williamson), Howard Witt (Aaronow/Levene)

A drama in 2 acts and 4 scenes. The action takes place at the present time in a Chinese restaurant, and in a real estate office.

*Still playing May 31, 1984. Recipient of 1984 Pulitzer Prize, NY Drama Critics Circle citation for Best American Play, and a "Tony" for Outstanding Featured Actor in a Play (Joe Mantegna)

†Succeeded by Howard Witt

Brigitte Lacombe Photos

Top: (L) Robert Prosky, J. T. Walsh, (R) Joe Mantegna, James Tolkan Below: Mike Nussbaum, Joe Mantegna

Joe Mantegna, James Tolkan, Robert Prosky

31

DEATH OF A SALESMAN

(BROADHURST THEATRE) By Arthur Miller; Director, Michael Rudman; Scenery, Ben Edwards; Costumes, Ruth Morley; Music, Alex North; Lighting, Thomas Skelton; Makeup, Ann Belsky; Hairstylist, Alan D'Angerio; Casting, Terry Fay; Production Associate, Doris Blum; General Manager, David Hedges; Stage Managers, Thomas A. Kelly, Charles Kindl, Patricia Fay; Props, Robert Saltzman; Wardrobe, James McGaha; Sound, Tom Morse; Presented by Robert Whitehead, Roger L. Stevens; Press, Patricia Krawitz. Opened Thursday, March 29, 1984.*

CAST

Willy Loman	Dustin Hoffman
Linda Loman	Kate Reid
Happy	Stephen Lang
Biff	John Malkovich
Bernard	David Chandler
Woman from Boston	Kathy Rossetter
Charley	David Huddleston
Uncle Ben	Louis Zorich
Howard Wagner	Jon Polito
Jenny	Patricia Fay
Stanley	Tom Signorelli
Miss Forsythe	Linda Kozlowski
Letta	Karen Needle
Waiter	Michael Quinlan

UNDERSTUDIES: Andrew Bloch (Biff/Happy), Bruce Kirby (Willy/Charley/Uncle Ben/Stanley), Anne McIntosh (Jenny/Miss Forsythe/Letta), Michael Quinlan (Bernard/Howard)

A drama in two acts. The action takes place in a 24-hour period in Willy Loman's house and yard, and in various places he visits in New York and Boston.

*Closed July 1, 1984 after limited engagement of 97 performances and 9 previews. Recipient of a 1984 "Tony" for Outstanding Reproduction of a Play. In 1949 it won the Pulitzer Prize as Best Play. It opened Feb. 10, 1049 at the Morosco Theatre and played 742 performances. The original cast included Lee J. Cobb, Mildred Dunnock, Cameron Mitchell and Arthur Kennedy. The 1975 revival at the Circle in the Square played 71 performances with George C. Scott, Teresa Wright, Harvey Keitel and James Farentino.

Inge Morath Photos

**Top Right: David Chandler, Stephen Lang,
Kate Reid, Dustin Hoffman, John Malkovich,
David Huddleston Below: Karen Needle, Stephen Lang, Linda Kozlowski
Right: Jon Polito, Dustin Hoffman**

Kate Reid, Dustin Hoffman

**Kate Reid, John Malkovich,
Dustin Hoffman, Stephen Lang**

THE HUMAN COMEDY

(ROYALE THEATRE) Music, Galt MacDermot; Libretto, William Dumaresq; From novel of the same title by William Saroyan; Director, Wilford Leach; Scenery, Bob Shaw; Costumes, Rita Ryack; Lighting, James F. Ingalls; Sound, Tom Morse; Makeup and Hairstylist, Marlies Vallant; Music Director/Orchestrator, Galt MacDermot; Conductor, Tania Leon; Associate Producer, Jason Steven Cohen; General Manager, Laurel Ann Wilson; Company Manager, David Conte; Projections, Wendall Harrington; Props, Solly Purnick, Don Nascia; Wardrobe, John Allen Guiteras; Stage Managers, Alan Fox, K. Siobhan Phelan; Presented by Joseph Papp and the Shubert Organization (Gerald Schoenfeld, Chairman/Bernard B. Jacobs, President); Press, Merle Debuskey, Richard Kornberg, Barbara Carroll, Bruce Campbell. Opened Thursday, April 5, 1984.*

CAST

Trainman	David Lawrence Johnson
Ulysses Macauley	Josh Blake
Mrs. Kate Macauley	Bonnie Koloc
Homer Macauley	Stephen Geoffreys
Bess Macauley	Mary Elizabeth Mastrantonio
Helen	Anne Marie Bobby
Miss Hicks	Laurie Franks
Spangler	Rex Smith
Thief	Christopher Edmonds
Mr. Grogan	Gordon Connell
Felix	Daniel Noel
Beautiful Music	Debra Byrd
Mary Arena	Caroline Peyton
Mexican Woman	Olga Merediz
Voice of Matthew Macauley	Grady Mulligan
Tobey	Joseph Kolinski
Soldiers	Kenneth Bryan, Louis Padilla, Michael Willson
A Neighbor	Kathleen Rowe McAllen
Diana Steed	Leata Galloway
Minister	Walter Hudson
Townspeople	Marc Stephen DelGatto, Lisa Kirchner, Vernon Spencer, Dan Tramon

STANDBYS & UNDERSTUDIES: Cass Morgan (Kate), Vernon Spencer (Trainman/Felix), Marc Stephen DelGatto (Ulysses), Lisa Kirchner (Kate/Mexican Woman), Dan Tramon (Homer), Donna Murphy (Bess/Mary Arena), Kathleen Rowe McAllen (Helen/Diana), Debra Byrd (Miss Hicks), Grady Mulligan (Marcus/Spangler), Walter Hudson (Spangler), Daniel Noel (Thief), David Vogel (Grogan/Swing), David Lawrence Johnson (Tobey)

MUSICAL NUMBERS: In a Little Town in California, Hi Ya Kid, We're a Little Family, The Assyrians, Noses, You're a Little Young for the Job, I Can Carry a Tune, Happy Birthday, Happy Anniversary, I Think the Kid Will Do, Beautiful Music, Cocoanut Cream Pie, When I Am Lost, I Said Oh No, Daddy Will Not Come Walking Through the Door, The Birds in the Sky, Remember Always to Give, Long Past Sunset, Don't Tell Me, The Fourth Telegram, Give Me All the Money, Everything Is Changed, The World Is Full of Loneliness

A musical in 2 acts and 10 scenes. The action takes place in 1943 in a little town in California.

*Closed Apr. 15, 1984 after 13 performances and 19 previews. It was transferred from the NY Shakespeare Festival's Public/Anspacher Theater where it had played 79 performances and 8 previews.

Martha Swope Photos

Top Right: Mary Elizabeth Mastrantonio, Caroline Peyton

Rex Smith, Gordon Connell, Stephen Geoffreys

SHIRLEY MacLAINE ON BROADWAY

(GERSHWIN THEATRE) Original Music and Lyrics, Marvin Hamlisch, Christopher Adler; Additional Material, Larry Grossman, Buz Kohan; Staged and Choreographed by Alan Johnson; Lighting, Ken Billington; Costumes, Pete Menefee; Musical Director, Jack French; Associate Lighting Designer, Jeffrey Schissler; Producer, Michael Flowers; Personal Management, Mort Viner; Technical Director, George Boyd; Company Manager, Steve Marquard; Wardrobe, Irene Ferrari; Production Assistant, Clare Culhane; Presented by Guber/Gross Productions and the Nederlander Organization; Press, Mark Goldstaub, Patt Dale, Phil Butler, Dan Kellachan, Will Pharis. Opened Thursday, April 19, 1984.*

CAST

Shirley MacLaine

Mark Reina	Jamilah Lucas
Larry Vickers	Antonette Yuskis

Gary Flannery (Swing)

A musical entertainment performed without intermission.

*Closed May 27, 1984 after limited engagement of 46 performances and 1 preview.

Martha Swope/Jay Thompson Photos

Left: Shirley MacLaine

Antonette Yuskis, Larry Vickers, Shirley MacLaine, Mark Reina, Jamilah Lucas

BEETHOVEN'S TENTH

(NEDERLANDER THEATRE) by Peter Ustinov; Director, Robert Chetwyn; Scenery, Kenneth Mellor; Costumes, Madeline Ann Graneto; Lighting, Martin Aronstein; Sound, Jim Morris; Production Associate, Karen Leahy; Mr. Ustinov's Costumes, John Fraser; Musical Sequences, Stephen Pruslin; General Managers, Robert A. Buckley, Douglas Urbanski, Karen Leahy; Company Manager, G. Warren McClane; Stage Managers, Jake Hamilton, Joe Cappelli; Props, Liam Herbert, George Salisbury; Wardrobe, Santos Ramos; Hairstylist, Joseph Blitz; Pianist, Susan Kingwill; Presented by Messrs. Buckley & Urbanski and Sandra Moss in association with the Baltimore Center for Performing Arts; Press, Marilynn LeVine, Merle Frimark, Meg Gordean. Opened Sunday, April 22, 1984.*

CAST

Stephen Fauldgate	George Rose
Jessica Fauldgate	Mary Jay
Irmgard	Gina Friedlander
Pascal Fauldgate	Adam Redfield
Ludwig	Peter Ustinov
Dr. Collis Jagger	Gwyllum Evans
Father	Anderson Matthews
Countess Giulietta Guiccardi	Leslie O'Hara
Count Robert Wenzel Gallenberg	Neil Flanagan

UNDERSTUDIES: John Messenger (Ludwig), John Swindells (Stephen/Count), Victoria Boothby (Jessica), Richard DeFabees (Pascal/Father), Marietta Mead (Giulietta/Irmgard), Neil Flanagan (Dr. Jagger)

A comedy in two acts. The action takes place at the present time in the London home of Stephen Fauldgate.

*Closed May 13, 1984 after 25 performances and 14 previews.

Martha Swope Photos

Top: (L) George Rose, Peter Ustinov
Below: Mary Jay, Ustinov, Adam Redfield
Top: (R) Gina Friedlander, Ustinov

Peter Ustinov

PLAY MEMORY

(LONGACRE THEATRE) By Joanna M. Glass; Director, Harold Prince; Scenery, Clarke Dunham; Costumes, William Ivey Long; Lighting, Ken Billington; Incidental Music, Larry Grossman; Presented by Alexander H, Cohen and Hildy Parks in association with Samuel Klutznick; Co-presented by Bernard Gersten; Casting, Joanna Merlin; Hairstylist, Richard Allen; General Manager, Howard Haines; Stage Managers, Francis X. Kuhn, Marc Schlackman, Glen Gerdali; Props, George Green, Robert Bostwick; Wardrobe, Elonzo Dann; Press, Merle Debuskey, David Roggensack, Sid Garfield, Rebecca Robbins. Opened Thursday, April 26, 1984.*

CAST

Cam MacMillan	Donald Moffat
Ruth MacMillan	Jo Henderson
Jean MacMillan	Valerie Mahaffey
Billy	Jerry Mayer
Ken	Edwin J. McDonough
Roy	James Greene
Miss Halverson	Marilyn Rockafellow
Mike Melzewski	Tom Brennan
Duncan	Rex Robbins
Ross	Curt Williams
Ernest	Steven Moses

STANDBYS & UNDERSTUDIES: Rex Robbins (Cam), Marilyn Rockafellow (Ruth), Lizbeth Mackay (Jean), Edwin J. McDonough (Duncan), Jerry Mayers (Ross/Mike), Curt Williams (Roy/Billy/Ken), Glen Gardali (Ernest)

A drama in two acts. The action takes place in the city of Saskatoon, Saskatchewan, Canada, from 1939 to 1968.

*Closed April 29, 1984 after 5 performances and 7 previews.

Martha Swope Photos

Jo Henderson, Valerie Mahaffey, Donald Moffat
Top Right: Donald Moffat

OLIVER!

(MARK HELLINGER THEATRE) Book/Music/Lyrics, Lionel Bart; Director, Peter Coe; Design, Sean Kenny; Lighting, Andrew Bridge; Sound, Jack Mann; Musical Director, John Lesko; Orchestrations, Eric Rogers; Casting, Johnson-Liff; Associate Director, Geoffrey Ferris; Executive Producers, R. Tyler Gatchell, Jr., Peter Neufeld; Presented by Cameron Mackintosh, Carole J. Shorenstein, James M. Nederlander by arrangement with The Southbrook Group; General Management, Gatchell & Neufeld; Production Manager, Paul MacKay; Company Manager, Steven H. David; Stage Managers, Sam Stickler, Bethe Ward, Richard Jay-Alexander; Assistant Musical Director, Arthur Wagner; Props, George Green, Jr., Abe Einhorn; Wardrobe, Adelaide Laurino; Hairstylist, Angela Gari; Design Associates, David Chapman (Scenery), Ruth Roberts (Lighting), Charles Schoonmaker (Costumes); Press, Fred Nathan, Anne Abrams, Leslie Anderson, Ted Killmer, Bert Fink. Opened Sunday, April 29, 1984.*

CAST

Oliver Twist	Braden Danner
Mr. Bumble, the Beadle	Michael McCarty
Mrs. Bumble, the Matron	Elizabeth Larner
Mr. Sowerberry, the Undertaker	Roderick Horn
Mrs. Sowerberry, his wife	Frances Cuka
Charlotte, their daughter	Andi Henig
Noah Claypole, their apprentice	Alan Braunstein
Fagin	Ron Moody
The Artful Dodger	David Garlick
Nancy	Patti LuPone
Bet	Sarah E. Litzsinger
Bill Sikes	Graeme Campbell
Bullseye	Vito/Buffy
Mr. Brownlow	Michael Allinson
Dr. Grimwig	Louis Beachner
Mrs. Bedwin	Elizabeth Larner

WORKHOUSE BOYS/FAGIN'S GANG: Robert David Cavanaugh, Samir Chowdhury, Ruben Cuevas, Roshi Handwerger, Cameron Johann, Mark Manasseri, Michael Manasseri, Kipp Marcus, Shawn Morgal, Brian Noodt, Roy Nygaard, R. D. Robb, Dennis Singletary, Zachary A. Stier.
LONDONERS: Diane Armistead, Louis Beachner, Alan Braunstein, Frances Cuka, W. P. Dremak, Gregg Edelman, Tony Gilbert, Eleanor Glockner, Beth Guiffre, Andi Henig, Roderick Horn, Jan Horvath, Michael McCarty, William McClary, Marcia Mitzman, Martin Moran, Barbara Moroz, Cheryl Russell, Clark Sayre, Jane Strauss, Susan Willis.
STANDBYS & UNDERSTUDIES: Stephen Hanan (Fagin), Cameron Johann (Oliver), Zachary A. Stier (Oliver), Marcia Mitzman (Nancy), Tony Gilbert (Bill), Eleanor Glockner (Mrs. Bumble), Louis Beachner (Brownlow), Kipp Marcus (Artful Dodger), Michael Manasseri (Artful Dodger), Andi Henig (Bet), Diane Armistead (Mrs. Bedwin), W. P. Dremak (Grimwig), Jane Strauss (Charlotte), William McClary (Sowerberry), Martin Moran (Noah), Susan Willis (Mrs. Sowerberry), Swings: Edward Prostak, Carrie Wilder, Joe Anthony Wright.
MUSICAL NUMBERS: Food Glorious Food, Oliver!, Boy for Sale, That's Your Funeral, Where Is Love, Consider Yourself, You've Got to Pick a Pocket or Two, It's a Fine Life, I'd Do Anything, Be Back Soon, Oom-pah-pah, My Name, As Long as He Needs Me, Who Will Buy?, Reviewing the Situation, Finale.

A musical in 2 acts and 10 scenes. The action takes place about 1850 in the North of England and in London.

*Closed May 13, 1984 after 17 performances and 12 previews. Original production opened Jan. 6, 1963 at the Imperial Theatre and played 774 performances. In the cast were Clive Revill, Georgia Brown, Danny Sewell and Bruce Prochnik.

Martha Swope Photos

Top Right: Ron Moody, Braden Danner
Below: Ron Moody

Patti LuPone (c), Ron Moody (r)

A MOON FOR THE MISBEGOTTEN

(CORT THEATRE) By Eugene O'Neill; Director, David Leveaux; Scenery and Costumes, Brien Vahey; Lighting, Marc B. Weiss; Original Music, Stephen Endelman; Casting, Soble/LaPadura; General Manager, Robert Kamlot; Company Manager, Max Allentuck; Props, Dick Hodgins; Stage Managers, Sally J. Jacobs, Philip Cusack; Wardrobe, Ellen Lee; Presented by The Shubert Organization (Gerald Schoenfeld, Chairman/Bernard B. Jacobs, President) and Emanuel Azenberg; Press, Bill Evans, Sandra Manley. Opened Tuesday, May 1, 1984.*

CAST

Josie Hogan	Kate Nelligan
Mike Hogan	John Bellucci
Phil Hogan	Jerome Kilty
James Tyrone, Jr.	Ian Bannen
T. Stedman Harder	Michael Tolaydo

STANDBYS: Giulia Pagano (Josie), Donald Gantry (James/, T. Stedman Harder), Michael Tolaydo (Mike), George Hall (Phil)

A drama in two acts. The action takes place in Connecticut at the home of tenant farmer Phil Hogan, between the hours of noon on a day in early September of 1923 and sunrise of the following day.

*Closed June 9, 1984 after 40 performances and 19 previews. Original production opened May 2, 1957 at the Bijou Theatre and played 68 performances with Wendy Hiller, Franchot Tone and Cyril Cusack; The 1973 revival at the Morosco Theatre played 313 performances with Colleen Dewhurst, Ed Flanders and Jason Robards.

Christopher Little Photos

Top: Kate Nelligan, Jerome Kilty

Kate Nelligan, Ian Bannen

SUNDAY IN THE PARK WITH GEORGE

(BOOTH THEATRE) Music and Lyrics, Stephen Sondheim; Book, James Lapine; Director, Mr. Lapine; Scenery, Tony Straiges; Costumes, Patricia Zipprodt, Ann Hould-Ward; Lighting, Richard Nelson; Special Effects, Bran Ferren; Sound, Tom Morse; Hairstylist/Makeup, LoPresto/Allen; Movement, Randolyn Zinn; Musical Direction, Paul Gemignani; Orchestrations, Michael Starobin; Casting, John S. Lyons; Set and Costume Designs adapted from the Georges Seurat painting entitled "Sunday Afternoon on the Island of the Grand Jatte"; General Manager, Robert Kamlot; Company Manager, Richard Berg; Stage Managers, Charles Blackwell, Fredric H. Orner, Loretta Robertson; Props, Jan Marasek, Timothy Abel; Wardrobe, Nancy Schaefer; Presented by The Shubert Organization and Emanuel Azenberg by arrangement with Playwrights Horizons; Press, Fred Nathan, Leslie Anderson, Anne Abrams, Ted Killmer, Bert Fink. Opened Wednesday, May 2, 1984.*

CAST

ACT I:

George, an artist	Mandy Patinkin
Dot, his mistress	Bernadette Peters
Old Lady	Barbara Bryne
Her Nurse	Judith Moore
Franz, a servant	Brent Spiner
Boy Bathing in the river	Danielle Ferland
Young Man sitting on the bank	Nancy Opel
Man lying on the bank	Cris Groenendaal
Jules, another artist	Charles Kimbrough
Yvonne, his wife	Dana Ivey
Boatman	William Parry
Celeste #1	Melanie Vaughan
Celeste #2	Mary D'Arcy
Louise, daughter of Jules and Yvonne	Danielle Ferland
Frieda, a cook	Nancy Opel
Louis, a baker	Cris Groenendaal
Soldier	Robert Westenberg
Man with bicycle	John Jellison
Little Girl	Michele Rigan
Woman with baby carriage	Sue Anne Gershenson
Mr.	Kurt Knudson
Mrs.	Judith Moore

ACT II:

George, an artist	Mandy Patinkin
Marie, his grandmother	Bernadette Peters
Dennis, a technician	Brent Spiner
Bob Greenberg, museum director	Charles Kimbrough
Naomi Eisen, composer	Dana Ivey
Harriet Pawling, patron of the arts	Judith Moore
Billy Webster, her friend	Cris Groenendaal
Photographer	Sue Anne Gershensen
Museum Assistant	John Jellison
Charles Redmond, visiting curator	William Parry
Alex, an artist	Robert Westenberg
Betty, an artist	Nancy Opel
Lee Randolph, publicist	Kurt Knudson
Blair Daniels, art critic	Barbara Bryne
Waitress	Melanie Vaughan/Joanna Glushak
Elaine	Mary D'Arcy

UNDERSTUDIES: Robert Westenberg (George), Joanna Glushak (Dot/Marie), Sara Woods (Old Lady/Blair/Nurse/Mrs./Harriet), Cris Groenendaal (Franz/Dennis/Soldier/Alex), Ray Gill (Soldier/Alex, Randolph/Franz/Dennis/Man/Louis/Billy), Michele Rigan (Boy/Louise), Sue Anne Gershenson (Young Man/Frieda/Betty/Celeste #2/Elaine), John Jellison (Man/Louis/Billy/Jules/Greenberg/Boatman/Redmond)

MUSICAL NUMBERS: Sunday in the Park with George, No Life, Color and Light, Gossip, The Day Off, Everybody Loves Louis, Finishing the Hat, We Do Not Belong Together, Beautiful, Sunday, It's Hot Up Here, Chromolume #7, Putting It Together, Children and Art, Lesson #8, Move On

ACT I takes place on a series of Sundays form 1884 to 1886 and alternates between a park on an island in the Seine just outside of Paris, and George's studio.
ACT II takes place in 1984 at an American art museum, and on the island in the Seine.

*Still playing May 31, 1984. Recipient of NY Drama Critics Circle as well as Drama Desk citation for Best Musical, 1984 "Tonys" for Outstanding Scenic Design, and for Outstanding Lighting Design.

Martha Swope Photos

Top Right: Mandy Patinkin (with sketch pad),
Bernadette Peters (3rd from right)
Below: Company

Mandy Patinkin, Bernadette Peters

Barbara Rush

A WOMAN OF INDEPENDENT MEANS

(BILTMORE THEATRE) By Elizabeth Forsythe Hailey based on her novel; Director, Norman Cohen; Incidental Music, Henry Mancini; Scenery, Roy Christopher; Lighting, Martin Aronstein; Costumes, Garland Riddle; Sound, Jon Gottlieb, Production Associate, Karen Leahy; Associate Producers, Robert Michael Geisler, John Roberdeau; General Managers, Robert A. Buckley, Douglas Urbanski; Company Manager, Susan Bell; Stage Managers, Warren Crane, Joanne Dalsass; Props, Liam Herbert; Wardrobe, Claudia Kaneb; Presented by Messrs. Buckley & Urbanski, James Hansen, with Della Koenig, Sandra Moss, Warren Cowan; Press, Solters/Roskin/Friedman, Joshua Ellis, Louise Ment, Cindy Valk, Jackie Green. Opened Thursday, May 3, 1984.*

CAST

Bess Steed Garner .... Barbara Rush

A solo performance, spanning a woman's life from 1899 to 1977.

*Closed May 13, 1983 after 13 performances and 12 previews.

Martha Swope, Ed Krieger Photos

Top: Barbara Rush

END OF THE WORLD

(THE MUSIC BOX) By Arthur Kopit; Director, Harold Prince; Scenery, Clarke Dunham; Costumes, William Ivey Long; Lighting, Ken Billington; Incidental Music, Larry Grossman; Sound, Rob Gorton; Projections, Clarke Dunham, Lisa Podgur; Assistant to Mr. Prince, Ruth Mitchell; General Management, Howard Haines; Casting, Joanna Merlin; Company Manager, John Caruso; Stage Managers, Beverley Randolph, Steven Kelley; Props, Andrew Acabbo, William F. Garvey; Hairstylist, Richard Allen; Wardrobe, Stephanie Cheretun; Production Assistant, Robert Ackerman; Presented by Kennedy Center and Michael Frazier; Press, Mary Bryant, Becky Flora, Mark Shannon. Opened Sunday, May 6, 1984.*

CAST

Michael Trent	John Shea
Philip Stone	Barnard Hughes
Audrey Wood	Linda Hunt
Paul Cowan	Richard Seff
Merv Rosenblatt	David O'Brien
Stella	Elaine Petricoff
General Wilmer	David O'Brien
Stanley Berent	Jaroslav Stremien
Pete	Peter Zapp
Jim	Nathaniel Ritch
Ann	Elaine Petricoff
Trent's Son	Wade Raley
Charles	Larry Pine

STRANGERS, WAITERS, WAITRESSES, ATTACHE, CUSTOMERS: Elaine Petricoff, Nathaniel Ritch, Peter Zapp, Frank Hankey, Larry Pine
STANDBYS & UNDERSTUDIES: Lee Bryant (Audrey Wood), Frank Hankey (Michael Trent/Jim), Larry Pine (Cowan/Wilmer/Cowan/Berent)

A play in three acts: The Commission, The Investigation, The Discovery.

*Closed June 2, 1984 after 33 performances and 13 previews.

Martha Swope Photos

Richard Seff, Linda Hunt, David O'Brien
Above: John Shea, Linda Hunt, Barnard Hughes

John Shea, Barnard Hughes
Top: Linda Hunt, John Shea

THE BABE

(PRINCESS THEATRE) By Bob and Ann Acosta; Director, Noam Pitlik; Scenery, Ray Recht; Lighting, F. Mitchell Dana; Costumes, Judy Dearing; Makeup, Steve LaPorte; General Manager, Paul B. Berkowsky; Company Manager, Jerry Livengood; Stage Managers, Doug Laidlaw, John O'Neill; Wardrobe, Toni Reed; Presented by Corniche Productions, Ltd.; Producer, Peter F. Buffa; Press, Max Eisen, Barbara Glenn, Maria Somma. Opened Thursday, May 17, 1984.*

CAST

George Herman "The Babe" Ruth .... Max Gail

Performed without intermission in three scenes: 1923, 1935, 1948.

*Closed May 20, 1984 after 5 performances and 9 previews.

Carol Rosegg Photos

Top: Max Gail

Max Gail

THE WIZ

(LUNT-FONTANNE THEATRE) Book, William F. Brown; Music & Lyrics, Charlie Smalls; Director, Geoffrey Holder; Choreography and Musical Staging, George Faison; Scenery, Peter Wolf; Costumes, Geoffrey Holder; Lighting, Paul Sullivan; Orchestrations, Harold Wheeler; Musical Direction/Vocal Arrangements, Charles H. Coleman; Dance Arrangements, Timothy Graphenreed; Sound, Gary M. Stocker; General Management, American Theatre Productions (George MacPherson/Jay Brooks/Jan Mallow); Company Manager, Daryl T. Dodson; Stage Managers, Jack Welles, Luis Montero, Nate Barnett; Props, Randy Moreland, Jude Timlin; Hairstylist/Makeup, Marylou Faherty; Wigs and Hair Styles, Ray Iagnocco; Presented by Tom Mallow, James Janek and the Shubert Organization; Press, Max Eisen, Barbara Glenn, Maria Somma, Madelon Rosen. Opened Thursday, May 24, 1984.*

CAST

Aunt Em	Peggie Blue
Toto	Toto
Dorothy	Stephanie Mills
Uncle Henry	David Weatherspoon
Tornado	Daryl Richardson
Munchkins	Carol Dennis, Ada Dyer, Lawrence Hamilton, Sam Harkness, David Weatherspoon
Addaperle	Juanita Fleming
Yellow Brick Road	Alfred L. Dove, Germaine Edwards Dwight Leon, David Robertson
Scarecrow	Charles Valentino
Sunflowers	Carol Dennis, Ada Dyer, Sam Harkness, David Weatherspoon
Crows	Paula Anita Brown, Marvin Engran, Jasmine Guy
Tinman	Howard Porter
Lion	Gregg Baker
Strangers	Carol Dennis, Sam Harkness, David Weatherspoon
Kalidahs	Marvin Engran, Jasmine Guy, Lawrence Hamilton, Raymond C. Harris, Gigi Hunter, Martial Roumain
Poppies	Sharon Brooks, Paula Anita Brown, Carla Earle, Tanya Gibson, Gigi Hunter, Daryl Richardson
Chief of Field Mice	Ada Dyer
Field Mice	Lawrence Hamilton, David Weatherspoon
Royal Gatekeeper	Sam Harkness
Head of Society of Emerald City	Sharon Brooks
The Wiz	Carl Hall
Evillene	Ella Mitchell
Lord High Underling	Lawrence Hamilton
Soldier Messenger	Marvin Engran
Winged Monkey	Germaine Edwards
Glinda	Ann Duquesnay

EMERALD CITY CITIZENS: Paula Anita Brown, Roslyn Burrough, Carol Dennis, Alfred L. Dove, Ada Dyer, Carla Earle, Germaine Edwards, Marvin Engran, Tanya Gibson, Jasmine Guy, Lawrence Hamilton, Sam Harkness, Raymond C. Harris, Gigi Hunter, Dwight Leon, Daryl Richardson, David Robertson, Martial Roumain, David Weatherspoon

UNDERSTUDIES: Ada Dyer (Dorothy), Ann Duquesnay (Aunt Em), Sharon Brooks (Glinda/Tornado), Carol Dennis (Addaperle), Juanita Fleming (Evilline), Germaine Edwards (Scarecrow), Sam Harkness (Lion), David Weatherspoon (Wiz), Lawrence Hamilton (Tinman), Alfred L. Dove (Winged Monkey), John Simmons (Assistant Musical Director), Swing Dancers/Singers: Sheri Moore, Eugene Little

MUSICAL NUMBERS: The Feeling We Once Had, Tornado Ballet, He's the Wizard, Soon as I Get Home, I Was Born on the Day before Yesterday, Ease on Down the Road, Slide Some Oil to Me, Mean Ole Lion, Kalidah Battle, Be a Lion, Lion's Dream, Emerald City Ballet (Psst), So You Wanted to Meet the Wizard, What Would I Do If I Could Feel, No Bad News, Funky Monkeys, Wonder Why, Everybody Rejoice, Who Do You Think You Are?, If You Believe, Y'All Got It!, A Rested Body Is a Rested Mind, Home

A musical in 2 acts and 15 scenes.

*Closed June 3, 1984 after 13 performances and 7 previews. Original production opened Jan. 5, 1975 at the Majestic Theatre (later moving to the Broadway Theatre) and played 1672 performances with Stephanie Mills as Dorothy.

Kenn Duncan Photos

Top Right: Stephanie Mills, Gregg Baker, Howard Porter (Tinman), Charles Valentino Below: Ann Duquesnay (atop melon)

Stephanie Mills (c)

A CHORUS LINE

(SHUBERT THEATRE) Conceived, Choreographed and Directed by Michael Bennett; Book, James Kirkwood, Nicholas Dante; Music, Marvin Hamlisch; Lyrics, Edward Kleban; Co-Choreographer, Bob Avian; Musical Direction/Vocal Arrangements, Don Pippin; Associate Producer, Bernard Gersten; Set, Robin Wagner; Costumes, Theoni V. Aldredge; Lighting, Tharon Musser; Sound, Abe Jacobs; Music Coordinator, Robert Thomas; Orchestrations, Bill Byers, Hershy Kay, Jonathan Tunick; Assistant to Choreographers, Baayork Lee; Musical Director, Robert Rogers; Wardrobe, Alyce Gilbert; Production Supervisor, Jason Steven Cohen; Original cast album by Columbia Records; A New York Shakespeare Festival production; Presented by Joseph Papp in association with Plum Productions; General Manager, Robert Kamlot, Laurel Ann Wilson; Company Manager, Bob MacDonald; Stage Managers, Tom Porter, Wendy Mansfield, Morris Freed, Bradley Jones, Ronald Stafford; Press, Merle Debuskey, William Schelble, Richard Kronberg. Opened Friday, July 25, 1975*

CAST

Roy	Evan Pappas
Kristine	Christine Barker
Sheila	Jane Summerhays †1
Val	Mitzi Hamilton
Mike	Danny Herman †2
Butch	Roscoe Gilliam
Larry	Brad Jeffries †3
Maggie	Pam Klinger
Richie	Kevin Chinn †4
Tricia	Kiel Junius †5
Tom	Frank Kliegel
Zach	Steve Boockvor †6
Mark	Chris Marshall
Cassie	Pamela Sousa †7
Judy	Melissa Randel
Lois	Laurie Gamache
Don	Michael Danek
Bebe	Pamela Ann Wilson
Connie	Lily-Lee Wong †8
Diana	Loida Santos
Al	Buddy Balou'
Frank	Fraser Ellis
Greg	Ronald A. NaVarre †9
Bobby	Matt West
Paul	Tommy Aguilar †10
Vicki	Ann Louise Schaut
Ed	Morris Freed
Jarad	Troy Garza
Linda	Catherine Cooper
Sam	Sam Piperato
Ralph	Bradley Jones
Hilary	Karen Ziemba †11

UNDERSTUDIES: Roxann Cabalero (Diana/Maggie/Connie), Catherine Cooper (Cassie/Sheila/Val), Michael Danek (Zach), Fraser Ellis (Mark/Bobby/Don), Morris Freed (Mark), Laurie Gamache (Kristine/Bebe/Judy/Cassie), Troy Garza (Mike/Mark/Paul/Larry/Al), Roscoe Gilliam (Richie), J. Richard Hart (Mike), Bradley Jones (Bobby/Greg), Frank Kliegel (Don/Zach/Bobby), Robin Lyon (Bebe/Diana/Val/Maggie), Evan Pappas (Mark/Al/Paul/Larry), Sam Piperato (Mike/Larry/Bobby), Ann Louise Schaut (Cassie/Sheila/Kristine/Judy), Pamela Ann Wilson (Val/Judy)

MUSICAL NUMBERS: I Hope I Get It, I Can Do That, and . . ., At the Ballet, Sing!, Hello 12 Hello 13 Hello Love, Nothing, Dance 10 Looks 3, Music and the Mirror, One, Tap Combination, What I Did for Love, Finale.

A musical performed without intermission. The action takes place in 1975 during an audition in the theatre.

*Still playing May 31, 1984. Cited as Best Musical by NY Drama Critics Circle, winner of 1976 Pulitzer prize, 1976 "Tonys" for Best Musical, Best Book, Best Score, Best Direction, Best Lighting, Best Choreography, Best Musical Actress (Donna McKechnie), Best Featured Actor and Actress in a Musical (Sammy Williams, Kelly Bishop), and a Special Theatre World Award was presented to each member of the creative staff and original cast. See THEATRE WORLD VOl. 31. On Thursday, Sept. 29, 1983 it celebrated its 3389 performance, becoming the longest running show in Broadway history. Members of original, national and international companies (332) appeared on stage for the memorable occasion.

†Succeeded by: 1. Susan Danielle, Kelly Bishop, Kathryn Ann Wright, 2. Don Correia, 3. J. Richard Hart, 4. Reggie Phoenix, 5. Robin Lyon, 6. Eivind Harum, 7. Cheryl Clark, Wanda Richert, 8. Sachi Shimizu, 9. Ronald A. NaVarre, Michael-Day Pitts, Justin Ross, 10. Sammy Williams, 11. Roxann Cabalero

Top Right: Sammy Williams (original Paul) with nine other Pauls

Above: Pamela Sousa, Ann Louise Schaut, Wanda Richert, Deborah Henry, Donna McKechnie, Cheryl Clark, Vicki Frederick (all played Cassie)

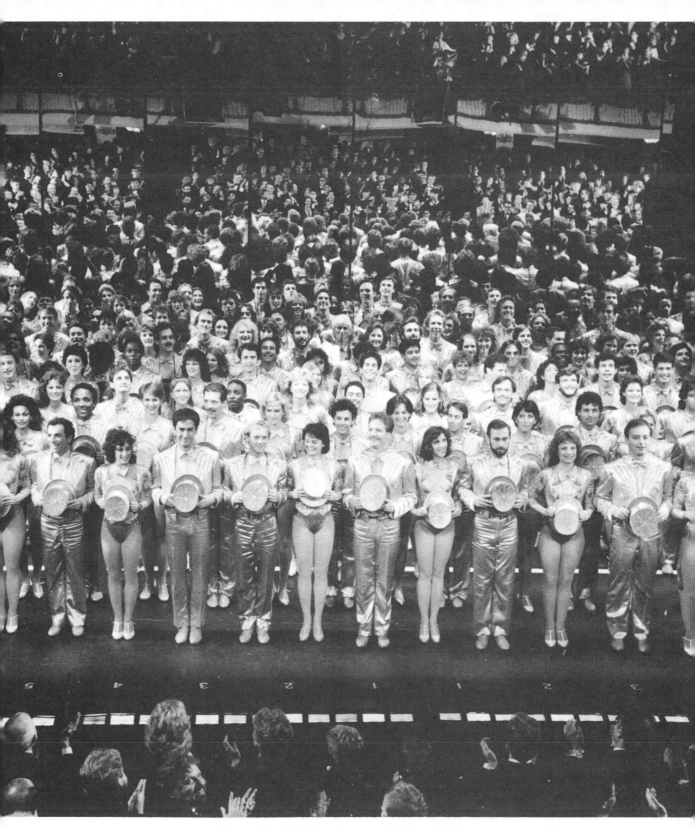

Curtain Call at the 3,389 performance of "A Chorus Line"

OH! CALCUTTA!

(EDISON THEATRE) Devised by Kenneth Tynan; Conceived and Directed by Jacques Levy; Contributors, Robert Benton, David Newman, Jules Feiffer, Dan Greenberg, Lenore Kandel, John Lennon, Jacques Levy, Leonard Melfi, Sam Shepard, Clovis Trouille, Kenneth Tynan, Sherman Yellen; Music and Lyrics, Robert Dennis, Peter Schickele, Stanley Walden, Jacques Levy; Choreography, Margo Sappington; Musical Director, Stanley Walden; Scenery/Lighting, Harry Silverglat Darrow; Costumes, Kenneth M. Yount; Supervised by James Tilton; Musical Conductor, Barry Harwood; Sound, Sander Hacker; Assistant to Director, Nancy Tribush; Projected Media Design, Gardner Compton; Live action film, Ron Merk; Assistant Musical Conductor, Dan Carter; Technical Directors, Thomas Healy, Charles Moran; Wardrobe, Mark Bridges; Props, James Tilton; Presented by Hillard Elkins, Norman Kean, Robert S. Fishko; Company Manager, Doris J. Buberl, Tobias Beckwith; Stage Managers, Maria DiDia, Ron Nash; Press, Les Schecter, Barbara Schwei. Opened June 17, 1960 at the Eden Theatre, and Sept. 24, 1976 at the Edison.*

CAST

Deborah Bauers	Cheryl Hartley
Nannette Bevelander	David Heisey
Michael A. Clarke	Mary Kilpatrick
Charles E. Gerber	James E. Mosiej

MUSICAL NUMBERS AND SKITS: Taking Off the Robe, Will Answer All Sincere Replies, Playin', Jack and Jill, The Paintings of Clovis Trouille, Delicious Indignities, Was It Good for You Too?, Suite for Five Letters, One on One, Rock Garden, Spread Your Love Around, Four in Hand, Coming Together Going Together

An "erotic musical" in two acts.

*Still playing May 31, 1984. For original production, see THEATRE WORLD, Vol. 33

FORTY-SECOND STREET

(WINTER GARDEN moved March 30, 1981 to MAJESTIC THEATRE) Music, Harry Warren; Lyrics, Al Dubin; Book, Michael Stewart, Mark Bramble from novel by Bradford Ropes; Direction/Choreography, Gower Champion; Scenery, Robin Wagner; Costumes, Theoni V. Aldredge; Lighting, Tharon Musser; Musical Direction, Philip Fradkin; Orchestrations, Philip J. Lang; Dance Arrangements, Donald Johnston; Vocal Arrangements, John Lesko; Sound, Richard Fitzgerald, Hairstylist, Ted Azar; Casting, Feuer & Ritzer; Presented by David Merrick; Props, Leo Herbert; Wardrobe, Gene Wilson, Kathleen Foster; Assistant Musical Director, Bernie Leighton; Company Manager, Leo K. Cohen; Stage Managers, Steve Zweigbaum, Barry Kearsley, Jane E. Neufeld, Debra Pigliavento, Jack Timmers, Janet Friedman, Dennis Angulo; Press, Solters/Roskin/Friedman, Joshua Ellis, David LeShay, Louise Ment, Cindy Valk. Opened Monday, Aug. 25, 1980*

CAST

Andy Lee	Danny Carroll
Oscar	Robert Colston
Mac/Thug/Doctor	Stan Page
Annie	Clare Leach †1
Maggie Jones	Jessica James
Bert Barry	Joseph Bova
Billy Lawlor	Lee Roy Reams †2
Peggy Sawyer	Lisa Brown †3
Lorraine	Ginny King †4
Phyllis	Jeri Kansas †5
Julian Marsh	Jerry Orbach †6
Dorothy Brock	Elizabeth Allen †7
Abner Dillon	Don Crabtree
Pat Denning	Steve Elmore
Thugs	Stan Page, Ron Schwinn
Doctor	Stan Page

ENSEMBLE: Dennis Angulo, Carlo Banninger, Dennis Batutis, Paula Joy Belis, Gail Benedict, Pam Cecil, Ronny DeVito, Rob Draper, Yvonne Dutton, Brandt Edwards, Mark Frawley, Cathy Greco, K. Craig Innes, Jack Karcher, Billye Kersey, Karen Klump, Terri Ann Kundrat, Neva Leigh, Gail Lohla, Maureen Mellon, Gwendolyn Miller, Ken Mitchell, Beth Myatt, Bill Nabel, Sheila O'Conner, Gail Pennington, Don Percassi, Rosemary Rado, Michael Ricardo, Lars Rosager, Linda Sabatelli, Ron Schwinn, Pamela S. Scott, Yveline Semeria, Allison Sherve, Roger Spivy, Cynthia Thole

UNDERSTUDIES: Connie Day (Dorothy/Maggie), Steve Elmore/Stan Page (Julian), Pam Cecil (Peggy), Rob Draper (Billy), Bill Nabel (Bert), Ron Schwinn (Bart/Mac), Don Percassi (Andy), Stan Page (Abner/Pat), Billye Kersey (Annie), Linda Sabatelli (Annie), Oscar-Bernie Leighton (Mac), Lizzie Moran/Debra Ann Draper (Phyliss/Lorraine), Ensemble: Debra Ann Draper, Patrice McConachie, Ida Gillams, Dennis Angulo, Christopher Lucas, Lizzie Moran

MUSICAL NUMBERS: Audition, Young and Healthy, Shadow Waltz, Go into Your Dance, You're Getting to Be a Habit with Me, Getting Out of Town, Dames, I Know Now, Sunny Side to Every Situation, Lullaby of Broadway, About a Quarter to 9, Shuffle Off to Buffalo, 42nd Street

A musical in 2 acts and 16 scenes. The action takes place during 1933 in New York City and Philadelphia.

*Still playing May 31, 1984. Recipient of 1981 "Tonys" for Best Musical and for Outstanding Choreography. For original production, see THEATRE WORLD VOl. 37.
†Succeeded by: 1. Billye Kersey, Dorothy Stanley, 2. James Brennan, 3. Karen Ziemba, Gail Benedict, 4. Gail Lohla, 5. Gail Pennington, 6. Stephen G. Arlen during vacation, 7. Millicent Martin, Anne Rogers

Top Right: (c) James Brennan, Karen Ziemba
Below: Jerry Orbach, Anne Rogers

(front) Joseph Bova, Karen Ziemba, Danny Carroll,
(back) James Brennan, Jerry Orbach

47

Terry Burrell, Sheryl Lee Ralph,
Loretta Devine

Julia McGirt   Hinton Battle

DREAMGIRLS

(IMPERIAL THEATRE) Book and Lyrics, Tom Eyen; Music, Henry Krieger; Direction/Choreography, Michael Bennett; Co-Choreographer, Michael Peters; Sets, Robin Wagner; Costumes, Theoni V. Aldredge; Lighting, Tharon Musser; Sound, Otts Munderloh; Musical Supervision/Orchestrations, Harold Wheeler; Musical Director, Yolanda Segovia, Paul Gemignani; Vocal Arrangements, Cleavant Derricks; Hairstylist, Ted Azar; Production Supervisor, Jeff Hamlin; Technical Coordinator, Arthur Siccardi; Props, Michael Smanko; Wardrobe, Alyce Gilbert, Stephanie Edwards; Assistant to Choreographers, Geneva Burke; Production Assistant, Charles Suisman; Assistant Conductor, Nick Cerrato; Casting, Olaiya, Johnson/Liff; Original cast album on Geffen Records and Tapes; General Management, Marvin A. Krauss, Eric L. Angelson, Gary Gunas, Steven C. Callahan, Joey Parnes; Stage Managers, Zane Weiner, Frank DiFilia, Jake Bell; Presented by Michael Bennett, Bob Avian, Geffen Records, the Shubert Organization; Press, Merle Debuskey, Diane Judge. Opened Sunday, December 20, 1981*

CAST

The Stepp Sisters	Deborah Burrell †1, Vanessa Bell †2, Tenita Jordan †3, Brenda Pressley
Charlene	Cheryl Alexander †4
Joanne	Linda Lloyd †5
Marty	Vondie Curtis-Hall
Curtis Taylor, Jr.	Ben Harney †6
Deena Jones	Sheryl Lee Ralph
M.C.	Larry Stewart †7
Tiny Joe Dixon/Nightclub Owner	Joe Lynn
Lorrell Robinson	Loretta Devine †8
C. C. White	Obba Babatunde †9
Effie Melody White	Jennifer Holliday †10
Little Albert & the Tru-Tones/James Early Band	Charles Bernard, Wellington Perkins, Jamie Patterson, Eric Riley, Charles Randolph-Wright, Frank Mastrocola, Richie Abanes, Barry Bruce, Bobby Daye, Sean Walker
James Thunder Early	Cleavant Derricks †11
Edna Burke	Sheila Ellis †12
Wayne	Tony Franklin †13
Dave & the Sweethearts	Paul Binotto †14, Candy Darling, Carol Logen †15
Press Agent Frank	David Thome †16
Michelle Morris	Deborah Burrell †17
Morgan	Larry Stewart †18
Film Executives	Paul Binotto, Scott Plank †19, Weyman Thompson †20
The Five Tuxedos	Charles Bernard, Jamie Patterson, Charles Randolph-Wright, Eric Riley, Larry Stewart
Les Style	Cheryl Alexander †4, Ethel Beatty †21, Mary Denise Bentley, Brenda Pressley

ANNOUNCERS, FANS, GUESTS, ETC.: Richie Abanes, Ethel Beatty, Paul Binotto, Mary Denise Bentley, Barry Bruce, Candy Darling, Bobby Daye, Ronald Dunham, Christopher Gregory, Nina Hennessey, Khandi Alexander, Hal Miller, Brenda Pressley, Eric Riley, Graciela Simpson, Leon Summers, Jr., Gina Taylor, Buddy Vest, Sean Walker, Swings: Charles Bernard, Brenda Braxton, Milton Craig Nealy, Allison Williams

UNDERSTUDIES: Brenda Pressley/Roz Ryan (Effie), Terry Burrell (Lorrell), Ethel Beatty/Brenda Pressley (Deena/Michelle), Vondie Curtis-Hall/Tony Franklin (Curtis), Tony Franklin (Early), Wellington Perkins (C. C.), Milton Craig Nealy (Marty/M.C./Morgan), Hal Miller (Dave/Jerry/Frank), Charles Bernard (Wayne/Tiny)

MUSICAL NUMBERS: I'm Looking for Something, Goin' Downtown, Takin' the Long Way Home, Move, Fake Your Way to the Top, Cadillac Car, Steppin' to the Bad Side, Party, I Want Your Baby, Family, Dreamgirls, Press Conference, Only the Beginning, Heavy, It's All Over, And I Am Telling You I'm Not Going, Love Love You Baby, I Am Changing, One More Picture Please, When I First Saw You, Got to Be Good Times, Ain't No Party, Quintette, The Rap, I Miss You Old Friend, One Night Only, I'm Somebody, Faith in Myself, Hard to Say Goodbye My Love

A musical in 2 acts and 20 scenes. The action takes place in the early 1960's and 1970's.

*Still playing May 31, 1984. Winner of 1982 "Tonys" for Best Book, Lighting, Choreography, Supporting Actor (Cleavant Derricks), Best Actor and Actress in a Musical (Ben Harney, Jennifer Holliday)
†Succeeded by: 1. Terry Burrell, 2. Graciela Simpson, 3. Gina Taylor, 4. Khandi Alexander, 5. Ethel Beatty, 6. Vondie Curtis-Hall during vacation, 7. Leon Summers, Jr., 8. Cheryl Alexander, Adriane Lenox, 9. Tony Franklin, Wellington Perkins, 10. Vanessa Townsell, Julia McGirt, Roz Ryan, 11. Hinton Battle, Cleavant Derricks, David Alan Grier, 12. Julia McGirt, Allison Williams, 13. Wellington Perkins, Eric Riley, 14. Richard Poole during vacation, 15. Nina Hennessey, 16. Buddy Vest, 17. Terry Burrell, 18. Leon Summers, Jr., 19. Hal Miller, 20. Eric Riley, 21. Allison Williams

TORCH SONG TRILOGY

(THE LITTLE THEATRE/re-named HELEN HAYES THEATRE) By Harvey Fierstein; Director, Peter Pope; Sets, Bill Stabile; Costumes, Mardi Philips; Lighting, Scott Pinkney; Musical Direction/Arrangements, Ned Levy; Original Music, Ada Janik; Producers, Kenneth Waissman, Martin Markinson, John Glines, Lawrence Lane with BetMar and Donald Tick; Associate Producer, Howard Perloff; Assistant Director, Judy Thomas; Technical Supervisor, Jeremiah J. Harris; Sound, Richard Fitzgerald, John Sullivan; Wardrobe, Kathy Powers, Larry Tarzy; Hairstylist, Andre Tavernise; Production Assistant, George Phelps; General Assistant, David Kratz, Barbara Hodgen; Casting, Hughes/Moss; General Management, Theatre Now; General Manager, Edward H. Davis; Props, Ronnie Lynch, Sr.; Stage Managers, Herb Vogler, Billie McBride; Press, Betty Lee Hunt, Maria Cristina Pucci, James Sapp. Opened Thursday, June 10, 1982.*

CAST

Lady Blues	Susan Edwards
Arnold Beckoff	Harvey Fierstein †1
Ed	Court Miller †2
Laurel	Diane Tarleton
Alan	Paul Joynt †3
David	Fisher Stevens †4
Mrs. Beckoff	Estelle Getty †5

STANDBYS AND UNDERSTUDIES: Susan Edwards (Laurel), Diane Tarleton (Lady Blues), Jeffrey Rogers (Alan/David), Sylvia Kauders (Mrs. Beckoff), Roger Leonard (Keyboard), Charles Adler (Arnold), Peter Ratray (Ed)

A play in 3 acts, and 10 scenes. Part 1: "The International Stud" takes place backstage, in a bar, Ed's apartment, Arnold's apartment at the present time from January to November. Part 2: "Fugue in a Nursery" a year later in Arnold's apartment, and in various rooms of Ed's farmhouse. Part 3: "Widows and Children First" five years later in Arnold's apartment, and on a bench in the park.

*Still playing May 31, 1983. Awarded 1983 "Tonys" for Best Play, and Best Actor in a Play (Harvey Fierstein).
†Succeeded by: 1. Richard DeFabees, Donald Corren, Jonathan Hadary, David Garrison, Philip Astor, Harvey Fierstein, Jonathan Hadary, 2. Robert Sevra, Peter Ratray, David Orange, Court Miller, Jared Martin, Court Miller, Raymond Baker, 3. Christopher Stryker, Craig Sheffer, 4. Jon Cryer, Christopher Collett, Mathew Vipond, 5. Chevi Colton

Jonathan Hadary, Mathew Vipond, Raymond Baker
Top Left: Jonathan Hadary, Chevi Colton

49

CATS

(WINTER GARDEN) Based on "Old Possum's Book of Practical Cats" by T. S. Eliot; Music, Andrew Lloyd Webber; Director, Trevor Nunn; Associate Director/Choreography, Gillian Lynne; Design, John Napier; Lighting, David Hersey; Sound, Martin Levan; Musical Director, Rene Wiegert; Production Musical Director, Stanley Lebowsky; Presented by Cameron Mackintosh, The Really Useful Company, David Geffen, The Shubert Organization; Executive Producers, R. Tyler Gatchell, Jr., Peter Neufeld; Casting, Johnson/Liff; Orchestrations, David Cullen, Andrew Lloyd Webber; Original cast album on Geffen Records; Company Manager, James G. Mennen; General Management, Gatchell & Neufeld; Associate Musical Directors, Keith Herrmann, Kevin Farrell; Production Assistant, Nancy Hall Bell; Wardrobe, Adelaide Laurino; Makeup, Candace Carell; Hairstylists, Leon Gagliardi, Ann Miles, Charles McMahon, Richard Orton, Fred Patton, Thelma Pollard, Frank Paul; Assistant Choreographer, Jo-Anne Robinson; Stage Managers, David Taylor, Lani Sundsten, Sally J. Greenhut, Jeff Lee, Donald Walters, Sherry Cohen; Production Dance Supervisor, T. Michael Reed; Props, George Green, Jr., Merlyn Davis, George Green III; Press, Fred Nathan, Eileen McMahon, Anne S. Abrams, Leslie Anderson, Bert Fink, Ted Killmer. Opened Thursday, Oct. 7, 1982*

CAST

Alonzo	Hector Jaime Mercado †1
Bustopher Jones/Asparagus/Growltiger	Stephen Hanan †2
Bombalurina	Donna King †3
Carbucketty	Steven Gelfer
Cassandra	Rene Ceballos †4
Coricopat/Mungojerrie	Rene Clemente †5
Demeter	Wendy Edmead †6
Etcetera/Rumpleteazer	Christine Langner †7
Grizabella	Betty Buckley †8
Jellylorum Griddlebone	Bonnie Simmons
Jennyanydots	Anna McNeely
Mistoffolees	Timothy Scott †9
Munkustrap	Harry Groener †10
Old Deuteronomy	Ken Page †11
Plato/Macavity/Rumpus Cat	Kenneth Ard †12
Pouncival	Herman W. Sebek †13
Rum Tum Tugger	Terrence V. Mann
Sillabub	Whitney Kershaw †14
Skimbleshanks	Reed Jones †15
Tantomile	Janet L. Hubert †16
Tumblebrutus	Robert Hoshour
Victoria	Cynthia Onrubia
Cats Chorus	Walter Charles †17, Susan Powers, Carol Richards †18, Joel Robertson

STANDBYS AND UNDERSTUDIES: Alonzo: Herman W. Sebek, Bob Morrisey, Brian Andrews, Rene Clemente, Claude R. Tessier, Mark Frawley, Jack Magrady; Bustopher: Steven Gelfer, Joel Robertson; Bombalurina: Marlene Danielle, Rene Ceballus, Nora Brennan, Deborah Henry; Carbucketty: Steven Hack, Claude R. Tessier, Brian Andrews, Jack Magrady; Cassandra: Diane Frantantoni, Marlene Danielle, Nora Brennan, Deborah Henry; Coricopat: Steven Hack, Herman W. Sebek, Rene Clemente, Claude R. Tessier, Mark Frawley, Jack Magrady; Demeter: Janet L. Hubert, Marlene Danielle, Denise DiRenzo, Deborah Henry, Valerie C. Wright; Etcetera: Diane Frantantoni, Jane Bodle, Denise DiRenzo; Grizabella: Janet L. Hubert, Colleen Fitzpatrick, Diane Fratantoni, Deborah Henry; Jellylorum: Diane Fratantoni, Susan Powers, Dodie Pettit; Jennyanydots: Susan Powers, Jane Bodle, Denise DiRenzo, Dodie Pettit; Mistoffelees: Rene Clemente, Guillermo Gonzalez, Herman W. Sebek, Joe Anthony Cavise, Michael Scott Gregory; Munkustrap: Bob Morrisey, Robert Hoshour, Bubba Dean Rambo, Jack Magrady, Brian Sutherland; Old Deuteronomy: Walter Charles, Erick Devine; Plato: Hector Jaime Mercado, Brian Andrews, Brian Sutherland; Pouncival: Steven Hack, Brian Andrews; Rum Tum Tugger: Bob Morrisey, Bubba Dean Rambo, Claude R. Tessier; Sillabub: Diane Fratantoni, Jane Bodle, Denise DiRenzo, Dodie Pettit, Valerie C. Wright; Skimbleshanks: Bob Morrisey, Claude R. Tessier, Mark Frawley, Jack Magrady; Tantomile: Marlene Danielle, Whitney Kershaw, Jane Bodle, Denise DiRenzo, Nora Brennan, Valerie C. Wright; Tumblebrutus: Brian Andrews, Steven Hack, Scott Wise; Victoria: Whitney Kershaw, Paige Dana, Sundy Leigh Leake, Christine Langner, Dodie Pettit, Valerie C. Wright

MUSICAL NUMBERS: Jellicle Songs for Jellicle Cats, The Naming of Cats, Invitation to the Jellicle Ball, Old Gumbie Cat, Rum Tum Tugger, Grizabella the Glamour Cat, Bustopher Jones, Mungojerri and Rumpleteazer, Old Deuteronomy, The Awefull Battle of the Pekes and Pollicles, Marching Song of the Pollicle Dogs, Jellicle Ball, Memory, Moments of Happiness, Gus the Theatre Cat, Growltiger's Last Stand, Skimbleshanks, Macavity, Mr. Mistoffolees, Journey to the Heaviside Layer, The Ad-Dressing of Cats.

A musical in 2 acts and 21 scenes.

*Still playing May 31, 1984. Winner of 1983 "Tonys" for Best Musical, Best

Laurie Beechman, Kevin Marcum
Top: Terrence V. Mann

Musical Book, Best Musical Score, Best Musical Director, Best Supporting Musical Actress (Betty Buckley), Best Costume Design, Best Lighting Design.

†Succeeded by: 1. Brian Sutherland, 2. Timothy Jerome, 3. Marlene Danielle, 4. Christina Kumi Kimball, Nora Brennan, 5. Guillermo Gonzalez, Joe Antony Cavise, 6. Jane Bodle, 7. Paige Dana, 8. Laurie Beechman, 9. Herman W. Sebek, 10. Claude R. Tessier, 11. Kevin Marcum, 12. Scott Wise, 13. Ramon Galindo, 14. Denise DiRenzo, 15. Michael Scott Gregory, 16. Sundy Leigh Leake, 17. Erick Devine, 18. Colleen Fitzpatrick

ON YOUR TOES

(VIRGINIA THEATRE) Book, Richard Rodgers, Lorenz Hart, George Abbott; Music, Richard Rodgers; Lyrics, Lorenz Hart; Director, George Abbott; Original Choreography, George Ballanchine; Additional Ballet Choreography, Peter Martins; Musical numbers choreographed by Donald Saddler; Design, Zack Brown; Lighting, John McLain; Original Orchestrations, Hans Spialek; Musical Director/Conductor, John Mauceri; Casting, Hughes/Moss; Presented by Alfred de Liagre, Jr., Roger L. Stevens, John Mauceri, Donald R. Seawell, Andre Pastoria; Coordinating Producer, Charlene Harrington; Props, Richard King, Jr.; Sound, Jan Nebozenko; Wardrobe, Dean Jackson, Rose Ann Moran; Production Associate, Jean Bankier; Production Assistant, Terry Wuthrich; Assistant Musical Director/Conductor, Paul Schwartz; Musical Contractor/Conductor, John Kim Bell; Makeup/Wigs, Charles Elsen, Dennis Bergevin; General Management, Charlene Harrington, C. Edwin Knill; Company Manager, Edwin Blacker; Hairstylist, Charles LoPresto; Press, Jeffrey Richards, C. George Willard, Robert Ganshaw, Ted Killmer, Ben Morse, Helen Stern, Richard Humleker; Stage Managers, William Dodds, Amy Pell, Sarah Whitham, Dennis Honeycutt; Original cast album on Polydor Records. Opened Sunday, March 6, 1983*

CAST

Phil Dolan/II/Oscar .... Eugene J. Anthony
Lil Dolan/Reporter .... Betty Ann Grove
Phil Dolan III/Junior .... Philip Arthur Ross
Stage Manager .... Dirk Lumbard †1
Lola .... Mary C. Robare
Junior (15 years later) .... Lara Teeter
Miss Pinkerton .... Michaela K. Hughes
Sidney Cohn .... Peter Slutsker
Frankie Frayne .... Christine Andreas
Joe McCall .... Jerry Mitchell
Vera Baronova .... Natalia Makarova †2
Anushka .... Tamara Mark †3
Peggy Porterfield .... Dina Merrill †4
Sergei Alexandrovitch .... George S. Irving
Konstantine Morrosine .... George de la Pena †5
Stage Doorman .... David Gold
Dimitri .... Chris Peterson
Ivan .... Don Steffy
Louie .... George Kmeck

"Princess Zenobia Ballet": Natalia Makarova (Zenobia), George de la Pena (Beggar), George Kmeck (Kringa Khan), Eugene J. Anthony (Ali Shar), David Gold (Ahmud), Michael Vita (Hank) "On Your Toes Ballet" Alexander Filipov †6, Starr Danias (Ballet Leaders), Dirk Lumbard, Dana Moore (Tap Leaders), Michael Vita (Cop), Bill Badolato (Messenger) "Slaughter on Tenth Ave. Ballet": Lara Teeter (Hoofer), Natalia Makarova (Stripper), Michael Vita (Big Boss), Jerry Mitchell (Cop)
ENSEMBLE: Teresa De Rose, Melody A. Dye, Marguerite Hickey, Jane Lanier, Dana Moore, Mary C. Robare, Marcia Watkins, Leslie Woodies, Sandra Zigars, Bill Badolato, David Gold, Malcolm Grant, Wade Laboissonniere, Dirk Lumbard, Robert Meadows, Jerry Mitchell, Chris Peterson, Don Steffy, Kirby Tepper, James Walski
UNDERSTUDIES: Dana Moore (Lil), Dirk Lumbard (Junior), Marcia Watkins (Frankie), Kirby Tepper (Sidney), Starr Danias (Vera), David Gold (Sergei), Leslie Woodies (Peggy), Jerry Mitchell (Louie), Don Steffy (Constantine)
MUSICAL NUMBERS: Two a Day for Keith, Questions and Answers, It's Got to Be Love, Too Good for the Average Man, The Seduction, There's a Small Hotel, Princess Zenobia Ballet, The Heart Is Quicker Than the Eye, Glad to Be Unhappy, Quiet Night, On Your Toes, Slaughter on Tenth Avenue

A musical in 2 acts and 12 scenes. The action takes place about 1920.

*Closed May 20, 1984 after 505 performances and 7 previews. Recipient of 1983 "Tonys" for Best Revival, Best Actress in a Musical (Natalia Makarova). Original production opened Apr. 11, 1936 at the Imperial Theatre and played 315 performances. Tamara Geva and Ray Bolger were starred.

†Succeeded by: 1. Robert Meadows, 2. Galina Panova, Valentina Kozlova (2 weeks), 3. Leslie Woodies, 4. Kitty Carlisle Hart, 5. Leonid Kozlov (3 weeks), Terry Edelfsen, 6. Malcolm Grant

Top Right: Philip Arthur Ross, Betty Ann Grove,
Eugene J. Anthony Below: Kitty Carlisle Hart,
George S. Irving

Lara Teeter, Galina Panova

BRIGHTON BEACH MEMOIRS

(**ALVIN THEATRE** name changed June 29, 1983 to **NEIL SIMON THEATRE**) By Neil Simon; Director, Gene Saks; Set, David Mitchell; Costumes, Patricia Zipprodt; Lighting, Tharon Musser; Presented by Emanuel Azenberg, Wayne M. Rogers, Radio City Music Hall Productions in association with Center Theatre Group/Ahmanson; Casting, Marilyn Szatmary, Jane E. Cooper, Hank McCann; Technical Supervisors, Arthur Siccardi, Pete Feller; Props, Jan Marasek, Arthur Hoaglund; Wardrobe, Nancy Schaefer, Mary Eno; Assistant to Producers, Leslie Butler; Assistant to Director, Jane E. Cooper; General Manager, Jose Vega, Robert Kamlot; Company Managers, Maria Anderson, Jane Robinson, Bruce Birkenhead; Stage Managers, Martin Herzer, Barbara-Mae Phillips, Lani Ball; Press, Bill Evans, Sandra Manley. Opened Sunday, March 27, 1983*

CAST

Eugene	Matthew Broderick [1]
Blanche	Joyce Van Patten [2]
Kate	Elizabeth Franz [3]
Laurie	Mandy Ingber [4]
Nora	Jodi Thelen [5]
Stanley	Zeljko Ivanek [6]
Jack	Peter Michael Goetz [7]

STANDBYS: Donna Haley/Dorothy Holland (Kate/Blanche), Robin Morse/Marissa Chibasi (Nora), Timothy Busfield/Roger Raines/Jon Cryer/Nicholas Strouse (Eugene), Timothy Busfield/J. Patrick Breen/Stanley Tucci (Stanley), Pamela Segall/Sarah Rose Kasowitz (Laurie), Stefan Gierasch/Robert Levine (Jack)

A comedy in two acts. The action takes place during September 1937 in the home of Jack and Kate Jerome in Brighton Beach, Brooklyn, NY.

*Still playing May 31, 1984. Selected by NY Drama Critics Circle as Best Play of the Season. Mr. Broderick received a "Tony" Award as Best Supporting Actor in a Play, and Mr. Saks received a "Tony" for Best Director of a Play.

[†] Succeeded by: 1. Doug McKeon, Fisher Stevens, Roger Raines, Jon Cryer, 2. Kathleen Widdoes, Anita Gillette, 3. Barbara Tarbuck, 4. Theresa Diane, Elizabeth Ward, Royana Black, 5. Marissa Chibas, 6. J. Patrick Breen, 7. Dick Latessa

J. Patrick Breen, Fisher Stevens Top Right: (seated) Royana Black, Kathleen Widdoes, J. Patrick Breen, Marilyn Chris, Fisher Stevens (front), (back) Marissa Chibas, Peter Michael Goetz

MY ONE AND ONLY

(ST. JAMES THEATRE) Music, George Gershwin; Lyrics, Ira Gershwin; Book, Peter Stone, Timothy S. Mayer; Staged and Choreographed by Thommie Walsh, Tommy Tune; Associate Choreographer, Baayork Lee; Scenery, Adrianne Lobe; Costumes, Rita Ryack; Associate Director, Phillip Oesterman; Musical/Vocal Direction, Jack Lee; Lighting, Marcia Madeira; Sound, Otts Munderloh; Musical Concept/Dance Arrangements, Wally Harper; Orchestrations, Michael Gibson; Dance Arrangements, Peter Larson; Casting, Hughes/Moss; Presented by Paramount Theatre Productions, Francine LeFrak, Kenneth-Mark Productions, in association with Jujamcyn Theatres, Tams-Witmark Music Library; Musical Consultant, Michael Feinstein; A King Street Production; Produced by Lewis Allen; Associate Producer, Jonathan Farkas; Technical Supervisor, Arthur Siccardi; Props, Paul Biega; Wardrobe, William Campbell; Production Assistant, Tom Santopietro; Wigs, Paul Huntley; Makeup, Anthony Clavet; Movie Sequence, Kenneth Leigh Hunter; General Management, Joseph P. Harris, Peter T. Kulok, Steven E. Goldstein; Stage Managers, Peter von Mayrhauser, Robert Kellogg, Betty Lynd; Press, Judy Jacksina, Glenna Freedman, Marcy Granata, Susan Chicoine, Mari H. Thompson, Marc Thibodeau, Kevin Boyle, Barbara MacNeish. Opened Sunday, May 1, 1983*

CAST

New Rhythm Boys	David Jackson, Ronald Dennis, Ken Leigh Rogers
Captain Billy Buck Chandler	Tommy Tune
Mickey	Denny Dillon
Prince Nicolai Erraclyovitch Tchatchavadze	Bruce McGill
Flounder	Nana Visitor †1
Sturgeon	Susan Hartley
Minnow	Stephanie Eley †2
Prawn	Jill Cook †3
Kipper	Niki Harris †4
Anchovie	Karen Tamburrelli †5
Edith Herbert	Twiggy
Rt. Rev. J. D. Montgomery	Roscoe Lee Browne
Reporter	Jill Cook
Mr. Magix	Charles "Honi" Coles
Policeman/Stage Doorman	Paul David Richards †6
Mrs. O'Malley	Ken Leigh Rogers
Conductor	Adrian Bailey
Achmed	Bruce McGill
Ritz Quartet	Casper Roos, Paul David Richards, †6 Carl Nicholas, Will Blankenship
Dancing Gentlemen	Adrian Bailey, Bar Dell Conner, Ronald Dennis, David Jackson, Alde Lewis, Jr., †7 Bernard Manners, Ken Leigh Rogers

STANDBYS AND UNDERSTUDIES: Ronald Young (Billy/Magix), Stephanie Eley/Susan Hartley (Edith), Judd Jones (Montgomery), Kerry Casserly/Jill Cook (Mickey), Walter Hook (Prince), Luther Fontaine (Magix), Jeff Calhoun (Billy), Swings: Patti D'Beck, Luther Fontaine, Walter Hook, Marilee Magnuson, Melvin Washington

MUSICAL NUMBERS: I Can't Be Bothered Now, Blah Blah Blah, Boy Wanted, Soon, High Hat, Sweet and Low-Down, Just Another Rumba, He loves and She Loves, "S Wonderful, Strike Up the Band, In the Swim, What Are We Here For, Nice Work If You Can Get It, My One and Only, Kickin' the Clouds Away, How Long Has This Been Goin' On?, Finale

A musical in 2 acts and 15 scenes. The action occurs during 1927.

*Still playing May 31, 1984. Winner of 1983 "Tony's" for Best Choreography, Best Actor and Best Supporting Actor in a Musical (Tommy Tune, Charles "Honi" Coles).

†Succeeded by 1. Jill Cook, 2. Niki Harris, 3. Stephanie Eley, 4. Sandra Menhart, 5. Kerry Casserly, 6. Adam Petroski, 7. Shaun Baker-Jones

Kenn Duncan, Schiarone Photos

Top Right: Tommy Tune, Twiggy, Below: Alde Lewis, Jr., Bernard Manners, Adrian Bailey, Bar Dell Conner, Ken Leigh Rogers, Ronald Dennis

Denny Dillon, Tommy Tune, Roscoe Lee Browne

OFF-BROADWAY PRODUCTIONS FROM PAST SEASONS THAT PLAYED THROUGH THIS SEASON

(SULLIVAN STREET PLAYHOUSE) Tuesday, May 3, 1960 and still playing May 31, 1984. Lore Noto presents the world's longest running musical: **THE FANTASTICKS** with Book and Lyrics by Tom Jones; Music, Harvey Schmidt; Suggested by Edmund Rostand's play "Les Romanesques"; Associate Producers, Sheldon Baron, Dorothy Olim, Jules Field, Robert Alan Gold; Original cast recording by MGM Records; Assistant Producer, Bill Mills; Production Assistant, John Krug; Stage Managers, Geoffrey Brown, James Cook, Jim Charles; Press, Bill Shuttleworth.

CAST

The Narrator .... Sal Provenza
The Girl .... Virginia Gregory
The Boy .... Howard Paul Lawrence
The Boy's Father .... Lore Noto
The Girl's Father .... Gordon Jones †1
The Old Actor .... Robert Molnar †2
The Man Who Dies/Indian .... Robert R. Oliver
The Mute .... Glenn Davish †3
At the piano .... Jeffrey Klotz †4
At the harp .... Winifred W. Starks
Understudies: Jim Charles (Narrator/Boy), Joan Wiest (Girl), William Tost (Boy's Father)

MUSICAL NUMBERS: Try to Remember, Much More, Metaphor, Never Say No, It Depends on What You Pay, Soon It's Gonna Rain, Rape Ballet, Happy Ending, This Plum Is Too Ripe, I Can See It, Plant a Radish, Round and Round, They Were You

A musical in two acts.

†Succeeded by: 1. William Tost, 2. Bryan Hull, 3. Jim Charles, 4. Jeffrey Saver

(back) William Tost, Sal Provenza, Jim Charles, Lore Noto, (front) Robert R. Oliver, Virginia Gregory, Howard Paul Lawrence, Bryan Hull Top Left: Howard Paul Lawrence, Virginia Gregory (*Martha Swope Photos*)

Jan Neuberger, Doug Voet
**Right: Jan Neuberger, Patrick Quinn,
Marilyn Pasekoff, Doug Voet**

(PALSSON'S) Opened Friday, January 15, 1982 and still playing May 31, 1984.
Playkill Productions (Sella Palsson, Executive Producer) presents:
FORBIDDEN BROADWAY with concept and Lyrics by Gerard Alessandrini;
Associate Producers, Peter Brash, Melissa Burdick; Director, Gerard Alessandrini;
Costumes, Chet Ferris; Photographer, Henry Grossman; Press, Becky Flora

CAST

Gerard Alessandrini
Bill Carmichael
Nora Mae Lyng
Fred Barton

Succeeded during the season by Chloe Webb, Jason Alexander, Jeff Etjen, Brad
Garside, Ann Leslie Morrison, Marilyn Pasekoff, Jan Neuberger, Larry Small,
Patrick Quinn, Doug Voet

A musical satire in two acts.

Henry Grossman Photos

**Marilyn Pasekoff, Patrick Quinn, Jan Neuberger,
Doug Voet (kneeling)**

55

Fyvush Finkel, Brad Moranz
Left Center: Audrey II Top: Jennifer Leigh
Warren, Leilani Jones, Sheila Kay Davis

(ORPHEUM THEATRE) Opened Tuesday, July 27, 1982 and still playing May 31, 1984.* WPA Theatre (Kyle Renick, Producing Director), David Geffen, Cameron Mackintosh, the Shubert Organization present:
LITTLE SHOP OF HORRORS with Book and Lyrics by Howard Ashman; Based on film by Roger Corman;

CAST

Chiffon	Leilani Jones
Crystal	Jennifer Leigh Warren
Ronnette	Sheila Kay Davis
Mushnik	Fyvush Finkel
Audrey	Marsha Skaggs
Seymour	Brad Moranz
Derelict	Anthony B. Asbury †
Orin/Bernstein/Snip/Luce	Robert Frisch
Audrey II	
Manipulation	Anthony B. Asbury †
Voice	Ron Taylor

STANDBYS: Suzzanne Douglas/Melodee Savage (Chiffon/Crystal/Ronnette), Michael Pace (Seymour/Orin/Bernstein/Snip/Luce/Audrey II Voice), Lynn Hippen/Francis Kane (Derelict/Audrey II Manipulation); Arn Weiner (Mushnik), Katherine Meloche (Audrey)
MUSICAL NUMBERS: Prologue, Skid Row, Da-Doo, Grow for Me, Don't It Go to Show Ya Never Know, Somewhere That's Green, Closed for Renovations, Dentist!, Mushnik & Son, Git It!, Now It's Just the Gas, Call Back in the Morning, Suddenly Seymour, Suppertime, The Meek Shall Inherit, Don't Feed the Plants.

A musical in two acts.

*Received 1983 citation from NY Drama Critics Circle as Best Musical.
†Succeeded by Lynn Hippen

Peter Cunningham Photos

Brad Moranz, Marsha Skaggs

(CHERRY LANE THEATRE) Opened Sunday, Oct. 17, 1982.* Harold Thau and Wayne Adams and Kenneth-John Productions, in association with Robert Courson, Jay J. Miller, Richard Sturgis present:

TRUE WEST by Sam Shepard; Director, Gary Sinise; Set, Kevin Rigdon, Deb Gohr; Lighting, Kevin Rigdon; Casting, McCorkle Sturtevant; General Management, Proscenium Services (Kevin W. Dowling); Company Manager, Suzanne VanderSaden, Patricia A. Butterfield; Assistant to Producers, Bruce Detrick; Props, Elliot Fox, Curtis Laseter, Robert K. Sherer; Wardrobe, Bruce Detrick; Hairstylist, Carlo Collazo; Stage Managers, Larry Bussard, Tom W. Picard; Press, Solters/Roskin/Friedman, Joshua Ellis, Cindy Valk.

CAST

Lee	John Malkovich [†1]
Austin	Gary Sinise [†2]
Saul Kimmer	Sam Schact [†3]
Mom	Margaret Thomson [†4]

Understudies: Clardy Malugen (Mom), Jere Burns (Men)

A drama in two acts. The action occurs at the present time in a house in a Southern California suburb.

[†]Succeeded by: 1. Bruce Lyons, James Belushi, Randy Quaid, Daniel Stern, Peder Melhuse, 2. Richmond Hoxie, Dan Butler, Gary Cole, Dennis Quaid, Tim Matheson, Erik Estrada, 3. Peder Melhuse, Bruce A. Jarchow, Francis Guinan, 4. Mary Copple, Sonja Lanzener
*Closed Aug. 4, 1984 after 762 performances and 10 previews. For original NY production, see THEATRE WORLD Vol. 37.

Martha Swope/Susan Cook Photos

Right: John Malkovich, Gary Sinise

Dennis Quaid, Randy Quaid
Above: Daniel Stern, Tim Matheson

James Belushi, Gary Cole

(CIRCLE REPERTORY THEATRE moved Wednesday, Nov. 30, 1983 to DOUGLAS FAIRBANKS THEATRE) Opened Wednesday, May 18, 1983 and still playing May 31, 1984. Circle Repertory Co. (Marshall W. Mason, Artistic Director) presents the Magic Theatre of San Francisco production of:
FOOL FOR LOVE by Sam Shepard; Director, Mr. Shepard; Set, Andy Stacklin; Costumes, Ardyss L. Golden; Lighting, Kurt Landisman; Sound, J. A. Deane; Company Manager, Lynn Landis: Associate Director, Julie Hebert; Production Manager, Kate Stewart, Alex Baker; Stage Managers, Suzanne Fry, Jody Boese, Red Reinglas; Press, Richard Frankel, Reva Cooper

CAST

May	Kathy Whitton Baker †1
Eddie	Ed Harris †2
Martin	Dennis Ludlow †3
Old Man	Will Marchetti †4

A drama performed without intermission. The action takes place at the present time in a motel room on the edge of the Mojave Desert.

†Succeeded by: 1. Ann Gentry, Moira McCanna Harris, 2. Will Patton, Bruce Willis, Aidan Quinn, 3. Stephen Mendillo, 4. John Nesci, Tom Aldredge, J. D. Swain, Richard Hamilton, John Seitz, Page Johnson

**Right: (front) Aidan Quinn, Moira McCanna Harris,
(back) Page Johnson, Stephen Mendillo**
(Gerry Goodstein Photos)

Will Patton, Moira McCanna Harris

David Andrews, Frances Fisher

58

OFF-BROADWAY PRODUCTIONS

(MERCER STREET THEATER) Thursday, June 2–26, 1983 (20 performances). The Facemakers in association with the Fanfare Theatre Ensemble present: **ENTER LAUGHING** by Joseph Stein; Adapted from the novel by Carl Reiner; Newly revised by the author; Director, Elisa Loti; Set, Robert Franklin; Costumes, Jennie Cleaver; Lighting, Mitch Goldstein; Technical Director, Michael Golden; Producers, Owen Thompson, David H. Hamilton; Press, Milly Schoenbaum, David LeShay. CAST: Paul Michael Cassidy, Frank Costanza, Gina Gold, David H. Hamilton, Elisa Loti, Bill MacNulty, Marianne McIsaac, Paul Rosson, Joan Shepard, Oscar Stokes, Michael P. Stultz, Owen Thompson, Stuart Zagnit.

(SARGENT THEATRE) Friday, June 3–18, 1983 (12 performances) StageArts Theater Company (Neil Robinson, Ruth Ann Norris, Artistic Directors) present: **THIRTEEN** by Lynda Myles; Director, Nell Robinson; Sets, Dan Conway; Costumes, Mary L. Hayes; Lighting, Bob Bessoir; Technical Director, Dickson Lane; Stage Managers, Richard Haunstein, Dennis Cameron; Press, Shirley Herz, Sam Rudy, Peter Cromarty. CAST: Joan Shangold (Jo), Roger DeKoven (Marcus), Mimi Turque (Honey), Elaine Princi (Eleanor), Anne O'Sullivan (Patsy), Peter Marklin (Norman). A play in 2 acts and 13 scenes. The action takes place in the early 1950's.

(PERRY STREET THEATRE) Friday, June 3–26, 1983 (20 performances) PACT (Public Arena for Communicative Theatre) presents: **MURDER WITHOUT CRIME** by J. Lee Thompson; Director, Geoffrey Sadwith; Costumes, Catherine Greitzer; Lighting, John Conway; Setting, Robert Kracik; Graphics, Althea Bodenheim; Music, Alva Nelson; Sound Effects, Paul Garrity; Stage Managers, Steven Miller, Barbara Arbeit; Executive Producer, Dean Silvers; Producers, Gregory T. Brennan, Peter J. Brennan; Associate Producer, Peter Accetta; Press, Burnham-Callaghan, Lynda C. Kinney. CAST: Doug Stevenson (Stephen), Lisa Loring (Grena), Carla Borelli (Mildred), Linda Gates (Jan). A drama in 3 acts and 5 scenes. The action takes place at the present time in Stephen's apartment in Mildred's Brownstone in Greenwich Village, NYC.

(ATA/CHERNUCHIN THEATRE) Saturday, June 4–18, 1983 (13 performances). Polaris Theatrical Productions and Jack O. Scher present: **BIRD OF PARADISE** conceived by Judy Geller Warner, Susan Nier; Book, Susan Nier; Director, George Margo; Music and Lyrics, Judy Geller Warner, Susan Nier; Choreography, Eddie Wright; Musical Direction/Orchestrations/Vocal & Dance Arrangements, Richard Honoroff; Costumes, Randall Ouzts; Lighting, Benay D. Forrest; Stage Manager, Allan Sobek. CAST: Jeff Keller, Bill Kuchon, Lou Miranda, Roberta Powell, Victoria Rowett, Karl Barbee, Jeff Bates, Alan Onickel, Mercedes Perez, Deborah Smith.

(INNER CIRCLE) Sunday, June 5–26, 1983 (6 performances) **THIS WEEK IN THE SUBURBS** with music by Douglas Cohen; Lyrics, Susan DiLallo; Musical Director, David Gaines; Vocal Arrangements, Stephen Flaherty; Choreographer, Jenny Seham. CAST: Terri Beringer, Denise Moses, Ron Orbach, Norman Kline. Performed without intermission.
MUSICAL NUMBERS: Welcome to the Neighborhood, Suburban Calendar, Car Pool Mother of the Year, Tennis, Chalktalk, I'm the Best Volunteer, 300 Meter, Newspaper Boy, Stacy Ann, I Met Him at the Mall, Used, Waiting for the 5:03, Jogging, Community Theatre, For the Children, Real Estate, The Day That We Say I Don't, It's Better in the Burbs.

(ACTORS PLAYHOUSE) Wednesday, June 8–12, 1983 (6 performances and 8 previews). Mark Beigelman, Susan Albert Loewenberg, and L.A. Theatre Works present: **GREEK** by Steven Berkoff; Directed by Mr. Berkoff; Set/Lighting, Gerry Hariton, Vicki Baral; Costumes, Peter Mitchell; General Manager, Albert Poland; Company Manager, Mary C. Miller; Stage Managers, Duane Mazey, John Francis Harries; Presented in association with Michel Kleinman Productions and Lorin Theatrical Productions; Press, Jeffrey Richards, Robert Ganshaw, C. George Willard, Ben Morse, Richard Humleker, Mary Ann Rubino. CAST: Georgia Brown (Mum/Waitress/Sphinx), Ken Danziger (Dad/Manager), Mary Denham (Doreen/Waitress/Wife), John Francis Harries (Eddie/Fortune Teller). The action takes place at the present time in England.

Top Right: Owen Thompson, David H. Hamilton, Elisa Loti in "Enter Laughing" *(Feldman-Shevett Photo)*

(ATA OUTDOOR THEATRE) Thursday, June 9–25, 1983 (12 performances and 4 previews). American Theatre of Actors (James Jennings, Artistic Director) presents: **RICHARD II** by William Shakespeare; Director, James Jennings; Set/Lighting, Joe Ray; Costumes, Melanie Samuels; Stage Manager, Diane Greenberg; Press, David Lipsky. CAST: James Judy, Herman Petras, Brian Muehl, Kevin Anderson, Robert Hefley, Virginia Robinson, Everett MacLerman, Todd Jamison, Vincent Nieman, Jonathan Ginsberg, Jeffrey West, David Carlyou, Christopher Horton, Ian Rose, Jonathan Croy, Charles Scotland, Alan Levine, Jack Fahey, Gregg Houston, Carol Ann Ryan, Michael Jones, Maureen McGuinness, Joan Mann, Lawrence Paone, Bruce Barton, Anthony Picciano, Daniel Crozier, Steve Ensore.

(HARTLEY HOUSE THEATRE) Thursday, June 9–25, 1983 (12 performances). Playwrights Preview Productions presents: **NEW ENGLAND ECLECTIC** 3 one-act plays by New England playwrights; Press, Susan Bloch and Company. "The Open Meeting" by A. R. Gurney; Director, Paul Dervis; CAST: Peter Waldren, Jayne Chamberlin, Nick Salamone. "Incoming" by Christopher S. Romano; Director, Paul Dervis; CAST: Mary Miller, Julia Kelly. "An Afternoon in the Park" by Sheryl North; Director, Frances Hill; CAST: Barbara Skor, Douglas Stender.

(RIVERWEST) Thursday, June 9–26, 1983 (12 performances) Riverwest Theatre (Nat Habib, June Summers, Producers) presents: **DO NOT DISTURB** an evening of one-act plays; Technical Director, Christopher Cole; Props, Tanya Harris; Rossana D'Orazio; Sets, Christopher Cole; Lighting, Matt Ehlert; Costumes, Sheila Berman; Sound, Peter McKinney; Stage Managers, Jonathan Shulman, Bronwyn O'Shaughnessy, Amy Coombs; Press, June Summers. CAST: "Shapes of Midnight" by Saul Zachary; Director, Linda Nerine; with Larry Goodsight (Morty), Jeffrey Holt Gardner (Harold), Bruce Vernon Bradley (Wallace), Catherine Carlen (Mrs. Friedlander), The action takes place in 1978 in the lobby of a closed hotel in Atlantic City at the end of the season. "Traveler's Rest" by William Wise; Director, Jeff Martin; with Natalie Ross (Joanne Peterson), Dan Lounsbery (Andy Milligan). The action takes place in October of last year in a motel room in Pennsylvania.

Georgia Brown, John Frances Harries, Mary Denham, Ken Danziger in "Greek" *(Peter Cunningham Photo)*

59

(ENTERMEDIA THEATRE) Thursday, June 9, 1983–January 8, 1984 (245 performances and 10 previews). Richard Seader, Maurice Levine, Sonny Fox, Joanne Cummings, Arleen Kane, Anthony Kane, Sally Sears present:
TAKING MY TURN with Music by Gary William Friedman; Lyrics, Will Holt; Based on writings by people in their prime; Adapted and Directed by Robert H. Livingston; Musical Staging, Douglas Norwick; Casting, Hughes/Moss; Scenery, Clarke Dunham; Lighting, David F. Segal; Costumes, Judith Dolan; Arrangements/Orchestrations, Gary William Friedman; Musical Direction, Barry Levitt; General Management, Sylrich Management; Stage Managers, Bethe Ward, Jane Robertson; Wardrobe, Linda C. Schultz; Dance Supervisor, Jane Robertson; Press, Jeffrey Richards, Robert Ganshaw, C. George Willard, Eileen McMahon. CAST: Mace Barrett (Eric), Marni Nixon (Edna), Victor Griffin (John), Cissy Houston (Helen), Tiger Haynes (Charles), Margaret Whiting (Dorothy), Ted Thurston (Benjamin), Sheila Smith (Janet), Understudies: Irving Barnes (Charles), Bob Carroll/Edward Penn (Eric/John/Benjamin), Sis Clark (Edna/Helen/Dorothy/Janet). A musical in two acts. The action takes place during the course of one year . . . this year.
MUSICAL NUMBERS: This Is My Song, Somebody Else, Fine for the Shape I'm In, Janet Get Up, Two of Me, I Like It, I Never Made Money from Music, Vivaldi, Do You Remember, In April, Pick More Daisies, Taking Our Turn, Sweet Longings, I Am Not Old, The Kite, Good Luck to You, In the House, It Still Isn't Over, This Is My Song

(TOMI TERRACE THEATRE) Monday, June 13–25, 1983 (12 performances and 4 previews). Mark deSolla Price and John Van Ness Philip present:
TALLULAH based on the life of actress Tallulah Bankhead; Lyrics, Mae Richard; Music, Arthur Siegel; Book, Tony Lang; Director/Choreographer, David Holdgreiwe; Assistant Choreographer, Alan Coats; Sets, Roger Mooney; Costumes, Neil Bieff; Lighting, Norman Coates; Hairstylist/Makeup, Jim Nelson; Music Director/Arranger, Bruce Coyle; Assistant Music Director, Jim Rice; General Management, Richard Horner Assocs.; General Manager, Leonard Soloway; Company Manager, Brian Dunbar; Casting, Liz Shafer; Stage Managers, Mark Baltazar, Tracy A. Crum; Press, FLT/Francine Trevens, Penny Landau. CAST: Helen Gallagher (Tallulah), Joel Craig (John Barrymore/John Emery), Robert Dale Martin (Will Bankhead), Tom Hafner, Eric Johnson, Richard Larson, Patrick Parker, Rick Porter, Fran Barnes (understudy for Tallulah)
MUSICAL NUMBERS: Darling, Tallulah, When I Do a Dance for You, Down Home, I've Got to Try Everything Once, You're You, I Can See Him Clearly, Tallulahbaloo, The Party Is Where I Am, Stay Awhile, It's a Hit, Tango, Love Is on Its Knees, Don't Ever Book a Trip on the IRT, You Need a Lift!, Finale

(ACTORS OUTLET) Saturday, June 11–26, 1983 (17 performances). Eccentric Circles Theatre (Janet Bruders, Barbara Bunch, Rosemary Hopkins, Paula Kay Pierce, Producing Directors) presents:
BURNSCAPE by Jo Coudert; Director, Paula Kay Pierce; Production Manager, Gary Miller; Associate Producer, Constance Carey; Set, Thomas Stoner; Lights, Ed Wernick; Costumes, Maureeen Frey; Props, Lenore Slade; Stage Manager, Rome Neal; Press, Patt Dale, Jim Baldissare. CAST: Jeffrey Bingham (Russell), J. J. Cole (Ellis), Lewis Cole (Various Male Clients), Allen Davison (Lou), Brenda Denmark (Beatie), David H. Kieserman (Sidney), Karen Lynne-Smith (Young Woman/Pearl McKay), Mercy Monet (Mrs. Rojas/Old Lady), Lex Monson (Clarence), Rome Neal (Crowd), Amy Jo Phillips (Blossom), L. V. Ross (Newscaster), Hershey Snyder (Dr. Horowitz), Kim Weston-Moran (Erica). A play in two acts.

(HAROLD CLURMAN THEATRE) Wednesday, June 15, 1983–April 15, 1984 (344 performances). The Harold Clurman Theatre (Jack Garfein, Artistic Director) and Lucille Lortel present:
SAMUEL BECKETT PLAYS: "Ohio Impromptu," "Catastrophe," "What Where"; Director, Alan Schneider; Settings/Lighting, Marc D. Malamud; Costumes, Carla Kramer; General Management, Judy Baldwin; Company Manager, Rita Tiplitz; Assistant Director, Valerie Lambroso; Press, Joe Wolhandler; Stage Managers, Charles Kindl, Daniel Wirth. CAST: "Ohio Impromptu" with David Warrilow succeeded by Alvin Epstein and Daniel Wirth (Reader), Rand Mitchell (Listener); "Catastrophe" with Margaret Reed succeeded by Leigh Taylor-Young (His Assistant), Donald Davis succeeded by Kevin O'Connor (The Director), Rand Mitchell (Luke), David Warrilow succeeded by Alvin Epstein and Daniel Wirth (Protagonist); "What Where" with Donald Davis succeeded by Kevin O'Connor (Bam), David Warrilow succeeded by Alvin Epstein and Daniel Wirth (Bom), Rand Mitchell (Bim), Daniel Wirth (Bem), Donald Davis (Voice of Bam)

(ATA/CHERNUCHIN THEATRE) Wednesday, June 22,–July 16, 1983 (16 performances). American Theatre of Actors presents:
WITHIN THE YEAR by Sheila Walsh; Director, Walter Scholz; Set, Christopher Scholz; Producer, James Jennings; Sound, George Jacobs; Stage Managers, D. C. Rosenberg, Meryl Jacobs, Rhonda Beaudette; Press, David Lipsky. CAST: Catherine Burns (Jessie), Rocky Parker (Edna), David Krasner (Ted), Leo Ferstenberg (Murray), Lee Billington (Judy). A play in three acts. The action takes place in an apartment in NYC's East 60's, at the present time and covers a year from November to November.

Top Right: Tiger Haynes, Margaret Whiting,
Marni Nixon, Cissy Houston, Mace Barrett
Below: Victor Griffin, Sheila Smith,
Ted Thurston in "Taking My Turn"

Tom Hafner, Patrick Parker, Rick Porter, Eric Johnson,
Helen Gallagher in "Tallulah"
(Feldman/Shevett Photo)

(432 THEATRE ROW) Thursday, July 7–31, 1983 (20 performances). Champ Productions presents:
OLD FRIENDS AND ROOMMATES by W. R. Miller; Director, Mr. Miller; Set, Drew Miller; Lighting, Steven E. Shelley; Stage Manager, Gay Isaacs; Company Manager, Charmaine Henninger. CAST: Kay L. Colburn (Kristin), Susanna Frazer (Jill), Lawrence Hubbell (Charlie), William Ernest Peterson (Bill). A comedy in 2 acts and 10 scenes. The action takes place at the present time in a New York apartment.

(THEATRE STUDIO) Friday, July 8–26, 1983 (17 performances). The Theatre Studio presents:
THE GREAT CITY in three short plays by James Purdy; Adapted by John Uecker; Director, Ann Raychel; Producers, Ann Raychel, John Uecker, Gary C. Walter; Design, Doug Ball, Doris Mezler-Andelberg; Lighting, David Higham; Technical Director, John A. Holt; Stage Manager, Karen Lee; Press, Gary Murphy. CAST: "Scrap of Paper" with Lucille Patton (Mrs. Bankers), Saundra McPherson (Naomi Green); "Don't Call Me by My Right Name" with Michael Beckett (Frank Klein), Virginia Cotts (Lois Klein), Herb Farnham (Older Man), Joey Werzinger (Younger Man); "What Is It, Zach?" with Micahel Santoro (Pete), John Uecker (Zach).

(JOYCE THEATER) Sunday, July 10, 1983 (1 performance and 42 previews). Stuart Ostrow presents:
AMERICAN PASSION with Book by Fred Burch; Music, Willie Fong Young; Lyrics, Willie Fong Young, Fred Burch; Direction/Choreography, Patricia Birch; Costumes, William Ivey Long; Lighting, Richard Winkler; Sound, Otts Munderloh; Musical Director/Orchestrations/Arrangements, Timothy Graphenreed; Casting, Johnson-Liff; General Management, Joseph P. Harris Associates; Technical Supervisor, Jeremiah Harris; Wardrobe, Michael Davies; Assistant Director/Choreographer, Greg Rosatti; Hairstylist, Angela Gari; Stage Managers, Perry Cline, Helena Andreyko; Press, John Springer, Meg Gordean, Gary Springer. CAST: Laura Dean (Patty), Robert Downey (Jackson), Todd Graff (Johnny), Taryn Grimes (Mary), Joie Gall (Understudy), Brian Kaman (Understudy), Don Kehr (Nick), Liza Lauber (Kathy), Sam Slovick (Joel), Christal Wood (Joy), Rosko (Sam).
MUSICAL NUMBERS: American Passion, Romance Is the Way, There Ain't No Virgins in Queens, The Gospel according to Rock, Limo to the Plaza, Trashin & Tourin', Loud Enough, Concert Tonight, Balcony of the Faithful, Shirts, In the Hallway, We'll Sleep with the Radio On, Hi, I Light a Light. The action takes place at the present time in New York City, and is performed without intermission.

(DOUGLAS FAIRBANKS THEATRE) Tuesday, July 12,–Aug. 14, 1983 (40 performances). The Acting Company (John Houseman, Producing Artistic Director; Margot Harley, Executive Producer; Artistic Directors, Michael Kahn, Alan Schneider) presents its alumni in:
THE CRADLE WILL ROCK by Marc Blitzstein; Director, John Houseman; Producer, Margot Harley; Sets, Mark Fitzgibbons; Lighting, Dennis Parichy; Assistant Director, Christopher Markle; Costumes, Judith Dolan; Musical Director, Michael Barrett; Consultant on Musical Staging, Denny Shearer; Stage Managers, Don Judge, Kathleen B. Boyette; Technical Director, J. Austin; Press, Fred Nathan, Anne Abrams, Eileen McMahon, Leo Stern, Bert Fink. CAST: David Anglin (Clerk/Pianist), Brooks Baldwin (Yasha), Lisa Banes (Moll), Casey Biggs (Cop/Gus), Daniel Corcoran (Steve/Prof. Scoot/Reporter), Leslie Geraci (Sister Mister/Reporter), James Harper (Rev. Salvation/Prof. Trixie), Laura Hicks (Sadie/Reporter), Randle Mell (Dauber/Larry), Brian Reddy (Prof. Mamie/Harry Druggist), Tom Robbins (Gent/Editor Daily), Mary Lou Rosato (Mrs. Mister), David Schramm (Mr. Mister), Charles Shaw-Robinson (Dr. Specialist/Bugs), Henry Stram (Dick/Junior Mister), Paul Walker (Pres. Prexy), Michele-Denise Woods (Ella Hammer), John Houseman succeeded by Randle Mell (Narrator). A musical in 2 acts and 10 scenes. The action takes place in Steeltown, U.S.A., on the night of a union drive.

(ACTORS PLAYHOUSE) Tuesday, July 12,–Sept. 4, 1983 (64 performances) and returned Tuesday, Dec. 27, 1983–Jan. 22, 1984 (28 performances). Ross & Timm Productions and Michael R. Hirtz present:
AN EVENING WITH QUENTIN CRISP (The Naked Civil Servant). Setting, Kenneth Cook; Lighting/Stage Manager, Pamela C. Ross; Press, Mark Goldstaub, Patt Dale, Daniel Kellachan. During the first part of the evening, Mr. Crisp explains his secrets for surviving, and in the second half he answers questions from the audience.

(NYC PARKS) Friday, July 15,–Aug. 7, 1983 (12 performances). Fronte-Page Productions (Albert Malafronte, Elizabeth Page, Artistic Directors) presents:
JULIUS CAESAR by William Shakespeare; Director, Elizabeth Page. CAST: Anthony Apolinario, Peter Bogyo, Richard Thomas Hawk, Mark Hirschfield, David Hughes, Chuck Kates, Bruce Kronenberg, Robert Laconi, Mary Lum, Albert Malafronte, Albert Neal, Katherine Neville, David Pendleton, Woody Regan, Don R. Richardson, JD Rosenbaum, Robert Sopher, Xenophon Theophall, Craig Allan Wichman, Ron Wier

Top Right: Cast of "American Passion"
(Peter Cunningham Photo)
Below: Mary Lou Rosato, James Harper
in "The Cradle Will Rock"
(Martha Swope Photo)

Quentin Crisp

(THE BALLROOM) Wednesday, July 27,–Aug. 20, 1983 (16 performances) The Ballroom presents:
AN EVENING OF SHOLOM ALEICHEM stories by the Yiddish writer; Translated by Joseph Singer; Director, Richard Maltby, Jr.; Costumes, Pegi Goodman; Set, Ron Placzek; Lighting, Mimi Sherrin. CAST: Murray Horwitz (Sholom Aleichem)

(PERRY STREET THEATRE) Thursday, Aug. 4–20, 1983 (9 performances and 7 previews). Provincetown Theater Ensemble in Exile presents:
DOGS with Book by James Stewart Bennett and Charles G. Horne; Music and Lyrics, James Stewart Bennett; Director, Charles Horne; Set, Jack Kelly; Lighting, Edward RF Matthews; General Manager, Richard Bennett; Stage Managers, Glen Cruz Mariano, Mark Menard; Costume Coordinator, Peyton Smith; Press, Howard Atlee. CAST: Valerie Santuccio (Dawn), Lanny Green (Human), Terry Blaine (Sally), Caroline Cox (Judi), Mark Enis (Butchy), Kathryn Hunter (Poco), Linda Marie Larson (Duney), Neil Lyons (Rex), Nicholas Searcy (Boomie), David Vaughn (Sammy). A musical in 2 acts and 5 scenes.
MUSICAL NUMBERS: Welcome to Googies, Tricks, Humpin' Hips, Dawn's Employment History, Keep It Cook, Tough Dogs/Chic Dogs, Jail Song, Somehow I Must Find a Way, I Hate Dogs, Masters Song, I'm the Master of the City, Dance at the Ritz, Awkward Walse, I Got a Plan, Bureau of Mutual Affairs, Don't Take Away All My Friends, Finale.

(ACTORS OUTLET) Thrusday, Aug. 4–21, 1983 (14 performances). Family Institute, Glenn Deigan, Al D'Andrea, Patricia Wing Tobias present:
FREUD a one-man play by Harvey White; Adapted from the letters and writings of Sigmund Freud; Director, Al D'Andrea; Scenery, Eva Brenner; Costumes, Jennifer Ruscoe; Lighting, David Arrow; Sound, Bob Goldberg; Voices, David Landau; Stage Manager, Regina Paleski; Press, Krista Altok. CAST: Mark Zeller (Sigmund Freud)

(T.O.M.I. TERRACE THEATRE) Thursday, Aug. 11–28, 1983 (12 performances). F/H Productions in association with the T.O.M.I. Theatre presents:
LIFE BENEATH THE ROSES by Gene Franklin Smith; Director, Richard Beck-Meyer; Design, Andrew Rubenoff; Costumes, Tamara Sachs; Stage Managers, Bert Michaels, Bill Watkins. CAST: Karen Braga (Jennie), James Winston Elwell (Andrew Steward), Michael Golding (Nick), Will Jeffries (Tony), Sarah Hall (Laura), Susan G. Stone (Elizabeth Steward). A play in three acts. The action takes place in late October in the Cape Cod home of Tony and Laura Cooper of Chatham, MA.

(VINEYARD THEATRE) Tuesday, Aug. 16,–Sept. 11, 1983 (24 performances). Waldron Productions presents:
AND THINGS THAT GO BUMP IN THE NIGHT by Terrence McNally; Director, Libby Lyman; Set/Lighting, Jefferson Sage; Sound/Slides, Catherine Rush; Costumes, Linda Melloy; Stage Manager, Pamela Edington; Props, Lynn Homa; Press, Rosanna Gamson. CAST: Alison Brunell (Ruby), Phillip Cimino (Clarence), Joseph Jamrog (Fa), John Mawson (Grandfa), Scott Renderer (Sigfrid), Catherine Rush (Lakme). A play in three acts.

(ATA/SARGENT THEATRE) Wednesday, Aug. 17,–Sept. 3, 1983 (12 performances). American Theatre of Actors presents:
WHO'S THERE? by Melba LaRose; Directed by Ms. LaRose; Set, David McNitt; Lighting, David Bean, Jane Sanders; Sound, Holly DeKam; Technical Director, David Bean; Costumes, Linda Vigdor; Original Music, Clark Gardner; Props, Fran Akawie, Lorene Farnsworth; Press, Lee Ann Thomas. CAST: Clark Gardner (Harold Wayne), Jennifer Williams (Natasha), Larry Swansen (Cramden), Herman Petras (Winthrop R. Renfield), Ruby Payne (Abigail), Marion Hunter (Sandra), Dana Delcastro (Dora). A play in two acts. The action takes place at the present time in Devonshire, England.

(QUAIGH THEATRE) Wednesday, Aug. 17,–Sept. 11, 1983 (32 performances) Dorothy Chansky with the Bridge Theatre Production Co. presents:
THE BROOKLYN BRIDGE with Music by Scott Maclarty; Book and Lyrics, Dorothy Chansky; Director, Marjorie Melnick; Musical Director, Harrison Fisher; Sets, Terry Bennett; Lights, Leslie Spohn; Costumes, Karen Gerson; Choreography, Missy Whitchurch; Art Direcor, Cheryl Gross; General Management, Maria DiDia, Jim Fiore; Props, Cheryl Gross, Paul Naish; Stage Managers, Steven Shaw, John McNamara; Press, Patt Dale, James Baldassare. CAST: Bijou Clinger (Emily), Anne Gartlan (Mrs. O'Malley), David Higlen (Man in the street), Nick Jolley (Kingsley), Paul Merrill (Murphy), Jack Sevier (John Roebling), John Leslie Wolfe (Washington Roebling). A musical in 2 acts and 11 scenes with a prologue and epilogue. The action takes place from 1865 to 1983.
MUSICAL NUMBERS: Brooklyn, Love Means, Can I Do It All, Bridge to the Future, Cash Politics, The Roebling Plan, Keep Me Out of the Caisson, When You're the Only One, Ain't No Women There, Every Day for Four Years, The Man in the Window, All That I Know, Finale.

Susan Dow, John Scherer, James Gedge, Karyn Quackenbush,
Tom Hafner, Tudi Roche, Bob Walton,
Dennis Bailey in "Preppies" *(Peter Cunningham Photo)*

(PROMENADE THEATRE) Thursday, Aug. 18,–Oct. 2, 1983 (52 performances and 9 previews). Anthony Fingleton and Carlos Davis present:
PREPPIES with Book by David Taylor, Carlos Davis; Music and Lyrics, Gary Portnoy, Judy Hart Angelo; Direction and Choreography, Tony Tanner; Sets, David Jenkins; Costumes, Patricia McGourty; Lighting, Richard Winkler; Sound, Tom Gould; Musical Direction/Vocal Arrangements, Jeff Lodin; Dance Music/Orchestrations, Peter Larson; Associate Producer, Valerie Gordon; General Management, Dorothy Olim; Company Manager, George Elmer; Wardrobe, Cathay Brackman; Casting, Lynn Kressel; Stage Managers, Melissa Davis, Marc Schlackman; Press, Jeffrey Richards, C. George Willard, Robert Ganshaw, Ben Morse, Richard Humleker, Mary Ann Rubino, Naomi Grabel. CAST: Dennis Bailey (Bogsy), Kathleen Rowe McAllen (Muffy), Bob Walton (Cotty), Beth Fowler (Marie), Michael Ingram (Joe), David Sabin (Endicott/Authority Figure), Susan Dow (Lallie), James H. Gedge (Skipper/Atwater), Tom Hafner (Jinks/Lawyer), Karyn Quackenbush (Steffie), Tudi Roche (Bitsy/Mrs. Atwater), John Scherer (Bookie) Tia Riebling (Dance Captain/Understudy). A musical in 2 acts and 19 scenes.
MUSICAL NUMBERS: People Like Us, The Chance of a Lifetime, One Step Away, Summertime, Fairy Tales, The Parents Farewell, Bells, Moving On, Our Night, We've Got Each Other, Gonna Run, No Big Deal, Worlds Apart, Bring on the Loot, Finale.

(T.O.M.I.) Friday, Aug. 26,–Sept. 3, 1983 (12 performances). Michael Gill and Robert Attermann present:
MIGHTY FINE MUSIC! written and directed by Brent Wagner; Music, Burton Lane; Lyrics, Harold Adamson, Dorothy Fields, Ralph Freed, Ira Gershwin, E. Y. Harburg, Alan Jay Lerner, Frank Loesser, Ted Koehler, Edward Pola; Choreography/Musical Staging, Linda Sabo; Music Direction/Arrangements/Keyboard, Ted Kociolek; Set/Lighting, Fritz Szabo; Costumes, Julie Schwolow; Assistant Choreographer, Kevin Halpin; Stage Manager/Assistant Director, Craig Butler; Press, Fred Hoot, David Mayhew, Chris Kimble. CAST: Greg Carter, Peter DePietro, Leslie Klein, David Lowenstein, Lisa Merrill McCord, Jane Michener, Suzanne Morey, Jennifer S. Myers, Laura Rockefeller, Paul P. Smith, Michael S. Stanchak, Timothy Thayer, Douglas Tompos. A revue of the songs of Burton Lane performed in 2 acts and 8 scenes.

Burton Lane (c) with "Mighty Fine Music"
cast: Jane Michener, Suzanne Morey,
Michael S. Stanchak, Douglas Tompos,
Leslie Klein *(Ken Howard Photo)*

(RIVERWEST THEATRE) Monday, Aug. 29,–Oct. 16, 1983 (48 performances; re-opened Thursday, May 10, 1984 at the Ballroom, and still playing May 31, 1984). CHS Productions and Greentrack Entertainment in association with Riverwest Management Co. present:
NITE CLUB CONFIDENTIAL by Dennis Deal; Directed and Staged by Dennis Deal; New Music/Lyrics, Dennis Deal, Albert Evans; Music Supervision, Albert Evans; Created by Dennis Deal with Albert Evans and Jamie Rocco; Costumes, Stephen Rotondaro; Lighting, Richard Latta; Technical Director, Christopher Cole; Sound, Michael Verbil; Stage Managers, Bronwyn O'Shaughnessy, Jeffrey Holt Gardner; Press, FLT/Francine L. Trevens, Penny Landay, David Lotz. CAST: Fay DeWitt (Kay Goodman), Stephen Berger (Buck Holden), Denise Nolin (Dorothy Flynn), Tom Spiroff (Sal), Doug Schneider succeeded by Steve Gideon (Mitch Dupre). A musical in two acts. The action takes place in various nightclubs during the Eisenhower era. Original Songs: Nite Club Confidential, Put the Blame on Mamie, The Canarsie Diner, Crazy New Words, Club au Revoir, Dressed to Kill, Nite Club Heaven

(TOP OF THE GATE) Wednesday, Sept. 14–25, 1983 (15 performances and 14 previews). Christopher Hart, Mike Houlihan, Eileen McMahon present:
BASEMENT TAPES by Erik Brogger; Director, Robert Engels; Set, Mark Haack; Costumes, Kristina Watson; Lighting, Bonnie Ann Brown; General Management, Mike Houlihan; Stage Manager/Sound, Kevin Mangan; Press, Patt Dale, Jim Baldassare. CAST: David Wohl (G. Gordon Liddy), Bill Schoppert (Gerald R. Ford), Michael Laskin (Richard M. Nixon). A comedy in two acts. The action takes place at the present time in Ferald Ford's basement recreation room in Palm Springs, CA.

(ACTORS OUTLET/CENTER STAGE II) Thursday, Sept. 8–18, 1983 (10 performances). Lone Wolfe Productons presents:
TWELFTH NIGHT by William Shakespeare; Director, Stephen A. Brown; Design, Vicki Romaine; Music, Donald L. Foster; Lighting, Maureen Fenwick; Associate Director, Marc Weinblatt; Assistant Director, Ross MacKenzie; Stage Manager, David D. Bauer; Press, Carol Fineman. CAST: Bernadette Cancelliere (Olivia), William Cannon (Feste), Pete Filiaci (Priest), William Gruneberg (Gentleman), Bruce Hamilton (Orsino), Benjamin Hart (Fabian), Nicholas Haylett (Sea Captain), Cynthia Hopkins (Maria), Bill Jacob (Gentleman), Wyatt James (Antonio), Robert Anthony Kelly (Sir Toby Belch), Joan Lader (Viola), Raymond Laudo (Gentleman), Ross MacKenzie (Sir Andrew Aguecheek), Michael Perez (Malvolio), John W. Wible (Sebastian). Performed in two acts.

(LA MAMA ANNEX) Sunday, Sept. 11,–Oct. 2, 1983 (25 performances). La Mama E.T.C. presents:
UNCLE VANYA by Anton Chekhov; New English version by Jean-Claude van Itallie; Director, Andrei Serban; Set/Costumes, Santo Loquasto; Lighting, Jennifer Tipton; Stage Managers, Richard Jakiel, Virlana Tkacz; Wardrobe, Mary Ann Monforton; Press, Bruce Cohen. CAST: F. Murray Abraham (Astrov), James Cahill (Serebryakov), Joseph Chaikin (Vanya), Shami Chaikin (Nanny), Frances Conroy (Sonya), Mohammed Ghaffari (Tyelyegin), Beatrice Manley-Blau (Mariya), Diane Venora (Yelyena). Scenes from a country life in four acts and performed without an intermission.

(LA MAMA E.T.C.) Wednesday, Sept. 7,–Oct. 2, 1983 (20 performances). La Mama in association with The Shaliko Co. presents:
THE ARBOR by Andrea Dunbar; Director, Leonardo Shapiro; Set, Bil Mikulewicz; Lighting, Arden Fingerhut; Costumes, Sally Lesser; Associate Producer, Christopher McCann; Stage Managers, Susanne Jul, Veronica Worth; Press, Bruce Cohen. CAST: Helen Nicholas (Girl), Christian Baskous (Boy/Steven/Chris/Chris' Dad/Policeman), Catherine Tambini (Sister/Neighbor/Nun/Karen/Yousaf's Sister), Peter Rogan (Father/Policeman/Paddy/Peter/Foreman), Leslie Lyles (Mother/Mrs. Rennish/Neighborhood/Elsie/Cath), Elizabeth Perkins (Ann Green/Neighbor/Nurse/Maureen), Paul Walker (Billy/Irishman/Sam), Steven Marcus (Fred/Policeman/David), Gary Easterling (Policeman/Conductor/Yousaf). A drama in two acts. The action takes place between April and November of 1977, and April and November of 1979 in an under-privileged neighborhood outside London, England.

(ASTOR PLACE THEATRE) Tuesday, Sept. 13–25, 1983 (15 performances and 17 previews). Dasha Epstein presents:
A WEEKEND NEAR MADISON by Kathleen Tolan; Dirctor, Emily Mann; Set, Thomas Lynch; Costumes, Karen Gerson; Lighting, Craig Miller; Sound, Tom Gould; General Management, Dorothy Olim, George Elmer; Company Manager, David Musselman; Wardrobe, Ginger Blake; Stage Managers, Neal Ann Stephens, Cathy B. Blaser; Press, Milly Schoenbaum, Kevin Patterson, Solters/Roskin/Friedman. CAST: Randle Mell (Jim), Robin Groves (Doe), Bill Mesnik (David), Mary McDonnell (Nessa), Holly Hunter (Samantha). A drama in 2 acts and 3 scenes. The action takes place in Wisconsin in the early autumn.

Stephen Berger, Tom Spiroff, Doug Schneider, Denise Nolin, Fay DeWitt(c) in "Nite Club Confidential" *(Paul Greco Photo)*

(O'NEAL'S CABARET) Monday, Sept. 26, 1983– Jill Larson and Marisa Smith present:
SERIOUS BIZNESS a comedy revue written by Jennifer Allen, Don Perman, David Babcock, Winnie Holzman; Music, David Evans; Director, Phyllis Newman; Set, Loren Sherman; Costumes, Cynthia O'Neal; Lights, Mal Sturchio; Associate Producer, Jeffrey Matthews; Musical Director, Frederick Weldy; Stage Manager, C. Myron Moore. CAST: David Babcock, Jill Larson, Don Perman, Nealla Spano. Performed without intermission.

(LA MAMA) Wednesday, Sept. 14,–Oct. 9, 1983 (20 performances) La Mama E.T.C., The Overtone Theatre, and New Writers at the Westside present:
SUPERSTITIONS/THE SAD LAMENT OF PECOS BILL ON THE EVE OF KILLING HIS WIFE by Sam Shepard; Director, Julie Hebert; Music for "Superstitions" by the Overtone Theatre, for "Pecos Bill" by Sam Shepard and Catherine Stone; Musical Director, Catherine Stone; Set, Katen Schulz; Lighting, Anne Militello; Costumes, Rita Yovino, Sound, J. A. Deane; Production Manager, Chris Silva; Production Associate, Jon Goldwater; Stage Manager, Ruth Kreshka Moran; Press, Burnham-Callaghan Associates. CAST: Mark Petrakis, O-Lan Shepard.

(WEST BANK CAFE) Saturday, Sept. 24,–Nov. 5, 1983 (19 performances and 8 previews). Lily Turner presents:
DICK DETERRED with Music by William Schimmel; Book and Lyrics, David Edgar; Director, George Wolf Reily; Set, Ted Reinert; Costumes, Marla R. Kaye; Choreography, Mary Pat Henry; Production Assistant, Michael Schindelheim; Wardrobe, Betty Berkowitz; Stage Manager, Marjorie Golden; Press, Jeffrey Richards Associates, Ben Morse. CAST: Mary Kay Dean (Anne/Martha/Singer), Elf Fairservis (Plantagenet/York/Singer), Malcolm Gray (McClarence/Citizen/Tyrell/Forrest/Stanley), Richard Litt (Hastings), Steve Pudenz (Richard), Sylvester Rich (Buckingham), Rhonda Rose (Elizabeth/Lady Jackie/Singer), Carl Williams (Murderer/Dighton/Ely/Richmond). A Watergate Musical Parody of "Richard III" in 2 acts.
MUSICAL NUMBERS: Welcome Washington, Gonna Win, Don't Let Them Take Checkers Away, You Are Bugging Me, Hostess with the Mostess of Them All, The Huck Stops Here, Expletive Deleted, I'm Leaving, It's the End

Mary McDonnell, Robin Groves (front), Bill Mesnik, Holly Hunter, Randle Mell in "A Weekend Near Madison" *(Peter Cunningham Photo)*

63

(SILVER LINING) Thursday, Sept. 15–Oct. 1, 1983 (18 performances and 5 previews). Daniel and Geraldine Abrahamsen with Silver Lining present:
THE GREAT AMERICAN BACKSTAGE MUSICAL with Music nd Lyrics by Bill Solly; Book, Bill Solly, Donald Ward; Musical Direction/Arrangements, Fred Barton; Direction/Choreography, Bob Talmage; Costumes, George Potts; Lighting, Gregg Marriner; Stage Manager, Franklin O. Davis; Hairstylist, Andrew Reese; Press, Shirley Herz, Peter Cromarty. CAST: Mark Fotopoulos (Johnny Brash), Suzanne Dawson (Sylvia), Joe Barrett (Harry), Paige O'Hara (Kelly Moran), Bob Amaral (Banjo), Maris Clement (Constance Duquette). The action takes place in New York, London and the battlefields of Europe from 1942–1945.
MUSICAL NUMBERS: Backstage, The Girls in Short Supply, Nickel's Worth of Dreams, I Got the What?, This Isn't Tomorrow, Pie and Coffee, Being Made Love To, The Star of the Show, When the Money Comes In, News of You, I Could Fall in Love, Ba-Broom, I'll Wait for Joe, Finale.

(NEW VIC THEATRE) Sunday, Sept. 18,–Oct. 12, 1983 (16 performances). Nickell Productions presents:
DUSA, FISH, STAS AND VI by Pam Gems; Director, Jane Mandel; Stage Manager, Kathleen Marsters; Press, Susan Jordan. CAST: Annie La Russa (Vi), Susan Jordan (Dusa), Robin Willis (Stas), Denise Lanctot (Fish). The action takes place in London in the 1970's.

(T.O.M.I. TERRACE THEATRE) Sunday, Sept. 18,–Oct. 2, 1983 (15 performances and 15 previews). Val Evans presents:
FLIRTATIONS by Fred Kolo; Director, Jack Allison; Casting, William T. Gardner, Ben Evans; Assistant Director, Fred Greene; Set, Dean Taucher; Lighting, Kirk Bookman; Costumes, Jay Embree, Woody Lane; General Manager, Kate Harper; Stage Managers, Scott Allen, Joe Miloscia; Press, Hunt/Pucci Associates. CAST: Graham Beckel (Sammy), Elizabeth Burkland (She), Kenneth Cory (Bruce), Joseph Culliton (Martin), John Dukakis (Young Man), W. H. Macy (He), Mercedes Ruehl (Joyce), Tom Spackman (Waiter/Understudy), Catherine Butterfield (Understudy). Presented in 2 acts and 4 scenes. The action takes place at the present time.

David Huddleston, Robin Howard
in "Big Maggie"

(BILLIE HOLIDAY THEATRE) Thursday, Sept. 22, 1983–Jan. 15, 1984 (98 performances). Billie Holliday Theatre (Marjorie Moon, Producer) presents:
FRIENDS by Samm-Art Williams; Director, Mikell Pinkney; Set, Felix E. Cochren; Costumes, Vicki Jones; Lighting, Tim Phillips; Associate Producer, Ron McIntyre; Wardrobe, Regina Watkins; Stage Manager, Maurice Carlton; Press, Howard Atlee. CAST: Valera Drummond (Amanda Sage), Avan Littles (Isaac Hansley), Helmar Augustus Cooper (Herman Barksdale), Carol Mitchell-Smith (Michelle "Mickey" Corbett). A play in 2 acts and 5 scenes. The action takes place at the present time at the home and adjacent apartment of Amanda Sage in Philadelphia, PA, on a weekend in early October.

(ACTORS & DIRECTORS THEATRE) Monday, Sept. 26,–Oct. 16, 1983 (20 performances and 3 previews). B/TRU Productions presents:
EVE IS INNOCENT by Leonard Melfi; Director, Alice Spivak; Scenery, James Fenhagen; Lighting, Betsy Adams; Costumes, Michele Reisch; Sound, Tom Gould; Producer, Gilbert Rogers Trunkett; Press, FLT/Francine L. Trevens, David Lotz. CAST: Peggy Bruen (Olympia O'Leary), Ellen Foley (Kim Dolphin), Steve Beach (Bobby Ruggero). A play in two acts. The action takes place in Olympia's new skylight apartment.

(DOUGLAS FAIRBANKS THEATRE) Wednesday, Sept. 28, 1983–Nov. 6, 1983 (45 performances and 9 previews) David J. Bell and Louis Roberts in association with Hugh O'Lunney, Lester Osterman (Executive Producer) present:
BIG MAGGIE by John B. Keane; Director, Donal Donnelly; Scenery, David Potts; Costumes, Judith Dolan; Lighting, Andrea Wilson; Sound, Tom Gould; General Management, Dorothy Olim, George Elmer; Company Manager, Colin Fraser; Stage Managers, Bill McComb, Ralph Wakefield; Wardrobe, Terry Lavada; Press, Jeffrey Richards, Robert Ganshaw; C. George Willard, Ben Morse, Richard Humleker. CAST: Robin Howard (Maggie Polpin), David Huddleston succeeded by Donal Donnelly (Byrne), Hope Cameron (Old Woman), Anne Clay (Mrs. Madden), Juliana Donald (Gert Polpin), Terry Finn (Katie Polpin), James Handy (Teddy Heelin), Kevin McGuire (Mick Polpin), Scott Schofield (Old Man), Maura Vaughn (Mary Madden), Robert Walsh (Maurice Polpin). A drama in 2 acts and 6 scenes.

(ACTORS PLAYHOUSE) Thursday, Sept. 29,–Nov. 26, 1983 (80 performances). The Gero Organization and Frank M. Zollo in association with Clifford Adler, Paul D'Addario and Vincent P. Rigolosi present:
FUNHOUSE conceived, written, directed and performed by Eric Bogosian; Co-Director, Joanne Bonney; Lighting, Jeffrey McRoberts; Set, Reagan Cook; Design Supervision, Eric Bogosian; General Manager, Randy Finch; Company Manager, Woji Gero; Stage Manager, Jason Gero; Press, Warren Knowlton. A solo performance by Eric Bogosian presented in two parts with one intermission.

(ACTORS OUTLET THEATRE II) Sunday, Oct. 2-16, 1983 (13 performances and 3 previews). Robert Landau presents.
MARMALADE SKIES by M. Z. Ribalow; Director, Thomas Babe; Scenery/Costumes, Mike Boak; Lighting, Gregory C. MacPherson; Technical Director, Jane Tomlinson; Costume Coordinator, Beba Shamash; Stage Managers, Nancy Rifkind, Mark Bagnall. CAST: Mark Arnott (Spence), Catherine Butterfield (Michelle), Kathryn Dowling (Julia), Alanna Hamill (Samantha), Chris Lutkin (Dennis). A comedy in two acts. The action takes place in a dormitory room on a college campus on May 30, 1970, and in an apartment on West 71 Street just off Central Park West on December 8, 1980.

(ACTORS CORNER THEATRE) Wednesday, Oct. 5-30, 1983 (16 performances). Empire Stages presents:
DAYDREAMS by Deborah Novak; Director, Lance Hewett; Set, Alex Polner; Costumes, Dolores DeCrisanti; Lighting, Bret Landow; Stage Manager/Props, Gina Serraino; Press, Milton Brooks, Deborah Hanna. CAST: Nora Baetz (Debbie), Michael Clarke (Malloy), Roz Dunn (Fran), Warner Schreiner (Mr. Brickelman), Dorothy Sterling (Dottie O'Connell)

(INTAR II) Wednesday, Oct. 5-29, 1983 (16 performances)
OFF BEAT by Lee Dunne; Director, Linda Pakri; Designer, Andres Mannik; Lighting, Jonathan Thaler; Sound, George Jacobs; Stage Manager, Marybeth Ward; Press, Fred Hoot, David Mayhew. CAST: Jaan Kusse (Myles Lonergen), Andrea Mead (Sally), Paul Taylor Robertson (Johnny Dolan), Mary Tierney (Donna Keyes). A play in 2 acts and 5 scenes. The action takes place at the present time in New York City.

Top Left: Avan Littles, Carol Mitchell-Smith
in "Friends" *(Bert Andrews Photo)*

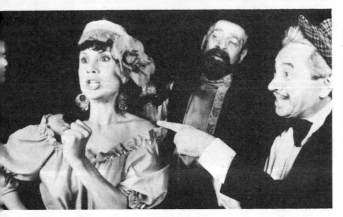

(PROVINCETOWN PLAYHOUSE) Wednesday, Oct. 5–9, 1983 (7 performances and 7 previews). Bellwether Productions and Bella Rosenberg present:
A LITTLE MADNESS by Gerald Zipper; Director, Norman Gevanthor; Set, John Kasarda; Lighting, Spencer Mosse; Costumes, Oleksa; General Manager, Harvey Elliott; Stage Managers, Marc Elliott Field, Anne S. King; Props, Marleen Marta, Maria Villa; Press, Arthur Cantor Associates. CAST: David Falkner (Harry Garden), Pamela Burrell (Elissa Garden), John LaGioia (Eddie), Kathleen Doyle (Lorelei), Sam Gray (Max), Ron Siebert (Donny), Robert Silver (Albie). A play in two acts. The action takes place at the present time in an upper West Side Manhattan apartment in winter.

(PERRY STREET THEATRE) Monday, Oct. 17–23, 1983 (13 performances). Key Productions (Mickey Rolfe, Producer) presents:
SECOND PRIZE: TWO MONTHS IN LENINGRAD by Trish Johnson; Director, Gus Kaikkonen; Set, Bob Barnett; Lighting, William Armstrong; Costumes, Martha Hally; Sound, Tom Gould; Stage Managers, James Bohr, David Higlen, Rosemary Keough; Casting, Jason LaPadura; Press, Howard Atlee, Barbara Atlee. CAST: Daniel Ahearn (Tom), John Bowman (Joey), Sarah Chodoff (Janice), Edmond Genest (Dr. Sherman), Kim Greist (Katya), Susan Sandler (Valentina), J. Smith-Cameron (Mary Alice), Mark Soper (Andrei), Victor Talmadge (Martin) Bruce Tracy (Leonard). A comedy in 2 acts and 4 scenes. The action takes place in a dormitory room for foreign students in Leningrad in the early 1970's.

(T.O.M.I. PARK ROYAL THEATER) Thursday, Oct. 6–9, 1983 (6 performances and 6 previews). Joan Schuster presents:
BRANDY BEFORE BREAKFAST by Max G. Weine; Director, T. Newell Kring; Scenery, Lloyd M. Jeffords; Props, Christine White; Costumes, Valerie Porr; Stage Managers, T. Newell Kring, Mark McQuown; Press, David Lipsky. CAST: Shirley Brandon Bays (Vicki), Sarah Daly (Jennifer), Ellen Dano (Maureen), Katherine Liepe (Trudie), Victor Raider-Wexler (Tommy), Debra Whitfield (Denise). A comedy in 2 acts and 10 scenes. The action takes place at the present time in the living room of a Riverside Drive apartment on the upper West Side of Manhattan.

**Rebecca Dobson, Elizabeth Lawrence,
Richard Hoyt-Miller in "Children"**
(A. A. Murphy Photo)

(TOWN HALL) Sunday, Oct. 9,–Dec. 26, 1983 (65 performances and 5 previews). Shalom Yiddish Musical Comedy Theatre (Raymond Ariel, Producer) presents:
THE JEWISH GYPSY with Book by Mordechai Mandel; Music, Martin Moskowitz; Lyrics, Moshe Sachar; Musical Director, Renee Solomon; Director, Michael Greenstein; Dances/Musical Numbers Staged by Derek Wolshonak; Scenery, Adina Reich, Abraham Mordoh; Costumes, Clare Gosney; English Narration, Bella Mysell Yablokoff; Additional Music, Dan Blitenthal; Production Supervisor, Sandy Levitt; Stage Manager/Lighting/Sound, F. Robin Rosenthal; Press, Max Eisen, Madelon Rosen. CAST: Mary Soreanu (Palashka), Yankele Alperin (Shmerl), Reizl Bozyk (Chaya), Diane Cypkin (Tzirl), David Ellin (Danilo), Stewart Figa (Berl), Sandy Levitt (Hirsh), Shifee Lovitt (Paya), Michael Michalovic (Shloime), David Montefiore (Yosl), Ensemble: Catherine Caplin, Carolyn Goor, Tara Tyrrell, Bill Badolato (Captain), Stanley Kramer, John Milne. A musical in two acts. The action takes place in early Czarist Russia.
MUSICAL NUMBERS: Ballade, Play Gypsy, My Yiddish Gypsy, Lord in Heaven, A Good Week, I Don't Agree, What a Pair, Bessarabia, Yearning, Russian Waltz, To Your Health, Let There Be Peace, When Love Calls, Life Is So Beautiful, The Dream, No! No! No!, Wish Me Luck, Together, I Want to Be a Jewish Girl, Finale

(FOLKSBIENE PLAYHOUSE) Saturday, Oct. 22, 1983–Mar. 31, 1984 (61 performances and 2 previews). The Folksbiene Playhouse (Ben Schechter, Manager; Morris Adler, Chairman) presents:
IT'S HARD TO BE A JEW by Sholom Aleichem; Adapted and Directed by Israel Beker; Music, Alexander Yampolsky; Musical Direction, Zalmen Mlotek; Set, J. Ben-Miriam; Technical Director, Zeev W. Neuman; Lighting, Paul McDonach; Costumes, Kulyk Costumes; Stage Manager, Jacques Brawer. CAST: I. W. Firestone (Shneyerson/Hersh Movshovitz), Alexander Sirotin (Ivanov/Ivan Ivanovitch), Ibi Kaufman (Betty), Paula Teitelbaum (Siomke), Jack Rechtzeit (Ketzele), Zypora Spaisman (Sarah), Leon Liebgold (David), Jacob Gostinsky (Makar), Yosef Toomim (Rabbi), Jacques Brawer (Policeman), David Braun (Understudy)

(WEST SIDE ARTS CENTER) Thursday, Oct. 20,–Dec. 4, 1983 (30 performances and 2 previews). American Kaleidoscope (Artistic Directors, Rebecca Dobson, Joan Rice Franklin; Managing Director, Richard Bell) presents:
CHILDREN by A. R. Gurney, Jr.; Director, Norris Houghton; Suggested by a John Cheever story; Set, Ernest Allen Smith; Costumes, Andrew B. Marlay; Lighting, Robert Strohmeier; Sound, Robert A. Kraemer; Production Manager, Arthur Bryant; Technical Director, Cliff Lane; Props, Varda Appleton; Stage Managers, Carolyn Caldwell, John J. Owens; Press, Arthur Cantor/Harvey Elliott. CAST: Rebecca Dobson (Barbara), Richard Hoyt-Miller (Randy), Elizabeth Lawrence (Mother), Christie Virtue (Jane). A play in 2 acts and 8 scenes. The action takes place at the present time at a beach house.

(NAC GALLERY PLAYHOUSE) Saturday, Oct. 22–23, 1983 (3 performances). The President, Board of Governors, the Joseph Kesselring Award Committee of the National Arts Club present:
BLESS ME FATHER by William Hathaway; Director, Michael Parva; Set, Dean Tschetter; Lighting, Craig Kennedy; Costumes, D. V. Thompson; Sound, Robert Lochow; Stage Manager, Kathy Uhler. CAST: Robert Bailey (Fr. Michael Mosely), Vince Carroll (Fr. James O'Brien), Ann Ducati (Divine Barbara), Paul Hebron (Fr. Robert Kane), David Labiosa (Norman Rivera), Marcella Lowery (Officer Crowley), Carol Rosenfeld (Mr. Joan Lucas), Eric van Valkenburg (Robert), Rick van Valkenburg (Thomas), Frederick Walters (Arthur Lucas), Judith Yerby (Maggie Lucas). A play in two acts. The action takes place in various locales in and around Detroit, MI.

(VINEYARD THEATRE) Monday, Oct. 24,–Nov. 13, 1983 (21 performances). Vineyard Theatre (Barbara Zinn, Artistic Director; Douglas Aibel, Associate Artistic Director) presents:
FAITH HEALER by Brian Friel; Director, Dann Florek; Set, William John Aupperlee; Lighting, Richard Lund; Costumes, Deborah Shaw; Sound, Steven Baker; Production Coordinator, Susan Wilder; Technical Director, Kate Mennone; Stage Managers, Crystal Huntington, Vicki de Wolfe; Press, Bruce Cohen. CAST: J. T. Walsh (Frank), Kathleen Chalfant (Grace), Martin Shakar (Teddy). A drama in two acts.

**Top Left: David Montefiore, Mary Soreanu, David Ellin,
Yankele Alperin in "The Jewish Gypsy"**
(Gerry Goodstein Photo)

(THEATRE AT ST. PETER'S CHURCH) Monday Oct. 24–30, 1983 (8 performances and 8 previews). Donald Rubin presents:
WEEKEND with Book, Music and Lyrics by Roger Lax; Directed and Choreographed by David H. Bell; Set, Ursula Belden; Costumes, Sally Lesser; Lighting, Toni Goldin; Sound, Paul Garrity; Musical Director, William Lewis; Orchestrations, Robby Merkin; General Manager, Albert Poland; Company Manager, Susan L. Falk; Stage Managers, Tom Capps, Bill "Lee" Lewis; Props, Cathy Poppe; Wardrobe, Donna Hattin; Photographer, Ken Howard; Casting, David Courier; Production Associates, Paul Callens, Joe Hunt; Press, Solters/Roskin/Friedman, Milly Schoenbaum, Kevin Patterson. CAST: Louise Edeiken (Louise), Gregg Edelman (Timothy), Justin Ross (Justin), Carole-Ann Scott (Sally), Standbys: John Ganzer, Rosalyn Rahn. A musical in two acts. The action takes place at the present time in New York City.
MUSICAL NUMBERS: Thank God It's Friday, Lip Service, This Song's for You, Big Date Tonight, Lover Sweet Lover, The Man Next Door, What's On?, Let's Have Dinner and Dance, Hangin' Out the Window, Saturday is Just Another Day, Lucky Woman, It's Sad to Say, Once You Take the Feeling Out, See What Happens, Where Is She Now?, Cuddle In, Baby It Must Be Love, Wake-Up Call, A Man Wakes Up, Seven Years Later, I Have Me, I'll Never Want You Again, Word Gets Around, Dragon Lady, What Time Is It?, Sunday Makes a Difference

(JEWISH REPERTORY THEATRE) Tuesday, Oct. 25–Nov. 6, 1983 (12 performances and 12 previews). The Jewish Repertory Theatre (Ran Avni, Artistic Director) presents:
UP FROM PARADISE with Book and Lyrics by Arthur Miller; Music, Stanley Silverman; Director, Ran Avni; Sets, Michael C. Smith; Costumes, Marie Anne Chiment; Lighting, Dan Kinsley; Musical Director, Michael Ward; Stage Managers, G. Franklin Heller, Gay Smerek; Press, Richard Kornberg. CAST: Len Cariou (God), Raymond Murcell (Azrael), Avery J. Tracht (Raphael), Richard Frisch (Uriel), Austin Pendleton (Adm), Alice Playten (Eve), Walter Bobbie (Lucifer), Paul Ukena, Jr. (Cain), Lonny Price (Abel). A musical in two acts.
MUSICAL NUMBERS: The Lord Is a Hammer of Light, How Fine It Is, When Night Starts to Fall, Bone of Thy Bones, Hallelujah, The Center of Your Mind, It's Just Like I Was You, Recitative, But If Something Leads to Good, I'm Me We're Us, Curses, Lonely Quartet, How Lovely Is Eve, I Am the River and Waltz, All of That Made for Me, As Good as Paradise, It Was So Peaceful Before There Was Man, It Comes to Me, I Don't Know What Is Happening to Me, Why Can't I See God?, All Love, Passion, Nothing's Left of God, Never See the Garden Again

(AMERICAN THEATRE OF ACTORS) Wednesday, Oct. 26,–Nov. 20, 1983 (31 performances and 17 previews). Katherine & Shelby Bryan and Tejas Theatrical Productions present:
THE LAST OF THE KNUCKLEMEN by John Powers; Director, Peter Masterson; Assistant Director, Carlin Glynn; Associate Producer, John Roddick; Set/Lighting, Kevin Hickson; Costumes, Susan Sayers; Flight Director, Normand Beauregard; General Manager, Leonard A. Mulhern; Company Manager, James Hannah; Stage Managers, Lewis Rosen, Joel Anderson; Props, Doug Zigler; Press, Susan L. Schulman, G. Theodore Killmer. CAST: David Kimball (Mad Dog), Tony Rizzoli (Horse), Ben George (Pansy), John Finn (Tassie), Thick Wilson (Methusalah), Dennis Quaid (Tom), K. C. Kelly (Monk), Kevin O'Connor (Tarzan), Bill Fagerbakke (Carl), Understudies: Joel Anderson, William Hardy, John Finn. A drama in 3 acts and 5 scenes. The action takes place in the bunkhouse at the present time in a Northwest Australian mining camp where the average temperature is 120 degrees.

(JASON'S PARK ROYAL THEATRE) Thursday, Oct. 27,–Nov. 20, 1983 (20 performances) Jeff Golding, Marshall H. Kozinn present:
LONDON DAYS & NEW YORK NIGHTS with Music by Jason McAuliffe; Lyrics by Chuck Abbott, Henry Avery, John Paul Hudson, Jay Jeffries, Bill Jones, Bel Kaufman, Fran Landesman, Jeff Golding; Director, Jeff Golding; Musical Director, Rick Lewis; Choreographer, Marcia Milgrom Dodge; Stage Manager, Larry Pelligrini; Press, Max Eisen, Madelon Rosen. CAST: Nancy Johnston, Joseph Kolinski, Scott Robertson.
MUSICAL NUMBERS: London Days and NY Nights, Yankee Doodle Londoner, Jaywalkin', A Song Whose Time Has Come, Against the Time, I'll Sing a Different Song Tomorrow, May the Force Be With You, I Will Never Be the Same, Best Way to Have the Blues, One Night Stand, Code of theWest, I Live in a Dive, Half-Remembered Melody, When Did the End Begin?, Who's New, A Permanent Romance, Brief Encounter, There's Something Worse Than Living Alone, Ending Up Alone, Dying a Little A Lot Alone, Big Dreams, Where Have I Been All My Life?, Crystal Palaces, Best of Friends

Top Right: Len Cariou, Austin Pendleton, Alice Playten,
Paul Ukena, Jr., Walter Bobbie, Lonny Price in "Up from Paradise"
(Inge Morath Photo)

(MARQUEE THEATRE) Thursday, Oct. 27,–Nov. 20, 1983 (16 performances). Returned Monday, Jan. 23,–Feb. 12, 1984 for 21 performances. Shelter West (Judith Joseph, Artistic Director) presents:
FLESH, FLASH & FRANK HARRIS by Paul Stephen Lim; Director, Judith Joseph; Assistant Director, Arthur Brooks; Set/Costumes, Tatiana De Stempel; Lighting, David Tasso; Props, Eric Achacoso; Stage Managers, Penny Weinberger, Perry Barden; Press, David H. Tasso. CAST: David Clarke (Old Frank), Ray Iannicelli (Middle Frank), John Barone (Young Frank), Margot Avery (Nita/Yolanda/Erika), Norma Jean Griffin (Laura/Princess Alice), Keely Eastley (Nellie), Arthur Brooks (Wm. Harris/Frank Scully/Prince of Wales), June White (Mrs. Mayhew/Emily/Old Kate), Richard Boddy (George Bernard Shaw), Anthony Dinovi (Byron), Perry Barden (Reporter/Servant), Bruce Mohat (Rev. Vershoyle/Priest/Sumner), Martin Thompson (Oscar Wilde). A play in two acts. The action takes place in the apartment of Frank Harris in Nice (and elsewhere in his memories) in late August of 1931.

(RIVERWEST THEATRE) Thursday, Oct. 27,–Nov. 20, 1983 (16 performances) CHS Productions and Riverwest Theatre present:
BENTLEY'S WAR by Elliott Caplin; Director, Joseph Gilford; Set, Thomas Stoner; Lighting, Matthew Ehlert; Technical Director, Christopher Cole; Stage Managers, Bronwyn O'Shaughnessy, Eleanor Gillmeister; Press, June Summers. CAST: Phil Matteson (Seaman Halverson), Malcolm Smith (Yeoman Wesley Waycroft), Allen Davison (Stewards Mate Robert Lovell), W. T. Martin (Ensign (JG) Reece Bentley), Mark Hofmaier (Ens. John Gorman), Mark Fleischman (Lt. Cmdr. Warren Martineau), James McDonnell (Lt. Rudolf Spanell), Matt Nichols (Yorimoto Muraski). A drama in two acts. The action takes place on board a U. S. Navy Minesweep (AM 365 from July 1944 through October 1945.

Thick Wilson, David Kimball, Dennis Quaid, Bill Fagerbakke,
Kevin O'Connor, Ben George, K. C. Kelly,
Tony Rizzoli, John Finn in "Last of the Knucklemen"
(Martha Swope Photo)

66

(WESTSIDE ARTS CENTER/CHERYL CRAWFORD THEATRE) Sunday, Oct. 30,–Dec. 6, 1983 (42 performances and 19 previews). Mark deSolla Price, John Van Ness Philip, Leonard Soloway in association with David Susskind present:
TALLULAH with Book by Tony Lang; Music, Arthur Siegel; Lyrics, Mae Richard; Direction/Choreography, David Holdgrive; Scenery/Costumes, John Falabella; Miss Gallagher's Gowns, Neil Bieff; Musical Director/Arrangements, Bruce W. Coyle; Lighting, Ken Billington; Projections, Stanley Topliff; Assistant Choreographer, William Alan Coats; Assistant Musical Director, Jim Rice; General Management, Richard Horner, Lynne Stuart; Stage Managers, Mark Baltazar, Tracy A. Crum, William Alan Coats; Conductor, Bruce W. Coyle; Wardrobe, Nancy Young; Wigs, Paul Huntley; Hairstylist, David H. Lawrence; Casting, Elizabeth Shafer; Press, FLT/Francine L. Trevens, Penny M. Landau, David Lotz. CAST: Helen Gallagher (Tallulah), Russell Nype (Will Bankhead), Joel Craig (John Barrymore/John Emery), Tom Hafner, Eric Johnson, Ken Lundie, Patrick Parker, Clark Sterling; Understudies: Eric Johnson (Will), Ken Lundie (Barrymore/Emery), William Alan Coats (all men/ Dance Captain). A musical in two acts based on the life of actress Tallulah Bankhead.
MUSICAL NUMBERS: Darling, Tallulah, When I Do a Dance for You, Home Sweet Home, I've Got to Try Everything Once, You're You, I Can See Him Clearly, Tallulahbaloo, The Party Is Where I Am, Stay Awhile, It's a Hit, If Only He Were a Woman, Love Is on Its Knees, Don't Ever Book A Trip on the IRT, You Need a Lift!, Finale

(18th STREET PLAYHOUSE) Thursday, Nov. 3–20, 1983 (12 performances). Autumn Productions presents:
CROSSROADS CAFE with Music and Lyrics by John C. Introcaso; Director, Carole Start; Choreography, Dick Shell; Set, Tony Damiano; Costumes, Jennie Weidmann; Stage Manager, Cathy Sonneborn White; Production Manager, Debbie Keyser; Props, Dolores and Susan Lomega; Lighting, Richard Clausen. CAST: Diane Disque (McKinley), Tommy Re (Tommy), Annie Joe Edwards (Pearl), Lynne McCall (Alyson), Gale Gallione (Lacy), Susan Berkson (Mama), Frank M. Rosner (Sal), John C. Introcaso (Jarrett), Ken-Michael Stafford (Johnson). A musical in two acts.
MUSICAL NUMBERS: Ain't Doin' Nothin' Wrong, Searching for That Sunset, Rainy Day Blues, Lovely Ladies, Fool Inside of Me, Give Before You Die, Three O'Clock in the Mornin', You Wanna Go to Broadway, Tell My Troubles to, Woman's Work Ain't Never Done, When I Dream, Good Mornin' Mr. Sunshine, Crossroads Cafe

(ACTORS OUTLET) Thursday, Nov. 3–20, 1983 (16 performances and 2 previews). StageArts Theatre Co. (Nell Robinson, Ruth Ann Norris, Artistic Directors) presents:
ZOOLOGY by Martin Jones; Director, Licia Colombi; Set, Peter Harrison; Costumes, Sheila Kehoe, Lighting, Whitney Quesenbery; Stage Managers, Dennis Cameron, Allan Babuska; Press, Shirley Herz, Sam Rudy, Peter Cromarty, Jane Shannon. CAST: Jean Bruno (Sophie), Eleanor Garth (Lenore), Nan Wilson (Rose), Gregg Daniel (Rollo), Art Kempf (Murphy), Giulia Pagano or Mary Ann Chance (Sally), Alice White (C.J.). A play in two acts. The action takes place at the present time in Chicago's Lincoln Park Zoo.

(VILLAGE GATE DOWNSTAIRS) Monday, November 7, 1983 (1 performance and 13 previews). Diane de Mailly presents:
SUNSET with Music by Gary William Friedman; Words, Will Holt; Director, Andre Ernotte; Choreography, Buzz Miller; Set, Kate Edmunds; Costumes, Patricia Zipprodt; Lighting, Robert Jared; Sound, Paul Garrity; Orchestrations/Vocal Arrangements, Gary William Friedman; Musical Director, Donald York; Casting, Julie Hughes, Barry Moss; Stage Managers, Duane F. Mazey, Ron Woodall, Jessica Molaskey; General Manager, Albert Poland; Company Manager, Pamela Hare; Wardrobe, Cathay Brackman; Press, Solters/Roskin/Friedman, Milly Schoenbaum, Kevin Patterson. CAST: Tammy Grimes (Lila Halliday), Ronee Blakley (Marta Gibson), Kim Milford (Danger Dan Hardin), Walt Hunter (Jamie), Standbys: Ellen Hanley (Lila), Jessica Molaskey (Marta), Eric Hansen (Dan/Jamie). A musical in two acts. The action takes place at the present time in Los Angeles, CA.
MUSICAL NUMBERS: Sunset City, La Bamba, Nothing But, Funky, Destiny, Back with a Beat, Standing in Need, Rock Is My Way of Life, Sunset Dreams, Rap, Cheap Chablis, Stuck on the Windshield of Life, 1945, Retreat, I Am the Light, Moments, Old Times Good Times, This One's for Me

(PROVINCETOWN PLAYHOUSE) Tuesday, Nov. 8,–Dec. 18, 1983 (47 performances and 9 previews). Robert Altman and Sandcastle 5 Productions present the Los Angeles Actors Theatre (Bill Bushnell, Producing Artistic Director) production of:
SECRET HONOR: The Last Testament of Richard M. Nixon by Donald Breed and Arnold M. Stone; Director, Robert Harders; Set/Lighting, Russell Pyle; General Management, Dorothy Olim Associates, George Elmer; Stage Manager, John Brigleb; Wardrobe, Lori Steinberg; Press, Jeffrey Richards, Robert Ganshaw, C. George Willard, Ben Morse, Eileen McMahon, Richard Humleker. CAST: Philip Baker Hall (Mr. Nixon). Performed without intermission; The action takes place in the 1980's in the study of Richard M. Nixon.

Ronee Blakley, Tammy Grimes
in "Sunset" *(Martha Swope Photo)*

(ASTOR PLACE THEATRE) Tuesday, Nov. 8–27, 1983; transferred to AMDA Theatre, Friday, Dec. 2–18, 1983 (43 performances and 16 previews). Judith Finn Haines and John Adams Vaccaro present:
LEFTOVERS conceived, written and performed by Marcia Kimmell, Deah Schwartz, Anne Wilford; Directorial Consultant, Barbara Harris; Set, Robert F. Strohmeier; Costumes, Tamara Melcher, Gregory Reeves; Lighting, Arwin Bittern, Vivian Leone; General Management, Maria DiDia, Jim Fiore; Stage Manager, Arwin Bittern; Production Assistant, Mary E. Lawson; Press, Betty Lee Hunt, Maria Cristina Pucci, James Sapp. Performed without intermission.

(BAM/CAREY PLAYHOUSE) Tuesday, Nov. 8–20, 1983 (14 performances) and returned for two additional weeks, Thursday, Dec. 15–31, 1983 (16 performances). Re-opened at Houston, TX, Grand Opera. Presented by the Brooklyn Academy of Music in association with Liza Lorwin and the Walker Art Center.
THE GOSPEL AT COLONUS adapted and directed by Lee Breuer; Based on an adaptation of Sophocles' "Oedipus at Colonus" in the version by Robert Fitzgerald, and incorporation passages from both Sophocles' "Oedipus Rex" and "Antigone" in versions by Dudley Fitts and Robert Fitzgerald; Music composed an arranged by Bob Telson; Set, Alison Yerxa; Costumes, Ghretta Hynd, Alison Yerxa; Sound, Otts Munderloh; Lighting, Julie Archer, Alison Yerxa; Special Effects, Esquire Jauchem, Gregory Meeh; Company Manager, Debbie Lepsinger; Stage Managers, Sal Rasa, Rob Brenner; Press, Ellen Lampert, Susan Spier, Jerri Brown. CAST: Morgan Freeman (Messenger), Clarence Fountain (Oedipus), Isabell Monk (Antigone), Carl Lumbly (Theseus), Jevetta Steele (Ismene), Robert Earl Jones (Creon), Kevin Davis (Polyneices) Chorus: Clarence Fountain and the Five Blind Boys of Alabama, J. J. Farley and the Original Soul Stirrers, J. D. Steele Singers, The Institutional Radio Choir. Performed in two parts.

Morgan Freeman in "The Gospel at Colonus"
(Johan Elbers Photo)

(WONDERHORSE THEATRE) Wednesday, Nov. 9–27, 1983 (17 performances). TRG REPERTORY (Marvin Kahan, Artistic Director) presents: **AN EVENING OF ADULT FAIRY TALES:** "Miss Chicken Little" with Music by Alec Wilder and Libretto by William Engvick; "The Journey of Snow White" with Libretto and Music by Al Carmines; Director, William Hopkins; Musical Director, Ernest Lehrer; Choreographer, Jerry Yoder; Set, Peter Harrison; Costumes, Christopher Cole; Lighting, Carol Graebner; Stage Manager, Ellen Sontag; Press, Jan Greenberg. CAST: Bob Arnold, Frank D'Ambrosio, Karen Merchant, Zoelle Montgomery, R. G. Moore, Donna Robinson, Hank Schob, Scott Sigler, Lee Teplitzky, Megan Lynn Thomas, Beth Williams. Performed with two intermissions.

(THEATRE FOUR) Tuesday, Nov. 15, 1983–Jan. 1, 1984. The Negro Ensemble Company (Douglas Turner Ward, Artistic Director; Leon B. Denmark, Managing Director) presents: **PUPPETPLAY** by Pearl Cleage; Director, Clinton Turner Davis; Set, Llewellyn Harrison; Costumes, Judy Dearing; Lighting, William H. Grant III; Sound, Bernard Hall; Stage Manager, Jesse Wooden, Jr.; Wardrobe, Marie McKinney; Props, Lisa L. Watson; Press, Irene Gandy, Porcia Howard. CAST: Wendell Brooks (Saxophonist), Seret Scott (Woman One), Phylicia Ayers-Allen (Woman Two), Brad Brewer (Puppeteer), Understudy: S. Epatha Merkerson. Performed without intermission.

(PLAYHOUSE 46) Tuesday, Nov. 15–26, 1983 (10 performances). The Lifecatchers Co. and the Long Island Theatre Co. present: **PAHOKEE BEACH** by Leo Rost; Music, Jimmy Horowitz; Lyrics, Jimmy Horowitz, Leo Rost; Director, Georgia McGill; Producer, Jimmy Wisner; Set, Ernest Allen Smith; Lighting, Susan Roth; Costumes, Vern Yates; Musical Director, Jeff Bates; Assistant Director, Joe Hayes; Stage Managers, Stacey Fleisher, Pierce Bihm; Technical Director , Rob Oakly; Press, Jeffrey Richards Associates. CAST: Sylvia Davis (Mrs. Entemans), Nancy Deering (Sarah), Ted Forlow (George), Curt Harpel (Lance), Kyle-Scott Jackson (Chez), Joe Muligan (Chris), Chris Seiler (Woody), Terry Urdang (Lisa). A play with music in two acts. The action takes place at the present time in a beach town, in George's beachhouse and Chez's rendezvous.

(OHIO SPACE) Thursday, Nov. 17–Dec. 11, 1983 (16 performances). Jon Teta presents: **PERICLES** by William Shakespeare; Director, Jon Teta; Assistant Director, Frankee McManus; Music, Richard Atkins; Choreography, Jerri Garner; Sets/Props, Blu Stratton; Costumes, Jon Teta/Yoland; Lighting, A. Merv Bornstein; Movement, Tony LoPresti; Stage Manager, Garwood. CAST: Blu Stratton, Robert Rosario, Suzanne Delahunt, Tom Deming, Edward Hyland, Lauren Cloud, J. Michael von Bose, Frankee McManus, Joyce Korn, Richard Rescigno, Frederic Goldberg, John Patrick Hurley (Pericles), Robert Boles, Muriel Fleit, David LeSueur, Kirby Hall, J. Patrick O'Sullivan, Tony LoPresti, Kevin Osborne, Joel Parsons, Vernon Morris, Terry Ashe Croft, Jeffrey Woodson, Susan Sparrow, Anthony Kane, Jeanne Morrissey, Lisa Cosman. Performed with one intermission.

(LAMB'S THEATRE) Tuesday, Nov. 22, 1983–May 20, 1984 (206 performances and 9 previews). Elizabeth I. McCann, Nelle Nugent, Ray Larsen, Lee Guber, Shelly Gross present the Second Stage Production of: **PAINTING CHURCHES** by Tina Howe; Director, Carole Rothman; Set, Heidi Landesman; Costumes, Linda Fisher; Lighting, Frances Aronson; General Management, McCann & Nugent; Production Coordinator, Mary Nealon; Company Manager, David Musselman; Press Consultant, Richard Kornberg; Stage Managers, Loretta Robertson, Barbara Schneider; Props, David Murdock; Wardrobe, Martha V. Blake; Press, Solters/Roskin/Friedman, Joshua Ellis, Louise Ment, Cindy Valk. CAST: Marian Seldes (Fanny Church), George N. Martin (Gardner Church), Elizabeth McGovern succeeded by Joanne Camp (Margaret Church), Understudies: Lily Lodge, Frances McDormand. A play in 2 acts and 5 scenes. The action takes place at the present time in the Church's home on Beacon Hill in Boston, MA.

(HARTLEY HOUSE) Saturday, Nov. 26,–Dec. 11, 1983 (12 performances). Playwrights Preview Productions presents three one-act plays: **THE SERMON** by David Mamet; Director, Larry Conroy; CAST: Daryl Edwards (Clergyman). **INCOMING** by Christopher Romano; Director, Paul Dervis; CAST: Mary Miller (Irene), Julia Kelly (Emy). **THE OPEN MEETING** by A. R. Gurney, Jr.; Director, Paul Dervis; CAST: Jayne Chamberlin (Verma), Nick Salamone (Eddie), Peter Waldren (Roy)

(MITZI E. NEWHOUSE THEATER) Wayne Adams, Sherwin M. Goldman, Martin Markinson in association with Westport Productions (Willian Twohill, Executive Producer) present: **AND A NIGHTINGALE SANG . . .** by C. P. Taylor; Director, Terry Kinney; Set, David Jenkins; Costumes, Jess Goldstein; Lighting, Kevin Rigdon; Sound, David Budries; General Management, Sherwin M. Goldman Productions; Company Manager, Thomas Shovestull; Technical Director, Richard Borman; Stage Managers, Dorothy J. Maffei, Zoya Wyeth; Assistant Director, Sari Ketter; Press, Betty Lee Hunt, Maria Cristina Pucci, James Sapp. CAST: Joan Allen (Helen Stott), Moira

McCann Harris succeeded by Jeanine Morick (Joyce Stott), John Carpenter (George Stott), Beverly May (Peggy Stott), Robert Cornthwaite succeeded by George Hall (Andie), Francis Guinan (Eric), Peter Friedman (Norman). A play in 2 acts and 6 scenes. The action takes place in Newcastle-on-Tyne during the years of World War II.

(LUCILLE LORTEL THEATRE) Monday, Nov. 28,–Dec. 31, 1983 (36 performances and 13 previews). Lucille Lortel, Elizabeth I. McCann, Nelle Nugent, Wiliam P. Suter present: **THE LADY AND THE CLARINET** by Michael Cristofer; Director, Gordon Davidson; Set, Heidi Landesman; Costumes, William Ivey Long; Lighting, Beverly Emmons; Company Manager, Kim Sellon; Stage Managers, Franklin Keysar, Ron Nguvu; Props, Debra Schutt; Wardrobe, Terry LaVada; Press, Solters/Roskin/Friedman, Joshua Ellis, Louise Ment, Cindy Valk, Daved E. Spangler. CAST: Jay Dryer (Clarinet Player), Stockard Channing (Luba), Kevin Geer (Paul), Paul Rudd (Jack), Josef Sommer (George), Standbys: Valorie Armstrong (Luba), Mark Moses (Paul), Ed Gilmore (Clarinetist), Eric Booth/Dan Desmond (Jack/George). A play without intermission. The action takes place at the present time.

(SOUTH STREET THEATRE) Tuesday, Nov. 29,–Dec. 11, 1983 (12 performances and 14 previews). The William and Mary Greve Foundation and Merry Enterprises Theatre ((Norman Marshall, Artistic Director) present: **BHUTAN** by Jane Stanton Hitchcock; Director, John Bird; Producer, Tony Kiser; Set, Tom Barnes; Costumes, Cynthia O'Neal; Lighting, Betsy Adams; General Management, Gail Bell, J. A. Whitcomb; Stage Managers, Laura Heller, Rosemary Keough; Props, Nan Siegmund; Casting, Stanley Soble, Jayson LaPadura; Press, Jeffrey Richards, Ben Morse, C. George Willard, Robert Ganshaw, Eileen McMahon, Richard Dahl, Mary Ann Rubino. CAST: Zach Grenier (Monk), N. Erick Avari (Samden), Marcus Smythe (Mark), Cynthia Crumlish (Ann), Patricia Hodges (Peggy), Doug Stender (Sidney), Victor Talmadge (Shepherd), Standbys: Rosemary Keough, Ed Power. A play in 2 acts and 4 scenes. The action takes place at the present time in the Taksung Monastery in the tiny kingdom of Bhutan.

(NO SMOKING PLAYHOUSE) Thursday, Dec. 1–30, 1983 (24 performances) **DESIREE** by Norman Ph. de Palm; Director/Designer, Felix R. de Rooy; Lighting, Felix de Rooy/Brett Landow; Press, Patt Dale. CAST: Marian Rolle (Desiree). A drama created from the newspaper item "Woman Burns Baby to Death."

(JEISH REPERTORY THEATRE) Tuesday, Dec. 6–25, 1983 (27 performances and 3 preivews) **GIFTED CHILDREN** by Donald Margulies; Director, Joan Vail Thorne; Set, Jeffrey Schneider; Costumes, Laura Drawbaugh; Lights, John Tomlinson; Stage Managers, Lue Douthit, Tracy Thorne. CAST: Zohra Lampert (Bernice Seidman), Dinah Manoff (Jill), Ben Siegler (David Horowitz). A play in 2 acts and 5 scenes. The action takes place in Bernice's apartment on Manhattan's Upper West Side.

(JOYCE THEATER) Wednesday, Dec. 21–31, 1983 (13 performances). Lee Gross Associates presents: **ONE MORE SONG/ONE MORE DANCE** Created and Staged by Grover Dale; Musical Director, Joel Silberman; Set, Lawrence Miller; Costumes, Albert Wolsky; Sound, Charles Bugbee III; Dance/Vocal Arrangements, Mark Hummel; New Dance/Vocal Arrangements, Joel Silberman; Special Material, Barbara Schottenfeld; General Manager, Frank Scardino Associates; Managerial Associate, Phil Leach; Technical Supervisor, Jeremiah Harris; Assistant Choreographer/Director, Stephen Jay; Wardrobe, Lillian Henderson; Stage Managers, Ed Preston, Lola Shumlin, Randall Whitescarver; Press, Mark Goldstaub, Jim Baldassare, Philip Butler, Daniel Kellachan. CAST: Ann Reinking, Gary Chryst, Jeff Calhoun, Stephen Jay, Gregory Mitchell, Brian Sutherland, Robert Warners, Nick Harvey (Swing). A musical entertainment in two acts.

(WESTSIDE ARTS CENTER/CHERYL CRAWFORD THEATRE) Tuesday, Dec. 27, 1983–Jan. 15, 1984 (24 performances). Woodie King, Jr., Raymond L. Gaspard, Martin Markinson, Mary Card, Ashton Springer (Executive Producer) present: **DINAH! QUEEN OF THE BLUES** written by Sasha Dalton, Ernest McCarty; Director, Woodie King, Jr.; Set/Lighting, Llewellyn Harrison; Costumes, Judy Dearing; Sound, Brian Penny; Musical Director, Bruce Townsend; Arrangements, Corky McLerkin; Additional Arrangements, Ernest McCarty; General Manager, Sheila Phillips-Murph; Stage Manager, Richard Douglass; Dance Movement, Sloan Robinson; Wigs, Breelun Daniels; Wardrobe, Bruce C. Edwards; Production Associates, Trudy Brown, Betsy C. Jackson; Press, Michael Alpert, Ruth Jaffe. CAST: Sasha Dalton (Dinah Washington). A musical in two acts. The action takes place backstage and at showtime at the famous jazz club Birdland in 1963. **MUSICAL NUMBERS:** I Wanna Be Loved, Dinah Washington, Blow Soft Winds, Dream, Lover Come Back to Me, Salty Papa Blues, Evil Gal Blues, I Don't Hurt Anymore, The Blues Ain't Nothing, This Can't Be Love, Blow Top Blues #1, Mixed Emotions, I Could Write a Book, Teach Me Tonight, This Bitter Earth, Love for Sale, Am I Asking Too Much, Medley, Make Someone Happy, What a Difference a Day Made, Unforgettable

Josef Sommer, Paul Rudd, Stockard Channing,
Kevin Geer in "The Lady and the Clarinet"
(Henry Grossman Photo) Top: George Martin, Joanne Camp,
Marian Seldes and Below: Seldes, Martin,
Elizabeth McGovern in "Painting Churches"
(Martha Swope/Susan Cook Photos)

Dinah Manoff, Zohra Lampert in "Gifted Children"
(Adam Newman Photo) Above: Joan Allen,
Peter Friedman in "And a Nightingale Sang"
(Lanny Nagler Photo) Top: Ann Reinking
in "One More Song/One More Dance"

**Vivienne Lenk, Reily Hendrickson, Joseph McCaren,
Suzanne Toren, Donald Brooks Ford, Robert Sukerman
in "French Toast"**

(ACTORS & DIRECTORS THEATRE) Wednesday, Jan. 11–29, 1984 (16 performances). American Folk Theater (Dick Gaffield, Artistic Director) presents: **WILLIE** by Leslie Lee; Director, Robert Maitland; Sets, Marc D. Malamud; Lighting, William J. Plachy; Costumes, David Toser; Assistant Director, Elaine Jones Lee; Stage Managers, Brian Evaret Chandler, Leon McMichael; Choreography, Louanna Gardner; Press, Kristin Jones. CAST: Thomas Anderson (Rev. Mosley/Dr. Stargell), Donald Buka (Paul), Herb Downer (Willie), Lawrence Evans (Tippet/Leonard), Jill Kotler (Chris/Amelia/Dancer), Phillip Lindsay (Pop), Carol London (Mom/Dorothy/Carrie), Saundra McClain (Alice/Marie), Nefretete Rasheed (Pamela/Wanda/Dancer), Mary Rausch (Jane Shelton), Bruce Strickland (Dr. Stargell), Jim Stubbs (Rick/Leonard). A play in two acts. The action takes place in the present and the past in various places and cities.

(AMERICAN THEATRE OF ACTORS) Tuesday Jan. 17, 1984–
MY FATHER'S HOUSE by James Jennings; Director, Ed. Setrakian; Set, Marc Beres; Costumes, Jeffrey L. Robbins; Lighting, James D'Asaro; General Manager, Lisa Lipsky; Press, David Lipsky. CAST: Joanne Hamlin (Margot), Katie Grant (Linda), Henderson Forsythe (Case), Ted Zurkowski (Jerry), James Nixon (Michael). A drama in two acts. The action takes place at the present time in mid-December in a small town in Kansas.

(JOYCE THEATER) Tuesday, Jan. 17,–Feb. 26, 1984 (48 performances). The Living Theatre Co. (Julian Beck, Judith Malina, Directors) in association with the Joyce Theater Foundation present in repertory:
THE ARCHEOLOGY OF SLEEP by Julian Beck,
THE ANTIGONE OF SOPHOCLES by Bertolt Brecht,
THE YELLOW METHUSELAH by Hanon Reznikov,
THE ONE AND THE MANY by Ernst Toller. COMPANY: Isha Manna Back, Julian Beck, Raaja Fischer, Rain House, Mina Lande, Henriette Luthi, Judith Malina, Catherine Marchand, Antonia Matera, Maria Nora, Karsten Nyvang, Horacio Martin Palacios, Hanon Reznikov, Stephan Schulberg, Nicolas Serrano, Dirk Szuszies, Ilion Troya, Serena Urbani, Christian Vollmer, Thomas Walker.

(TOMI PARK ROYAL THEATRE) Friday, Jan. 20,–Feb. 5, 1984 (15 performances and 5 previews). Presented by the Raven Production Co.
KING LEAR by William Shakespeare; Director, Jordan Deitcher; Sets, David Raphel; Costumes, Lare Schultz; Lights, Victor En Yu Tan; Sound, Philip Campanella; Press, David Lotz. CAST: Jane Kessler Bassin, Terry Donnelly, Timothy Hall, Dennis Lavalle, Philip Lombardo, Ron Martell, Maxim Mazumdar, Ciaran O'Reilly, Meghan Robinson, Paul Rosa, Wesley Stevens, Mark Torres

(TOMI PARK ROYAL THEATRE) Sunday, Jan. 22–29, 1984 (8 performances). The Festival Theatre Foundation (Robert O'Rourke, Artistic Director) presents: **FRENCH TOAST** by Frances Eliot Mitchell and Robert O'Rourke; Costumes, Susan L. Gomez; Lighting, Katy Orrick; Stage Managers, Sally Jane Gellert, Alicia Sapienza; Wardrobe, Helen Krumm. CAST: Joseph McCaren (Henri Des Prunelle), Vivienne Lenk (Cyprienne Des Prunelle), Robert Zukerman (Clavignac/Pierre/Policeman), Suzanne Toren (Josepha/Mme. De Brionne/Waiter/Policeman), Donald Brooks Ford (Adhemar De Gratignan), Reily Hendrickson (Mlle. De Lusignan/Waiter/Inspector). A comedy in two acts and three scenes. The action takes place in the spring of 1880 in the home of Des Prunelles, just outside Paris, and in a private dining room at Maxim.

(UPSTAIRS AT GREENE STREET) Thursday, Jan. 19,–March 31, 1984 (33 performances). Daisy Chain Productions presents:
BALL by John Jiler; Director, Daniel Wilson; Original Music and Lyrics, Richard Vitzhum; Musical Director, Lauriann Greene; Choreographer, Margarite Winer; Costumes, Susan Frances; Lighting, Peggy Eisenhauer; Stage Manager, Lisa Kirsch; Hairstylist/Makeup, Shannon Harrington; Press, Jeffrey Richards Associates. CAST: Phillip Goodwin (Lord Armbruster), Mary Irey (Lady Bottomley), Mike Lisenco (Ralph Greenbaum), Marcia McIntosh (Nora Greenbaum), Michael McKenzie (Count Hun), Martha Horstman (Countess Hun), Susan Morgenstern (Duchess of Trent), Paul Mullins (Lord Bottomley). A musical satire. The action takes place in England just prior to the first World War.

(18th STREET PLAYHOUSE) Sunday, Jan. 1,–Feb. 29, 1984 (24 performances) Eccentric Circles Theatre (Paula Kay Pierce, Rosemary Hopkins, Barbara Bunch, Janet Bruders, Producers) presents its third annual series of original one-act plays written and directed by women. Executive Producer, Paula Kay Pierce; Production Manager, Gary Miller; Assistant Production Manager, Ed Wernick; Lighting, Richard Clausen; Photographer, Denise De Mirjian; Press, Patt Dale Associates. CAST: "A Stranger in a Strange Land" by Jolene Goldenthal; Director, Janet Bruders; with Albert Makhtsier (Joseph), Yanni Sfinias (Simon), Jean Brookner (Millie). "Triple Exposure" by Shirley Guy; Director, Gary Miller; with Lory Marcosson (Anne), Maggie Suter (Emily), Georgia Heaslip (Sarah). "Bloodfeud" written and performed by Judith Morley. "The Confessional" by Judy Montague; Director, DeeDee Sandt; with Diane Boardman (Dot), Randie Jean Davis (Lola), David Gianopoulos (Buddy), Jacob Terry (Dr. Healy). "Foxy and John"/"234 and 235" by Edna Morris; Director, Laurie Eliscu; with Viola Borden (Foxy), John McLearen (John), Michael Lisenco (Policeman), Kin Weston-Moran (Receptionist), Denise Simone (Mary), Robert Boardman (Michael). "Challah and Raspberries" by June Calender; Director, Diana Barth; with Mary Francina Golden (Sandy), Vera Lockwood (Esther). "Today's Children" by Judith Knox; Director, Nina Mende; with Al Sperduto (Phil), Susan Schwirck (Evelyn), William Ellis (Hal), Joan Kendall (Frieda), Pamela Title (Debby), Robert Boardman (Peter). "A Double Scoop" by Leslie Ava Shaw; Director, Marianne Murphy; with Bill Johnson (Bob), Ken Womble (Jim), Rosemary Hopkins (Shirley), Melissa Hurst (Susan), Marie O'Donnell (Linda). "Fry Canyon, Pop. 3" by Vicki Rosen; Director, Mollie David; with Fred Sugerman (Ric), John Bukovec (Skipper), George Buck (Les), Marion Hunter (Dorothy), Meg Van Zyl (Tisha). "Patty and Josh" by Toni Press; Director, Denise De Mirjian; with Beth Williams (Patty), Michael Lazarus (Josh), Les Forshey (Policeman). "The Soul of a Stripper" by Ilsa Gilbert; Director, Eleonore Treiber; with Thomas J. Brogan (Dandy Deathpit), Lorna Lable (Extra Vaganza), James Bormann (Waiter), Art Pingree (Dandy Deathpit/inner person), Martha Nazzaro (Extra Vaganza/inner person). "Free Falling in Manhattan" written and performed by Brownlee. "Carrie" by Jean Nuchtern; Director, Melanie Sutherland; with Judith Heineman, Amy Beth Williams, Catherine Way, Sally Frances, Pattie Tierce. "Romped out 84!" written and performed by C. J. Critt, with additional actors David May, Jan Hunter, Paul Dunlap, William E. Peterson.

(ACTORS OUTLET) Thursday, Jan. 26,–Feb. 19, 1984 (30 performances). Artists Unlimited (David Charles Keeton, Executive Producer; Karen Lesley-Lloyd, Producer) presents:
UNCOMMON HOLIDAYS by John Crabtree; Director, Arnold Willens; Set, Victor Dinapoli; Lighting, Randall C. McAndrews; Costumes, Jeanne Bosse; Stage Managers, Tom Langford, Avril Hordyck; Photographer, Victor Dinapoli; Press, FLT/Francine L. Trevens, Penny Landau. CAST: "Ready for the Ritz" with Brian Evers (Brendan), Tobey (Hudson), "Still Life with Phoenix AD" with David Schachter (First Man), Nole Cohen (Second Man), "Billy Angel" with James Mathers (David), Robert Mason (Billy).

Hudson Plumb, Brian Evers in "Uncommon Holidays"
(Victor D'Napoli Photo)

Roy Brocksmith, Jessica Harper, David Patrick Kelly in "Dr. Selavy's Magic Theatre"

(ST. CLEMENT"S THEATRE) Friday, Jan. 27,–Feb. 18, 1984 (20 performances and 3 previews). Music-Theatre Group/Lenox Arts Center (Lyn Austin, Producing Director; Diane Wondisford, Managing Director) and Ontological-Hysteric Theatre present:
DR. SELAVY'S MAGIC THEATRE conceived and directed by Richard Foreman; Music, Stanley Silverman; Lyrics, Tom Hendry; Musical Director, Michael Ward; Scenery, Richard Foreman, Nancy Winters; Costumes, Lindsay W. Davis; Lighting, Pat Collins; Stage Managers, Cathy B. Blaser, Patrick D'Antonio; Props, Gaby Aarons; Press, Monina von Opel. CAST: Roy Brocksmith, Annie Golden, Jessica Harper, David Patrick Kelly, George McGrath, Kathi Moss, Dara Norman, Charlie O'Connell, John Vining. A musical in two acts.

(RIVERWEST THEATRE) Thursday, Feb. 2–26, 1984 (15 performances and 5 previews). CHS Productions and Roderick Cook in association with Riverwest Theatre present:
THE NINTH STEP by Tom Ziegler; Director, Roderick Cook; Set, Thomas Lynch; Lighting, F. Mitchell Dana; Costumes, Karen Gerson; Technical Director, Christopher Cole; Stage Managers, David K. Rodger, Jeanne Ward; Casting, Jack Kelly/Ronnie Yeskel; Photographer, Mike Burrows; Press, FLT/Francine L. Trevens, Penny M. Landau. CAST: Gerrianne Raphael (Joanna Wheeler), Jennie Ventriss (Eleanor Houser), Kim Ameen (Maria), Lynn Goodwin (Melissa Wheeler), Karen Tull (Tracy Smithfield). A play in two acts. The action takes place at the present time on a Friday in spring, in the attic apartment of Joanna Wheeler, located in Hyde Park, not far from the University of Chicago.

(BEACON THEATRE) Sunday and Monday, Feb. 5 & 6, 1984 (2 performances). Kazuko Hillyer presents:
NOH-KYOGEN the National Theatre of Japan: Kongo Noh School and Shigeyama Kyogen; Tour Manager, Richard Fried; Press, Shirley Herz, Sam Rudy, Pete Sanders. PROGRAM: Yashima (Yashima Bay), Uri Nusubito (The Melon Thief), Hagoromo (The Robe of Feathers). Presented in two parts.

(THEATRE FOUR) Wednesday, Feb. 1 The Negro Ensemble Company (Douglas Turner Ward, Artistic Director; Leon B. Denmark, Managing Dirctor) presents:
AMERICAN DREAMS by Velina Houston; Director, Samuel P. Barton; Set, Daniel Proett; Lighting, Shirley Prendergast; Costumes, Judy Dearing, Sound, Bernard Hall; Stage Manager, Jerry Cleveland. CAST: Walter Allen Bennett, Jr. (Lawrence), Count Stovall (Manfred Banks), Sandra Reaves-Phillips (Freddie Banks), Reuben Green (Creed Banks), Nancy Hamada (Setsuko Banks), Ron Auguste (Policeman/Military Officer), Kim Yancey (Blue River Banks), Janet League (Alexis Morgan), Ching Valdes (Fumiko Brennan); understudy: Lynette Chun (Setsuko/Funiko). A play in two acts. The action takes place on Manhattan's lower East Side in early fall of 1955.

(SOUTH STREET THEATRE) Tuesday, Feb. 7–12, 1984 (6 performances and 4 previews). Dudley Field Malone presents:
MADEMOISELLE by Arthur Whitney; Director, Cliff Goodwin; General Manager/Associate Producer, Mary Sutton; Design, Salvatore Tagliarino; Lighting, Vivien Leone; Stage Managers, Laura Heller, David Carlyon; Photography, Arthur Whitney; Press, Jeffrey Richards, C. George Willard, Robert Ganshaw, Ben Morse, Richard Dahl. CAST: Nick Demetrius (Mike), Sylvia Davis (Mademoiselle), David Carlyon/Peter Filiaci (Lurkers). A drama in 2 acts and 6 scenes. The action takes place in Mademoiselle's room in a S.R.O. hotel in Miami, Florida, at the present time in late spring.

(TERRACE THEATRE) Wednesday, Feb. 8–25, 1984. (12 performances). Aranrhod Productions
THE BONE GARDEN by Peter Maeck; Director/Producer, Geoffrey Shlaes; Set, David Emmons; Costumes, Beba Shamash; Sound, Paul Schierhorn; Lighting, John Hastings; General Manager, Allan Francis; Production Manager/Technical Director, Mark Wallace; Casting, Susan LaFollette; Stage Managers, Parker Young, Mark Wallace, James Thomas; Press, Shirley Herz Associates, Pete Sanders. CAST: Robert John Frank (Cootie), Ron Harper (Trump), Jack Wetherall (Pip), David Clarke (Leo), Richard Mazza (Bobo), Harry Spillman (Dr. Crabb), Maggie Greer (Zinnia), James Thomas (Attendant). A play in 2 acts and 4 scenes. The action takes place at the present time in a locker room.

(WONDERHORSE THEATRE) Thursday, Feb. 9–26, 1984 (20 performances). Cherubs Guild Corporaton (Carol Avila, Executive Director; Hillary Wyler, Artistic Director) presents:
THE BEAUTIFUL LA SALLES by Michael Dinwiddie; Director, Hillary Wyler; Set, Bob Phillips; Lighting, Jo Mayer; Costumes, Martin Pakledinaz; Stage Managers, Sharon Stover, Randi Zimmerman; Production Coordinators, Carol Avila, Rebecca Taylor; Technical Director, Edmond Ramage; Casting, David Connell; Makeup, Laurie Lombardi; Press, Walter Vatter. CAST: Ethel Ayler (Emilie Josephine LaSalle), Hazel J. Medina (Nantucket Dorene LaSalle), Charles H. Patterson (Kenny "Bobo" Laker), Joan B. Pryor (Wilhelmina "Willie" Lewis), Michael Yanez (Rafael "Raffy"), Arthur French (Joseph "Cliptoe" Bradley). A comedy-drama in two acts. The action takes place in the LaSalles' Riverside Drive apartment in Harlem in late August of the present time.

(SAMUEL BECKETT THEATRE) Thursday, Feb. 16,–Apr. 22, 1984 (78 performances and 8 previews). The Harold Clurman Theatre (Jack Garfein, Artistic Director) and Lucille Lortel present:
ROCKABY by Samuel Beckett; Director, Alan Schneider; Set/Lighting, Rocky Greenberg; Costumes, Carla Kramer; General Manager, Erik Murkoff; Company Manager, Jonathan Stuart Cerullo; Assistant Director, Valerie Lumbroso; Technical Director, Marc Malamud; Stage Managers, Tham Mangan, Greg Petitti; Press, Jeffrey Richards, Robert Ganshaw, Ben Morse, C. George Willard, Richard Dahl. CAST: "Enough" a dramatic reading of the Beckett short story by Billie Whitelaw. "Footfalls" by Mr. Beckett with Billie Whitelaw (May), Sybil Lines (Mother's Voice). "Rockaby" Billie Whitelaw (Woman and Voice)

(AMERICAN RENAISSANCE THEATRE) Saturday, Feb. 11,–March 4, 1984 (20 performances). The American Stage Co. (Anita Khanzadian, Artistic Director) presents:
SAVAGE AMUSEMENT by Peter Flannery; Director, Pierre Epstein; Set/Lighting, Steven T. Howell; Costumes, Steven L. Birnbaum; Stage Manager, Virginia Jones; Press, Richard Kornberg. CAST: Christopher Wells (Stephen), Marc Epstein (Fitz), Rob Knepper (Olly), Kelly Pino (Ali), Brenda Daly (Hazel). A drama in two acts, set in Manchester, England.

(PROVINCETOWN PLAYHOUSE) Wednesday, Feb. 15,–March 3, 1984 (23 performances and 9 previews). Arthur Cantor, Brad Hall, Bruce Ostler, Paul Barrosse, Bonnie Nelson Schwartz present The Practical Theatre Co. (Bapul Barrosse, Brad Hall, Artistic Directors; Angela Murphy, Producing Director) production of:
BABALOONEY with Original Music by Larry Schanker and the Practical Theatre Co.; Director, Brad Hall; Setting, Louis DiCrescenzo; Sketches developed improvisationally by and for The Practical Theatre Co.; Lighting, Tom Larson; Costumes, Iwo Jima, Jen Crawford; Stage Manager, Wolf Larson; General Manager, Harvey Elliott; Company Manager, Bruce Ostler; Press, Arthur Cantor Associates. CAST: Rush Pearson, Jamie Baron, Bekka Eaton, Uncle Charlie, Jane Muller, Paul Barrosse.

Billie Whitelaw in "Rockaby"

71

Bill Cwikowski, John Danelle in "Split Second"
(Austin Trevett Photo)

**Tom Ligon, Robin Thomas, Kathy McNeil
in "Clean Sweep"** *(Carol Rosegg Photo)*

**Percy Mtwa, Mbongeni Ngema
in "Woza Albert!"**
(Chris Bennion Photo)

(INTAR STAGE 2) Wednesday, Feb. 15,–March 11, 1984 (20 performances). Re-opened at Theatre 4 on Wednesday, May 23, 1984 and still playing. Amistad World Theatre and McDonald-Fleming Productions present:
SPLIT SECOND by Dennis McIntyre; Director, Samuel P. Barton; Set/Lighting, Leo Bambacorta; Composer, Cornelia J. Post; Sound, Full House Productions; Stage Managers, Max Storch, Gordon T. Skinner; Managing Director/Press, Shirley Fishman. CAST: Helmar Augustus Cooper (Parker), Bill Cwikowski (Willis), John Danelle (Val Johnson), Peter Jay Fernandez (Charlie), Norman Matlock (Rusty Johnson), Michele Shay (Alea Johnson). A drama in two acts. The action takes place at the present time on July 4th.

(PERRY STREET THEATRE) Thursday, Feb. 16,–March 18, 1984 (35 performances). PACT/Public Arena for Communicative Theatre presents:
CLEAN SWEEP by Joel Gross; Director, Brian Hurley; Set, Cabot McMullen; Costumes, David Toser; Lighting, Curt Ostermann; Stage Manager, Patrick McCord; Hairstylist, Mark Taylor; Sound, Will Austen; Wardrobe, Adrienne Mason; Press, Burnham-Callaghan Associates, David Lotz. CAST: Robin Thomas (Stu), Kate McNeil (Diane), Tom Ligon (Bobby), Carole Chase (Marta). A comedy in 2 acts and 6 scenes. The action takes place at the present time in Stu's luxury apartment in New York City.

(VINEYARD THEATRE) Friday, Feb. 17,–March 11, 1984 (21 performances). Vineyard Theatre (Barbara Zinn, Executive Director; Douglas Aibel, Artistic Director) presents:
SHADOW MAN by Michael Wright; Director, Mary B. Robinson; Set, Johniene Papandreas; Lighting Richard Lund; Costumes, Muriel Stockdale; Sound, Laura Larsen; Stage Managers, Crystal Huntington; Press, Bruce Cohen. CAST: Christopher Marcantel (Sonny), Christine Jansen (Amy), Frank Girardeau (Ray), Keith Reddin (Warren). A drama in two acts and five scenes. The action takes place in the spring of 1981 in a tract house in Dundale, a suburb of Baltimore, MD.

(JEWISH REPERTORY THEATRE) Tuesday, Feb. 21,–March 11, 1984 (20 performances). JRT presents:
THE HOMECOMING by Harold Pinter; Director, Anthony McKay; Set, Mike Boyer; Costumes, Janetta Turner; Lighting, Dan Kinsley; Stage Manager, G. Franklin Heller; Press, Bruce Cohen. CAST: Joe Silver (Max), Mark Arnott (Lenny), Charles Randall (Sam), Howard Sherman (Joey), WIlliam McNulty (Teddy), Cheryl McFadden (Ruth). A drama in two acts. The action takes place at the present time in an old house in the North of London.

(LUCILLE LORTEL THEATRE) Thursday, Feb. 23,–May 6, 1984 (79 performances and 5 previews). Elliot Martin, Arnold Bernhard, Columbia Artists Theatrical Corp. in association with Lucille Lortel present the Market Theatre Company's production of:
WOZA ALBERT! by and with Percy Mtwa and Mbongeni Ngema who created the play with the Director, Barney Simon; Set, Barney Simon; Lighting, Mannie Manin; Executive Producer, Gary McAvay; General Management, Leonard A. Mulhern/ Gail Bell/James Hannah; Stage Managers, Joseph DePauw, Dixon Setlhare Malele; Press, Jeffrey Richards, Ben Morse, Robert Ganshaw, C. George Willard, Richard Dahl.

(NAT HORNE THEATRE) Friday, Feb. 24–26, 1984 (5 performances); returned Friday, May 4–6, 1984 for 3 additional performances. The Off Center Theatre in association with Yaffa Productions II present:
SPIRIT, BLACK AND FEMALE directed by Denise Hamilton; Musical Director, Jimi Foster; Choreographer, Bruce Hawkins; Costumes, Ron Harris; Lighting, Ulric O'Flaherty; Set/Lighting, Pete Caldwell; Production Manager, Lynda Doubille. CAST: Linda Hazel Humes with percussionists Jack Scavella, Montego Joe.

(ALL SOULS FELLOWSHIP HALL) Friday, Feb. 24,–March 10, 1984 (8 performances). The All Souls Players present:
JUDY: A GARLAND OF SONGS created and staged by Jeffrey K. Neill; Musical Adaptations and Direction, Wendell Kindberg; Set, Robert Edmonds; Costumes, Charles W. Roeder; Lighting, Dorian Bernacchio; Sound, Ira Stoller; Stage Manager, Ruth E. Kramer; Producers, Suzanne Kaszynski, Jeffery K. Neill, Howard Van Der Meulen; Wardrobe, Elaine H. and Selma M. Hirsch; Technical Directors, Janice Matteucci, Cindy Dobie, Press, Marie Landa. CAST: Diana Daniel, Edwin Decker, Helen Eckard, Steven Fickinger, Debra Kelman, Richard K. Smith, Standbys: Craig Shepherd, Mary E. P. Young. A musical celebration of Judy Garland and her career, performed in two acts.

(TOP OF THE VILLAGE GATE) Sunday, Feb. 26,–March 11, 1984 (5 performances).
CUMMINGS & GOINGS with Poetry by E. E. Cummings; Music, Ada Janik; Orchestrations/Additional Songs, Steven Margoshes; Directed and Staged by Nina Janik; General Manager, Ruth Goldblatt; Stage Manager, Diane Ward; Technical Adviser, Carl Seltzer; Press, G. Theodore Kilmer. CAST: Sharon Brown, Elisa Fiorillo, Nina Hennessey, Bruce Hubbard, Raymond Patterson. A special musical event in two acts.

Kaye Ballard in "Hey, Ma . . . Kaye Ballard"
(Martha Swope Photo)

**Thomas A. Carlin, Louisa Flaningam, James Greene
in "Pigeons on the Walk"** *(Carol Rosegg Photo)*

**Isabella Hofmann, Mike Hagerty, Richard Kind,
John Kapelos, Rick Thomas, Meagen Fay
in "Orwell That Ends Well"**

(PROMENADE THEATRE) Monday, Feb. 27,–Apr. 22, 1984 (62 performances and 16 previews). Karl Allison and Bryan Bantry present:
HEY, MA . . . KAYE BALLARD with concept, original music and lyrics by David Levy, Leslie Ebenhard; Written by Kaye Ballard; Director, Susan H. Schulman; Set, Linda Hacker; Costumes, William Ivey Long; Lighting, Ruth Roberts; Musical Supervision/Direction, Robert Billig; Orchestrations, Robby Merkin; Special Musical Arrangement, Arthur Siegel; Associate Producer, Paul Bellardo; General Management, Jay Kingwill, Lawrence Goossen; Company Manager, Susan Sampliner; Production Associate, Michael Bethea; Props, Val Medina; Hairstylist/Wardrobe, Ron Frederick; Stage Manager, Marjorie Horne; Press, Henry Luhrman, Terry M. Lilly, Keith Sherman, Kevin P. McAnarney, Bill Miller. CAST: Kaye Ballard as herself. Performed in two acts. Musical Numbers: Up There, Someone Special, Nana, You Made Me Love You, Thinking of You, Supper Club, Without a Song, Nobody but You, Teeny Tiny, Hey, Ma, Lazy Afternoon, Always You, You Don't Need It, Down in the Depths, Cookin' Breakfast, Old Tunes, All the Magic Ladies

(UPSTAIRS AT GREENE STREET) Wednesday, March 7, – Risa Bramon, Joseph Kleinmann, Mark Krantz and the Ensemble Studio Theatre (Curt Dempster, Artistic Director; David S. Rosenak, Managing Director) present:
STRANGE BEHAVIOR by Neil Cuthbert; Director, Charles Karchmer; Music, Michael Bramon; Stage Manager, Kit Liset; Costumes, Deborah Shaw; Press, Bruce Cohen, Jim Baldassare. CAST: Wende Dasteel, Christine Farrell, Jack Gilpin, Ilene Kristen, Bob Lesser, Peter Zapp. A cabaret comedy in 26 scenes.

(DOUGLAS FAIRBANKS THEATRE/UPSTAIRS) Thursday, March 1,–18, 1984 (24 performances). Eric Krebs presents:
CIRCUS GOTHIC with music by Marsha Coffee; Book and Lyrics, Jan Kudelka; Musical Director, Kenneth Lundie; Director, Alex Dmitriev; Set, Doug McLean; Costumes, Chris Sanders; Lighting, Phil Monat; Press, Jeffrey Richards Associates, Ben Morse. CAST: Jana Robins in a solo performance.

(VILLAGE GATE DOWNSTAIRS) Thursday, March 1,–June 3, 1984 (110 performances and 10 previews). Bernard Sahlins and Art D'Lugoff present the original Chicago Second City Company in:
ORWELL THAT ENDS WELL with Music by Fred Kaz; Director, Bernard Sahlins; Associate Producer, Joyce Sloane; Stage Manager, Craig Taylor; House Manager, Neal Haynes; General Manager, Art D'Lugoff; Production Supervisor, Robert Strohmeier; Press, Max Eisen, Maria Somma, Madelon Rosen. CAST: Meagen Fay, John Kapelos, Mike Hagerty, Richard Kind, Isabella Hofmann, Rick Thomas. A revue in two acts. Repertoire: Reunion, Job Interview, Rendezvous, Editorial, Nothingness and Being, Culture Quiz, Oh America!, Personals, Pirates, Bernardin, Love Story, Oh Chicago!, Double Exposure, Domesticity, Home Study, Uses of Television, Growing Up, Margaret Thatcher, Who Gives a Damn

(McGINN/CAZALE THEATRE) Tuesday, March 6,–April 7, 1984 (10 performances and 20 previews). The Second Stage (Robyn Goodman/Carole Rothman, Artistic Directors) presents:
ALL NIGHT LONG by John O'Keefe; Director, Andre Gregory; Set, Adrianne Lobel; Lighting, James F. Ingalls; Costumes, Susan Hilferty; Sound, Gary Harris; Hairstylist, Antonio Soddu; Score, Bruce Coughlin; Stage Managers, Charles Otte, Susanne Jul; Production Supervisor, Kim Novick; Press, Richard Kornberg. CAST: Michael Riney (Eddy), Mary McDonnell (Jill), Gerry Bamman (Jack), Catherine Coray (Tammy), Alyssa Jayne Milano (Terry), A comedy in two acts. The action takes place at the present time in Jack's suburban home.

(ACTORS OUTLET THEATRE CENTER) Sunday, March 11,–April 14, 1984 (20 performances). StageArts Theatre Company (Nell Robinson/Ruth Ann Norris, Artistic Directors) presents:
PIGEONS ON THE WALK by Andrew Johns; Director, Nell Robinson; Set, Joseph A. Varga; Costumes, Sheila Kehoe; Lighting, Bob Bessoir; Technical Director, John Saltonstall; Saxophone Music written and played by Hugo Napier; Stage Managers, Dennis Cameron, Renee Porte, Allan Babuska; Press, Shirley Herz, Sam Rudy, Peter Cromarty. CAST: Stephen Bradbury (Cowboy), Dorothy Brooks (Susan), Peter Brouwer (Walter), Erma Campbell (Adolph), Thomas A. Carlin (Victor), Joseph Dobish (Albert), Flloyd Ennis (Frank), Kevin Eshelman (Kid), Louisa Flaningam (Irene), James Greene (Richie), Ariana Johns (Girl), Peter Marklin (Steve), Bernie Passeltiner (Louis). A comedy in 2 acts and 3 scenes. The action takes place at the present time on a Sunday in a New York City Off Track Betting Parlor.

(RIVERWEST THEATRE) Monday, March 12,–April 29, 1984 (48 performances). CHS Productions in association with RiverWest Theatre presents the New York premiere of:
THE PATRICK PEARSE MOTEL by Hugh Leonard; Director, Robert Bridges; Set, James Noone; Costumes, Karen Gerson; Lighting, Matt Ehlert; Technical Director, Christopher Cole; Sound, Edward Fitzgerald; Stage Manager, D. C. Rosenberg; Press, FLT/Francine L. Trevens; Ballad composed and sung by John Didrichson. CAST: Janet Bell (Grainne Gibbon), William Ferriter (James Usheen), James Gleason (Dermod Gibbon), Madelyn Griffith-Haynie (Miss Manning), Richard Merrell (Fintan Kinmore), Ron Randell (Hoolihan), Judith Tillman (Niamh Kinnore). An Irish farce in 2 acts and 3 scenes. The action takes place in 1968 in the living-room of the Gibbon home in a fashionable suburb of Dublin, and in the Patrick Pearse Motel.

(MANHATTAN COMMUNITY COLLEGE PERFORMING ARTS CENTER) Thursday, March 15–28, 1984 (12 performances and 4 previews). Richard Allen Center for Culture and Art (Shirley J. Radcliffe, Executive Producer) in association with Performing Arts Center (William Spencer Reilly, Executive Director) presents: **TAKE ME ALONG** with Book by Joseph Stein; Adapted from Eugene O'Neill's "Ah, Wilderness"; Music and Lyrics, Bob Merrill; Direction and Choreography, Geraldine Fitzgerald, Mike Malone; Arrangements/Musical Direction/Additional Music, Coleridge Taylor Perkinson; Additional Choreography, Dianne McIntyre; Musical Director/Pianist, Frederic Gripper; Set, James Wolk; Lighting, Toshiro Ogawa; Costumes, Myrna Colley-Lee; Stage Manager, Otis White; Press, Howard and Barbara Atlee. CAST: Duane Jones (Nat), Mary Alice (Essie), Rhetta Hughes (Lily), Mario Van Peebles (Arthur), Marchand Odette (Mildred), Jeffrey V. Thompson (Sid), Mark Wade (Richard), Robert Kya-Hill (Dave), Michael Darden (Wint), Vanessa Bell (Belle), Kirk Taylor (Bartender), Sandy Williams (Muriel), Olivia Ward (Mrs. McComber). A musical in 2 acts. The action takes place on the 4th and 5th of July circa 1906 in the Miller home in Centerville, CT.
MUSICAL NUMBERS: Oh Please, Sid Ol' Kid, I'm Staying Young, The Hurt They Write About, I Get Embarrassed, Take Me Along, We're Home, The Company of Men, That's How It Starts, A Slight Detail, Little Green Snake, I Would Die.

(WONDERHORSE THEATRE) Thursday, March 15,–April 1, 1984 (16 performances). TRG Repertory (Marvin Kahan, Artistic Director; Anita Pintozzi, Associate Producer) presents:
SILENT NIGHT, LONELY NIGHT by Robert Anderson; Director, William Hopkins; Set, Peter Harrison; Costumes, Christopher Cade; Lighting, Carol Graebner; Stage Manager, Robert Foreman; Production Coordinator, Marion Mackles; Technical Director, Allan Sporing; Press, Jan Greenberg. CAST: Lillian Byrd (Janet), Brian Evers (John), Steven Haft (Jerry), Katherine Jay-Carroll (Katherine), Ruby Payne (Mae), Robert B. Putnam (Philip). A drama in 2 acts and 4 scenes. The action takes place in a colonial inn in a New England town in 1959.

(INTERART THEATRE) Friday, March 16,–May 6, 1984 (56 performances). Interart Theatre (Margot Lewitin, Artistic Director; Sam Sweet, Managing Director) and Mabou Mines present:
THROUGH THE LEAVES by Frank Xaver Kroetz; Translated by Roger Downey; Director, Joanne Akalaitis; Dramaturg, Colette Brooks; Set, Douglas Stein; Costumes, Kurt Wilhelm; Lighting, Frances Aronson; Sound, L. B. Dallas; Company Manager, Cynthia Hedstrom; Stage Manager, Paula Gordon; Supervising Producer, Byeager Blackwell; Technical Director, Richard Meyer; Props, Susan Block; Press, Fred Hoot, David Mayhew. CAST: Ruth Maleczech (Annette), Frederick Neumann (Victor). Performed without intermission. The action takes place in a butcher shop and its squalid backroom parlor.

(THE CUBICULO) Monday, March 19,–April 15, 1984 (20 performances and 5 previews). New York Theatre Workshop (Jean Passanante, Artistic Director) presents:
GREATE DIVIDE by Robert Litz; Director, David Rotenberg; Set, Peter David Gould; Costumes, V. Jane Suttell; Lighting, John Hickey; Sound, Tommy Hawk, Stan Metelits; Technical Director, Bill Wells; Props, Terrence Hart; Production Assistant, Jarmila Packard; Stage Manager, Lawrence Eaton; Press, Fred Hoot, David Mayhew. CAST: (In Wisdon, Montana at the present) William Newman (Early), Kevin Geer (Marle), Sloane Shelton (Madge), (In Caledonia County, Vermont in the 1930's) Sloane Shelton (Edna), Kevin Geer (Earl), William Newman (James), J. Smith-Cameron (Ruth), (In a small city in Upstate New York in 1982) William Newman (John), Kevin Geer (Moll), J. Smith-Cameron (Julie), Sloane Shelton (Marge), William Newman (Mountain Man). A play in two acts.

Brian Evers, Robert B. Putnam, Lillian Byrd,
Katherine Jay-Carroll in "Silent Night, Lonely Night"

Pat Russell, David Finklestein, Terry Greiss,
Christina Sluberski in "Ethan Frome"
(John Stahle Photo)

(BEACON THEATRE) Monday, March 19–25, 1984 (9 performances). Kazuko Hillyer in association with Concert Arts Society presents the New Vic Theatre of London in:
DRACULA or a Pain in the Neck by Phil Woods with Michael Bogdanon; Director, Michael Bogdanon; Assistant Director, John Labanowski; Designer, Marty Flood; Lighting, Chic Reid, Nicholas Cavallaro; Company Managers, Shirley Escott, Christina Giannelli; Wardrobe, Irma Hager, Cayte Thorpe; Producers, Tony Milner, Micky O'Donoughue; Press, Shirley Herz, Sam Rudy, Peter Cromarty, Pete Sanders. CAST: Anthony Milner (Dracula), Derek Hollis (Sir Jonathan Harker), Chris Barnes (Dr. Seward), Micky O'Donoughue (Renfield), John Darrell (Van Hesling), Moira Brooker (Lady Lucy), Colette Stevenson (Mina Harker). A farce in two acts.

(IRONDALE THEATRE) Friday, March 23,–April 15, 1984 (20 performances and 2 previews). The Irondale Ensemble Project (James Louis Niesen, Artistic Director) presents:
ETHAN FROME adapted from the Edith Wharton novel by Owen and Donald Davis; Director, James Louis Niesen; Set, Kennon Rothchild; Lighting, Richard Dorfman; Costumes, Elena Pellicciaro; Stage Managers, Penny Marks, Kate Chad; Press, G. Theodore Killmer. CAST: Terry Greiss (The New Englander), David Finkelstein (Ethan Frome), Barbara Mackenzie-Wood (Zeena Frome), Christina Sluberski (Mattie Silver), Women of Starkfield: Karen Cook, Pat Russell, Aviva Twersky. A drama in 3 acts and 10 scenes with a prologue and an epilogue. The action takes place in Northern New England during the winter.

(WESTSIDE ARTS THEATRE/DOWNSTAIRS) Wednesday, March 21,–April 15, 1984 (25 performances and 12 previews). Hendrix Productions (Gayle Stants Hendrix, Producer) and John Van Ness Philip present:
THE FLIGHT OF THE EARLS by Christopher Humble; Director, Allen R. Belknap; Scenery, Lawrence Miller; Costumes, Susan A. Cox; Lighting, Richard Winkler; Stage Managers, Mark Baltazar, Tracy Crum; Company Manager, Alice Bernstein; Wardrobe, Lillian Landeo; Casting, Elizabeth Shafer, Fight Choreography, Charles Conwell; Press, Betty Lee Hunt, Maria Cristina Pucci, James Sapp, Robert Larkin. CAST: Guy Paul (Ian Earl), Reed Birney (Timothy Strain), Timothy Landfield (Michael Earl), Carol Teitel (Kate Earl), Christine Estabrook (Brigitte Earl), Peggy Schoditsch (Claire Strain), Kenneth Meseroll (Keith Earl). A play in 2 acts and 6 scenes. The action takes place in the Earl family home in County Tyrone, in September of 1971.

(VILLAGE PERFORMERS THEATRE) Thursday, March 22,–April 15, 1984 (16 performances and 2 previews). The Village Performers (Reena Heenan, Artistic Director) present:
I'LL BE BACK BEFORE MIDNIGHT by Peter Colley; Director, Marc Field; Lighting, David Ferri; Set, Jesse Rosenthal; Costumes, Stephanie Maslansky; Company Manager, Gina Freschet; Stage Managers, Melissa Heenan, Shirley Winters. CAST: Dawn Davis (Laura), Clifford Allen Goodman (Robert Willoughby), Randy Kelly (Greg), Donna Moryn (Jan), Bob Snider (George Willoughby). A play in two acts. The action take place in a cabin in a remote part of the woods.

(CIRCLE IN THE SQUARE DOWNTOWN) Thursday, March 22,–April 29, 1984 (56 performances and 10 previews). M Square Entertainment (Mitchell Maxwell, Alan J. Schuster, Fred H. Krones) and the Ensemble Studio Theatre (Curt Dempster, Artistic Director; David S. Rosenak, Managing Director) present:
TO GILLIAN ON HER 37th BIRTHDAY by Michael Brady; Director, Pamela Berlin; Associate Producer, Andrew R. Morse; Set, Robert Thayer; Lights, Allen Lee Hughes; Costumes, Deborah Shaw; Sound, Bruce Ellman; Music Robert Dennis; General Management, Dorothy Olim, George Elmer; Wardrobe, Cathay Brackman; Production Assistant, Victoria Maxwell; Associate Producer, Billy Hopkins; Stage Managers, Richard Costabile, Kerstin Kilgo; Press, Bruce Cohen, Jim Baldassare. CAST: David Rasche (David), Noelle Parker (Cindy), Sarah Jessica Parker (Rachel), Frances Conroy (Kevin), Richmond Hoxie (Paul), Jean De Baer (Esther), Cheryl McFadden (Gillian). A play in two acts. The action takes place at the present time on a small island off the coast of New England on a weekend in August.

(PROVINCETOWN PLAYHOUSE) Monday, March 26,–April 1, 1984 (8 performances and 10 previews). Yentl Productions (George Schapiro, Producer) presents:
THE ACTORS' DELICATESSEN by Murray Mednick and Priscilla Cohen; Director, Julie Hebert; Set, Ernie A. Smith; Costumes, Donna Granata; Lighting, Novella Smith; Presented in association with Chris Silva, Sari E. Weisman; Stage Manager, M. A. Howard; Press, Burnham-Callaghan, David Lotz. CAST: Marilyn Sokol (Maggie), David Garfield (Mendel). A comedy in two acts. The action takes place in Maggie and Mendel's backstage dressing room.

(ST. CLEMENT'S THEATRE) Tuesday, March 27,–April 14, 1984 (16 performances). Pierre Cardin and Music-Theatre Group/Lenox Arts Center (Lyn Austin, Producing Director) present:
THE GARDEN OF EARTHLY DELIGHTS with Music by Richard Peaslee; Conception and Direction, Martha Clarke; Lighting, Paul Gallo; Costumes, Jane Greenwood; Flying by Foy; Consultant, Peter Beagle; Production Manager, F. Cameron MacRae; Stage Managers, Nora Percival, David Carriere; Wardrobe, Kai Lofton; Press, Monina von Opel. CAST: Robert Barnett, Felix Blaska, Robert Faust, Marie Fourcaut, Margie Gillis, Polly Styron. A dramatization of Hieronymus Bosch's painting of the same title.

(WESTSIDE ARTS CENTER/CHERYL CRAWFORD THEATRE) Tuesday, March 27,–April 8, 1984 (16 performances and 16 previews). The Gero Organization in association with Michael Bennahum presents:
A HELL OF A TOWN by Monte Merrick; Director, Allan Carlsen; Set, Ray Recht; Lighting, F. Mitchell Dana; Costumes, Pamela Scofield; Sound, Nic Minetor; Stage Managers, Louis D. Pietig, Jason Gero; General Management, Gero Communications; Company Manager, Roger Gindi; Wardrobe, Donna McGehean; Props, Thomas Scott Lilly, Susan Selig; Press, Shirley Herz, Sam Rudy, Peter Cromarty, Pete Sanders. CAST: Joanna Gleason (Jill), Peter Riegert (Sandy). A comedy in 2 acts and 7 scenes. The action takes place at the present time in an apartment on the Upper West Side of New York City in early October.

(TERRACE THEATRE AT TOMI) Wednesday, March 28,–April 22, 1984 (20 performances). The Open Space Theatre Experiment (Lynn Michaels, Artistic Director) presents:
ANOTHER PARADISE by Donna Spector; Director, Nancy Gabor; Set/Lighting, Robert E. Briggs; Music, Carolyn Dutton; Costumes, Mary Huessy; Stage Managers, Christopher Willamson, Rachel Griffin; Press, Hunt/Pucci Associates. CAST: Lauren Klein (Neva), Allison Brennan (Birdie Mae), Ralph Elias (Hiram), Anne O'Sullivan (Sal Henry). The action takes place in Paradise, Kentucky in early 1900. Performed without intermission.

Joanna Gleason, Peter Riegert
in "A Hell of a Town"
(Carol Rosegg Photo)

Frances Conroy, David Rasche in "To Gillian
on Her 37th Birthday" *(Carol Rosegg Photo)*

(SOUTH STREET THEATRE) Wednesday, April 4,–May 13, 1984 (20 performances and 6 previews). American Theatre Alliance (Aaron Levin, Artistic Director; Robert J. Weston, Managing Director; Jerold Barnard, Associate Director) under the patronage of the Consul General of France (Bertrand de La Taillade) presents:
SUZANNA ANDLER by Marguerite Duras; Translation, Barbara Bray; Director, Aaron Levin; Set, John Kasarda; Lighting, Jeffrey Beecroft; Costumes, Richard Hornung; Opening and Closing Music, Philip Glass; Sound, Michael DeMayo; Props, Marleen Marta; Wardrobe, Ron Berliner; Stage Managers, Alan Mann, Erica Stevens; Press, Fred Nathan, Leslie Anderson, Anne Abrams, Ted Killmer, Bert Fink. CAST: Herman Petras (Riviere), Barbara Andres (Suzanna Andler), Nicholas Cortland (Michel Cayre), Janet League (Monique Combes). A play in two acts. The action takes place at the present time in a beach house at St. Tropez, out of season.

(UPSTAIRS AT GREENE STREET) Thursday, April 5,–June 28, 1984 (24 performances).
NOT SO NEW FACES OF '84 conceived and directed by Stuart Ross; Musical Director, John Spalla; Choreography, Edmond Kresley; Costumes, Carol Wenz; Production Manager, Ellyn Williams; Lighting, Jeffrey McRoberts; Stage Manager, Myron Moore; Press, Burnham-Callaghan; Music, Lyrics and Sketches by Robin Batteau, Abra Bigham, David Buskin, Michael Feingold, Ellen Fitzhugh, Larry Grossman, Jay Jeffries, Jason McAuliffe, Alan Menken, Scott Oakley, Bob Ost, Jim Ricketts, Stuart Ross, Joel Saltzman, Michael Sartor, David Sinkler, Karen Trott, David Zippel, and the cast: Nancy Ringham, John Spalla, Mary Testa, William Thomas, Jr.

(SOUTH STREET THEATRE) Thursday, April 5–15, 1984 (16 performances).
THE ME NOBODY KNOWS with Music by Gary William Friedman; Lyrics, Will Holt; Adapted by Robert H. Livingston and Herb Schapiro from the book of same title edited by Stephen M. Joseph; Original idea by Herb Schapiro; Director, Robert H. Livingston; Musical numbers staged by Rael Lamb; Set/Costumes, John Falabella; Lighting, Jeff Davis; Conductor, Jefrey Silverman; Additional Lyrics, Herb Schapiro; Arrangements/Orchestrations, Gary William Friedman; Press, Shirley Herz, Sam Rudy, Peter Cromarty. CAST: Sonia Bailey (Rhoda), Tisha Campbell (Lillian), Jose Martinez (Carlos), Kia Joy Goodwin (Lillie), Donald Acree (Benjamin), Jessie Janet Richards (Catherine), Pamela Harley (Melba), Jaison Walker (Lloyd), Stephen Fenning (Donald), Keith Amos (Clorox), Deborah Smith (Nell). A musical in two acts.

(TOMI PARK ROYAL THEATRE) Thursday, April 5,–May 6, 1984 (17 performances). The Open Space Theatre Experiment (Lynn Michaels, Artistic Director) presents:
ALL THE NICE PEOPLE by Hugh Leonard; Director, Alex Dmitriev; Set, James Morgan; Costumes, Barbara Weiss; Lighting, Ann Wrightson; Stage Managers, Crystal Huntington, Eric Hall, Jaime McIntosh; Press, Hunt/Pucci Associates. CAST: Cara Duff-MacCormick (Fran Corish), David Clarke (Old Heegan), W. T. Martin (Charlie Lambert), Marilyn McIntyre (Christine Lambert), Mildred Clinton (Mrs. Corish), Kathleen Chalfant (Lily Heegan), Peter Rogan (Bertie Totterdel), Dermot McNamara (Humphries), James Harper (Mick Humphries), Dan Strimer (Colm Corish), Eric Hall (Terrance), Jaime McIntosh (Kathleen). A play in two acts. The action takes place at the present time in the County Dublin in Dalkey.

Jayne Haynes, John Vickery, Paul Guilfoyle,
Elizabeth Berridge (on shoulders),
Graham Beckel, Anne Twomey in "The Vampires"
(Martha Swope Photo)

(HARTLEY HOUSE) Friday, April 6–22, 1984 (16 performances and 1 preview). Playwrights Preview Productions (Frances Hill, Artistic Director, Paul Dervis, Managing Director) presents:
LITKO/SHOEHORN two one-act plays; Sets, Barry Axtell; Lighting, Richard Comfort; Costumes, Leigh Daniel; Sound/Production Coordinator, Adelle Sardi; Props, Sarah Hill; Wardrobe, Ann Shepphird; Assistant Dirctor/Stage Manager, Linda Shary; Stage Managers, Robert Thierren, Jim Horton; Press, Hunt/Pucci Associates. CAST: "Litko" written and directed by David Mamet; Performed by Larry Conroy. "Shoehorn" by Mark Weston; Director, Laurence Conroy; with Fred Burrell (Don Davis), Annette Hunt (Helen Davis), Jayne Chamberlin (Corliss Unger), Lynn Fitzpatrick (Rhoda Powers).

(ASTOR PLACE THEATRE) Wednesday, April 11–29, 1984 (22 performances and 10 previews). Stephen Graham presents:
THE VAMPIRES by Harry Kondoleon; Directed by the playwright; Set, Adrianne Lobel; Costumes, Rita Ryack; Lighting, William Armstrong; Sound, Paul Garrity; Fight Direction, Randy Kovitz; Company Manager, Erik Murkoff; General Management, Albert Poland; Casting, Mary Colquhoun; Props, Kevin Allen; Wardrobe, Bill "Lee" Lewis; Press, David Powers, Leo Stern. CAST: John Vickery (Ian), Jayne Haynes (CC), Anne Twomey (Pat), Graham Beckel (Ed), Elizabeth Berridge (Zivia), Paul Guilfoyle (Porter). A comedy in two acts. The action takes place at the present time during the month of June in a house off the Hudson River.

(JACK LAWRENCE THEATRE) Thursday, April 12,–May 6, 1984 (29 performances and 15 previews). Nicholas Benton, Stanley Flink, Brent Peek, Force Ten Productions present:
THE GOLDEN AGE by A. R. Gurney, Jr.; Director, John Tillinger; Set, Oliver Smith; Costumes, Jane Greenwood; Lighting, Arden Fingerhut; Suggested by "The Aspern Papers" by Henry James; General Management, Brent Peek Productions; Production Associate, Scott Green; Company Manager, Claire Abel; Props, Gene O'Donovan; Stage Managers, Franklin Keysar, Jody Boese; Press, David Powers, Leo Stern. CAST: Stockard Channing (Virginia), Jeff Daniels (Tom), Irene Worth (Isabel Hastings Hoyt). A comedy in two acts. The action takes place at the present time during spring and summer in the front room of the second floor of a brownstone house on the Upper East Side of New York City.

(JEWISH REPERTORY THEATRE) Thursday, April 12,–May 6, 1984 (23 performances and 5 previews).
ESCAPE FROM RIVERDALE by Donald Wollner; Director Lynn Polan; Set/Costumes, Leslie Taylor; Lighting, Jackie Manassee; Stage Manager, Gay Smerek; Press, Bruce Cohen, Rosemary Cunningham. CAST: Lisa Goodman (Candy Raymond), Stephen Hamilton (Gregory Lewin), Peter Berkrot (Marty Feinberg), Rob Morrow (Stuart Miller), Michael Albert Mantel (Vincent Katz), David Saint (Korey Sonder). A comedy in two acts.

(WEST SIDE Y ARTS CENTER) Saturday, April 14,–May 6, 1984 (17 performances and 3 previews). American Kaleidoscope (Joan Rice Franklin, Rebecca Dobson, Nicholas Benton, Richard Bell, Producing Artistic Directors) presents:
A RAISIN IN THE SUN by Lorraine Hansberry; Director, Shauneille Perry; Set, Louanne Gilleland; Lighting, Jayne Dutra; Costumes, Judy Dearing; Sound, Janet Wilson; Stage Managers, Richard Douglass, James Carter; Props, Mark Jerrick; Company Manager, Edward Hambleton; Production Manager, Arthur Bryant; Press, FLT/Francine L. Trevens, John Fisher. CAST: Phylicia Ayers-Allen (Ruth), William Lancelot Bowles III (Travis), Charles Weldon (Walter Lee), Kim Weston-Moran (Beneatha), Louise Stubbs (Lena), Lou Ferguson (Joseph), Kim Sullivan (George), Nick Smith (Bobo), Joe Ponazecki (Karl), Lloyd Frazier (Moving Man)

(AUDREY WOOD THEATRE) Sunday, April 15–29, 1984 (27 performances and 17 previews). Haila Stoddard, Joy Klein, Maggie Minskoff present:
LOVE with Book by Jeffrey Sweet; Based on play "Luv" by Murray Schisgal; Music, Howard Marren; Lyrics, Susan Birkenhead; Scenery/Costumes, Kevin Rupnik; Director, Walton Jones; Musical Staging, Ed Nolfi; Musical Direction/Vocal and Dance Arrangements, Uel Wade; Orchestrations, Robby Merkin; Lighting, Ruth Roberts; Associate Producers, John Kenley, Vincent Curcio, Tarquin Jay Bromley; General Manager, Victor Samrock; Company Manager, Kerrin K. Clark; Props, Nicki Wilson; Wardrobe, Rose Keough; Stage Managers, Richard Lombard, Gus Kaikkonen; Press, Solters/Roskin/Friedman, Joshua Ellis, Louise Ment, Cindy Valk, Jackie Green. CAST: Nathan Lane (Harry), Stephen Vinovich (Milt), Judy Kaye (Ellen); Gus Kaikkonen (Understudy). A musical in two acts. The action takes place on a bridge on an October evening, and one year later.
MUSICAL NUMBERS: Don't Make Me Laugh, Polyarts U, Paradise, Carnival Ride, The Chart, Ellen's Lament, Somebody, Yes I Love You, Love, What a Life!, Lady, If Harry Weren't Here, My Brown Paper Hat, Do I Love Him?, Harry's Resolution

(WESTSIDE ARTS THEATRE) Wednesday, April 18,–June 3, 1984 (54 performances). Dann Byck, Wendell Cherry, the Shubert Organization and Frederick M. Zollo present:
'NIGHT, MOTHER by Marsha Norman; Director, Tom Moore; Set and Costumes, Heidi Landesman; Lighting, James Ingalls; Press, Hunt/Pucci Associates. CAST: Anne Pitoniak (Thelma Cates), Kathy Bates (Jessie Cates). A drama performed without intermission. The action takes place at the present time in Thelma Cates' relatively new house built way out on a country road.

(WALTER McGINN/JOHN CAZALE THEATRE) Thursday, April 19,–May 20, 1984 (12 performances and 18 previews). The Second Stage (Robyn Goodman, Carole Rothman, Artistic Directors) presents:
LANDSCAPE OF THE BODY by John Guare; Director, Gary Sinise; Set, Loren Sherman; Lighting, Kevin Rigdon; Costumes Jess Goldstein; Sound, Gary Harris; Hairstylist, Antonio Soddu; Words and Music, John Guare; Incidental Music, Jeremy Kahn; Production Manager, Kristina Kinet; Stage Managers, Barrie Moss, Stacey Fleischer; Choreography, Eddie Castrodad; Casting, Meg Simon, Fran Kumin; Press, Richard Kornberg. CAST: Alison Bartlett (Joanne), Eddie Castrodad (Donny), Reg E. Cathay (Masked Man/Dope King/Bank Teller), Mary Copple (Rosalie), Maddie Corman (Margie), Dann Florek (Holahan), Christine Lahti (Betty), Frank Maraden (Peach), Christian Slater (Bert), Ted Sod (Raulito)

Jeff Daniels, Irene Worth, Stockard Channing
in "The Golden Age" *(Peter Cunningham Photo)*
Above: Judy Kaye, Stephen Vinovich, Nathan Lane
in "Love" *(Martha Swope Photo)*

**Dawn Kreizer, Ron Meier, Court Miller,
Anne Meara, Tom Noonan in "Spookhouse"**

(PLAYHOUSE 91) Wednesday, May 2–6, 1984 (6 performances and 55 previews). Terry Allen Kramer and Harry Rigby present:
SPOOKHOUSE by Harvey Fierstein; Director, Eric Concklin; Set, Bill Stabile; Costumes, Randy Barcelo; Lighting, Craig Miller; Sound/Special Effects, Bran Ferren; Sound, Bob Kerzman; Associate Producer, Frank Montalvo; General Manager, Alan C. Wasser; Associate Manager, Mark Kruger; Props, Jay Aiken; Wardrobe, Mary Lou Rios; Technical Coordinator, T. Wiley Bramlett; Stage Managers, James Long, Leonard Finger; Press, Henry Luhrman, Terry M. Lilly, Keith Sherman, Kevin P. McAnarney. CAST: Ron Meier (Max Janik), Court Miller/Michael Sacks in previews (Sam Wilbur), Anne Meara (Connie Janik), Dawn Kreizer (Claire Janik), Ron Meler (Wayne Janik), Tom Noonan/Mark Gordon in previews (Rube Janik); Standbys: Cora Buono (Claire), Alice Spivak (Connie), Philip Richard Allen (Sam/Rube). A drama in two acts. The action takes place at the present time on a Friday morning in June in an apartment above the Spookhouse at Coney Island.

(TOMI TERRACE THEATRE) Friday, May 4–21, 1984 (12 performances). Peterson's Productions presents:
FAMILY SNAPSHOTS by Sam Henry Kass; Director, Peter Kass; Lighting, Gregory MacPherson; Set, Bill Wood; Casting, Karen Cellini; Wardrobe, Julie Merz; Press, Douglas & Reichardt Associates. CAST: Roger Serbagi (Mike Heaton), Kevin Gray (Danny Heaton). A play in two acts. The action takes place in Mike Heaton's apartment in Hoboken, NJ, on a Sunday in the spring of 1982.

(THEATRE 55) Sunday, May 6–20, 1984 (12 performances). Windowpane Productions (Van Santvoord, Producer) presents:
BURDEN PIE by Bob McAndrew and Earl Hagan in collaboration with the cast; Director, Bob McAndrew; Set, Daniel Proett; Costumes, Miriam Nieves; Lighting, Rick Butler; Technical Director, Van Santvoord; Stage Manager, Jill Merzon; Managing Director/Press, Kim Kuhlmann. CAST: Antonia Banewicz (Becky), Earl Hagan, Jr. (Blake), Linda Freitag (Bonnie), L. R. Hults (Joe), Van Santvoord (Billy), Edward Breen (Dad/Catcher). The action of the play takes place at the present time in the Burden household in South Bend, IN.

(LAMB'S THEATRE) Sunday, May 6–23, 1984 (16 performances). The Lamb's Theatre Company (Carolyn Rossi Copeland, Executive Director) presents:
COURAGE by John Pielmeier; Dirctor, Susan Gregg; Set, Patricia Woodbridge; Costume, Karen Gerson; Lighting, Karl Haas; Stage Manager, Lois Taylor; Press, Fred Hoot, David Mayhew. CAST: Paul Collins as Sr. James M. Barrie. A monodrama in two acts, adapted from the writings of J. M. Barrie.

(THE CUBICULO) Monday, May 7–27, 1984 (12 performances and 3 previews). New York Theatre Workshop (Jean Passantine, Artistic Director) presents:
SOUVENIRS by Sheldon Rosen; Director, Stephen Katz; Set, Loy Arcenas; Lighting/Projections, John Gisondi; Costumes, Deborah Shaw; Sound, Tommy Hawk; Composer/Cellist, Michael Bacon; Murals, Gerard P. Bourcier; Production Manager, Moss Hassell; General Manager, Alison Clarkson; Company Manager, Nina Katzander; Casting, David Tochterman; Technical Director, Bill Wells; Props, Charlie Eisenberg; Wardrobe, Jarmila Packard; Photography, Bob Stern; Stage Manager, Nicholas Dunn; Press, Fred Hoot, David Mayhew. CAST: Joe Morton (Peter), David Purdham (John Purvis), John Milligan (Ralph Cloot), Delphi Lawrence (Mrs. Evelyn Harold), Gilbert Cole (Daniel), Ellen Barber (Vicki), Larry Block (Hotel Manager). A drama in two acts. The action takes place at the present time on the island of Lacona during late summer in a middle-class, mid-priced hotel.

(THE NEW THEATRE) Wednesday, May 9–28, 1984 (29 performances in repertory). City Theatre Festival's New Plays in May (John Morrison, Artistic Director; Patricia Hunter, Executive Director) presents:
DIVINE RIGHT by John Morrison; Director, Mr. Morrison; Set and Lighting, Hank Cartwright; Stage Manager, Ann Minski. CAST: Leslie Minski (Allman), Art Kempf (Jack Keating), Lindsay Borden (Riley Keating), Michael Clarke (Phil), Melissa Hurst (Kieran Keating), Matthew Gallagher (Donny Armaio).
VICTORY BONDS by Anson Campbell; Director, Jack L. Davis; Set, Mr. Davis; Costumes, Joel Vig; Lighting, Hank Cartwright; Stage Manager, Joe Dahman. CAST: Patricia Hunter (May), Jean Barker (Dedda Stuart), Tony Carlin (Martin Stuart), Laura Pierce (Ginger), Jim Fyfe (Guy Stuart), Daniel Pollack (Troy), David Kelly (Sergeant), Curtis Anderson (Corporal)

(THE BALLROOM THEATER) Thursday, May 10–Sept. 23, 1984 (165 performances). CHS Productions and Greentrack Entertainment in association with Sidney L. Shlenker, Joseph Stein, Jr., Barbara M. Friedman present:
NITE CLUB CONFIDENTIAL by Dennis Deal; Conceived by Dennis Deal, Albert Evans, Jamie Rocco; New Songs/Arrangements, Dennis Deal, Albert Evans; Directed/Staged by Dennis Deal; Set, Christopher Cole; Lighting, Richard Latta; Costumes, Stephen Rotondaro; Sound, Stuart Schwartz; Music Supervision, Albert Evans; General Management, Dorothy Olim, George Elmer; Company Manager, Colin Fraser; Stage Managers, J. R. MacDonald, Marcus Neville; Wardrobe, Jeanne Ward, Donna Lee Katz; Press, Jeffrey Richards, Robert Ganshaw, C. George Willard, Ben Morse, Richard Humleker. CAST: Stephen Burger (Buck Holden), Tom Spiroff (Sal), Denise Nolin (Dorothy Flynn), Steve Gideon (Mitch Dupre), Fay DeWitt (Kay Goodman), Understudies: Nancy Hillner, Marcus Neville. A musical in 2 acts and 14 scenes with a prologue and epilogue. The action takes place during the Eisenhower era.
MUSICAL NUMBERS: Nite Club, Comment Allez-Vous, Something's Gotta Give, Love Isn't Born It's Made, Goody Goody, Nothing Can Replace a Man, I Thought About You, Put the Blame on Mamie, Canarsie Diner, Saturday's Child, Bonjour, French with Tears, That Old Black Magic, Crazy New Words, Black Slacks, The Long Goodbye, Ev'rybody's Boppin', Cloudburst, The Other One, Yodelin' Dixieland, Dressed to Kill, Dead End Street.

(ST. CLEMENT'S THEATRE) Tuesday, May 15,–June 2, 1984 (21 performances). Music-Theatre Group/Lenox Arts Center (Lyn Austin, Producing Director) and Jack Curtis present:
STREET DREAMS by Mitchell Ivers; Music, William Eaton; Direction and Choreography, Peter Gennaro; Assistant Choreographer, Don Bonnell; Music Directors, Nick Diminno, Grant Sturiale; Set, Nancy Winters; Lighting, Marilyn Rennagel; Costumes, Joan V. Evans; Sound, Gary Harris; Stage Managers, Robert I. Cohen, Susan Whelan; Wardrobe, Drew Rosenberg; Casting, Jim Mulkin, Terry Fay, Ira Weitzman, David Tochterman; Press, Joe Wolhandler Associates, Monina von Opel. CAST: Ray Contreras (Lincoln), Christopher Cowley (Monkey), Ali Hernandez (Peeper), Benjamin Hernandez (Cas-Bah), Marishka Phillips (Leesha), Clayton Prince (Super-Ru), Kevin Ramsey (Calvin), Tico Wells (Prophet), Harold Williams (Bug), Lucky Williams (Jelly)

**Joe Morton, Delphi Lawrence
in "Souvenirs"**
(Martha Swope/Carol Rosegg Photo)

77

(PAPER MOON CABARET) Friday, May 18,–June 9, 1984 (20 performances and 2 previews). Chris Adams and David Agress present:
BROADWAY BABYLON - the Musical That Never Was! Conceived and created by Christopher Adams and David Agress; Staged and Choreographed by Susan Stroman; Musical Director, Eric Diamond; Set, Salvatore Taliarino; Costumes, Carol Wenz; Associate Producer, Roni Gallion; Stage Manager, David Combs; General Manager, Maria DiDia; Press, Shirley Herz, Sam Rudy, Peter Cromarty, Pete Sanders. CAST:Scott Bakula, Jossie De Guzman, Melinda Gilb.
MUSICAL NUMBERS: A Broadway Musical, You Mustn't Be Discouraged, Where Was I When They Passed Out Luck?, Everybody Needs Something, Quiet Thing, Go Visit, Yente Power, You I Like, He Touched Me, Once Upon a Time, What's New at the Zoo?, Lawyers, 10 Percent, I Like What I Do, It's an Art, Be Happy, Go to Sleep Early, Dance a Little Closer, This Is a Great Country

(ACTORS PLAYHOUSE) Tuesday, May 22,–July 1, 1984 (47 performances and 5 previews). Irish Arts Center in association with Ross and Timm Productions, Carol Giannone, Charlotte Moore and Bruce Saul present:
THE SHADOW OF A GUNMAN by Sean O'Casey; Director, Jim Sheridan; Set, David Raphel; Lighting, Victor En Yu Tan; Costumes, Randall Ouzts, Mary G. Dixon; Stage Managers, Patrick Folan, Siobhan Kennedy; Press, FLT/Francine L. Trevens, Caroline Cornell, Andrew Shearer, Ann Edwards. CAST: Ciaran O'Reilly (Davoren), Chris O'Neill succeeded by Peter Rogan (Shields), Mickey Kelly (McGuire/Auxilliary), John William Short (Landlord), Freda Kavanagh (Minnie), Shane O'Neill (Tommy), Carmel O'Brien (Mrs. Henderson), Chris Keeley (Gallagher), Terry Donnelly (Mrs. Grigson), Maurice Kehoe (Grigson). A drama in two acts. The action takes place in an Irish rooming house, in the 1920's.

(NAMELESS THEATRE) Wednesday, May 23,–June 10, 1984 (18 performances and 6 previews). Irondale Productions (James Louis Niesen, Artistic Director) presents:
THE GOOD WOMAN OF SETZUAN by Bertolt Brecht; English version by Eric Bentley; Director, James Louis Niessen; Music/Additional Lyrics, Lara Crete; Set, Kennon Rothchild; Lighting, Richard Dorfman; Costumes, Elena Pellicciaro; Musical Direction, Lara Crete; Choreographer, Annie B. Parson; Stage Manager, Crystal Huntington; Technical Director, Sylvia Pierce; Press, G. Theodore Killmer. CAST: Josh Broder (Wong), David Finkelstein, Terry Greiss, Paul Lazar (Three Gods), Barbara Mackenzie-Wood (Shen Te), Lynn Anderson (Mrs. Shin; Mrs. Mi Tzu), David Finkelstein (Unemployed Man/Carpenter/Policeman), Paul Lazar (Yang Sun), Kate Chad, Lynn Anderson (Whores), Pat Russell, Paul Lazar (Old Couple), Terry Greiss (Priest/Shu Fu/Barber), Pat Russell (Mrs. Yang). A play in three acts. The action takes place in the half Westernized city of Setzuan.

(UNIVERSITY THEATRE) Wednesday, May 23–25, 1984 (5 performances). La Maison Francaise of NYU and the French Institute/Alliance Francaise with the cooperation of the Program in Education and Theater at NYU present:
THE HUMAN VOICE by Jean Cocteau; Direction and Design, Simone Benmussa; Lighting, Genevieve Soubirou, Stephen Palestrant; A new translation by Susannah York; Slide for painting, Antoni Taule. CAST: Susannah York as The Woman, and the recorded voice of Michael Lonsdale.

(TOMI TERRACE THEATRE) Thursday, May 31,–June 16, 1984 (21 performances). Double Image Theatre (Helen Waren Mayer, Executive/Artistic Director) presents:
JUST LIKE THE LIONS by Patrick Meyers; Director, Max D. Mayer; Set, G. W. Mercier; Costumes, Michael Krass; Lighting, William Armstrong; Sound, Gary Harris; Managing Director, Leslie Urdang; Administrative Director, Grace L. Jones; Props, Victoria Mourafchan; Technical Director, David Tasso; Wardrobe, Lynn Marie E. Lentz, Filomena Dobbins; Stage Manager, Neal Ann Stephens; Press, David Low. CAST: Jana Schneider (Adrian), Diane Davidson-Porter (Martha), Gregory Beecroft (Roy), Lizzie Miller (Cat), Dan Moran (Kenneth), Ralph Marrero (Martin), David Thornton (Peter/Carl), Daniel Carey (Preacher), Scott Renderer (Gary), Tony Todd (Myron). A play in 2 acts. The action takes place in 1969 in a living room in Southern California, and in 1979 in the dayroom of Atascadero State Mental Institution for the Criminally Insane.

Top Right: Melinda Gilb, Scott Bakula
in "Broadway Babylon" *(Dan Strickler Photo)*
Below: Ciaran O'Reilly, Mickey Kelly, Peter Rogan in
"Shadow of a Gunman" *(Feldman/Shevett Photo)*

Susannah York
in "the Human Voice"
(Phil Gallo Photo)

78

OFF-BROADWAY SERIES

AMAS REPERTORY THEATRE

Rosetta LeNoire, Founder/Artistic Director
Fifteenth Season
Administrator/Business Manager, Gary Halcott; Administrator/Press, Jerry Lapidus
Thursday, October 27,–November. 20, 1983 (16 performances)
THE BUCK STOPS HERE! conceived by Richard A. Lippman; Book, Norman J. Fedder; Music and Lyrics, Richard A. Lippman; Additional Lyrics, Norman J. Fedder; Director, Regge Life; Musical Director, Lea Richardson; Choreographer, Tim Millett; Set, Kalina Ivanov; Lighting, Gregg Marriner; Costumes, Eiko Yamaguchi; Stage Managers, Ken Nixon, Jim Griffith, Kuan Bennett; Technical Director, Kieran Kelly; Wardrobe, Cindy Boyle; Additional Music, Lea Richardson; Arrangements, Jack Engler, Lea Richardson.
CAST: Scott Banfield (John Snyder/MacArthur), Mary Dunn (Martha Truman), Andrew Gorman (Charlie Ross/Eddie Jacobson), Janet Hayes (Tilly Brown/Reporter), Paul Hewitt (Reporter), Janice L. Holt (Reporter), Laurel Lockhart (Madge Wallace), Fredric Marco (Bob Hannegan), Jim McNickle (Eddie McKim/Grand Wizard), Kimberly Mucci (Young Bess Wallace/Young Margaret Truman), Ilona Papp (Reporter), Brian Pew (Young Harry Truman), Paul Hewitt (Tom Pendergast), Stephanie M. Pope (Reporter), Alexana Ryer (Bess Wallace Truman), Harris Shore (Harry S. Truman), Paul Tardi (Lloyd Stark), Jacqueline Trudeau (Margaret Truman).
A musical in 2 acts and 31 scenes. The action takes place between 1894 and 1953, primarily in and around Independence, MO, and Washington, DC.
MUSICAL NUMBERS: The 33rd President, If You Try, My Best Friend, That Boy's Not Good Enough for You, Haberdashery Blues, When Will You Learn, I Believe in the Man, The Buck Stops Here, My One Day, Dear Dad, Simple But Not an Ordinary Man, Never Look Back, This Time We're Clapping for You.
Thursday, February 9,–March 4, 1984 (16 performances)
SING ME SUNSHINE! based on "Peg O' My Heart" by J. Hartley Manners; Book, Robert E. Richardson, Johnny Brandon; Music and Lyrics, Johnny Brandon; Director, Jack Timmers; Choreography, Henry Le Tang; Music and Vocal Arrangements/Musical Director, Thom Bridwell; Costumes, Gail Cooper-Hecht; Lighting, Paul Sullivan; Sets, Robert Lewis Smith; Dance Arrangements, Timothy Graphenreed; Book Adaptation, Michael Sawyer; Production Manager, Ken Nixon; Technical Directors, Gary Sullivan, Kieran Kelly; Wardrobe, Cindy Boyle; Stage Managers, Kuan Bennett, Jim Griffith, Lynda Field.
CAST: Sal Biagini (Roger), George Bohn (Jenkins/Reggie/Sir Horace), Leonard Drum (Jarvis), Rod Ferrone (Claude/Footman), Andrea Frierson (Peg), Joanne Genelle (Mrs. Wentworth), Marta Hedges (Celia/Lady Cholmondeley), Jan Horvath (Ethel), Glenn Kramer (Hawkes), Mary Anne Prevost (Maid), Rose Roffman (Mrs. Chichester), Scott Willis (Jerry).
A musical in 2 acts and 19 scenes. The action takes place in and around the Chichester Manor House in a small country town in Hertfordshire, England, during late spring of 1934.
MUSICAL NUMBERS: The H'Elegant Homes of H'England, Ruined, A Long Long Time, When a Gentleman's Well Dressed, Nothing Like a Friend, All Alone, The Education of Peg, That's What Living's All About, Where Is Away?, You Can Do It, Changes, Down My Street, That Is What I Give You, Peg, Sing Me Sunshine, Where Do I Stand?, Finale.
Thursday, April 19,–May 13. 1984 (16 performances)
BLACKBERRIES conceived by Joseph George Caruso; Book, Mr Caruso; Sketches, Billy K. Wells; Additional Material/Dialogue, Andre De Shields; Direction/Choreography, Andre De Shields; Co-Choreographer, Gui Andrisano; Set, Edward Goetz; Costumes, Mardi Philips; Lighting, Deborah Tulchin; Musical Direction/Arrangements, John McMahon; Musical Supervision, Joel Silberman; Production Manager, Ronald L. McIntyre; Technical Director, Kirk Madsen; Stage Managers, Kuan Bennett, Jim Griffith; Hairstylist, Thelma L. Pollard; Special Effects, Barry Goldfarb, Paul Goldberg; Wardrobe, Cindy Boyle; Press, Merle Frimark.
CAST: Steven Bland (Georgia Berry), Anthony Bova (Virigina Berry), Clent Bowers (Mr. Interlocutor Berry), Christina Britton (North Carolina Berry), Marion Caffey (Florida Berry), Ellia English (South Carolina Berry), Janice Holt (Tambo Berry), Allynne Johnson (Arkansas Berry), Lynda Joy (Mississippi Berry), Cynthia Pearson (Maryland Berry), Mardi Philips (Tennessee Berry), Gary Sullivan (Kentucky Berry), Steve Tapp (Alabama Berry), Tug Wilson (Texas Berry), Andrea Wright (Bones Berry).
A minstrel-vaudeville spectacular celebrating the enormous contributions made to our American musical comedy, in 2 acts and 16 scenes.

Joanne Genelle, Glenn Kramer, Rod Ferrone,
Marta Hedges, George Bohn, Mary Ann Prevost
in "Sing Me Sunshine" *(JWL Photo)*

"Blackberries"
(JWL Photo)

79

AMERICAN JEWISH THEATRE

Stanley Brechner, Artistic Director
Fourth Season

Business Manager, Raymond T. Grant; Resident Director, Dan Held; Production Supervisor, Stewart Shneck; Technical Director, Bern Gautier; Casting Director, France Burke; Press, Lois Cohn, Helene Davis

(92nd STREET Y) Saturday, September 24,–November 20, 1983 (45 performances).

MADE IN HEAVEN! by Edward Belling; Director, Stanley Brechner; Set, Jeffrey Schneider; Costumes, Barbara Weiss; Lighting, Jenny Ball; Props, Nan Siegmund; Stage Manager, Patrice Thomas.

CAST: Vera Lockwood (Rose Rothenberg), Maurice Sterman (Jack Rothenberg), Estelle Kemler (Bunny Gross), Reuben Schafer (Milton Gross), Lauren White (Ellen Rothenberg), David Chandler (Richard Rothenberg).

A comedy in 2 acts and 5 scenes. The action takes place at the present time in Richard and Ellen's apartment on the upper East Side of Manhattan.

Saturday, December 3, 1983–January 22, 1984 (35 performances)

I AM A CAMERA by John Van Druten; Director, Geoffrey Sherman; Set, Paul Wonsek; Lighting, Sid Bennett; Costumes, Don Newcomb; Production Supervisor, Stewart Schneck; Technical Director, Bern Gautier; Wardrobe, Harriet Robinson; Production Assistant, Alice Perlmutter; Casting, France Burke; Play adapted from Christopher Isherwood's "Berlin Stories"; Stage Manager, Anita Ross; Press, Lois Cohn.

CAST: Tom Spackman (Christopher Isherwood), Lois Markle (Fraulein Schneider), Max Chalawsky (Fritz Wendel), Cherry Jones (Sally Bowles), Alexandra O'Karma (Natalia Landauer), Richard Maxfield (Clive Mortimer), Betty Low (Mrs. Watson-Courtneidge).

A play in 3 acts and 7 scenes. The action takes place in a room in Fraulein Schneider's flat in Berlin in 1930 before the rise of the Hitler regime.

Saturday, February 11,–April 8, 1984 (43 performances)

IT'S HARD TO BE A JEW by Sholom Aleichem; Translated and adpated by Isaiah Sheffer; Director, Dan Held; Set, John Kenny; Costumes, Barbara Blackwood; Lighting, Greg Chabay; Production Supervisor, Lori M. Doyle; Production Consultant, Stewart Schneck; Production Assistant, Alice Perlmutter; Stage Manager, John N. Concannon.

CAST: Max Chalawsky (Vanya Ivanov), Avi Hoffman (Hershel Shneourson), David Breitbarth (Student/Greensburg/Porter), Mitchell Green (Student/Hurevich/Policeman), James Lish (Student/Fratkin/Sexton), Michael Vaughn (Student/Policeman), Norman Golden (Ketzele/Ravbi Halpern), K. Lype O'Dell (Police Chief), Rosalind Harris (Sarah Shapiro), Nancy Travis (Betty Shapiro), Mitchell Allan (Siomka Shapiro), Steven Gilborn (David Shapiro).

A play in 3 acts and 4 scenes. The action takes place between 1913 and 1914.

Saturday, April 21,–June 17, 1984 (40 performances)

ANDORRA by Max Frisch; Translated into English by Michael Bullock; Director, Dan Held; Set, Kalina Ivanov; Costumes, Muriel Stockdale; Sound, Tim Roberts; Lighting, Greg Chabay; Production Supervisor, Lori Doyle; Technical Director, Bern Gautier; Production Assistants, Alice Perlmutter, Constance Trapani; Casting, Ronnie Yeskel; Stage Manager, Patrice Thomas.

CAST: Larry Singer (Andri), Kelly Curtis (Barblin), Frank Anderson (Teacher), Bryarly Lee (Mother), Karen Kondazian (Senora), Dimo Condos (Priest), Michael Kuhn (Soldier), M. Patrick Hughes (Innkeeper), Fredric Cook (Carpenter), John Bennes (Doctor), Craig Sisler (Journeyman), Frank Trezza (Somebody), Clark Middleton (Jew Detector/Idiot), Soldiers: Bob Barnes, Jacob Kritenberg, Michael Vaughn.

A play in 2 acts and 12 scenes. The action takes place in and around the main square of the small country of Andorra.

**Top Left: Tom Spackman, Cherry Jones
in "I Am a Camera"**
(Gerry Goodstein Photo)

**Steven Gilborn, Avi Hoffman
in "It's Hard to Be a Jew"**

Kelly Curtis, Robert Porter, Larry Singer, Karen Kondazian
in "Andorra" *(Ken Howard Photo)* Top: Maurice Sterman, Vera Lockwood,
Estelle Kemler, Reuben Schafer in "Made in Heaven" *(Gerry Goodstein Photo)*

81

AMERICAN PLACE THEATRE

Wynn Handman, Director
Julia Miles, Associate Director
Twentieth Season

General Manager, Scott Allison; Literary Manager, C. Lee Jenner; Photographer, Martha Holmes; Press, Jeffrey Richards, Robert Ganshaw, Ben Morse, C. George Willard, Richard Humleker.

(AMERICAN PLACE THEATRE) Wednesday, June 1–11, 1983 (12 performances). The Women's Project (Julia Miles, Director) presents:

HEART OF A DOG written and performed by Terry Galloway; Director, Suzanne Bennett; Set, Maxine Willi Klein; Costumes, Mimi Maxmen; Lighting, Joni Wong; Sound, Jane Pipik; Production Coordinator, Nancy Harrington; Dramaturg, C. Lee Jenner; Radio Voices: Dale Christopher, David Shuman, Alice Gordon, Elizabeth Ferguson, Suzanne Bennett.

Sunday, June 5–12, 1983 (9 performances and 4 previews). The Women's Project presents:

TERRITORIAL RITES by Carol K. Mack; Director, Josephine Abady; Set, David Potts; Lighting, Frances Aronson; Costumes, Mimi Maxmen; Sound, Gary Harris; Casting, Elissa Myers; Stage Managers, Laura deBuys, Filomena Dobbins; Technical Director, Seth Jacobs; Props, Pat Kaufman; Wardrobe, Susan M. Schifano.

CAST: Robin Groves (Catherine), Michael Gross (Sam), Kim Hunter (Margaret), Penelope Milford (Genevieve).

A play in 2 acts and 6 scenes. The action takes place on a weekend in February.

Thursday, June 16–26, 1983 (12 performances and 8 previews)

GREAT DAYS by Donald Barthelme; Director, J. Ranelli; Set, Neil Peter Jampolis; Lighting, Arden Fingerhut; Costumes, David C. Woolard; Stage Manager, Nancy Harrington; Technical Director, Dennis Moyes.

CAST: Penelope Allen, Catherine Byers, Paul Collins, James Greene, Jeanne Ruskin, Robert Stattel.

A play in 2 acts and 7 scenes.

Tuesday, October 4–16, 1983. (14 performances)

THE VI-TON-KA MEDICINE SHOW an authentic recreation of an American theatrical tradition; Project Director, Glenn Hinson; Associate Director, C. Lee Jenner; Staging and Design Consultant, Brooks McNamara; Sets and Lights, Marco A. Martinez-Galarce; Production Supervisor, Nancy Harrington; Wardrobe, Susan Schifano, Susan Gibney; Production Assistants, Susan Gibney, Michelle Kroczynski.

CAST: Fred F. Bloodgood, James "Goober" Buchanan, Colonel Buster Doss, Ernest W. Hayes, DeWitt "Snuffy" Jenkins, Tommy Hizziah, Harold Lucas, Randy Lucas, Dale Madden, Sr., Dale "Boots" Madden, Mary Smith McClain, Connie Mills, Homer "Pappy" Sherrill, LeRoy Watts.

Friday, January 6–24, 1984 (21 performances)

BREAKFAST CONVERSATIONS IN MIAMI by Reinhard Lettau; Director, Gordon Edelstein; Set, Neil Peter Jampolis; Costumes, David C. Woolard; Lights, Jane Reisman; Dramaturg, Alisa Solomon; Stage Manager, Renee Lutz, Tom Carson; Assistant Director, Liz Diamond; Wardrobe, Winsome McCoy; Production Assistant, Richard Hester; Technical Director, Peter Bendevski.

CAST: William Meyers (Gen. Juan Bugoslawsky), Jeremiah Sullivan (Gen. Wessin), Pierre Epstein (Colonel Jesu: Schneider), Humbert Allen Astredo (President Armulio Manuel Rosa), Arthur Brooks (Professor), Tom Carson (Gen. Miguel Mimosa), Robert Silver (Gen. Davila/Lincoln Cellini/Gen. Torrijos).

Performed without intermission. The action takes place at the present time in the breakfast froom of an old hotel in Miami.

Wednesday, January 11–19, 1984.

DO LORD REMEMBER ME by James De Jongh; Director, Regge Life; Set, Julie Taymor; Lighting, Sandra L. Ross; Costumes, Judy Dearing; Stage Managers, Nancy Harrington, Celestine DeSaussure; Technical Director, Earl Vedder; Wardrobe, Anita Ellis.

CAST: Giancarlo Esposito, Frances Foster, Ebony Jo-Ann, Lou Myers, Roger Robinson, Celestine DeSaussure (Standby).

The memories of slaves, recorded as interviews in the 1930's constitute the raw material for this play.

Top Right: Kim Hunter in "Territorial Rites"
(Martha Holmes Photos) **Below: James Greene, Paul Collins in "Great Days"**

**Frances Foster, Lou Myers, Ebony Jo-Ann
in "Do Lord Remember Me"**

82

Friday, February 24,–March 11, 1984 (12 performances). Moved Friday, March 30, 1984 to the Village Gate where it was still playing May 31, 1984.

A....MY NAME IS ALICE conceived and directed by Joan Micklin Silver, Julianne Boyd; Choreography, Edward Love; Set, Adrianne Lobel; Costumes, Mimi Maxmen; Lighting, Ann Wrightson; Music Direction, Michael Skloff; Casting, Elissa Myers; General Manager, David Lawlor; Stage Managers, Renee F. Lutz, Randy Graff; Wardrobe, Winsome McKoy; Wardrobe, Anita Ellis; Presented by Anne Wilder, Douglas F. Goodman and Rosita Sarnoff by special arrangement with The Women's Project; Press, Shirley Herz, Sam Rudy, Peter Cromarty, Pete Sanders.

CAST: Roo Brown, Randy Graff, Mary Gordon Murray, Alaina Reed, Charlaine Woodard.

MUSICAL NUMBERS AND SCENES: All Girl Band, A....My Name Is Alice, At My Age, Trash, For Women Only Poems, Good Thing I Learned to Dance, Welcome to Kindergarten Mrs. Johnson, Ms. Mae, Good Sports, Harbour Lady, Bluer Than You, Pretty Young Men, Demigod, The French Song, I Sure Like the Boys, Hot Lunch, I Am Woman, Emily the M.B.A., Sisters, Honeypot, Friends.

Performed in two acts.

Sunday, March 11–18, 1984 (20 performances)

THE DANUBE by Maria Irene Fornes; Director, Ms. Fornes; Scenery, Ms. Fornes; Costumes, Gabriel Berry; Lighting, Anne E. Militello; Puppet, Esteban Fernandez; Stage Manager, Nancy Harrington; Casting, Joan Fishman; Technical Director, Mark Tambella; Wardrobe, Anita Ellis.

CAST: Sam Gray (Sandor), Richard Sale (Paul Green), Kate Collins (Eve Sandor-Green), Thomas Kopache (Kovacs/Waiter/Doctor/Barber), W. Scott Allison (English Tape), Stephan Balant (Hungarian Tape).

Tuesday, March 20,–April 1, 1984 (33 performances). The Women's Project presents:

FESTIVAL OF ONE-ACT PLAYS: "Special Family Things" by Ara Watson, Mary Gallagher; Director, Page Burkholder; with Sharon Chatten, Lois Smith. "The Only Woman General" by LaVonne Mueller; Director, Bryna Wortman; with Colleen Dewhurst, John Connolly; "Old Wives Tale" by Julie Jensen; Director, Alma Becker; with Donna Davis, Jane Hickey, Kenna Hunt, Helen Stenborg; "Aye Aye Aye I'm Integrated" by Anna Deavere Smith; Director, Billie Allen; "Candy and Shelley Go to the Desert" by Paula Cizmar; Director, Carey Perloff; "The Longest Walk" by Janet Thomas; Director, Claudia Weill.

Wednesday, March 21,–April 1, 1984 (12 performances). The Women's Project presents:

TO HEAVEN IN A SWING by Katharine Houghton; Director, Joan Vail Thorne; Scenery, Rosaria Sinisi; Costumes, David Toser; Lighting, Anne E. Militello; Production Supervisor, Nancy Harrington; Stage Manager, Sally A. Lapiduss; Technical Director, Mark Tambella.

CAST: Katharine Houghton as Louisa May Alcott.

Performed with one intermission.

Tuesday, April 24, 1984– . American Place Theatre's American Humorists Series presents:

PAY ATTENTION with music and script by Doug Skinner; Director, Wynn Handman; Slide show drawings, Doug Roesch; Slide show photographs, John Sangalli; Voiceover, Janeen Wyatt.

CAST: Doug Skinner and Eddie Gray (His dummy)

Wednesday, April 25,–May 6, 1984 (14 performances and 12 previews). Playwrights Horizons and the American Place Theatre present:

TERRA NOVA by Ted Tally; Director, Gerald Gutierrez; Set, Douglas Stein; Costumes, Ann Emonts; Lighting, Paul Gallo; Sound, Scott Lehrer; Film Design, John Pieplow; Stage Managers, Kate Pollock, Carroll Cartwright III; Props, Jim Feng; Wardrobe, Lisa Locurto; Hairstylist/Makeup, Peg Shierholz.

CAST: Robert Foxworth (Scott), Anthony Zerbe (Amundsen), Christine Healy (Kathleen), Ian Trigger (Bowers), Daniel Gerroll (Oates), Simon Jones (Wilson), Michael Countryman (Evans).

A drama in two acts. In the winter of 1911–12, five Britons and five Norwegians raced each other to the bottom of the earth, and only the five Norwegians returned. This is the story of the Britons.

Top Right: Charlaine Woodard, Mary Gordon Murray,
Roo Brown, Randy Graff, Alaina Reed in "A . . . My Name
Is Alice" *(Carol Rosegg Photo)* Below: Richard Sale,
Kate Collins in "The Danube" *(Martha Holmes Photo)*

(front) Ian Trigger, Michael Countryman, (back) Simon Jones,
Daniel Gerroll, Robert Foxworth in "Terra Nova"
(Peter Cunningham Photo)

83

APPLE CORPS THEATRE

John Raymond, Artistic Director
Fifth Season
Business Manager, Neal Arluck; Scenic Design, Larry Brodsky; Press, Aviva Cohen
Thursday, June 9,–July 3, 1983 (20 performances)
THE HOUND OF THE BASKERVILLES adapted by Tim Kelly from Sir Arthur Conan Doyle's novel; Director, Fred Weiss; Set, Patrick Dearborn; Costumes, Greg Jones; Lighting, Alan Sporing; Sound, Elliott Forrest; Stage Manager, Doug Salzinger.
CAST: Stockman Barner (Barrymore), Skip Corris (Dr. Watson), Samuelle Easton (Parkins), Richard Fancy (Sherlock Holmes), Helen Marcy (Mrs. Barrymore), Rica Martens (Lady Agatha Mortimer), Donna Moryn (Kathy), Richard Payne (Sir Henry), Jeremy Stuart (Jack Stapleton), Debra Whitfield (Laura Lyons)
Thursday, August 4–
APPOINTMENT WITH DEATH by Agatha Christie; Director, John Raymond; Set, Jim Feng; Lighting, William Plachy; Costumes, Gregory L. Jones; Stage Manager, Pamela Edington.
CAST: Charlotte Jones (Mrs. Boyton), Janes Koenig (Ginevra), Dick Turmall (Lennox), Judith Scarpone (Nadine), Robert McFarland (Higgs), Mary Orr (Lady Westholm), Helen Marcy (Amabel), Bob Del Pazzo (Dr. Gerard), Debra Whitfield (Sarah), Curt Williams (Jefferson), Steve Tschudy (Raymond), Spencer Cherashore (Dragoman), Neal Arluck (Clerk/Col. Carbery).
A drama in three acts. The action takes place in the King Solomon Hotel in Jerusalem.
Thursday, August 25,–September 18, 1983 (20 performances)
THE STRANGE CASE OF DR. JEKYLL AND MR. HYDE by Colston Corris; Adapted from story by Robert Louis Stevenson; Director, Christopher Catt; Set, Larry Brodsky; Costumes, Gregory L. Jones; Lighting, Wayne S. Lawrence; Sound, Elliott Forrest; Stage Manager, Deborah Constantine.
CAST: Bill Gorman (Dr. Lanyon), Peter Murphy (Canon Carew), Val Dufour (Gabriel John Utterson), Orson Bean (Dr. Henry Jekyll), Jeremy Stuart (Richard Enfield), Debra Whitfield (Margaret Jekyll Drew), Rica Martens (Mrs. Poole), Eric Booth (Edward Hyde).
Thursday, November 3–28, 1983 (16 performances and 2 previews)
STRICTLY DISHONORABLE by Preston Sturges; Director, John Raymond; Scenery, Rick Dennis; Costumes, Gregory L. Jones; Lighting, Deborah Constantine; Sound, Elliott Forrest; Stage Manager, Doug Salzinger.
CAST: Spencer Cherashore (Mario), Bob Del Pazzo (Tomasso), Eric Douglas (Henry), Michael Guido (Gus), Heather Holmes (Isabelle), John Jamiel (Giovanni), Sherman Lloyd (Judge Dempsey), Fredrick Walters (Mulligan).
A comedy in 2 acts and 3 scenes. The action takes place in the speakeasy of Tomaso Antiovi on West 49th Street, and the rear apartment, in New York City.
Thursday, February 2–26, 1984 (20 performances
VERDICT by Agatha Christie; Director, Tom Carroll; Costumes, Maryann D. Smith; Sound, Judy Baldwin; Stage Manager/Lighting, Deborah Constantine.
CAST: David Babbitt (Lester Cole), Ann Barrett (Lisa Koletzky), Lauren Brecher (Helen Rollander), P. L. Carling (Sir William Rollander/Det. Insp. Ogden), Francine Farrell (Anya), Helen March (Mrs. Roper), Peter Murphy (Dr. Stoner), Nick Stannard (Prof. Hendryk).
A mystery in 2 acts and 5 scenes. The action takes place in the living room of Prof. Hendryk's flat in Bloomsbury.
Thursday, May 24,–June 17, 1984 (20 performances). Debut production in the Apple Corps' new theatre.
THE LAND IS BRIGHT by Edna Ferber and George S. Kaufman; Director, John Raymond; Set, Sally Locke; Lighting, Rick Petit; Costumes, Maryann D. Smith; Sound, Elliott Forrest; Makeup, Daniel Frye; Stage Manager, Joseph Millett.
CAST: Annie Abbott (Ellen), Marvin Beck (Lacey), J. P. Chartier (Theodore/Lacey II), Cress Darwin (Carlock/Tonetti), Bob Del Pazzo (Blake/Dorset/Bennett), Samuelle Easton (Deborah/Perk/Greta), George Holmes (Czarniko/Waldemar), Pat Karpen (Tana), Mare Kenney (Ellen II), John Anthony Lack (Frawley/Bart), Lynne McCall (Clare), Nicole Orth-Pallavicini (Anne), Robert B. Putnam (Pritchard/Jerry), Ronald Siebert (Grant), Jessie Speart (Flora), Andrew Teheran (Timothy), Steve Tschudy (Wayne), Juanita Walsh (Letty), Debra Whitfield (Linda).
A play in three acts. The action takes place in the sitting room of the Kincaid mansion on Fifth Avenue in New York City in the 1890's, the 1920's and 1940.

Austin Trevett Photos

Top Left: P. L. Carling in "Verdict"

Eric Douglas, Sherman Lloyd
in "Strictly Dishonorable"

P. L. Carling, Nick Stannard, also top with Peter Murphy
in "Verdict" *(Austin Trevett Photos)*

ARK THEATRE COMPANY

Sixth Season

Directors, Bruce Daniel, Donald Marcus, Lisa Milligan; Associate Director, Rebecca Guy; Casting, Jason LaPadura, Stanley Soble; Literary Managers, Melissa Whitcraft, Daniel Wilson; Press, Jeffrey Richards Associates

Thursday, November 3–27, 1983 (16 performances)

MACBETH by William Shakespeare; Director, Rebecca Guy; Set, Kalina Ivanov, Loy Arcenas; Costumes, Donna Zakowski; Sound, Daryl Bornstein; Lighting, Betsy Adams; Fights, B. H. Barry, Ellen Saland; Stage Manager, Michelle E. Tatum; Assistant Director, Jon Larson; Composer/Musician, P. Morghean McPhail; Technical Director, Kevin West; Props, Mary Svoboda; Hairstylist, John-Michael Carter; Wardrobe, Mary Marsicano.

CAST: David Carlyon (Witch/Murderer/Doctor), Michael Cerveris (Malcolm), Michael Charter (Macduff's son), Stephanie Copeland (Macduff's daughter), Randy Danson (Lady Macbeth), Robert Emmet (Sgt./Servant/Murderer/Messenger), John Griesemer (Servant/Porter/Seyton), Harriet Harris (Witch/Lady Macduff), Myvanwy Jenn (Witch/Gentlewoman), John Christopher Jones (Macbeth), Christopher McHale (Banquo), Ryland Merkey (Duncan/Old Man/Siward), Charles Morey (Ross), Brett Porter (Lennox), Jamey Sheridan (Macduff), Charles Simon (Fleance/Young Siward).

Performed with one intermission.

Thursday, March 8,–April 1, 1984 (16 performances)

THE MAN WHO COULD SEE THROUGH TIME by Terri Wagener; Director, Carey Perloff; Set, Loy Arcenas; Costumes, Martha Kelly; Lighting, David N. Weiss; Sound, Daryl Bornstein; Music, Raymond Benson; Sculptor/Consultant, Hilarie Johnston; Stage Managers, Diane Ward, Mary Svoboda; Wardrobe, Connie Culbertson.

CAST: Bob Cunton (Prof. Mordecai Bates), Leslie Geraci (Ellen Brock).

A play in two acts and 7 scenes. The action takes place at the present time in Prof. Bates' classroom and in his apartment

Thursday, May 10,–June 10, 1984 (18 performances)

THE TRANSPOSED HEADS by Sidney Goldfarb and Julie Taymor; Adapted from Thomas Mann's novella; Director, Julie Taymor; Scenery, Atsushi Moriyasu; Costumes, Donna Zakowski; Lighting, David N. Weiss; Puppetry Design, Julie Taymor; Original Music, Yukio Tsuji, Masa Imamura; Songs, Yukio Tsuji, Masa Imamura, Sheila Dabney; Dance Consultant, Arundhati Chattopadhya; Assistant Director, Leslie Gifford; Lightscapes, Caterina Bertolotto; Stage Managers, Chris Fielder, Gretchen Taylor; Wigs, Scott Farley.

CAST: Sheila Dabney (Narrator), Harry Streep (Shridaman), Mark Morales (Nanda), Yamil Borges (Sita), Puppeteers: Kerry Burke, Stephen Kaplin, Barbara Pollitt, Gretchen Taylor.

A drama in two acts.

Yamil Borges in "The Transposed Heads"
(Martha Swope/Carol Rosegg Photo)

Harry Streep, in "The Transposed Heads"
(Martha Swope/Carol Rosegg Photo)

**Top: Bob Gunton, Leslie Geraci
in "The Man Who Could See Through Time"**
(Ken Schwenker Photo)

CIRCLE REPERTORY COMPANY

Marshall W. Mason, Artistic Director
Fifteenth Season

Managing Director, Richard Frankel; Acting Artistic Director, B. Rodney Marriott; Associate Artistic Director, Tanya Berezin; Literary Manager, Robert Meiksins; Assistant to Mr. Mason, Glenna Clay; Business Manager, Sharon Rupert; Production Manager, Kate Stewart; Resident Stage Managers, Fred Reinglas, Jody Boese, Tim Morse; Technical Director, Jesse Gardner; Props, Richard Lollo, Marguerite Montelo; Wig/Wardrobe, Miriam Nieves; Photographer, Gerry Goodstein; Wigs, Paul Huntley; Press, Richard Frankel, Reva Cooper

(AMERICAN PLACE THEATRE) Thursday, November 17,–December 11, 1983 (21 performances and 26 previews)

THE SEA GULL by Anton Chekhov; Translated by Jean-Claude van Itallie; Director, Elinor Renfield; Sets, John Lee Beatty; Costumes, Jennifer von Mayrhauser; Lighting, Dennis Parichy; Sound, Chuck London Media/Stewart Werner; Original Music, Norman L. Berman; Production Supervisor, Tanya Berezin; Stage Manager, Fred Reinglas.

CAST: Michael Ayr (Medvedenko), Robin Bartlett (Masha), Barbara Cason (Arkadina), Katherine Cortez (Nina), Colleen Davenport (Maid), Michael Higgins (Sorin), Judd Hirsch (Trigorin), Nancy Killmer (Paulina), Bruce McCarty (Yakov), Dennis Patrick (Dorn), Richard Seff (Shamraev), Richard Thomas (Treplev), Beryl Towbin (Cook), Understudies: Colleen Davenport (Nina/Masha), Beryl Towbin (Arkadina/Paulina), David Fellows (Yakov), Matthew Lewis (Sorin/Dorn/Shamraev).

A drama in four acts performed with one intermission. The action takes place in Russia at the turn of the century.

(CIRCLE REPERTORY THEATRE) Thursday, December 29, 1983–January 22, 1984 (47 performances)

FULL HOOKUP by Conrad Bishop, Elizabeth Fuller; Director, Marshall W. Mason; Set, David Potts; Costumes, Laura Crow; Lighting, John P. Dodd; Sound, Chuck London Media/Stewart Werner; Associate Director, B. H. Barry; Stage Manager, Ginny Martino.

CAST: Steve Bassett (Ric), Sharon Schlarth (Beth), Jacqueline Brookes (Rosie), Lynne Thigpen (Joellen), Edward Seamon (Les), Understudies: Mick Weber (Ric), Tom Smith (Les), Colleen Davenport.

A drama in two acts. The action takes place at the present time in Omaha, Nebraska.

Gerry Goodstein Photos

Richard Thomas, Barbara Cason, Judd Hirsch in "The Sea Gull"
Top Right: Jacqueline Brookes, Edward Seamon in "Hookup"

(CIRCLE REPERTORY THEATRE) Sunday, February 12,–March 11, 1984 (47 performances)
LEVITATION by Timothy Mason; Director, B. Rodney Marriott; Set, David Potts; Costumes, Laura Crow; Lighting, Dennis Parichy; Original Music, Norman L. Berman; Sound, Chuck London Media/Stewart Werner; Stage Manager, Jody Boese.

CAST: Adam Davidson (Tom), Trish Hawkins (Jean), Matthew Lewis (Wright), Bruce McCarthy (Ira), Lenka Peterson (Ada), Eric Schiff (Michael), Ben Siegler (Joe), Helen Stenborg (Inga), Understudies: Tom Smith (Joe), Mick Weber (Arthur/Wright), Colleen Davenport (Ada/Jean/Inga), David Fellows (Michael/Ira).

A drama performed without intermission. The action takes place in 1979 in a residential section of Minneapolis, MN.

(CIRCLE REPERTORY THEATRE) Wednesday, March 21,–April 29, 1984 (47 performances)
THE HARVESTING by John Bishop; Director, Mr. Bishop; Set, Loren Sherman; Costumes, Ann Emonts; Lighting, Mal Sturchio; Sound, Chuck London Media/Stewart Werner; Associate Director, Chris Silva; Dramaturg, Milan Stitt; Stage Manager, Fred Reinglas.

CAST: Kiya Ann Joyce (Carol Ann), Timothy Carhart (Tommy Heisler), Lionel Mark Smith (Curtis Gibson), Jimmie Ray Weeks (John Torski), Paul Butler (Walter Hollins), Jane Fleiss (Joyce Miller), James McDaniel (Gary Majors), Edward Seamon (Bim Miller), S. Epatha Merkerson (Louise Cline), Colleen Davenport, Tom Smith (Police Officers).

A drama in two acts. The action takes place July 1st through 4th of 1970 in Mansfield, Ohio.

(CIRCLE REPERTORY THEATRE) Thursday, May 31, 1984– The Circle Repertory Company and the Steppenwolf Theatre Ensemble of Chicago present the Steppenwolf Theatre Company's production of:
BALM IN GILEAD by Lanford Wilson; Director, John Malkovich; Set/Lighting, Kevin Rigdon; Costume Supervision, Glenne Headly; Sound, John Malkovich; Stage Manager, Teri McClure.

CAST: Paul Butler (John), Giancarlo Esposito (Ernesto), Lazaro Perez (Carlo), Debra Engle (Babe), Billie Neal (Rust), Tanya Berezin succeeded by Lynne Thigpen (Bonnie), Terry Kinney (Fick), Jeff Perry (Franny), Brian Tarantina (David), James McDaniel (Tig), James Pickens, Jr. (Rake), Jonathan Hogan succeeded by Christopher Goutman (Martin), Bruce McCarty (Bob), Zane Lasky (Frank), Burke Pearson (Al), Laurie Metcalf (Darlene), Gary Sinise (Dopey), Betsy Aidem (Kay), Danton Stone (Joe), Karen Sederholm (Terry), Glenne Headly (Ann), Tom Zanarini (Xavier), Tom Irwin (Stranger), Mick Weber (Tim), Charlotte Maier (Judy), Children: Adam Davidson, Eben Davidson, Ernnisse Heuer, Samantha Kostmayer.

A drama in two acts. The action takes place in October of 1972 in an all-night coffee shop and the street corner outside on upper Broadway in New York City.

Jimmie Ray Weeks, Paul Butler, Edward Seamon in "The Harvesting" Left Center: Timothy Carhart, Jane Fleiss in "The Harvesting" Top: Michael Higgins, Ben Siegler in "Levitation" *(Gerry Goodstein Photos)*

Laurie Metcalf, Danton Stone, and Top: Paul Butler, James McDaniel, Glenne Headly,
Brian Tarantina in "Balm in Gilead" *(Gerry Goodstein Photos)*

CSC/CITY STAGE COMPANY

Christopher Martin, Artistic Director
Seventeenth Season

Formerly Classic Stage Company; Managing Director, Dan J. Martin; Business Manager, Caroline F. Turner; Administrative Assistant, Byron Johns; Associate Director/Dramaturg, Karen Sunde; Resident Composer, Noble Shropshire; Assistant Artistic Director, Craig Kinzer; Stage Manager, Bonnie L. Becker; Costumes, Miriam Nieves; Lighting, Richard Butler; Production Manager, Peter Ollquist; Development Director/Press, Will Maitland Weiss
COMPANY: Christopher Martin, Karen Sunde, John Camera, Ginger Grace, Thomas Lenz, Mary Eilenn O'Donnell, Charles H. Patterson, Helene Rose, Noble Shropshire, Gary Sloan, Tom Spiller, Amy Warner, Donn Youngstrom
PRODUCTIONS: (in repertory from October 6, 1983–May 20, 1984) Big and Little/Scenes, Hamlet, Baal, Faust (Parts I & II), Dance of Death

Gerry Goodstein Photos

Right: Karen Sunde in "Big and Little/Scenes"

**Ginger Grace as Ophelia
in "Hamlet"**

**Noble Shropshire
as Hamlet**

90

THE CLASSIC THEATRE

Executive Director, Nicholas John Stathis; Artistic Director, Maurice Edwards, Production Director, Robert Anthony; Production Coordinator, Jerry Roth; Casting Consultant, Sonia Dressner

Saturday, September 24,–October 16, 1983 (16 performances)
A NEW WAY TO PAY OLD DEBTS by Philip Massinger; Director, Maurice Edwards; Set, Jon Teta; Costumes, Henri Ewaskio; Lighting, David Landau; Music, Max Hammock; Stage Manager, Sandra M. Bloom.
CAST: Owen S. Rackleff (Sir Giles Overreach), Edward Baran, John L. Bader, John Barrett, Stephen Byers, Alfred Casas, Rob Gomes, Sid R. Gross, Max Hammock, Gloria Harper, Harry H. Kunesch, Lee DeLond, Arlene Nadel, Joseph O'Brien, Bernie Rubin, Rosemary Sykes, Nancy Ward.
Performed with one intermission.

Saturday, October 29,–November 13, 1983 (12 performances) Director, Jonathan Amacker;
PELICANS PLEASE MUTE three short plays from the French avant-garde of the 1920's; Set, Brian Kelly; Costumes, Bernice Boucher; Lighting, Jay Johnson; Assistant Director, Sonia Dressner; Stage Manager, Leslie Loeb. "The Pelicans by Raymond Radiguet, "If You Please" by Andre Breton and Philippe Soupault, "Humulus the Mute" by Jean Anouilh and Jean Aurenche.
CAST: Edward Baran, Kay L. Colburn, Muriel Gould, Siobhan Kennedy, Eric Kramer, Bill Maloney, Ray Virta

Wednesday, November 23,–December 11, 1983 (15 performances)
THE LIFE I GAVE YOU by Luigi Pirandello; Translated by Frederick May; Director, Maurice Edwards; Set, Gene D'Onofrio; Costumes, Catharine Bray; Lighting, Jay Johnson; Music, Max Hammock; Stage Manager, Philip Stone.
CAST: Vera Visconti Lockwood (Donn'Anna), Patricia Mauderi (Lucia), Tamara Reed (Freancesca), Virginia Aquino (Fiorina), Maurice Sterman (Giorgio), Elizabeth De Ono (Lida), Max Hammock (Flavio), Irma St. Paule (Elisabetta), William DaPrato (Giovanni), Dolores McCullough, Irma St. Paule, Elizabeth De Ono (Neighborhood Women).
A play in three acts with one intermission. The action takes place in a lonely villa in the Tuscan countryside about 1924.

Thursday, January 12,–February 5, 1984 (16 performances)
THE BARBER OF SEVILLE by Beaumarchais; Adapted and Directed by Jerry Ross; Set, B. Rogers; Lighting, Jayne Dutra; Costumes, Janet Moody; Original Music, Eric Rausch; Assistant Directors, John Bruno, Keith Miller; Stage Manager, Leslie Loeb.
CAST: Mark de Veer (Almaviva), Clifford Mason (Figaro), Elek Hartman (Bartholo), Shelley Hoffman (Rosine), Bill Maloney (Basile), Keith Miller (Notary), Eric Rausch (Musician).
A comedy in two acts.

Thursday, February 16,–March 11, 1984 (16 performances)
HELEN by Euripides; Director, Douglas Tow; Choreography, Livia Ann; Set, Ed Farley; Costumes, Leigh George Odom; Lighting, David Bergstein; Sound, Elliott Forrest; Adaptation, Douglas Tow; Assistant Director, Quinton Wiles; Stage Manager, Paul A. Kochman.
CAST: Patricia Murray (Helen), Richard Rohan (Teucer/Messenger), Raphael Nash (Menelaus), Greg Gerard (Old Woman/Messenger), Loretta Toscano (Theonoe), Drew Tillotson (Theoclymenus), Chorus: Theresa Aceves, Mary Dollarhide, Lisa Simon Conley, Stacy Smith.
A romantic comedy in two acts. The action takes place in Egypt seventeen years after the Trojan War.

Thursday, March 22,–April 8, 1984 (12 performances)
ARIA DA CAPO by Edna St. Vincent Millay; Director, Michael Jason; Music, Jose Luis Greco; Costumes, Inya Schoenvaelder; Set/Lighting, Rinaldo Sartore; Stage Manager, Jeffrey L. Hilburn.
CAST: James Castagna (Makeup Man), Curtis Harwell (Pierrot), Tom McClary (Director), Suzette Reiss (Set Designer), Autry Davis Ratliff (Cothurnis), Mike Maher (Thyrsis), Peter Smith (Corydon), Diane Cremisio (Columbine).
The action takes place at the present time in the Classic Theatre. Performed with one intermission.

Saturday, April 21,–May 13, 1984 (16 performances)
TOSCA 1943 by Victorien Sardou; Adapted and Directed by Owen S. Rackleff; Set, Mr. Rackleff; Lighting, Cora Sangree; Costumes, Leigh George Odom; Stage Managers, Robert Verini, Ned Snell.
CAST: Martitia Palmer (Floria Tosca), Edward Baran (Mario Cavaradossi), Dan Lutzky (Baron Scarpia), Nicholas L. Eastman (Cesare), Ned Snell (Gennarino), James Kissane (Scristan/Composer), Vincent Bossone (Sciarrone), Alfred Casas (Spoletta), Patric Flynn (Marquis Attavanti), Nelson Bradshaw (Capt. Brockhaus).
A drama in 2 acts and 6 scenes. The action takes place in Rome during July of 1943.

Wednesday, May 23,–June 10, 1984 (16 performances)
ROUNDHEADS AND PEAKHEADS by Bertolt Brecht; Director, Jerry Roth; Musical Director/Original Music, Charles Robbin Mills; Lyrics, Bertolt Brecht; Assistant Director, Keith Miller; Choreography, Livia Ann; Set, Pamela Renee; Costumes, Donna Parish; Masques/Heads/Makeup, Tom Wilson; Lighting, Jeff. L. Hilburn; Stage Manager, Cathy Lee Crane.

Patricia Mauceri, Vera Visconti Lockwood
in "The Life I Gave You" (*S. Epstein Photo*)

Vincent Bossone, Edward Baran, Patrick Flynn,
Dan Lutzky, Martita Palmer in "Tosca 1943"
(*H. Rosenkranz Photo*) Above: Rosemary Sykes, Owen Rackleff,
Arlene Nadel in "A New Way to Pay Old Debts"

CAST: Livia Ann (Mme. Tomaso), Elizabeth Bove (Mme. Cornamontis), Amy Brentano (Nanna), Ned Butikofer (Regent/Lord Chief Justice), Sam Clay (Inspector), Lee DeLong (Mother Superior), Elise Dewsberry (Peakhead "Czich" Lawyer), Paul Edwards (Hua I), William Kramer (Emanuel), Jud Lawrence (Parr), Doug Lothes (Callamassi), Bill Maloney (Callas), Grace Millo (Isabella), Dennis Pallante (Missena), Kristin Reeves (Roundhead "Czuch" Lawyer), Jodi Shaw (Hua II), Laura G. Stammers (Iberin), Mark Stefanik (Saz), Barry Thompson (Palmosa/Lopez).
A play with music in 2 acts and 11 scenes.

ENSEMBLE STUDIO THEATRE

Curt Dempster, Artistic Director
Twelfth Season
Managing Director, David S. Rosenak; Associate Producer, Billy Hopkins; Literary Manager, Stuart Spencer; Production Manager, Teresa Elwert; Technical Director, Jack Wikoff; Production Coordinator, John W. Magness; Casting, Billy Hopkins, Marion Chamow; Business Manager, Joyce Farra; Press, Bruce Cohen
Sunday, October 23,–December 18, 1983 (46 performances. Re-opened Tuesday, March 13, 1984 at Circle in the Square Downtown)
TO GILLIAN ON HER 37th BIRTHDAY by Michael Brady; Director, Pamela Berlin; Set, Robert Thayer; Lighting, Allen Lee Hughes; Costumes, Deborah Shaw; Composer, Robert Dennis; Sound, Bruce Ellman; Stage Managers, Richard Costabile, Derek Hodel; Props, Joseph M. Petrillo, Jr.
CAST: James Rebhorn (David), Sarah Jessica Parker (Rachel), Noelle Parker (Cindy), Heather Lupton (Kevin), Richmond Hoxie (Paul), Jean De Baer (Esther), Cheryl McFadden (Gillian).
A drama in two acts. The action takes place during a weekend in August of the present time on a small island off the coast of New England.
Friday, February 10,–March 18, 1984 (28 performances)
BROKEN EGGS by Eduardo Machado; Director, James Hammerstein; Set, Keith Gonzales; Costumes, Deborah Shaw; Lighting, Cheryl Thacker; Sound, Bruce Ellman; Stage Managers, Amy Pell, Carol A. Impaglia; Props, Nan Siegmund; Wardrobe, Denise Laffer.
CAST: Leonardo Cimino (Alfredo), Julie Garfield (Miriam), Baxter Harris (Osvaldo), Karen Kondazian (Sonia), Theresa Saldana (Mimi), Michael Sandoval (Oscar), Sol (Manuela), Ann Talman (Lizette).
A play in two acts. The action takes place on a hot January day in Los Angeles in 1979.
Saturday, May 5,–June 17, 1984 (46 performances in repertory)
ONE-ACT PLAY MARATHON '84 : Series A: Producer, Billy Hopkins; Sets, Mark Fitzgibbons; Lighting, Karl E. Haas; Costumes, Deborah Shaw; Sound, Bruce Ellman; Production Manager, Teresa Elwert; Stage Managers, Kit Liset, Dara O'Brien, Amy L. Vining, Ted Altschuler, Lisa Kirsch, Susan Selig. "House" by Danny Cahill; Director, Bruce Ornstein; with Kevin O'Keefe (Mark), Scott Burkholder (Patrick), Joe Cerwin (Michael), Margaret Colin (Debbie). "Bite the Hand" by Ara Watson; Director, David Margulies; with Lois Smith (Reba), Judith Yerby (April), Frank Girardeau (Frank). "Remember Crazy Zelda?" by Shel Silverstein; Director, Art Wolff; with Jane Hoffman (Bea), Richard Woods (Alex). Series B: Sets, Mark Fitzgibbons; Lighting, Karl E. Haas; Costumes, Isis C. Mussenden; Stage Managers, Richard Heeger, John Henry Lipscomb, Diane B. Greenberg, G. Roger Abell, Robert Kaplan, Denise Laffer, Tracy Foster, Karen Cohen. "Blood Bond" by Gina Barnett; Director, Melodie Somers; with Novella Nelson (Flo), Samatha Atkins (Karen). "At Home" by Richard Dresser; Director, Jerry Zaks; with Carolyn Mignini (Janet), Dan Ziskie (Dick), John Goodman (Ted), Mary Catherine Wright (Jackie), Jeff Brooks (Don), Melodie Somers (Ronnie). "Fine Line" by Janice Van Horne; Director, Harris Yulin; with Roxanne Hart (Doty), Jill Eikenberry (Zee). "Slam!" by Jane Willis; Director, Shirley Kaplan; with Rob Morrow (Lincoln), Evan Handler (Mel). Series C: Sets, Jane Muskyl; Lighting, Karl E. Haas; Costumes, Hilary Rosenfeld; Stage Managers, Kit Liset, Amy L. Vining, Susan Selig, Anne Singer, Charles Otte. "Jazz" by Elizabeth Albrecht; Director, Elaine Petricoff; with Gina Barnett (Charlotte), Harrison Avery (Leo). "Been Taken" by Roger Hedden; Director, Billy Hopkins; with Corey Parker (John), Perry Lang (Dennis), Anna Levine (Margaret), Ric Martino (Steve); Assistant Director, Houston Demere. Series D: Sets, Jane Musky; Costumes, Linda Vigdor; Stage Managers, Richard Heeger, Denise A. Laffer, Cornelia Twitchell, Ted Altschuler. "Saxophone Music" by Bill Bozzone; Director, Risa Bramon; Musician, Louis Belogenis; Assistant Director, Mark Gordon; with Ned Eisenberg (Hector), David Strathairn (Emil), Ilene Kristen (Margo), Mary Davenport (Mrs. Firestone). "Ariel Bright" by Katharine Long; Director, John Schwab; with Bill Swikowski (Hiley), Melodie Somers (Ariel Bright). "Raving" by Paul Rudnick; Director, Peter Mark Schifter; with Winnie Holzman (Edie), Nathan Lane (Patrick), Jack Gilpin (Archie)

Carol Rosegg Photos

**Top Right: Cheryl McFadden (top), James Rebhorn,
Sarah Jessica Parker in "To Gillian on Her 37th
Birthday" Below: Julie Garfield, Leonardo Cimino
in "Broken Eggs"**

**Richard Woods, Jane Hoffman
in "Remember Crazy Zelda"**

EQUITY LIBRARY THEATRE

George Wojtasik, Managing Director
Forty-first Season

Producing Director, Lynn Montgomery; Informals Producer, Rebecca Kreinen; Production Coordinator, Stephanie Brown; Technical Director, Michael Yarborough; Wardrobe, JoEllen Bendall; Sound, Hal Schuler; Staff Photographer, Gary Wheeler; Press, Lewis Harmon

(MASTER THEATRE) Thursday, September 22,–October 9, 1983 (30 performances)

THE LADY'S NOT FOR BURNING by Christopher Fry; Director, Kip Rosser; Set, James Wolk; Costumes, Colleen Muscha; Lighting, Deborah E. Matlack; Original Music, Polly Pen; Stage Managers, James R. Sabo, Carolyn DeMaggio.
CAST: Lynn Archer (Margaret), Lisabeth Bartlett (Jennet), Stephen Burks (Richard), Callan Egan (Matthew Skipps), Peggy Harmon (Alizon Eliot), Charles Michael Howard (Humphrey Devise), Leonard Kelly-Young (Thomas Mendip), Gerald Lancaster (Tappercoom), James Leach (Nicholas Devise), Robert Molnar (Hebble), Zeke Zaccaro (The Chaplain).

A play in 3 acts. The action takes place in the house of Hebbie Tyson, mayor of the small market town of Cool Clary during the 15th Century, either more or less or exactly.

(MASTER THEATRE) Thursday, October 27,–November 20, 1983 (30 performances)

THE MUSIC MAN with Book, Music and Lyrics by Meredith Willson; Story, Meredith Willson, Franklin Lacey; Director, Worth Howe; Choreography, Diana Baffa-Brill; Musical Director, Ken Uy; Scenery, Roger Benischek; Lighting, Clarke W. Thornton; Stage Managers, J. Francis Fisher, John Calder III, Becca Bean; Associate Musical Director, Edward Reichert; Props, Andrew Ness; Wardrobe, Jamie DeLorenzo.
CAST: Lowell Alecson (Oliver), James Anthony (Harold Hill), John Barone (Ewart), Joanna Beck (Maud), Dick Decareau (Marcellus), Leonard Drum (Mayor Shinn), Ari Gold (Winthrop), Lynne Goldsman (Effie), Jessica Houston (Alma), Irma Larrison (Eulalie), Brett Larson (Barney), Suzanne Lukather (Eunice), Kimberly Meyers (Bertha), Dan Mojica (Linus), Cheryl Montelle (Gracie), Mary Rausch (Mrs. Paroo), Sarah Rice (Marian), Joseph Rice (Tommy), Terry Runnels (Charlie), Whitney Anne Savage (Amaryllis), Eric Schussler (Olin), Susan Secunda (Ethel), Mollie Smith (Zaneeta/Dance Captain), Alan Stuart (Davey), Skip Zipf (Jacey).

A musical in 2 acts and 17 scenes. The action takes place in the past in River City, Iowa.

MUSICAL NUMBERS: Rock Island, Iowa Stubborn, Trouble, If You Don't Mind My Saying So, Goodnight My Someone, Columbia the Gem of the Ocean, 76 Trombones, Sincere, Sadder but Wiser Girl, Pick-a-little Talk-a-little, Goodnight Ladies, Marian the Librarian, My White Knight, Wells Fargo Wagon

(MASTER THEATRE) Thursday, December 1–18, 1983 (22 performances)

FOR THE USE OF THE HALL by Oliver Hailey; Director, Margaret Denithorne; Set, Alex Polner; Lighting, Eric Cornwell; Paintings, Roxanne Amico; Costumes, Karen Eifert; Stage Managers, Roger Kent Brechner, Mark Wallace, David Munnell; Sound, Hal Schuler; Wardrobe, Jann Kratz; Photographer, Gary Wheeler.
CAST: Helen Lloyd Breed (Bess), William Wise (Allen), Nancy Linehan (Charlotte), Myra Turley (Terry), Linda Christian-Jones (Alice), John P. Connolly (Martin).

A play in two acts. The action takes place in a summer house on Long Island in the future with flashbacks to the winter of 1973.

Thursday, January 5–29, 1984 (24 performances)

RED, HOT AND BLUE! with Music and Lyrics by Cole Porter; Book, Howard Lindsay, Russel Crouse; Director, Christopher Catt; Set, Bryan Johnson; Lighting, Natasha Katz; Costumes, Konnie Kittrell; Dance Arrangements, Stephen Flaherty; Assistant to Director, Lynnette Barkley; Musical Direction/Vocal Arrangements, Jeffrey L. Patterson; Choreography, Patti D'Beck, Jerry Yoder; Stage Managers, Clark Taylor, Alane Brown, Bruce Greenwood; Assistant Musical Director, Paul Johnson; Hairstylist, Thomas Garcia; Wardrobe, Kathleen M. Mulligan; Props, Bruce Greenwood, Clark Taylor.
CAST: Christine Anderson (Peaches), Stanley Bojarski (O'Shaughnessy), Robert Buntzen (Ratface Dugan/Marine), Susan Cella (Nails), Anne Connors (Vivian/Francine), Michael Di Fonzo (Bill), Tracy Dodrill (Natalie/Pansy), Tom Flagg (Pinkle), Becky Garrett (Arnita/Dance Captain), Kristie Hannum (Grace), Matthew Kwiat (Malvinsky), Steven Minning (Loie the Louse), Diana Myron (Irene/Dr. Bandersnatch), Steve Owsley (Jeff), Carol Schuberg (Olive), Philip Shultz (Senator Delgrasso), Tom Schumacher (Babyface Metelli), Gordon Stanley (Fingers), Karen Toto (Betty/Celia), A. C. Weary (Bob Hale).

A musical in two acts. The action takes place in 1936.

MUSICAL NUMBERS: I'M Throwing a Ball Tonight, Down in the Depths on the 90th Floor, Red Hot and Blue, A Little Skipper from Heaven Above, You're a Bad Influence on Me, How'm I Ridin'?, You've Got Something, It's De-Lovely, Goodbye Little Dream Goodbye, Let's Do It, When All's Said and Done, Dizzy Baby, Finale.

Gary Wheeler Photos

Top Right: Lynn Archer, Peggy Harmon, Stephen Burks, Charles Michael Howard, James Leach in "The Lady's Not for Burning" Below: James Anthony (c) and chorus in "The Music Man"

Myra Turley, John P. Connolly, William Wise, Linda Christian-Jones in "For the Use of the Hall"

93

(MASTER THEATRE) Thursday, February 9–26, 1984 (22 performances)
A THURBER CARNIVAL by James Thurber; Music, Don Elliott; Muscial Director/Vocal Adaptation/Arrangements, Mike Huffman; Director, J. Barry Lewis; Choreography/Musical Staging, Matthew Diamond; Scenery, J. Robin Modereger; Costumes, Andrea Carini; Lighting, David Lee Crist; Stage Managers, Lawrence Rosenthal, Melody E. KirkWagner, Penny Marks; Props, Geoffrey Allen; Wardrobe, Brian Grace.
CAST: Peter Bartlett, Joy Bond, Linda Gelman, Stephen Gleason, Mitchell Greenberg, Evelyn Joan Halus, Jim McNickle, Hardy Rawls, Kate Weiman, Mike Huffman at the piano. ACT I: Overture, Word Dance Part I, The Night the Bed Fell, The Wolf at the Door, The Unicorn in the Garden, The Little Girl and the Wolf, If Grant Had Been Drinking at Appomattox, Casuals of the Keys, The Macbeth Murder Mystery, Gentlemen Shoppers, The Last Flower. ACT II: The Pet Department, File and Forget, Mr. Preble Gets Rid of His Wife, Take Her Up Tenderly, The Secret Life of Walter Mitty, Word Dance Part II.
(MASTER THEATRE) Thursday, March 8,–April 1, 1984 (30 performances)
UP IN CENTRAL PARK with Book by Herbert and Dorothy Fields; Lyrics, Dorothy Fields; Music, Sigmund Romberg; Director, John Sharpe; Choreography, Gerald Teijelo; Musical Direction/Additional Dance and Choral Arrangements, Jerald B. Stone; Scenery, Carl A. Baldasso; Lighting, Karl E. Haas; Costumes, Mary F. Marsicano; Stage Managers, Sondra R. Katz, Gail A. Burns, Peggy L. Hess; Hairstylist, Thomas Garcia; Props, Sarah Higgins.
CAST: Martha E. Arnold (Gertrude), Mark Basile (Vincent), Richard Blair (Danny), Jon Brothers (Peter), David Bryant (Thomas), Nick Corley (Joe), Robert DeLeon (Billy), Jim Donahoe (Timothy), George K. Emch (Mayor Hall), Nicole Flender (Essie), Craig Frawley (Richard), Mimi Froom (Ethel), Joe Giuffre (Newsboy), Cliff Goulet (Dutton), David Inloes (Joe), Nick Jolley (Boss Tweed), James Judy (Mathews), Luke Lynch (Munroe), Jeremy Mann (Lotta's brother), Barbara McCulloh (Rosie), Corinne Melancon (Can-Can Girl), Meredith Murray (Bessie), Judy Anne Nelson (Lotta), Kelly Patterson (Headwaiter), Lisa Peters (Fanny), Marjorie Smith (Clara), Cheryl Stern (Mildred), Joe S. Wyatt (George).
A musical in 2 acts and 10 scenes. The action takes place from 1870–1872 at various places in New York City.
MUSICAL NUMBERS: You Can't Get Over the Wall, Up from the Gutter, Carousel in the Park, It Doesn't Cost You Anything to Dream, Boss Tweed, Christmas Eve, When She Walks in the Room, Currier and Ives, Skaters Dance, Close as Pages in a Book, Opening, Fireman's Bride, When the Party Gives a Party for the Party, Big Back Yard, April Snow, Bessie's Wedding Day, The Birds and the Bees.
(MASTER THEATRE) Thursday, April 12–29, 1984 (22 performances)
A TOUCH OF THE POET by Eugene O'Neill; Director; Yvonne Ghareeb; Set, Dennis Bradford; Costumes, JoEllen Bendall; Lighting, Craig Van Tassel; Stage Managers, Elizabeth Katherine Carr, Virginia Jones; Hairstylist, Scott A. Mortimer; Wardrobe, Debbie Rosen; Production Assistant, Geoffrey Allen.
CAST: Andrew Gorman (Mickey Maloy), Don Perkins succeeded by Peter J. Saputo (Jamie Cregan), Kay Walbye (Sara Melody), Helen-Jean Arthur (Nora Melody), Gerald J. Quimby (Cornelius Melody), John F. Degen (Dan Roche), Carl A. Northgard (Paddy O'Dowd), Rod Houts (Patch Riley), Joanne Dorian (Deborah), John Armstrong (Nicholas Gadsby).
A drama in 2 acts and 4 scenes. The action takes place on July 27, 1828 in the dining room of Melody's Tavern in a village a few miles from Boston, MA.
(MASTER THEATRE) Thursday, May 10,–June 3, 1984 (32 performances)
PAL JOEY with Music by Richard Rodgers; Lyrics, Lorenz Hart; Book, John O'Hara; Scenery, Joel Fontaine; Costumes, Daria Wheatley; Musical Direction, Francis P. Minarik; Director, Bill Herndon; Lighting, Randy Becker; Choreography, Piper Pickrell; Stage Managers, Travis DeCastro, Peter Wolf, Meryl Simone Jacobs; Wardrobe, Jacqueline Owens, Maureen Frey; Props, Geoffrey Allen, Shasti O'Leary.
CAST: Melanie Backer (Society Lady), Brantley Bardin (Waldo), David Berk (Mike), Cathy Brewer-Moore (Vera), Melinda Buckley (Janet/Dream Vera), Irving Burton (Ernest), Jerry Colker (Ludlow), Colleen Dodson (Tilda), Christopher Edmonds (Stage Manager), Spence Ford (Gladys), Mark Fotopoulos (Joey), Gale Gallione (Terry), Greg Ganakas (Victor/Dream Joey), David Horwitz (Hoople), Lydia Laurans (Valerie), Michele Minailo (Diane), Rusty Riegelman (The Kid/Dream Linda), Susan Schaumberg (Society Lady/Dance Captain/Swing), Jay Schneider (Louis), Mary Lou Shriber (Linda), Elizabeth Stover (Claire), Marijane Sullivan (Melba), William Walsh (Commissioner O'Brien), Kevin Brooks Winkler (Herman).
A musical in 2 acts and 12 scenes. The action takes place in Chicago in the late 1930's.
MUSICAL NUMBERS: A Great Big Town, You Mustn't Kick It Around, I Could Write a Book, That Terrific Rainbow, What Is a Man?, Happy Hunting Horn, Bewitched, Pal Joey, Dream Ballet, The Flower Garden of My Heart, Zip, Plant You Now Dig You Later, Den of Iniquity, Do It the Hard Way, Take Him

Gary Wheeler Photos

Top Left: A. C. Weary, Christine Anderson,
Tom Flagg in "Red, Hot and Blue!" Below:
Hardy Rawls, Joy Bond, Peter Bartlett,
Kate Weiman in "A Thurber Carnival"

Barbara McCulloh, Meredith Murray, Richard Blair,
Jim Donahoe in "Up in Central Park"

EQUITY LIBRARY THEATRE INFORMALS

Rebecca Kreinen, Producer
(Bruno Walter Auditorium/Lincoln Center) Each production presented for three performances. September 26–28, 1983: "Be Still Thunder" By Shirley Hardy-Leonard; Director, Shelley Raffle; CAST: William Jay, Edythe Davis, Minnie Gentry, David Sotolongo, Joan Valentina, Allen Barone, Mitchell Bonta. October 17–19, 1983: "The Men's Group" by David St. James; Director, Kent Thompson; CAST: Janet Aldrich, Jeffrey West, Jonathan Slaff, Leo Schaff, Jerry Lee. November 21–23, 1983: "Trading Places" Original Concept, Jeff Veazey, Susan Stroman; Director, Dennis Deal;
CAST: Jeff Veazey, Susan Stroman, Nancy Hillner, Chris Ranck, Patti Wyss. December 19–21, 1983: "Dickens' Reflections on the Carol" adapted by Philip William McKinley; Music and Lyrics, Suzanne Buhrer, Philip William McKinley; Director, Stephen Bonnell; Choreography, Piper Pickrell; Musical Direction, Jeffrey Klotz; CAST: Frank Ventura, David Trim, Hope W. Sacharoff, Nona Waldeck, Kim Ivan Motter, Barbara Surosky, Thomas Ikeda, Michael Shane Rogers, Stephen Moser, Dan Jinks, Michele Rigan, Glory Crampton, Kathryn Wilson, Aldene Kelly. January 16–18, 1984; "The Middlemen" by Glen Merzer; Director, David Dorwart; Assistant Director, Cheryl Aden; CAST: Pattie Tierce, Kent Thompson, Stan Lachow, Paul Edwards, Arthur Strimling. February 27–29, 1984: "Romantic Arrangements" by Alan M. Brown; Director, Morgan Sloane; CAST: Lachlan Macleay, Linda Cook, Nona Waldeck, Daniel Allen Kremer, Stephen Ahern. March 26–28, 1984: "A Good Year for Roses" by Susan Kander; Director, Stan Lachow; CAST: Rosemary McNamara, Kathleen Claypool, William R. Riker, Jay Devlin, Dee Ann McDavid. May 21–23, 1984: "American Power Play" by Judith Brussell; Director, Dinah Gravel; Musical Director, John Mulcahy; CAST: J. D. Cedillo, Lynne Charnay, Eileen Engel, Saunder Finard, Doug Franklin, Nancy Hamada, Laura Neal, Mark Proctor, Nicholas Saunders, Robin Westphal, Betsy Wingfield, Steve Wise

Gary Wheeler Photos

**Left: Mark Fotopoulos, Cathy Brewer-Moore
in "Pal Joey"**

Kay Walbye, Gerald J. Quimby in "A Touch of the Poet"

HUDSON GUILD THEATRE

David Kerry Heefner, Producing Director
Daniel Swee, Associate Director
Ninth Season

Workshops Director, Erika Goodman; Stage Manager, Brian A. Kaufman; Production Manager/Technical Director, Edward R. F. Matthews; Marketing and Development Director, John Blinstrub Fisher; Business Manager, Lucinda Marker; Photographer, Charles Marinaro; Press, Jeffrey Richards, Robert Ganshaw, C. George Willard, Ben Morse, Richard Dahl

Sunday, June 5–26, 1983 (9 performances and 18 previews)
ACCOUNTS by Michael Wilcox; Director, Kent Paul; Set, Jane Clark; Costumes, Mariann Verheyen; Lighting, Phil Monat; Dance Consultant, Anthony Abbriano; Props, Susan Izatt.
CAST: Kathleen Nolan (Mary Mawson), Josh Clark (Andy Mawson), Kevin Conroy (Donald Mawson), Allan Carlsen (James Ridley-Bowes), Frank Girardeau (John Duff).

A drama in two acts. The action takes place during 1979 and 1980 in various locations in the border region of Scotland.

Wednesday, October 12,–November 6, 1983 (28 performances)
SAND DANCING by Kenneth Pressman; Director, Robert Moss; Set/Lighting, Paul Wonsek; Costumes, Jeanne Button; Sound, Edward R. Fitzgerald; Props, Becca Bean.
CAST: John Abajian (Kyle Foote), Stephen Burleigh (John Burgess), Willie Reale (Jeremy Hubbell), Kristin Griffith (Carol Stoddard), Michael Earl O'Connor (Walter), Lynn Milgrim (Miranda Castigan).

A drama in two acts. The action takes place the week after Labor Day on the beach at Shell Island in the Chesapeake Bay.

Sunday, December 4–18, 1983 (28 performances)
WEDNESDAY by Julia Kearsley; Director, Geraldine Fitzgerald; Set, Ron Placzek; Costumes, Mariann Verheyen; Lighting, Phil Monat; Production Assistant, Bob Hallman; Technical Director, Michael J. Kondrat; Props, Andrew Ness.
CAST: John Bowman (David), Sada Thompson (Sal), Mia Dillon (Lillian), John Cunningham (Arthur).

A drama in two acts. The action takes place at the present time in the livingroom of a semi-detached bungalow in Lancashire, England.

Wednesday, January 25,–February 19, 1984 (28 performances)
GETTING ALONG FAMOUSLY by Michael Jacobs; Director, Joan Darling; Set, James Leonard Joy; Costumes, Mariann Verheyen; Lighting, Phil Monat; Props, Mary Beth McCabe.
CAST: Ted Flicker (Harry Leeby), Beverly Nero (Lori Leeby), Tom Aldredge (Sandy Castle), Edward Power (Justin Dean), John Bowman (Offstage Voices).

A play in two acts. The action takes place at the present time in the brownstone mansion of Harry Leeby in New York City.

Wednesday, March 28,–April 22, 1984 (28 performances)
LOVE LETTERS ON BLUE PAPER by Arnold Wesker; Director, Kenneth Frankel; Set, Paul Wonsek; Costumes, Mariann Verheyen; Lighting, Jeff Davis; Sound, Ed Fitzgerald; Sculpture, H. A. Pope; Production Assistant, Carol A. Impaglia.
CAST: Josef Sommer (Victor Marsden), Pauline Flanagan (Sonia Marsden), Jeffrey Jones (Maurice Stapleton), Christopher Curry (Trade Union Official).

A drama performed without intermission. The action takes place in the home of Victor Marsden, a retired trade union official, in the suburbs of an English industrial city, spring through fall of a recent year.

Wednesday, May 23–June 24, 1984 (35 performances)
BROWNSTONE by Josh Rubins, Peter Larson, Andrew Cadiff; Music, Peter Larson, Josh Rubins; Lyrics, Josh Rubins; Set/Lighting, Paul Wonsek; Costumes, Tom McKinley; Orchestrations, Hal Serra; Choreography, Cheryl Carty; Musical Direction, Yolanda Segovia; Assistant Musical Director, Norma Curley; Production Assistant, Carol A. Impaglia; Props, Chris Mealey; Wardrobe, Elizabeth Griffith; Hairstylist, Michael deCesare.
CAST: Loni Ackerman (Claudia), Ralph Bruneau (Stuart), Kimberly Farr (Joan), Maureen McGovern (Mary), Lenny Wolpe (Howard).

A musical in 2 acts and 7 scenes with an epilogue. The entire action takes place in and around a Manhattan brownstone at the present time.
MUSICAL NUMBERS: Someone's Moving In, I Just Want to Know, The Tonight Show, There She Goes, Should We Talk?, Camouflage, Thanks a Lot, Procrastination, Water Through the Trees, Don't Tell Me Everything, One of Them, See That Lady There, Spring Cleaning, Some Things Change, Since You Stayed Here, We Came Along Too Late, A Letter in the Mail, The Books, It's a Funny Thing, Did You Ever Fall?, Someone's Moving Out

Charles Marinaro Photos

Top Left: Josh Clark, Kathleen Nolan,
Kevin Conroy in "Accounts" Below: Sada Thompson,
John Cunningham, John Bowman in "Wednesday"

Ralph Bruneau, Loni Ackerman
in "Brownstone"

Maureen McGovern, Loni Ackerman in "Brownstone" Top: (L) Pauline Flanagan, Jeffrey Jones in "Love Letters on Blue Paper" (R) Ted Flicker, Tom Aldredge in "Getting Along Together"

INTERNATIONAL ARTS RELATIONS/ INTAR

Max Ferra, Artistic Director/Founder

Managing Director, Dennis Ferguson-Acosta; Development Director, Joanne Pottlitzer; Adminstrator, Mark Johnson; Literary Manager, Dolores Prida; Press, Bruce Cohen

(INTAR THEATRE) Wednesday, January 18,–February 19, 1984 (35 performances)

SARITA with Book and Lyrics by Maria Irene Fornes; Music, Leon Odenz; Set, Donald Eastman; Lighting, Anne E. Militello; Costumes, Gabriel Berry; Musical Direction/Arrangements, Leon Odenz; Director, Maria Irene Fornas; Stage Managers, Kate Mennone, Bernado Solano; Technical Director, Mark Tambella.

CAST: Blanca Camacho (Yeye), Sheila Dabney (Sarita), Carmen Rosario (Fela), Rodolfo Diaz (Fernando), Michael Carmine (Julio), Tom Kirk (Marc), Juan Vega (Jose).

A musical in two acts. The action takes place in the South Bronx from 1939 to 1949.

MUSICAL NUMBERS: He Was Thinking of You, I'm Pudding, Holy Spirit Good Morning, I'm Lonely, A Woman Like You, Lo Que Me Gusta a Mi, You Are Tahiti, A Little Boo Boo, To Ochun, His Wonderful Eye, Here Comes the Night, Papi No, The Letter.

Wednesday, March 14,–April 8, 1984 (34 performances)

EQUINOX by Mario Diament; Translated by Simone Z. Karlin, Evelyn Strouse; Director, Moni Yakim; Set, Don Coleman; Casting, Janet L. Murphy; Lighting, Lisa Grossman; Sound, Ray Hopper; Costumes, K. L. Fredericks; Stage Managers, Michael Verbil, Judith Granite, Lindanell Rivera; Technical Director, Phil Miller; Press Bruce Cohen, Jim Baldassare.

CAST: Ricardo Velez (Guido), Maria Cellario (Amanda), Fran Anthony (Ireme), Lindanell Rivera (Matilda), Judith Granite (Sophie), Lisa Vidal (Mariela), Boaz Yakim (Voice of man in 3C).

A play in two acts.

Wednesday, May 2–27, 1984 (23 performances)

THE CUBAN SWIMMER/DOG LADY by Milcha Sanchez-Scott; Director, Max Ferra; Sets, Ming Cho Lee; Costumes, Connie Singer; Sound, Paul Garrity; Stage Managers, Anne Marie Hobson, Manuel Rivera, Marcella White; Technical Director, Pete Ollquist; Movement/Mime, Pilar Garcia.

CAST: "Dog Lady" with Manuel Rivera (Raphael), Carlos Carrasco (Orlando), Jeannette Mirabel (Rosalinda), Graciela LeCube (Rosalinda's Mother), Lillian Hurst (Luisa Ruiz/Dog Lady), Elizabeth Pena (Jesse), Marcella White (Mrs. Amador), Percussionists: Daniel Barrajanos, Arto Tuncboyaci. "The Cuban Swimmer" with Jeannette Mirabel (Margarita the swimmer), Carlos Cestro (Her Father), Manuel Rivera (Her Brother), Lillian Hurst (Her Mother), Graciela LeCube (Her Grandmother), Carlos Carrasco (Newscaster), Elizabeth Pena (Newscaster)

Lindanell Rivera, Judith Granite, Fran Anthony, Maria Cellario, Ricardo Velez in "Equinox"
Top Right: Lillian Hurst, Carlos Cestero in "The Cuban Swimmer" *(Carol Rosegg Photos)*

98

MANHATTAN PUNCH LINE

Steve Kaplan, Artistic Director
Sixth Season

Executive Director, Mitch McGuire; Producing Directors, Jerry Heymann, Richard Erickson; Development Director, Ferne A. Farber; Production Manager, Pamela Singer; Casting, Holly Carlin; Business Manager, Trisha Hanger; Assistant to Artistic Director, Robin Saex; Press, Gary Murphy

(LION THEATRE) Thursday, June 2–26, 1983 (18 performances)

A KISS IS JUST A KISS by Paul Foster; Director, Don Scardino; Set, Production Value; Scenic Coordinator, Charles McCarry; Lighting, Joshua Dachs; Costumes, Julie Schwolow; Sound, Aural Fixation; Stage Manager, Jane MacPherson; Hairstylist, Scott Mortimer; Press, Jeffrey Richards Associates.

CAST: Elizabeth Austin (Alice), Shelby Brammer (Martha), Stephen Ahern (Ted), Kevin O'Connor (Bogart).

Performed without intermission. The action takes place in a Greenwich Village movie theatre.

(LION THEATRE) Monday, November 7,–December 4, 1984 (24 performances)

SYMPATHY by Dana Coen; Director, Steven D. Albrezzi; Setting, Production Value; Costumes, Julie Schwolow; Lighting, Joshua Dachs; Sound, Aural Fixation; Stage Managers, Kate Hancock, Kate Dale; Assistant Director, Lee Bloomrosen; Production Assistant, Brandy Berman.

CAST: Laurie Heineman (Barbara), Bernard Barrow (Phillip Adelman), Joan Kaye (Millie Krantz), Frances Chaney (Myra Adelman), Gil Kashkin (Marshall Krantz), Susan Heldfond (Paula Hickman), Lee Shepherd (Alan Hickman), Stephen Singer (Howard Levy), Joey Rigol, Adam Rose (Barbara's Children).

A drama in two acts. The action takes place at the present time in Barbara's house in suburban Long Island, NY.

(LION THEATRE) Monday, December 12, 1983–January 15, 1984 (38 performances)

JUNE MOON by Ring Lardner and George S. Kaufman; Director, Steve Kaplan; Settings, Production Value; Costumes, Amanda J. Klein; Lighting, Joshua Dachs; Sound, Aural Fixation; Musical Coordinator, Gordon G. Jones; Production Consultants, Ring Lardner, Jr., Anne Kaufman Schneider; Assistant Director, Nancy Lawrence; Technical Director, Marc D. Malamud; Stage Managers, Judy Martel, Suzanne Wakamoto.

CAST: Michael Countryman (Fred Stevens), Susan Dow (Edna Baker), Stephan Weyte (Paul Sears), Mercedes Ruehl (Lucille), Joanne Camp (Eileen), David Berk (Maxie), Robin Westphal (Goldie), Gordon G. Jones (Window Cleaner), F. L. Schmidlapp (Man Named Brainard), Joel Bernstein (Benny Fox), William Lawrence (Mr. Hart), Laura Margolis (Miss Rixey).

A comedy in 3 acts with prologue. The action takes place in a parlor car, Paul Sears' place, and a room at Goebel's

**Cast of "June Moon" Top Right: Shelby Brammer, Kevin O'Connor
in "A Kiss Is Just a Kiss" Below: Cast of "Sympathy"**
(Cathryn Williams Photos)

(LION THEATRE) Monday, February 6–26, 1984 (24 performances)
THE RIVALS by Richard Brinsley Sheridan; Director, Tom Costello; Sest, Toby Corbett/Production Value; Costumes, David Loveless; Lighting, Gregory Mac-Pherson; Music, Margaret R. Pine; Production Manager, Pamela Singer; Stage Managers, Anne Singer, Lora Manning; Assistant Directors, Doug Block, Sheryl Kaller; Technical Director, Michael Moran.
CAST: Jeanne Cullen (Lucy), Arthur Erickson (Bob Acres), Joanne Jarvis (Maid/Boy), Jerry Mayer (Sir Lucius), Dennis J. McLernon (Servant), John Michalski (Faulkland), Michael P. Moran (Sir Anthony), Richard Niles (David), Alexander Peck (Servant), Angela Pietropinto (Mrs. Malaprop), Larry Pine (Capt. Absolute), Debora Pressman (Julia), Richard M. Davidson (Fag), Wendy Rosenberg (Lydia), Jerry Winsett (Thomas).

A comedy performed in two acts. The action takes place in Bath, a city outside London on one day in the past.

(LION THEATRE) Friday, March 9,–April 1, 1984 (24 performances)
HACKERS by Mike Eisenberg; Director, Jerry Heymann; Settings, Jane Musky; Costumes, David Loveless; Lighting, Scott Pinkney; Sound, Gary Harris; Stage Managers, Neal Fox, Lora Manning; Technical Director, Marc D. Malamud.
CAST: Tim Choate (Martin), Michael Curran (Chris), Peter Basch (KJ), Sabrina LeBeauf (Mary).

A comedy in two acts. The action takes place at the present time in the basement of a college computer center somewhere in New England.

(LION THEATRE) Monday, April 9,–May 6, 1984 (24 performances)
LAUGHING STOCK by Romulus Linney; Director, Ed Howard; Sets, Paul Bryan Eads; Costumes, Sally Lesser; Lighting, Judy Rasmuson; Sound, Gary Harris; Stage Managers, Pamela Singer, Kate Hancock, Suzanne Wakamoto; Wardrobe, Karen Jo Prager; Production Assistant, Lora Manning.
CAST: "Goodbye, Howard": Timothy Wilson (Charles), Peggity Price (Nurse), Helen Harrelson (Edna), Jane Connell (Alice), Frances Sternhagen (Sarah), Harold Guskin (Dr. Bailey).

The action takes place in the spring of 1965 in a hospital waiting room in Durham, NC. "F.M.": Frances Sternhagen (Constance Lindell), Jane Connell (May Ford), Peggity Price (Suzanne LaChette), Leon Russom (Bufford Bullough).

The action takes place in the fall of 1981 in a small Southern college near Birmingham, AL. "Tennessee": Peggity Price (Mary), Leon Russom (Hershel), Timothy Wilson (Cardell), Frances Sternhagen (Old Woman), Harold Guskin (Griswold Plankman), Helen Harrelson (Neighbor).

The action takes place in 1880 in the Appalachian Mountains of North Carolina.
(LION THEATRE) Thursday, May 17,–June 10, 1984 (22 performances) Manhattan Punch Line in association with Manhattan Center Stage presents:
RICH GIRLS by Philip Magdalany; Director, Robert Moss; Set, Rick Dennis; Costumes, Michael Krass; Lighting, Gregory MacPherson; Sound, Gary Harris; Production Assistant, Eric Moreland; Hairstylist, Laura Christine Habrack; Stage Managers, Andrew Feigin, Suzanne Wakamoto.
CAST: Gwyda DonHowe (Minerva), Lisa Lonergan (Melanie), Louise Troy (Sally).

The action takes place at the present time on the terrance of Club Femme, an exclusive resort on Grand Cayman Island in the Caribbean.

Frances Sternhagen, Helen Harrelson, Jane Connell in "Laughing Stock" Top: Jerry Mayer, Jeanne Cullen, Angela Pietropinto in "The Rivals" Below: Gwyda DonHowe, Louise Troy in "Rich Girls" *(Karen Moody Photo)*

MANHATTAN THEATRE CLUB

Lynne Meadow, Artistic Director
Twelfth Season

Managing Director, Barry Grove; General Manager, Connie L. Alexis; Casting Director, Donna Isaacson; Business Manager, Victoria B. Bailey; Associate Artistic Director, Jack Temchin; Literary Manager, Jonathan Alper; Production Manager, Tom Aberger; Technical Director, Nicholas R. Miller; Props, Claudia Kavenagh; Wardrobe, Kate Amendola; Photographer, Gerry Goodstein; Press, Virginia P. Louloudes, Kim Kuhlmann, Abigail Evans

(MTC/DOWNSTAGE) Thursday, October 13,–November 20, 1983 (64 performances)

THE PHILANTHROPIST by Christopher Hampton; Director, Andre Ernotte; Set, Kate Edmunds; Costumes, Linda Fisher; Lighting, F. Mitchell Dana; Sound, Eric Rissler Thayer; Stage Managers, Dianne Trulock, Mindy K. Farbrother; Wardrobe, James Latus.

CAST: David McCallum (Philip), Anthony Heald (Donald), Brent Spiner (John), Glenne Headly (Celia), Benjamin Hendrickson (Braham), Robin Bartlett (Araminta), Cherry Jones (Liz), Standbys: Rob Knepper (John), William Kux (Donald), Jeremiah Sullivan (Philip/Braham).

A play in two acts. The action takes place in a university town in the near future.

(MTC/UPSTAGE) Tuesday, October 18,–November 27, 1983 (47 performances)

BLUE PLATE SPECIAL with Book by Tom Edwards; Music, Harris Wheeler; Lyrics, Mary L. Fisher; Set, David Jenkins; Costumes, David Murin; Lighting, Arden Fingerhut; Orchestration/Arrangements, Robby Merkin; Musical Director, Jimmy Roberts; Director, Art Wolff; Choreography, Douglas Norwick; Stage Managers, Steven Adler, Lauren Class Schneider.

CAST: Gretchen Cryer (Della Juracko), Ron Holgate (Preacher Larry), Tina Johnson (Ramona), Mary Gordon Murray (Connie Sue), Gordon Paddison (Ronnie Frank), David Strathairn (Ricky Jim).

A musical in two acts. The action takes place at the present time in a continuing daytime drama broadcast from Morning Glory Mountain, Tennessee.

MUSICAL NUMBERS: Morning Glory Mountain, At the Bottom Lookin' Up, Ramona's Lament, Never Say Never, Halfway to Heaven, Satisfaction Guaranteed, Blue Plate Special, Twice as Nice, All American Male, Side of Fries, Honky Tonk Queens, I Ain't Looking Back, I'm Gonna Miss Those Tennessee Nights

(MTC/DOWNSTAGE) Tuesday, January 10–22, 1984 (48 performances)

FRIENDS by Lee Kalcheim; Director, Barnet Kellman; Set, David Jenkins; Costumes, Patricia McGourty; Lighting, Ian Calderon; Sound, Eric Rissler Thayer; Fights, B. H. Barry; Stage Managers, Karen Armstrong, Chris Fielder; Wardrobe, Alice Hale.

CAST: Craig T. Nelson (Harold "Okie" Peterson), Ron Silver (Mel Simon), Standbys: David Berman (Mel), Brian Evers (Okie).

A play in three acts. The action takes place at the present time in a cabin in Vermont.

(MTC/UPSTAGE) Tuesday, December 13, 1983–January 29, 1984 (48 performances)

A BACKERS' AUDITION conceived by Martin Charnin, Douglas Bernstein, Denis Markell; Book/Music/Lyrics, Douglas Bernstein, Denis Markell; Director, Martin Charnin; Choreography, Janie Sell; Musical Direction, William Ray; Set, Ray Recht; Costumes, Linda Fisher; Lighting, Marc B. Weiss.

CAST: Barbara Barrie, Douglas Bernstein, Mary D'Arcy, Bill Fagerbakke, Scott Robertson, William Roy, Dana Vance, Nicholas Woodeson.

A musical in two acts. The action takes place at the present time in the living room of a wealthy Park Avenue "angel" who is producing her first Broadway show.

Gerry Goodstein Photos

**Top Right: Cherry Jones, Anthony Heald, David McCallum,
Benjamin Hendrickson, Glenne Headly in "The Philanthropist"
Below: Gretchen Cryer, Ron Holgate, David Strathairn,
Tina Johnson, Mary Gordon Murray, Gordon Paddison
in "Blue Plate Special"**

Craig T. Nelson, Ron Silver in "Friends"

(MTC/DOWNSTAGE) Saturday, February 11,–March 18, 1984 (40 performances)
MENSCH MEIER by Franz Xaver Kroetz; Translated by Roger Downey; Director, Jacques Levy; Set, Ray Recht; Costumes, Susan Hilferty; Lighting, Robert Jared; Paintings, Clayton Campbell; Stage Managers, G. Roger Abell, Marianne Cane; Wardrobe, Colleen Cosgrove.
CAST: Stephen McHattie (Otto Meier), Barbara eda-Young (Martha Meier), Thor Fields (Ludwig Meier), Standbys; George Bartenieff (Otto), Scott Tiler (Ludvig).

A drama in two acts. The action takes place recently in Munich, West Germany.
(MTC/UPSTAGE) Thursday, February 28,–April 15, 1984 (48 performances)
PARK YOUR CAR IN HARVARD YARD by Israel Horovitz; Director, Lynne Meadow; Set, John Lee Beatty; Costumes, Jennifer von Mayrhauser; Lighting, Marc B. Weiss; Sound, Stan Metelits; Stage Manager, Chris Fielder.
CAST: Burgess Meredith succeeded by James Greene (Jacob Brackish), Ellen Burstyn (Kathleen Hogan), Michael McNamara (Voice of Byron Weld).

A play in two acts. The action takes place in the front rooms of the home of Jacob Brackish, East Gloucester, MA., from February through May of the following year.
(MTC/DOWNSTAGE) Tuesday, April 3,–May 20, 1984 (48 performances)
OTHER PLACES three plays by Harold Pinter; Director, Alan Schneider; Set, John Lee Beatty; Costumes, Jess Goldstein; Lighting, Rocky Greenberg; Stage Managers, James Bernardi, Anne S. King; Wardrobe, Amy J. Goldfarb.
CAST: "Victoria Station" with Henderson Forsythe (Controller), Kevin Conway (Driver). "One for the Road" with Kevin Conway (Nicolas), Greg Martyn (Victor), David George Polyak (Nicky), Caroline Lagerfelt (Gila). "A Kind of Alaska" with Dianne Wiest (Deborah), Henderson Forsythe (Hornby), Caroline Lagerfelt (Pauline).
(MTC/UPSTAGE) Tuesday, May 1–Aug. 25, 1984 (131 performances)
THE MISS FIRECRACKER CONTEST by Beth Henley; Director, Stephen Tobolowsky; Set, John Lee Beatty; Costumes, Jennifer von Mayrhauser; Lighting, Dennis Parichy; Sound, Stan Metelits; Wardrobe, Winsome McKay, Brian James Grace; Stage Managers, Wendy Chapin, Daniel Kanter, Marianne Cane.
CAST: Holly Hunter (Carnelle Scott), Belita Moreno (Popeye Jackson), Patricia Richardson (Elain Rutlege), Mark Linn-Baker (Delmount Williams), Budge Threlkeld (Mac Sam), Margo Martindale (Tessy Mahoney).

A play in two acts. The actions takes place at the present time in Brookhaven, MS, a small southern town at the end of June and the beginning of July.

Gerry Goodstein Photos

102   Ellen Burstyn in "Park Your Car in Harvard Yard" Top Right: Stephen McHattie, Thor Fields, Barbara eda-Young in "Mensch Meier"

Holly Hunter, Patricia Richardson in "The Miss Firecracker Contest" Above: Dianne Weist, Caroline Lagerfelt in "Other Places"

MEAT & POTATOES COMPANY

Neal Weaver, Artistic Director
Eighth Season

Administrative Director, Marilys Ernst; Lighting Design, David L. Arrow; Sets, Toru Shimakawa; Costumes, Carol Van Valkenberg; Photographer, Herbert Fogelson; Press, Karli Dwyer

(ALVINA KRAUSE THEATRE) Thursday, June 30,–July 31, 1983 (20 performances)

SPIDER'S WEB by Agatha Christie; Director, Neal Weaver; Props, Lanny Green; Set, Edmond Ramage; Costumes, Mary Young-Gonzales; Stage Manager, Becca Bean.

CAST: Joe Bev (Elgin), Carl Brown (Jeremy), Barbary Callander (Pippa), Ed Easton (Henry), Ed Hyland (Oliver), Jan Meredith (Mildred), Vernon Morris (Inspector), Joel Parsons (Sir Rowland), Terri Price (Clarissa), Henry J. Quinn (Hugo), Joseph Scott (Constable).

A mystery in 3 acts and 4 scenes.
Thursday, August 4–21, 1983 (20 performances)

WAR GAMES written and directed by Neal Weaver; Set, Neal Weaver; Art Work, Tom Starce; Costumes, Carol Van Valkenberg.

CAST: Gram Slaton (John Flagstad), Tony Genfan Brown (Mrs. Moylan), Michael Raymond (Ted), Elliott Landen (Gen. Flagstad), Terry Ashe Croft (Mrs. Flagstad), Barbara Callander (Sandra Cates).

A play in 2 acts and 4 scenes. The action occurs in a furnished room near the University in Toronto, Canada, in the 1960's.
September 1,–October 2, 1983 (20 performances)

THE CHERRY ORCHARD by Anton Chekhov; Director, Neal Weaver; Set, Bruce Brown; Stage Managers, Becca Bean, Tom Farrell.

CAST: Stephanie Beswick (Dunyasha), Joe Cattelona (Yepihodov), Lisa Cosman (Charlotta), Ed Hyland (Pyetia), Nancy Killmer (Lyubov), Barbara Leto (Varya), Michael Levine (Semyonov-Pishchick), Vernon Morris (Gayev), Debra O'Leary (Servant), Kevin Osborne (Yasha), Jack Parrish (Lopakhin), Alfonso Ramos (Station Master/Servant), Tom Sleeth (Firs), Robert Sopher succeeded by Raymond Barrie (Tramp/Clerk/Servant), Lynn Weaver (Anya).

A drama in three acts and four scenes. The action occurs in 1904 on the estate of Mme. Ranyevsky in a rural part of central Russia.
Wednesday, October 12,–November 6, 1983 (20 performances)

ON APPROVAL by Frederick Lonsdale; Director, Herbert DuVal; Set, Joe Varga; Costumes, Barbara Gerard; Stage Managers, Garwood, Dana Reedy.

CAST: Ellisa Napolin (Helen), Tanny McDonald (Maria), David Deardorff (Richard), Michael Raymond (George).

A comedy in 3 acts. The action takes place during the fall of 1927 in London and in Scotland.
Thursday, November 17,–December 18, 1983 (20 performances)

TOWARDS ZERO by Agatha Christie; Director, Neal Weaver; Costumes, Madeleine Doran-McEvoy, Star Gabrielle; Stage Managers, David Keats, Dana Reedy, Jill Larmett.

CAST: Jeff Beach (Royde), Stephanie Beswick (Audrey), Ron Brooks (Latimer), Joe Cattelone (Inspector), Jean Gennis (Mary), Lanny Green (Battle), David Keats (Benson), Janet Meyer (Lady Tressilian), Henry J. Quinn (Treves), Dana Reedy (Miss Barrett), Jean Tafler (Kay), Douglas Werner (Nevile).

A mystery in 3 acts and 6 scenes. The action takes place in the drawing room of Lady Tressilian's house at Saltcreek, Cornwall, England.
Thursday, January 12,–February 12, 1984 (20 performances)

MRS. WARREN'S PROFESSION by George Bernard Shaw; Director, Neal Weaver; Stage Manager, Becca Bean; Set, Joe Varga; Costumes, Madeleine McEvoy, Star Gabrielle.

CAST: Elissa Napolin (Vivie), Vernon Morris (Praed), Martha Schlamme (Mrs. Kitty Warren), Henry J. Quinn (Sir George), Jack Armstrong (Frank), Joel Parsons (Rev. Samuel Gardner). A play in 3 acts and 4 scenes. The action occurs in 1894 in England.
Wednesday, February 22,–March 18, 1984 (20 performances)

THE MARQUISE by Noel Coward; Director, David Perry; Costumes, Madeleine McEvoy; Set, Jim Gilmartin; Lighting, Janet Herzenberg; Stage Manager, Rob Brindley.

CAST: Reb Buxton (Father Clement), Edwin De Asis (Miguel), Frances Ford (Eloise), Ernesto Gonzalez (Esteban), Kathryn Layng (Adrienne), Joe Parsons (Hubert), William Perley (Raoul), Peter Toran (Jacques), Janet Villas (Alice).

A comedy in three acts. The action occurs in September of 1735 in the drawing room of the Chateau de Vriaac, a few hours from Paris.
Thursday, March 29,–April 29, 1984 (20 performances)

Right Center: Martha Schlamme surrounded by Vernon Morris, Henry J. Quinn, Joel Parsons, Elissa Napolin in "Mrs. Warren's Profession"

KING RICHARD II by William Shakespeare; Director, Neal Weaver; Costumes, Phyllis Maximilien; Stage Managers, Jill Larmett, Tom Farrell.

CAST: David Bahr (Abbott/Herald), Loren Bass (Green/Archbishop), Robert Boles (Bushy/Gardener), Robert Caccomo (Salisbury/Fitzwater), Frank Faranda (Scroop/Groom), Tom Farrell (Servant/Gardener), Pascal Grieco (Gardener/Keeper), Casey Kizziah (Richard II), Elliott Landen (Willoughby/Lord Marshall), Jill Larmett (Lady), Michael McGuinness (Aumerle), Joseph O'Brien (Ross), Toby O'Brien (Berkeley), Michael Earl O'Connor (Norfolk/Percy), Donald Pace (Duke of York), Joe Parsons (John of Gaunt), Dana Reedy (Lady), Henry J. Quinn succeeded by Neal Weaver (Earl of Northumberland), Alfonso Ramos (Pierce/Welsh Capt.), Mary Quinn (Duchess of Gloucester/Duchess of York), Michael Raymond (Bolingbroke), Ryan Sexton (Bagot), Jean Tafler (Queen Isabel).

Performed in three acts
Thursday, May 10,–June 10, 1984 (20 performances)

THE PLAY'S THE THING by Ferenc Molnar; Adapted by P. G. Wodehouse; Set/Direction, Neal Weaver; Stage Manager, Richard Meier.

CAST: Neal Canavan (Albert), Tom Deming (Johann), Herbert DuVal (Turai), Gwendolyn Lewis (Ilona), Vernon Morris (Almady), Richard Meier (Footman), Philip Tatum (Footman).

A comedy in 3 acts. The action passes in a room of a castle on the Italian Riviera on a Saturday in the summer of 1926.

Herb Fogelson Photos

**William Perley, Frances Ford, Ernesto Gonzalez
in "The Marquise"**

MIRROR REPERTORY COMPANY

Sabra Jones, Artistic Director
First Season

Executive Consultant, Porter Van Zandt; Administrator, Barbara Leep; Development Director, Carol True Palmer; Business Manager, Patti White; Stage Managers, Alan R. Traynor, Kathleen Blair Costello; General Management, McCann/Nugent; Press, Solters/Roskin/Friedman, Josh Ellis, Louise Ment, Cindy Valk; Casting, Albert Tavares, Nancy Nayor; Wardrobe, Callee Frith, Dorothy Duncan; Photography, Martha Swope

(THE REAL THEATRE/THEATRE AT ST. PETER'S CHURCH) Saturday, December 10, 1983, and played in repertory until July 1, 1984.

COMPANY: Mason Adams, Haru Aki, Margaret Barker, Kristofer Batho, Peter Bloch, Tom Brennan, W. B. Brydon, Frank Camacho, Maxwell Caulfield, Randy William Charnin, Bryan Clark, Matthew Coles, David Cryer, Terry Finn, Clement Fowler, Francois de la Giroday, Rose Gregorio, William Ha'o, Baxter Harris, Ann Hillary, Anthony Hopkins, Meg Hosey, Timothy Jenkins, Sabra Jones, Tad Jones, Lilah Kan, Jose Kendall, Jim Knobeloch, Sofia Landon, Joan MacIntosh, David May, Clark Middleton, Juliet Mills, F. J. O'Neil, Jess Osuna, Geraldine Page, James Pritchett, Ellis Rabb, James Rebhorn, Charles Regan, Madeleine Sherwood, Fred G. Smith, Michael O. Smith, Victor Slezak, Denise Stephenson, John Strasberg, Thomas G. Waites, Todd Waring, Steven Weber. Directors: Ellis Rabb, John Strasberg, Porter Van Zandt, Austin Pendleton. Designers: Ron Placzek (Sets), Mal Sturchio (Lighting), Rob Gorton (Sound), Heidi Hollmann (Costumes).

REPERTOIRE: "The Inheritors" by Susan Glaspell, "Paradise Lost" by Clifford Odets, "Rain" by John Colton, "Ghosts" by Henrik Ibsen; translated by Eva LeGallienne, "The Hasty Heart" by John Patrick.

Martha Swope Photos

**Left: Juliet Mills, Maxwell Caulfield
In "Paradise Lost"**

Juliet Mills, Geraldine Page, Mason Adams in "Paradise Lost"

104

Geraldine Page in "Ghosts"
Top: Brian Clark, Geraldine Page
in "Paradise Lost"

Victor Slezak, Sofia Landon
in "The Hasty Heart"

105

NEW FEDERAL THEATRE

Woodie King, Jr., Producer

Executive Vice President, Michael Frey; Production Manager, Llewellyn Harrison; Production Coordinator, Bill Harris; Technical Director, Janice A. Matteucci; Sound, James Wooden, Jr.; Press, Warren Knowlton, Michael Alpert, Ruth Jaffe (HARRY DeJUR HENRY STREET SETTLEMENT PLAYHOUSE) Wednesday, July 20,–August 7, 1983 (11 performances for each play in repertory). The New Federal Theatre, and New York Shakespeare Festival (Joseph Papp, Producer) present: THE WOMEN'S SERIES: Associate Producer, Barbara Tate; GAMES by Joyce Walker-Joseph; Director, Elizabeth Van Dyke; Set, Bob Edmonds; Lighting, Shirley Prendergast; Costumes, Karen Perry; Stage Manager, Richard Douglass; with Dan Barbaro (Tony), Gylan Kain (Piggott), Dianne Kirksey (Sylvia), Kim Weston-Moran (Gin), Nadyne Cassandra (Vivian), Kumbha Alouaba (Robin). A play in 2 acts and 9 scenes. The action occurs late spring in the 1970's in a studio apartment in Brooklyn. PARTING by Nubia Kai; Director, Bette Howard; Original Music, Dianaruthe Wharton; Set, May Callas; Lights, Bill Grant; Costumes, Vicki Jones, Props, Ron Davis; Stage Manager, Fai Walker; with Brenda Denmark (Sherrie), Lanyard A. Williams (Sudan). The action is continous for 3 days and 2 nights. HOSPICE by Pearl Cleage; Director, Frances Foster; Set, Llewellyn Harrison; Light, Bill Grant; Costumes, Vicki Jones; Stage Manager, Jerry Cleveland; with Lee Chamberlin (Alice Anderson), Joan Harris (Jenny Anderson). The time is early morning. INCANDESCENT TONES by Rise Collins; Director, Marjorie Moon, Set/Lights, Llewellyn Harrison; Costumes, Rise Collins; Stage Manager, Elizabeth Omilami; with Rise Collins, Terria Joseph, S. Epatha Merkerson, Pamela Poitier. The action occurs at the present time on Earth Plane.

Thursday, September 8–25, 1983 (15 performances)

BASIN STREET with Book by Michael Hulett, G. William Oakley; Music, Turk Murphy; Lyrics, Michael Hulett; Director, G. William Oakley; Musical Conductor, Thom Bridwell; Choreography, Michael Gorman; Musical Supervision, Danny Holgate; Choral Arrangements, Carl Maultsby; Orchestrations, Turk Murphy, Danny Holgate; Set, Robert Edmonds; Lights, Jeremy Johnson; Costumes, Judy Dearing; Sound, Brian Penney; Stage Managers, Alan R. Traynor, Richard Douglass.

CAST: Jeff Bates (Umbrella Man), Kevin Devoe (Spasm Kid), J. Lee Flynn (Tom), Clebert Ford (Joe), Gloria Jones (Spasm Kid), Shaun Jones (Aberdeen), Sandra Reaves-Phillips (Harmony), Charles H. "Chuck" Patterson (Chauncey), Michael Potter (Creese Malceau), Alexana Ryer (Adele), Tamara Tunie (Yvette), Keith Darious Williams (Spasm Kid), Pat Yankee (Lulu), Lawrence Vincent (Rev. Hapgood/Pelligrew), Ensemble: George Bernhard, Diana Blue, Jeffrey Bryan, Erik Geier, Patrice Hollrah, Mary Ann Lamb, Stephanie M. Pope, Lise Simms, James Young.

A musical in two acts. The action takes place in September 1917 in the Storyville District of New Orleans.

MUSICAL NUMBERS: Chauncey's Tune, Call the Children Home, All That It Takes, Penny Whistle Sweet, After, The Sporting House Professor Blues, Blue Book, Soldiers of the Lord, Song of My Fathers, Lady Gets Me There, Miss Lulu White, Razzy Dazzy, Ragtime Man, Chicago Drag, The Ham Kick, Don't Much Matter Any More, The Naked Dance, Elegy.

(LOUIS ABRONS ARTS FOR LIVING CENTER) Thursday, October 6,–November 6, 1983 (24 performances). Chelsea Theater Center (Robert Kalfin, Artistic Director; Joseph V. Melillo, Associate Producer; Steven Gilger, General Manager) and Henry Street Settlement's New Federal Theatre (Woodie King, Jr., Producer) present:

SHADES OF BROWN by Michael Picardie; Director, Joan Kemp-Welch; Set, Loren Sherman; Company Manager, Steven Gilger; Stage Managers, Leslie Moore, Stephen Powell; Technical Director, Randy Hartwig; Props, Stephen Powell, Barbara Perkins; Press, Susan Bloch and Company, Adrian Bryan-Brown, Bill Gosewisch, Ellen Zeisler.

CAST: Count Stovall (Jannie Veldsman), Michael O'Hare (Capt. Jaap Van Tonder).

A play in two acts. The action takes place at the present time in Veldsman's consulting room, a shanty in a Western coloured township, Johannesburg, S.A.

Thursday, October 20,–November 20, 1983 (24 performances) The Frank Silvera Writers' Workshop production of:

THE TRIAL OF ADAM CLAYTON POWELL, JR. by Billy Graham; Director, Dianne Kirksey; Costumes, Karen Perry; Set, Billy Graham; Lights, Zebedee Collins; Sound, Bernard Hall; Production Manager, Lew Harrison; Company Manager, Linda Herring; Stage Manager, Malik.

CAST: Timothy Simonson (Adam Clayton Powell, Jr.), Eldon Bullock (Chuck), Dan Barbaro (Celler), Richard Mooney (Teague), Bill Canyon (Pepper), Charles Harley (Conyers), Barry Ford (Moore), Christine Campbell (Roberts), Mizan Nunes (Mrs. Adam Clayton Powell, Jr.).

A play in two acts.

Top Right: Joyce Walker Josephs, Gylan Kain, Nadyne Cassandra Spratt in "Games"
(Bert Andrews Photo)

Count Stovall, Michael O'Hare in "Shades of Brown"
(Martha Swope Photo)

(LOUIS ABRON ARTS FOR LIVING CENTER) Thursday, February 16,–March 4, 1984 (15 performances)
SELMA with Book/Music/Lyrics/Musical and Choral Arrangements, Thomas Isaiah Butler; Director, Cliff Roquemore; Choreography, Charles Lavont Williams; Musical Director, Neal Tate; Light, William H. Grant III; Costumes, Judy Dearing; Stage Managers, Malik, Fai Walker.
CAST: Ernie Banks (Rev. Abernathy), James Curt Bergwall (Rev. Graetz), Jonathan Carroll (Young Boy/Black Panther), Daryl E. Copeland (Drunk/Black Panther), Cora Lee Day (Mama Sweets), J. Lee Flynn (Sheriff Barnside), Pat Franklin (Jackie/Nurse/Klansman), Michael French (Bus Driver/Deputy/Ensemble), Rita Graham-Knighton (Coretta), Joyce Griffen (Child/Klansman), Levern (Ensemble), Paul M. Luksch (Deputy), George E. Morton III (Tillman), Cynthia I. Pearson (Teacher/Klansman), Sherrie Strange (Rosa), Pamala Tyson (Miss Anne/Ensemble), Ronald Wyche (Woody).
A musical in 2 acts and 17 scenes.
MUSICAL NUMBERS: Nature's Child, Working in the Name of King, Celebration, Martin Martin, Niggerwoman, Precious Memories, The Time Is Now, Wash Your Sings, Pull Together, You're My Love, Isn't It Wonderful, Freedom Liberation, Jesus Christ, Tell Us Martin, Where's That Martin Boy?, Do You Lie?, Pick Up Your Weapon, Boycott Trial Song, I Can Feel Him, When Will It End, Klansmen Song, Prison Song, Higher, I Hate Colored People, Children of Love, Poison Hiding, Burn, Listen to Me Jesus, Selma, Selma March, We Shall Overcome.
Thursday, February 9–26, 1984 (15 performances)
BECOMING GARCIA by Tato Laviera; Director, Esteban Vega; Set, Pete Caldwell; Costumes, Karlos; Light, William H. Grant III; Sound, Willie Correa; Stage Manager, Casandra Scott.
CAST: Hector Quinones (JJ Garcia), Carlos Carrasco (John Garcia), Gerta Grunen (Rose), Raul Davila (Don Juan), Geisha Otero (Julia), Ilka Tanya Payan (Shirley), Elizabeth Pena (Jane).
A play in three acts. The action takes place on the Lower East Side of Manhattan in the early 1980's.
Thursday, March 15,–April 2, 1984 (15 performances)
TWENTY YEAR FRIENDS by J. E. Gaines; Director, Andre Mtumi; Set, Terry Chandler; Costumes, Celia Bryant; Light, Jeffery Richardson; Sound, Garland Thompson, Jr.; Stage Manager, Herman Fitzgerald.
CAST: Louise Stubbs (Stell), Joyce Joseph (Dee), Jack Neal (Harry), Juanita Clark (Inez), Clebert Ford (Blue), Roscoe Orman (Money).
A play in 3 acts and 9 scenes. The action takes place at the present time in the home of Estelle and Harry, and in the apartment of Blue and Inez.
(COLONNADES THEATRE) Thursday, March 22,–April 8, 1984 (15 performances)
FRATERNITY by Jordan Budde; Director, Gideon Y. Schein; Set, Jane Clark; Light, Victor En Yu Tan; Costumes, Judy Dearing; Sound, Tom Gould; Casting, David Tochterman; Stage Manager, Nicholas Dunn.
CAST: Kevin Carrigan (Bubba Seaton), Robert Downey (Rusty), Donald E. Fischer (Grey), Steve Hofvendahl (Pierson), Mark Moses (Reese).
A play in 2 acts and 8 scenes. The action takes place at the present time at Southern Methodist University.
(COLONNADES THEATRE LAB) Tuesday, May 1–20, 1984 (15 performances)
EVERY GOODBYE AIN'T GONE by Bill Harris; Director, Nathan George; Set, Llewellyn Harrison; Costumes, Vicki Jones; Lights, William H. Grant III; Sound, Sande Knighton; Stage Manager, Imani.
CAST: Denzel Washington (Frank), S. Epatha Merkerson (Rula).
HOSPICE by Pearl Cleage; Director, Frances Foster.
CAST: Lee Chamberlin (Alice Anderson), S. Epatha Merkerson (Jenny)
(HARRY DeJUR HENRY STREET SETTLEMENT PLAYHOUSE) Thursday, May 3–20, 1984 (15 performances)
THE LAST DANCEMAN by Alan Foster Friedman; Director, John Pynchon Holms; Set/Lights, Richard Harmon; Music, Alan Foster Friedman; Sound, Tom Gould; Costumes, Shelia Kehoe; Choreography, Lynnette Barkley; Stage Manager, Peggy Hess.
CAST: Joel Rooks (Rabbi), Hy Anzel (Billy "Man" Danceman), Anthony Inneo (Billy "Boy" Danceman), Norma Novak (Mama Nettie), Jerry Matz (Papa Jacob), Steve Coats (Deo), Leslie Carroll (Addie).
A play in two acts. The action occurs on Sunday, July 20, 1969, on the sixth floor of a storage warehouse on the upper West Side of Manhattan.
(LOUIS ABRONS ARTS FOR LIVING CENTER) Friday, May 4–20, 1984 (15 performances)
THE HOOCH by Charles Michael Moore; Director, Chuck Smith; Costumes, Karen Perry; Sound, Bernard Hall; Stage Manager, Malik.
CAST: Kevin Hooks (Lance Cpl. Promus), Cortez Nance (Sgt. Aston), Hubert B. Kelly, Jr. (Pvt. Brown), Jaime Perry (Seaman Willie Pride), Clifton C. Powell (Pfc John Holloway), Jeffrey Howard Kaufman (Cpl. DeWight Seebold), Neal Arluck (Cpl. Blankenship), Ching Valdes (Hoo).
A play in two acts. All the action takes place in a hooch on October 31, 1968 in Chu Lei, South Viet Nam.
(LOUIS ABRONS ARTS FOR LIVING CENTER) Thursday, June 7–24, 1984 (15 performances)

Top Right: Gerta Grunen, Raul Davila
in "Becoming Garcia"

Leslie Carroll, Hy Anzell, Anthony Inneo
in "The Last Danceman"

OH! OH! OBESITY! with Lyrics/Music/Story by Gerald W. Deas; Script Collaboration/Direction, Bette Howard; Set, May Callas; Costumes, Vicki Jones; Choreography, Ronn Pratt; Stage Manager, Malik.
CAST: Sandra Reaves-Phillips (Fat Momma), Karen Langerstrom (Ms. Knosh), Reginald Vel-Johnson (Fat Daddy), Stuart D. Goldenberg (Blimpie), Mennie F. Nelson (Fatsie), Jacquelyn Bird Smith (Church Sisters).
A musical in 2 acts and 13 scenes.

Bert Andrews Photos

107

NEW YORK SHAKESPEARE FESTIVAL PUBLIC THEATER

Joseph Papp, Producer
Seventeenth Season

General Manager, Robert Kamlot succeeded by Laurel Ann Wilson; Company Manager, Robert Reilly; Casting, Rosemarie Tichler; Associate Producer, Jason Steven Cohen; Production Manager, Andrew Mihok; Technical Director, Mervyn Haines, Jr.; Props, Bill Dreisbach, James Gill; Press, Merle Debuskey, Richard Kornberg, Barbara Carroll, Bruce Campbell.

(PUBLIC/MARTINSON) Friday, June 3–19, 1983 (21 performances)
GOODNIGHT LADIES! Devised by the company; Artistic Director, Geraldine Pilgrim; Lighting, Tom Donnellan; Sound, John Darling; Management, Sophia Caldwell; Stage Manager, D. W. Koehler; Wardrobe, Bruce Brumage.
CAST: Lizza Aiken, Alex Mayro, Andrzej Borkowski, Rick Fisher

(PUBLIC/MARTINSON) Thursday, June 23,–July 16, 1983 (16 performances)
FUNHOUSE a solo piece written and performed by Eric Bogosian
(PUBLIC/MARTINSON) Thursday, June 23,–July 15, 1983 (8 performances) returned Thursday, August 11–27, 1983 (9 performances)
EMMETT: A ONE MORMON SHOW written, directed and performed by Emmett Foster.

(PUBLIC/NEWMAN) Tuesday, August 2,–October 2, 1983 (60 performances and 25 previews)
ORGASMO ADULTO ESCAPES FROM THE ZOO by Franca Rame and Dario Fo; Directed by Franca Rame, Estelle Parsons; Costumes, Ruth Morley; Lighting, Jennifer Tipton; Scenic Consultant, Santo Loquasto; Stage Managers, Elizabeth Holloway, John Masterson; Props, Garry Shepherd; Wardrobe, April Briggs.
CAST: Estelle Parsons, John Masterson.
 A series of eight pieces performed with one intermission: Waking Up, A Woman Alone, We All Have the Same Story, Contrasto for a Solo Voice, Monologue of a Whore in a Lunatic Asylum, The Freak Mama, It Happens Tomorrow, Medea

(PUBLIC/OTHER STAGE) Friday, September 23,–October 23, 1983 (16 performances and 19 previews)
MY UNCLE SAM by Len Jenkin; Director, Mr. Jenkin; Scenery, John Anone; Lighting, Frances Aronson; Costumes, Kurt Wilhelm; Choreography, Catlin Cobb; Stage Managers, Jan Hubbard, G. Roger Abell; Props, Frances Smith, Tom Perry; Wardrobe, Hannah Murray.
CAST: Laura Innes (Darlene/Little Person/Ensemble), Olek Krupa (Bottler/Ensemble), Kathleen Layman (Lila/Ensemble), Mark Margolis (Uncle Sam), John Nesci (Jake/Prof. Finley/Golf Manager/Ensemble), Kristine Nielsen (Sacristan/Assistant Travel Agent/Ensemble), Rocco Sisto (Capability Brown/Mexican Doctor/Ensemble), Scott Wentworth (Travel Agent/Detective Agent Instructor/Ensemble), Margaret Whitton (Miss Simmons/Stella/Ensemble), R. Hamilton Wright (Young Sam), Ray Xifo (Mr. Fleagle/M.C./Lighthouse Keeper/Ensemble)

(PUBLIC/LUESTHER HALL) Friday, October 21, 1983–January 1, 1984 (63 performances and 12 previews)
SOUND & BEAUTY by David Henry Hwang; Director, John Lone; Assistant Director, Lenore Kletter; Music, Lucia Hwong; Musical Direction/Choreography, John Lone; Scenery, Andrew Jackness; Costumes, Lydia Tanji; Lighting, John Gisondi; Wigs/Makeup, Marlies Vallant; Stage Managers, Alice Jankowiak, Annie Marie Hobson; Wardrobe, Susan Freel; Props, Tom Perry.
CAST: "The House of Sleeping Beauties": Ching Valdes (Michiko), Victor Wong (Kawabata), Elizabeth Fong Sung (Girl).
 The action takes place in Tokyo in 1972; 4 scenes.
"The Sound of a Voice": John Lone (Man), Natsuko Ohama (Woman), Ching Valdes, Elizabeth Fong Sung (Movement).
 The action takes place in a remote corner of a forest.

(PUBLIC/MARTINSON) Sunday, November 20, 1983–February 12, 1984 (95 performances and 14 previews)
A PRIVATE VIEW by Vaclav Havel; Translated by Vera Blackwell; Director, Lee Grant; Scenery, Marjorie Bradley Kellogg; Lighting, Arden Fingerhut; Costumes, Carol Oditz; Stage Managers, Michael Chambers, Anne King; Assistant Director, Milton Justice; Props, Frances Smith; Wardrobe, Dawn Johnson.
CAST: Barton Heyman (Head Maltster), Stephen Keep (Vanek), Concetta Tomei (Vera), Nicholas Hormann (Michael), Richard Jordan (Stanek).
 A drama in 2 acts and 3 scenes. The action takes place in Prague, Czechoslovakia in 1975 and 1978.

Martha Swope/Susan Cook Photos

Top Right: Estelle Parsons in "Orgasmo Adulto"
Below: Natsuko Ohama, John Lone
in "Sound and Beauty"

Stephen Keep, Richard Jordan
in "A Private View"

(PUBLIC/OTHER STAGE) Tuesday, November 15,–December 17, 1983 (32 performances)

SAMUEL BECKETT'S COMPANY by Samuel Beckett; Directors, Honora Fergusson, Frederick Neumann; Music, Philip Glass; Set, Gerald Marks; Lighting, Craig Miller, Sabrina Hamilton; Sound, L. B. Dallas; Music Produced and Recorded by Kurt Munkacsi; Conductor, Michael Riesman; Production Manager, Sabrina Hamilton; A Mabou Mines Production.
CAST: Frederick Neumann, Honora Fergusson (She).
Performed with one intermission.

(PUBLIC/NEWMAN) Wednesday, December 7, 1983–January 8, 1984 (20 performances and 14 previews).

LENNY AND THE HEARTBREAKERS by Kenneth Robins; Music, Scott Killian, Kim D. Sherman; Lyrics, Kenneth Robins, Scott Killian, Kim D. Sherman; Orchestrations, Kim D. Sherman; Additional Orchestrations, James McElwaine, Robert Kilgore; Scenery, Alwin Nikolais, Nancy Winters; Lighting, Alwin Nikolais, Peter Koletzke; Costumes, Lindsay W. Davis; Sound, Bill Dreisbach, John Kilgore; Film Sequences/Computer Graphic Slides, John Sanborn, Mary Perillo; Conductor, James McElwaine; Staged and Choreographed by Murray Louis, Alwin Nikolais; Stage Managers, Stephen McCorkle, Mitchell Lemsky; Props, Evan Canary; Wardrobe, Kathy Roberson; Hair/Wig/Makeup, Marlies Vallant.
CAST: Robert Joy or Michael Brian (Lenny), Darren Nimnicht (J. P. deMedici), Sally Williams (Alto Saint), James Wilson (Tenor Saint), Frank Nemhauser (Bass Saint), Nancy Ringham (Soprano Saint), Joanna Glushak or Sally Stotts (Angela), Dancers: Michael Blake, Janis Brenner, Betsy Fisher, Robert McWilliams, Margaret Morris, Danial Shapiro, Joanie Smith, Edward Akio Taketa, Understudies: Gary Harger (Lenny/Tenor), Raymond Murcell (J.P./Bass), Gloria Parker (Alto Saint), Janis Brenner (Angela/Soprano), Holly Schiffer (Swing Dancer)
MUSICAL NUMBERS: The First Last Supper, The Saints Come In—Flying In, Video Dreamboy, Study of the Human Figure, Video Bleeptones, Gimme-a-Break Heartbreak, Hockney-Blue Eyes, Art Machine #1, Video Enigma, A Light Thing, Lighter Than A Light Thing, Dissection Section, I'm A Rocket Tonight, Interesting Use of Space, Di Medici Cha Cha, Angela's Flight Drama, Angela's Tanga, There's Art in My Revenge, Lonely in Space, Lenny and the Heartbreakers.
Performed in two acts.

(PUBLIC/ANSPACHER) Tuesday, December 20, 1983–March 4, 1984 (79 performances and 8 previews). Re-opened on Broadway's Royale Theatre on Thursday, April 5, 1984. See Broadway Calendar for details of THE HUMAN COMEDY.

(PUBLIC/OTHER STAGE) Tuesday, January 17,–February 19, 1984 (16 performances and 14 previews). Joseph Papp presents The Second Stage (Robyn Goodman, Carol Rothman, Artistic Directors) production of:

SERENADING LOUIE by Lanford Wilson; Director, John Tillinger; Set, Loren Sherman; Lighting, Richard Nelson; Costumes, Clifford Capone; Sound, Gary Harris; Hairstylist, Antonio Soddu; Production Supervisor, Kim Novick; Casting, Simon & Kumin; Stage Managers, Kate Hancock, Anne Marie Kuehling; Technical Director, Dale Harris; Props, Kevin Lee Allen; Wardrobe, Rita Robbins; Managing Director, Rosa I. Vega; Associate Director, Andrew Farber; Production Associate, John Peter Weller (Alex), Lindsay Crouse (Mary).
A drama in two acts. The action takes place in a suburb north of Chicago.

(PUBLIC/LUESTHER) Monday, February 20,–April 8, 1984 (56 performances and 16 previews)

CINDERS by Janusz Glowacki; Translation, Christina Paul; Director, John Madden; Scenery, Andrew Jackness; Costumes, Jane Greenwood; Lighting, Paul Gallo; Incidental Music, Richard Peaslee; Music Director, Deena Kaye; Stage Managers, James Harker, Tracy B. Cohen; Fights, B. H. Barry; Props, Evan Canary; Wardrobe, Susan Freel; Hairstylist, Marlies Vallant.
CAST: Peter McRobbie (Inspector), George Guidall (Principal), Robin Gammell (Deputy), Lucinda Jenney (Cinderella), Dori Hartley (Prince), Greta Turken (Fairy Godmother), Eli Marder (Mouse), Melissa Leo (Stepmother), Martha Gehman (Father), Anna Levine and Johann Carlo (Ugly Sisters), Christopher Walken (Director), Kevin McClarnon (Electrician), Jonathan Walker (Cameraman), Peter McRobbie (Soundman).
A drama in two acts. The action takes place in a girls' reform school somewhere in Poland, not far from Warsaw.

(PUBLIC/NEWMAN) Sunday, March 4,–April 22, 1984 (59 performances and 10 previews)

FEN by Caryl Churchill; Director, Les Waters; Scenery/Costumes, Annie Smart; Lighting, Tom Donnellan; Stage Managers, Stephen McCorkle, Mitchell Lemsky; Fight Consultant, B. H. Barry; Dance Staging, Ara Fitzgerald; Production Assistant, Carolyn Warnick; Wardrobe, Dawn Johnson; Props, John Masterson; Original Music, Ilona Sekacz.
CAST: Robin Bartlett (Mrs. Hassett/Becky/Alice/Ivy), Linda Griffiths (Shirley/Shona/Miss Cade/Margaret), Ellen Parker (Val/Woman working in the field), Pamela Reed (Boy/Angela/Deb/Mrs. Finch), David Strathairn (Wilson/Frank/Tewson/Geoffrey), Concetta Tomei (Japanese Businessman/Nell/May/Mavis).
Performed without intermission. The Fens are rich farming areas less than a hundred miles north of London in the East of England.

Martha Swope Photos

**Top Right: Dianne Wiest, Peter Weller,
Jimmie Ray Weeks, Lindsay Crouse in "Serenading Louie"
Below: Lucinda Jenney, Christopher Walken
in "Cinders"**

Ellen Parker, Pamela Reed
in "Fen"

(PUBLIC/MARTINSON) March 8–11, 1984 (7 performances). Joseph Papp presents The Acting Company (John Houseman, Producing Artistic Director; Margot Harley, Executive Producer; Michael Kahn, Alan Schneider, Artistic Directors)

PIECES OF 8 conceived and directed by Alan Schneider; Settings, Mark Fitzgibbons; Costumes, Carla Kramer; Lighting, Richard Riddell; General Manager, Mary Beth Carroll; Stage Managers, Giles F. Colahan, Michael S. Mantel; Technical Director, David Byron Fish; Wardrobe, Laurel Frushour; Props, Doug Beebe.

CAST: Laura Brutsman, Jerome Butler, Terrence Caza, Libby Colahan, Jacqueline DeHaviland, David Fuller, Richard S. Iglewski, Jack Kenny, David Manis, Michael Manuelian, DeLane Matthews, Steven Mattila, Devenia McFadden, Phil Meyer, Anthony Powell, Gregory Welch.

Eight modern one-act plays presented with one intermission: "The Unexpurgated Memoirs of Bernard Mergendeiler" by Jules Feiffer, "The Black and White" by Harold Pinter, "The Tridget of Greva" by Ring Lardner, "The Sandbox" by Edward Albee, "The (15 Minute) Dogg's Troupe Hamlet" by Tom Stoppard, "Come and Go" by Samuel Beckett, "Foursome" by Eugene Ionesco, "I'm Herbert" by Robert Anderson.

(PUBLIC/MARTINSON) Tuesday, May 1–20, 1984 (12 performances and 12 previews) Joseph Papp presents the Foundation of the Dramatists Guild's production of: **THE YOUNG PLAYWRIGHTS FESTIVAL** with "Romance" by Catherine Castellani; Director, Elinor Renfield; Music, Louis Rosen; Performed by Catherine Ann Christianson, Rob Knepper. "Meeting the Bike Rider" by Juan Nunez; Director, Elinor Renfield; Music, Louis Rosen; Performed by Jeffrey Marcus, Corey Parker. "Fixed Up" by Patricia Durkin; Director, Shelly Raffle; Music, Michael Rubell, Whyte Lyte; Performed by Ellen Mareneck, Marc Epstein. "In the Garden" by Anne Harris; Director, James Milton; Performed by Etain O'Malley, Pamela Payton-Wright. "Tender Places" by Jason Brown; Director, Shelly Raffle; Performed by Carolyn Mignini, Stephen Vinovich, Knowl Johnson, Lois Diane Hicks.

(PUBLIC/ANSPACHER) Opened Friday, May 25, 1984 and still playing May 31, 1984.

FOUND A PEANUT by Donald Margulies; Director, Claudia Weill; Scenery, Thomas Lynch; Costumes, Jane Greenwood; Lighting, Beverly Emmons; Fight Direction, B. H. Barry; Sound, Chuck London/Stewart Werner; Incidental Music, Allen Shawn; Stage Managers, Susan Green, Johnna Murray; Hairstylist, Marlies Vallant; Props, Lisa Venezia.

CAST: Robert Joy (Mike 11), Evan Handler (Jeffrey Smolowitz 11), Robin Bartlett (Melody 8), Nealla Spano (Joanie 8), Peter MacNicol (Little Earl 5), Greg Germann (Scott 12), Jonathan Walker (Ernie 14), Kevin Geer (Shane 12).

Performed without intermission. The action takes place on Sunday, the last day of summer in 1962 at the back of an apartment building in Brooklyn.

(PUBLIC/OTHER STAGE) Wednesday, May 30,–June 24, 1984 (6 performances and 21 previews) Joseph Papp presents the Vietnam Veterans Ensemble Theatre Company (Thomas Bird, Artistic Director) production of:

ICE BRIDGE by John Forster; Director, Edward Cornell; Scenery, Salvatore Tagliarino; Costumes, Lee Entwisle; Lighting, Marcia Madeira, Terry Wuthrich; Production Supervisor, Cynthia Gold; Stage Managers, Sally B. Andrews, Anne Marie Hobson; Bear conceived and constructed by Paull Mantell; Production Assistant, Maggie Levine; Technical Director, Pat Freni.

CAST: Brian Delate (Polar Bear), James Handy (Thor), Tom Jenkins (Mick), Ray Robertson (Terry), Anthony Chisholm (Snow), R. J. Bonds (Ike), David Adamson (Voice of Teller).

A drama in two acts. The action takes place at the present time in a weather station and missile launch site in Greenland 1500 miles above the Arctic Circle.

(PUBLIC/NEWMAN) Wednesday, May 30,–July 22, 1984 (46 performances and 17 previews)

THE NEST OF THE WOOD GROUSE by Victor Rozov; Translated by Susan Layton; Director, Joseph Papp; Scenery, Loren Sherman; Costumes, Theoni V. Aldredge; Lighting, Arden Fingerhut; Stage Managers, Ellen Raphael, Barbara Abel; Props, Nathaniel Hussey.

CAST: Mary Beth Hurt (Iskra), Ricky Paull Goldin (Prov), Julie Cohen (Zoya), Anne Jackson (Natalya Gavrilovna), Dennis Boutsikaris (Georgy Samsonovich Yasyunin), Ernesto Gasco (Zirelli), Jacqueline Bertrand (Julia), Rebecca Schull (Valentina Dmitrievna), Phoebe Cates (Ariadna Koromyslova), Christian Baskous (Zolotarev), Rosemary DeAngelis (Vera Vasilyevna), Gene Lewis, Afemo Omilami (Foreign Vistors).

A play in two acts. The action takes place in Moscow in the early 1970's.

Top Left: Laura Brutsman, Anthony Powell,
Libby Colahan, Jack Kenny in "The Sandbox"
(Louisa Johnson Photo)

**Robin Bartlett, Nealla Spano, Peter MacNicol
in "Found a Peanut"** *(Martha Swope Photo)*

Ricky Paull, Anne Jackson, Mary Beth Hurt, Dennis Boutsikaris, Eli Wallach
in "The Nest of the Wood Grouse" *(Christopher Little Photo)* Top: Brian Delate, Anthony Chisholm,
James Handy in "Ice Bridge" *(Carol Rosegg/Martha Swope Photo)*

PAN ASIAN REPERTORY THEATRE

Tisa Chang, Artistic/Producing Director
Seventh Season

General Manager, Elizabeth A. Hyslop; Development Associate, Jon Nakagawa; Administrative Assistant, Lesli-Jo Morizono; Technical Director, Bill Schafner; Photographers, Carol Rosegg, Gene Moy; Stage Manager, Jon Nakagawa; Press, G. Theodore Killmar

(47th STREE THEATRE) Sunday, June 12,–October 30, 1983 (138 performances and 3 previews)

YELLOW FEVER by R. A. Shiomi; Co-conceived by Marc Hayashi; Director, Raul Aranas; Set, Christopher Stapleton; Costumes, Eiko Yamaguchi; Lighting, Dawn Chiang; Technical Director, Ronald L. McIntyre; Wardrobe, Ali Davis; Music Coordinator, Raul Aranas; Stage Managers, Paul Schneeberger, Eddas Bennett; Press, Shirley Herz, Sam Rudy, Peter Cromarty.

CAST: Donald Li succeeded by Ernest Abuba (2 weeks) and Mako (4 weeks) (Sam Shikaze), Carol A. Honda (Rosie), James Jenner (Goldberg), Henry Yuk (Chuck Chan), Freda Foh Shen (Nancy Wing), Jeffrey Spolan succeeded by Gerald Lancaster (Sgt. Mackenzie), Ernest Abuba succeeded by Ron Nakahara (Capt. Kenji Kadota), James Jenner (Supt. Jameson).

A comedy-drama in two acts. The action occurs in March of 1970 on Powell Street in Vancouver, British Columbia, in Rosie's Cafe and Sam's office.

(ACTORS OUTLET) Wednesday, November 30,–December 23, 1983 (24 performances)

A SONG FOR A NISEI FISHERMAN by Philip Gotanda; Director, Raul Aranas; Set, Atsushi Moriyasu; Lighting, Victor En Yu Tan; Costumes, Eiko Yamaguchi; Music, Yukio Tsuji, Chin Suzuki; Stage Manager, Jon Nakagawa.

CAST: Stanford Egi (Mosan/Robert), Wai Ching Ho (Kachan), Mariye Inouye (Michiko), Alvin Lum (Kats), Tom Matsusaka (Tochan), Ron Nakahara (Fisherman), Barbara Pohlman (Taxi Dancer/WAC), Ann C. Stoney (Taxi Dancer), Ronald Yamamoto (Jeffrey).

Performed without intermission.

(ACTORS OUTLET) Wednesday, February 29,–March 25, 1984 (28 performances)

THE FACE BOX by Wakako Yamauchi; Director, Ron Nakahara; Set, Ron Kajiwara; Costumes, Eiko Yamaguchi; Lighting, Toshiro Ogawa; Stage Manager, David Lober; Music, Chin Suzuki; Wardrobe, Susan Sayers.

CAST: Michael G. Chin (Doug), Kati Kuroda (Joanne), Natsuko Ohama (Marie/Mariko), Koji Okamura (The Man).

A play in two acts. The action takes place at the present time in Marie's apartment.

(ACTORS OUTLET) Wednesday, April 25,–June 3, 1984 (42 performances)

EMPRESS OF CHINA by Ruth Wolff; Director, Tisa Chang; Set, Bob Phillips; Lighting, Victor En Yu Tan; Costumes, Eiko Yamaguchi; Composer, Robert Pace; Movement, Yung Yung Tsuai; Stage Managers, James D'Asaro, Lesli-Jo Morizono.

CAST: Mel D. Gionson (Shen Tai the Actor), Tom Matsusaka (Li Lien-Ying, Chief Eunuch), Tina Chen (Tzu-Hsi the Empress Dowager), Lester J. N. Mau (Kuang-Hsu the Emperor), Ernest Abuba (Kang Yu-Wei the Tutor), Carol A. Honda (Lung-Yu the Empress), Mary Lee (Pearl Concubine), Alvin Lum (Gen. Jung Lu).

A drama in two acts. The action occurs in the Forbidden City, Peking, China, between 1898 and 1900.

Carol Rosegg Photos

**Top Left: Freda Foh Shen, Donald Li
in "Yellow Fever"**

**Ron Nakahara, Mariye Inouye
in "A Song for a Nisei Fisherman"**

112

Barbara Pohlman, Stanford Egi, Ron Nakahara, Ann C. Stoney in "A Song for a Nisei Fisherman"
Top: (L) Natsuko Ohama, Kati Kuroda in "The Face Box" (R) Carol Honda, Tina Chen, Mary Lee in
"Empress of China" *(Carol Rosegg Photos)*

PLAYWRIGHTS HORIZONS

Andre Bishop, Artistic Director
Paul Daniels, Managing Director
Thirteenth Season
Production Manager, Pat DeRousie; Casting Director, John Lyons; Development, Cynthia Gold; Business Manager, Rory Vanderlick; Wardrobe, James Nadeaux; Press, Bob Ullman, Louise Ment

Thursday, June 2–12, 1983 (14 performances and 17 previews). Playwrights Horizons in association with New York Theatre Workshop presents:
CHRISTMAS ON MARS by Harry Kondoleon; Director, Andre Ernotte; Setting, Andrew Jackness; Lighting, James F. Ingalls; Costumes, Rita Ryack; Stage Manager, J. Thomas Vivian; Production Assistant, Blake Malouf, Nancy Robillard; Props, V. A. Nourafchan; Wardrobe, Mireya Hepner.
CAST: Michael O'Keefe (Bruno), Harriet Harris (Audrey), Joe Pichette (Nissim), Marie Cheatham (Ingrid).

A comedy in two acts. The action takes place in an apartment in a city.
Sunday, June 26,–July 31, 1983 (46 performances)
THAT'S IT, FOLKS! by Mark O'Donnell; Director, Douglas Hughes; Settings, Loren Sherman; Costumes, Ann Emonts; Lighting, Rachel Budin; Sound, Gary Harris; Stage Manager, Barbara Abel; Production Assistant, Grace Cornish; Wardrobe, Lynn Nickels; Props, Susan D. Andrews.
CAST: Alice Playten (Eden), David Pierce (Otis), Cynthia Darlow (Penny), Peter G. Morse (Darryl), Jerome Collamore (Billy), James McDonnell (Zed), Steve Massa (Satanist/Radio Voice 1), Arthur Howard (Satanist/Radio Voice 2).

A comedy in two scenes performed wihout intermission. The action takes place on the last day on earth in the living room in a bad neighborhood, or possibly somewhere inside the human body.
Wednesday, July 6–30, 1983 (26 performances) Presented in association with the Herrick Theatre Foundation.
SUNDAY IN THE PARK WITH GEORGE with Music and Lyrics by Stephen Sondheim; Book, James Lapine; Director, James Lapine; Musical Director, Paul Gemignani; Set, Tony Straiges; Costumes, Patricia Zipprodt, Ann Hould-Ward; Lighting, Richard Nelson; Sound, Scott Lehrer; Stage Managers, Frederik H. Orner, Loretta Robertson; Props, Susan D. Andrews; Wardrobe, James Nadeaux; Hair and Wig Designs, Charles LoPresto.
CAST: Christine Baranski (Clarissa), Ralph Byers (Jules), Danielle Ferland (Louise), Kelsey Grammer (Young Man/Soldier/Alex Savage), Bradley Kane (Boy), Kurt Knudson (Mr. Robert Blackmun), Kevin Marcum (Louis/Photographer), Mary Elizabeth Mastrantonio (Celeste #2), Carmen Mathews (Old Lady), Judith Moore (Nurse/Mrs.), Nancy Opel (Bette), William Parry (Boatman), Mandy Patinkin (George), Bernadette Peters (Dot), Brent Spiner (Franz), Melanie Vaughan (Celeste #1).

Tuesday, November 8, 1983–January 15, 1984 (84 performances 16 previews)
BABY WITH THE BATHWATER by Christopher Durang; Director, Jerry Zaks; Sets, Loren Sherman; Costumes, Rita Ryack; Lighting, Jennifer Tipton; Sound, Jonathan Vall; Stage Managers, Esther Cohen, Diane Ward; Wardrobe, Martha Corbin Eddison; Props, Stephen Caldwell.
CAST: Christine Estabrook (Helen), W. H. Macy (John), Dana Ivey (Nanny/Woman in park/Principal) succeeded by Kate McGregor-Stewart, Mary Louise Wilson, Cynthia Darlow, Keith Reddin (Young Man), Leslie Geraci (Cynthia/Woman in park/Miss Pringle/Susan), Understudies: Melodie Somers, William Kux

Thursday, December 15, 1983–June 17, 1984 (223 performances) Re-opened Wednesday, June 20, 1984 at Lucille Lortel Theatre.
ISN'T IT ROMANTIC by Wendy Wasserstein; Director, Gerald Gutierrez; Set, Andrew Jackness; Costumes, Ann Emonts; Lighting, James F. Ingalls; Sound, Scott Lehrer; Music Coordinator, Jack Feldman; Dance Sequences, Susan Rosenstock; Stage Managers, J. Thomas Vivian, Toby Simpkins; Wardrobe, Joy Alpern; Props, Clayton Campbell.
CAST: Cristine Rose (Janie Blumberg), Lisa Banes (Harriet Cornwall), Chip Zien succeeded by Mitchell Greenberg, Tom Robbins (Marty Sterling), Betty Comden succeeded by Marge Kotlisky, Barbara Barrie (Tasha Blumberg), Stephen Pearlman succeeded by Steven Gilborn (Simon Blumberg), Jo Henderson succeeded by Peg Murray, Scotty Bloch (Lillian Cornwall), Jerry Lanning (Paul Stuart), Tom Robbins succeeded by Gerald Gutierrez, Alan Rosenberg (Vladimir), Stagehands: Peter Becker, Ralph Marrero, Robert Verlacque, David Boor, Understudies: Lynn Cohen, John Carroll, Sally Faye Reit.

A comedy in two acts. The action takes place at the present time in New York City.
Thursday, February 16,–March 4, 1984 (22 performances and 17 previews)
FABLES FOR FRIENDS by Mark O'Donnell; Director, Douglas Hughes; Set, Christopher Nowak; Costumes, Linda Fisher; Lighting, David Noling; Music, Paul Sullivan; Stage Managers, Barbara Abel, Vincent A. Feraudo; Assistant Director, David Saint; Wardrobe, Susan Selig; Production Assistants, Francesca Dow, Susan Selig.
CAST: Debra Cole (Beth/Sarah/Lynn/Tishy/Evie), Timothy Daly (Trevor/Chris/Nicky/Victor/Eddie), Cynthia Darlow (Libby/Jill/Deirdre/Peggy/Ginny), Laura Hughes (Liz/Pandy/Patty/Nan), Paul McCrane (Chick/Kit/Vinnie/Bernard/Clay/Andy), Brian Tarantina (Skeeter/Trip/Ray/Danny/Cappy)

Christine Estabrook, Leslie Geraci, Mary Louise Wilson
in "Baby with the Bathwater" *(Gerry Goodstein Photo)*
Top: Michael O'Keefe, Harriet Harris, Joe Pichette in
"Christmas on Mars" *(Susan Cook Photo)*

114

Left Center: David Pierce, Peter Morse, Steve Massa, Cynthia Darlow,
Arthur Howard, Alice Playten, James McDonnell
in "That's It, Folks!" *(Peter Cunningham Photo)*

Chip Zien, Cristine Rose, and Top: Lisa Banes, Jerry Lanning
in "Isn't It Romantic" *(Peter Cunningham Photos)*

THE PRODUCTION COMPANY

Norman René, Artistic Director
Seventh Season

Managing Director, Abigail Franklin; Production Supervisor, Margi Rountree; Promotional Manager, Andrew Shearer; Technical Director, Derald Plumer; Assistant to Artistic Director, Andrea Corney; Assistant to Production Supervisor, Jody Altman; Photographers, Anita Feldman, Steve Shevett; Press, Fred Nathan Associates, Ann Abrams

(THEATRE GUINEVERE) Thursday, October 13,–November 12, 1983 (42 performances)

DEMENTOS conception and lyrics, Robert I.; Music, Marc Shaiman; Book, Sebastian Stuart, Robert I.; Direction/Choreography, Theodore Pappas; Set, Loy Arcenas; C stumes, Steven L. Birnbaum; Lighting, Debra J. Kletter; Orchestrations, Marc Shaiman, Michael Holmes; Production Assistant, Stacey Eichel; Wardrobe, Deborah Berold; Stage Manager, M. A. Howard.

CAST: Joanne Beretta (Irene), Pi Douglass (Maria), Jane Galloway (Marcie), Annie Golden (Spike), Patrick Jude (Ruby), Jimmy Justice (Leon), Roger Lawson (Charles), Charlaine Woodard (Precious).

A musical in two acts.

MUSICAL NUMBERS: Crazy Crazy, Hotel Del Rio, I Saw God, Hustlers Hookers Whores, It's a Job, Lowlife, Dreams, I'd Like to Spray the World, High Class Bums, Just Like You, Woolworth's, Never Had a Home, Let Me Out, What If, New York Is a Party, Shopping Bag Man, God Save the City

(THEATRE GUINEVERE) Saturday, November 12–28, 1983 (16 performances)

SECOND LADY by M. Kilburg Reedy; Director, Carey Perloff; Set, Loy Arcenas; Costumes, James Delaney Collum; Lighting, Debra J. Kletter; Stage Manager, Michael Daniels; Sound, Karen Zabinsky; Wardrobe, Stacey Eichel.

CAST: Judith Ivey (Mrs. Joseph Erskine, wife of a U.S. Senator who is running for Vice-President of the U.S.).

The action takes place at a luncheon meeting of the League of Women Voters in Philadelphia, Pa., in October of the next presidential election year.

(THEATRE GUINEVERE) Sunday, January 15,–February 12, 1984 (42 performances). The Production Company by special arrangements with David S. Singer Productions presents:

CRIMINAL MINDS by Robin Swicord; Director, David Trainer; Set, Karen Schultz; Lighting, Dennis Parichy; Costumes, David Murin; Stage Manager, M. A. Howard.

CAST: Pamela Reed (Billy Marie), Leo Burmester (Eddie Ray), John Glover (Renfroe).

A play performed without intermission. The action takes place in March of the present in Panama City Beach, Florida.

(THEATRE GUINEVERE) Tuesday, March 13,–April 21, 1984 (42 performances). The Production Company by special arrangement with Norman Twain presents:

THE ROAD TO HOLLYWOOD with Book by Michael Pace; Music, Rob Preston; Lyrics, Michael Pace, Rob Preston; Director, Word Baker; Choreography, Lynnette Barkley; Musical Direction/Dance and Vocal Arrangements, Rob Preston; Scenery, Kate Edmunds; Costumes, Sally J. Lesser; Lighting, Debra J. Kletter; Orchestrations, Robby Merkin; Stage Managers, Mark Kalfin, Jodi Klosner; Props, Marlene Marta; Wardrobe, Julie Nichols; Press, Jeffrey Richards Associates.

CAST: Michael Pace (Beau Hartman), Kay Cole (Babs/Maybelle), Scott Fless (Frankie/Sheik), Haskell Gordon (Mr. Fritz), Gary Herb (Tappy Butler), Camille Saviola succeeded by Nora Mae Lyng (Nun/Diva Rita), Bebe Neuwirth (Princess Dorothy), D. Peter Samuel (Dick Stickler), Ron Lee Savin (Shiny/Reporter/Announcer), Maggie Task (Queen Minnie), Michael DiFonzo (Understudy).

A musical in two acts with a prologue. The action takes place in January of 1941 in Springfield, IL, and in Chicago.

MUSICAL NUMBERS: I Can't Sit Still, 56 Cities, Schleppin', Welcome to the Calmer House, Loumania, Talent, Hey Kid, The Beast in Me, Hot Ice, Don't Spill the Beans, Mr. Flatfoot, I've Got My Eye on You, When the Right One Comes Along, Opening Night, I Don't Care, She's a Star, Frankie's Return, Finale.

(GUINEVERE THEATRE) Monday, May 28, 1984–

BLUE WINDOW by Craig Lucas; Director, Norman Rene; Set, Loy Arcenas; Costumes, Walker Hicklin; Lighting, Debra J. Kletter; Stage Manager, M. A. Howard; Assistant Directors, Christian Angermann, Mark Ramont; Press, Jeffrey Richards Associates.

CAST: Maureen Silliman (Emily), Lawrence Joshua (Tom), Randy Danson (Libby), Matt Craven (Norbert), Christine Estabrook succeeded by Sophia Landon (Boo), Brad O'Hare succeeded by Mark Metcalf (Griever), Margo Skinner (Alice).

**Top Left: Charlaine Woodard, Roger Lawson
in "Dementos"** *(Feldman-Shevett Photo)*
Below: Judith Ivey in "Second Lady"
(George Connolly Photo)

Leo Burmester, John Glover, Pamela Reed
in "Criminal Minds" *(Carol Rosegg Photo)*

Brad O'Hare, Randy Danson, Lawrence Joshua, Maureen Silliman in "Blue Window"
Top: Gary Herb, Michael Pace, Kay Cole in "The Road to Hollywood"
(Peter Cunningham Photos)

PUERTO RICAN TRAVELING THEATRE

Miriam Colon Edgar, Executive Producer
Seventeenth Season

Managing Director, Christopher Manson; Office Manager, Vera Ryan; Technical Director, Ed Bartosik; Sound, Paul Garrity; Photographer, Martha Swope; Press, Max Eisen, Maria Somma.

Wednesday, January 11,–February 5, 1984 (28 performances alternating in Spanish and English)

THE MASSES ARE ASSES by Pedro Pietri; Director, Alba Oms; Set/Lighting, Robert Strohmeter; Translator, Alfredo Matilla; Stage Manager, John W. Calder III. CAST: Ivonne Coll (The Lady), Alex Colon (English) or Mike Robelo (The Gentleman), Offstage Voices: Marcela White, Eric Sabater.

The action takes place in a fancy restaurant or an empty apartment sometime last week, and performed without intermission.

Wednesday, February 22,–April 1, 1984 (42 performances alternating in Spanish and English).

"O.K." by Isaac Chocron; Director, Alba Oms; Set, Carl A. Baldasso; Lighting, Craig Kennedy; Translator, Pilar Zalamea; Stage Manager, Leslie Moore. CAST: Sheila MacRae (English) or Elisa de la Roche (Mina), Christofer De Oni (Franco), Isabel Segovia (Angela).

A play in two acts. The action occurs in a Latin American country today.

Wednesday, April 18,–June 3, 1984 (48 performances alternating in Spanish and English).

THE ACCOMPANIMENT by Carlos Gorostiza/
THE MANAGEMENT WILL FORGIVE A MOMENT OF MADNESS by Rodolfo Santana; Sets, Carl A. Baldasso; Lighting, Craig Kennedy; Costumes, Paul Harold Gindhart; Translator, Pilar Zalamea; Speech Consultant, Elaine Eldridge; Props, Stephen Powell; Stage Manager, Leslie Moore.
CAST: "The Accompaniment" with Freddy Valle (Tuco), Jorge Luis Ramos (Sebastian).

The action takes place anywhere at any time.

"The Management Will Forgive a Moment of Madness" with Sully Diaz (Psychologist), Norman Briski (English) or David Zuniga (Orlando Nunez).

The action takes place in a Latin American country today.

Martha Swope Photos

**Right: Sheila MacRae, Chris DeOni
in "O.K."**

**Freddy Valle, Jorge Luis Ramos
in "The Accompaniment"**

**Sully Diaz, David Zuniga in "The Management
Will Forgive a Moment of Madness"**

118

QUAIGH THEATRE

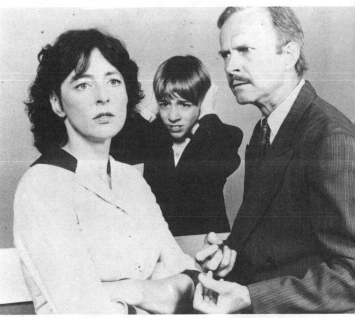

Will Lieberson, Artistic Director
Ninth Season

Managing Director, Peggy Ward; Staff Directors, Terence Cartwright, Dennis Lieberson; Photographer, Steve Stevett; Development Director, Iris Posner; Sound, George Jacobs; Artistic Consultant, Albert Brower; Administrative Consultant, Joyce R. Korbin; Producer, Leslie Middlebrook; Press, Max Eisen, Maria Somma

Wednesday, July 13,–August 6, 1983 (20 performances)
CHRISTOPHER BLAKE by Moss Hart; Director, June Prager; Set, Raegan Cook; Lighting, Heather Carson; Costumes, Lillian Pan; Stage Managers, Nancy Rutter, Glenn Gilbert.
CAST: Herman O. Arbeit (Announcer/Judge/Doorman), Andrew Cassese (Christopher Blake), Michael-Eliot Cooke (Aide/Caldwell/Upton/Janitor/Old Man), David Lanton (Johnny), Leslie Lyles (Evie Blake), Richard Marr (President/Kurlick/Headmaster/Superintendent), Lee Moore (Kenneth Blake), Susan Orem (Miss Holly/Miss McIntyre/Old Lady).

A drama in two acts. The action takes place in New York City in Judge Adamson's courtroom and in Christopher's imagination.

Saturday, December 31, 1983–January 2, 1984 (56 continous hours of theatrical entertainment).
Producer, Will Lieberson; Associate Producer, Michelle E. Tatum; Production Consultants, Barbara Barnett, Adam Kraar, Al Brower, Crystal Brown; Lighting, E. St. John Villard; Sound, George Jacobs; Production Coordinator, Valerie Harris; Stage Managers, Anne Cowett, Mark D. Goodwin, Robert McDuffie, Meg McSweeney, Elise Pearlman, Fred Ruiz, Andrew Warshaw, Tom Wilson, Barbara Williams.

Friday, January 20,–February 18, 1984 (24 performances)
BITTERSUITE a new musical by Mike Champagne and Elliot Weiss; Director, Bert Michaels; Production Coordinator, Ruth Preven; Set, Geoffrey Hall; Lighting, Eric Cornwell; Costumes, Eric Newland; Stage Manager, Liz Hopper.
CAST: Claudine Casson, Del Green, Anthony Mucci, Theresa Rakov, Richard Roemer.

A musical in two acts.
MUSICAL NUMBERS: Let's Do It Right, The Life That Jack Built, Ice Cream, Our Favorite Restaurant, You're Not Getting Older, Meg and Joe, The Influence of Scotch, The Recipe, I'll Be There, 20th Reunion, Mama Don't Cry, Narcissism Rag, Snap Back, John's Song, Soap Opera, Apology, Pretty Lady, Pay the Piper, Cliche, Win and Lose, Fathers and Sons, How Little We've Learned, Dream Like a Child

Tuesday, May 15,–June 10, 1984 (20 performances)
YEATS three one-act plays by William Butler Yeats; Direction and Design, Sam McReady; Choreography, Christopher Fleming; Music, Joe Morra; Lighting, Susan Chute; Costumes, Christopher Fleming; Coordinator, Ruth Preven; Associate Producer, Timothy Productions; Stage Managers, Sandy Pace, Richard Van Patten; Press, Howard Atlee, Barbara Atlee.
CAST: "At the Hawk's Well" with Todd Oleson (Old Man), Brooke Myers (Guardian), Michael Stacy (Young Man). "The Dreaming of the Bones" with Kevin Gardiner (Young Man), Michael Stacy (Dermot), Brooke Myers (Dervogilla). "King of the Great Clock Tower" with Todd Oleson (King), Brooke Myers (Queen), Kevin Gardiner (Attendant), Michael Stacy (Stroller)

Anita Feldman-Shevett Photos

**Top Right: Leslie Lyles, Andrew Cassese,
Lee Moore in "Christopher Blake"
Below: Andrew Cassese, Herman O. Arbeit
in "Christopher Blake"**

**Michael Stacy, Brooke Myers
in "The Dreaming of the Bones"**

119

**Bertram Ross, Laurine Towler
in "The Tempest"**

RIVERSIDE SHAKESPEARE COMPANY

W. Stuart McDowell, Artistic Director
Seventh Season

Executive Director, Gloria Skurski; Assistant Artistic Director, Timothy Oman; Associated Director, John Clingerman; Production Manager, H. Bradford Johnson; Technical Director, Alex LaBianca; Costumes, Joseph Church, Michael Canick; Press, Jane Badgers.

(NEW YORK CITY PARKS) Wednesday, July 13,–August 7, 1983 (20 performances). Presented by Joseph Papp and the New York Shakespeare Festival.
THE MERRY WIVES OF WINDSOR by William Shakespeare; Director, Timothy Oman; Assistant Director, Linda Masson; Set, Peter R. Feuche; Costumes, David Pearson; Props and Masks, Catherine Policella, Georgette Franzone; Choreography, Linda Reiff; Music Director/Composer, Deena Kaye; Percussion Patterns, Bill Gerstel; Technical Director, Daniel E. Geoffrey; Stage Managers, Mary Ellen Allison, H. Bradford Johnson.
CAST: C. B. Anderson (Shallow), Waguih Takla (Sir Hugh Evans), Maurice Kehoe (Slender), Daniel Daily (Sir Page), Joseph Reed (Sir John Falstaf), Roger Cox (Bardoph), Jonathan Fuller (Pistol), Gay Reed (Nym), Michael Landsman (Robin), Leslie Block (Anne Page), Sonja Lanzener (Mistress Ford), Norma Fire (Mistress Page), Dan Bedard (Simple), Warren Sweeney (Host), Anna Deavere Smith (Mistress Quickly), Pat Kennerly (John Rugby), Shelly Desai (Dr. Caius), Paul Hebron (Fenton), Douglas Broyles (Master Ford), H. Bradford Johnson (John), L. Robert Johnson (Robert).
The action takes place in 1875 at the Mardi Gras in New Orleans.

(SHAKESPEARE CENTER) Tuesday, October 18–22, 1983 (4 performances, 4 seminars, 17 workshops)
The Alliance for Creative Theatre and Educational Research (University of California/Santa Barbara) and the Riverside Shakespeare Company present five actors from the Royal Shakespeare Company in residence for THE SHAKESPEARE PROJECT: Heather Canning, John Kane, Christopher Ravenscroft, Edwin Richfield, Jennie Stoller performing "Under Milk Wood" by Dylan Thomas, "The Tarnished Phoenix" by D. H. Lawrence, and "The Merchant of Venice" by William Shakespeare; Sets, Kevin Lee Allen; Lighting, Julia Ruben; Music, Joseph Church; Stage Manager, Lee Davis Knight.

(SHAKESPEARE CENTER) Tuesday, November 15,–December 11, 1983 (20 performances)
THE TEMPEST by William Shakespeare; Director, Robert Mooney; Choreography/Movement, Shela Xoregos; Set, Kevin Lee Allen; Costumes, David P. Pearson; Lighting, Whitney Quesenbery; Stage Manager, Sondra R. Katz.
CAST: Paul Batchelor (Adrian), Ellen L. Cleghorne (Juno), Alexander Cook (Antonio), Stephen Fitzgerald (Ship's Master/Spirit), Kevin Harris (Boatswain/Spirit), Eric Hoffmann (Caliban), Elmore James (Ferdinand), Michael Mauldin (Sebastian), Joe Meek (Trinculo), Dale Linx Orrin (Dancer), Herman Petras (Alonso), Jessica Rausch (Miranda), John Reese (Gonzalo), Bertram Ross (Prospero), Myra Taylor (Ceres), Laurine Towler (Ariel), Steven Van Benschoten (Stephano), Sarah Durand (Iris).
Performed with one intermission.

Wednesday, February 29,–March 25, 1984 (20 performances)
CAESAR by William Shakespeare; Adapted and Directed by W. Stuart McDowell; Music, Michael Canick; Set, Kevin Lee Allen; Costumes, David Pearson; Lighting, Jayne Dutra; Stage Managers, Jane MacPherson, Sharon Veselic; Associate Director, Linda Masson.
CAST: Dan Johnson (Flavius/Trebonius/Titinius), Andrew Achsen (Carpenter/Cinna/Octavius), Paul Hebron (Marullus/Metellus/Messala/Messenger), Ronald Lew Harris (Cobbler/Cinna the Poet/Popilius/Clitus), Robert Walsh (Antony), James Maxson (Soothsayer/Messenger/Claudio), Harold Scott (Brutus), Alexander Cook (Cassius), Jeff Shoemaker (Decius/Lucillius), Warren Sweeney (Publius/Lepidus/Cicero/Artimedorus), Michael Golding (Lucius), Mary Lowry (Portia).
Performed with one intermission.

Wednesday, May 9,–June 3, 1984 (20 performances)
HENRY V by William Shakespeare; Director, Timothy Oman; Music, Sanchie Bobrow; Set/Lighting, Norbert U. Kolb; Fight Director, Conal O'Brien; Costumes, David Pearson; Stage Manager, Jane MacPherson; Props, Valerie Kuehn, Martha Tack; Wardrobe, Angelo Banuchi, Denise Manning-Craven; Production Manager, James L. Kottwinkel; Technical Director, Kerry Smith.
CAST: Lee Corghan (Chorus), Joseph Reed (Archbishop/Bedford), Gene Santarelli (Bishop/Gloucester), Frank Muller (Henry V), Evan Thompson (Duke of Exeter), John Boylan (Westmoreland/Bates/Bretagne), Ronald Lew Harris (Montjoy/Court), William Prosser (Bardolph/Grey/Bourbon), Time Winters (Nym/Cambridge/Orleans/York), Jere O'Donnell (Pistol/Scroop/Grandpere), Norma Fire (Quickly/Queen Isabel), Franklin Brown (French King), Phillipe Ruskin (Dauphin/Williams), Kevin Sullivan (Constable/Warwick), Pat Kennerly (Gower), David Adamson (Fluellen), Jeffrey Rhys (Capt. MacMorris/French Solider), W. Stuart McDowell (Capt. Jamy), Dene Nardi (Katharine), Sandi Shackelford (Alice), Jim Pratzon (Duke of Clarence).
Performed with two intermissions.

Elizabeth Colley Photos

**Top Left: Joe Reed, Sonja Lanzener in "The Merry
Wives of Windsor" Below: John Kane, Heather Canning,
Christopher Ravenscroft, Jennie Stoller,
Edwin Richfield in "Shakespeare Project"**

Norma Fire, Dene Nardi, Frank Muller in "Henry V"
Top: "Julius Caesar"

ROUNDABOUT THEATRE

Gene Feist, Producing Director
Eighteenth Season

Managing Director, Todd Haimes; Executive Associate, Erica Evans; Technical Director/Production Manager, Eddie R. Feldman; Musical Director/Resident Composer, Philip Campanella; Costumes Supervisor, Richard Hieronymus; Props, Debra Levine; Casting Consultant, Cindy Leiter; Press, Susan Bloch and Co., Adrian Bryan-Brown, Ron Jewell, Ellen Zeisler.

(HAFT THEATER) Tuesday, June 14,–July 24, 1983 (48 performances)

AH, WILDERNESS! by Eugene O'Neill; Director, John Stix; Scenery, Kenneth Foy; Lighting, Ron Wallace; Costumes, Gene K. Laskin; Music, Philip Campanella; Stage Managers, Victoria Merrill, Scott Gordon Miller.

CAST: Philip Bosco (Nat Miller), Dody Goodman (Essie), John Dukakis (Arthur), Scott Burkholder (Richard), Kelly Wolf (Mildred), Mark Scott Newman or Tommy Harris (Tommy), Robert Nichols (Sid Davis), Laurinda Barrett (Lily Miller), Joseph Leon (David McComber), Liane Langland (Muriel McComber), Robert Curtis-Brown (Wint Selby), Jean Hackett (Belle), Bernadette Quigley (Nora), Robert Curtis-Brown (Bartender), Scott Gordon Miller (Salesman).

A comedy in 2 acts and 7 scenes. The action takes place in the Miller home in a smalltown in Connecticut on July 4, 1906 and the next day, and in the backroom of a small hotel bar, and a boathouse on the harbor.

(ROUNDABOUT STAGE ONE) Tuesday, June 21,–September 11, 1983 (96 performances)

THE KNACK by Ann Jellicoe; Director, Peter Gordon; Set, Douglas Stein; Lighting, Ronald Wallace; Costumes, Jane Clark; Sound, Philip Campanella; Stage Manager, Kathy J. Faul.

CAST: Daniel Gerroll (Tom), Mark Arnott (Colin), John Abajian (Tolen), J. Smith-Cameron (Nancy).

A comedy in two acts. The action takes place in 1962 in a room in London, England.

(HAFT THEATRE) Thursday, August 4,–September 4, 1983 (37 performances and 11 previews). Presented by Roundabout Theatre in association with Lawrence N. Dykun, Michael J. Needham, Robert L. Sachter.

JEEVES TAKES CHARGE by P. G. Wodehouse; Conceived and Adapted by Edward Duke; Design, Carl Toms; Lighting, Ronald Wallace; Costumes, Una-Mary Parker; Choreography, Susan Holderness; Director, Gillian Lynne; Stage Manager, Cosmo P. Hanson; Wardrobe, Scott Wiscamb; Props, Howard Munford, Teresa Buckley.

A one-man performance by Edward Duke presented in two acts and four scenes with prologue.

(STAGE ONE) Thursday, September 20,–December 4, 1983 (88 performances)

THE MASTER BUILDER by Henrik Ibsen; Director, David Hammond; Set, Roger Mooney; Lighting, Judy Rasmuson; Costumes, Eloise Lunde; Stage Manager, Kathy J. Faul.

CAST: Edward Seamon (Halvard Solness), Joan Potter (Aline Solness), Tom Klunis (Dr. Herdal), Maury Cooper (Knut Brovik), Keith Reddin (Ragnar Brovik), Susan Pellegrino (Kaia Fosli), Laurie Kennedy (Hilda Wangel).

A drama in 2 acts and 3 scenes. The action takes place in 1892 in the Solness home in Christiania, Norway.

(SUSAN BLOCH THEATRE) Tuesday, November 1, 1983–March 18, 1984 (195 performances)

THE KILLING OF SISTER GEORGE by Frank Marcus; Director, Allen R. Belknap; Set, Roger Mooney; Lighting, Ron Wallace; Costumes, Susan A. Cox; Sound, Philip Campanella; Choreographer, D. J. Giagni; Dialect Coach, Lileen Mancell; Stage Manager, Kurt Wagemann.

CAST: Tandy Cronyn succeeded by Cynthia Dozier (Alice "Childie" McNaught), Aideen O'Kelly (June Buckridge/Sister George), Ruby Holbrook (Mrs. Mercy Croft), Elizabeth Owen (Madame Xenia).

A play in 3 acts and 4 scenes. The action takes place in the late 1950's in the living room of June Buckridge's flat on Devonshire Street in London, England.

Martha Swope Photos

Top Left: (c) Philip Bosco, and clockwise:
Dody Goodman, Kelly Wolf, John Dukakis, Scott Burkholder,
Mark Scott Newman in "Ah, Wilderness!"
Below: J. Smith-Cameron, Daniel Gerroll
in "The Knack"

Edward Duke as Bertie and Jeeves
in "Jeeves Takes Charge"

Aideen O'Kelly, Tandy Cronyn in "The Killing of Sister George" Top: Edward Seamon (front), Maury Cooper, Keith Reddin, Susan Pellegrino, Tom Klunis, Laurie Kennedy, Joan Potter in "The Master Builder" *(Martha Swope Photos)*

(STAGE ONE) Tuesday, December 20, 1983–March 4, 1984 (98 performances)
OLD TIMES by Harold Pinter; Director, Kenneth Frankel; Set, Marjorie Bradley Kellogg; Costumes, Linda Fisher; Lighting, Judy Rasmuson; Production Assistant, Tammy Taylor; Stage Manager, Kathy J. Faul.
CAST: Anthony Hopkins (Deeley), Marsha Mason (Kate), Jane Alexander (Anna).
  The action takes place at the present time in a converted farmhouse in England on an autumn night.
(STAGE ONE) Tuesday, March 20,–June 3, 1984 (82 performances)
DESIRE UNDER THE ELMS by Eugene O'Neill; Director, Terry Schreiber; Set, Michael Sharp; Costumes, Eloise Lunde; Lighting, Robert F. Strohmeier; Stage Manager, Kathy J. Faul; Press, Adrian Bryan-Brown.
CAST: Lenny Von Dohlen succeeded by Patrick Meyers (Eben Cabot), Tom Spiller (Simeon Cabot), Patrick Meyers succeeded by Gregory Salata (Peter Cabot), Lee Richardson succeeded by Marco St. John (Ephraim Cabot), Kathy Whitton Baker succeeded by Jeanne Ruskin (Abbie Putnam Cabot), Tom Spiller (Sheriff). A drama in two acts.
  The action takes place in and around the Cabot farmhouse in New England in 1950.
(SUSAN BLOCH THEATRE) Tuesday, March 27,–September 16, 1984 (200 performances)
ON APPROVAL by Fredrick Lonsdale; Director, Daniel Gerroll; Set, Holmes Easley; Lighting, Ronald C. Wallace; Costumes, Richard Hieronymus; Stage Manager, Matthew Mundinger.
CAST: Cynthia Dozier (Helen), Jane Summerhays succeeded by LeClanche du Rand (Maria), Mark Capri (George, Duke of Bristol), John Cunningham succeeded by Gordon Gould (Richard).
  A comedy in 2 acts and 4 scenes. The action takes place in Helen's house in Mayfair, London, in September 1926, and in Maria's house in Scotland in October of 1926.

**Left: Marsha Mason, Anthony Hopkins,
Jane Alexander in "Old Times"**

**Marsha Mason, Anthony Hopkins, Jane Alexander
in "Old Times"** *(Martha Swope Photos)*

Jane Summerhays, Cynthia Dozier, Mark Capri, John Cunningham in "On Approval"
Top: (L) Lee Richardson, Kathy Whitton Baker, Lenny von Dolen, and (R) Patrick Meyers,
Jeanne Ruskin in "Desire under the Elms"

125

SOHO REPERTORY THEATRE

Ninth Season

Artistic Directors, Jerry Engelbach, Marlene Swartz; Production/Casting Director, Brian Chavanne; Business/Stage Management, Deborah A. Friedman; Dramaturg, Victor Gluck.

Thursday, October 27,–November 20, 1983 (20 performances)

UNDER THE GASLIGHT by Augustin Daly; Director, Stephen Wyman; Set, Robert E. Briggs; Costumes, Martha Kelly; Lighting, David Noling; Assistant Director, Dinah Gravel; Fight Choreography, Doug Franklin; Stage Managers, Brian Chavanne, Deborah A. Friedman; Musical Direction/Song Arrangements/Incidental Music, Michael John La Chiusa.

CAST: Andrew Barnicle (Trafford), Joyce Leigh Bowden (Pearl), Suzanne Ford (Laura), Peter Waldren (Martin/DeMilt/Justice Bowling/Sgt./Signal), Dustin Evans (Snorkey), Evan Thompson (Byke), Laura Neal (Mrs. Van Dam/Old Judas), Julia Glender (Sue/Bermudas), Laura-Jean Schwartau (Check Girl/Peanuts), Joan Shangold (Peachblossom).

Thursday, December 1–18, 1983 (15 performances of short plays in repertory)

WOOD PAINTING by Ingmar Bergman; Director, Alan Wynroth; Costumes, Donna Zakowski.

YES IS FOR A VERY YOUNG MAN by Gertrude Stein; Director, Rob Barron; Set, Dorian Vernacchio; Costumes Jeremy Stuart Fishberg.

BERTHA/GEORGE WASHINGTON CROSSING THE DELAWARE both by Kenneth Koch; Director, Steven Brant; Costumes, Stephanie Kerley.

THE BUSINESS OF GOOD GOVERNMENT by John Arden; Directors, Jerry Engelbach, Matthew N. Couglin; Costumes, Susan Kanaly; Music Direction, Michael John La Chiusa; Technical Director, Brian Chavanne; Lighting, Bruce A. Kraemer; Stage Managers, Susan Hall, Don Loper.

CAST: (the permanent acting corps) James Caulfield, Laura Picard, Michael French, Matthew Gottlieb, Sharon Rubin, Cliff Weissman, Valerie DeJose, John Finch.

Friday, January 27,–February 19, 1984 (20 performances)

CATCHPENNY TWIST by Stewart Parker; Music, Shaun Davey; Lyrics, Stewart Parker; Director, Marlene Swartz; Musical Director/Arrangements, Michael John LaChiusa; Set, Tarrant Smith; Costumes, Mary L. Hayes; Lighting, Heather Carson; Stage Managers, Pamela Edington, Brian Chavanne; Assistant Director, Kirsten Sanderson; Dialect Coach, Peter Hirsch.

CAST: Steven Culp (Roy), Deborah Walsh (Marie), Gerald Finnegan (Man), Jennifer Sternberg (Woman), Katherine Leask (Girl), Michael John La Chiusa (Keyboards).

A play with songs in two acts.

Friday, March 16,–April 1, 1984 (14 performances)

THE DWARFS by Harold Pinter; Director, Jerry Engelbach; Set/Slide Projections, Mr. Engelbach; Lighting, Bruce A. Kraemer; Costumes, cast and director; Stage Manager, Dolores R. Miller.

CAST: Matthew Gottlieb (Len), James Caulfield (Pete), John Finch (Mark).

A play without intermission. Preceded by "Dwarfs: A Survey of Folklore" with slides, narration and sound by Jerry Engelbach.

Friday, April 13,–May 6, 1984 (20 performances)

MANDRAKE with Book and Lyrics by Michael Alfreds; Based on "Mandragola" by Machiavelli; Music, Anthony Bowles; Director, Mr. Bowles; Muscial Director, Michael Rafter; Set, Joseph A. Varga; Costumes, Steven L. Birnbaum; Lighting, David Noling, Michael Bergfield; Assistant Director, Nina Stachenfeld; Stage Managers, Mark Wallace, Deborah A. Friedman.

CAST: Steve Sterner (Siro), Helen Zelon (Genevieve), Kim Moerer (Callimaco), Suzanne Ford (Lucrezia), Mary Rocco (Sostrata), Mary Eileen O'Donnell (Widow), Mary Testa (Doria), Sharon Watroba (Chaperone), Tory Alexander (Fra Timoteo), Jeff Etjen (Novice), Jim Denton (Nicia), Andrew Barnicle (Ligurio).

A musical in two acts. The action takes place in Florence during the early 16th Century.

Friday, May 18,–June 3, 1984 (12 performances)

LENZ by Mike Stott; Based on story by Georg Buchner; Director, Alma Becker; Set, Bill Wolf; Costumes, Paige Southard; Lighting, David M. Shepherd; Stage Manager, Dolores R. Miller.

CAST: John Finch (Jacob Lenz), Matthew Gottlieb (Johann Oberlin), Maris Heller (Anna Oberlin), Connie Culbertson (Magda Schoenfeld), James Caulfield (Sebastian Scheidecker), Steve Kollmorgen (Christoph Kaufman).

A drama in two acts. The action occurs in Germany in 1778.

Joseph Schuyler Photos

Top Right: James Caulfield, Matthew Gottlieb, John Finch in "The Dwarfs"

Suzanne Ford in "Mandrake"

THEATRE OFF PARK

Ninth Season

Producing Director, Bertha Lewis; Artistic Director, Albert Harris; Managing Director, Trevor Thomas; Press, Anita Kroll, Margaret Sabo, Burnham-Callaghan Associates.

Tuesday, October 11–29, 1983 (16 performances)
PROMENADE with Book and Lyrics by Maria Irene Fornes; Music, Al Carmines; Director, Albert Harris; Musical Director, John R. Williams; Costumes, Tony Chase; Scenery, Leo B. Meyer; Lighting, Martin Friedman; Makeup/Hairstylist, Kathleen Reilly; Wardrobe, Fontella Boone; Technical Director, James Whelan; Stage Managers, Paul Bowen, John M. Atherlay.
CAST: Bill Buell (Jailer), Judith Cohen (Miss Cake), Connie Coit (Miss O), Georgia Creighton (Mother), Tim Ewing (106), Susan Feldon (Miss I), Jason Graae (105), Michael Halpern (Mr. R), Jim Hindman (Dishwasher/Injured Man/Soldier), Mitchell Jason (Mayor), Mark McGrath (Mr. T), Robert McNamara (Waiter/Driver/Soldier), Regina O'Malley (Servant), Hal Robinson (Mr. S), Marcie Shaw (Miss U).
A musical in 2 acts and 7 scenes.
MUSICAL NUMBERS: Promenade Theme, Dig Dig Dig, Unrequited Love, Isn't That Clear?, Don't Eat It, Four, Chicken Is He, The Moment Has Passed, A Flower, Apres Vous I, Bliss, Cigarette Song, Thank You, Clothes Make the Man, Two Little Angels, Passing of Time, Capricious and Fickle, Crown Me, Mr. Phelps, Madeline, Spring Beauties, Poor Man, Why Not, Finger Song, Now That You Are Mine, Little Fool, Listen I Feel, Laughing Song, Mother's Love, I Saw a Man, All Is Well in the City

Thursday, November 8,–December 3, 1983 (16 performances)
FIRST TIME ANYWHERE! by Leo Meyer; Director, Louis Rackoff; Set, Philip Louis Rodzen; Lighting, Todd Lichtenstein; Visuals, Wendall Harrington, Stage Manager, Roy Harris.
CAST: Ted Van Griethuysen in a one-man portrait of P. T. Barnum, the fabulous Show Prince. Presented in two acts.

Friday, December 9–24, 1983 (16 performances)
HENRY CHINASKI IN HOW TO BE A GREAT WRITER created from the works of Charles Bukowski; Music and Lyrics, John Roby; Director, Mina E. Mina; Set/Lights, James Knight; Sound, Peter Jamison; Stage Manager, Rosalyn Renken.
CAST: Mina E. Mina (Henry Chinaski), John Roby (Piano Man).
A protrait of Henry Chinaski in two acts.

Thursday, March 8–25, 1984 (16 performances)
PUNCH-IN PUNCH-OUT: "Until Further Notice . . . Tomorrow Is Cancelled" by Elyse Nass, James Struthers; Director, Bob Luke; "The Real Wife Beater" by Elyse Nass; Director, Toni Dorfman; Technical Director, Jerry Bell; Set, Craig Kennedy; Lighting, David Tasso; Costumes, Fontella Boone; Stage Manager, Peter Jamieson.
CAST: Edward Canaan (#3), Steven Field (Timothy Jade), Bert Fraser (MC/Sweeney/Messenger), Timothy Hall (#2), Anna Heins (Janis/Mrs. Orville), Diane Jean-George (Candace), Richard Litt (Gordon Bing/Thurkfield/Granado), Bob Luke (Byron/Mickey), Susan Mackin (Vivian/Casey/Model), Barbara Nicoll (Ethel), Thom Zimerle (#1)

Thursday, June 7–30, 1984 (16 performances)
HOT SAUCE by Karmyn Lott; Director, Toni Dorfman; Set/Lighting, Richard Harmon; Costumes, Katherine Roberson; Sound, Kenn Dovel; Stage Managers, Brenda D. Brown, Richard Wood.
CAST: Wayne Elbert (Lester Hankins), Sharon Hope (Ruby Hankins), Marchand Odette (Loretta Hankins), Katherine Price (Bebe Hankins).
A play in 2 acts and 3 scenes.

Top Right: Tim Ewing, Regina O'Mally, Jason Graae in "Promenade"

**Ted van Griethuysen
in "First Time Anywhere!"**

127

THEATER FOR THE NEW CITY

Thirteenth Season

Artistic Directors, George Bartenieff, Crystal Field; Development Director, Harvey Seifter; General Manager, Steven Miller; Administrator, Philip Hackett; Aide to Directors, Walter Corwin; Press, Bruce Cohen

Thursday, November 10,–December 11, 1983 (16 performances)

SUCCESS AND SUCCESSION by Ronald Tavel; Director, Michael Hillyer; Composer, Don Crusor; Set, Rick Dennis; Costumes, Natalie B. Walker; Lighting, Craig Kennedy; Sound, Paul Garrity; Production Manager, Linda Chapman; Stage Managers, Larry Frenock, Suzanne Carreiro; Technical Director, John Saltonstall; Wardrobe/Props, Fran Fore.

CAST: John Fitzgibbon (Richard), Tony Hoty (Glenn), Lola Pashalinski (Jenny), Elizabeth Chin (Luk), John Henry Redwood (White), Tom Mardirosian (Barton), Joan Matthiessen (Jolene).

A play in 3 acts and 8 scenes. The action takes place on the main floor of a New York brownstone during a November and December in the mid-1980's.

Sunday, November 20,–December 22, 1983 (16 performances)

MUD written and directed by Maria Irene Fornes; Set, Diann E. Duthie; Lighting, Anne E. Militello; Costumes, Gabriel Berry; Stage Manager, Peter Kisiluk.

CAST: Michael Sollenberger (Lloyd), Patrick Mattick (Mae), Alan Nebelthau (Henry).

A play in 2 acts and 17 scenes.

Thursday, March 1,–April 1, 1984 (16 performances)

THE LAST OF HITLER by Joan Schenkar; Director, Ms. Schenkar; Set, Reagan Cook; Lighting, Heather Carson; Costumes, Jessica Fasman; Sound, Phil Lee.

CAST: Marylouise Burke, David Florek, Peter Saputo, Susan Stevens, Martin Treat, Diane Zaremba, Robert Zukerman.

Thursday, May 17,–June 17, 1984 (16 performances)

ZONES OF THE SPIRIT by Amlin Gray; Director, Sharon Ott; Sets, Kate Edmunds; Costumes, Colleen Muscha; Lighting, Rachel Budin, David Higham; Stage Manager, Richard Lollo.

CAST: "Outlanders" with Bill Moor (Askanius), Leslie Geraci (Karin), Peter Crook (Apothecary), James Pickering (Ekerot). "Wormwood" with Leslie Geraci (Marika), Peter Crook (Johan), Bill Moor (Malachi), James Pickering (Ossian).

Thursday, May 24,–June 24, 1984 (16 performances)

DELICATE FEELINGS with Book and Lyrics by Rosalyn Drexler; Music, Steve and Franne Rosenthal; Director, George Ferencz; Set, Bill Stabile; Costumes, Sally J. Lesser; Lighting, Blu; Sound, Phil Lee; Assistant Director, Virlana Tkacz; Stage Manager, Sandy Crimmins; Fight Choreography/Stage Manager, Kitty Pedone.

CAST: Bobby Faust (Fingers), Bill Nunnery (Mike), Leslie Levinson (Rosa Carlo), Martha Whitehead (Lee Darling), Tino Juarez (Paul Ortiz).

A play in 2 acts, with music.

Patricia Mattick, Michael Sollenberger in "Mud" *(Carol Halebian Photo)* Top Left: Elizabeth Chin, Tony Hoty in "Success and Succession" *(Carol Rosegg Photo)*

**Bill Moor, Leslie Geraci in "Zones of the Spirit" Top: (L) Susan Stevens,
Martin Treat in "The Last of Hitler" (R) Bobby Faust, Bill Nunnery
in "Delicate Feelings"** *(Carol Rosegg Photos)*

WPA THEATRE

Kyle Renick, Artistic Director
Seventh Season

Managing Director, Wendy Bustard; Casting, Darlene Kaplan; Resident Designer, Edward T. Gianfrancesco; Lighting, Craig Evans; Technical Director, Ross A. Wilmeth; Production Assistant/House Manager, Leah Menken; Photographer, Ken Howard; Press, Fred Hoot, David Mayhew

Thursday, October 20,–November 20, 1983 (21 performances and 4 previews)
THE ALTO PART by Barbara Gilstrap; Director, Zina Jasper; Costumes, Don Newcomb; Sound, Michael Kartzmer; Musical Direction/Piano Arrangements, Guy Strobel; Props, Rachel Kaufman; Stage Manager, Mary Fran Loftus.
CAST: Elizabeth Council (Hattie), Kit Flanagan (Florence), Jane Hoffman (Ethyl), Carole Monferdini (Ola Belle), Marisa Morrell (Wanda), Jennifer Walker (Althea).
A play in 2 acts and 7 scenes. The action takes place in 1955 in Sparta, Texas.
Sunday, January 8,–February 5, 1984 (20 performances)
LA BREA TARPITS by Alan Gross; Director, Stephen Zuckerman; Set, James Fenhagen; Lighting, Phil Monat; Costumes, Mimi Maxmen; Sound, Aural Fixation; Stage Manager, Mary Fran Loftus.
CAST: Roxanne Hart (Gayle), Peter Riegert (Marty).
A play in two acts. The action takes place for some twelve hours in and around Los Angeles, California.
Thursday, March 15,–April 15, 1984 (25 performances)
THIN ICE by Jeffrey Haddow; Director, Dann Florek; Set, Tom Schwinn; Lighting, Phil Monat; Costumes, Don Newcomb; Sound, Aural Fixation; Stage Manager, Mary Fran Loftus.
CAST: William Carden (Skreeb), Caitlin Clarke (Jo), Dave Florek (Bill), Anne DeSalvo (Smith).
A play in 2 acts and 4 scenes. The action takes place at the present time in a loft in Tribeca in New York City.
Wednesday, May 9,–June 10, 1984 (30 performances)
MR. & MRS. by Kevin Wade; Director, David Trainer; Set, David Gropman; Lighting, Paul Gallo; Costumes, David Murin; Sound, Paul Garrity; Props, Craig Palanker; Stage Manager, Mary Fran Loftus.
CAST: Peter Friedman (Sam Dawkins), Mark Metcalf (Jake Marlowe), Polly Draper (Blake Upton), Pamela Brook (Alexandra Mulwray).
A play in 2 acts and 8 scenes. The action takes place at the present time, and a year earlier.

Elizabeth Council, Jane Hoffman, Marisa Morell, Jennifer Walker, Carole Monferdini, Kit Flanagan
in "The Alto Part" Top Left: Polly Draper, Mark Metcalf, Peter Friedman, Pamela Brook (seated)
in "Mr. & Mrs." *(Ken Howard Photos)*

130

Anne DeSalvo, Caitlin Clarke in "Thin Ice" *(Ken Howard Photo)* **Top: Roxanne Hart, Peter Riegert in "LaBrea Tarpits"** *(Ross Cameron/KLH Photo)*

YORK THEATRE COMPANY

Janet Hayes Walker, Producing Director
Fifteenth Season

(CHURCH OF THE HEAVENLY REST) Friday, November 18,–December 4, 1983 (20 performances)

NUDE WITH VIOLIN by Noel Coward; Director, William Prosser; Set/Graphics, James Morgan; Lighting, Mary Jo Dondlinger; Costumes, Michael J. Krass; Music, Stephen Hoffman; Hairstylist/Makeup, Laura Christine Hobrack; Technical Director, Deborah Alix Martin; Production Manager, Molly Grose; Stage Managers, Marianne Cane, Renee Picard, Francesca de Mauri; Wardrobe, Robert Swasey; Press, Keith Sherman.

CAST: Kevin Anderson (Fabrice), Jacqueline Barnett (Marie-Celeste), Lynne Charnay (Anya), Edward Conery (Sebastien), Roger Cox (George), Jeffrey D. Eiche (Colin), Catherine Haun (Pamela), David S. Howard (Jacob Friedland), Katherine Leask (Jane), Raphael Nash (Obadiah), Rende Rae Norman (Cherry-May), Bertram Prosser (Stotesbury), Gavin Troster, Jr. (Clinton), Janet Hayes Walker (Isobel).

A comedy in three acts. The action takes place in Paul Sorodin's studio in Paris.

(CHANCEL OF THE CHURCH OF HEAVENLY REST) Thursday, January 19–28, 1984 (11 performances).

MASS APPEAL by Bill C. Davis; Director, Austin Pendleton; Set, James Morgan; Lighting, Mary Jo Dondlinger; Costumes, Robert Swasey; Technical Director, Deborah Alix Martin; Production Manager, Molly Grose; Stage Manager, Sarah Marshall.

CAST: E. G. Marshall (Father Tim Farley), Scott Burkholder (Mark Dolson).

A play in two acts. The action takes place at the present time in Father Tim Farley's office and in St. Francis' Church in autumn.

(CHURCH OF THE HEAVENLY REST) Tuesday, March 27,–April 14, 1984 (20 performances)

PACIFIC OVERTURES with Music and Lyrics by Stephen Sondheim; Book, John Weidman; Additional Material, Hugh Wheeler; Director, Fran Soeder; Scenery, James Morgan; Lighting, Mary Jo Dondlinger; Costumes, Mark Passerell; Technical Director, Deborah Alix Martin; Production Manager, Molly Grose; Movement Consultant, Ernest Abuba; Fight Choreographer, Khin-Kyaw; Musical Director, James Stenborg; Choreography, Janet Watson; Stage Managers, Elisabeth Farwell, Jean Davis, Yvonna Mestrovic, Judith Zolan; Press, Keith Sherman.

CAST: Ernest Abuba (Reciter/Shogun/Jonathan Goble/Emperor Meiji), Tony Marino (Lord Age/First Officer), Henry Ravelo (John Manjiro), Thomas Ikeda (Councilor/Merchant's Mother/Physician/Madam/Noble Merchant), Tom Matsusaka (Shogun's Mother/Fisherman/Imperial Priest), Eric Miji (Councillor/Thief/Soothsayer/Warrior/Russian Admiral/British Sailor), Kevin Gray (Kayama Yesaemon), Lester J. N. Mau (Tamate/Shogun's Wife/French Admiral), Ronald Yamamoto (Merchant/Sumo Wrestler/Geisha), Alan Tung (Merchant's Wife/Confucian/Geisha/Noble/Fencing Master's Daughter), John Bantay (Merchant's Son/Cmdr. Perry/Geisha), Tim Ewing (Observer/First Officer/Sumo Wrestler/British Admiral/British Sailor), John Baray (Observer/Sumo Wrestler/Old Man/American Admiral), Francis Jue (Confucian/Geisha/Boy/Dutch Admiral/British Sailor), Khin-Kyaw Maung (Officer/Storyteller/Fencing Master/Old Samurai/Samurai); Stagehands: Gerri Igarashi, Gayln Kong, Khin-Kyaw Maung, Diane Lam, Jennifer Lam.

A musical in two acts. The action takes place in Japan in July 1853 and from then on. . . .

MUSICAL NUMBERS: The Advantages of Floating in the Middle of the Sea, There Is No Other Way, Four Black Dragons, Chrysanthemum Tea, Poems, Welcome to Kanagawa, Someone in a Tree, Lion Dance, Please Hello, A Bowler Hat, Pretty Lady, Next.

(CHANCEL OF THE HEAVENLY REST) Wednesday, May 23,–June 2, 1984 (16 performances)

ELIZABETH AND ESSEX with Book by Michael Stewart and Mark Bramble; Based on Maxwell Anderson's play "Elizabeth the Queen"; Music, Douglas Katsaros; Lyrics, Richard Engquist; Staged and Directed by Sondra Lee; Set, James Morgan; Lighting, Mary Jo Dondlinger; Costumes, Willa Kim; Technical Directors, Deborah Alix Martin, Sally Smith; Choreography, Onna White; Musical Direction, Douglas Katsaros; Stage Managers, Victor Lukas, Lisa Ledwich.

CAST: Paul Blankenship (Courier), David Bryant (Fool), Nora Colpman (Lady Charlotte), George Dvorsky (Armin), Willy Falk (Herbert), David Hart (Marvel), Evelyn Lear (Queen Elizabeth), Jennifer Naimo (Lady Ann), Dennis Parlato (Essex), Jan Pessano (Penelope), Paul David Richards (Raleigh), D. Peter Samuel (Bacon), Barbara Scanlon (Martha), Gordon Stanley (Cecil), Lisa Vroman (Lady Wicket), Sally Yorke (Ireland Lady).

A musical in two acts. The action takes place in the Palace, on its grounds, and in Ireland.

MUSICAL NUMBERS: Opening, As You Are, Cheers, I'll Be Different, Gloriana, Gossip, The First to Know, Ireland, Love Knots, Not Now, It Takes a Woman, She's a Woman, The Lady Lies, All I Remember Is You, Fool's Song, The Last Encounter, Conclusion, Finale.

Carol Rosegg Photos

**Top Left: Janet Hayes Walker, Edward Conery
in "Nude with Violin"**

**Gavin Troster, Janet Hayes Walker
in "Nude with Violin"**

John Baray, and Top: Ernest Abuba,
Tom Matsusaka in "Pacific Overtures"

Evelyn Lear, Dennis Parlato in "Elizabeth
and Essex" Top: Scott Burkholder, E. G. Marshall
in "Mass Appeal"

NATIONAL TOURING COMPANIES
(Failure to submit material necessitated omissions)

AGNES OF GOD

By John Pielmeier; Director, Michael Lindsay-Hogg; Set, Eugene Lee; Lighting, Roger Morgan; Costumes, Carrie Robbins; General Management, Theatre Now; General Manager, Edward H. Davis; Company Manager, Hans Hortig; Production Supervisor, Jere Harris; Props, Kevin Schwanke; Wardrobe, Mary Beth Regan; General Assistant, Barbara Hodgen; Casting, Hughes/Moss; Stage Manager, Frank Marino; Press, Betty Lee Hunt, Maria Cristina Pucci, James Sapp; Presented by Kenneth Waissman, Lou Kramer, Paramount Theatre Productions. Opened Wednesday, Aug. 17, 1983 at the Curran Theatre in San Francisco, CA., and closed Feb. 19, 1984 at the Fox Theatre in San Diego, CA. For original Broadway production, see THEATRE WORLD Vol. 39.

CAST

Dr. Matha Livingstone .... Elizabeth Ashley
Mother Miriam Ruth .... Mercedes McCambridge
Agnes .... Maryann Plunkett

Understudies: Susan Riskin, Judith Yerby

A drama in two acts. The action takes place at the present time.

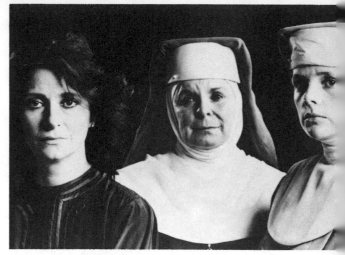

Elizabeth Ashley, Mercedes McCambridge,
Maryann Plunkett in "Agnes of God"

Peggy Cass, Susan Strasberg
in "Agnes of God"

AGNES OF GOD

By John Pielmeier; Original Michael Lindsay-Hogg direction re-staged by Larry Forde; Set, Eugene Lee; Costumes, Carrie Robbins; Lighting, Roger Morgan; Sound, Gary M. Stocker; Casting, Hughes/Moss; General Management, James Janek, George MacPherson, Jay Brooks, Jan Mallow; Company Manager, John Pasinato; Wardrobe, Tina Ryan; Production Assistant, Brian Callanan; Presented by Tom Mallow and James Janek by arrangement with Kenneth Waissman, Lou Kramer and Paramount Theatre Productions; Stage Managers, Jane Neufeld, Steve Wappel; Press, Max Eisen, Barbara Glenn, Maria Somma. Opened Tuesday, Jan. 24, 1984 at the University Theatre, Athens, OH, and closed at the American Theatre in St. Louis, MO, on April 1, 1984. For original Broadway production, see THEATRE WORLD Vol. 39.

CAST

Dr. Martha Livingstone .... Susan Strasberg
Mother Miriam Ruth ....Peggy Cass
Agnes .... Lynn Chausow

Understudies: Marilyn Alex, Sally Prager

A drama in two acts. The action takes place at the present time.

ALBERT EINSTEIN: THE PRACTICAL BOHEMIAN

Written by Ed Metzger, Laya Gelff; Director/Producer, Laya Gelff; Artistic Coordinator, Sully Boyar; Presented by MC Square Productions; Tour began in November of 1983, and closed in May of 1984.
A solo performance by Ed Metzger portraying the character and ideas of Albert Einstein in two acts: The Years in Europe, The Years in America.

Ed Metzger
as Albert Einstein

AMADEUS

By Peter Shaffer; Director, Roger Williams; Production, Peter Hall; Design, John Bury; Associate Scenic Designer, Ursula Belden; Associate Costume Designer, John David Ridge; Associate Lighting Designer, Beverly Emmons; Music Director/ Arrangements, Harrison Birtwistle; Presented by Tom Mallow in association with James Janek; General Manager, James Janek; Company Manager, Daryl Dodson; Stage Managers, Charles Collins, Alice Dewey, William Campbell; Production Supervisor, Ellen Raphael; Props, Robert Michael; Wardrobe, Al Costa, Jude Timlin; Casting, Johnson/Liff; Sound, Jack Mann; Wigs/Hairstylist, Paul Huntley; Press, Max Eisen, Barbara Glenn, Maria Somma. Opened Friday, Oct. 8, 1982 at Masonic Temple in Scranton, PA, and closed Feb. 4, 1984 at the Royal Alexandra Theatre in Toronto, CAN. For original Broadway production, see THEATRE WORLD Vol. 37.

CAST

Antonio Salieri	Daniel Davis[†1]
Venticelli	Ronald Sopyla, W. P. Dremak
Salieri's valet	Stuart Rudin
Salieri's cook	Donald L. Norris
Joseph II, Emperor of Austria	Philip Pleasants[†2]
Johann Kilian von Strack	Jonathan Farwell[†3]
Count Orsini-Rosenberg	Charles Rule
Baron van Swieten	Keith Perry
Priest	Fred Melamed[†4]
Giuseppe Bonno	Kevin Sullivan[†5]
Teresa Salieri	Bonnie Bowers
Katherina Cavalieri	Mary Jo Salerno[†6]
Constanze Weber	Tanya Pushkine[†7]
Wolfgang Amadeus Mozart	Peter Crook[†8]
Major Domo	Ron Keith
Valets	Peter Kingsley, Walker Hicklin, Peter Toran, William Campbell, Paul Maisano, Arnie Burton

CITIZENS OF VIENNA: Frank Borgman, Bonnie Bowers, W. P. Dremak, Jean Fitzgibbons, Joel Fredrickson, Dan Handley, Walker Hicklin, Jack Honor, Ron Keith, Robert Langdon Lloyd, Jonathan Miller, Donald L. Norris, Keith Perry, Alyssa Roth, Ken Rubenfeld, Stuart Rudin, Charles Rule, Ronald Sopyla, Kevin Sullivan
UNDERSTUDIES: Jack Honor (Mozart), Alyssa Roth (Constanze), Ron Keith (Joseph II), Walker Hicklin (Venticello), Kevin Sullivan (Van Swieten/Valet), Frank Borgman (Count/Cook), Jean Fitzgibbons (Theresa/Katherina), Dan Handley (Major Domo), Joel Fredrickson (Valets)

A drama in two acts. The action takes place in Vienna in November 1823 and in recall the decade 1781–1791.

†Succeeded by: 1. Jonathan Farwell, 2. Robert Langdon Lloyd, 3. Kevin Sullivan, 4. Frank Borgman, 5. Walker Hicklin, 6. Alyssa Roth, 7. Mary Jo Salerno, 8. Ed Hodson

Tanya Pushkine, Daniel Davis,
Peter Crook in "Amadeus"

BLUES IN THE NIGHT

Conceived and Directed by Sheldon Epps; Choreography, Mercedes Ellington; Producing Director, Mitchell Maxwell; Vocal Arrangements, Chapman Roberts; Musical Orchestrations/Arrangements, Sy Johnson; Musical Director, Clem Moorman; Vocal Direction, David Brunetti; Set, Randel Wright; Costumes, Patty Greer McGarity; Lighting, Doug Kolbo; Company Manager, Andrea Ladik; Production Supervisor, Bruce Kagel; Associate Producer, Elaine Brownstein; General Management, M2 Entertainment; Technical Director, Peter Hanson; Sound, Jerry O'Donnell; Production Assistant, Douglas Kane; Wardrobe, Jeanne Trevor; Presented by Blues Tours Inc. and Bill Fegan Attractions. For original Broadway production, see THEATRE WORLD Vol. 39.

CAST

The Girl with a date ....Neva Small
The Woman of the world ....Cynthia White
The Lady from the road ....Della Reese
The Saloon Singer ....Clem Moorman

Standby: Jeanne Trevor

MUSICAL NUMBERS: Blue Blues, Four Walls and One Dirty Window Blues, I've Got a Date with a Dream, New Orleans Hop Scop Blues, Stompin' at the Savory, Taking a Chance on Love, It Makes My Love Come Down, Lush Life, Take Me for a Buggy Ride, Wild Women Don't Have the Blues, Lover Man, Willow Weep for Me, Kitchen Man, Low, Take It Right Back, Jam Session, Blues in the Night, Dirty No-Gooder's Blues, Baby Doll, Nobody Knows You When You're Down and Out, I Gotta Right to Sing the Blues

A musical in two acts. The action takes place in Chicago in the late 1930's: Three women and a saloon singer in a cheap hotel, and the music that get them through the long lonely night.

Cynthia White, Della Reese, Neva Small
in "Blues in the Night"

Jonathan Silverman (front), Joan Copeland, Elizabeth Perkins,
Olivia Laurel Mates, Mark Nelson, Charles Cioffi,
Barbara Caruso

BRIGHTON BEACH MEMOIRS

By Neil Simon; Director, Gene Saks; Set, David Mitchell; Costumes, Patricia Zipprodt; Lighting, Tharon Musser; Company Manager, Jane Robison; Props, Patrick Harmeson; Wardrobe, Jeanne Frisbie; Casting, Meg Simon/Fran Kumin; General Manager, Robert Kamlot; Production Supervisor, Martin Herzer; Technical Supervisor, Theatrical Services; Stage Managers, Thomas P. Carr, Lisa M. Hogarty; Press, Bill Evans, Sandra Manley, Harry Davies. Opened Monday, Nov. 21, 1983, and still touring May 31, 1984. For original Broadway production, see THEATRE WORLD Vol. 39.

CAST

Eugene ....Jonathan Silverman
Blanche ....Barbara Caruso
Kate ....Joan Copeland
Laurie ....Olivia Laurel Mates
Nora ....Elizabeth Perkins
Stanley ....Mark Nelson
Jack ....Charles Cioffi

STANDBYS: Geoffrey Sharp (Eugene/Stanley), Wendy Gazelle (Nora), Judy Unger (Laurie), Rocky Parker (Kate/Blanche), Jack R. Marks (Jack)

A play in two acts. The action takes place in Brighton Beach, Brooklyn, NY, during September of 1937 in the home of Jack and Kate.

CATS

Based on "Old Possum's Book of Practical Cats" by T. S. Eliot; Music, Andrew Lloyd Webber; Presented by Cameron Mackintosh, The Really Useful Co., David Geffen and the Shubert Organization; Executive Producers, R. Tyler Gatchell, Jr., Peter Neufeld; Casting, Johnson/Liff; Orchestrations, David Cullen, Andrew Lloyd Webber; Production Musical Director, Stanley Lebowsky; Musical Director, Thomas Helm; Sound, Martin Levan; Lighting, David Hersey; Design, John Napier; Associate Director/Choreographer, Gillian Lynne; Director, Trevor Nunn; Production Supervisor, David Taylor; Dance Supervisor, T. Michael Reed; Company Manager, Martin Cohen, Nina Lannan; Assistant Musical Director, Susan Anderson; General Management, Gatchell & Neufeld; Production Assistant, Jay Raibourn; Props, George Green, Jr., John Alfredo, Sr, Paul Bach; Wardrobe, Adelaide Laurino, Robert Daily; Hairstylists, Leon Gagliardi, Wayne Herndon, Jodi Denn, Linda Goggin; Wigs, Paul Huntley; Makeup, Candace Carell; Stage Managers, Jake Bell, Dan Hild, Maureen C. Donley; Press, Fred Nathan, Leslie Anderson, Anne Abrams, Ted Killmer, Bert Fink; Opened in Boston's Shubert Theatre on Wednesday, Dec. 21, 1983 and still touring May 31, 1984. For original Broadway production, see THEATRE WORLD Vol. 39.

CAST

Alonzo/Rumpus Cat	Jamie Patterson
Bustopher Jones/Asparagus/Growltiger	Sal Mistretta
Bombalurina	Cindi Klinger
Cassandra	Charlotte d'Amboise
Coricopat	Allen Hidalgo
Demeter	Pamela Blasetti
Grizabella	Diane Fratantoni
Jellylorum/Griddlebone	Jennifer Butt
Mistoffelees	Jaime Torcellini
Munkustrap	Mark Dovey
Old Deuteronomy	Calvin E. Remsberg
Plato/Macavity	Russell Warfield
Pouncival	Barry K. Bernal
Rum Rum Tugger	Rich Hebert
Rumpleteazer	Kelli Ann McNally
Sillabub	Tina Decker
Skimbleshanks	Anthony Whigas
Tantomile	Tori Brenno
Tumblebrutus	Thomas McManus
Victoria	Susan Zaguirre
Cats Chorus	John Dewar, Janene Lovullo, Bill Nolte, Susanna Wells

STANDBYS & UNDERSTUDIES: Joseph Konicki, Greg Minahan, Scott Dainton (Alonzo/Rumpus), John Dewar (Bustopher/Asparagus/Growltiger), Tori Brenno, Frankie Cassady, Nancy Hess (Bombalurina), Nancy Hess/Lily-Lee Wong (Cassandra), John Crutchman, Joseph Konicki, Danny Rounds, Greg Minahan (Coricopat), Tori Brenno, Frankie Cassady, Nancy Hess (Demeter), Janene Lovulla, Pamela Blasetti (Grizabella), Susanna Wells, Cindy Benson (Jellylorum), Susanna Wells, Jennifer Butt (Jennyanydots), Barry K. Bernal, Thomas McManus (Mistoffelees), John Crutchman, Danny Rounds, Greg Minahan (Mungojerrie), Scott Dainton, Greg Minahan (Munkustrap), Bill Nolte (Old Deutoronomy), Joseph Konicki, Jamie Patterson, Greg Minahan (Plato/Macavity), John Crutchman, Danny Rounds (Pouncival), Scott Dainton, Greg Minahan (Rum Tum Tugger), Cathy Carson (Rumpleteazer), Cathy Carson, Frankie Cassady, Tori Brenno (Sillabub), Danny Rounds, Greg Minahan (Skimbleshanks), Frankie Cassady, Nancy Hess, Lily-Lee Wong (Tantomile), John Crutchman, Joseph Konicki (Tumblebrutus), Cathy Carson, Lily-Lee Wong (Victoria)
MUSICAL NUMBERS: see Broadway calendar

Martha Swope Photos

Right Center: Diane Fratantoni

Jennifer Butt, Sal Mistretta

CHAPLIN

Book, Music and Lyrics, Anthony Newley, Stanley Ralph Ross; Director/Choreographer, Michael Smuin; Co-Choreographer, Claudia Asbury; Scenery, Douglas W. Schmidt; Costumes, Willa Kim; Lighting, Ken Billington; Sound, John McClure; Orchestrations, Bill Byers, Chris Boardman, Angela Morley; Dance Arrangements, David Black; Hairstylist, Howard Leonard; Music Supervised/Arranged/Conducted by Ian Fraser; Presented by Raymond Katz, Sandy Gallin, James M. Nederlander, Arthur Rubin in association with David Susskind; General Managers, Joseph Harris, Ira Bernstein; Associates, Peter T. Kulok, Steven E. Goldstein; Company Manager, Mitzi Harder; Technical Supervisor, Jeremiah Harris; Props, Paul Biega; Sound, Jim Morris; Wardrobe, Mario Brera, Ingrid Ferrin; Assistant Conductor, David Black; Stage Managers, Martin Gold, Parker Young, William Vosburgh; Press, Solters/Roskin/Friedman, Lisa Kasteler, Gail Browne, Gail Block. Opened at Dorothy Chandler Pavilion in Los Angeles on Saturday, Aug. 13, 1984 and closed there on Sept. 24, 1983.

CAST

Charlie	Anthony Newley
Hannah/Miss Peterson	Mary Leigh Stahl
Young Charlie	Scott Grimes
Young Sydney	Ricky Segall
Charles Senior/Hearst	Kenneth H. Waller
Oona/Paulette Goddard/Lita	Andrea Marcovicci
Victoria	Kathy Andrini
Grudgewick/Picklebrain	Jack Ritschel
Matron/Chee Chee San/Lillian	Marsha Bagwell
Grown Sydney	Michael Byers
Teen Sydney	Thom Keeling
Teen Charlie	John Allee
Karno/Butzi/Carl Robinson	S. Marc Jordan
Reeves/Fatty Arbuckle/Oliver Hardy	Ric Stoneback
Stan Laurel/Willhartz	Jim MacGeorge
M.C./Mack Sennett/Edwin	Lyle Kanouse
Mabel Normand	Sheri Cowart
Dubczek	Ric Stoneback
Kojo	Thom Sesma

PEOPLE WHO TOUCHED CHARLIE'S LIFE: Kathy Andrini, K. T. Brown, Sheri Cowart, Nikki D'Amico, Dennis Daniels, Kathleen Dawson, Michael Estes, Michael Jay Lawrence, Aaron Lohr, Bridget Michele, Barbara Moroz, Roger Spivy, Chance Taylor, Swings: Adam Hurley, Frank Kopyc, Alice Anne Oakes, J. Thomas Smith

UNDERSTUDIES: Michael Byers (Charlie), Alice Anne Oakes (Oona/Lita/Paulette), Michael Jay Lawrence (Young Charlie), Frank Kopyc (Stan/Willhartz)

MUSICAL NUMBERS: A Little Bit of Powder and Paint, Me and You, Joyeux Noel, Love, Sydney's Hymn, Heel Toe and Away We Go, Funny Man, Madame Butterfingers, Doing the Charlie Chaplin, If Only You Were Here, My Private Life, Thanks for Nothing, Dinner with W. R., One Man Band, The American Dream, Remember Me

A musical in 2 acts and 40 scenes. The action takes place from 1895 to the present.

Anthony Newley (center) Top Left: Andrea Marcovicci, Anthony Newley in "Chaplin" *(Alan Berliner Photos)*

CRIMES OF THE HEART

By Beth Henley; Director, James Pentecost; Set, John Lee Beatty; Costumes, Patricia McGourty; Lighting, Dennis Parichy; Casting, Shirley Rich; Associate Producer, Ethel Watt; General Management, McCann/Nugent; Company Manager, Alexander Holt; Production Coordinator, Mary Nealon; Props, Mel Saltzman; Wardrobe, Kevin Woodworth; Stage Managers, Rick Ralston, Gregory Johnson; Press, Betty Lee Hunt, Maria Cristina Pucci, James Sapp; Opened at Boston's Shubert Theatre, Saturday, Oct. 8, 1983 and closed Mar. 25, 1984 at the DuPont Playhouse, Wilmington, DE. For original Broadway production, see THEATRE WORLD Vol. 38.

CAST

Lenny MaGrath	Caryn West
Chick Boyle	Dawn Didawick
Doc Porter	Tom Stechschulte
Meg MaGrath	Kathy Danzer
Babe Botrelle	Cyd Quilling
Barnette Lloyd	David Allison Carpenter

UNDERSTUDIES: Debra Dean (Babe/Chick), Patricia Miller (Meg/Lenny), David Reinhardsen (Doc/Barnette)

A comedy in three acts. The action takes place in Hazelhurst, Mississippi, five years after Hurricane Camille.

Left: (front) Cyd Quilling, Caryn West, Kathy Danzer, (back) David Allison Carpenter, Tom Stechschulte

Kathy Danzer, Caryn West, Cyd Quilling

DANCIN'

Direction/Choreography re-created by Gail Benedict from the original by Bob Fosse; Music and Lyrics, Ralph Burns, George M. Cohan, Neil Diamond, Jerry Leiber/Mike Stoller, Bob Haggert, Ray Bauduc, Gil Rodin/Bob Crosby, Johnny Mercer/Harry Warren, Louis Prima, John Philip Sousa, Barry Mann/Cynthia Weil, Felix Powell/George Asaf, Sigmund Romberg/Oscar Hammerstein II, Cat Stevens, Jerry Jeff Walker; Scenery, Peter Larkin; Costumes, Willa Kim; Lighting, Jules Fisher; Sound, Abe Jacob; Music Arrangements, Gordon Lowry Harrell; Orchestrations, Ralph Burns, Michael Gibson; Musical Director, David Firman; Presented by Tom Mallow/James Janek; Company/Stage Manager, Nick Bromley; Musical Director, Randy Booth; Company Manager, Sue Frost; Wardrobe, Tina Ryan; Hairstylist, Romaine Greene; Stage Managers, Mark S. Krause, Karen DeFrancis, Quin Baird; Press, Max Eisen, Barbara Glenn; General Management, American Theatre Productions; Opened at Milwaukee's Performing Arts Center on Tuesday July 29, 1980 and closed Jan. 28, 1984 at London's Drury Lane Theatre. For original Broadway production, see THEATRE WORLD Vol. 34.

CAST

Quin Baird, Robin Cleaver, Andre De La Roche, John De Luca, Spence Ford, Heather Lea Gerdes, Raymond Charles Harris, Joseph Konicki, Manette LaChance, Diana Laurenson, Fred C. Mann III, Daniel May, Joanie O'Neill, Peggy Parten, Shan Reece, Lynne Savage, David Thome, Cheryl Yamaguchi

PROGRAM: Hot August Night, Crunchy Granola Suite, Mr. Bojangles, Percussion, I Wanna Be a Dancin' Man, Big Noise from Winnetka, I've Got Them Feelin' Too Good Today Blues, Was Dog a Doughnut, Sing Sing Sing, Here You Come Again, America Medley

A musical in 3 acts.

DREAMGIRLS

Book & Lyrics, Tom Eyen; Music, Henry Krieger; Direction/Choreography, Michael Bennett; Co-Choreographer, Michael Peters; Scenery, Robin Wagner; Costumes, Theoni V. Aldredge; Lighting, Tharon Musser; Sound, Otts Munderloh; Musical Supervision/Orchestrations, Harold Wheeler; Musical Director, Steven Cagan; Vocal Arrangements, Cleavant Derricks; Hairstylist, Ted Azar; Production Supervisor, Jeff Hamlin; General Manager, Marvin A. Krause; Original Cast Album on Geffen Records and Tapes; Presented by Michael Bennett, Bob Avian, David Geffen and the Shubert Organization; Press, Merle Debuskey, Diane Judge, Judy Davidson; Opened at the Shubert Theatre in Los Angeles, CA, on Sunday, Mar. 20, 1983 and still touring May 31, 1984. For original Broadway production, see THEATRE WORLD Vol. 38.

CAST

The Stepp Sisters ....Deborah Burrell, Tyra T. Ferrell,
LuCinda RamSeur, Johnnie Teamer
Charlene .... Betty K. Bynum
Joanne .... Susan Beaubian
Marty .... Weyman Thompson
Curtis Taylor, Jr. ....Larry Riley
Deena Jones .... Linda Leilani Brown
M.C./Mr. Morgan .... Ron Richardson
Tiny Joe Dixon/Nightclub Owner .... Roy L. Jones
Lorrell Robinson .... Arnetia Walker
C. C. White ....Lawrence Clayton
Effie Melody White ....Jennifer Holliday [†]
Little Albert & the Tru-Tones .... Rudy Huston, Abe Clark,
Vincent M. Cole, Thomas Scott Gordon, Gordon J. Owens
James Thunder Early .... Clinton Derricks-Carroll
Edna Burke .... Edwina Lewis
James Early Band .... Abe Clark, Vincent M. Cole,
Rudy Huston, Gordon J. Owens, Stephen Terrell
Wayne .... Maurice Felder
Dave & the Sweethearts ....Ray Benson, Delyse Lively,
Candi Milo
Press Agent Frank .... Tim Cassidy
Michelle Morris .... Deborah Burrell
Five Tuxedos ....Abe Clark, Vincent M. Cole,
Thomas Scott Gordon, Gordon J. Owens, Ron Richardson
Les Style .... Susan Beaubian, Betty K. Bynum,
Candi Milo, Johnnie Teamer
Film Executives .... Ray Benson, Donn Simione, Abe Clark

FANS, REPORTERS, GUESTS, ETC: Susan Beaubian, Ray Benson, Betty Clark, Tim Cassidy, Abe Clark, Lawrence Clayton, Vincent M. Cole, Tyra T. Ferrell, Thomas Scott Gordon, Rudy Huston, Roy L. Jones, Edwin Lewis, Delyse Lively, Candi Milo, Gordon Owens, LueCinda RamSeur, Ron Richardson, Angel Rogers, Donn Simione, Johnnie Teamer, Stephen Terrell, Kristi Tucker, Derryl Yeager, Swings: Sharon Brooks, Helen Castillo, Phillip Gilmore
MUSICAL NUMBERS: see Broadway Calendar

A musical in 2 acts and 20 scenes. The action takes place during the early 1960's and the early 1970's.

Deborah Burrell, Linda Leilani Brown, Arnetia Walker
Top Right: Lillias White *(Martha Swope Photos)*

141

FORTY-SECOND STREET

See credits for previous listing; Musical Direction, Jim Coleman; General Manager, Leo K. Cohen; Company Manager, John Corkill; Stage Managers, George Martin, John Grigas, William O'Brien, Luke Stallings; Props, Leo Herbert, Edward Schneck; Wardrobe, Dorothy Priest, Richard Romero; Assistant Muscial Director, Bill Elton; Press, Solters/Roskin/Friedman, Lisa Kasteler, Ken Werther, Laura Gold, Joshua Ellis, Louise Weiner Ment, Cindy Valk. Opened Friday, Feb. 3, 1984 in the Shubert Theatre in Los Angeles, CA, and still playing May 31, 1984.

CAST

Andy Lee	James Dybas
Oscar	Bob Gorman
Mac	Lonnie Burr
Annie	Rose Scudder
Maggie Jones	Carole Cook
Bert Barry	Matthew Tobin
Billy Lawlor	Lee Roy Reams
Peggy Sawyer	Nana Visitor
Phyllis	Nancy Bickel
Lorraine	Marla Singer
Julian Marsh	Jon Cypher
Dorothy Brock	Millicent Martin
Abner Dillon	Iggie Wolfington
Pat Denning	Gary Holcombe
Thugs	Lonnie Burr, Alan Bardsley
Doctor	Lonnie Burr

ENSEMBLE: Charles E. Baker, Alan Bardsley, Cheryl Baxter, John Bazzell, Steve Belin, Marcella Betz, Nancy Bickel, Jim Carey, Karen Chase, Sterling Clark, Keith Clifton, Janie Dale, Dennis Daniels, Margie Cenecke, Teri DeOntine, Kathy Donavan, Keith Ellinger, Lloyd Gordon, Jill B. Gounder, Kenneth Jezek, Victoria Kent, Paul Latchaw, Terry Mason, Mark McGee, Denise McKenna, Dawn Merrick, Kim Meyer, Julie O'Connell, Anne Marie Roller, Debra Seitz, Marla Singer, Pam Souders, Julie Tea, Truett Wright, Cathy Wydner, Norine Xavier
UNDERSTUDIES & STANDBYS: Joy Claussen (Dorothy/Maggie), Terry Mason (Dorothy), Rose Scudder (Maggie), Gary Holcombe (Julian), Jim Carey (Julian), Cathy Wydner (Peggy), Keith Ellinger (Billy), Paul Latchaw (Bert), Steve Belin (Andy), Lonnie Burr (Abner/Pat), Karen Chase (Annie), Alan Bardsley (Mac), April Clawson (Phyllis/Lorraine), Donalin Patton (Phyllis/Lorraine), Ensemble: April Clawson, Jon Engstrom, Donalin Patton, Elaine Pepparde, Pamela Prescott, Luke Stallings
MUSICAL NUMBERS: see Broadway Calendar

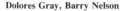
Dolores Gray, Barry Nelson

Nana Visitor, Lee Roy Reams

FORTY-SECOND STREET

Book, Michael Stewart/Mark Bramble; Based on novel by Bradford Ropes; Music, Harry Warren; Lyrics, Al Dubin; Choreography, Gower Champion; Reproduced by Karin Baker/Randy Skinner; Directed by Lucia Victor from Gower Champion's original; Set, Robin Wagner; Musical Direction, Stephen Bates; Vocal Arrangements, John Lesko; Costumes, Theoni V. Aldredge; Orchestrations, Philip J. Lang; Hairstylist, Anne Sampogna; Casting, Hughes/Moss; Lighting, Tharon Musser; Dance Arrangements, Donald Johnston; Sound, Jan Nebozenko; General Manager, Leo K. Cohen; Company Manager, Kim Sellon; Props, Leo Herbert, Cheri Herbert; Wardrobe, Robin B. Robillard; Presented by David Merick; Stage Managers, Harold Goldfaden, Pat Trott, David Hansen, Paul Del Vecchio; Press, Solters/Roskin/Friedman, Joshua Ellis, Cindy Valk, Lisa Kasteler, Gail Browne. Opened at the Forrest Theatre, Philadelphia, Tuesday, Nov. 8, 1983 and still touring May 31, 1984. For original Broadway production, see THEATRE WORLD, Vol. 37.

CAST

Andy Lee	Barry Preston
Oscar	Chuck Hunnicutt
Mac/Thug/Doctor	Igors Gavon
Annie	Beth Leavel
Maggie Jones	Bibi Osterwald
Bert Barry	Don Potter
Billy Lawlor	Jim Walton
Peggy Sawyer	Clare Leach
Lorraine	Sandra Yarish
Phyllis	Bonnie Patrick
Julian Marsh	Barry Nelson
Dorothy Brock	Dolores Gray
Abner Dillon	J. Frank Lucas
Pat Denning	Randy Phillips
Thug	Al Micacchion

ENSEMBLE: David Askler, Marietta Clark, Jeffrey Cornell, Kelly Crafton, Debbie DiBiase, Barbara Early, Judy Ehrlich, Russell Giesenschlag, Eileen Grace, Terri Griffin, Suzie Jary, Cathy Jones, Kim Larese, Patricia Lockery, Bobby Longbottom, Susan McGonegle, Al Micacchion, Doug Okerson, Bonnie Patrick, Marc Pluf, Russell Rhodes, Richard Lee Ruth, Ann Rutter, John Salvatore, Greg Schanuel, Jeanna Schweppe, Karen Sorensen, Susanne Leslie Sullivan, Nikki Summerford, Sandra Yarish
UNDERSTUDIES & STANDBYS: Marjorie Sires (Dorothy/Maggie), Randy Phillips (Julian), Vickie Taylor (Peggy), Russell Rhodes (Billy), Paul Del Vecchio (Bert), Marc Pluf (Andy), Igors Gavon (Abner/Pat), Sandra Yarish (Annie), Al Micacchion (Mac), Jay Alger (Oscar), Barbara Early/Ann Rutter (Phyllis/Lorraine), Ensemble: Paul Del Vecchio, Lynn Marlowe, Tony Parise, Brenda Pipik
MUSICAL NUMBERS: see Broadway Calendar

Martha Swope Photos

I DO! I DO!

Book and Lyrics, Tom Jones; Music, Harvey Schmidt; Based on "The Fourposter" by Jan de Hartog; Directed and Staged by Lucia Victor; Music Director, Gordon O. Brown; Costumes, Michael Bottari, Ronald Case; Set, Oliver Smith; Associate Conductor, Leo P. Carusone; Lighting, Ray Dooley; Presented by Theatre Management Inc.; Wigs/Hairstylist, Paul Huntley; Stage Managers, Ben Strobach, Patricia Drylie; Company Manager, Keith Dodge; Opened Tuesday, July 26, 1983 at Dallas Music Hall, and closed Sept. 25, 1983 at the Morris Mechanic Theatre in Baltimore, MD. For original Broadway production, see THEATRE WORLD Vol. 23.

CAST

She (Agnes) ....Lucie Arnaz
He (Michael) ....Laurence Luckinbill

Understudies: Beth Leavel, Dale Radunz

MUSICAL NUMBERS: Prologue, Good Night, I Love My Wife, Something Has Happened, My Cup Runneth Over, Love Isn't Everything, Nobody's Perfect, A Well Known Fact, Flaming Agnes, The Honeymoon Is Over, Where Are the Snows?, When the Kids Get Married, The Father of the Bride, What Is a Woman?, Someone Needs Me, Roll Up the Ribbons, This House

A musical in two acts. The action takes place in a bedroom and covers fifty years of marriage, beginning just before the turn of the century.

Laurence Luckinbill, Lucie Arnaz
(Marc Raboy Photo)

Andrea McArdle, Leslie Uggams, Jerry Herman, Carol Channing Above: Channing, Uggams

JERRY'S GIRLS

Music and Lyrics, Jerry Herman; Concept, Jerry Herman, Larry Alford; Staged and Directed by Larry Alford; Choreography, Sharon Halley; Set, Hal Tine; Costumes, David Dille; Lighting, Michael Newton-Brown; Musical Supervisor, Donald Pippin; Musical Conductor, Janet Glazener; Pianist, Maida Libkin; Orchestrations, Joseph Gianono, Christopher Bankey; General Management, Theatre Now; Sound, Peter J. Fitzgerald; Casting, Mark Reiner; Presented by Zev Bufman, Sidney Shlenker, Allen J. Becker, Barry Lewis, Miles Wilkin, and Nederlander Producing Co., Produced in association with Charles Lowe Productions; Associate Producers, Bruce Michael, Neil Fleckman; Stage Manager, Patrick Tolson; Press, Charles Cinnamon Associates. Opened at Royal Poinciana Playhouse in Palm Beach, FL. on Tuesday, Feb. 28, 1984 and still touring May 31, 1984.

CAST

Carol Channing	Leslie Uggams
Andrea McArdle	
Ellyn Arons	Suzanne Ishee
Laura Soltis	Diana Myron
Deborah Graham	Helena-Joyce Wright

MUSICAL NUMBERS: Jerry's Girls, Put on Your Sunday Clothes, It Only Takes a Moment, Wherever He Ain't, We Need a Little Christmas, I Won't Send Roses, Tap Your Troubles Away, Two-a-Day, Bosom Buddies, The Man in the Moon, So Long Dearie, I Wanna Make the World Laugh, Shalom, Milk and Honey, Show Tune, If He Walked into My Life, Hello Dolly, Just Go to the Movies, Movies Were Movies, Look What Happened to Mabel, Nelson, Time Heals Everything, It's Today, Mame, Kiss Her Now, The Tea Party, That's How Young I Feel, Gooch's Song, Before the Parade Passes By, I Don't Want to Know, La Cage aux Folles, Song on the Sand, I Am What I Am, The Best of Times

A musical entertainment in two acts.

THE KING AND I

Music, Richard Rodgers; Book and Lyrics, Oscar Hammerstein 2nd; Based on novel "Anna and the King of Siam" by Margaret Landon; Producer-Director, Mitch Leigh; Jerome Robbins' original choreography reproduced by Rebecca West; Scenery, John Jay Moore, Costumes, Stanley Simmons; Lighting, Ruth Roberts; Musical Director, Lawrence Brown; Production Supervisor, Conwell Worthington II; Costumes based on original by Irene Sharaff; Executive Producer, Milton Herson; Associate Producer, Manny Kladitis; Company Manager, Abbie M. Strassler; General Manager, Manny Kladitis, Props, Sam Bagarella, John Godsey; Wardrobe, Becky Denson, Gigi Nelson; Hairstylists, Burt Pitcher, Michael Gouty; Stage Managers, Kenneth L. Peck, John M. Galo, Charles Reif; Press, John A. Prescott. Opened at the Lyric Theatre in Baltimore, MD, Tuesday, Feb. 21, 1984 and still touring May 31, 1984. For original Broadway production, see THEATRE WORLD Vol. 7.

CAST

Captain Orton	Burt Edwards
Louis Leonowens	Jeffrey Bryan Davis
Anna Leonowens	Mary Beth Peil
Interpreter	Jae Woo Lee
Kralahome	Christopher Wynkoop
The King	Yul Brynner
Tuptim	Patricia Welch
Lady Thiang	Irma-Estel LaGuerre
Prince Chulalongkorn	Douglas Klaif
Princess Ying Yaowalak	Yvette Laura Martin
Lun Tha	Thomas Heath
Sir Edward Ramsey	Edward Crotty
Eliza/Lead Royal Dancer	Kathy Lee Brynner
Simon	Rebecca West
Angel/Fan Dancer	Patricia Weber
Topsy	Deborah Harada
Uncle Thomas	Hope Sogawa
Little Eva	Evelina Deocares
Royal Princess	Kathy Nghiem
Royal Prince	David Seaman

ENSEMBLE: Alis-Elaine Anderson, Marla F. Bingham, Gregg Busch, Joyce Campana, Mariann Cook, Kaipo Daniels, Carolyn DeLany, Evelina Deocares, Gary Bain Domasin, Deborah Harada, Stanley Earl Harrison, Janet Jordan, Thom Cordeiro Kam, Valerie Lau-Kee, Cornel Chan, Nancy Latuja, Andre Lengyel, Suzen H. Murakoshi, Siana, Hope Sogawa, Ron Stefan, Sylvia Yamada

STANDBYS & UNDERSTUDIES: Christopher Wynkoop (King), Mariann Cook (Anna), Edward Crotty (Orton), David Seaman (Louis), Kaipo Daniels (Interpreter), Jae Woo Lee (Kralahome), Carolyn DeLany (Tuptim), Joyce Campana (Thiang), Kathy Nghiem (Princess Ying), Gregg Busch (Lun Tha), Burt Edwards (Ramsey), Deborah Harada (Angel/Fan Dancer), Evelina Deocares (Lead Dancer), Sylvia Yamada (Eliza), Thom Cordeiro Kam (Simon), Siana (Topsy), Marla F. Bingham (Uncle Thomas), Nancy Latuja (Little Eva), Swings: Siana, Thom Cordeiro Kam

MUSICAL NUMBERS: I Whistle a Happy Tune, My Lord and Master, Hello Young Lovers, March of the Siamese Children, A Puzzlement, The Royal Bangkok Academy, Getting to Know You, We Kiss in a Shadow, Shall I Tell You What I Think of You?, Something Wonderful, Finale

A musical in two acts. The action occurs in and around the King's place in Bangkok in the 1860's.

Ernest Haas Photos

Top Left: Yul Brynner

"Small House of Uncle Thomas"

Lena Horne

LENA HORNE: THE LADY AND HER MUSIC

Concept by Lena Horne and Sherman Sneed; Musical Conductor, Linda Twine; Scenery, David Gropman; Lighting, Thomas Skelton; Miss Horne's Wardrobe, Giorgio Sant'Angelo; General Manager, Veronica Claypool; Overture orchestrated and arranged by Frank Owens; Production by arrangement with James Nederlander, Michael Frazier, Fred Walker in association with Jack Lawrence; Company Manager, Young Hughley; Assistant Conductor, Larry Nash; Presented by Shepperton, Ltd., Lavabrook Productions, Sherman Sneed (Executive Producer); Stage Managers, Clinton Turner Davis, Ron Nguvu; Press, Solters/Roskin/Friedman, Joshua Ellis, Cindy Valk, Irene Gandy. Opened Saturday, Sept. 11, 1982 at San Francisco's Golden Gate Theatre, and still touring May 31, 1984. For original Broadway production, see THEATRE WORLD Vol. 37.

COMPANY

Lena Horne   Stanley Perryman
Marva Hicks   Janice Harrison
Janet Powell   C. E. Smith

LENA'S QUINTET: Larry Nash (Keyboards), Rodney Jones (Guitar), Benjamin Franklin Brown (Bass), Ron Bridgewater (Reeds), Vinnie Johnson (Drums)
MUSICAL NUMBERS: A Lady Must Live, As Long as I Live, But Not for Me, Can't Help Lovin Dat Man, Copper Colored Gal of Mine, Day In Day Out, Deed I Do, Fly, From This Moment On, Honeysuckle Rose, I Got a Name, If You Believe, Just One of Those Things, Lady with a Fan, Let Me Be Your Mirror, Life Goes On, I Want to Be Happy, Push de Button, Raisin' the Rent, Stormy Weather, Where or When, Yesterday When I Was Young

A musical entertainment performed with one intermission.

Christian Steiner Photo

LYNDON

By James Prideaux; Based on the book "Lyndon" by Merle Miller; Director, George Schaefer; Set, Roy Christopher; Costumes, Al Lehman; Lighting, Marcia Madeira; General Managers, Theatre Now, Allan Francis; Associate Producers, Jerry Felix, Brian K. Gendece; Presented by Henry T. Weinstein, Robert W. Whitmore, Yale Wexler, Lester Osterman in association with Warner Bros. and Leslie Srager; Company Manager, Leonard Soloway; Production Supervisor, Jeremiah J. Harris; Props, Abe Einhorn; Makeup, Charles Schram; Wig, Ziggy; Stage Managers, Bill McComb, Peter Taylor; Press, Solters/Roskin/Friedman, Milly Schoenbaum, Kevin Patterson, Lisa Kasteler, Gail Brown. Opened Friday, Jan. 17, 1984 at the Playhouse in Wilmington, DE, and closed in Philadelphia's Shubert Theatre on Feb. 26, 1984.

CAST

Lyndon Baines Johnson .... Jack Klugman

A candid portrait of Lyndon Baines Johnson and his turbulent career as President of the United States.

Jack Klugman as Lyndon Johnson

145

NINE

Book, Arthur Kopit; Music/Lyrics/Choral Composition/Musical Continuity, Maury Yeston; Adaptation from the Italian by Mario Fratti; Director, Tommy Tune; Scenery, Lawrence Miller; Costumes, William Ivey Long; Lighting, Marcia Madeira; Orchestrations, Jonathan Tunick; Musical Supervision, Tommy Crasker; Choreography, Thommie Walsh, JoAnn Ogawa; General Management, Theatre Now; Sound, Jack Mann; Hairstylist, Angela Gari; Musical Conductor, Richard Parrinello; Casting, Hughes/Moss; Assistant Director, Bruce Lumpkin; Company Manager, Steven Suskin; Production Supervisor, Jeremiah J. Harris; Props, Edward Horton; Wardrobe, Sydney Smith; Production Associate, Susan L. Falk; Assistant Conductor, Norman Weiss; Production Assistant, Laura Balboni; Stage Managers, Roger Allan Raby, J. Marvin Crosland, Angie Wheeler; Press, Molly Smyth. Opened Saturday, Mar. 31, 1984 in the Opera House at JFK Center in Washington, DC, and still touring May 31, 1984. For original Broadway production, see THEATRE WORLD Vol. 38.

CAST

Guido Contini	Sergio Franchi
Guido at an early age	Danny Barak
Luisa	Diane M. Hurley
Carla	Karla Tamburrelli
Foofie	Murphey Nash
Claudia	Lauren Mitchell
Guido's Mother	Leigh Beery
La Fleur	Jacqueline Douguet
Ishi Darling	Chikae Ishikawa
Stephanie Necrophorus	Kathryn Skatula
Our Lady of the Spa	O'Hara Parker
Mama Maddelena	Holly Lipton Nash
Saraghina	Camille Saviola
Maria	Candace Rogers
Venetian Gondolier	Dorothy Kiara
Giulietta	Louise Edeiken
Annabella	Nancy McCall
Francesca	Barbara Walsh
Diana	Margareta Arvidsson
Renata	Pegg Winter
Gretchen von Krupf	Mary Stout
Heidi von Sturm	Mary Chesterman
Olga von Sturm	Lou Ann Miles
Ilsa von Hesse	Melody Jones
Young Guido's Schoolmates	Jason Dinter, Jonathan H. Florman, Philip Maranges

STANDBYS & UNDERSTUDIES: David Brummel (Guido), Chikae Ishikawa (La Fleur), O'Hara Parker (Claudia), Dorothy Kiara (Carla), Nancy McCall (Mother), Patrice Pickering (Our Lady/Ishi), Pegg Winter (Stephanie), Lou Ann Miles (Saraghina), Mary Stout (Mama), Leigh Finner (Germans), Patrice Pickering (Italians)

MUSICAL NUMBERS: Overture Delle Donne, Spa Music, Not Since Chaplin, Guido's Song, Coda di Guido, Germans at the Spa, My Husband Makes Movies, A Call from the Vatican, Only with You, Nine, Follies Bergeres, Ti Voglio Bene/Be Italian, Bells of St. Sebastian, A Man Like You, Unusual Way, Now's the Moment, Grand Canal, Simple, Be On Your Own, I Can't Make This Movie, Getting Tall, Long Ago

A musical in two acts.

Martha Swope Photos

Top Right: Sergio Franchi, Danny Barak, Leigh Beery

Lauren Mitchell, Jacqueline Douguet, Leigh Berry, Karla Tamburrelli surround Sergio Franchi

ON YOUR TOES

Music, Richard Rodgers; Lyrics, Lorenz Hart; Book, Rodgers & Hart, George Abbott; Director, George Abbott; Original Choreography, George Balanchine; Musical Numbers Staged by Donald Saddler; Additional Ballet Choreography, Peter Martins; Sets/ Costumes, Zack Brown; Lighting, John McLain; Original Orchestrations, Hans Spialek; Associate Producer/Musical Supervisor, John Mauceri; Musical Director, Scott Oakley; Sound, Jan Nebozenko; General Management, Theatre Now; Casting, Hughes/Moss; Presented by Zev Bufman, Sidney Shlenker, Allen J. Becker, Barry Lewis, Miles Wilkin, Nederlander Producing Co.; Company Manager, Helen V. Meier; Production Supervisor, Jeremiah J. Harris; Props, Chester Perry II; Wardrobe, Dean Jackson, Louis Fata; Stage Managers, Steven Beckler, Mark Rubinsky, Phil DiMaggio; Press, Marilynn LeVine, Merle Frimark, Meg Gordean. Opened Wednesday, March 21, 1984 in Miami Beach's Theatre of the Performing Arts, and closed April 29 at the Majestic Theatre in Dallas, TX. For original Broadway revival see THEATRE WORLD Vol. 39.

CAST

Phil Dolan II/Oscar	Terry Eno
Lil Dolan/Reporter	Margery Beddow
Phil Dolan III/(Junior)	Thom Keeling
Stage Manager/Joe/Cop	Richard Reuter-Smith
Lola	Michelle O'Steen
Junior (15 years later)	Michael Kubala
Sidney Cohn	N. A. Klein
Frankie Frayne	Susan Bigelow
Vera Baronova	Leslie Caron
Anushka	Tarry Caruso
Peggy Porterfield	Frances Bergen
Sergei Alexandrovitch	Stephen Pearlman
Konstantine Morrosine	Alexander Filipov
Stage Doorman	Michael O'Carroll
Dimitri	Alexander Kramarevsky
Ivan	Thomas Condon
Louie/Hank Jay Smith	William Ryall
Messenger Boy	Richard Stafford

"Princess Zenobia Ballet": Leslie Caron (Zenobia), Alexander Filipov (Beggar), William Ryall (Kinga Kahn), Michael O'Carroll (Ali Shar), Terry Eno (Ahmud Ben B'Du), "On Your Toes Ballet": Ballet Leaders: Alexander Kramarevsky, Rebecca Wright, Tap Leaders: Christopher d'Amboise, Michelle O'Steen, "Slaughter on Tenth Avenue Ballet": Michael Kubala (Hoofer), Leslie Caron (Strip Tease Girl), Richard Reuter-Smith (Big Boss), George P. Saunders (Cop), Barry Ramsey (Plainclothesman), Thomas Condon, Alexander Kramarevsky, Barry Ramsey (Police)
ENSEMBLE: Tarry Caruso, Thomas Condon, Christine Cookson, Christopher d'Amboise, Diana Gonzalez, Michaela Hughes, Thom Keeling, Kristine Kepright, Alexander Kramarevsky, David Lowenstein, Michael O'Carroll, Michelle O'Steen, Barry Ramey, Richard Reuter-Smith, William Ryall, George P. Saunders, Richard Stafford, Ellen Troy, Rebecca Wright, Swings: Quin Aluni, Troy Myers, Amy O'Brien, Claudia Shell
UNDERSTUDIES: Rebecca Wright (Vera), Christopher d'Amboise (Junior), Michael O'Carroll (Sergei), Michaela Hughes (Peggy), Alexander Kramarevsky (Konstantine), Christine Cookson (Frankie), Richard Stafford (Phil II/Oscar), Tarry Caruso (Lil/Reporter), Thom Keeling (Cohn), George P. Sanders (Stage Manager/Joe/Cop), Thomas Condon (DiMitri), Richard Reuter-Smith (Louis/Hank), Ellen Troy (Ballet Leader)
MUSICAL NUMBERS: see Broadway Calendar

A musical in 2 acts and 12 scenes.

Martha Swope Photos

Top Right: Leslie Caron, Michael Kubala

Michael Kubala, Susan Bigelow

A SENSE OF HUMOR

By Ernest Thompson; Director, Robert Greenwald; Scenery/Lighting, Gerry Hariton/Vicki Baral; Costumes, Len Marcus; Miss Parson's Costumes, Ruth Morley; Special Artwork, D. J. Hall; Associate Producer, James Hansen; General Management, Joseph P. Harris Associates; Company Manager, John Caruso; Technical Director, Robert Routolo; Props, Steve Rapollo; Wardrobe, Eddie Dodds; Incidental Music, Shelly Manne; Casting, Johnson/Liff, Dinman Co.; Presented by Robert Fryer and Frank von Zerneck in association with Center Theatre Group/Ahmanson Theatre, Los Angeles; Stage Managers, A. Robert Altshuler, Jerry Trent; Press, Fred Nathan, Anne Abrams, Leslie Anderson, Bert Fink. Opened Wednesday, Nov. 16, 1983 in Denver's Auditorium Theatre, and closed Feb. 26, 1984 in San Francisco's Curran Theatre.

CAST

Richard Dale ....Jack Lemmon
Elizabeth Dale .... Estelle Parsons
Abe Manning .... Clifton James
Jean Manning .... Polly Holliday

Standbys: Warren Munson, Liz Sheridan

A drama in 2 acts and 4 scenes: Nonsense, Innocents, Ascents of Decency, A Sense of Humor.

Martha Swope Photos

Estelle Parsons, Polly Holliday, Jack Lemmon, Clifton James
Top Left: Jack Lemmon, Estelle Parsons

Adolph Caesar, Larry Riley

A SOLDIER'S PLAY

By Charles Fuller; Director, Douglas Turner Ward; Set, Felix E. Cochren; Costumes, Judy Dearing; Lighting, Allen Lee Hughes; Stage Manager, Janice C. Lane; Opened Friday, June 3, 1983 at the Goodman Theatre in Chicago, and closed May 20, 1984 at the Coconut Grove Playhouse in Coconut Grove, Florida.

CAST

Sgt. Waters	Graham Brown
Capt. Charles Taylor	Danny Goldring
Cpl. Bernard Cobb	Ruben Hudson
PFC Melvin Peterson	O. L. Duke
Cpl. Ellis	Cedric Turner
Pvt. Louis Henson	Robert Gossett
Pvt. James Wilkie	Steven A. Jones
Pvt. Tony Smalls	Lanyard A. Williams
Capt. Richard Davenport	Geoffrey Ewing
Pvt. C. J. Memphis	Ben E. Epps
Lt. Byrd	Gary Armagnac
Capt. Wilcox	Stephen Zettler

Bert Andrews Photos

Adolph Caesar, Larry Riley

TORCH SONG TRILOGY

By Harvey Fierstein; Director, Peter Pope; Sets, Bill Stabile; Costumes, Mardi Philips; Lighting, Martin Aronstein; Musical Director, Rick Jensen; General Management, Theatre Now; Musical Supervision/Arrangements, Ned Levy; Original Music, Ada Janik; Associate Producer, Howard Perloff; General Manager, Edward H. Davis; Company Managers, Thomas W. Parlett, David Wyler; Props, Richard LaRose; Wardrobe, Jan Edwards; Stage Managers, John Weeks, Clifford Schwartz, Raymond Gin; Press, Betty Lee Hunt, Maria Cristina Pucci, James Sapp, Spittel & Kephart. Opened Tuesday, June 21, 1983 in San Francisco's Theatre on the Square, and closed in Los Angeles at the Huntington Hartford Theatre on June 2, 1984. For original Broadway production, see THEATRE WORLD Vol. 39.

CAST

Lady Blues ....Meg Mackay
Arnold Beckoff ....Donald Corren [1]
Ed ....Brian Kerwin [2]
Laurel ....Meg Mackay
Alan ....Marc Poppel [3]
David ....Christopher Collet [4]
Mrs. Beckoff ....Sylvia Kauders [5]

STANDBYS & UNDERSTUDIES: Jerry Pavlon (Alan/David), Alison Bevan (Lady Blues/Laurel), Fritzi Burr (Mrs. Beckoff), J. David Krassner (Arnold/played matinees), John Seeman (Ed/played matinees)

[†]Succeeded by: 1. Jonathan Hadary, Harvey Fierstein, 2. Jared Martin, 3. Paul Joynt, 4. Jon Cryer, 5. Estelle Getty

A play in three acts.

Right: Donald Corren, Marc Poppel
(Ron Scherl Photo)

Jonathan Hadary, Estelle Getty
(Gerry Goodstein Photo)

THE WIZ

Music & Lyrics, Charlie Smalls; Book, William F. Brown; Based on "The Wonderful Wizard of Oz"; Direction/Costumes, Geoffrey Holder; Scenery, Peter Wolf; Lighting, Paul Sullivan; Orchestrations, Harold Wheeler; Musical Direction/Vocal Arrangements, Charles H. Coleman; Dance Arrangements, Timothy Graphenreed; Choreography and Musical Numbers staged by George Faison; Sound, Gary M. Stocker; General Management, American Theatre Productions; Company Manager, Daryl T. Dodson; Props, Robert Michaels; Wardrobe, Linda Berry, Jude Timlin; Makeup, Joseph McDevitt; Wigs/Hairstyles, Ray Iagnocco; Presented by Tom Mallow, James Janek and the Shubert Organization; Stage Managers, Jack Welles, Luis Montero, Nate Barnett; Press, Max Eisen, Barbara Glenn, Maria Somma; Opened at Boston's Shubert Theatre on Friday, Sept. 16, 1983 and still touring May 31, 1984. For original Broadway production, see THEATRE WORLD Vol. 31.

CAST

Aunt Em	Juanita Fleming
Dorothy	Stephanie Mills
Uncle Henry	David Weatherspoon
Tornado	Sharon Brooks
Munchkins	Ada Dyer, Lawrence Hamilton
	Sam Harkness, David Weatherspoon, Carol Dennis
Addaperle	John-Ann Washington
Yellow Brick Road	Germaine Edwards, David Robertson,
	Alfred L. Dove, Dwight Leon
Scarecrow	Charles Valentino
Sunflowers	Ada Dyer, Carol Dennis,
	David Weatherspoon, Sam Harkness
Crows	Paula Anita Brown, Jasmine Guy,
	Marvin Roberson
Tinman	Howard Porter
Lion	Gregg Baker
Strangers	David Weatherspoon, Carol Dennis,
	Sam Harkness
Kalidahas	Marvin Roberson, Jasmine Guy,
	Gigi Hunter, Lawrence Hamilton, Martial Roumain
Poppies	Sharon Brooks, Paula Anita Brown,
	Daryl Richardson, Tanya Gibson
Chief of the Field Mice	Ada Dyer
Royal Gatekeeper	Sam Harkness
Head of the Society of Emerald City	Carol Dennis
The Wiz	Carl Hall
Evillene	Ella Mitchell
Lord High Underling	Lawrence Hamilton
Soldier Messenger	Marvin Roberson
Winged Monkey	Germaine Edwards
Glinda	Ann Duquesnay

EMERALD CITY CITIZENS: Sharon Brooks, Paula Anita Brown, Alfred L. Dove, Ada Dyer, Germaine Edwards, Tanya Gibson, Jasmine Guy, Lawrence Hamilton, Sam Harkness, Gigi Hunter, Dwight Leon, Daryl Richardson, Marvin Roberson, David Robertson, Martial Roumain
UNDERSTUDIES: Ada Dyer (Dorothy), Ann Duquesnay (Aunt Em), Sharon Brooks (Glinda), Carol Dennis (Addaperle), Juanita Fleming (Evillene), Germaine Edwards (Scarecrow), Sam Harkness (Lion), David Weatherspoon (Wiz), Lawrence Hamilton (Tinman), Alfred L. Dove (Winged Monkey), Daryl Richardson (Tornado), Swing: Sheri Moore, De Lawrence J. Young
MUSICAL NUMBERS: The Feeling We Once Had, Tornado Ballet, He's the Wizard, Soon as I Get Home, I Was Born on the Day Before Yesterday, Ease on Down the Road, Slide Some Oil to Me, Mean Ole Lion, Kalidah Battle, Be a Lion, Lion's Dream, Emerald City Ballet, So You Wanted to Meet the Wizard, What Would I Do If I Could Feel, No Bad News, Funky Monkeys, Wonder Why, Don't Cry Girl, Everybody Rejoice, Who Do You Think You Are?, If You Believe, Y'all Got It!, A Rested Body Is a Rested Mind, Home

A musical in 2 acts and 16 scenes.

Kenn Duncan Photos

**Top Right: Stephanie Mills, Gregg Baker (Lion),
Howard Porter (Tinman), Charles Valentino (Scarecrow)
Below: (c) John-Ann Washington, Stephanie Mills**

Carl Hall (center)

WOMAN OF THE YEAR

Book, Peter Stone; Based on MGM Film by Ring Lardner, Jr. and Michael Kanin; Music, John Kander; Lyrics, Fred Ebb; Direction and Choreography, Joe Layton; Sets, Tony Walton; Costumes, Theoni V. Aldredge; Lighting, Marilyn Rennagel; Sound, Abe Jacob; Musical Direction, Jay Blackton; Orchestrations, Michael Gibson; Vocal Arrangements, Donald Pippin; Dance Arrangements, Glen Roven; Animations, Michael Sporn; General Manager, Marvin Krauss; Hairstylist, Masarone; Casting, Hughes/Moss; Production Associate, Denny Shearer; Company Manager, Bob Skerry; Props, Charles Zuckerman, Munro Gabler, William Garvey; Wardrobe, Max Hager, Ellen Lee; Miss Bacall's wardrobe by Halston; Presented by Lawrence Kasha, David S. Landay, James M. Nederlander, Warner Theatre Productions/Claire Nichtern, Carole J. Shorenstein, Steward F. Lane; Stage Managers, Jay B. Jacobson, Jeanne Fornadel, Victor Lukas; Press, Solters/Roskin/Friedman, Joshua Ellis, Cindy Valk, Gail Browne, Lisa Kasteler, Gail Block. For original Broadway production, see THEATRE WORLD Vol. 37.

CAST

Tess Harding	Lauren Bacall
Chairperson	Helon Blount
Floor Manager	Timm Stetzner
Chip Salisbury	John Hammil
Gerald	Emory Bass
Helga	Kathleen Freeman
Abbott Canfield	Dennis Parlato
Phil Whitaker	William H. McDonald
Pinky Peters	Bill Bateman
Ellis McMaster	Ted Agress
Sam Craig	Harry Guardino
Tony	Gene Castle
Maury	Michael Norris
Prescott	Michael Laughlin
Gordon	Fitzhugh G. Houston
Alexi Petrikov	James P. Hogan
Ballet Mistress	Sybil Scotford
Prima Ballerina	Sheryll Fager-Jones
Jan Donovan	Marilyn Cooper
Larry Donovan	Del Hinkley

ENSEMBLE: Belle Calaway, Sheryll Fager-Jones, Fitzhugh G. Houston, Michael Laughlin, Donna Monroe, Michael Norris, Sybil Scotford, Denny Shearer, Timm Stetzner, Swings: Greg Mowry, Cathy Susan Pyles
UNDERSTUDIES: Greg Mowry (Alexi), Sybil Scotford (Helga), Michael Norris (Chip), Belle Calaway (Tess), Del Hinkley (Sam), Cathy Susan Pyles (Jan), Michael Laughlin (Abbott/Ellis), Denny Shearer (Pinky), Fitzhugh G. Houston (Phil), Bill Bateman (Gerald), Dennis Parlato (Larry)
MUSICAL NUMBERS: Woman of the Year, See You in the Funny Papers, When You're Right You're Right, Shut Up Gerald, So What Else Is New, Poker Game, One of the Boys, Table Talk, The Two of Us, It Isn't Working, I Told You So, I Wrote the Book, Happy in the Morning, Sometimes a Day Goes By, The Grass Is Always Greener, Open the Window Sam, Finale

A musical in 2 acts and 14 scenes.

Lauren Bacall, Marilyn Cooper

Alan Berliner Photos

Top: Bill Bateman, Lauren Bacall, Ted Agress, Dennis Parlato, William H. McDonald

152

PROFESSIONAL RESIDENT COMPANIES

ABSOLUTE THEATRE COMPANY

Chicago, Illinois
October 1983–July 1984
Artistic Director, Warner Crocker; General Manager, Wes Payne; Associate Director, Michael Leavitt; Marketing Director, Ellen Taylor; Stage Manager, Peggy Miller; Literary Manager, Cheri Chenoweth; Sets, John Story II; Costumes, Donna Marr

COMPANY: Larry Baldacci, Elaine Carlson, Cheri Chenoweth, Steven Fedoruk, Alex Kerr, Nicholas R. Kusenko, Michael Leavitt, Peggy Miller, Mary Peterson, David Puszkiewicz, Robert Rothman, James Winfrey, *Guest Artist* Michael Nowak
PRODUCTIONS: Happy End, Six Characters in Search of an Author, A Cry of Players, Come Back to the 5 and Dime, Jimmy Dean, Jimmy Dean

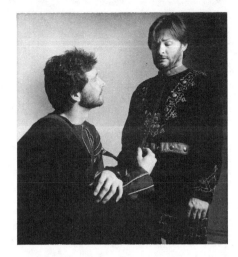

**Right: Nicholas Kusenko, David Puski
in "Ironhand"** *(Jennifer Gerard Photo)*

ACT: A CONTEMPORARY THEATRE

Seattle, Washington
May 3, 1983–May 26, 1984
Nineteenth Season
Producing Director, Gregory A. Falls; Producing Manager, Phil Schermer; Administrative Manager, Susan Trapnell Moritz; Stage Managers, Joan Kennedy, Julie Anderson; Development, Ann-Marie Spata; Press, Michael Eagan, Jr.

PRODUCTIONS AND CASTS
THE DRESSER by Ronald Harwood; Director, Jay Broad; Set, Shelley Henze Schermer; Costumes, Susan Min; Lighting, Jody Briggs; Sound, Carmine Simone. CAST: Dick Arnold, Jahnna Beecham, Robert Blumenfeld, Lee Corrigan, Donald Ewer, Livia Genise, Jerry Harper, Gwen Jackson, Robert Loper, Anthony Motzenbacker, Nelsen Beim Spickard
THE DINING ROOM by A. R. Gurney, Jr.; Director, Lou Salerni; Set, Scott Weldin; Costumes, Marian Hill Cottrell; Lighting, Christopher Beardsley. CAST: Jahnna Beecham, Malcolm Hillgartner, Suzy Hunt, Peggy Schoditsch, Bill terKuile
CRIMES OF THE HEART by Beth Henley; Director, M. Burke Walker; Set, Bill Forrester; Costumes, Shay Cunliffe; Lighting, Donna Grout. CAST: Kathy Danzer, Brian Faker, Suzanna Hay, Malcolm Hillgartner, Patricia Miller, Rebecca Wells
EDUCATING RITA by Willy Russell; Director, Sharon Ott; Set, Robert Dahlstrom; Costumes, Shay Cunliffe; Lighting, Jeff Robbins; Sound, Carmine Simone. CAST: Gale Garnett, Eberle Thomas
A SOLDIER'S PLAY by Charles Fuller; Performed by the touring Negro Ensemble Company cast.
CLOUD 9 by Caryl Churchill; Director, Jeff Steitzer; Set, Bill Raoul; Costumes, Sally Richardson; Lighting, Phil Schermer. CAST: Keith Langsdale, William O'Leary, Jeanne Paulsen, Rex Rabold, Richard Riehle, Peggy Schoditsch, Nina Wishengrad, Kevin Loomis
A CHRISTMAS CAROL by Charles Dickens; Adapted by Gregory A. Falls; Music, Robert MacDougall; Director, Mr. Falls; Set, Bill Forrester; Costumes, Nanrose Buchman; Lighting, Jody Briggs; Choreographer, Valerie Dunne; Stage Manager, Bonita M. Ernst. CAST: John Gilbert, Ben Tone, Brian Martin, Tony Soper, Michael Schauermann, Vern Taylor, Noah Marks, Amy Steltz, Noya Jacobson, Mary Van Arsdel, Ben Silver, Alvin Lee Sanders, Rich Rand, Christopher Marks, Terres Unsoeld, Nina Wishengrad, David Colacci, Adam Silver, Kathleen Worley, Robert John Zenk
THE FLYING KARAMAZOV BROTHERS: Timothy Daniel Furst, Paul David Magid, Randy Nelson, Howard Jay Patterson, Sam Williams, Wow, Flutter
AMADEUS by Peter Shaffer; Director, Jeff Steitzer; Set, Shelley Henze Schermer; Costumes, Sarah Nash Gates; Lighting, Phil Schermer; Sound, Lindsay Smith; Stage Manager, Bonita M. Ernst. CAST: John Gilbert, James W. Monitor, David Pichette, R. A. Farrell, Peter Silbert, Jerry Harper, Frank Borgman, Rick Tutor, Larry Paulsen, Rod Pilloud, Jeanne Paulsen, Helene McCardle, Ki Gottberg, Gwynne Rhynedance, Brian Hargrove, Kevin C. Loomis, Joshua Gillow, Rex E. Allen, Helene McCardle, Larry Paulsen, Rod Pilloud

Chris Bennion Photo

**John Gilbert (center left), Brian Hargrove
(center) in "Amadeus"** *(Chris Bennion Photo)*

ACTORS THEATRE OF LOUISVILLE

Louisville, Kentucky
Twentieth Season

Producing Director, Jon Jory; Administrative Director, Alexander Speer; Associate Director, Marilee Hebert-Slater; Press, Jenan Dorman, Mina S. Davis, Chris Boneau; Assistant to Mr. Jory, Corey Beth Madden; Business/Management, Patrick Michae; James Roemer, Jake Studebaker; Festival Coordination, Marcia Tarbis Tofteland, Melanie L. Morehouse; Company Manager, Frazier W. Marsh; Directors, Kent Broadhurst, Tom Bullard, Larry Deckel, Oskar Eustis, Ray Fry, Ken Jenkins, Jon Jory, Barnet Kellman, Frazier W. Marsh, Laszlo Marton, Vaughn McBride, Adale O'Brien, John Pielmeier, Robert Spera, Anthony Taccone, Patrick Tovatt; Stage Managers, Susanna M. Banks, C. A. Clark, Richard A. Cunningham, Jeff Hill, Benita Hofstetter, Bob Hornung, Cynthia A. Hood, Elizabeth Ives, George Kimmel, Mark Luking, Barbara A. Lutz, Frazier W. Marsh, Janice Neustedter, Sandra Strawn, Craig Weindling, Frank Wicks; Sets, Paul Owen, Sandra Strawn, Miklos Fehrer; Costumes, Marcia Dixcy, Karen Gerson, Kurt Wilhelm, Katherine Bonner; Lights, Jeff Hill, Karl Haas, Geoffrey T. Cunningham, Joe Ragey; Sound, James M. Bay; Technical Director, Tom Rupp; Costumiere, Leslie Miller

COMPANY: Andy Backer, Bob Burrus, Ray Fry, Michael Kevin, Bruce Kuhn, Frederic Major, Vaughn McBride, Adale O'Brien, Steve Rankin, Fred Sanders, Dierk Torsek, John C. Vennema

GUEST ARTISTS: Joseph Adams, Katherine Borowitz, Dennis Boutsikaris, Fran Brill, Thomas Martell Brimm, Kent Broadhurst, Dorothy Brooks, Cheryl Lynn Bruce, Susan Bruyn, Margaret Castleman, Jude Ciccollela, Lynn Cohen, Shelley Crandall, Gloria Cromwell, Dawn Didawick, Beth Dixon, Lee Anne Fahey, Clarence Felder, Lanny Flaherty, J. E. Freeman, Sylvia Gassel, Georgine Hall, Marilyn Hamlin, Jan Leslie Harding, Suzanna Hay, Deborah Hedwall, Laura Hicks, Lorri Holt, Patrick Husted, Ken Jenkins, Robert Judd, Christian Kauffman, Caroline Kava, George Kimmel, Susan Kingsley, Ruth Livingston, Margo Martindale, Theresa Merritt, Nancy Mette, Dana Mills, Debra Monk, Elizabeth Moore, Tania Myren, Basia McCoy, Tanny McDonald, Sally Parrish, Natalie Ross, Shyrl Ryanhartt, David Sabin, Nancy Niles Sexton, Joan Shangold, Mary Shelley, Anne Shropshire, Barbara Sohmers, John Spencer, Fritz Sperberg, June Stein, Hal Tenny, Ellen Tobie, John Turturro, Gretchen West

PRODUCTIONS: A Midsummer Night's Dream, Holy Ghosts, A Christmas Carol, Of Mice and Men, A Coupla White Chicks Sitting Around Talking, Dial M for Murder, The Middle Ages, The Gift of the Magi, The Three Sisters, Extremities, Cemetery Man, Rupert's Birthday, Rodeo, Twirler, Bartók as Dog, Clear Glass Marbles, Cheek to Cheek, Goober's Descent, The Laundromat, Gervelles au Beurre Noir

'83 SHORTS: Businessman's Lunch by Michael David Quinn, Well Learned by Andrew J. Bondor, Creative Pleas by Fred Sanders, What Comes after Ohio? by Daniel Meltzer, Approaching Lavendar by Julie Beckett Crutcher, The Renovation by Susan Sandler, Coastal Waters by Corey Beth Madden, Girl in Green Stockings by Kenneth Pressman, Graceland by Ellen Byron, Husbandry by Patrick Tovatt, The Death of King Philip by Romulus Linney, Couvade by Sallie Bingham, A Gothic Tale by John Pielmeier, Cuffs by Lee Eisenberg, Arts and Leisure by Paul Rudnick, Sweet Sixteen by David Bradley, Five Ives Gets Named by Roy Blount, Jr., American Tropical by Richard Ford, Shasta Rue by Jane Martin

HUMANA FESTIVAL OF NEW AMERICAN PLAYS: Danny and the Deep Blue Sea by John Patrick Shanley, Independence by Lee Blessing, The Octette Bridge Club by P. J. Barry, Execution of Justice by Emily Mann, Lemons by Kent Broadhurst, The Undoing by William Mastrosimone, 007 Crossfire by Ken Jenkins

David S. Talbott Photos
Top: Mary Shelley, Lynn Cohen, Sylvia Gassell,
Sally Parrish in "The Octette Bridge Club"

John Vennema, Susan Kingsley
in "A Gothic Tale" Top: June Stein,
John Turturro in "Danny and the Deep Blue Sea"

154

ALASKA REPERTORY THEATRE

Anchorage/Fairbanks, Alaska
October 13, 1983–March 25, 1984
Eighth Season

Artistic Director, Robert J. Farley; Producing Director, Paul Brown; Associate Artistic Directors, John Going, Walton Jones; Managing Director, Mark Somers; Production Manager, Bennett Taber; General Manager, Dan Dixon; Sets, Karen Gjelsteen, Michael Stauffer, David Potts, Kevin Rupnik; Costumes, Cathleen Edwards, Michael Olich, William Schroder, Dunya Ramicova; Lighting, Judy Rasmuson, Michael Stauffer, Dennis Parichy, Donald Thomas, Michael Chybowski; Sound, Stephen Bennett, Bill Henderson; Stage Managers, Carol Chiavetta, Pam Guion; Press, Erick Borland, Patricia Eckert; Photographers, Christopher Arend, David Predeger.

PRODUCTIONS:

ALL MY SONS by Arthur Miller. CAST: Thomas Carson, Nora Chester, Sid Conrad, Elliott Gagnon, Terry Layman, Gary McGurk, Nancy Nichols, Charles Shaw Robinson, Dorothy Stinnette, Jana Schneider

WINGS by Arthur Kopit. CAST: Nicola-Maria Barthen, Nora Chester, Jerry Harper, Annie Stokes Hutchinson, Gary McGurk, Mary Nell Santacroce, Mary Lou Spartz, Tony Vita, Gerald Wilson

THE PHILADELPHIA STORY by Philip Barry. CAST: Joseph Culliton, Larking Ford, Susie Foster, Vanya Franck, Jerry Harper, Tim James, Bram Lewis, Jay Louden, James McDonnell, Monica Merryman, Michael Mitchell, Perrin Morse, Kate Mulgrew, Jim Oyster, Susan Reilly, Pete Sugden

TARTUFFE by Moliere. CAST: Maury Cooper, Susie Foster, Conan McCarty, Peter MacNicol, Jane Murray, Patricia Norcia, Michael Paul, Marina Posvar, Gavin Reed, Ellen Schafroth, John Shuman, Paul Thomas, Mary Van Dyke

Lorna Erickson, Edward Billups, Jack Hoffman in "Threepenny Opera" *(Charles Rafshoon Photo)*

ALLIANCE THEATRE COMPANY

Atlanta, Georgia
September 7, 1983–June 17, 1984
Fifteenth Season

Artistic Director, Fred Chappell; Managing Director, Andrew Witt; Press, Kim Resnik, Brock Haley; Literary Manager, Sandra Deer; Development Director, Betty Blondeau; Production Manager, Billings Lapierre; Associate Director, Kent Stephens

A STREET CAR NAMED DESIRE by Tennessee Williams; Director, Fred Chappell; Set, Philip Jung; Lighting, Michael Stauffer; Costumes, Susan Hirschfeld; Stage Managers, Pat F. Waldorf, Gretchen Van Horne. CAST: Sharlene Ross (Neighbor), Jill Jane Clements (Eunice), John Homa (Stanley), Della Cole (Stella), Al Hamacher (Steve), Tracy Griswold (Mitch), Jan Maris (Merican Woman/Nurse), Linda Stephens (Blanche), Rudy Goldschmidt (Young Collector), Jim Peck (Doctor)

IN THE SWEET BYE AND BYE by Donald Driver; Director, Kent Stephens; Set, Mark Morton; Lighting, William Duncan; Costumes, Susan Mickey; Stage Managers, Gretchen van Horne, Pat Flora. CAST: Bella Jarrett (Jessie), John Sterling Arnold (Hagen), Al Hamacher (Lamar Shooler), Ellen Heard (Neva), Craige Christensen (Carmel), Jon Kohler (Bill)

THE MUSIC MAN with Book/Music/Lyrics by Meredith Willson; Story, Meredith Willson, Frank Lacey; Set, Mark Morton; Costumes, Susan Hirschfeld; Lighting, Jason Kantrowitz; Musical Director, Michael Fauss; Choreography, Dennis Dennehy; Director, Edward Stone; Stage Managers, Pat Flora, Gretchen van Horne. CAST: Traveling Salesmen: Brent Black, Ken Ellis, Kenny Gannon, Rob Roper, Darren Stephens, Brian White, Adrian Elder (Charlie), Steven Olsen (Conductor), Jeff Keller (Harold Hill), Adrian Elder (Mayor), Jon Kohler (Marcellus), Betty Leighton (Eulalie), Leslie Hicks (Marian), Jill Jane Clements (Mrs. Paroo), Tricia Grant (Amaryllis), Zack Finch (Winthrop), Ken Ellis (Jacey), Kenny Gannon (Ewart), Steven Olsen (Oliver), Bob Roper (Olin), Wayne Lancaster (Tommy), Bridget Knox (Gracie), Kay McClelland (Alma), Jan Maris (Alma), Judy Longofrod (Maud), Roberta Illg (Ethel), Megan McFarland (Hazel), Robby Pressy (Avis), Brent Black (Constable), Townspeople and Kids: Kristin Galloway, Kim Guenther, Merle Halliday, Dawn Hopper, Robert Mackey, B. J. McGroskey, Vince Pesce, Darren Stephens, David Sterner, Angela Pridgen, Brian White, Frank Wood

CRIMES OF THE HEART by Beth Henley; Director, Fred Chappell. CAST: Jill Jane Clements (Lenny), Ginny Parker (Chick), Dan Doby (Doc), Marianne Hammock (Meg), Tina Smith (Babe), Brooks Baldwin (Barnette)

THE THREEPENNY OPERA with Book/Lyrics, Bertolt Brecht; Music, Kurt Weill; English Adaptation, Marc Blitzstein; Director, Kent Stephens; Choreography, Rick Goss; Musical Director, Michael Fauss; Set, Michael Stauffer; Lighting, Cassandra Henning; Costumes, Susan Hirschfeld. CAST: Chandra Currelli (Streetsinger), Jack Hoffmann (Peachum), Lorna Erickson (Mrs. Peachum), Edward W. Billups III (Filch), Keith David (Macheath), Kay D. McClelland (Polly), Thos Shipley (Readymoney), Al Garrison (Crookfinger), Joseph Wise (Bob the Saw), Jihad Babatunde (Walt), Calvin Smith (Rev. Kimball), Eddie Lee (Tiger Brown), Olivia Virgil Harper (Jenny), Felicia Hernandez (Betty), Kathleen Jackson (Molly), Sharlene Ross (Dolly), Pat Harding (Coaxer), Jon Menick (Smith/Warden), Michele-Denise Woods (Lucy), Don Spalding/Brent Black (Policemen), Edward W. Billups III (Messenger), Sharon Caplan (Dancer/Singer)

JULIUS CAESAR by William Shakespeare; Director, Robert Woodruff; Composer/Arranger, William Harper; Lighting, Paulie Jenkins; Sound, David M. Lyons; Battle Choreographer, Susan Eldridge. CAST: Seth Allen (Marcus Brutus), William Russ (Cassius), Eddie Lee (Trebonius), Don Spalding (Decius Brutus), Jihad Babatunde (Metellus Cimber), John Purcell (Cinna), Skip Foster (Casca), Ken Strong (Octavius Caesar), Jamey Sheridan (Marcus Antonius), Bruce Evers (Lepidus), Neil Vipond (Julius Caesar), Tony Thomas (Cicero), Marc Clement (Flavius), Jack Hoffmann (Marullus), Stuart Culpepper (Artemidorus), Al Hamacher (Cinna the Poet), Marc Clement (Lucilius), Jack Hoffmann (Claudius), Brent Black (Varro), Don Spalding (Worker/Poet), Joey Chavez (Lucius), John Purcell (Pindarus), Hugh D. Cobb (Cobbler), Bruce Evers (Carpenter), Brent Black, Patricia Lundberg, B. James Hughes, Brent Plack (Servants), Linda Stephens (Calpurnia), Marianne Hammock), Messengers: Darren Stephens, B. James Hughes, Patricia Lundberg (Beggar Woman)

TRUE WEST by Sam Shepard; Director, Kent Stephens; Set, Nancy Margaret Orr; Lighting, P. Hamilton Shinn; Costumes, J. Thomas Seagraves; Stage Managers, Kathy Richardson, Dale C. Lawrence. CAST: Tom Fitzsimmons (Austin), Skip Foster (Lee), Sid Shier (Saul), Laura Whyte (Mom)

WORLD PREMIERES:

THE BOYS IN AUTUMN by Bernard Sabath; Director, Fred Chappell; Set, Johnny Thigpen; Lighting, Paul Ackerman; Costumes, Judy Winograd; Stage Manager, Kathy Richardson. CAST: Robert Blackburn (Henry Finnegan), Alan Mixon (Thomas Gray)

THE GRUBB CHRONICLES by Eddie Lee, Larry Larson; Directors, Kent Stephens, Skip Foster; Stage Manager, John Courtney. CAST: John Courtney (Fang/Klieg), Bill Nunn (Dinosaur/Tar Lady/Dragon/Alpo), Mary Lynn Owen (Grubb), Jackie Welch (Tang/Reena)

Left Center: Peter MacNicol, Jane Murray in "Tartuffe" *(Christopher Arend Photo)*

ALLEY THEATRE

Houston, Texas
October 20, 1983–August 26, 1984
Thirty-seventh Season
Artistic Director, Pat Brown; Managing Director, Tom Spray; Associate Artistic Director, George Anderson; Production Manager, Trevor Smith; Technical Director, Joe Kaplor; Sets, Keith Belli, Dale F. Jordan; Costumes, Ainslie G. Bruneau, Fortini Dimou, Lighting, Richard W. Jeter; Stage Managers, Richard Earl Laster, Katherine M. Goodrich, Glenn Bruner, Robert S. Garber, Ann Arganbright, Cathy A Frank; Wardrobe, Bernadette Schmeits, Sandra Flowers; Props, Suzanne Kaplor, Mary Conley, Megan McGavran; Sound, Tony Johnson; Press, Bob Feingold, Michael Tiknis

COMPANY: Ruth E. Adams, Timothy Arrington, Sue Batchelor, Steve Brush, John Cagan, Dante DiLoreto, Lillian Evans, Bettye Fitzpatrick, Ken Fowler, Bonnie Gallup, Melissa Ann Gray, Daydrie Hague, Anthony Hendrix, Richard Hill, Trent Jenkins, Kent Johnson, Cynthia Lammel, Dan LaRocque, Jo Marks, Lawr Means, Sarah Jane Moody, Karen Friman Morris, Robin Moseley, Bruce Norris, Patrick Nugent, Mitchell Patrick, Richard Poe, Beth Sanford, Brandon Smith, John Vreeke, John Woodson
PRODUCTIONS: The Dresser by Ronald Harwood, Donkeys' Years by Michael Frayn, All My Sons by Arthur Miller, Crimes of the Heart by Beth Henley, Uncle Vanya by Anton Chekhov, 'night, Mother by Marsha Norman, Winnie-the-Pooh by Beth Sanford, Cloud 9 by Caryl Churchill, True West by Sam Shepard, Angels Fall by Lanford Wilson, Cold Feet by Diane Corley, Little Bird by Mary Gallagher, Words from the Moon by Tom Ross, Conversations by Gloria Parkinson, Bad Bad Jo-Jo by James Leo Herlihy, Patio by Jack Heifner, Anna Akhmatova by Beth Sanford, and *Premiere* of Amateurs by Tom Griffin

**Joe Barrett, Tanny McDonald-Wright
in "Cloud 9"**

AMERICAN CONSERVATORY THEATRE

San Francisco, California
November 1, 1983–June 2, 1984
Eighteenth Season
General Director, William Ball; Conservatory Director, Allen Fletcher; Managing Director, Benjamin Moore; Treasurer, James B. McKenzie; Stage Directors, William Ball, Eugene Barcone, James Edmondson, Allen Fletcher, Edward Hastings, Lawrence Hecht, Janice Hutchins; Production Manager, John Brown; Lighting, Joseph Appelt; Scenery, Robert Blackman; Costumes, Martha Burke, Michael Casey, Cathleen Edwards; Sound, Christopher D. Moore; Stage Managers, James Haire, Eugen Barcone, James L. Burke, Karen Van Zandt, Sarah J. Eggleston; Wigs, Katharine E. Kraft, Rick Echols; Props, Oliver C. Olsen; Wardrobe, Donald Long-Hurst, Thea Heinz; Press, Marne Davis Kellogg, Kirsten Mickelwait

COMPANY: Linda Aldrich, Annette Bening, Joseph Bird, Peter Bretz, Nancy Carlin, Mimi Carr, John DeMita, Barbara Dirickson, Peter Donat, James Edmondson, Drew Eshelman, Allen Fletcher, Mark Harelik, John Hertzler, Nancy Houfek, Janice Hutchins, Johanna Jackson, Byron Jennings, Nicholas Kaledin, Anne Lawder, Douglas Martin, Dakin Matthews, Carolyn McCormick, William McKereghan, Anne McNaughton, DeAnn Mears, Frank Ottiwell, Tom O'Brien, William Paterson, Ray Reinhardt, Harold Surratt, Tynia Thomassie, Sydney Walker, Marrian Walters, J. Steven White, Bruce Williams, D. Paul Yeuell
PRODUCTIONS Arms and the Man by George Bernard Shaw, Dial "M" for Murder by Frederick Knott, John Gabriel Borkman by Henrik Ibsen, A Midsummer Night's Dream by William Shakespeare, Angels Fall by Lanford Wilson, The Sleeping Prince by Terence Rattigan, and the *World Premiere* of The Dolly by Lawrence Hecht

Larry Merkle Photos

AMERICAN MIME THEATRE

New York, New York
Thirty-first Year
Founder/Director, Paul J. Curtis; Administrator, Jean Barbour; Counsel, Joel S. Charleston

COMPANY: Jean Barbour, Charles Barney, Joseph Citta, Paul J. Curtis, Dale Fuller, Kevin Kaloostian, Erica Sarzin and Mr. Bones
REPERTOIRE: Dreams, The Lovers, The Scarecrow, Hurly-Burly, Evolution, Slude, Six, *World Premiere* of The Unitaur

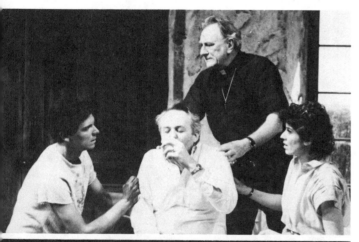

**John DeMita, Janice Hutchins, Carolyn McCormick,
Peter Bretz in "Midsummer Night's Dream"**

**Left Center: Peter Bretz, Dakin Matthews, Sydney Walker,
Barbara Dirickson in "Angels Fall"**

AMERICAN REPERTORY THEATRE

Nicole Shalhoub, Linda Lavin, Seth Goldstein,
Jeremy Geidt, Lise Hilboldt, Robert Stattel
in "Six Characters in Search of an Author"

Cambridge, Massachusetts
Fifth Season
Artistic Director, Robert Brustein; Managing Director, Robert J. Orchard; Literary Director, Jonathan Marks; Production Manager, Jonathan Miller; Marketing Director, Jeanne Broduer; Press, Jan Geidt; Technical Director, Donald R. Soule, Production Coordinator, Thomas C. Behrens; Stage Managers, John Grant-Phillips, Abbie Katz, Antony Rudie.

PRODUCTIONS AND CASTS:
MEASURE FOR MEASURE by William Shakespeare; Director, Andrei Belgrader; Sets, Douglas Stein; Costumes, Kurt Wilhelm; Lighting, Jennifer Tipton; Music, William Utley. CAST: Robert Stattel, Jeremy Geidt, Tony Shalhoub, Thomas Derrah, Hugh D'Autremont, Karen MacDonald, John Bottoms, Ben Halley, Jr., John Bellucci, Amy Brenneman, Ben Evett, Alden Jackson, Marianne Owen, Nina Bernstein, Richard Spore, Mark Driscoll, Harry S. Murphy, Nick Wyse
A MOON FOR THE MISBEGOTTEN by Eugene O'Neill; Director, David Leveaux; Set/Costumes, Brien Vahey; Lighting, Donald Edmund Thomas; Music, Stephen Endelman. CAST: Kate Nelligan, John Bellucci, Jerome Kilty, Ian Bannen, Thomas Derrah
SIX CHARACTERS IN SEARCH OF AN AUTHOR by Luigi Pirandello; Adapted and Directed by Robert Brustein; Set/Costumes, Michael H. Yeargan; Lighting, Jennifer Tipton. CAST: John Grant-Phillips, Antony Rudie, John Bottoms, Thomas Derrah, Karen MacDonald, Jeremy Geidt, Harry S. Murphy, Robert Stattel, Linda Lavin, Lise Hilboldt, Tony Shalhoub, Seth Goldstein, Nicole Shalhoub, Stephen Rowe
ANGEL CITY by Sam Shepard; Director, David Wheeler. CAST: John Bottoms, Thomas Derrah, Ben Halley, Jr., Karen MacDonald, Harry S. Murphy
WORLD PREMIERES:
TRAVELER IN THE DARK by Marsha Norman; Director, Tom Moore; Set, Heidi Landesman; Costumes, Robert Blackman; Lighting, James F. Ingalls. CAST: Damion Scheller, Sam Waterston, Phyllis Somerville, Hume Cronyn
BIG RIVER: THE ADVENTURES OF HUCKLEBERRY FINN with Music and Lyrics by Roger Miller; Book, William Hauptman; Director, Des McAnuff; Sets, Heidi Landesman; Costumes, Patricia McGourty; Lighting, James F. Ingalls; Sound, Randolph C. Head; Orchestrations/Vocal Arrangements/Musical Director, Michael S. Roth. CAST: Nina Bernstein, John Bottoms, Sandy Brown, Thomas Derrah, Mark Driscoll, Ben Evett, Jeremy Geidt, Ben Halley, Jr., Robert Joy, Jerome Kilty, Karen MacDonald, Harry S. Murphy, Marianne Owen, Tony Shalhoub, Alison Taylor
HOLY WARS by Allan Harvis; Director, Gerald Chapman; "The Road from Jerusalem" with Lise Hilboldt, Tony Shalhoub, Jeremy Geidt. "Morocco" with Tony Shalhoub, Ben Halley, Jr., Lise Hilboldt
STROKES by Leslie Glass; Director, Phillip Cates. CAST: Shirley Wilber, Mark Driscoll, Guy Strauss, Maggie Topkis

Richard Feldman Photos

"Twelfth Night"

AMERICAN THEATRE ARTS

Hollywood, California
November 17, 1983–April 14, 1984
Artistic Director, Don Eitner; Executive Director, Jim Hildebrandt; Production Manager, Tom Henschel; Conservatory Director, Bette Ferber; Company Manager, Barbara Stewart; Special Projects, Jeannie Sherry; Technical Director, John Calhoun; Literary Manager, Oren Curtis; Music Director, Bruce Ewen; Press, Todd Durwood; Directors, Don Eitner, Tom Henschel, Bette Ferber, Dianne Haak, Joe Ruskin, Ken Letner, Gene Nelson; Sets, Jim Agazzi, Bob Green, Don Eitner, Alex Stewart, Dale Barnhart, Betty Miller, W. Lansing Barbour; Costumes, Armand Coutu, Marianna Elliott, Elaine Ramirez, Elena Del Rio; Lighting, Robert Smitherman, Vance Sorrells, Ilya Mindlin, Nancy Schaefer; Stage Managers, Tom Coffey, Stevie Michaels, Freddye Chapman, Elaine Van Hogue, Lisa Berke; Press, Ken Letner, Dale Reynolds, Sharon Mazer

PRODUCTIONS & CASTS:
PERIOD OF ADJUSTMENT by Tennessee Williams; Director, Gene Nelson. CAST: Ross Clark, Daniel Grace, Linda Hammell, David Johnston, Carl Moebus, Catherine Perdue, Betty Ramey
THE TART FROM MONTMARTRE by Georges Feydeau. CAST: Howard Adler, Lynda Beattie, Earlene Davis, Rob Donohoe, Lou Fant, David Fulk, Bob Griffard, Ken Letner, Elaine Nalee, Tony Papenfuss
SHERLOCK HOLMES by Sir Arthur Conan Doyle and William Gillette; Director, Ken Letner. CAST: Greg Rusin, Sally Sommer, Bill Furnell, Maura Albertson, Andrew Pickwood, Janet Jones, John Terry Bell, Oren Curtis, Steve Yudson, Steve T. Matthews, Daniel Grace, Richard Moffitt, Tom Coffey, Lee Rossignol, June Ward, Victoria Herrick
THE AMERICAN SIGN LANGUAGE TWELFTH NIGHT by William Shakespeare; ASL Translation by Lou Fant, Tom Henschel, Lois Foraker, Gary Sanderson; English translation from the ASL by Tom Henschel and Lou Fant; Director, Don Eitner. CAST: Roxanne Baker, Barbara Bernstein, Jack Burns, Margo Cienik, Robert Daniels, Eric Davidove, Lou Fant, Tom Henschel, Jackie Kinner, Genni Klein, Lewis Merkin, Stevie Michaels, Bill Milestone, Kevin Mills, Rick Najera, Freda Norman, Rico Peterson, Pamela Printy, Dale Reynolds, Catherine Richardson, Michael Richardson, Frances Ripplinger, Dean Sheridan, Warren Teel, Elaine Vaan Hogue, Bobbie Williams
World Premier of HOW WE LIVED by Yale Gould; Director, Bette Ferber. CAST: Maura Albertson, Kelly Bailey, Keith Cox, Oren Curtis, Daniel Grace, Nancy Jeris, Don Mantooth, Lauren Peterson, Steve Weingartner

Richard Moffitt Photos

ARENA STAGE

Washington, D.C.
October 7, 1983–June 10, 1984
Sixteenth Season
Producing Director, Zelda Fichandler; Executive Director, Thomas C. Fichandler; Associate Producing Director, Douglas C. Wager; Administrative Director, JoAnn M. Overholt; Press, Richard Bryant: Development, Elspeth Udvarhelyi; Production Coordinator, Guy Bergquist; Technical Director, David M. Glenn; Literary Manager, John Glore; Stage Directors, Jacques Cartier, Zelda Fichandler, Gary Pearle, Richard Russell Ramos, Douglas C. Wager, Garland Wright; Sets, John Arnone, Karl Eigsti, David Jenkins, Thomas Lynch, Alexander Okun, Tony Traiges; Costumes, Laura Crow, Ann Hould-Ward, Mary Ann Powell, Marjorie Slaiman; Lighting, Frances Aronson, Arden Fingerhut, Paul Gallo, Allen Leee Hughes, William Mintzer, Nancy Schertler; Musical Directors, Robert Fisher, John McKinney; Stage Managers, Don Buschmann, Rita Calabro, Maxine Krasowski, Ann Matthews

COMPANY: Stanley Anderson, Richard Bauer, Marilyn Caskey, Kevin Donovan, Mark Hammer, Tom Hewitt, Charles Janasz, Christina Moore, Joe Palmieri, Henry Strozier, Halo Wines
GUEST ARTISTS: John Aller, Roger Alvarez, Jack Aranson, Pamela Bierly, Casey Biggs, Susan Blommaert, Diana Braak, James Cahill, Ron Canada, Michael Cone, Frances Conroy, Randy Danson, James Davies, Roger DeKoven, Abraham Dobkin, Franchelle Stewart Dorn, T. J. Edwards, Laura Gardner, Michael Genet, Martin Goldsmith, Bill Grimmett, Robin Groves, Chris Haley, Terry Hinz, Michelle Howard, Christopher Hux, Michael Jeter, Keith Johnson, Cherry Jones, Rita Karin, Madeleine le Roux, Kevin McClarnon, Frederica Meister, Stephen Mellor, Sheryl Melvin, Lynn Milgrim, Kevin Murray, Connie Nelson, David Perry, Susan Plaksin, William Preston, Lizabeth Pritchett, John Remme, John Rensenhouse, Judith Anna Roberts, Nanette Savard, Raymond Serra, J. Fred Shiffman, Henry Stram, Kathleen Weber, Jeffrey Wilkins, Nicholas Wyman
PRODUCTIONS: The Importance of Being Earnest by Oscar Wilde, Beyond Therapy by Christopher Durang, As You Like It by William Shakespeare, The Three Sisters by Anton Chekhov, Accidental Death of an Anarchist by Dario Fo adapted by Richard Nelson, Quartermaine's Terms by Simon Gray, Cloud 9 by Caryl Churchill, Happy End by Bertolt Brecht, Kurt Weill and adapted by Michael Feingold

**Michael Jeter, Richard Bauer
in "Accidental Death of an Anarchist"**
(Joan Marcus Photo)

"The Quilters"

ARIZONA THEATRE COMPANY

Tucson/Phoenix, Arizona
October 16, 1983–May 24, 1984
Artistic Director, Gary Gisselman; Managing Director, David Hawkanson; Associate Artistic Director, Ken Ruta; Director, Jon Cranney; Sets, Don Yunker, Jack Barkla; Costumes, Bobbi Culbert, Christopher Beesley, Jared Aswegan; Lighting, Donald Darnutzer, James Sale; Sound, Warren Hogan, Bob Bish; Composers, Charles Lewis, Roberta Carlson; Musical Directors, Roberta Carlson, David Brunetti; Development/Marketing, Barb Levy, Sharon Griggins; Press, Julie Devane

PRODUCTIONS & CASTS:
A STREET CAR NAMED DESIRE by Tennessee Williams. CAST: Helen Carey (Blanche), Carol Kuykendall (Stella), Casey Biggs (Stanley), Don West (Mitch), Judy Leavell (Eunice), Michael Ellison (Steve), Mark Hansen (Pablo), Ana Estrada (Neighbor), Oliver Cliff (Doctor), Dee Maaske (Nurse), Richard Howard (Young Collector)
BILLY BISHOP GOES TO WAR by John Gray and Eric Peterson. CAST: Casey Biggs (Billy Bishop), David Brunetti (Pianist)
OUR TOWN by Thornton Wilder and THE TAMING OF THE SHREW by William Shakespeare in repertory. CAST: Ken Ruta, Gary Clark, John Parra, John Conley, Richard Riehle, Dee Maaske, Judy Leavell, Newton-John Skinner, Michael Ellison, Richard Howard, Katie Taylor, Pamela Nyberg, Philip Rosenberg, J. C. Hoyt, Don West, Susan Wedekind, R. A. Farrell, Kathleen Todd, Oliver Cliff, Penny Metropulos, Hank Kendrick, Joseph Graves, Hank Gardner, David Marsh, Harriet Standring
'NIGHT, MOTHER by Marsha Norman. CAST: Fern Persons (Thelma), Kandis Chappell (Jessie)
QUILTERS by Mollie Newman and Barbara Damashek. CAST: Kimberly King (Dana), Becky Borczon (Jane), Penelope Miller (Jody), Marian Primont (Sarah McKendree Bonham), Barbara Davidson (Jenny), Suzy Hunt (Lisa), Cynthia Wells (Margaret), Musician Daughters: Maggie Lee, Carol Webb, Rose Marie Lowe, Margaret Leonard

Tim Fuller Photos

ASOLO STATE THEATER

Sarasota, Florida
June 1, 1983–May 31, 1984
Twenty-fifth Season

Executive Director, Richard G. Fallon; Managing Director, David S. Levenson; Artistic Director, John Ulmer; Musical Director, John Franceschina; Business Manager, Thomas Fordham; Press, Edith N. Anson; Sets, John Doepp, Bennet Averyt, Jeffrey W. Dean, Thomas Michael Cariello, Henry Swanson, Kenneth N. Kurtz, Robert Barnes; Costumes, Catherine King, Sally Kos Harrison; Lighting, Martin Petlock; Stage Managers, Marian Wallace, Stephanie Moss, Patricia Halpop, Dan Sedgwick; Technical Director, Victor Meyrich

PRODUCTIONS AND CASTS:

MAN WITH A LOAD OF MISCHIEF directed by Jim Hoskins. CAST: Nancy Johnston, John J. Martin, Maggie Task, Roy Alan Wilson, Mark Zimmerman
THE WINSLOW BOY directed by John Ulmer, **SHERLOCK HOLMES** directed by James Kirkland, **DARK OF THE MOON** directed by Sheldon Epps, in repertory. CAST: Barbara Barringer, George Gitto, Douglas Jones, Rory Kelly, Rob Knepper, Gretchen Lord, Phillip Pruneau, Karl Redcoff, Eric Tavares, Isa Thomas, Bradford Wallace, Colleen Smith Wallnau
ARMS AND THE MAN directed by Robert Falls, **WAITING FOR GODOT** directed by John Ulmer, and **THE GIN GAME** directed by John Gulley in repertory. CAST: Judith Ashe, Stephen Daley, Valery Daemke, Douglas Jones, Karl Redcoff, Eric Tavares, Isa Thomas, Bradford Wallace
PROMENADE, All! directed by John Ulmer. CAST: A. D. Cover, Richard Grubbs, Colleen Smith Wallnau, Carn N. Wallnau
DEATH OF A SALESMAN directed by John Ulmer. CAST: Lydia Bruce, Richard G. Fallon, Douglas Jones, Rory Kelly, Terry Layman, Karl Redcoff, Allan Stevens, Leon B. Stevens, Isa Thomas
THE DRUNKARD, RASHOMON, THE IMPORTANCE OF BEING EARNEST in repertory. CAST: Randy Clements, Kay Daphne, Daria Dolan, Joleen Fodor, Jayne Houdyshell, Richard Hoyt-Miller, Jerry Allan Jones, Katie Karlovitz, Marcie Stringer, Eric Tavares, Isa Thomas, Bradford Wallace, Carol Williard
ASSOCIATE COMPANY: Kevin Brief, Phillip Douglas, Suzanne Grodner, Kelley Hazen, Randy Hyten, Paul Kassel, Tom Kendall, Keith LaPan, Jerry Plourde, Brant Pope, Wendy Scharfman, Leslie J. Smith, Lizbeth Trepel, Diane C. Compton, Joan Crowe, Paul J. Ellis, Colleen Kane, Tim O'Neal Lorah, Patrick Manley, Holly Methfessel, Cynthia Newman, Pam Taylor, William L. Thomas, Jack Willis, Marc Ciokajlo, Jody Kielbasa, Susan Mannino, Carol Martini, Michael Piontek, Kenn Rapcynski, Karen Rasch, Kathryn Riedman, Jennifer Riggs, Cynthia Simpson, Steve Spender

Gary W. Sweetman Photos

Richard Fallon, Leon B. Stevens
in "Death of a Salesman"

**Chet Carlin, Edwin J. McDonough
in "Da"** (*Bill McKee Photo*)

BARTER THEATRE

Abingdon, Virginia
June 8, 1983–May 12, 1984
Fifty-first Season

Artistic Director/Producer, Rex Partington; Business Manager, Pearl Hayter; Promotion/Press, Lou Flanigan; Stage Managers, Don Buschmann, Champe Leary, Jeanne Oster; Directors, Ken Costigan, Harry Ellerbe, Pamela Hunt, William Van Keyser; Sets, Daniel Ettinger, John C. Lorrance, Lynn Pecktal; Costumes, Georgia Baker, Marianne Custer, Barbara Forbes, Sigrid Insull; Lighting, Al Oster

PRODUCTIONS AND CASTS:

BUS STOP by William Inge. CAST: Jeffrey Charles-Reese, Bob Horen, Catherine Coray, Richard Litt, Janet Maylie, Edwin J. McDonough, Victoria Page, Michael Patterson
FALLEN ANGELS by Noel Coward. CAST: Richard Bowden, Cleo Holladay, Victoria Page, Mary Shelley, Raymond Thorne
DA by Hugh Leonard. CAST: Richard Bowden, Chet Carlin, Cleo Holladay, Edwin J. McDonough, Leslie Lynn Meeker, Moultrie Patten, Michael Patterson, Mary Shelley
THE DINING ROOM by A. R. Gurney, Jr. CAST: Ken Costigan, Cleo Holladay, Edwin J. McDonough, Wendy Nute, Moultrie Patten
SIDE BY SIDE BY SONDHEIM by Stephen Sondheim with additional music by Leonard Bernstein and Jule Styne. CAST: Don Bradford, Marcy Degonge, Richard Kevlin-Bell, Roxie Lucus, Randy Barnett (Musical Director)
RELATIVELY SPEAKING by Alan Ayckbourn. CAST: Karen Braga, Douglas Fisher, Cleo Holladay, Michael Patterson
TINTYPES conceived by Mary Kyte with Mel Marvin and Gary Pearle. CAST: Ralph Braun, Barbara Niles, David Pevsner, Lynne Wieneke, Mary Yarbrough

BERKELEY REPRETORY THEATRE

Berkeley, California
June 9, 1983–May 20, 1984

Acting Artistic Director, Joy Carlin; Managing Director/Literary Manager, Mitzi Sales; Production Manager, Dennis Gill Booth; Technical Director, Richard G. Norgard; Stage Managers, Meryl Lind Shaw, Kimberly Mark Webb; Costumes, Toni M. Lovagilia; Props, Jerry Reynolds; Sound, James LeBrecht; General Manager, Barbara S. Miller; Marketing, Jim Royce; Press, Rhea Feldman; Resident Company: Hope Alexander-Willis, Tony Amendola, David Booth, Joy Carlin, Charles Dean, Irving Israel, Judith Marx, Michelle Morain, Richard Rossi, Brian Thompson, Michael Tulin

PRODUCTIONS AND CASTS (Guest Artists):
TOO TRUE TO BE GOOD with Scenery by Karen Gjelsteen; Costumes, Walter Watson; Lighting, Derek Duarte
AMERICAN BUFFALO: Director, John Dillon; Set, Ralph Funicello; Costumes, Kurt Wilhelm; Lighting, Dan J. Kotlowitz; Actors, Larry Shue (Donny), Abvi Spindell (Bobby)
THE WAY OF THE WORLD: Director, Albert Takazauckas; Set, Bernard Vyzga; Costumes, Deborah Dryden; Lighting, Greg Sullivan; Actors; Wayne Alexander (Mirabell), Amy K. Kimball (Betty), Holly Barron (Mrs. Marwood), Emily Heebner (Mincing), Barbara Oliver (Foible), Janice Cole (Peg), Lawrence Glass (Servant)
AWAKE AND SING!: Set, Jesse Hollis; Costumes, Michael Olich; Lighting, Derek Duarte; Actors: Roland Scrivner (Myron), Suzanne Shepherd (Bessie), Kimberly King (Hennie), Luis Oropeza (Schlosser), Joe Bellan (Morty)
FILUMENA: Set, Vicki Smith; Costumes, Sally Richardson; Lighting, Tom Ruzika; Actors: Luis Oropeza (Domenico), Barbara Oliver (Rosalia), Joe Bellan, Devin Binder (Waiters), Theresa Plikaitis (Lucia)
SEASON'S GREETINGS *(American Premiere):* Director, Douglas Johnson, Set, Karen Gjelsteen; Costumes, Merrily Murray-Walsh; Lighting, Derek Duarte; Actor: Emily Heebner (Pattie)
WORLD PREMIERES:
GEOFF HOYLE MEETS KEITH TERRY: Set/Costumes, Peggy Snider; Lighting, Derek Duarte; Actors: Geoff Hoyle, Keith Terry
THE MARGARET GHOST: Director, Edward Hastings; Set, Mark Donnelly; Costumes, Jeannie Davidson; Lighting, Greg Sullivan; Actor: Dan Cawthon (Ralph Waldo Emerson)

Ken Friedman Photos

Judith Marx, Luis Oropeza
in "Filumena"

Charles Nelson Reilly, Larry Hansen,
Alice Ghostley in "Bye Bye Birdie"

BURT REYNOLDS THEATRE

Jupiter, Florida
July 5, 1983–June 24, 1984

Producer/Vice President, Dudley Remus; Executive Director, Elaine Deacy; Associate Producer, Karen Poindexter; Press, Celeste Bennett, Morna Hessee; Artistic Coordinator, Michael Deal; Technical Director, James Hungerford; Stage Manager, Ken Williams; Costumes, Barbara Bell; Photography, Greg Allikas

PRODUCTIONS:
GEORGE M! directed by Tony Mordente and starring J. J. Jepson;
THE HASTY HEART directed by Bob Finkel and starring Robert Urich and Heather Menzies; The
PRISONER OF SECOND AVENUE directed by Charles Nelson Reilly and starring Vincent Gardenia and Carol Locatell;
ON BORROWED TIME directed by Dick Latessa and starring Richard Basehart;
BYE BYE BIRDIE directed by John Sharpe and starring Alice Ghostley and Charles Nelson Reilly;
IT HAD TO BE YOU directed by Robert Drivas and starring Joe Bologna and Renee Taylor;
SWEET CHARITY directed by Darwin Knight and starring Patricia Harty;
SORROWS OF STEPHEN directed by Alan Arkin and starring Adam Arkin;
THE SUPPORTING CAST directed by Tom Troupe and starring Fannie Flagg;
STOP THE WORLD I WANT TO GET OFF directed Frank Scardino and starring George Chakiris

Greg Allikas Photos

CALDWELL PLAYHOUSE

Boca Raton, Florida
July 13, 1983–April 29, 1984
Fourth Season

Artistic/Managing Director, Michael Hall; Guest Directors, Joe Warik, J. Randall Hugill; Sets, Frank Bennett, James Morgan, Marion Kolsby, Joe Gillie; Costumes, Brigid R. Bartlett; Lighting, Craig Ferraro, Laurel Shoemaker, Joyce Fleming; Stage Managers, Doug Fogel, Kenneth Kay, John Bjostad, Kate Powers; Press, Patricia Burdett; Photographers, Joyce Brock, Linda Bannister, Jeff Friedland

PRODUCTIONS AND CASTS:
LUNCH HOUR by Jean Kerr. CAST: Pat Nesbit, David Reinhardsen, Beth Taylor, Tom Tarpey, Kurt Schlesinger
CAT ON A HOT TIN ROOF by Tennessee Williams. CAST: Pat Nesbit, Will Osborne, James C. Cassidy, Justine Johnston, Annie Stafford, Jack Hrkach, Dennis Jones, Earle Edgerton, Sam Lindsey
THE BICYCLE MAN (World Premiere) by Edward J. Moore. CAST: Edward J. Moore, Kimberly Vaughan, Susan Riskin, Dick Boccelli
THE MIDDLE AGES by A. R. Gurney, Jr. CAST: Geoffrey Wade, Pat Nesbit, Donald Barton, Patricia O'Connell
BEDROOM FARCE by Alan Ayckbourn. CAST: Max Gulack, Deirdre Owens, Pat Nesbit, Jack Hrkach, Caroline McGee, Ralph Redpath, Barbara Bradshaw, Geoffrey Wade
THE DEADLY GAME by James Yaffe. CAST: Robert Fitzsimmons, Ronald Durling, Robert Cenedella, James Hillgartner, Bill Boss, Deborah Stern, Gary Goodson, Kay Brady
THE CIRCLE by Somerset Maugham. CAST: June Prud'Homme, Pat Nesbit, Derek Murcott, Geoff Garland, Mark McConnell, David Bulasky, Kay Brady, Jack Hrkach, Brigid Cleary
THE DECLINE AND FALL OF THE ENTIRE WORLD AS SEEN THROUGH THE EYES OF COLE PORTER by Ben Bagley; CAST: Debra Hauptman, Lucinda Hitchcock-Cone, Theresa Rakov, Patrick Hamilton, Paul Mack, Michael O'Flaherty

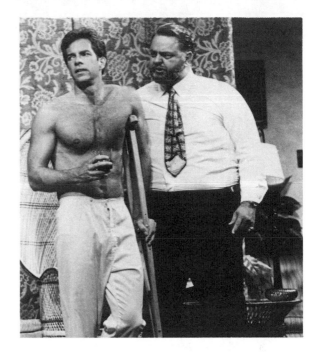

Top Right: Will Osborne, James C. Cassidy
in "Cat on a Hot Tin Roof"
(Jeff Friedland Photo)

CAPITAL REPERTORY COMPANY

Albany, N.Y.
October 29, 1983–April 15, 1984

Producing Directors, Bruce Bouchard, Peter H. Clough; Business Manager, Barbara Highter Smith; Press, Hilde Schuster; Literary Manager, Lou Rackoff; Company Manager, Peter Kindlon; Production Manager, David Yergan; Stage Manager, Patricia Frey; Technical Director, Darlene Murray; Costumes, Lloyd K. Waiwaiole; Props, Janet Storck; Photographer, Skip Dickstein

PRODUCTIONS AND CASTS:
THE GLASS MENAGERIE by Tennessee Williams; Director, Michael J. Hume; Set, Jeffrey Schneider; Costumes, Barbara Forbes; Lighting, Mal Sturchio. CAST: Chris Ceraso, Bobo Lewis, Shelley Rogers, Daren Kelly
HAPPY END with Lyrics by Bertolt Brecht; Music, Kurt Weill adapted by Michael Feingold; Director, Peter H. Clough; Set, Ray Recht; Lighting, Robert Thayer; Costumes, Lloyd K. Waiwaiole; Choreography, Lisa Hillyer; Musical Director, Andrea Goodzeit. CAST: Peter Johnson, James Goodwin Rice, Adam LeFevre, Jared Matesky, Michael J. Hume, Richard Council, Gloria Hodes, Kate Kelly, Kristin Jolliff, Melissa Hurst, Denise Carnell, Jack Mulvey, Jim Kidd, Phyllis Gottung, Kitty Jones, Pamela Tanner, Gregg Berrian, William Coulter, Jack Fris
TRANSLATIONS by Brian Friel; Director, Pamela Berlin; Set, Jeffrey Schneider; Costumes, Barbara Forbes; Lighting, Lary Opitz. CAST: William Carden, Peter Johnson, Laura MacDermott, Adam LeFevre, Anne O'Sullivan, William Kuhlke, John Griesemer, George Holmes, Jeff Leabow, Pat Titterton
LIVING TOGETHER by Alan Ayckbourn; Director, Lynn Polan; Set, Leslie Taylor; Costumes, Lloyd K. Waiwaiole; Lighting, David Yergan. CAST: Mary Baird, Michael Arkin, James Goodwin Rice, Kate Kelly, Michael J. Hume, Joan Grant
ALICE AND FRED (World Premiere) by Dan Ellentuck; Director, Gloria Muzio Thayer; Set, Ray Recht; Costumes, Lloyd K. Waiwaiole; Lighting, Robert Thayer; Original Music, George Andoniadis. CAST: Jan Leslie Harding, Jack Fris, Bruce Tracy, Chris Fracchiolla, Sarah Rush
THE WAKE OF JAMEY FOSTER by Beth Henley; Director, Bruce Bouchard; Set, Rick Dennis; Costumes, Martha Halley; Lighting, Lary Opitz. CAST: Jessie K. Jones, Bruce Tracy, Shaw Purnell, Adam LeFevre, Kate Kelly, Jan Leslie Harding, William Kuhlke

Skip Dickstein Photos

Richard Council, Gloria Hodes
in "Happy End"

CENTER STAGE

Baltimore, Maryland
September 30, 1983–June 10, 1984
Fifth Season

Artistic Director, Stan Wojewodski, Jr.; Managing Director, Peter W. Culman; Associate Artistic Director, Jackson Phippin; Associate Managing Director, Victoria Nolan; Dramaturg, Warren MacIsaac; Artistic Associates, Hugh Landwehr, Irene Lewis, Grace McKeaney, Eric Overmyer; Stage Managers, Amanda Mengden, Susan C. Guszynski; Press, Jean Brubaker, Mary E. Howell; Guest Directors, Stephen Zuckerman, Travis Preston, John Pasquin; Guest Designers, Mimi Maxmen, Richard Winkler, Tony Straiges, James F. Ingalls, Kate Edmunds, Jennifer Tipton, Bill Ballou, Dona Granata, Craig Miller, Douglas Stein, Jess Goldstein, Pat Collins, Linda Fisher, Judy Rasmuson

PRODUCTIONS AND CASTS:

CROSSING THE BAR *(World Premiere)* by Michael Zettler. CAST: William Mooney, Betsy Sue Aidem, Jay Devlin, Stan Lachow, Irwin Ziff, Bryan E. Clark, Tom Crawley, Tom Bade, William R. Riker

OUR TOWN by Thornton Wilder. CAST: Robert Gerringer, Robert Blackburn, Lance Lewman, Michael Tolaydo, Patricia Falkenhain, June Squibb, Peter Mackenzie, Sarah Hart, Zachary Knower, Lili Flanders, J. S. Johnson, Emery Battis, David O. Petersen, Brenda Wehle, William R. Riker, Daniel Chaney, Steven Arbonna, Steven Blanchard, Peter Crombie, Daniel Szelag

THE SLEEP OF REASON *(U. S. Premiere)* by Antonio Buero-Vallejo; Translated by Marion Peter Holt. CAST: John Gould Rubin, Michael Tolaydo, Emery Battis, Jennifer Harmon, David O. Petersen, Caris Corfman, Daniel Szelag, Steven Arbona, Steven Blanchard, Peter Crombie, Lance Lewman, Shannon Rye

YOU NEVER CAN TELL by George Bernard Shaw. CAST: Michael Tolaydo, Lili Flanders, Anne Cantler, Peter Mackenzie, Patricia Falkenhain, Helen Carey, Emery Battis, William Cain, David O. Petersen, Daniel Szelag

ANOTHER PART OF THE FOREST by Lillian Hellman. CAST: Caris Corfman, Gary Sloan, Anne Shropshire, Delores Mitchell, Biff McGuire, Ron Frazier, Emery Battis, Kevin O'Rourke, Sarah Chodoff, Daniel Szelag, Walter Pearthree, Nicolette Goulet, Erik Benjamin, Melanee Murray

OHIO TIP-OFF *(World Premiere)* by James Yoshimura. CAST: Tom Wright, William E. Kennedy, Bill Fagerbakke, Jay O. Sanders, Mark Kenneth Smaltz, Eugene Lee, Samuel L. Jackson, Walter Atamaniuk

Richard Anderson Photos

**Top Right: Nicolette Goulet, Kevin O'Rourke
in "Another Part of the Forest"**

CENTER THEATRE GROUP
AHMANSON THEATRE

October 7, 1983–May 27, 1984
Seventeenth Season

Artistic Director, Robert Fryer; Managing Director, Michael Grossman; Associate Artistic Director, James H. Hansen; Press, Rick Miramontez; Manager, Thomas Jordan; Executive Associate, Joyce Zaccaro; Management Associate, Michelle McGrath; Production Manager, Ralph Beaumont; Technical Director, Robert Routolo; Stage Managers, Jake Hamilton, Joe Cappelli, A., Robert Altshuler, Jerry Trent, Robert Charles Martin, Michael Foley, Michael Wolf, Michael McEowen

PRODUCTIONS AND CASTS

BEETHOVEN'S TENTH *(American Premiere* Friday, Oct. 7, 1983) by Peter Ustinov; Director, Robert Chetwyn; Set, Kenneth Mellor; Costumes, Madeline Ann Graneto, John Fraser; Lighting, Martin Aronstein; Produced in association with Duncan C. Weldon with Paul Gregg, Lionel Becker, Alexander H. Cohen. CAST: Fritz Weaver (Stephen), Mary Jay (Jessica), Adam Redfield (Pascal), Elizabeth Norment (Irmgard), Peter Ustinov (Ludwig), Gwyllym Evans (Dr. Jagger), Brad O'Hare (Father), Leslie O'Hara (Countess), John Devlin (Count), Understudies: Benjamin Stewart, John Devlin, Courtney Burr, Patricia Fraser, Marietta Meade, Neil Flanagan. See *Broadway Calendar* for NY production.

A SENSE OF HUMOR *(World Premiere,* Sunday Dec. 4, 1983) by Ernest Thompson; Director, Robert Greenwald; Set/Lighting, Gerry Hariton/Vicki Baral; Costumes, Len Marcus, Ruth Morley; Special Artwork, D. J. Hall; Produced by Robert Fryer and Frank von Zerneck in association with the CTG/Ahmanson Theatre; Associate Producer, James Hansen; Press, Fred Nathan, Ann Abrams, Leslie Anderson, Bert Fink; Company Manager, John Caruso. CAST: Jack Lemmon (Richard), Estelle Parsons (Elizabeth), Clifton James (Abe), Polly Holliday (Jean), Understudies: Warren Munson, Liz Sheridan

DETECTIVE STORY by Sidney Kingsley; Director, Paul Giovanni; Set, Douglas W. Schmidt; Costumes, Michael William Casey; Lighting, Martin Aronstein; Assistant Director, Marc Beckerman. CAST: Hugh Gillin (Lt. Monoghan), Joe George (Dakis), Frank McCarthy (Gallagher), John Schuck (Brody), Charlton Heston (McLeod), John Corey (Callahan), Chip Lucia (O'Brien), Beau Billingslea (Barnes), Scott Stevensen (Keogh), Matthew Kimbrough (Feeney), Daniel Trent (Baker), Mary Wickes (Willie), Ron Rifkin (Feinson), Candy Azzara (Shoplifter), Tim Barber succeeded by Thomas Harrison (Arthur), Keith Carradine (Charlie), Charles Whiteside (Lewis), Donald Hotton (Dr. Schneider), Martin LaPlatney (Sims), Lora Staley (Mrs. Bagatelli), Melora Marshall succeeded by Doran Clark (Susan), Claire Malis (Miss Hatch), William Lanteau (Pritchett), Mariette Hartley (Mary), Michael DeLano (Giacoppetti), Understudies: Peter Henry Schroedder, Robert Legionaire, Claire Malis, Daniel Trent, Frank McCarthy, Robert Ott Boyle, Robin Cantor, Lora Staley, Charles Whiteside, Matthew Kimbrough, Scott Stevensen

LIGHT COMEDIES by Peter Shaffer; Director, Paul Giovanni; Sets, Douglas W. Schmidt; Costumes, Michael William Casey; Lighting, Dawn Chiang; Assistant Director, Marc Beckerman. "The Public Eye" and "Black Comedy" CAST: Harry Groener (Julian/Brindsley), David Dukes (Charles/Harold), Melora Marshall (Belinda/Clea), Caitlin O'Heaney (Carol), Elizabeth Franz (Miss Furnival), Keene Curtis (Col. Melkett), Avery Schreiber (Schuppanzigh), Tommy Maurice McLoughlin (Bamberger), Understudies: Zale Kessler, Raymond Skipp, Gillian Eaton, Jack Blessing, Caitlin O'Heaney, Rosina Widdowson-Reynolds, Lora Staley

Jay Thompson Photos

**Charlton Heston, Mariette Hartley
in "Detective Story"**

CENTER THEATRE GROUP
MARK TAPER FORUM

August 11, 1983–August 19, 1984
Seventeenth Season

Artistic Director/Producer, Gordon Davidson; Managing Director, William P. Wingate; Associate Artistic Director, Kenneth Brecher; Producer Taper Too, Madeline Puzo; Staff Director ITP, Peter C. Brosius; Director in Residence, Ben Levit; Staff Director, John Frank Levey; Literary Manager/Producer, Russell Vandenbroucke; Press, Nancy Hereford, Karen Kruzich, Guy Giarrizzo, Robert Wildman, Phyllis Moberly-Fisher, Diana Moore; Lighting, Tharon Musser; Production Coordinator/Casting Director, Frank Bayer; Stage Managers, Jonathan Barlow Lee, James T. McDermott, Mary Michele Miner, Michael F. Wolf, Jill Johnson, Lynda A. Lavin, Daniel McPhee, Tami Toon; Richard Winnie; Technical Director, Robert Routolo.

PRODUCTIONS AND CASTS:

CAT ON A HOT TIN ROOF by Tennessee Williams; Director, Jose Quintero; Set, John Lee Beatty; Costumes, Noel Taylor; Lighting, Marilyn Rennagel; Assistant Director, John Frank Levey. CAST: Hank Rolike (Lacey), Helen Martin (Sookey), Kirstie Alley (Margaret), James Morrison (Brick), Patricia McCormack (Mae), Jason Hervey (Sonny), Peter Jurasik (Gooper), Alice Ghostley (Big Mama), Wendy Alpan (Dixie), Pat Hingle (Big Daddy), John Miranda (Rev. Tooker), George D. Wallace (Dr. Baugh), Susan Hinkebein (Trixie), Jeffrey B. Cohen (Buster), Joanne Oliver (Daisy), Art Evans (Brightie), Garret Davis (Small).

AN AMERICAN COMEDY (*World Premiere*) by Richard Nelson; Director, John Madden; Set, Andrew Jackness; Costumes, Julie Weiss; Lighting, James F. Ingalls. CAST: Mark Blum (Max Whitcomb), Bob Gunton (George Reilly), Bill Macy (Joe Williams), Melora Marshall (Julie Jackson), Jack Hallett (Tony Ricardo), David Downing (Freddy Hart), Lester C. Fletcher (Samuel Conklin), Demetra Arliss (Eva Rose), Robert Ellenstein (Col. Face).

QUILTERS by Molly Newman and Barbara Damashek; Music, Lyrics and Direction, Barbara Damashek; Set, Ursula Belden; Costumes, Marianna Elliott; Lighting, Allen Lee Hughes; Adapted in part from the book "The Quilters: Women and Domestic Art" by Patricia Cooper, Norma Bradley Allen; Musical Coordinator, Elizabeth Myers. CAST: Betty Garrett (Sarah McKendree Bonham), Suzanne Collins (Dana), Donna Fuller (Margaret), Sally Klein (Lisa), Laurie O'Brien (Jody), Jennifer Parsons (Jane), Teri Ralston (Jenny), Sands Hall, Melanie Sue Harby, Miriam Mayer, Kristina Olsen, Joseph A. Waterkotte.

THE GENIUS (*American Premiere*) by Howard Brenton; Director, Ben Levit; Set Douglas W. Schmidt; Costumes, Csilla Marki; Lighting, Tharon Musser; Sound, Stephen R. Shaffer; Dialect Coach, James Wilson. CAST: Andrew Robinson (Prof. Leo Lehrer), Mare Winningham (Gilly Brown), Jack Gwillim (Richard Weight), Roy Dotrice (Graham Hay), Suzanne Lederer (Virginia Hay), Ralph Drischell (Cliff Jones), Alison Price (Andrea Long), Charles Shaughnessy (Tom Dicks), Miriam Mayer (Skeleton), Susan Zimmerman (Greenham Woman), Air Force Guards: Steve Nevil, Eric Trules.

THREE PLAYS IN REPERTORY:

THE AMERICAN CLOCK: A MURAL FOR THE THEATRE a new version by Arthur Miller inspired in part by Studs Terkel's "Hard Times"; Director, Gordon Davidson; Set, Ralph Funicello; Costumes, Marianna Elliott; Lighting, Martin Aronstein; Original Music, Alex North; Production Coordinator, Frank Bayer; Assistant Director, Robert Berlinger; Musical Coordinator, Anita Leonard Nye; Slide Sequences, KMH Multi Media. CAST: Fred Applegate (Quinn/Sheriff/Bidder), Mark Blum (Lee Baum), Howland Chamberlin (Farmer), Joel Colodner (Taylor/Rudy), Cynthia Darlow (Doris/Isabel/Harriet), Gary Dontzig (Clayton/Margolies), Ralph Drischell (Dr. Rosman/Ryan), Charles Gregory (Charley/Graham/Ralph), Mark Harelik (Frank/Toland/Piano Player), Helen Martin (Irene/Farmer's Wife), Deborah May (Diana/Edie/Lucille), Thomas Oglesby (Joe/Brewster), Alan Oppenheimer (Grandpa/Kapush), Fred Pinkard (Louis/Farmer), John Randolph (Moe/Farmer), Michael Richards (Tony/Howard/Stanislaus), Eve Roberts (Rose/Farmer's Wife), Tom Rosqui (Jesse/Bush), Ken Ruta (Robertson/Farmer), David Sage (Durant/Judge/Dugan), John Wesley (Clarence/Isaac/Farmer), Erica Yohn (Fanny/Mrs. Taylor)

WILD OATS: A Romance of the Old West newly adapted from John O'Keeffe's play by James McLure; Director, Tom Moore; Set, Ralph Funicello; Costumes, Robert Blackman; Music Composed/Adapted/Arranged by Larry Delinger. CAST: Fred Applegate (Ike), Mark Blum (Harry), Howland Chamberlin (Cpl. Crow), Joel Colodner (Ephraim), Cynthia Darlow (Jane), Gary Dontzig (Sim), Ralph Drischell (Leko), Charles Gregory (Wilson), Mark Harelik (Jack), Deborah May (Kate), Thomas Oglesby (Muz), John Randolph (Kliegl), Michael Richards (Liberty), Eve Roberts (Amelia), Tom Rosqui (Morales), Ken Ruta (Col. Thunder), David Sage (Sheriff), Robert Webb (Piano Player), John Wesley (Angel Eyes).

MOBY DICK—REHEARSED by Orson Welles; An Adaptation of the novel by Herman Melville; Director, Edward Payson Call; Set, Ralph Funicello; Costumes, Robert Blackman. CAST: Joel Colodner (Starbuck), Mark Harelik (Ishmael), Ken Ruta (Capt. Ahab)

Right Center: Sally Klein, Jennifer Parsons, Donna Fuller, Betty Garrett, Teri Ralston, Suzanne Collins, Laurie O'Brien in "Quilters"
Jay Thompson Photos

NEW THEATRE FOR NOW
PRODUCTIONS: Dead End Kids: A History of Nuclear Power, Made in America, (*World Premiere*), Pass/Fail (*World Premiere*), Cakewalk (*World Premiere*), Beckett! Beckett! Beckett! ACTORS: Rhonda Aldrich, Carmen Argenziano, Remy Auberjonois, George Bartenieff, Earl Billings, Michael Bond, David Brisbin, Anne Gee Byrd, Shaun Cassidy, Ton Cayler, Valerie Curtin, Brian Dennehy, Theresa DePaolo, Lisa Eichhorn, Alvin Epstein, Mike Farrell, John Fistos, David Gale, Hershcel Garfein, Gerrit Graham, Wiley Harker, Ernesto Hernandez, Mark Herrier, Elizabeth Huddle, Dale Keever, Carol Kelley, Richard Lawson, Sybil Lines, Jay Louden, Ruth Maleczech, Ellen McElduff, Pat McNamara, Greg Mehrten, Ralph Meyering, Jr., Dan Monahan, John Napierala, Terry O'Reilly, Steven Peterman, Joel Polis, Kathleen Salamone, B-St. John Schofield, Scottie Snyder, Patrick Stack, Michael Talbott, Leigh Taylor-Young, David Warrilow, Billie Whitelaw
TAPER TOO PRODUCTIONS
Wire, The Regard of Flight, In the Belly of the Beast, A Private View ACTORS: Gretchen Almond, David Anglin, Paul Beard II, Raye Birk, Pendleton Brown, Pat Carey, Carl Franklin, Bruce French, Lita Gaithers, Kai Ganado, M. B. Gordy, Wayne Grace, Steve Hicks, Bill Irwin, Richard Jordan, Michael Keenan, Daniel McDonald, M. C. O'Connor, William Pasley, Andrew Robinson, Stuart K. Robinson, Sharon Jayne Scott, Doug Skinner, Joe Sorce, Olga Talyn, Monica Valdez, Laurnea Laurea Wilkerson, Andy Wood, Lynne Yoneyama

**Bill Macy, Bob Gunton
in "An American Comedy"**

163

"Godspell" Top: Angela Thornton, Gary Sandy
in "Sweet Bird of Youth" (Sandy Underwood Photo)

David Snizek, Lynn Watson
in "Let's Get a Divorce"

CINCINNATI PLAYHOUSE IN THE PARK

Cincinnati, Ohio
September 15, 1983–July 22, 1984
Producing Director, Michael Murray; Managing Director, Baylor Landrum; Stage Managers, Patricia Ann Speelman, Kimberly Osgood, William Slutz; Press, Charlaine Martin, Sue Ann Stein, Betty Schwartz; Photographer, Sandy Underwood

PRODUCTIONS AND CASTS:
TRUE WEST by Sam Shepard; Director, Don Toner; Set, Alison Ford; Lighting, Jay Depenbrock; Costumes, Rebecca Senske. CAST: Mary Diveny, Dave Florek, David Rosenbaum, Richard Zobel
SWEET BIRD OF YOUTH by Tennessee Williams; Director, Michael Murray; Set, Paul R. Shortt; Costumes, James Berton Harris; Lighting, William Mintzer. CAST: Linda Bennett, William Brenner, Gary Cookson, Buz Davis, Tony Darnell-Davis, Richard Dix, Dale Doerman, Tom Ford, Joseph Fuqua, Elizabeth Gregory, Richard Hagerman, Michael Hankins, Jeffery Hasler, Cheryl Hulteen, Robert Judd, Bobbi Jo Lathan, Don Martin, Dianne Neil, Cyrus Newitt, Michael Pollard, Richard Pruitt, Gary Sandy, J. D. Swain, Trinity Thompson, Angela Thornton
THEY DANCE TO THE SUN (World Premiere) by Leigh Podgorski; Director, Gloria Muzio Thayer; Set, David Ariosa; Costumes, Rebecca Senske; Lighting, Jay Depenbrock. CAST: Glynis Bell, Catherine Ann Christianson, Dave Florek, Jacklyn Maddux, Tania Myren, Donald Reeves
GODSPELL conceived by John-Michael Tebelak; Music/New Lyrics, Stephen Schwartz; Director/Choreographer, Darwin Knight; Musical Direction, Zalmen Mlotek; Set, Charles Caldwell; Lighting, F. Mitchell Dana; Costumes, Caley Summers. CAST: Jerry Bradley, Tom Ford, Olivia Virgil Harper, Todd Heughens, Tim Johnson, Lora Martens, Leilani Mickey, Cynthia I. Pearson, Eleanor Reissa, Todd Taylor
A SOLDIER'S PLAY by Charles Fuller; performed by the Negro Ensemble Company; Director, Douglas Turner Ward; Set, Michael Devine; Costumes, Judy Dearing; Stage Managers, Edward DeShae, Janice C. Lane. CAST: Gary Armagnac, Nick Bakay, Graham Brown, Adolph Caesar, O. L. Duke, Ben E. Epps, Danny Goldring, Robert Gossett, Ruben Hudson, Steven A. Jones, James Pickens, Jr., Cedric Turner, Lanyard A. Williams, Stephen Zettler
MONDAY AFTER THE MIRACLE by William Gibson; Director, Leonard Mozzi; Set, James Fenhagen. CAST: Denise Bessette, Thomas Carson, John Hardy, Charles Shaw Robinson, Mercedes Ruehl
JULIUS CAESAR by William Shakespeare; Director, Michael Murray; Set, Karl Eigsti; Lighting, Neil Peter Jampolis; Costumes, Kurt Wilhelm. CAST: C. B. Anderson, Robert Bell, Robert Browning, Monica Calhoun, Malcolm Richard Cochrane, Dick Collier, Peggy Cowles, Tony Darnell-Davis, Buz Davis, Lyn Dohaney, Herb Downer, Tom Ford, Peter Francis-James, Joseph Fuqua, Dick Hagerman, Jeffery Hasler, Jay Hinton, Tony Hoty, John Houston, Cheryl Hulteen, Charlotte Hunter, Marcia Isabel, Phillip Lindsay, Tom Maridrosian, Don Martin, Jim Moody, Cyrus Newitt, Ophelia, Robert Pescovitz, Michael Pollard, Ramon Ramos, Lynn Ritchie, Donald L. Rosenberg, Judith Sternlight, Jeremiah Sullivan, Lorraine Toussaint, Earl Christopher Williams, Melinda Wood
TRANSLATIONS by Brian Friel; Director, Don Toner; Set, David Ariosa. CAST: Nancy Boykin, Michael Burnham, James Handy, Terry Heck, Bram Lewis, Donald C. Moore, Gary Pollard, Charles Shaw Robinson, Steven Stahl, Judith Sternlight
HAY FEVER by Noel Coward; Director, Geoffrey Sherman; Set, Paul Wonsek; Costumes, William Schroder; Lighting, Paul Wonsek. CAST: Joyce Cohen, Mary Diveny, Warren Keith, Jessica Rausch, Sam Stoneburner, Angela Thornton, Robert Trumbull, Diana Van Fossen, Ray Virta
LOVES AND HOURS (World Premiere) by Stephen Metcalfe; Director, Michael Murray; Set, David Ariosa; Lighting, Jay Depenbrock; Costumes, Rebecca Senske. CAST: Dave Florek, Margaret Gibson, Don Toner
THE DINING ROOM by A. R. Gurney, Jr.; Director, Michael Hankins; Set, David Ariosa; Lighting, William Mintzer; Costumes, Kurt Wilhelm. CAST: Arthur Brooks, Chris Casady, Edward Conery, Debra Dean, Cliff Fetters, Marilyn Rockafellow

CLARENCE BROWN COMPANY

Knoxville, Tennessee
Artistic Director, Wandalie Henshaw; Associate Directors, Albert J. Harris, Robert Mashburn; Sets, Robert Cothran; Lighting, L. J. DeCuir, Leonard Harman; Costumes, Bill Black, Marianne Custer; Technical Director, Robert Field; Production Coordinator, Lisa Norman-Lay; Stage Manager, Phebe A. Day; Company Manager, Nancy Walther; Press, Angela Perez-Cisneros

COMPANY: James Berry, Richard Bowden, Raymond Clarke, Abigail Crabtree, Dale Dickey, George Maguire, Monique Morgan, Ellen Jane Smith, David Snizek, Jim Stubbs, Lynn Watson
PRODUCTIONS: Arms and the Man by George Bernard Shaw, A Doll's House by Henrik Ibsen, Engaged by W. S. Gilbert, Let's Get a Divorce by Victorien Sardou, A Shakespearean Miscellany

Marc Engel Photos

CLEVELAND PLAY HOUSE

Cleveland, Ohio
October 5, 1983–June 24, 1984
Sixty-eighth Season

Director, Richard Oberlin; Managing Director, Janet Wade; Business Manager, Nelson Isekeit; Press, Tony Mastroianni, David Kenley Frantz; Stage Directors, Paul Lee, Evie McElroy, William Rhys, William Roudebush; Guest Directors, Jim Corti, Philip Kerr, Woodie King, Jr., Michael Maggio, M. Seth Reines, Toby Robertson, Dennis Zack; Fight Choreographer, David Leong; Scenic Director, Richard Gould; Sets, James Irwin, Estelle Painter; Guest Designers, Gary Eckhart, Colleen Mucha, Dennis Parichy, Paul Rodgers; Music Director/Composer/Consultant, David Gooding; Production Manager, James Irwin; Stage Managers, Michael Stanley, Anthony Berg, Deborah A. Gosney, Richard Oberlin, Jim Hassert; Production Assistant, Dave Benson; Props, James A. Guy; Costumes/Wardrobe, Estelle Painter; Wardrobe, Sandy Hanlon; Photographer, CR Studio

COMPANY Kim Belsan, Norm Berman, Sharon Bicknell, Steven Breese, John Buck, Jr., Paul A. Floriano, Dion Graham, Jeffrey Green, Richard Halverson, James P. Kisicki, Allen Leatherman, Paul Lee, Catherine Long, Morgan Lund, John Mariano, Evie McElroy, Catherine McQueen, Kelly C. Morgan, Marcus Naylor, Richard Oberlin, Thomas S. Oleniacz, Si Osborn, Tracee Patterson, Robert D. Phillips, Carolyn Reed, William Rhys, James Richards, William Roudebush, Wayne S. Turney, Dan Westbrook, Cassandra Wolfe
GUEST ARTISTS: Peter Aylward, Cliff Bemis, Charles Brown, Joel Hammer, David Havsky, Lorey Hayes, Jill Hayman, Providence Hollander, David Jendre, Charles Keating, Edward Lee Kelly, Linda Leonard, Milledge Mosley, Austin Pendleton, Theresa Piteo, Jim Rupp, Bobbie Beth Scoggins, Nadyne Cassandra, James W. Sudik, Mary Colleen Vreeland, Barrie Youngfellow
PRODUCTIONS: Home, The Dining Room, The Tempest, among others not submitted.

CR Studio Photos

**Charles Brown, Nadyne Cassandra
in "Home"**

**Terence Knox, Kim Hunter, Edward Binns, Lois Chiles in
"Cat on a Hot Tin Roof"
*(Michelle Edelson Photo)***

COCONUT GROVE PLAYHOUSE

Coconut Grove, Florida
October 25, 1983–May 20, 1984

Artistic Adviser, Jose Ferrer; Managing Director, G. David Black; General Manager, Barry J. W. Steinman; Development, Ilene Zweig; Press, Susan Westfall; Production Manager, Marsha Hardy; Sets, David Trimble, William Schroder, Kenneth N. Kurtz, Felix E. Cochren; Costumes, Barbara A. Bell, Ellis Tillman, Maria Marrero, Debbie Ann Thompson, Judy Dearing; Lighting, David Goodman, Pat Simmons, Toni Goldin, James Riley, Allen Lee Hughes; Stage Managers, Rafael V. Blanco, Alexandra C. Fuller, Jay Tompkins, David M. Flasck, Lee Geisel, Janice C. Lane; Photographers, Michelle Edelson, Bill McPhearson

PRODUCTIONS AND CASTS:
LIGHT UP THE SKY by Moss Hart; Director, Jose Ferrer. CAST: Lois Nettleton (Irene), Mary Wickes (Stella), Gordon Chater (Carleton), Norma Davids (Miss Lowell), Harrigan Logan (Frances), Barrett Clark (Owen), Miguel Ferrer (Peter), Allen Swift (Sidney), Bill Hindman (Tyler), Jerry Hotchkiss (Max), Don Stout (Gallegher), Thomas Buckland (Sven/Cop).
A FUNNY THING HAPPENED ON THE WAY TO THE FORUM by Burt Shevelove and Larry Gelbart (Book) with music and lyrics by Stephen Sondheim; Director/Choreographer, Judith Haskell. CAST: Woody Romoff (Senex), Judith Moore (Domina), Keith Ryan (Hero), Phil Leeds (Hysterium), Jess Richards (Pseudolus), Charles Goff (Erronius), Tom McKinney (Miles Gloriosus), Steve Pudenz (Lycus), Randon Lo (Tintinabula), Kay Ostrenko (Panacea), Martie Dearmin, Barbara Gordon (The Geminae), Nancy Lyn Miller (Vibrata), Anna Cassady (Gymnasia), Suzanne Sloan (Philia), Danny Ettinger, Robb Hyman, Howard Wilkinson (Proteans).
CAT ON A HOT TIN ROOF by Tennessee Williams; Director, Jose Ferrer. CAST: Lois Chiles (Margaret), Terence Knox (Brick), James McGill (Tooker), Harold Bergman (Dr. Baugh), Kim Hunter (Big Mama), Tom McKinney (Gooper), Sandy Patton (Sookey), Edward Binns (Big Daddy), Margo Martindale (Mae), Clarence Thomas (Lacey), Erinn Acker, Joshua Goodwin, Michael Loeb, Vanessa Santiago, Trae Williamson (Children).
LIFE WITH FATHER by Howard Lindsay and Russel Crouse; Director, Jeremiah Morris. CAST: Kim Hunter (Vinnie), Emily Kairalla (Annie), Rafael Ferrer (Clarence), Ken Tibeau (John), Lon Jason (Whitney), Chad Ivan (Harlan), Jose Ferrer (Father), Jody Wilson (Margaret), Darcy Pulliam (Cora), Alicia Chambers (Mary), James McGill (Rev. Lloyd), Carol Cavallo (Nora), Harold Bergman (Dr. Humphreys), S. Alfred Carollo (Dr. Somers), Rhonda Flynn (Maggie/Delia).
DANCING IN THE END ZONE *(World Premiere)* by Bill C. Davis; Director, Stephen Hollis. CAST: Elaine Stritch (Madeleine Bernard), Tony Musante (Coach Dean), Mary Joan Negro (Jan Morrison), Fredric Lehne (James Bernard).
A SOLDIER'S PLAY by Charles Fuller; performed by the Negro Ensemble Company touring company.

THE CRICKET THEATRE

Minneapolis, Minnesota
October 19, 1983–May 12, 1984
Artistic Director, Lou Salerni; Managing Director, Rossi Snipper; Development, Sara Burstein, Glenn Skov; Associate Artistic Director, Sean Michael Dowse; Guest Artists, Vera Polvka-Mednikov (Set/Costumes), Christopher Beesely, Kristian Kraai (Costumes), Ton Butsch, Laura Cowell (Sets), Michael Vennerstrom, Lisa Johnson (Lighting), Robert Engels, Don Amendolia (Directors)

PRODUCTIONS:
CLARENCE DARROW by David W. Rintels. CAST: James J. Lawless
CLOUD 9 by Caryl Churchill. CAST: Don Amendolia, Diane Benjamin-Hill, Bruce Bohne, Shirley Venard Diercks, James Morrison, Jane Murray, Frederick Winship
GREATER TUNA by Jaston Williams, Joe Sears, Ed Howard. CAST: Robert Breuler, Frederick Winship
ANGELS FALL by Lanford Wilson. CAST: Robert Breuler, Camille D'Ambrose, Shirley Venard Diercks, Allen Hamilton, David Morgand, Frederick Winship
LONG DAY'S JOURNEY INTO NIGHT by Eugene O'Neill. CAST: Stephen D'Ambrose, Patricia Fraser, James Harris, James J. Lawless, Wendy Lawless
THE KEEPING OF PHILLIP (World Premiere) by Lawrence Kamarck. CAST: Nancy Bagshaw, Stephen D'Ambrose
SCHEHERAZADE by Marisha Chamberlain. CAST: Robert Breuler, Stephen D'Ambrose, Noreen Jeremiah, Peter Moore

Bruce Goldstein Photos

Left: Shirley Venard Diercks, James Morrison in "Cloud 9"

DALLAS THEATER CENTER

Dallas, Texas
December 6, 1983–September 2, 1984
Artistic Director, Adrian Hall; Design, Eugene Lee; General Manager, Albert Milano; Directors, Larry Arrick, Word Baker, Peter Gerety, Adrian Hall, Richard Jenkins, David Wheeler; Sets, Word Baker, Eugene Lee, James Maronek; Lighting, Zak Herring, Eugene Lee, Roger Morgan, Robert Shook; Costumes, Donna M. Kress; Stage Managers, Ken Bryant, Maureen F. Gibson, David Glynn; Press, Nancy Akers

COMPANY: Cointon Anderson, Susan Bayer, Bill Bolender, Candy Buckley, Sharon Bunn, Peggy Ann Byers, Jeanne Cairns, Bob Chapman, Melvin O. Dacus, R. Bruce Elliot, Hugh Feagin, John Figlmiller, Niki Flacks, Linda Gehringer, Peter Gerety, Robert Graham, Paul Haggard, Ann Hamilton, Dee Hannigan, John Henson, Ken D. Hornbeck, Stephen Kane, Tom Key, Jon Krause, Jo Livingston, Tom Matts, Norma Moore, Randy Moore, John Rainone, Martin Rayner, Dan Shackelford, David Stump, James Werner, Lou Williford, Dustye Winniford, Rudy Young
GUEST ARTISTS: Tom Bloom, Timothy Crowe, Patrick Hines, Richard Jenkins, David C. Jones, Richard Kavanaugh, Richard Kneeland, Becca Lish, Barbara Meek, Deirdre O'Connell, Steven Snyder, Cynthia Strickland, Daniel Von Bargen
PRODUCTIONS: Billy Bishop Goes to War, Galileo, The Wild Duck, Fool for Love, Seven Keys to Baldpate, Lady Audley's Secret, Cloud Nine, Tom Jones

Linda Blase Photos

Deirdre O'Connell, Richard Jenkins in "Fool for Love"
Above: Richard Kavanaugh, Becca Lish in "The Wild Duck"

166

Nancy Nichols, Harlan Foss, Robert Moyer,
Marion Pratnicki, Mary Munger, Howard Pinhasik in
"Man with a Load of Mischief"

DELAWARE THEATRE COMPANY

Wilmington, Delaware
October 26, 1983–March 24, 1984
Fifth Season
Artistic Director, Cleveland Morris; Managing Director, Raymond Bonnard; Business Manager, Raymond Barto; Development, Ann Schenck; Press, Marilyn Giammarco; Stage Manager, Patricia Christian; Technical Director, Eric Schaeffer; Sets, Howard P. Beals, Jr., Lewis Folden, Eric Schaeffer; Costumes, Teri Beals, E. Lee Florance; Lighting, Benjamin F. Levenberg; Sound, Alan Gardner

PRODUCTIONS AND CASTS
TRIPLE PLAY by Joseph Hart; Director, Peter DeLaurier. CAST: David Gray, Paris Peet, Scott Schofield, Vicki Shelton, F. Gregory Tigani, Ellis Skeeter Williams
MAN WITH A LOAD OF MISCHIEF by John Clifton and Ben Tarver; Director, Dorothy Danner; Musical Director, Judy Brown. CAST: Harlan Foss, Robert Moyer, Mary Munger, Nancy Nichols, Howard Pinhasik, Marion Pratnicki
DIAL "M" FOR MURDER by Frederick Knott; Director, Gavin Cameron-Webb. CAST: Charles J. Conway, William Denis, Terry Layman, Barry Mulholland, Bill Murphy, Paulette Sinclair
AIM FOR THE HEART *(World Premiere)* by Kenneth Rich; Director, Cleveland Morris. CAST: Jon Krupp, George Reinholt
THE PRIME OF MISS JEAN BRODIE by Jay Presson Allen from novel by Muriel Spark; Director, Cleveland Morris. CAST: Anna Ans, Lori Bellamy, Jarlath Conroy, Jennifer Michelle Cunha, Luba Dolgopolsky, le Clanche du Rand, Kathy Farkas, Donna Jo Furio, Aline Lathrop, Diane M. T. Lewis, Dottie Magner, Iliff McMahon, Edward Mortimer-Thomas, Barry Mulholland, Beatrice O'Donnell, Elizabeth Ryan, Irene K. Sroog

Richard Carter Photos

DENVER CENTER THEATRE COMPANY

Denver, Colorado
December 1, 1983–June 16, 1984
Fifth Season
Associate Artistic Director, Peter Hackett; Managing Director, Gully Stanford; Production Manager, Danny Ionazzi; Directing Associate/Casting Director, Dan Hiester; Stage Directors, John Broome, Wallace Chappell, Barbara Damashek, Caroline Eves, Peter Hackett, Walter Schoen, Jerry Zaks; Sets, Susan Benson, Robert Blackman, Mark Donnelly, Kent Dorsey, Christopher M. Idoine, Michael Stauffer; Lighting, Kent Dorsey, Allen Lee Hughes, Danny Ionazzi, James Sale; Music, Bruce Coughlin, Barbara Damashek, Bruce Odland; Sound, G. Thomas Clark, Bruce Odland, Brian Waters; Costumes, Susan Benson, Robert Blackman, Elizabeth Covey, Deborah Dryden, Christina Haatainen, Deborah Trout; Choreographer, Michael Sokoloff; Fight Choreographer, Mark Kincaid; Musical Directors, Bruce Coughlin, Michael Fauss; Stage Mangers, Kent Conrad, Corbey Rene Low, Jane Page, Lyle Paper, Pamela J. Young; Literary Manager/Resident Playwright, Peter Parnell; Company Manager, Mary Nelson; Business Manager, Sandra F. Dunning; Development/Press, Eleanor Glover; Photographers, Nicholas De Sciose, Larry Laszlo

COMPANY Kevin Bartlett, Duane Black, Frank Collison, Wayne Cote, Jeff Dinmore, George Ede, Lin Esser, Ken Fenwick, James Finnegan, Julian Gamble, Malcolm Hillgartner, Bob Horen, Jamie Horton, Paul James, Jason Kenny, Revina Krueger, Darrie Lawrence, Zoaunne LeRoy, Philip LeStrange, Yolanda Lloyd, Michael Maes, Gus Malmgren, Michael Mancuso, Kathy Mar, Mark McCoin, Joseph McDonald, Lisa McMillan, Gary Montgomery, Patricia Moren, Gregory Mortensen, Margery Murray, Caitlin O'Connell, David J. Partington, Peter J. Rivard, Linda O. Robinson, Robynn Rodriquez, Ruth Seeber, Jane Shepard, Archie Smith, Miles Stasica, Theodore Stevens, Glenn Tapley, Hal Terrance, James Tyrone-Wallace II, W. Francis Walters, Darline White, Melody Sue White
PRODUCTIONS: The Front Page by Ben Hecht and Charles MacArthur, The Night of the Iguana by Tennessee Williams, Romeo and Juliet by William Shakespeare, The Importance of Being Earnest by Oscar Wilde, Cyrano de Bergerac by Edmond Rostand, Spokesong by Stewart Parker, Trumpets and Drums by Bertolt Brecht, Crossfire by Theodore Faro Gross, Darwin's Sleepless Night by Merle Kessler, Door-Play by Sallie Laurie, On the Verge or The Geography of Yearning by Eric Overmyer, Hyde in Hollywood by Peter Parnell, Arms and the Man by George Bernard Shaw

Right Center: Robynn Rodriguez, Jamie Horton
"Spokesong" *(Nicholas de Sciose)*

Jamie Horton (seated), George Ede
in "Front Page" *(Larry Laszlo Photo)*

167

DETROIT REPERTORY THEATRE

Detroit, Michigan
November 3, 1983–June 24, 1984
Twenty-sixth Season
Artistic Director, Bruce E. Millan; Executive Director, Robert Williams; Press, Dee Andrus; Literary Manager/Fiscal Director, Barbara Busby; Music Director, Kelly Smith; Sets, Bruce E. Millan; Stage Managers, Dee Andrus, William Boswell; Costumes, Anne Saunders, Pamela Brown; Lighting, Kenneth R. Hewitt, Jr; Sound, Reuben Yabuku; Props, Dee Andrus, Monica Deeter; Production Assistant, Mark Murri

PRODUCTIONS AND CASTS:
VALESA, A NIGHTMARE by Jerzy Tymicki; Translated/Adapted/Introduced by Jeffrey Haddow, Maya Haddow; Director, Bruce E. Millan. CAST: Lea Charisse Woods, William Boswell, Willie Hodge, Dee Andrus, Robert Williams, Jose M. Quintero, Darius L. Dudley, Betty Lynn Marks, Andrew Dunn
CEREMONIES IN DARK OLD MEN by Lonne Elder III; Director, Dee Andrus. CAST: Duane R. Shepard, Sr., John H. McCants, Jr., Willie Hodge, Wilton Hurtt, Catrina Ganey, Robert Williams, Linda Quiroz
KEYSEARCHERS (U.S. Premiere)by Istvan Orkeny; Translated and adapted by Clara Gyorgyev; Director, Bruce E. Millan. CAST: Dee Andrus (Nellie), William Boswell (Oscar), Mack Palmer (Benedict), John Swain (Telephone Man), Mark Murri, Jim Sterner (Undertakers), Lea Charisse Woods (Kate), Catrina Ganey (Erica), James Griffin (Fodor), Robert Williams (Kovacs)
A DAY OUT OF TIME (Ellis Island 1906) by Alan Foster Friedman; Director, Bruce E. Millan. CAST: Darius L. Dudley, Dee Andrus, Jim Sterner, Camille Price, William Boswell, Bathsheba Garnett, Wilton Hurtt, Robert Rucker, Robert Williams, Alex McAlinden, Harry Carlson, James Griffin, Mark Murri

Duane R. Shepard, Sr., Willie Hodge, Wilton Hurtt,
Robert Williams in "Ceremonies in Dark Old Men"

EAST WEST PLAYERS

Los Angeles, California
October 5, 1983–August 5, 1984
Artistic Director, Mako; Administrator, Janet Mitsui; Literary Manager, Alberto Isaac; Producer, Keone Young; Technical Director, Jim Ishida; Press, Emily Kuroda; Photographers, E. Kuroda, Michael Burr, James Young

PRODUCTIONS AND CASTS
LIVE OAK STORE by Hiroshi Kashiwagi; Director, Shizuko Hoshi; Set, Fred Chuang; Lighting, Rae Creevey; Costumes, Terence Tam Soon; Producers, Jim Ishida, Keone Young; Stage Managers, Tim Dang, Susan Ioka. CAST: Keone Young, Betty Muramoto, Loren Miyake, Sala Iwamatsu, Jim Ishida, Michael Paul Chan, Tom Donaldson, Refugio A. Guevara, Michael Pujdak, Doug Yasuda
YOU'RE ON THE TEE/RIPPLES IN THE POND by Jon Shirota; Director, Dana Lee; Set/Lighting, Rae Creevey; Costumes, Sue Gee; Sound, Yuki Nakamura; Stage Manager, Jeanne Sakata. CAST: Lori Rika Inano, Timothy Dang, James Saito, Michael Pujdak, Refugio A. Guevara, Sab Shimono, Mary Rehbein, Keone Young
ASAGA KIMASHITA by Velina Houston; Director, Shizuko Hoshi; Set, Fred Chuang; Lighting, Rae Creevey; Stage Manager, Doug Yasuda. CAST: Emily Kuroda, Keone Young, Merv Maruyama, June Kim, Momo Yashima, Doreen Remo, Susan Haruye Ioka, Roger Aaron Brown
THE GRUNT CHILDE by Lawrence O'Sullivan; Director, Dana Lee; Set/Lighting, Rae Creevey; Costumes, Susan Gee; Flute Music, Will Salmon; Stage Manager, Yuki Nakamura. CAST: Bill Lee, Robert Curtin, Clay Miller, Prince A. Hughes, Doug Yasuda, Art Tizon, Peter Parros, Michael Conn, Peter Roderick, Steve Fifield, Eddie Pratt, Karin Strandjord, Lowell Gytri, Greg Rusin, Frantz Turner, Sab Shimono, Bill Wiley, Michael Paul Chan, Pat Li, Ping Wu, Charles Han, John Fife, Tex Donaldson, Don Sato
World Premieres of Paint Your Face on a Drowning on the River by Craig Kee Strete; Visitors from Nagasaki by Perry Miyake, Jr.

Sala Iwamatsu, Loren Miyake, Betty Muramoto,
Refugio A. Guevara in "Live Oak Store"
(Michael Burr Photo)

GEORGE STREET PLAYHOUSE

New Brunswick, New Jersey
October 18, 1983–May 19, 1984
Tenth Season

Producing Director, Eric Krebs; General Manager, Geoffrey Merrill Cohen; Press, Sharon Rothe; Development, Kim Nelson; Business Manager, Richard D. Granville; Literary Manager, Alexis Greene; Associate Artistic Director/Stage Manager, Maureen Heffernan; Technical Director, Reid Bartlett; Props, Dave Williams; Sound, Tom Gould; Sets, Daniel Proett; Costumes, Linda Reynolds; Lighting, Daniel Stratman

PRODUCTIONS AND CASTS
CHILDREN OF A LESSER GOD by Mark Medoff; Director, Sue Lawless. CAST: Bobbie Beth Scoggins (Sarah), Chuck Rosenow (James), Ron Trumble (Orin), Howard Brunner (Franklin), Mimi Cozzens (Mrs. Norman), Mary Beth Barber (Lydia)
THE OLD FLAG *(World Premiere)* by Vincent Canby; Director, John Schwab; Set, David Mitchell; Costumes, Hilary Rosenfeld. CAST: Paul Austin (Sgt. Bogle), Bill Pullman (Robinson), Afemo (Bent)
EMLYN WILLIAMS AS CHARLES DICKENS, a solo performance.
BEYOND THERAPY by Christopher Durang; Director, Maureen Heffernan; Set, Rob Hamilton. CAST: Garson Stine (Bruce), Marty Portser (Prudence), Richard Leighton (Dr. Framingham), Judith K. Hart (Dr. Wallace), Keith Curran (Bob), Bob Greene (Andrew)
MASTER HAROLD . . . and the boys by Athol Fugard; Director, Bob Hall. CAST: Sullivan Walker (Sam), Lowell Williams (Willie), Eric Schiff (Hally)

Suzanne Karp Krebs Photos

Lowell Williams, Eric Schiff, Sullivan Walker
in "Master Harold ... and the boys"

Carol Maillard, Heather MacRae, Pat Gorman
in "I'm Getting My Act Together" Above:
Valerie von Volz, Pirie MacDonald in "Uncle Vanya"

GeVa THEATRE

Rochester, New York
October 8, 1983–April 29, 1984

Producing Director, Howard J. Millman; General Manager, Timothy C. Norland; Marketing/Press, Adel Fico-McCarthy; Development, Gayle Porter; Literary Director, Ann Patrice Carrigan; Costumes, Pamela Scofield; Props, Nick Fici; Sets, Cynthia Sweetland; Technical Director, Robb L. Smith; Production Coordinator, Michael Powers; Stage Managers, James Sulanowski, Catherine Norberg

PRODUCTIONS AND CASTS:
I'M GETTING MY ACT TOGETHER AND TAKING IT ON THE ROAD with Book and Lyrics by Gretchen Cryer; Music, Nancy Ford; Direction/Choreography, Judith Haskell; Musical Director, Bob Goldstone; Set, Patricia Woodbridge; Costumes, Betsey Sherman Norland; Lighting, Phil Monat; Stage Manager, Catherine Norberg. CAST: Pat Gorman, Eric Hansen, Heather MacRae, Carol L. Maillard, William Van Hunter
UNCLE VANYA by Anton Chekhov; Director, Thomas Gruenewald; Set, William Barclay; Costumes, Pamela Scofield; Stage Manager, James Stephen Sulanowski. CAST: Saylor Creswell, Pirie MacDonald, Ceal Phelan, Miriam Phillips, John Quinn, Sonya Raimi, Gerald Richards, Colgate Salsbury, Valerie von Volz
THE DINING ROOM by A. R. Gurney, Jr.; Director, Beth Dixon; Set, Richard Hoover; Costumes, Martha Kelly; Lighting, Walter R. Uhrman; Stage Manager, Catherine Norberg. CAST: Amy Appleby, Arthur Burns, Saylor Creswell, Marlena Lustik, Beth McDonald, Robert Trumbull
A HELL OF A TOWN *(World Premiere)* by Monte Merrick; Director, Allan Carlsen; Set, Ray Recht; Costumes, Pamela Scofield; Lighting, F. Mitchell Dana; Stage Managers, James Stephen Sulanowski, Catherine Norberg. CAST: Joanna Gleason, John Monteith
QUILTERS by Molly Newman and Barbara Damashek with Music and Lyrics by Miss Damashek; Director, Howard J. Millman; Movement/Dances, Pilar Garcia; Musical Direction, Bob Goldstone; Set, Ursula Belden, Catherine Poppe; Costumes, Pamela Scofield. CAST: Marian Baer, Mara Beckerman, Barbara Broughton, Nora Chester, Mary Donnet, Kate Lohman, Marcia Nowik
BORN YESTERDAY by Garson Kanin; Director, Edward Stern; Set, Richard Hoover, Cynthia Sweetland; Stage Manager, Catherine Norberg; Costumes, Pamela Scofield. CAST: Jeff Brone, Alan Brooks, Saylor Creswell, Georgia Engel, Max Howard, Thora Nelson, John Quinn, Gerald Richards, Michael M. Ryan, Mary Stark, James Stephen Sulanowski

Wayne Calabrese Photos

169

GOODMAN THEATRE

Chicago, Illinois
September 23, 1983–July 8, 1984
Artistic Director, Gregory Mosher; Managing Director, Roche Schulfer; Associate Artistic Director, David Mamet; Sound, Michael Schweppe

PRODUCTIONS AND CASTS:
A RAISIN IN THE SUN by Lorraine Hansbury; Director, Thomas Bullard; Set, Karen Schulz; Costumes, Judy Dearing; Lighting, Dennis Parichy. CAST: Chuck Bailey, David Winston-Barge, Robert L. Curry, Allen Edge, Nancy Giles, Brent Jennings, Jr., Ernest Perry, Jr., Antoine Roshell, Jackie Taylor, Basil A. Wallace, Melva Williams
A CHRISTMAS CAROL adapted by Barbara Field from Charles Dickens' novel; Director, Tony Mockus; Choreographer, Gus Giordano; Set, Joseph Nieminski; Costumes, James Edmund Brady; Lighting, Robert Christen. CAST: Mark Anderson, Mary Best, Donald Brearly, Belinda Bremner, Del Close, Ralph Concepcion, Darci Dunbar, Melissa Geeting, Heather Gray, Tricia Grennan, Joseph Guzaldo, Geoffrey Herden, Dennis Kennedy, Michael A. Krawic, Molly Landgraf, Lauren Leeder, Tony Lincoln, Andrea Joy Miller, David Mink, Tony Mockus, Jr., Roger Mueller, Mark Nelson, William J. Norris, Joyce O'Brien, John Strander, Laurence Russo, Antoine Roshell, David Simpatico, Donald Thompson, Robert Thompson, Jamie Wild
CANDIDA by George Bernard Shaw; Director, Munson Hicks; Set, Joseph Nieminski; Costumes, Nan Cibula; Lighting, Robert Christen. CAST: Brad Bellamy, Wanda Bimson, Sara Botsford, James Hurdle, David Pierce, Danny Sewell
THE TIME OF YOUR LIFE by William Saroyan; Director, Donald Moffett; Set, Thomas Lynch; Sound, Christian Petersen; Choreographer, Gigi Buffington. CAST: Del Close, Nathan Davis, Kevin Dunn, Dennis Farina, Tim Halligan, Rufus E. Hill, Michael Hughes, Michael A. Krawic, Ted Levine, Catherine Martineau, Lindsay McGee, Amy Morton, Alan Novak, John Pankow, William L. Petersen, Stephen Prutting, Lee Sobczak, Natalie West, Tom White
THE ROAD (U.S. Premiere) by Wole Soyinka; Director, Wole Soyinka; Set, Patricia Woodbridge; Costumes, Judy Dearing; Lighting, Stephen Strawbridge. CAST: Paul Bates, Wilson Cain III, Lorenzo Clemmons, Bill Cobbs, Johnny Lee Davenport, Robert Jason, Razz Jenkins, Jay Lawson, Steven W. J. Long, Reggie Montgomery, Ivory Ocean, Tunji Ojeyemi, Sammy Kunle Oshin, Ernest Perry, Jr., Jeris L. Poindexter, Ving Rhames, Sam Sanders, Tony Stokes, Mark Townsend
THE THREE MOSCOWTEERS (World Premiere) adapted by the Flying Karamazov Brothers; Director, Robert Woodruff; Set, Kate Edmunds; Costumes, Susan Hilferty; Lighting, James F. Ingalls; Fight, Roy William Cox; Music, Douglas Wieselman. CAST: Steven Bernstein, Bud Chase, Laurel Cronin, Robert Dorfman, Chas Elstner, Danny Frankel, Timothy Daniel Furst, Jan Kirschner, Gina Leishman, Paul Magid, Daniel Mankin, Randy Nelson, Howard Jay Patterson, Eric Peterson, Jeff Raz, Mark Sackett, Sophie Schwab, Missy Whitchurch, Douglas Ieselman, Sam Williams
GLENGARRY GLEN ROSS (U.S. Premiere) by David Mamet; Director, Gregory Mosher; Set, Michael Merritt; Costumes, Nan Cibula; Lighting, Kevin Rigdon. CAST: Joe Mantegna, Mike Nussbaum, William Petersen, Robert Prosky, James Tolkan, Jack Wallace, J. T. Walsh
HURLYBURLY (World Premiere) by David Rabe; Director, Mike Nichols; Set, Tony Walton; Costumes, Ann Roth; Lighting, Jennifer Tipton. CAST: William Hurt, Judith Ivey, Harvey Keitel, Cynthia Nixon, Jerry Stiller, Christopher Walken, Sigourney Weaver
HEY, STAY A WHILE with plays and lyrics by John Guare; Music, Galt McDermot, Jan Warner, John Guare; Director, Larry Sloan; Musical Director, Margaret James. CAST: Kevin Anderson, William Dick, Nancy Giles, Megan Mullally
DIAGONAL MAN: THEORY AND PRACTICE written and directed by Peter Schumann and performed by the Bread and Puppet Theater.

"The Road" (Lascher Photo)

GOODSPEED OPERA HOUSE

East Haddam, Connecticut
June 1, 1983–May 31, 1984
Executive Director, Michael P. Price; Associate Producer, Warren Pincus; Musical Director, Lynn Crigler; Choreographer, Dan Siretta; Press, Kay McGrath; Technical Director, Jack Conant; Stage Managers, John J. Bonanni, Brennan Roberts; Company Manager, William S. Nagel; Casting, Warren Pincus, William S. Nagel; Props, Jennifer L. Baker; Wardrobe, John Riccucci; Hairstylist, Jerry Masarone; Production Assistant, Cindi-Marie Wanamaker

PRODUCTIONS AND CASTS
GAY DIVORCE with Book by Dwight Taylor, Kenneth Webb, Samuel Hoffenstein; Music/Lyrics, Cole Porter; Director, Robert Brink; Choreography, Helen Butleroff; Musical Director, Lynn Crigler; Book Adaptation, Bob Brittan; Dance Arrangements/Additional Orchestrations, David Schaefer; Special Consultant, Robert Kimball; Music Research Consultant, Alfred Simon; Sets, James Leonard Joy; Lighting, Craig Miller; Costumes, David Toser; Orchestrations, Hans Spialek, Robert Russell Bennett. CAST: Joe Masiell (Rudolfo), Debra Dickinson (Mimi), Leonard Drum (Waiter), Jonathan Freeman (Teddy), Bryan Harris (Octavius), Cynthia Meryl (Hortense), Krista Newmann (Barbara), Scott Willis (Guy), John Witham (Robert), Christine Gradly (Vivian), Kristie Hannum (Edith), Heather Holmes (Gladys), Connie Kunkle (Iris), Carol Marik (Doris), Kimberly Meyers (Pat), Bob Walton (Porter)
MISS LIBERTY with Music and Lyrics by Irving Berlin; Book, Robert E. Sherwood; Director, Bill Gile; Choreography, Daniel Levans; Musical Direction, Lynn Crigler; Set, Vittorio Capecce; Lighting, Jeff Davis; Costumes, David Toser; Orchestrations, Don Walker; Dance Arrangements, Donald Johnston; Assistant Musical Director, Patrick Vaccariello. CAST: Susan Browning (Maisie), Ray Gill (Pulitzer), Paula Laurence (Countess Dupont), Carole-Ann Scott (Monique), Michael Scott (Horace), Evan Thompson (Bennett), Paul Vincent (Batholdi), Roger Keller (Carthwright), Susanna Wells (Mary), Steven Minning (French Ambassador), Michael Lott (Richard Fox), Andrea Andresakis, Jack Doyle, David Gebel, Ann Heinricher, Bambi Jordan, Cindi Klinger, David Lang, Bruce Moore, Amy O'Brien, Daniel Pelzig
OH, BOY! with Music by Jerome Kern; Book/Lyrics, Guy Bolton, P. G. Wodehouse; Director, Thomas Gruenewald; Choreography/Musical Staging, Dan Siretta; Sets, James Leonard Joy; Lighting, Richard Winkler; Costumes, David Toser; Dance Music, G. Harrell; Assistant Choreographer, Lori Lynott. CAST: Susan Bigelow (Jackie), David-James Carroll (George), Dillon Evans (Briggs), Laurie Franks (Mrs. Carter), James Harwood (Judge Carter), Jack R. Marks (Constable), Julie Osburn (Lou Ellen), Joan Shepard (Penelope), David Staller (Jim), Colleen Ashton (Polly), David Fredericks (Ivan), Beth Guiffre (Sheila), Karen Harvey (Rhoda), Robert Kellet (Waiter), Gary Kirsch (Hugo), David Monzione (Phelan), Rhonda White (Lotta), Kyle Whyte (Olaf), Suzi Winson (Jane)
THE BOYS FROM SYRACUSE with Music by Richard Rodgers; Lyrics, Lorenz Hart; Book, George Abbott; Orchestrations, Hans Spialek; Director/Choreographer, Dennis Rosa; Musical Director, Lynn Crigler; Sets, James Leonard Joy; Lighting, Craig Miller; Costumes, David Toser. CAST: Judith Cohen (Luce), Ned Coulter (Sorcerer's Apprentice), Debra Dickinson (Adriana), Ken Jennings (Dromio of Ephesus), Jo Anna Lehmann (Courtesan), Lee Lobenhofer (Antipholus of Ephesus), James Mellon (Antipholus of Syracuse), Kathy Morath (Luciana), Michael Nostrand (Dromio of Syracuse), Richard Russell Ramos (Sorcerer), Ensemble: Deborah R. Bendixen, T. Michael Dalton, Lisa Guignard, Lester Holmes, Tony Jaeger, Steven Minning, Wendy Oliver, Carol Schuberg, Robin Taylor, Rebecca Timms, Zachary Wilde

Julie Osburn, David-James Carroll
in "Oh, Boy!" (Wilson H. Brownell Photo)

GUTHRIE THEATER

Minneapolis, Minnesota
June 10, 1983–March 11, 1984
Twenty-first Season
Artistic Director, Liviu Ciulei; Associate Artistic Director, Garland Wright; Managing Director, Donald Schoenbaum; Literary Manager/Associate Dramaturg, Mark Bly; Press, Dennis Behl, Timothy Streeter; Stage Directors, Edward Payson Call, Liviu Ciulei, Athol Fugard, Christopher Markle, Lucian Pintilie, Garland Wright; Sets, Jack Barkla, Radu Boruzescu, Liviu Ciulei, Ming Cho Lee, Michael Miller, Douglas Stein, Garland Wright, Paul Zalon; Costumes, Miruna Boruzescu, Jack Edwards, Gene Lakin, Carrie Robbins, Ann Wallace, Kurt Wilhelm; Lighting, William Armstrong, Frances Aronson, Dawn Chiang, Craig Miller, Richard Riddell, Paul Scharfenberger; Choreographers, Loyce Houlton, Robert Moulton, Randolyn Zinn; Musical Directors, David Bishop, Dick Whitbeck; Composer, Vasili Sirli

PRODUCTIONS AND CASTS
MASTER HAROLD. . . .and the boys with James Earl Jones, Delroy Lindo, Charles Michael Wright
THE THREEPENNY OPERA with Barbara Andres, Fred Applegate, Arminae Azarian, Charles Bari, Mark Baker, John Barone, Theodore Bikel, Joe Antony Cavise, Susanna Clemm, Mark Davis, Scott Elliot, John Fistos, Anne Gunderson, Thomas Griffith, Allen Hidalgo, Eleni Kelakos, Lee Lobenhofer, Laura McCarthy, Tony Mockus, Connie Nelson, Pamela Nyberg, Peggy O'Connell, Richard Ooms, Erica Paulson, Deirdre Peterson, Armin Schimerman, Eugene Troobnick, Henrietta Valor, Ralph Vucci, Claudia Wilkins, Dennis Warning, Danny Weathers, Jeffrey Wilkins, Stephen Yoakam
THE ENTERTAINER with Steve Coulter, Stephen D'Ambrose, Pauline Flanagan, George Hall, James J. Lawless, Lisa Naylor, Richard Ooms, Wendy Rosenberg, Christine Tschida
GUYS AND DOLLS with Fred Applegate, Arminae Azarian, Mark Baker, Charles Bari, John Barone, Joe Antony Cavise, Mark Davis, Madeleine E. Doherty, Scott Elliot, John Fistos, Thomas Griffith, Anne Gunderson, James Handy, Allen Hidalgo, Lee Lobenhofer, Mike Mazurki, Laura McCarthy, Bill McIntyre, Kathy Morath, Connie Nelson, Peggy O'Connell, Richard Ooms, Erica Paulson, Deirdre, Peterson, Barbara Sharma, Roy Thinnes, Ralph Vucci, Dennis Warning, Danny Weathers, Claudia Wilkins, Jeffrey Wilkins, Stephen Yoakam
THE SEAGULL with Oksana Bryn, Lynn Cohen, Michael Egan, Donald E. Fischer, Mary Beth Fisher, June Gibbons, George Hall, Allen Hamilton, Munson Hicks, Joel Lee, David Melmer, David Pierce, Lois Smith, Barbara Tirrell, Paul Walker
A CHRISTMAS CAROL with Julian Bailey, David E. Chadderdon, Stephen D'Ambrose, William Denis, Donald E. Fischer, Mary Beth Fisher, Kate Fuglei, June Gibbons, Jo Howarth, Kenneth LaZebnick, Patrick Leehan, David Melmer, Richard Ooms, Deirdre Peterson, John Rainer, Barbara Tirrell, Paul Walker, Danny Weathers, Stephen Willems
THE IMPORTANCE OF BEING EARNEST with Robert Burns, Robert Curtis-Brown, Michele Farr, June Gibbons, Richard Ooms, John Rainer, J. Smith-Cameron, Sylvia Short, Jane Smith
HEDDA GÁBLER with Munson Hicks, Laura Innes, Joan MacIntosh, Christopher McCann, Barbara Tirrell, David Warrilow, Joyce Worsley

Joe Giannetti Photos

**Theodore Bikel, Barbara Andres in "Threepenny
Opera" Top: J. Smith-Cameron, Robert Curtis-Brown in
"The Importance of Being Earnest"**

HARTFORD STAGE COMPANY

Hartford, Connecticut
October 4, 1983–June 3, 1984
Twenty-first Season
Artistic Director, Mark Lamos; Managing Director, William Stewart; Associate Artistic Director, Mary B. Robinson; Press, Robert P. Stein; Production Manager, Candice Chirgotis; Business Manager, Vera Furdas; Dramaturg, Helen Sheehy; Literary Manager, Constance Congdon; Stage Directors, Mark Lamos, Mary B. Robinson, Terry Kinney, Emily Mann, Clay Stevenson; Sets, David Jenkins, Michael Yeargan, Lowell Detweiler, Marjorie Bradley Kellogg, John Conklin, G. W. Mercier; Costumes, Jess Goldstein, Dunya Ramicova, Lowell Detweiller, Jennifer von Mayrhauser, G. W. Mercier; Lighting, David K. H. Elliot, Craig Miller, Paul Gallo, Pat Collins, Mimi Jordan Sherin; Stage Managers, Ruth Feldman, Wendy Chapin, Neal Ann Stephens, Candace J. Coons; Guest Artists, Playwrights Lanford Wilson, Jeffrey Sweet

PRODUCTIONS AND CASTS
AND A NIGHTINGALE SANG by C. P. Taylor. CAST: Joan Allen, John Carpenter, Robert Cornthwaite, Peter Friedman, Francis Guinan, Moira Harris, Beverly May
AS YOU LIKE IT by William Shakespeare. CAST: Nicole Baptiste, George Bowe, Robert Burr, Jeffrey Alan Chandler, Gilbert Cole, Lance Davis, Frank Groseclose, Jeffrey Hayenga, Laura Hughes, Scott Kealey, Mary Layne, Mark Lewis, Jonathan Moore, Mark Wayne Nelson, Mark O'Donnell, Kim Staunton, Saul Stein, Harley Venton
OF MICE AND MEN by John Steinbeck. CAST: Steve Carlisle, Jeffrey Alan Chandler, Eric Conger, Clifford Fetters, Kristin Griffith, Frank Groseclose, Damien Leake, Edward O'Neill, Victor Slezak, F. Allan Tibbetts
THE VALUE OF NAMES by Jeffrey Sweet. CAST: Larry Block, Alvin Epstein, Robin Groves
THREE SISTERS by Anton Chekhov (*World Premiere* translation by Lanford Wilson). CAST: Donna Agee, Robert Blumenfeld, Chris Ceraso, Jennifer Chudy, James Eckhouse, Monique Fowler, Frank Groseclose, Laura Hughes, Annalee Jefferies, Michael Kamtman, Nicholas Kepros, Mary Layne, Mark Wayne Nelson, Mark O'Donnell, Michael O'Hare, Alexander Scourby, S. Richard Simon
HOME by Samm-Art Williams. CAST: Olivia Virgil Harper, Delroy Lindo, Lorraine Toussaint

Cast of "Three Sisters"
(Lanny Nagler Photo)

171

HUNTINGTON THEATRE COMPANY

Boston, Massachusetts
October 1, 1983–June 10, 1984
Second Season
Producing Director, Peter Altman; Managing Director, Michael Maso; Marketing/Press, Marty Jones; Stage Directors, Ken Ruta, Larry Carpenter, Jacques Cartier, Edward Gilbert, Thomas Gruenewald; Sets, Richard M. Isackes, James Leonard Joy, David Jenkins; Costumes, Mariann Verheyen, Ann Wallace, James Berton Harris; Lighting, Marcus Dilliard, Frances Aronson, Roger Meeker, Pat Collins, Jeff Davis; Stage Manager, Peggy Peterson

PRODUCTIONS AND CASTS
DESIGN FOR LIVING by Noel Coward. CAST: Richard Council, Katherine Ferrand, Nicholas Kaledin, Hubert Kelly, Jr., Jeanette Landis, Ann-Sara Matthews, Kenneth Meseroll, James Walch, Pegge Winslow
UNCOMMON WOMEN AND OTHERS by Wendy Wasserstein. CAST: Sally Chamberlin, Jill Choder, Mary Donnet, Breon Gorman, Ronna Kress, Nataliji Nogulich, Viveca Parker, Lee Richardson, Ann Risley, Michele Seyler
CYRANO DE BERGERAC by Edmond Rostand; Translated by Brian Hooker. CAST: James Bodge, Susan Browning, Mark Capri, Sally Chamberlin, Max Deitch, Ray Dooley, Joyce Fideor, Dorothy Gallagher, J. S. Johnson, Henry J. Jordan, Leonard Kelly-Young, David Lawton, Samuel Maupin, William McManus, Cristal Miller, Kathleen Mulligan, Michael Pereira, Ramon Ramos, Paul Romero, David Rothauser, Claude-Albert Saucier, Ned Schmidtke, John Searles, Diana Stagner, Gail Wheeler, Aleksander F. Wierzbicki, Dester Witherell, Anthony Zerbe
PLENTY by David Hare. CAST: Clifford Arashi, Mark Lewis, Cynthia Mace, Katharine Manning, Anne Miyamoto, Al Mohrmann, Jonathan Moore, Julianne Moore, Gary Reineke, Claude-Albert Saucier, Ned Schmidtke, Doug Stender, Denise Stephenson
ON THE RAZZLE by Tom Stoppard; Adapted from a play by Johann Nestroy. CAST: Laurence Addeo, Gary Beach, Michael Chiklis, Dorothy Gallagher, Emily Heebner, Bella Jarrett, Christopher Johnston, Lohn Leighton, William McManus, Cristal Miller, Douglas Murray, Susan Pellegrino, Michael Pereira, Scott Rhyne, M. Lynda Robinson, Reid Shelton, Ingrid Sonnichsen, David Staller, Sam Tsoutsouvas, Valerie von Volz

Gerry Goodstein Photos

**Ethel Billig, Steve S. Billig in "Harry and
Thelma in the Woods"** *(Lynn Mannuell Photo)*

HERITAGE ARTISTS LTD.

Cohoes, New York
November 4, 1983–March 10, 1984
Managing Producer, William S. Campbell; Directors, Karla Koskinen, J. Barry Lewis, Vincent Telesco; Choreographer, Craig North; Musical Directors, Maida Libkin, Helen Gregory; Designers, Michael Daughtry, Chuck Noble; Stage Manager, Nancy E. Clark; Assistant to the Producer, Keith A. Shult

COMPANY: Zeva Barzell, Gary Dirda, Jaime Eisner, Andrew Hammond, Mitchell Kantor, Sarah Knapp, Danny Macrini, Jeremy Mann, Tom McClary, Richie McCall, Michele Murray, Richard Stegman, Barbara Wright, Tom Wyatt
PRODUCTIONS: Once Upon a Mattress, She Love Me, Perfectly Frank, Anything Goes, and *World Premiere* of Across the River, a new musical adaptation of Huckleberry Finn

Keith A. Shult Photos

Top Left: "She Loves Me"

**Richard Council, Katherine Ferrand,
Kenneth Meseroll in "Design for Living"**

ILLINOIS THEATRE CENTER

Park Forest, Illinois
September 30, 1983–April 29, 1984
Artistic Director, Steve S. Billig; Additional Directors, Dan LeMonnier, Etel Billig; Lighting, Richard Peterson; Costumes, Henriette Swearingen; Technical Director, Richard Poshard; Sets, Jonathan Roark; Choreographer, Mark Donaway; Photographers, Lynn Manuell, Lloyd de Grane

PRODUCTIONS AND CASTS
HAPPILY EVER AFTER (World Premiere) with Paula Markovitz, Richard Waterhouse, Etel Billig, Mark Donaway, Catherine Lord, Thomas Jan Roberts
THE MOST HAPPY FELLA by Frank Loesser. CAST: Paula Markovitz, M. Nunzio Cancilla, Etel Billig, Steve S. Billig, Mark Donaway, Sharon Ellis, Bonnie Jensen, Howard Hahn, Liz Shrake, Dan Moore, Lee Osteen, Cathy Bieber, David Saxe
HARRY AND THELMA IN THE WOODS (World Premiere) by Stan Lachow. CAST: Steve S. Billig, Etel Billig
DO LORD REMEMBER ME by James de Jongh. CAST: Pat Bowie, Razz Jenkins, Wandachristine, Tony Stokes, Albert McGhee
A LIFE by Hugh Leonard. CAST: Tim Murray, Steve S. Billig, Sharon Carlson, William A. Miles, Mark Donaway, Etel Billig, Cathy Bieber, Franette Liebow
TEIBELE AND HER DEMON by Issac Bashevis Singer and Eve Friedman. CAST: Andrea Cohen, Terry Bozeman, Dan LeMonnier, Cathy Bieber, Richard Poshard, Mark Donaway, M. Nunzio Cancilla, Bernard Rice

INTIMAN THEATRE COMPANY

Seattle, Washington
May 13, 1983–June 2, 1984
Eleventh Season
Artistic Director, Margaret Booker; General Manager, Simon Siegl; Business Manager, Jan Matheson; Development, Beatrice Wallace; Press, Lin Bauer, Kelly Allen; Production Manager, Peter W. Allen; Technical Director, Mark Putnam; Stage Managers, K. Kevyne Baar, Jane E. Maurer; Props, Carl P. Choquette; Wardrobe, Delia Mulholland

PRODUCTIONS AND CASTS
MISALLIANCE by George Bernard Shaw; Director, Margaret Booker. CAST: Terry Caza, R. Hamilton Wright, Mary Ewald, Margaret Hilton, John Gilbert, Glenn Mazen, Patrick Watkins, Jill Tanner, JV Bradley, Liann Pattison
DEAR LIAR by Jerome Kilty; Director, Robert Brink. CAST: Margaret Hilton, Ian Stuart
THE CRUCIFER OF BLOOD by Paul Giovanni; Director, Margaret Booker. CAST: David Mong, Peter Silbert, Laurence Ballard, R. Hamilton Wright, Brian Martin, Ruben Sierra, Marc Mayo, John Gilbert, Will Huddleston, Liann Pattison, Mark Jenkins, JV Bradley, Henry Tsu, Patrick Watkins, Brian Tyrrell, Amy Crumpacker
IN THE JUNGLE OF CITIES by Bertolt Brecht; Director, Christof Nel. CAST: Laurence Ballard, R. Hamilton Wright, Peter Silbert, John Gilbert, JV Bradley, David Mong, Richard Riehle, Mary Ewald, Ruben Sierra, Glenn Mazen, Marjorie Nelson, Amy Crumpacker, Mark Jenkins, Patrick Watkins, Michael Morgan-Dunne, Liann Pattison
THE RIBADIER SYSTEM by George Feydeau and Maurice Hennequin; Translated by Elizabeth Swain; Director, Nagle Jackson. CAST: David Mong, Suzy Hunt, Liann Pattison, Peter Silbert, Patrick Watkins, Laurence Ballard
THE SEAGULL by Anton Chekhov; Adapted by John Murrell; Director, Margaret Booker. CAST: Judith Roberts, David Mong, Glenn Mazen, Mary Ewald, Cal Winn, Mimi Carr, Suzy Hunt, Peter Silbert, John Gilbert, Laurence Ballard, Bill Watson, Toni Douglass, Amy Crumpacker
HOBSON'S CHOICE by Harold Brighouse; Director, James Moll; Costumes, Liz Covey. CAST: Terres Unsoeld, Jean Marie Kinney, Allison Studdiford, Daniel Mayes, Patrick Farrelly, Marjorie Nelson, Brian Thompson, David Mong, Richard Riehle, Amy Crumpacker, Brett Keogh, Michael Morgan-Dunne

Chris Bennion Photos

Will Huddleston, John Gilbert, Liann Pattison in "Crucifer of Blood"

LONG WHARF THEATRE

New Haven, Connecticut
October 6, 1983–June 16, 1984
Nineteenth Season
Artistic Director, Arvin Brown; Executive Director, M. Edgar Rosenblum; Press, Marta Mellinger; General Manager, John K. Conte; Sets, Hugh Landwehr, David Jenkins, Marjorie Bradley Kellogg, Robert Dahlstrom, Michael Yeargan, Andrew Jackness; Costumes, Noel Taylor, William Ivey Long, Sally Richardson, Bill Walker, Natasha Landau, David Murin; Lighting, Ron Wallace, Pat Collins, Judy Rasmuson; Stage Managers, Anne Keefe, George Darveris, Beverly J. Andreozzi

PRODUCTIONS AND CASTS
THE HOSTAGE by Brendan Behan; Director, Joseph Maher. CAST: Paddy Croft, Joseph Maher, Gavin Reed, James McDaniel, Mary Fogarty, Barbara Shannon, Charles Simon, Louis Beachner, John Braden, Joyce Ebert, Sean Griffin, Pippa Pearthree, Paul McCrane, Peter Rogan, Deborah Lapidus
ACCENT ON YOUTH by Samson Raphaelson; Director, Kenneth Frankel. CAST: Kathleen Quinlan, Mark Metcalf, Nancy Kulp, John Braden, Richard Venture, Richard Woods, Kimberly Farr, Marvin Greene, Peter Hydock
REQUIEM FOR A HEAVYWEIGHT by Rod Serling; Director, Arvin Brown. CAST: Tony Taddei, Kevin Carrigan, David Proval, Joseph Leon, Richard Dreyfuss, John Lithgow, Dominic Chianese, Daniel F. Keyes, Cosmo F. Allegretti, Joyce Ebert, John C. Moskoff, Bill Smitrovich, Maria Tucci, Ellis "Skeeter" Williams, John R. Conway, Kenneth R. Main
THE HOMESTEADERS by Nina Shengold; Director, John Pasquin. CAST: Jon DeVries, Sam McMurray, Nancy Elizabeth Kammer, Katherine Borowitz, Kelly Wolf
THE BATHERS *(World Premiere)* by Victor Steinbach; Director, Steven Robman. CAST: Bara-Cristin Hansen, Merwin Goldsmith, John Charles-O'Leary, Robin Leary, William Swetland, Richard E. Council, Tom Batten, Colin Fox, Kristine E. Nielsen, Jack Davidson, Robert Lansing, Colin Stinton
UNDER THE ILEX by Clyde Talmage; Director, Charles Nelson Reilly. CAST: Julie Harris, Leonard Frey
NOT QUITE JERUSALEM by Paul Kember *(American Premiere)*; Director, John Tillinger, CAST: Anthony Fusco, Daniel Gerroll, Cara Duff-MacCormick, Greg Martyn, Jon Korkes, Caitlin Clarke
SHIVAREE by William Mastrosimone; Director, Daniel Sullivan. CAST: Steven Flynn, John Procaccino, Diane Kagan, Lori Larsen, Maggie Baird

Gerry Goodstein Photos

Leonard Frey, Julie Harris in "Under the Ilex"

173

LOS ANGELES ACTORS' THEATRE

Los Angeles, California
June 16, 1983–July 14, 1984

Artistic/Producing Director, Bill Bushnell; Producer, Diane White; Consulting Director, Alan Mandell; Dramaturg/Associate Director, Adam Leipzig; Managing Director, Stephen Richard; Associate Director/Assistant to Artistic/Producing Director, R. S. Bailey; Wardrobe, Terri Emilio; Sound, Jon Gottleib; Press, Constance Harvey, Joy Lazo; Stage Managers, Donald David Hill, Chaz McEwan, Joan Toggenburger; Designer, Barbara Ling; Technical Director, David MacMurtry; Music Director/Composer, Fredric Myrow; Development, Carolyn Elliott; Photographers, Jan Deen, Rose Shoshana, Jim Farber, Demetrios Demetropoulos

PRODUCTIONS AND CASTS

NATIVE SPEECH (*World Premiere*) by Eric Overmyer; Director, John Olon; Set, A. Clark Duncan; Costumes, Fred Chuang; Choreography, Jerry Grimes; Sound Effects/Music, Sharon Smith. CAST: John Horn (Hungry Mother), Lisa Thayer (Loudspeaker), Candy Ann Brown (Freelance), Al Stevenson (Belly Up), Miguel Fernandes (Charlie), Billy Edgar (Johnny), Enrique Kandre (Jimmy/Crazy Joe), Robin Ginsburg (Janis), John LaFayette (Mook), Christine Avila (Freddy), Henry Bal (Hoover)

SURE FEELS GOOD (*World Premiere*) concept, music and lyrics by Fredric Myrow; Additional original lyrics, Mark Breyer, Martin Kibbee, Stuart Murphy, Susan Tyrrell; Director, Bill Bushnell; Costumes, Garland W. Riddle. CAST: Melissa Converse, Hannah Dean, Kim O'Kelley, Susan Tyrrell

VENUS AND ADONIS by William Shakespeare; Adapted and Performed by Benjamin Stewart.

ENEMY OF THE PEOPLE by Henrik Ibsen; *World Premiere* of Charles Marowitz adaptation; Director, Mr. Marowtiz. CAST: Peter Mitchel, Clifford A. Pellow, Barbara Tarbuck, Melissa Stern, Donald Thompson, Mathew French, Ford Rainey, Kurtwood Smith, Gerald Hiken, Robert Symonds, Tim Chic, David Hooks, Kenneth Benjamin, Larry Cort, Barbara Dab, Jackson Hughes, Mara Ivancovich, Todd Kutches, Pamela Lamont, Kate Noonan, Gregg Ostrin, William Pflueger, Marco Turbovich, Paul Ziegler, Sarah Zinsser

SUS by Barrie Keeffe; Director, Edmund J. Cambridge; Set/Lighting/Costumes, Timian. CAST: James Booth, Charles Shaughnessy, Glynn Turman succeeded by Carl W. Lumbly

SECRET HONOR: The Last Testament of Richard M. Nixon by Donald Freed and Arnold M. Stone; Director, Robert Harders; Set/Lighting, Russell Pyle. CAST: Philip Baker Hall (Mr. Nixon)

SADE-SACK or How to Live after the Asprocalisp by Pascal Vrebos; English Adaptation, Robert M. Hammond (*World Premiere*); Director, Adam Leipzig; Set, Leonard Degen. CAST: Rene Assa or Franklyn Seales

HAPPINESS/WALKING TO WALDHEIM by Mayo Simon; Set, Mary Angelyn Brown. CAST: Constance Sawyer, Manny Kleinmuntz, Walter Mathews, Blanche Bronte, Marvin Karon, Benny Baker, Lillian Adams, Marley Sims

THE CAGE by Rick Cluchey; Director, R. S. Bailey. CAST: Victor Arnold, Rudy Ramos, Ernie Hudson, Stephen Nichols

BILL AND EDDIE (*World Premiere*) by Robert Harders; Director, Bill Bushnell; Set, Arpad Petrass. CAST: Hal Bokar (Eddie), Thomas Newman (Bill), Peter Schreiner (Danny)

Jan Deen Photos

Barbara Tarbuck, Gerald Hiken, Robert Symonds
in "Enemy of the People" Top: John Larroquette,
Brian Farrell in "Bartok as Dog"

Janie Sell, Diana Verlain
in "Melody Sisters"

LOS ANGELES PUBLIC THEATRE

Los Angeles, California
October 1983–June 1984

Artistic Director, Peg Yorkin; General Manager, Suzan Miller; Sets, John Kavelin, Marjorie Bradley Kellogg; Costumes, Carol Brolaski, Marianna Elliott; Lighting, Barbara Ling; Stage Managers, Richard Winnie, Linda Hensley, Mary Michele Miner; Press, Judy Davidson, Tim Choy

PRODUCTIONS AND CASTS

BEYOND THERAPY by Christopher Durang; Director, Paul Benedict. CAST: David Clennon, Carol Morley, Robert Picardo, Linda Purl, Harry Shearer, Charles Van Eman

EXTREMITIES by William Mastrosimone; Director, Robert Allan Ackerman. CAST: Kim Darby, Meg Foster, Lauren Hutton, Kario Salem

THE DINING ROOM by A. R. Gurney; Director, Eve Brandstein. Cast not submitted.

MELODY SISTERS by Anne Commire (*World Premiere*); Directed by Miss Commire. Cast not submitted.

David Hiller Photos

MARRIOTT'S LINCOLNSHIRE THEATRE

"The Boys from Syracuse"
Top: "Gypsy"

Lincolnshire, Illinois
June 1, 1983–May 31, 1984
Producer, Kary M. Walker; Production Manager, Dyanne Earley; Development/Press, Peter R. Grigsby; Resident Director/Choreographer, David H. Bell; Stage Manager, Michael Hendricks; Sets, Jeffrey Harris; Lighting, Terry Jenkins; Costumes, Nancy Missimi; Musical Directors, Jeffrey Lewis, Kevin Stites; Props, Roy Hine; Wardrobe, Brigid Brown.

PRODUCTIONS AND CASTS
GIVE MY REGARDS TO BROADWAY (*World Premiere*) with Book, Lyrics, Direction and Choreography by David H. Bell; Music and Lyrics, George M. Cohan; Original Music, David Siegel; Musical Arrangements/Direction, Kevin Stites; Orchestrations, David Siegel; Set, Jeffrey Harris; Costumes, Doug Marmee; Lighting, Terry Jenkins; Sound, Todd Seisser. CAST: Scott Cervien (Tad), James W. Sudik (George M.), Mary Ernster (Josie), Mark Pence (Jerry), Peggy Roeder (Nellie), Kurt Johns (Stan), Carol Dilley (Maisy), Rob Rahn (Al/Dance Captain), Ross Lehman (Sam Harris), Barbara Robertson (Ethel Levy), Dana Kirk Sweeney (Pete), Peter Anderson, Quin Aluni (Pages).
CHICAGO with Book by Fred Ebb/Bob Fosse; Music, John Kander; Lyrics, Fred Ebb; Director/Choreographer, David H. Bell. CAST: Karen Curlee, Barbara Robertson, Rick Sparks, Dale Morgan, Vince Viverito, Susan Hart, Jill Walmsley, Judith T. Smith, Iris Lieberman, Suzanne Samorez, Alene Robertson, John Reeger, Susan Hart, Gordon McClure, Charles Lubeck, Vern Noparstak.
GYPSY with Book by Arthur Laurents; Music, Jule Styne; Lyrics, Stephen Sondheim; Director, Dominic Missimi; Choreography, Mark Hoebee. CAST: Alene Robertson, Vince Viverito, Paula Scrofano, Jill Walmsley, Barbi Jo Bersche, Jennifer Balen, Rob Rahn, Peggy Roeder, Judith T. Smith, Martina Vidmar, J. Neil Boyle, Marc S. Rabinowitz, James Kall, George Newbern, Mark Ward, Suzanne Samorez, Jamie Dawn Gangi, Katherine Lynne Condit, Michelle Kelly.
WINDY CITY (American Premiere) with Music by Tony Macaulay; Book and Lyrics, Dick Vosburgh; Based on play "The Front Page" by Ben Hecht and Charles Mac Arthur; Direction/Choreography, David H. Bell; Set, Jeffrey Harris; Costumes, Nancy Missimi. CAST: Ron Holgate (Burns), Kurt Johns (Hildy), Paula Scrofano (Natalie), Vanessa Shaw (Mollie), Chelcie Ross (Mayor), Frank Kopyc (Sheriff), Jimmy Sudik (Earl), Kim Strauss (Endicott), Lawrence Raiken (Schwartz), Dale Morgan (McCue), Tim Mathistad (Murphy), Bob Zrna (Kruger), Richard Storm (Bensinger), Jack Kyrieleison (Louie), Lawrence McCauley (Engelhoffer), Jim Perine (Oakland), Mary Ernster (June), Judith Riley (Jenny).
THE BOYS FROM SYRACUSE with Music by Richard Rodgers; Lyrics, Lorenz Hart; Book, George Abbott; Assistant Director, James W. Sudik; Director/Choreographer, David H. Bell. CAST: Kurt Johns, Rob Rahn, Gene Sager, Joel Sager, Mary Ernster, Kathryn Jaeck, Judith T. Smith, Nancy Voigts, Jack Kyrieleison, Bruce Falco, Mark Ward, Bob Lambert, Charles Lubeck, Rudy Hogen-Miller, Iris Lieberman

Lisa Ebright Photos

**William Wright, Barbara Barringer,
Joey L. Golden in "Candida"**

MEADOW BROOK THEATRE

Rochester, Michigan
October 6, 1983–May 13, 1984
General/Artistic Director, Terence Kilburn; Tour Director/Assistant General Director, Frank F. Bollinger; Stage Directors, Terence Kilburn, Charles M. Nolte, Carl Schurr, John Ulmer; Sets, Peter W. Hicks, Barry Griffith; Lighting, Reid G. Johnson, Barry Griffith, Deatra Smith; Stage Managers, Terry Carpenter, Thomas Spence; Technical Director, Barry Griffith; sound, Kim Kaufman; Costume Coordinator, Mary Lynn Crum; Wardrobe, Renee DiFilippo; Props, Mary Chmelko-Jaffe; Press, Jane U. Mosher.

PRODUCTIONS AND CASTS
CYRANO DE BERGERAC: Jerry Bacik, Loren Bass, Marjory Basso, Randall Forte, Jeff Scott Gendelman, George Gitto, Zdzislawa Gumul, Thom Haneline, Paul Hopper, Jayne Houdyshell, Roosevelt T. Johnson, Tom Kammer, Frederick Karn, Michael Kelley, Jeff King, Phillip Locker, John Michael Manfredi, Thomas Mahard, Maureen McDevitt, Charles McGraw, Matt Penn, Glen Allen Pruett, David Regal, John Roberts, Eric Travares, Peter Thomson
THE MAGNIFICENT YANKEE: Anthony Aiello, Peter Brandon, John Eames, George Gitto, Thom Haneline, Paul Hopper, Jayne Houdyshell, Robert Herrle, Frederick Karn, Jeff King, Melvin Kramer, Phillip Locker, Fran Loud, Thomas Mahard, Priscilla Morrill, Wayne David Parker, Matt Penn, Glen Allen Pruett, David Regal, Donald Schore, Peter Thomson
A CHRISTMAS CAROL: Marjory Basso, Bethany Carpenter, Booth Colman, Jenie Lynn Dahlmann, Jon Diskin, Thom Haneline, Roy Hall, Paul Hopper, Jayne Houdyshell, Sarah Huber, Luke Huber, Phillip Locker, Thomas Mahard, Maureen McDevitt, Wayne David Parker, Joseph Reed, John Manfredi, Anne Pringle, Jane Shaffmaster, David Sinkus, James Sterner, Peter Thomson, Larry Szafran, Cheryl Zeese
LONG DAY'S JOURNEY INTO NIGHT: Gregg Almquist, Bethany Carpenter, Deanna Dunagan, Joey L. Golden, Tony Mockus
THE DINING ROOM: Jeanne Arnold, Bethany Carpenter, Joey L. Golden, Jane Lowry, Donald Symington, Peter Thomson
THE HEIRESS: Mary Benson, Bethany Carpenter, Linda Gehringer, Thom Haneline, Jillian Lindig, Maureen McDevitt, Kathryn Paraventi, Donald Symington, Peter Thomson
CANDIDA: Mary Benson, Joey L. Golden, Thom Haneline, William LeMassena, William Wright
SIDE BY SIDE BY SONDHEIM: Jeanne Arnold, Connie Carmody, Gail Oscar, Robert Spencer, Terrence Sherman, Julie Kutosh, Jane Shaffmaster

Richard Hunt Photos

175

MERRIMACK REGIONAL THEATRE

Lowell, Massachusetts
November 5, 1983–April 15, 1984
Producing Director, Daniel L. Schay; Marketing/Press, Helene Desjarlais; Business Manager, Doris Hubert; Production Manager, Richard Rose; Technical Director, John McHugh; Stage Manager, Tom Clewell; Lighting, David Lockner; Costumes, Amanda Aldridge

PRODUCTIONS AND CATS
ARMS AND THE MAN by George Bernard Shaw; Director, Daniel L. Schay; Set, Edward Cesaitis; Costumes, Barbara Forbes. CAST: Patricia Charbonneau, Joan Kendall, Ann Crumb, Gary Armagnac, Donald Abodeely, William Miller, Richard Seguin, Richard Bekins.
A CHRISTMAS CAROL by Charles Dickens; Director, Larry Carpenter. CAST: Richard Bowne, Robin Chadwick (Scrooge), John Cruz, Edmund Davys, Elizabeth A. Dickinson, Angela Eiben, David Hilliard, Gerald Lancaster, William Miller, Janice Neri, Billy Peters, Brent Rourke, Susan Saunders, David Shanahan, Elizabeth Sheehy, Dina Veillette, Alice White
MASS APPEAL by Bill C. Davis; Director, Terence Lamude; Set, David Lockner. CAST: Edward McPhillips (Father Farley), Robert Walsh (Mark)
OF MICE AND MEN by John Steinbeck; Director, Brian Smiar; Set, Gary English. CAST: Ron Frazier, M. Patrick Hughes, William Sharp, Harold Bond, John Thomas Waite, Ariane Munker, Robert B. Johnson, John Savoia, Gregg Ward, David Connell
CHAPTER TWO by Neil Simon; Director, Gavin Cameron-Webb; Set, Alison Ford. CAST: Art Burns, Jay E. Raphael, Mary Chalon, Innes-Fergus McDade
WORKING by Studs Terkel; Adapted by Stephen Schwartz and Nina Faso; Director, Richard Rose; Set, Duke Durfee; Musical Director, Mike Huffman; Choreographer, Ronald Shepherd. CAST: Evan Bell, Stephen Crain, John Hickoc, Travis Hudson, Betsy Kiser, Michele Mais, Alberto Stevans, Frederick Walters, Suzi Winson, John Cruz, Lee Doyle, Allistair Former, Dian Veillette

John Fogel Photos

Gary Armagnac, Patricia Charbonneau, Richard Bekins in "Arms and the Man"

Ahvi Spindell, Tony Amendola, Larry Shue in "American Buffalo"

MILWAUKEE REPERTORY THEATER

Milwaukee, Wisconsin
September 23, 1983–May 20, 1984
Artistic Director, John Dillon; Managing Director, Sara O'Connor; Business Manager, Peggy Rose; Directors, Nick Faust, Sharon Ott, Stephen Katz, William Ludel, Eric Hill, Rob Goodman, Kristine Thatcher, Daniel Stein, Christopher Gibson; Sets, Ralph Funicello, Richard Hoover, Laura Maurer, Tim Thomas; Lighting, John Gisondi, Dan J. Kotlowitz, Spencer Mosse, Dennis Parichy; Costumes, Sam Fleming, Colleen Muscha, Carol Oditz, Patricia M. Risser, Kurt Wilhelm; Production Managers, Richard L. Rogers, Deborah Simon; Stage Managers, Rob Goodman, Diane Carlin-Bartel, Robin Rumpf; Wardrobe, Carol Jean Horaitis, Christine A. Cook; Props, Sandy Struth; Press, Philip Orkin

COMPANY: Eric Hill, Ellen Lauren, Daniel Mooney, James Pickering, Rose Pickering, Larry Shue
GUEST ARTISTS: Catherine Albers, Tony Amendola, Tobias Andersen, Laurence Ballard, Dana Barton, Jack Bittner, Tom Blair, Alan Brooks, Brendan Burke, Peter Callender, David E. Chadderdon, Kathleen Chalfant, Donald Christopher, Paul Collins, Edward Conery, David Coxwell, Montgomery Davis, Mary Fogarty, Robert Grossman, Davis Hall, Lois Holmes, Nicholas Hormann, David S. Howard, Jack Kyrieleison, Peter Lohnes, Jared Matesky, Ursula Meyer, Jeanne Paulsen, Burke Pearson, Wyman Pendleton, John Perkins, Mary Ed Porter, Rosemary Prinz, Rex Rabold, Victor Raider-Wexler, Peter Rybolt, Peter Silbert, Jonathan Smoots, Ahvi Spindell, William Stancil, Jack Stehlin, Daniel Stein, Edward Stevlingson, Theodore Swetz, Kristine Thatcher, Patricia Turney, Eloise Watt, Paul Zegler
PRODUCTIONS: Much Ado About Nothing by William Shakespeare, American Buffalo by David Mamet, The Splintered Wood *(World Premiere)* by William Stancil, The Forest by Alexander Ostorvsky *(World Premiere* of translation by Tom Cole), The Rules of the Game by Luigi Pirandelo, Translations by Brian Friel, A Christmas Carol by Charles Dickens and adapted by Nagle Jackson, Inclined to Agree by Daniel Stein and Christopher Gibson, Zones of the Spirit *(World Premiere)* by Amlin Gray, Antony and Me by Andrew Johns, The Frog Prince/The Revenge of the Space Pandas or Binky Rudich and the Two-Speed Clock by David Mamet

Mark Avery Photos

Left Center: "The Splintered Wood"

MONTANA REPERTORY THEATRE

Missoula, Montana
February 8,–April 28, 1984
Artistic Director/Executive Producer, Dr. James D. Kriley; Managing Director, Steve Wing; Press, Pam Ahern; Administrative Aide, Nancy Fuller; Wardrobe, Janet E. Smith; Stage Manager, Dale Kaufman; Lighting, Richard H. James; Costumes, Deborah J. Lotsof

PRODUCTIONS AND CASTS
TINTYPES conceived by Mary Kyte with Mel Marvin and Gary Pearle; Director, Randy Bolton; Scenery, Bill Raoul. CAST: Steve Abel (Charlie), Demetra Pittman (Susannah), Jeff Redford (T. R.), Patricia Britton (Anna), Julie Moore (Emma)
CHILDREN OF A LESSER GOD by Mark Medoff; Director, Cal Pritner; Set, Phil Peters. CAST: Stevie Kallos (Sarah), Jeff Redford (James), Steve Abel (Orin), Craig Kenyon Menteer (Mr. Franklin), Julie Moore (Mrs. Norman), Patricia Britton (Lydia), Demetra Pittman (Edna)

Jerry Kling Photos

Jeff Redford, Patricia Britton, Steve Abel,
Demetra Pittman, Julie Moore in "Tintypes"

NASSAU REPERTORY THEATRE

Rockville Centre, New York
October 18, 1983–June 10, 1984
Artistic Director, Clinton J. Atkinson; Managing Director, Kenneth E. Hahn; Executive Director, Sally Cohen; Technical Directors, Michael Sapsis, John Pender; Press, the Merlin Group, Cheryl Dolby, Doris Meadows; Stage Managers, David Wahl, Cornelia Twitchell, John W. Calder III; Lighting, John Hickey, Bob Bessoir; Props, Laura Kinnamon, Renee Porte, Gene Carey; Directors, Clinton J. Atkinson, Charles Karchmer; Sets, Dan Conway, David Weller, Ron Placzek, Jack Stewart; Costumes, Joan Vick, Felicia Hittner, Fran Rosenthal, Jose Lengson; Sound, Phil Lee

PRODUCTIONS AND CASTS
THE MARQUISE by Noel Coward. CAST: Tom McLaughlin, Ian Thomson, Edward Luther, Mary Portser, Robert Fitzsimmons, Ben Lemon, Tony Aylward, Delphi Harrington, Gaby Michaels
ROADSIDE by Lynn Riggs. CAST: Doug Baldwin, David H. Cohen, Lane Luckert, Don Reeves, Lee Sloan, Gaby Michaels, Kathleen Kellaigh, Will Osborne, William Sevedge, Jr., Adrian Sparks
JOURNEY'S END by R. C. Sherriff. CAST: Gene Carey, Frank Hamilton, Thomas Lawer, Elwood J. Howard, Alexander Reed, David H. Cohen, Hall Hunsinger, Ben Lemon, Mike O'Carroll, Lee Sloan, Zeke Zaccaro
THE MIDDLE AGES by A. R. Gurney, Jr. CAST: Mimi Cozzens, Kymberly Dakin, James Harder, Harley Venton
THE LITTLE FOXES by Lillian Hellman. CAST: Thomas Anderson, P. J. Barry, Pamela Burrell, David H. Cohen, Minnie Gentry, Eve Hall, Bjorn Johnson, Linda Kampley, John Newton, David Pursley

Cathy Blaivas Photos

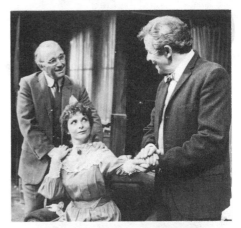

P. J. Barry, Pamela Burrell, John Newton
in "The Little Foxes"

NEW PLAYWRIGHTS' THEATRE

Washington, D. C.
July 1, 1983–June 30, 1984
Twelfth Season
Artistic Director, Harry M. Bagdasian; Managing Director, Todd Bethel; Literary Manager, E. Lloyd Rose; Production Manager, Jim Taylor; Press, Shelley M. Clark, Sarah Oram; Technical Director, Neil P. Wilson; Sets, Russell Metheny, Lewis Folden, Douglas A. Cumming; Lighting, Daniel M. Wagner, Lewis Folden, Nancy Schertler; Costumes, Mary Ann Powell, Jane Schloss Phelan

PRODUCTIONS AND CASTS
BEYOND YOUR COMMAND (*World Premiere*) by Ralph Pape; Director, Ron Canada. CAST: Franchelle Stewart Dorn, Roger Frazier, Ernie Meier, Lisa Mobley, Fred Strother, Bill Grimmett, Caron Tate
FLESH EATERS (*World Premiere*) by Ernest Joselovitz; Director, James C. Nicola. CAST: Christopher Hurt, Rosemary Walsh, Stephen Zazanis, Robert Lesko, Valdred Brown, Jeff Albert, David Ingram, Beau James
GROVES OF ACADEME/THE LIBRARY OF CONGRESS TALENT SHOW two one-act plays by Mark Stein; Director, Steve Albrezzi. CAST: Ernie Meier, Linda Hall, Carter Reardon
GARDENIA in repertory with **LYDIE BREEZE** by John Guare; Directors, James C. Nicola, E. Lloyd Rose. CAST: Laurie Spencer, Grover Gardner, Stanley Anderson, Ernie Meier, Carter Reardon, Kathleen Weber, Tami Tappen, Kevin Joseph, Steven Dawn, Cary Anne Spear, Brian Price, David Ingram, Jerry Paone

Doc Dougherty Photos

Bill Grimmett, Lisa Mobley, Fred Strother
in "Beyond Your Command"

NORTHLIGHT REPERTORY THEATRE COMPANY

Evanston, Illinois
October 5, 1983–July 1, 1984
Eighth Season
Artistic Director, Michael Maggio; General Manager, Eileen Tipton; Business Manager, Richard Schnackenberg; Marketing, Ellen Mittenthal; Development, Dan McKinley; Press, Marilyn Perlman; Stage Manager, James K. Tinsley; Technical Director, Teri McClure: Assistant Artistic Director, Jimmy Bickerstaff; Production Assistant, Carolyn Piper Zinner; Lighting, Bob Shook

PRODUCTIONS AND CASTS
SONDHEIM SUITE (World Premiere) by Michael Maggio and Wacker Drive; Director, Michael Maggio; Set, John Paoletti, Mary Grisweld; Costumes, Julie Jackson. CAST: Vivina Davis, Skip Hartstim, John Salewski
WHAT I DID LAST SUMMER by A. R. Gurney, Jr.; Director, Michael Maggio; Set, James Nieminski; Costumes, Kay Nottbusch. CAST: Laurel Cronin, Deanna Dunagen, Jeff Ginsberg, Joseph Guzaldo, Jeaning Morick, Meagan Mullally
MEETINGS by Mustapha Matura; Director, Jim O'Connor; Set, Jeffrey Bauer; Costumes, Rita Pietraszek; Props, Linda Samodral. CAST: Pat Bowie, Bruce Young, Celene Evans
BALLERINA (U.S. Premiere) by Arne Skouen; Director, Michael Maggio; Set, Linda Buchanen; Costumes, Kerry Fleming. CAST: Belinda Bremner, Ann Dowd, John Greenleaf, Dorothea Hammond, John Mahoney, Marian Reiter
THE PRICE by Arthur Miller; Director, Sheldon Patinkin; Set, Michael Merritt; Costumes, Julie Jackson; Lighting, Geoffrey Bushor. CAST: Caitlin Hart, Joe Lauck, John Mahoney, Bernie Landis
WHAT THE BUTLER SAW by Joe Orton; Director, Michael Maggio; Set, Joseph Neiminski; Costumes, Kerry Fleming; Technical Director, Debra Gohr. CAST: Jorge Cacheiro, Dennis Cockrum, Jodean Culbert, John Mahoney, Roger Mueller, Megan Mullally

Lisa Ebright Photos

**Caitlin Hart, Joe Lauck, John Mahoney,
Bernie Landis in "The Price"**

PAPER MILL PLAYHOUSE

Millburn, New Jersey
September 14, 1983–June 10, 1984
Executive Producer, Angelo Del Rossi; General Manager, Wade Miller; Administrative Director, Jim Thesing; Marketing, Debra Waxman; Press, Albertina Reilly; Production Manager, David Kissel; Sets, Michael Anania, Robert Barnes, Karl Eigsti, James M. Pouchard, Philip Rodzen; Costumes, Gail Cooper-Hecht, Guy Geoly, Arnold S. Levine, Julie Weiss; Lighting, Barry Arnold, Frances Aronson, Patricia Donovan, David Kissel; Stage Managers, Jerry Bihm, James Danford, Roy Meachum, Robert Neu, Robert C. Strickstein, Ben Strobach; Photographers, Terence A. Gili, Dalia Studio

PRODUCTIONS AND CASTS
ANNIE by Thomas Meehan, Charles Strouse, Martin Charnin; Director, Jerry Adler; Musical Director, Glen Clugston. CAST: Jennine Babo, Suzanne Bedford, Deborah Bendixon, Stanley Bojarski, Edwin Bordo, Dana Dawson, Dick Ensslen, Donald Hare, Gary Holcombe, Tammy Kauffman, Loren Kaufman, Danielle Kelly, Tara Kennedy, Marcia Lewis, David E. Mallard, Caroline McMahon, Moose, Dorothy Stanley, Sam Stoneburner, Swen Swenson, Donna Thomason, Mimi B. Wallace, Katy Winters
FIDDLER ON THE ROOF by Joseph Stein, Jerry Bock and Sheldon Harnick; Director, Frank Coppola; Musical Director, Michael Dansicker. CAST: Maurice Brenner, Elizabeth Cade, Lindsay Cain, Edward M. Carrion, Joe Cusanelli, Joel Dzarlinsky, Michael Howell Deane, Kevin Dearinger, Jason Edwards, Rhonda Farer, Carol Grant, Allen Gruet, Anna Marie Gutierrez, Daniel P. Hannafin, Goldie Harris, Mitchell Jason, Ruth Kaye, Kelby Kirk, Bryant Lanier, Elliot Levine, Davie E. Mallard, John T. O'Conner, Michele Pigliavento, Lee Raines, Tee Scatuorchio, Carlo Thomas, Laura Tubbs, Jeffrey Wilkins, Dolores Wilson, Phyllis Young, Emily Zacharias
THE GUARDSMAN by Ferenc Molnar; Director, David Rothkopf. CAST: Lucie Arnaz, Jane Connell, Michael Lipton, Laurence Luckinbill, Jane Prelinger, Richard Zavaglia
THE SHOW-OFF by George Kelly; Director, William H. Putch. CAST: Orson Bean, Lloyd Brass, Pamela Burrell, Sally Dunn, Wil Love, John Newton, Carl Schurr. P. Jay Sidney, Jean Stapleton
JOSEPH AND THE AMAZING TECHNICOLOR DREAMCOAT by Tim Rice and Andrew Lloyd Webber; Director, Tony Tanner; Musical Director, Michael Tornick. CAST: Bob Amore, Wayne Bryan, Elizabeth Cade, Tom Carder, Paul Cira, Marcy DeGonge, John Ganzer, James H. Gedge, Stephen Hope, Peter Kapetan, Liz Larsen, Ken Lundie, Robert McNeill, Jodi Marzorati, Lorena Palacios, Gordon Stanley, Carrie Waller, Elizabeth Gray Williams
THE DESERT SONG by Sigmund Romberg, Otto Harbach, Oscar Hammerstein II, Frank Mandel; Director, Robert Johanson; Musical Director, Phil Hall. CAST: John Anania, Cathleen Axelrod, Karen Bogan, Beth Bornstein, Merwin Foard, John Foster, Lillian Graff, Devin Gray, Ruth Gottschall, Randy Hansen, Ira Hawkins, Terence Hodges, Patrice Hollrah, Kathryne Jennings, Kenneth Kantor, Bryant Lanier, Kirk Lawson, Brent Maroon, Gene Masoner, David Miles, Judith McCauley, Jean McClelland, Philip William McKinley, Monte Ralstin, Stephen Allen Roberts, Keith Ryan, Kelly Sanderbeck, Brad Scott, Michael Craig Shapiro, Richard White, Elizabeth Gray Williams, Roy Alan Wilson, Carol Wolfe

**Sally Dunn, Orson Bean, Jean Stapleton,
Lloyd Bass in "The Show-Off"**
(Terence A. Gili Photo)

OLD GLOBE THEATRE

San Diego, California
January 7,–October 2, 1983
Thirty-fourth Season
Executive Producer, Jack O'Brien; Artistic Director, Jack O'Brien; Managing Director, Thomas Hall; Press, Bill Eaton

PRODUCTIONS AND CASTS

THE SKIN OF OUR TEETH by Thornton Wilder; Director, Jack O'Brien; Set, Douglas W. Schmidt; Costumes, Robert Morgan; Composer, Conrad Susa; Lighting, Gilbert V. Hemsley, Jr.; Sound, Dan Dugan; Stage Manager, Douglas Pagliotti. CAST: Blair Brown (Sabina), Sada Thompson (Mrs. Antrobus), Sean Sullivan (Dinosaur), Michael Lueders (Mammoth), Gary Dontzig (Telegraph Bay), Monique Fowler (Gladys), Jeffrey Combs (Henry), Harold Gould (Mr. Antrobus), Bill Geisslinger (Doctor), Larry Drake (Professor), G Wood (Judge/Tremayne), Bonnie-Campbell Britton (Miss T Muse), Renee Brooks (Miss M Muse), Diana Bellamy (Miss E Muse), Jonathan McMurtry (Fitzpatrick), John Houseman (Newscaster), Rue McClanahan (Fortuneteller), Rosina Widdowson-Reynolds (Hester), Diana Bellamy (Ivy), John Eames (Fred Baily)

MASS APPEAL by Bill C. Davis; Director, David McClendon; Set, Mark Donnelly. CAST: Tom Lacy (Father Farley), Andrew Stevens (Mark Dolson)

TERRA NOVA by Ted Tally; Director, Gerald Gutierrez; Set, Douglas Stein. CAST: Benjamin Hendrickson (Scott), Michael MacRae (Amundsen), Christine Healy (Kathleen), James Coyle (Bowers), Larry Drake (Oates), Jonathan McMurtry (Wilson), Mark Harelik (Evans)

WINGS by Arthur Kopit; Director, Eve Roberts; Set/Lighting, Kent Dorsey. CAST: Teresa Wright (Emily), Tamu Gray (Amy), Robert Ellenstein (Brownstein), Ellen Drexler (Mrs. Timmins), John Procaccino (Billy), G Wood, Paul Hebron (Doctors), Diane Rodriquez, Joan Synder (Nurses)

CLAP YOUR HANDS (*World Premiere*) by Ellis Rabb; Text developed in collaboration with Nicholas Martin; Director, Ellis Rabb; Set, Robert Morgan, Kent Dorsey. CAST: G Wood (Darling), Patricia Conolly (Wendy), Ralph Williams (Peter)

THE DINING ROOM by A. R. Gurney, Jr.; Director, Craig Noel; Set, Alan K. Okazaki; Costumes, Sally Cleveland. CAST: Jonathan McMurtry, Kandis Chappell, Michael Byers, Deborah Taylor, Jay Bell, Caroline Smith

TWELFTH NIGHT by William Shakespeare; Director, Jack O'Brien; Set, Douglas W. Schmidt; Costumes, Robert Morgan. CAST: Jack Wetherall (Orsino), Henry J. Jordon (Sebastian), Von Schauer (Antonio), Alex Starr (Sea Captain), Joseph Drago (Valentine), Will Dalley (Curio), Jonathan McMurtry (Sir Toby), Jeffrey Alan Chandler (Sir Andrew), Tom Lacy (Malvolio), Sean Sullivan (Fabian), G Wood (Feste), Katherine McGrath (Olivia), Marsha Mason (Viola), Christine Healy (Maria), Jean M. Lesmeister, Eva Wielgat (Attendants), Derek Harrison Hurd, Alex Starr (Officers), Derek Harrison Hurd, Reed Maroc (Servants)

HENRY IV PART I by William Shakespeare; Director, James Dunn; Set, Steven Rubin; Costumes, Alan Armstrong. CAST: Thomas Hill succeeded by Thomas S. Oleniacz (Henry IV), Mark Moses (Prince of Wales), Michael Cadigan (Prince John), Thomas S. Oleniacz succeeded by Robert Curry (Westmoreland), Mark Rasmussen (Sir Walter), Robert Strane (Thomas Percy), Larry Drake (Earl of Northumberland), Stephen McHattie (Hotspur), Michael Masterson (Mortimer), James Carpenter (Vernon), David Ogden Stiers (Falstaff), Christopher Brown (Poins), Robert Curry (Gadshill), Laurence Kaiser (Peto), Bertram Tanswell (Bardolph), Mark Hofflund (Francis), Deborah Taylor (Lady Percy), Christie Botkin (Lady Mortimer), Diana Bellamy (Mrs. Quickly), Matthew Downham (Page), Jay Jones, Anne Lilly, Donald Martin, JoAnn Johnson Patton, Cecilia Rathburn, Barry Sherman

TALLEY'S FOLLY by Lanford Wilson; Director, Andrew J. Traister; Set, Kent Dorsey; Costumes, Robert Morgan. CAST: Robert Darnell (Matt), Monique Fowler (Sally)

ARSENIC AND OLD LACE by Joseph Kesselring; Director, Craig Noel; Set, Richard Seger; Costumes, Deborah Dryden. CAST: Elizabeth Kerr (Abby), Robert Strane succeeded by William Roesch (Rev. Harper), Thomas S. Oleniacz (Teddy), Von Schauer (Brophy), Michael Cadigan (Klein), Helen Page Camp (Martha), Deborah Allison (Elaine), Scott Stevensen (Mortimer), Andrew J. Traister (Gibbs), Larry Drake (Jonathan), Jeffrey Alan Chandler (Einstein), James Carpenter, (O'Hara), Navarre T. Perry (Rooney), Bertram Tanswell (Witherspoon)

THE RIVALS by Richard Brinsley Sheridan; Director, Joseph Hardy; Set/Costumes, Steven Rubin. CAST: Paxton Whitehead (Anthony Absolute), Jack Wetherall (Jack Absolute), Mark Moses (Faulkland), Jonathan McMurtry (Acres), David Ogden Stiers (Sir Lucius), Tom Lacy (Fag), Sean Sullivan (Boy), Michael Masterson (David), Bertram Tanswell (Thomas), Katherine McGrath (Mrs. Malaprop), Harriet Hall (Lydia), Caitlin O'Heaney (Julia), Deborah Taylor (Lucy), Christy Botkin, Robert Curry, Joseph Drago, Mark Hofflund, Laurence Kaiser, Jean Lesmeister, JoAnn Johnson Patton, Alex Starr, Eva Wielgat

MACBETH by William Shakespeare; Director, Jack O'Brien; Set, Kent Dorsey; Costumes, Robert Morgan. CAST: Andra Akers (Lady Macbeth), Christopher Brown (Lennox), Monique Fowler (Malcolm), Christine Healy (Lady Macduff), Henry J. Jordan (Banquo), Stephen McHattie (Macduff), Mark Rasmussen (Ross/Siward), Jack Sydow (Duncan/Porter/Doctor), Anthony Zerbe succeeded by Jonathan McMurtry (Macbeth)

Robert Burroughs Photos

Monique Fowler, Sada Thompson, Jeffrey Combs,
Sean Sullivan, Harold Gould in
"The Skin of Our Teeth"

Jack Wetherall, Paxton Whitehead, Katherine McGrath,
Harriet Hall in "The Rivals"

Jack Wetherall, Marsha Mason
in "Twelfth Night"

PENNSYLVANIA STAGE COMPANY

Allentown, Pennsylvania
September 28, 1983–June 3, 1984
Producing Director, Gregory S. Hurst; General Manager, Gary C. Porto; Associate Director/Literary Manager, Pam Pepper; Sets, Quentin Thomas, Richard Hoover, William Barclay, Curtis Dretsch, Russell Smith, Karen Schulz, Robert Thayer; Costumes, Johanna Forte, Karen Gerson, Colleen Muscha, Martha Kelly, Karen Schulz, Ann Hould-Ward; Lighting, Quentin Thomas, Richard Hoover, Phil Monat, Curtis Dretsch, William Frein, Stephen Strawbridge, Robert Thayer; Stage Managers, Dennis Blackledge, Peter S. Del Vecho; Press, Joan Nowak; Marketing, William Coyne; Development, Donna B. Rovito; Business Manager, Paul E. Davison; Production Manager, Peter Wrenn-Meleck

PRODUCTIONS AND CASTS
SLEUTH by Anthony Shaffer; Director, Stephen Rothman. CAST: Jack Aranson, Sam Maupin
ALL MY SONS by Arthur Miller; Director, Gregory S. Hurst. CAST: Arch Johnson, Victoria Boothby, Stephen Stout, Margaret Reed, James Maxwell, Dallas Greer, Maggie Tucker, Brian Reddy, Tammie McKenzie, John Henry Pearce
A CHRISTMAS CAROL by Charles Dickens; Adapted by Pam Pepper; Director, Pam Pepper. CAST: Robert Davis, Susan Decker, Stanley Flood, Kay Foster, Diane Kamp, Barbara Marineau, James Maxwell, Michael John McGann, Tammie McKenzie, Robbie Miller, John Scanlan, David Smith, Elaine Swenson, William Van Hunter, Lesley Vogel, Joyce Worsely, Ray Xifo, Michael Zibers
COPPERHEAD (World Premiere) by Erik Brogger; Director, Gregory S. Hurst. CAST: Paul Guilfoyle, Ann Wedgeworth, Arch Johnson, Dennis Bailey
CHILDREN OF A LESSER GOD by Mark Medoff; Director, Robert Livingston. CAST: Mary Beth Barber, Robin Bartholiek, Mimi Bensinger, Candace Broeker, Don Gantry, Tammie McKenzie, Chuck Rosenow, Joan Ulmer
THE FURTHER ADVENTURES OF SALLY (World Premiere) by Russell Davis; Director, Tony Giordano. CAST: Sheree North, Gary Tacon, Gary McCleery
I DO, I DO with Book and Lyrics by Tom Jones; Music, Harvey Schmidt; Director, Julianne Boyd; Musical Direction, Vicki Carter; Choreography, Yvonne Adrian. CAST: Kathleen Marsh, Robert Stoeckle

Gregory M. Fota Photos

**Top Right: Sandy and Dennis Bailey
in "Copperhead"**

**Sheree North, Gary Tacon
in "Further Adventures of Sally"**

PHILADELPHIA DRAMA GUILD

Philadelphia, Pennsylvania
October 6, 1983–May 13, 1984
Producing Director, Gregory Poggi; Business Manager, Mark Bernstein; Marketing, Barbara Konik; Development, Tom Sherman; Press, Mary P. Packwood; Sets, Barry Robison, John Jensen, John Falabella, Daniel P. Boylen; Costumes, James Edmund Brady, Constance R. Wexler, Frankie Fehr, Jess Goldstein; Lighting, William Armstrong, Jeff Davis, Ann Wrightson, F. Mitchell Dana; Stage Managers, Ralph Batman, Donna E. Curci; Director Playwrights Projects, Steven Schachter

PRODUCTIONS AND CASTS
TEIBELE AND HER DEMON by Isaac Bashevis Singer, Eve Friedman; Director, Steven Schachter. CAST: Cristine Rose, Timothy Landfield, Paul Harman, Suzanne Toren, Dominic Chianese, Jeff Natter, Michael P. Stoltz
THE MEMBER OF THE WEDDING by Carson McCullers; Director, William Woodman. CAST: Esther Rolle, Jane Jones, Roshi Handwerger, Matthew Ashford, Kelly Curtis, Donald Gantry, Sandi Shackelford, Rama Atkins, Claire Kelly, Helen Craig Malloy, Robert Colston, Dorwey Wright, Thomas Vallette
THE DINING ROOM by A. R. Gurney, Jr.; Director, Charles Karchmer. CAST: Scotty Bloch, Richmond Hoxie, Miles Chapin, Alice Nagel, Christine Farrell, Jonathan Moore
BLACK COMEDY by Peter Shaffer; Director, Jerry Zaks. CAST: Stephen Stout, Jill Rose. Anita Dangler, Michael Egan, Richard Peterson, Jerry Zaks, Margot Dionne, Charles Techman
THE FATHER by August Strindberg; New translation/adaptation (World Premiere) by Oliver Hailey, Ann. B. Weissman; Director, William Woodman. CAST: Stephen Joyce, Adrian Sparks, James McConnell, Mark Lewis, Betsy Palmer, Jonathan Moore, Ruth Nelson, Katherine Leask

Kenneth Kauffman Photos

**Stephen Joyce, Betsy Palmer
in "The Father"**

PLAZA THEATRE

Dallas, Texas
September 21, 1983–May 13, 1984
Premiere Season

Executive Director, Kjehl Rasmussen; Artistic Director, Dale AJ Rose; Assistant Executive Director, Joe Calk; Business Manager, Randy Brown; Production Manager, Douglas Parker; Props, A. Dale Nally; Wardrobe, Jan Allison, Sarajane Milligan; Casting, Pat McCorkle; Press, Bonnie Leslie; Photographer, Tom Geddie

PRODUCTIONS AND CASTS

THE PALACE OF AMATEURS by John Faro PiRoman; Director, Walton Jones; Set, G. W. Mercier; Costumes, Susan Hilferty; Lighting, Ann Wrightson; Sound, Rick Peeples; Stage Manager, Richard Lombard. CAST: Louisa Flaningam, Richard Frank, John Goodman, Mariel Hemingway, Alan Rosenberg, Ben Siegler, Florence Stanley

CRIMES OF THE HEART by Beth Henley; Director, Dale AJ Rose; Set, G. W. Mercier; Costumes, Colleen Muscha; Lighting, David Martin Jacques; Sound, Rick Peeples; Stage Manager, Steve Zorthian. CAST: Gregory Grove, Annalee Jefferies, Debbie Leigh Jones, Alexa Kenin, Wesley A. Pfenning, Gary Roberts

THE DINING ROOM by A. R. Gurney, Jr.; Director, Mesrop Kesdekian; Set, William Eckart; Costumes, Patty Greer McGarity; Lighting, C. Dall Brown; Stage Manager, Steve Zorthian. CAST: Laurinda Barrett, Kermit Brown, Donna Bullock, Dwain Fail, Lizbeth Mackay, Scott Waara

MASTER HAROLD . . . and the boys by Athol Fugard; Director, Mr. Fugard; Set, Jane Clark; Costumes, Sheila McLamb; Lighting, David Noling; Company Manager, Sandy Carlson; Stage Manager, Naomi Wexler. CAST: Zakes Mokae, Ray Aranha, Evan Handler

THE ACTING COMPANY (John Houseman, Producing Artistic Director) presents in repertory: THE CRADLE WILL ROCK by Marc Blitzstein, THE MERRY WIVES OF WINDSOR by William Shakespeare, and PERICLES by William Shakespeare. CAST: Charles Berigan, Laura Brutsman, Jerome Butler, Terrence Caza, Libby Colahan, Jacqueline DeHaviland, David Fuller, Richard S. Iglewski, Jack Kenny, David Manis, Michael Manuelian, DeLane Matthews, Steven Mattila, Davenia McFadden, Phil Meyer, Anthony Powell, Gregory Welch

Tom Geddie Photos

**Top Right: Richard Frank, Mariel Hemingway,
Ben Siegler in "The Palace of Amateurs"**

**Kermit Brown, Lizbeth Mackay,
Scott Waara in "The Dining Room"**

**(clockwise) Catherine Gaines, Michael McCarty,
Lucinda Hitchcock Cone, Gail Grate,
Randy Brenner in "Tintypes"**

REPERTORY THEATRE OF ST. LOUIS

St. Louis, Missouri
September 7, 1983–April 13, 1984

Acting Artistic Director/Managing Director, Steven Woolf; Assistant Managing Director, Jane E. Bryan; Development/Press, Anne B. DesRosiers, Barbara Harris, Dorothy A. Brockhoff, Sharon Salomon; Directors, Timothy Near, Marita Woodruff, Pamela Hunt, Edward Stern, Gregory Boyd, Ian Trigger, Milton R. Zoth, Larry Lillo; Sets, Carolyn L. Ross, Dorothy L. Marshall, John Roslevich, Jr., Tim Jozwick, Bill Schmiel, Michael Ganio; Costumes, Carolyn L. Ross, Dorothy L. Marshall, Michael Ganio, Bonnie J. Cutter, Steven Epstein; Lighting, Max De Volder, Peter E. Sargent, Glenn Dunn; Stage Managers, Glenn Dunn, T. R. Martin, Rachael Lindhart, M. Gregory Murphy

PRODUCTIONS AND CASTS

THE GLASS MENAGERIE by Tennessee Williams. CAST: Rosemary Prinz, Peter Webster, Susan Greenhill Victor Slezak

THE DINING ROOM by A. R. Gurney, Jr. CAST: Jillian Lindig, Alan Clarey, Cordis Heard, Brian Hohlfeld, Lee Patton Hasegawa, John Michalski

TINTYPES by Mary Kyte, Mel Marvin, Gary Pearle. CAST: Randy Brenner, Lucinda Hitchcock Cone, Catherine Gaines, Gail Grate, Michael McCarty

SLEUTH by Anthony Shaffer. CAST: Robert Burr, Michael Rothhaar

MEDEA by Euripides; Robinson Jeffers adaptation. CAST: Ronnie Gilbert, James Paul, Martha Miller, Julia Jonathan, Lynn Ann Leveridge, Judith Anna Roberts, Peter Johl, Alexander Spencer, Ian Stuart, Roscoe F. Carroll, Gregory Michael Sporleder

THE IMPORTANCE OF BEING EARNEST by Oscar Wilde. CAST: Dennis Bacigalupi, Alan Clarey, Anthony Fusco, Paddy Croft, Laura MacDermott, Jeanette Landis, Christa Germanson, Brendan Burke, Wayne Salomon

TRUE WEST by Sam Shepard. CAST: John Spencer, Jonathan Fuller, James Paul, Janet Ward

KILLER'S HEAD/THE UNSEEN HAND by Sam Shepard. CAST: Chris Limber, Barron Winchester, Joneal Joplin, Dan Marderosian, Maxwell Beaver

TONGUES with Ronnie Gilbert, William Uttley

SAVAGE/LOVE with Ronnie Gilbert, William Uttley, Robert DeBellis

Scott Dine Photos

SEATTLE REPERTORY THEATRE

Seattle, Washington
October 25, 1983–May 19, 1984

Producing Director, Peter Donnelly; Artistic Director, Daniel Sullivan; Associate Artistic Director, Douglas Hughes; Technical Director, Robert Scales; Production Manager, Vito Zingarelli; Press, Marnie Andrews, Juli Ann Rae; Marketing, Jerry Sando; Development, Frank Self; Wardrobe, Sally Roberts; Stage Manager, Mary Hunter; Sound, Michael Holten; Photographers, Chris Bennion, Nick Gunderson, Don Hamilton

PRODUCTIONS AND CASTS

THE BALLAD OF SOAPY SMITH *(World Premiere)* by Michael Weller; Director, Robert Egan; Sets, Eugene Lee; Costumes, Robert Blackman; Musical Score, Norman Durkee. CAST: Roderick Aird, Denis Arndt, John Aylward, Kurt Beattie, JV Bradley, James Brousseau, Scott Caldwell, Karen Kay Cody, Christopher Cooper, Frank Corrado, Lee Corrigan, Clayton Corzatte, Toni Cross, Ted D'Arms, Corky Dexter, Norman Durkee, Tina Marie Goff, Mark Jenkins, Brian Martin, Kate Mulgrew, Marjorie Nelson, William P. Ontiveros, Rod Pilloud, Richard Riehle, Gretchen Runbaugh, Michael Santo, Michael J. Smith, Kevin Tighe, Kathleen Worley

THE ADVENTURES OF HUCKLEBERRY FINN *(World Premiere)* by James Hammerstein, Christopher Harbon; Director, James Hammerstein; Sets, Robert Dahlstrom; Costumes, Liz Covey; Lights, Arden Fingerhut; Music, Ralph Affoumado; Musical Director, Daniel Brinbaum; Musical Staging, Nancy Cranbourne; Stage Manager, Marc Rush. CAST: Karen Kay Cody, Frank Corrado, Ted D'Arms, Corky Dexter, Brian Faker, Michael Beer, Tamu Gray, Mark Jenkins, Susan Ludlow, Robert Macnaughton, Glenn Mazen, Kathryn Mesney, Marjorie Nelson, Keith Nicholai, William O'Leary, John Procaccino, Carl August Sander, Michael Santo, Steve Sneed, David Toney, Sharon Ullrick

MAKE AND BREAK by Michael Frayn; Director, Daniel Sullivan; Sets, Hugh Landwehr; Costumes, Robert Wojewodski; Lights, Pat Collins; Stage Manager, Diane DiVita. CAST: Denis Arndt, Christian Burz, Veronica Castang, Clayton Corzatte, Ted D'Arms, Tony DeBruno, Gale McNeeley, Michael Santo, R. Hamilton Wright, William Wright

THE MISANTHROPE by Moliere; Richard Wilbur translation; Director, Garland Wright; Set, Paul Zalon; Costumes, Kurt Wilhelm; Lights, Jennifer Tipton; Stage Manager, Marc Rush. CAST: Brian Cousins, Ted D'Arms, Daniel Davis, Mary Ewald, Dennis R. J. Fox, Michael Geer, David Hunter Koch, Kate Mulgrew, Jeff Natter, Mary Lou Rosato, Michael Santo, Jean Sherrard, Kevin Spacey, R. Hamilton Wright

MASTER HAROLD . . . and the boys by Athol Fugard; Director, Paul Weidner; Set, Ralph Funicello; Costumes, Sally Richardson. CAST: David Downing (Sam), William Jay (Willie), John Leonard (Hally)

AS YOU LIKE IT by William Shakespeare; Director, Daniel Sullivan; Scenery, Robert Dahlstrom; Costumes, Kurt Wilhelm; Lights, Dennis Parichy; Music, Kenneth Benshoof. CAST: Roderick Aird, Jeff Allin, JV Bradley, Jane Bray, Christina Burz, Clayton Corzatte, Ted D'Arms, Jim Dean, Thomas H. Diggs, C. R. Gardner, Carolyn Hurlburt, Mark Jenkins, Susan Ludlow, Douglas Marney, Todd Moore, Gun-Marie Nilsson, Philip Pleasants, Barry M. Press, Rex Rabold, Michael Santo, Kevin Spacey, Bill terKuile, Paul C. Thomas, R. Hamilton Wright

SHIVAREE *(World Premiere)* by William Mastrosimone; Director, Daniel Sullivan; Set, Robert Dahlstrom; Costumes, Sally Richardson; Lights, Michael Davidson; Stage Manager, Diane DiVita. Cast not submitted.

Steven Flynn, Maggie Baird in "Shivaree"
Top: Ted D'Arms, John Procaccino,
Robert Macnaughton, David Toney in "The Adventures
of Huckleberry Finn" *(Chris Bennion Photos)*

STAGEWEST

Springfield, Massachusetts
December 15, 1983–July 1, 1984

Producing Director, Stephen E. Hays; Production Manager, Ken Denison; Administrative Manager, Paul J. Horton; Marketing/Development, Sheldon Wolf

PRODUCTIONS AND CASTS

THE MISER by Moliere; Director, Ron Lagomarsino; Set, Jeffrey Struckman; Costumes, John Carver Sullivan; Lighting, Barry Arnold, Music, John Clifton; Stage Manager, Kaz J. Reed. CAST: Michael Connolly, Steve Hofvendahl, Deborah Taylor, Mark Hattan, Jeff Brooks, J. D. Rosenbaum, Richard Karn, Roman Alis, Maria Ricossa, Mary Beth Lerner, John Clarkson, Christopher Wynkoop

CANDIDA by George Bernard Shaw; Director, Donald Hicken, Set, Jeffrey Struckman; Costumes, Bill Walker; Lighting, Jeff Davis; Stage Manager, Robert Stevenson. CAST: Maria Ricossa, Adrian Sparks, Thomas Apple, John Clarkson, Tana Hicken, Thomas Nahrwold

HANNIBAL BLUES *(World Premiere)* by Bernard Sabath; Director, Thomas Gruenewald; Set, James Leonard Joy; Costumes, Mariann Verheyen; Lighting, Barry Arnold; Composer, John Clifton; Stage Manager, Kaz J. Reed. CAST: Jane Hoffman, Gregory Chase, Jon Matthews, Betty Williams

ALL MY SONS by Arthur Miller; Director, Timothy Near; Set, Tom Lynch; Costumes, Jeffrey Struckman; Lighting, Robert Jared; Stage Manager, Bob Stevenson. CAST: Joseph Warren, Anna Minot, Mark Metcalf, Donna Snow, William Mesnik, Deborah Strang, Jeanne Morrissey, Brian Connors, Gregory Chase, Steven Marasi, Timothy Woodward

THE GIN GAME by D. L. Coburn; Director, Ted Weiant; Set/Lighting, Joseph W. Long; Costumes, Georgia M. Carney; Stage Manager, Kaz J. Reed. CAST: Mary Fogarty, David O. Petersen

MAN WITH A LOAD OF MISCHIEF with Music and Lyrics by John Clifton, Ben Tarver; Musical Director, Herb Kaplan; Director, Ted Weiant; Set/Costumes, Jeffrey Struckman; Lighting, Ned Hallick. CAST: Maureen Sadusk, Ray Cox, Alan Brasington, SuEllen Estey, Polly Pen, Charles Hudson

THE UNEXPECTED GUEST by Agatha Christie; Director, Timothy Near; Set, Jane Clark; Costumes, Jeffrey Struckman; Lighting, Ned Hallick. CAST: Doug Stender, Leslie Hicks, Lachlan Macleay, Sally Parrish, Jace Alexander, Janet Ward, Basil Wallace, Charles Hudson

Carl Bartels Photo

Polly Pen, SuEllen Estey
in "Man with a Load of Mischief"

STUDIO ARENA THEATRE

Buffalo, New York
September 23, 1983–May 20, 1984
Nineteenth Season

Artistic Director, David Frank; Managing Director, Michael P. Pitek III; Associate Director/Dramaturg, Kathryn Long; Marketing, J. Dennis Rich; Press, Blossom Cohan; Development, Gail Leacy Kratt; Company Manager, Liane M. Gray; Stage Managers, Debra A. Acquavella, Christine Michael; Production Coordinator/Technical Director, Brett Thomas; Wardrobe, Gail Evans; Props, Jolene Obertin; Sound, Rick Menke

PRODUCTIONS AND CASTS

WHAT I DID LAST SUMMER by A. R. Gurney, Jr.; Director, David Frank; Set, Patricia Woodbridge; Costumes, Donna Langman; Lighting, Robby Monk. CAST: Eric Schiff, Michael Albert Mantel, Etain O'Malley, Kari Jenson, Helene Udy, Sylvia Short

CABARET by Joe Masteroff, John Kander, Fred Ebb; Director, Carl Schurr; Musical Director, Terrence Sherman; Choreography, Mary Jane Houdina; Sets, Gary C. Eckhart; Costumes, John Carver Sullivan; Lighting, Robby Monk. CAST: Robert Spencer, John Buscaglia, Carolyn Ferrini, Gerry Burkhardt, Jeffrey Dreisbach, Michael McAssey, Corinne Melancon, Pegg Winter, Becca Greene, Lynn Safrit, Suzanne Kennedy, Blake Atherton, Jim DeMunn, Robert Lund, Brad Scott, Mary McMahon, Kathleen Conry, John Didrichsen, Timothy Meyers, Richard Fanning, Evelyn Page, Maureen Sadusk, Stan Rubin

WAIT UNTIL DARK by Frederick Knott; Director, Kathryn Long; Set/Lighting, Paul Wonsek; Costumes, Janice I. Lines. CAST: Ving Rhames, John Tormey, Timothy Meyers, Janet Zarish, Tony Pasqualini, Sandra Weiss, Kelly Wright, Brian LaTulip, Evan Parry

THE DRESSER by Ronald Harwood; Director, Geoffrey Sherman; Set, Paul Wonsek; Costumes, Marian Verheyen; Lighting, Michael Orris Watson. CAST: Robert Spencer, Jeannie Carson, Lois Diane Hicks, Biff McGuire, Julianne Moore, Timothy Meyers, John Curless, Howard P. Wyrauch, Donald Grant, Walter Barrett, Jack Hunter

TERRA NOVA by Ted Talley; Director, Kathryn Long; Set, John Scheffler; Costumes, Catherine B. Reich; Lighting, Robby Monk. CAST: Jacob Brooke, Rand Bridges, Giulia Pagano, Timothy Meyers, David Hude-Lamb, John Curless, Richard Hoyt-Miller

ARMS AND THE MAN by George Bernard Shaw; Director, David Frank; Set/Costumes, Robert Morgan; Lighting, Brett Thomas. CAST: Mary Hara, Kristin Griffith, Claudia Wilde, James Maxwell, Jack Hunter, Timothy Meyers, Moultrie Patten, Kelsey Grammer

A PLACE TO STAY (World Premiere) by Richard Culliton; Director, Ron Lagomarsino; Set/Costumes, Lowell Detweiler; Lighting, Curt Ostermann. CAST: Steve Hofvendahl, Deborah Taylor

K. C. Kratt Photos

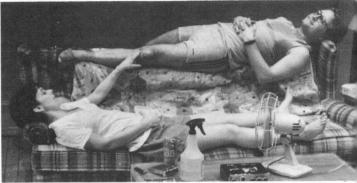

**Deborah Taylor, Steve Hofvendahl
in "A Place to Stay" Top: Robert Spencer, Biff McGuire,
Lois Hicks in "The Dresser"**

**John Cullum, Lisabeth Bartlett (above),
Marcus Smythe in "Cyrano de Bergerac"**

SYRACUSE STAGE

Syracuse, New York
October 21, 1983–May 13, 1984
Eleventh Season

Producing Director, Arthur Storch; Managing Director, James Clark; Business Manager, Betty Starr; Development, Shirley Lockwood; Press, Jenifer Breyer, Zoe Tolone; Marketing, Barbara J. Beckos; Production Manager, Bob Davidson; Stage Managers, Cynthia Poulson, Lauren Class Schneider; Technical Director, Donald R. Fassinger; Sound, Steve Shapiro; Props, Gretchen Gregg; Costumer, Maria Marrero; Wardrobe, Trish Gryczka

PRODUCTIONS AND CASTS

THE SHADOW OF A GUNMAN by Sean O'Casey; Director, George Ferencz; Set, John Doepp; Lighting, Judy Rasmuson; Costumes, Sally J. Lesser. CAST: Eva Charney, Yolanda Childress, Andrew Clark, Earle Edgerton, Sylvia Harman, Randal Masters, Dermot McNamara, Stephen Mellor, John Milligan, James Newcomb, Patrick Tull

THE SHOW-OFF by George Kelly; Director, William H. Putch; Set, James M. Fouchard; Costumes, Arnold S. Levine; Lighting, Judy Rasmuson. CAST: Pamela Burrell, Jean Stapleton, Sally Dunn, Carl Schurr, John Newton, Lloyd Brass, Orson Bean, P. Jay Sidney, Wil Love

CYRANO DE BERGERAC by Edmond Rostand; Adapted by Emily Frankel; Music, Michael Jay; Director, Arthur Storch; Set, Victor A. Becker; Lighting, Michael Newton-Brown; Costumes, Jennifer von Mayrhauser; Fight Choreography, Erik Fredricksen; Sound, Michael Jay. CAST: John Cullum, Walter Atamanluk, Lisabeth Bartlett, Gerrit DeBeer, Shirl Bernheim, John P. Connolly, Richard Cottrell, Timothy Davis-Reed, Sean G. Griffin, Andrew Grose, Christine Hechinger, Lisa Merrill McCord, Gerard E. Moses, John Perkins, Marcus Smythe, Paul Tracey, Cliff Weissman

'NIGHT, MOTHER by Marsha Norman; Director, Claudia Weill; Set, John Doepp; Costumes, Davelle E. DeMarco; Lighting, William T. Paton. CAST: Florence Stanley, Kit Flanagan

THE DINING ROOM by A. R. Gurney, Jr.; Director, Susan Einhorn; Set, Bob Davidson; Costumes, Maria Marrero; Lighting, Victor En Yu Tan. CAST: Cynthia Crumlish, Daniel Ahearn, Brenda Pentland, John Short, Jill Larson, Gregg Almquist

THE DOUBLE BRASS (American Premiere) by Patrick Suskind; Director, Arthur Storch; Set, Charles Cosler; Costumes, Maria Marrero; Lighting, F. Mitchell Dana; Sound, Steve Shapiro. CAST: Alan Brasington

Susan Piper Kublick Photos

THEATRE BY THE SEA

Portsmouth, New Hampshire
September 22, 1983–May 27, 1984
Artistic Director, Tom Celli; Assistant Artistic Director, Sharon Fentiman; President, Nancy Beck; Business Manager, Jean Barter; Stage Manager, John Becker; Press, Ann Cole; Stage Directors, Tom Celli, Peter Bennett, Derek Wolshonak, John Fogle, Richard Hughes, Malcolm Morrison, John Montgomery; Sets, Robert Phillips, Mark Pirolo, Kathie Iannicelli; Lighting, Michael Watson, David Weiss, Harry Sangmeister; Costumes, Kathie Iannicelli

COMPANY Dori Arnold, Joanne Baum, Peter Bennett, Bonnie Black, Natalie Brown, Catherine Caplin, Tom Celli, Ronda Click, Connie Coit, Anne Connors, Steve Coulter, Roger Curtis, Peter DeLaurier, Bob DuSold, Felicia Farone, Susanna Frazer, Jay Freer, Ashly Gardner, Dean Gardner, Lauren Goler, Gerry Goodman, Bernard Granville, Rhoda Griffis, Tripp Hanson, Randal Harris, Peter Haydu, James Huston, Kelby Kirk, William Lyman, Terrence Markovich, Michael McCormick, Michael McGrath, Vance Mizelle, Roxann Parker, Michael Perrier, K. Lype O'Dell, Richard Sabellico, Ben Scranton, Jane Seaman, Scott Severance, Donna Sorbello, Guy Stroman, Maxine Taylor-Morris, Edward Trotta, Christine Toy, Stephanie Voss, Christopher Walsh, Eric Zwemer
PRODUCTIONS: The Passion of Dracula, The Diary of Anne Frank, Equus, Betrayal, Good Evening, Stop the World I Want to Get Off

Andrew Edgar Photos

**Guy Stroman in "Stop the World—
I Want to Get Off"**

TRINITY SQUARE REPERTORY COMPANY

Providence, Rhode Island
June 1, 1983–May 31, 1984
Twenty-first Season
Director, Adrian Hall; Managing Director, E. Timothy Langan; Assistant to Mr. Hall, Marion Simon; General Manager, Michael Ducharme; Musical Directors, Richard Cumming, Daniel Birnbaum; Press, Scotti DiDonato; Sets, Eugene Lee, Robert D. Soule; Lighting, Eugene Lee, John F. Custer; Costumes, William Lane; Technical Direcor, David Rotondo; Props, William Wieters, Robert Schleinig, Sandra Nathanson; Production Manager, William Radka; Stage Managers, Maureen F. Gibson, Ken Bryant, Mary O'Leary; Choreographer, Sharon Jenkins; Stage Directors, Adrian Hall, Philip Minor, David Wheeler, Patrick Hines, Paul Benedict, George Martin, William Radka; Photographers, Tom Bloom, Constance Brown, Mark Morelli, John Fogle, John C. Meyers

COMPANY: Hoda Baron, Tom Bloom, Barbara Blossom, Dan Butler, James Carruthers, Vince Ceglie, Timothy Crowe, Richard Cumming, Timothy Daly, William Damkoehler, Maurice Dolbier, Richard Ferrone, Peter Gerety, Paul Haggard, Ed Hall, Richard Jenkins, Keith Jochim, David C. Jones, Melanie Jones, Richard Kavanaugh, David Kennett, Richard Kneeland, Geraldine Librandi, Becca Lish, Howard London, Margaret Marx, Ruth Maynard, Brian McEleney, Derek Meader, Barbara Meek, Philip Minor, Deirdre O'Connell, Barbara Orson, Ricardo Pitts-Wiley, Alyssa Roth, Ken Rubenfeld, Charles Scovil, Anne Scurria, Stephen Snyder, Sylvia Ann Soares, David P. B. Stephens, Cynthia Strickland, Patricia Ann Thomas, Amy Van Nostrand, Daniel Von Bargen, Rose Weaver, Robert Whitney
PRODUCTIONS: Tintypes, Billy Bishop Goes to War, Bus Stop, Galileo, The Wild Duck, A Christmas Carol, Fool for Love, Cloud 9, Amadeus, Crimes of the Heart, and *World Premiere* of Jonestown Express by James Reston, Jr.

**Barbara Orson, Richard Kneeland
in "Jonestown Express"** *(John C. Meyers Photo)*

**Left Center: Deidre O'Connell, Richard Jenkins
in "Fool for Love"** *(Tom Bloom Photo)*

VIRGINIA MUSEUM THEATRE

Richmond, Virginia
October 7, 1983–May 26, 1984
Twenty-ninth Season
Artistic Director, Tom Markus; Managing Director, Ira Schlosser; Associate Artistic Director, Terry Burgler; Associate Artistic Director for Musical Theatre, Darwin Knight; Business Manager, Edward W. Rucker; Marketing, Phil Crosby; Press, Don Dale; Sets, James Burbeck, Charles Caldwell, Elizabeth K. Fischer, Joseph A. Varga; Costumes, Bronwyn J. Caldwell, Emelle Holmes, Julie Keen, Susan Tsu; Lighting, F. Mitchell Dana, Lynne M. Hartman, Richard Moore; Stage Managers, Doug Flinchum, Hazel Norris, Donna Stanley

PRODUCTIONS AND CASTS
SHINE-THE HORATIO ALGER MUSCIAL *(World Premiere)* by Richard Seff, Richard Altman, Roger Anderson, Lee Goldsmith; Direction/Choreography, Darwin Knight; Musical Director, Sand Lawn. CAST: Maggie Anderson, George Lee Andrews, Marshall Borden, Randy Brenner, Martile Bucklew, Tempy Cornelius-Fisk, William Doan, Nathan Fairman, David Franklin, Randy Hansen, Maj-Lis Jalkio, Richard Kinter, Alexandra Korey, John McNamara, Milica Govich Miller, Suzanne Murphy, John Newton-Fletcher, David Pursley, Todd Rodriquez, Anne Russell, Todd Taylor, Valerie Toth, Geoffrey Weglarz, Eric Weitz
MACBETH by William Shakespeare; Directors, Terry Burgler, Tom Markus. CAST: Bev Appleton, Lenny Brisendine, Donald Christopher, Lucien Douglas, Maury Erickson, David Franklin, Max W. Jacobs, Maj-Lis Jalkio, Daniel Timothy Johnson, Daniel Leith Lafoon, Tom Markus, Milica Govich Miller, Jane Moore, Ryan Morgan, Robert Ousley, J. C. Palmore, Adrian Rieder, Granville Scott, Conor Shiel, Sherry Skinker, Rob Storrs, Ian Stuart, Nan Wray
A CHRISTMAS CAROL by Charles Dickens; Adapted by Tom Marcus; Director, Terry Burgler; Musical Director, R. L. Rowsey. CAST: Bev Appleton, Nancy Boykin, Susan Brandner, Donald Christopher, Lucien Douglas, Judith Drake, Christy Michelle Fairman, Nathan Fairman, Robert Foley, David Franklin, Tracy O'Neil Heffernan, Maj-Lis Jalkio, Daniel Timothy Johnson, Milica Govich Miller, Jessica Printz, Walter Rhodes (succeeded by Terry Burgler), Adrian Rieder, Todd Rodriquez, Emily Skinner, Rob Storrs, John Winn III, Nan Wray
A PERFECT GENTLEMAN by Herbert Appleman; Director, Tom Marcus. CAST: Michael Allinson, Robert Foley, Richard Gustin, I. M. Hobson, Jean McNally, Johanna Morrison, John Sefton, Jean Sincere, Douglas Wing
MASS APPEAL by Bill C. Davis; Director, Terry Burgler. CAST: Jerry Bradley, Donald Christopher
SLEUTH by Anthony Shaffer; Director, Josephine R. Abady. CAST: Brian Petchey, Peter Webster
THE DINING ROOM by A. R. Gurney, Jr.; Director, Tom Marcus. CAST: Jo Ann Cunningham, Lucien Douglas, Tracy O'Neil Heffernan, John Michalski, Dana Mills, Jane Moore
AT THIS EVENING'S PERFORMANCE written and directed by Nagle Jackson. CAST: Barry Boys, Robin Chadwick, Jay Doyle, Gerald Lancaster, Stacy Ray, Penelope Reed, Greg Thornton

VMT Photos

Todd Taylor in "Shine"

VIRGINIA STAGE COMPANY

Norfolk, Virginia
October 14, 1983–May 19, 1984
Fifth Season
Artistic Director, Charles Towers; Managing Director, Randy Adams; Development, Nancy Kauffman; Press, Katie Lincoln-Lively; Business Manager, Nikki Thompson; Administrative Assistant, Ann Garbler; Sets/Lighting, Joe Ragey; Costumes, Carrie Curtis, Ann Marie Wright; Stage Managers, Nancy K. Uffner, Ann S. Ostermayer; Props, Christine Martis; Scenic Artist, Steve Sysko

PRODUCTIONS AND CASTS
ISLAND conceived and developed by Brent Nicholson; Music/Lyrics, Peter Link; Additional Lyrics, Joe Bravaco, Larry Rosler; Director, Peter Link; Musical Director, Alan Smallwood. CAST: Clare Bathe, Victoria Blumenthal, Michael Calkins, Byron Utley
BETRAYAL by Harold Pinter; Director, Charles Towers. CAST: C. R. Gardner, David Lively, David Mong, Peggy Schoditsch
A CHRISTMAS CAROL by Charles Dickens; Adapted and Directed by Jamie Brown; Musical Direction, Leon Odenz. CAST: Virginia Downing, Earle Edgerton, John Leighton, David Lively, Lium O'Begley, Chris Rhodes, Janet Stanford, Mona Stiles, Larry Swansen, Grey Buccella, John Durham, Scott Elliott, Erick Gallun, Wayne Henry, Paul James, Leslie Joelle, Andrew McCoy, Sara Noah, Tonye Patano, Aubrey Simonds, Lance Spellerberg, Rebecca Steinberg, Henry Tenney
ARTICHOKE by Joanna Glass; Director, Jamie Brown. CAST: David Combs, C. R. Gardner, Leslie Joelle, Paul Milikin, Lium O'Begley, Nicola Sheara, Larry Swansen
THE NIGHT OF THE IGUANA by Tennessee Williams; Director, Charles Towers. CAST: Kelley Bishop, C. R. Gardner, Sylvia Harman, John Leighton, Maeve McGuire, Paul Milikin, Larry Swansen, Gregory Buccella, Joseph Giardina, Su Hyatt, Leslie Joelle, Lance Spellerberg, Henry Tenney, Donna Wyant
A LESSON FROM ALOES by Athol Fugard; Director, Bill Partlin. CAST: Joseph Costa, Delroy Lindo, Nicola Sheara
THE DINING ROOM by A. R. Gurney, Jr.; Director, Jamie Brown. CAST: David Falkner, Hamilton Gillett, Stanja Lowe, Kathleen Masterson, Nicola Sheara, Larry Swansen
TRUE WEST by Sam Shepard; Director, Charles Towers. CAST: Jock MacDonald, David Penhale, David Rosenbaum, Margaret Thomson

Ellen Forsyth Photos

**C. R. Gardner, Kelly Bishop
in "Night of the Iguana"**

WHOLE THEATRE COMPANY

Montclair, New Jersey
October 11, 1983–April 8, 1984
Artistic Director, Olympia Dukakis; Managing Director, Patricia K. Quinn; General Manager, Laurence Feldman; Marketing, Lynn Gialanella; Production Coordinator, Mary C. Orme; Press, Rita Perello; Sets, Loren Sherman, Paul Dorphley, Richard Harmon, Michael Miller; Lighting, Rachel Budin, Carol Rubinstein, Richard Moore; Costumes, Galen M. Logsdon, Sigrid Insull, Richard Harmon, Sam Fleming; Stage Managers, Tom Brubaker, Edward Neuert

PRODUCTIONS AND CASTS
NOBODY STARTS OUT TO BE A PIRATE *(World Premiere)* Book/Lyrics, Fred Tobias; Music, Stanley Lebowski; Musical Direction/Orchestrations, Arnold Gross; Director, Arnold Mittelman. CAST: Evalyn Baron, James Brennan, Rex D. Hays, Harve Presnell, Joe Silver, Ken Jennings, Dawn Spare, Sara Wiedt, Kim Zimmer
A SOLDIER'S PLAY by Charles Fuller. Performed by the Negro Ensemble Company
ALTERATIONS by Leigh Curran; Director, Tom Brennan. CAST: Dortha Duckworth, Alexandra Gersten, Carlin Glynn, Stephen Newman, Kate Purwin
TALLEY'S FOLLY by Lanford Wilson; Director, Olympia Dukakis. CAST: Apollo Dukakis, Erika Petersen
BLITHE SPIRIT by Noel Coward; Director, Stuart Howard. CAST: Apollo Dukakis, Olympia Dukakis, Frank Grimes, Jennifer Harmon, Lisby Larson, Debra Jo Rupp, Susan Willis

Jim Chambers Photos

**Stephen Newman, Carlin Glynn
in "Alterations"**

YALE REPERTORY THEATRE

New Haven, Connecticut
October 4, 1983–May 24, 1984
Eighteenth Season
Artistic Director, Lloyd Richards; Managing Director, Benjamin Mordecai; Sets Adviser, Ming Cho Lee; Costumes Adviser, Jane Greenwood; Lighting Adviser, Jennifer Tipton; Lighting Director, William B. Warfel; Dramaturgs, Gitta Honegger, Barbara Davenport, Joel Schechter; Press, Rosalind Heinz; Photographers, William B. Carter, George G. Slade

PRODUCTIONS AND CASTS
MAJOR BARBARA by George Bernard Shaw; Director, Lloyd Richards; Set, Michael Yeargan; Costumes, Dunya Ramicova. CAST: Barbara Baxley, Ivar Brogger, Sheila Coonan, Roy Cooper, Robert Curtis-Brown, Regina David, Bruce Hurlbut, John Little, Guilia Pagano, Don Plumley, Laila Robins, Kenneth Ryan, Gabriele Schafer, Norman Snow
A RAISIN IN THE SUN by Lorraine Hansberry; Director, Dennis Scott; Set, Robert M. Wierzel; Costumes, Richard F. Mays. CAST: Mary Alice, Tim Douglas, LaMar James Fredrick, Dennis Green, Delroy Lindo, Sharon Mitchell, Mansoor Najee-Ullah, Joe Ponazecki, Beah Richards, Troy Streater, Courtney Vance, Tyrone Wilson
RICHARD II by William Shakespeare; Director, David Hammond; Set, Derek McLane; Costumes, Catherine Zuber; Lighting, Robert M. Wierzel. CAST: Steven R. Blye, Julie Boyd, Dominic Chianese, Christian Clemenson, Bill Cohen, Jonathan Emerson, Allen Evans, Clarence Felder, Steven Gefroh, Cordelia Gonzalez, Paul Guilfoyle, Tom Isbell, David Jaffe, Ron Johnston, Warren Manzi, Ken Marks, Don Plumley, Tom Rolfing, Reno Roop, Gabriele Schafer, Rebecca Schull, Sloane Shelton, John Straub, Joseph Urla, John Vickery
WINTERFEST IV: Three *World Premieres* presented in rotating repertory.
THE DAY OF THE PICNIC by Russell David; Director, Tony Giordano; Set, Peter Maradudin; Costumes, Charles Henry McClennahan; Lighting, Tom Roscher; Sound, Robert Chase. CAST: Lori Tan Chinn, Patricia Clarkson, Ron Faber, Margaret Hilton, James Earl Jones, Carl Low, Theresa Merritt
THE SWEET LIFE by Michael Quinn; Director, Robert Alford II; Set, Andrew Carter; Costumes, James D. Sandefur; Lighting, William J. Buck; Sound, Peter Bartholomew. CAST: William Andrews, John Finn, Dennis Green, David Jaffe, Alan Mixon, Al Mancini, Joseph Siravo, Tyrone Wilson, Joseph Urla
CHOPIN IN SPACE by Philip Bosakowski; Director, James Simpson; Set, Michael H. Yeargan; Costumes, Candice Donnelly; Lighting, William B. Warfel; Sound, Mike Nolan. CAST: Robin Bartlett, Christian Clemenson, Bill Cohen, Jonathan Emerson, Allen Evans, Dann Florek, Robert Lesser, Laila Robins
NIGHT IS MOTHER TO THE DAY *(American Premiere)* by Lars Noren; Director, Goran Graffman; Translated from Swedish by Harry G. Carlson; Set, Richard F. Mays; Costumes, Catherine Zuber; Lighting, Robert M. Wierzel; Fights, B. H. Barry. CAST: Keith Charles, Greg Germann, Anita Gillette, Christopher McHale
MA RAINEY'S BLACK BOTTOM *(World Premiere)* by August Wilson; Director, Lloyd Richards; Set, Charles Henry McClennahan; Costumes, Daphne Pascucci; Lighting, Peter Maradudin; Musical Direction, Dwight Andrews. CAST: Steven R. Blye, Lou Criscuolo, Richard M. Davidson, Charles S. Dutton, Leonard Jackson, Robert Judd, Theresa Merritt, Sharon Mitchell, David Wayne Nelson, Joe Seneca
THE ROAD TO MECCA *(World Premiere)* Written and Directed by Athol Fugard; Set, Elizabeth Doyle; Costumes, Derek McLane; Lighting, William B. Warfel. CAST: Tom Aldredge, Carmen Mathews, Marianne Owen

**Theresa Merritt in "Ma Rainey's Black Bottom"
Above: Tom Aldredge, Carmen Mathews, Marianne Owen in
"The Road to Mecca"** *(Wm. Carter Photo)*

ANNUAL SHAKESPEARE FESTIVALS

ALABAMA SHAKESPEARE FESTIVAL

Anniston, Alabama
July 10, - August 21, 1983
Twelfth Season

Artistic Director, Martin L. Platt; Managing Director, Jim Volz; Production Manager, Dena Kirkland; Sets, Michael Stauffer, Charles J. Kilian, Jr.; Costumes, Susan M. Rheaume, Susan A. Cox, April Parke; Lighting, Lauren MacKenzie Miller, Paul Valoris; Composer/Musical Director, Philip Rosenberg; Fight Choreographer, Bruce Cromer; Choreographer, Louise Crofton; Stage Managers, Carol Chiavetta, Gretchen Van Horne; Technical Directors, Charles J. Kilian, Jr., Stuart Rosenstein; Props, Dennis A. Lockhart, T. C. LaBiche; Wardrobe, Greg McMahan; Company Manager, Sammy Ledbetter; Press, Patricia S. Lavender
COMPANY: Carol Allin, Charles Antalosky, Zander Brietzke, Kermit Brown, Robert Browning, Evelyn Carol Case, A. D. Cover, Bruce Cromer, James Donadio, Daryl Donley, Michele Farr, Larry E. Greer, Jr., Arthur Hanket, William Todd Jeffries, John-Frederick Jones, Mark D. Jones, David Meaders Klein, Bruce H. Laks, David Landon, Betty Leighton, Lilene Mansell, Michael McKenzie, John W. Morrow, Jr., Annemarie E. Potter, Sally W. Pressly, Frank Raiter, Clarinda Ross, Clay Rouse, Charles E. Sanders, Jean Sterrett, David Wheeler, Cal Winn, Jerri Zoochi
PRODUCTIONS: King Lear, All's Well That Ends Well, Arms and the Man, Mass Appeal (all directed by Martin L. Platt), The Taming of the Shrew (directed by Allen R. Belknap), The Comedy of Errors (directed by John-Frederick Jones)

Michael Doege Photos

**Carol Allin, John-Frederick Jones, Lilene Mansell in
"Taming of the Shrew"**
(Michael Doege Photo)

CAMDEN SHAKESPEARE COMPANY

Camden, Maine
June 24, - September 5, 1983

Artistic Director, William James Kelly; Managing Director, Mary F. Rindfleisch; Directors, Charles Kondek, Stephen White; Costumes, Martin Thaler; Lighting/Technical Director, Kenton Yeager; Stage Manager, Candace Lo Frumento; Public Relations, Alexa Fogel; Press, Katrinka Wilder
COMPANY: John Brady, Julian Bailey, Richard Boddy, Michael Connolly, Susanne Egli, Michael Endy, Patrick Frawley, Darian Harris, Michael McGuinness, Lawr Means, Kenneth Metivier, Martin Moran
PRODUCTIONS: The Taming of the Shrew, Julius Caesar, Dear Liar by Jerome Kilty, Tartuffe by Moliere (translated by Richard Wilbur), Androcles and the Lion by Aurand Harris

Richard Watherwax Photos

AMERICAN PLAYERS THEATRE

Spring Green, Wisconsin
June 7, - October 9, 1983
Fourth Season

Artistic Director, Randall Duk Kim; Resident Director, Anne Occhiogrosso; Directors, Mik Derks, Fred Ollerman; Executive Director, Charles J. Bright; General Manager, Thomas Mason; Movement, Jerry Gardner; Props, Larry Henke; Costumes, Budd Hill, Nanalee Raphael; Lighting, Elizabeth Green; Stage Managers, Dana Graham, Linda Harris, Rhoda F. Nathan; Production Manager, Robert Wood; Press, Jean Louise Sassor, Karen Johnson.
COMPANY: John Aden, Paul Bentzen, David Cecsarini, Victoria Constan, Lee Elmer Ernst, Steven Helmeke, Stephen Hemming, Lucas G. Hendrickson, Jonathan Herold, James Hulin, Terry Kerr, Peter Kettler, Randall Duk Kim, Ray Lonergan, Marie Mathay, Alexandra Mitchell, Drew C. Noll, Anne Occiogrosso, Robert Pescovitz, Arleigh Richards, JoAnn Rome, William Schlaht, Jonathan Smoots, Charles Stransky, Theodore Swetz, Peter Syvertsen, Michael Tezla, Thomas Winslow
PRODUCTIONS: The Taming of the Shrew, Tambourlaine the Great Part I, A Midsummer Night's Dream, Love's Labour's Lost, Romeo and Juliet.

Left Center: Randall Duk Kim, Arleigh Richards in "Romeo and Juliet"
(John Barry Photo)

**Susanne Egli, Michael Endy, Julian Bailey
in "Taming of the Shrew"**

187

GREAT LAKES SHAKESPEARE FESTIVAL

Cleveland, Ohio
June 24–October 30, 1983
Twenty-second Season

Producing Director, Vincent Dowling; Managing Director, Mary Bill; Design/Associate Director, John Ezell; Musical Director, Daniel Hathaway; Costumes, Mary-Anne Aston, Paul Costelloe, Gene Lakin, Lewis D. Rampino; Lighting, Kirk Bookman, Toni Goldin; Stage Managers, Andrew Feigin, Peter Muste, Mimi Appel; Press, Walt Sado

COMPANY: Bonnie Black, Bob Breuler, David Purham, Sara Woods, Richard C. Brown, Jill Holden, Nicola Shearer, Clive Rosengren, Michael Thompson, George Maguire, Michael Haney, Richard Gustin, Larry Sherwood, John Greenleaf, John Q. Bruce, Suzanne Petri, Bernard Canepari, Holmes Osborne, Gale Fury Childs, Madylon Branstetter, Leta Anderson, Bairbre Dowling, Glenna Forde, Clare Giblin, Christine Malik, Barbara McGreevy, Ann Timmons, James Glossman, Robert Elliott, Jill Tanner, William Youmans, Jack Milo, Colm Meaney, J. S. Johnson, Robert Van Horn, Dan Westbrook, Jonathan Gillard, Michael Swain, Barry Boys

PRODUCTIONS: "Merry Wives of Windsor: by Shakespeare, "Blanco!" a musical based on "The Shewing Up of Blanco Posnet" by George Bernard Shaw, Samuel Beckett's "Waiting for Godot," Shakespeare's "Henry V," "The Life and Adventures of Nicholas Nickleby" adapted from Charles Dickens by David Edgar

Mark C. Schwartz Photos

David Purdham and cast in "The Life and Adventures of Nicholas Nickleby"
Left: Annalee Jefferies, John Hertzler, Clay Cornog in "Edward IV"

NEW JERSEY SHAKESPEARE FESTIVAL

Madison, New Jersey
June 28, 1983 - January 1, 1984
Nineteenth Season

Artistic Director, Paul Barry; Producing Director, Ellen Barry; Production Manager, Jon P. Ogden; Stage Managers, Richard Dorfman, John Pietrowski; Assistant Director, John Pietrowski; Lighting, Richard Dorfman, Jon P. Ogden; Sets, Michael Sharp; Costumes, Kathleen Blake, Heidi Hollmann, Jayne A. Serba; Musical Director/Composer, Deborah Martin; General Manager, Donna M. Gearhardt; Press, Kate Wisniewski, Deidre Jacobson; Photographer, Jerry Dalia; Technical Director, Christopher R. Galbraith; Technical Coordinator/Props, Carolyn Enz; Stage Directors, Paul Barry, Dan Held

COMPANY: William Andrews, Lisa Barnes, Ellen Barry, Paul Barry, Deveren Bookwalter, Victoria Boothby, Kate Collins, Ed Dennehy, Clement Fowler, Donald Gantry, Davis Hall, John Hertzler, David S. Howard, J. C. Hoyt, Annalee Jefferies, Eve Johnson, Jeff King, Dane Knell, Richard Lee, Don Leslie, Tom McLaughlin, John O'Hurley, Don Perkins, William Pitts, Brett Porter, Andrew Potter, Margery Shaw, Geddeth Smith, Richard Sterne, Michael Tolaydo, Eric Tull, Virginia White

Soshanah Aborn, Jeff Becker, Nancy-Anna Bull, Bill Chappelle, Karen Case Cook, Clay Cornog, Susan L. Coromel, Patrick Crea, Diane Dreux, David Duffield, Michelle-Suzette Eberts, Susan Epstein, Blair Fell, Dominic Fico, Kevin Finney, Edward L. Furs, Stu Goldman, Michael Stuart Haupt, Susan C. Hoffer, Kevin Hogan, Meg Inglima, Maureen Jammo, Jeff Janus, Diane Jones, Laura Jones, Kathleen Kimber, Elliot Lanes, Alan Levine, Mary MacDonald, Wayne Markover, Barbara Ann Martin, Rebecca Martinez, Dennis McLernon, Bergin Michaels, Michael S. Monroe, Anita Namar, Richard A. O'Brien, Michele Ortlip, Suzanne Pietrowski, Phil Prestamo, Lee Robin, Malerie Rose, Sandie Rowe, Michael Rubenstein, Jonathan Sherman, Judith Sternlight, Polly Stone, Elizabeth Striker, Michael Sutton, Mark Henry Tonyan, Aviva Twersky, David von Salis, David Waggett, Scott Winters

PRODUCTIONS: War of the Roses: Henry VI Parts I, II, III and Richard III performed as Henry VI, Edward IV and Richard III, Let's Get a Divorce by Victorien Sardou, Born Yesterday by Garson Kanin, Beyond the Fringe by Jonathan Miller and Dudley Moore, and Bill C. Davis' "Mass Appeal."

Jerry Dalia Photos

Michael Tolaydo, Polly Stone, Margery Shaw
in "Richard III"

NEW YORK SHAKESPEARE FESTIVAL

Joseph Papp, Producer
Delacorte Theatre/Central Park
Twenty-eighth Season

Thursday, June 30, - July 31, 1983 (30 performances)
RICHARD III by William Shakespeare; Director, Jane Howell; Set/Costumes, Santo Loquasto; Music, Richard Peaslee; Lighting, Pat Collins; Fight Sequences, B. H. Barry; General Manager, Robert Kamlot; Production Manager, Andrew Mihok; Technical Director, Mervyn Haines, Jr.; Props, Joe Toland; Stage Managers, Bonnie Panson, Bill McComb; Hairstylist/Makeup, J. Roy Helland; Wardrobe, Dawn Johnson; Company Manager, Robert Reilly; Associate Producer, Jason Steven Cohen; Press, Merle Debuskey, Richard Kornberg, Barbara Carroll, Bruce Campbell.
CAST Gerry Bamman (Buckingham), Scott Becker (Page), Ivar Brogger (Rivers/Bourchier), Reg E. Cathey (Keeper of Tower/Messenger/Brandon), Maurice Copeland (Brakenbury/Bishop of Ely/Earl of Surrey), Jonathan Croy (Berkeley/Penker/Urswick), Philip Cruise (Understudy), Steven Culp (Dorset), Bruce Davison (Clarence), Paul R. Duke (Messenger), Roc Dutton (Lord Mayor), Peter Francis-James (Helberdier/Lovell), Richard Greene (Catesby), David Alan Grier (Murderer/Richmond), Mark Hammer (Stanley/Derby), John Harnagel (Tressel/Shaa), Kevin Kline (Richard), Tom Klunis (Grey/Archbishop of York/Sheriff of Norfolk), Sandra Laub (Mistress Shore), Christopher McCann (Ratcliffe), Betty Miller (Duchess of York), Katherine Neuman (Duke of Clarence's daughter), Terrance O'Quinn (King Edward IV/Scrivener/Tyrrell/Blunt), Michael Pearlman (Duke of York), Madeleine Potter (Lady Anne), Ving Rhames (Hastings/Herbert), Ed Rubeo (Priest/Body of Henry VI), Ward Saxton (Duke of Clarence's son), John Seitz (Hastings), Marian Seldes (Queen Margaret), Concetta Tomei (Queen Elizabeth), Mathew Vipond (Edward), Christopher Wertz (Murderer/Vaughan/Messenger); Ensemble: Christian Baskous, Jonathan Croy, Paul R. Duke, Roc Dutton, John Harnagel, Brian Jackson, William E. Kennedy, Robert E. Quinn, Ving Rhames, Ed Rubeo, Dana Smith, Malcolm Smith, John C. Talbot, Susan Titman, Jonathan Walker, Christopher Wertz. Performed with one intermission.

Tuesday August 9, - September 4, 1983 (21 performances)
NON PASQUALE by Gaetano Donizetti and Giovanni Ruffini; Based on "Don Pasquale"; Music adapted by William Elliott; Director, Wilford Leach; Musical Direction/Vocal Arrangements, William Elliott; New Libretto, Nancy Heikin, Anthony Giles; Choreography, Margo Sappington; Set, Bob Shaw/Wilford Leach; Lighting, Jennifer Tipton; Costumes, Nan Cibula; Conductor, William Elliott; Associate Producer, Jason Steven Cohen; Stage Managers, Stephen McCorkle, Ginny Martino; Hairstylist, Marlies Vallant; Makeup, J. Roy Helland; Technical Director, Sebastian Schulherr; Props, John Doyle; Wardrobe, Dawn Johnson; General Manager, Robert Kamlot; Company Manager, Robert Reiliy
CAST Carol Dennis (Nina), James Dunne (Dance Captain), Ernesto Gasco (Cousin Cesario), Susan Goodman (Pinta), Joe Grifasi (Trumpet), Ron Leibman (Don Pasquale), Priscilla Lopez (Norina), Joe Masiell (Malatesta), Joe Pichette (Valet), James Rich (Cousin Alfredo), Kipp Tozzi (Ernesto), Ensemble: Kevin Berdini, Joyce Leigh Bowden, Katharine Buffaloe, Charlotte d'Amboise, Christopher d'Amboise, Carol Dennis, Bruce Falco, Ernesto Gasco, Susan Goodman, N. A. Klein, Paul Nunes, Caroline Peyton, Joe Pichette, James Rich, Kathy Robinson, David Sanders, Alan Sener, Charlie Serrano, Marcie Shaw, Lauren Tom, Michael Willson. Performed with one intermission.

Marian Seldes, Kevin Kline in "Richard III"
(Martha Swope/Susan Cook Photo)

OREGON SHAKESPEARE FESTIVAL

Ashland, Oregon
February 22 - October 31, 1983
Forty-eighth Season

Founder, Angus L. Bowmer; Artistic Director, Jerry Turner; Executive Director, William W. Patton; Directors, Denis Arndt, Robert Benedetti, Dennis Bigelow, J. H. Crouch, Richard Geer, James Moll, Pat Patton, Jerry Turner; Choreographers, Judith Kennedy, Thomas Arthur Scales; Fight Choreographer, Christopher Villa; Lighting, Peter W. Allen, Robert Peterson, James Sale; Music Director/Composer, Todd Barton; Scenery, William Bloodgood, Richard L. Hay; Production Manager, Pat Patton; Technical Directors, Tom Snapp, Le Hook; Wardrobe, Lynn M. Ramey; Wig Maker/Hairstylists, Ranny Beyer, Laurie Theodorou; Props, Paul-James Martin, Kevin Boog; Sound, Douglas K. Faerber; Stage Managers, Peter W. Allen, Kirk M. Boyd, Lee Alan Byron, Jana Hislop, Mary Steinmetz, Edward D. O'Connell; General Manager, Paul E. Nicholson; Press, Margaret Rubin, Sally K. White
COMPANY: Tobias Andersen, Denis Arndt, John Aylward, Wayne Ballantyne, Gayle Bellows, Jack Wellington Cantwell, Robert Chase, Todd Cohen, Megan Cole, Phyllis Courtney, Philip Davidson, Richard Denison, Richard Elmore, Richard Esterbrook, James Fields, Timothy Glenn, Bruce T. Gooch, Wesley Grant, Hugh Hastings, Judson L. Hoyt, Brenda Hubbard, Gregg Johnson, Jill Jones, William Keeler, Michael Kevin, Barry Kraft, Priscilla Hake Lauris, Zoaunne LeRoy, Owen Lewis, Gregg Loughridge, Kevin Lynch, David M. LoVine, Helen Machin-Smith, Douglas Markkanen, Steven Martin, Daniel Mayes, William McKereghan, Ivars Mikelson, Jarion Monroe, Mark Murphy, Allen Nause, Charles Noland, Paul Vincent O'Connor, Greg Pake, Greg Patnaude, Shirley Patton, Amy Potozkin, Bill Ritchie, Craig Rovers, Robert Sicular, Joan Stuart-Morris, Mary Ellen Thomas, Mary Turner, Joe Vincent, Susan Wands
PRODUCTIONS: Much Ado about Nothing, Cymbeline, Hamlet, Richard III by William Shakespeare, Man and Superman, Don Juan in Hell by Bernard Shaw, Ah, Wilderness! by Eugene O'Neill, What the Butler Saw by Joe Orton, Dracula by Richard Sharp, the Entertainer by John Osborne, Dreamhouse by Stuart Duckworth

Zoaunne LeRoy, Tobias Andersen
in "Cymbeline" *(Hank Kranzler Photo)*

PULITZER PRIZE PRODUCTIONS

1918-Why Marry? 1919-No award, 1920-Beyond the Horizon, 1921-Miss Lulu Bett, 1922-Anna Christie, 1923-Icebound, 1924-Hell Bent fer Heaven, 1925-They Knew What They Wanted, 1926-Craig's Wife, 1927-In Abraham's Bosom, 1928-Strange Interlude, 1929-Street Scene, 1930-The Green Pastures, 1931-Alison's House, 1932-Of Thee I Sing, 1933-Both Your Houses, 1934-Men in White, 1935-The Old Maid, 1936-Idiot's Delight, 1937-You Can't Take It with You, 1938-Our Town, 1939-Abe Lincoln in Illinois, 1940-The Time of Your Life, 1941-There Shall Be No Night, 1942-No award, 1943-The Skin of Our Teeth, 1944-No award, 1945-Harvey, 1946-State of the Union, 1947-No award, 1948-A Streetcar Named Desire, 1949-Death of a Salesman, 1950-South Pacific, 1951-No award, 1952-The Shrike, 1953-Picnic, 1954-The Teahouse of the August Moon, 1955-Cat on a Hot Tin Roof,

1956-The Diary of Anne Frank, 1957-Long Day's Journey into Night, 1958-Look Homeward, Angel, 1959-J. B., 1960-Fiorello!, 1961-All the Way Home, 1962-How to Succeed in Business with Really Trying, 1963-No award, 1964-No award, 1965-The Subject Was Roses, 1966-No award, 1967-A Delicate Balance, 1968-No award, 1969-The Great White Hope, 1776, 1970-The Effect of Gamma Rays on Man-in-the-Moon Marigolds, Borstal Boy, Company, 1971-Home, Follies, The House of Blue Leaves, 1972-That Championship Season, 1974-No award, 1975-Seascape, 1976-A Chorus Line, 1977-The Shadow Box, 1978-The Gin Game, 1979-Buried Child, 1980-Talley's Folly, 1981-Crimes of the Heart, 1982-A Soldier's Play, 1983-'night, Mother, 1984-Glengarry Glen Ross

NEW YORK DRAMA CRITICS CIRCLE AWARDS

1936-Winterset, 1937-High Tor, 1938-Of Mice and Men, Shadow and Substance, 1939-The White Steed, 1940-The Time of Your Life, 1941-Watch on the Rhine, The Corn is Green, 1942-Blithe Spirit, 1943-The Patriots, 1944-Jacobowsky and the Colonel, 1945-The Glass Menagerie, 1946-Carousel, 1947-All My Sons, No Exit, Brigadoon, 1948-A Streetcar Named Desire, The Winslow Boy, 1949-Death of a Salesman, The Madwoman of Chaillot, South Pacific, 1950-The Member of the Wedding, The Cocktail Party, The Consul, 1951-Darkness at Noon, The Lady's Not for Burning, Guys and Dolls, 1952-I Am a Camera, Venus Observed, Pal Joey, 1953- Picnic, The Love of Four Colonels, Wonderful Town, 1954-Teahouse of the August Moon, Ondine, The Golden Apple, 1955-Cat on a Hot Tin Roof, Witness for the Prosecution, The Saint of Bleecker Street, 1956-The Diary of Anne Frank, Tiger at the Gates, My Fair Lady, 1957-Long Day's Journey into Night, The Waltz of the Toreadors, The Most Happy Fella, 1958-Look Homeward Angel, Look Back in Anger, The Music Man, 1959-A Raisin in the Sun, The Visit, La Plume de Ma Tante, 1960-Toys in the Attic, Five Finger Exercise, Fiorello! 1961-All the Way Home, A Taste of Honey, Carnival, 1962-Night of the Iguana, A Man for All Seasons, How to Succeed in Business without Really Trying, 1963-Who's Afraid of Virginia Woolf?,

1964-Luther, Hello Dolly!, 1965-The Subject Was Roses, Fiddler on the Roof, 1966-The Persecution and Assassination of Marat as Performed by the Inmates of the Asylum of Charenton under the Direction of the Marquis de Sade, Man of La Mancha, 1967-The Homecoming, Cabaret, 1968-Rosencrantz and Guildenstern Are Dead, Your Own Thing, 1969-The Great White Hope, 1776, 1970-The Effect of Gamma Rays on Man-in-the-Moon Marigolds, Borstal Boy, Company, 1971-Home, Follies, The House of Blue Leaves, 1972-That Championship Season, Two Gentlemen of Verona, 1973-The Hot l Baltimore, The Changing Room, A Little Night Music, 1974-The Contractor, Short Eyes, Candide, 1975-Equus, The Taking of Miss Janie, A Chorus Line, 1976-Travesties, Streamers, Pacific Overtures, 1977-Otherwise Engaged, American Buffalo, Annie, 1978-Da, Ain't Misbehavin', 1979-The Elephant Man, Sweeney Todd, 1980-Talley's Folly, Evita, Betrayal, 1981-Crimes of the Heart, A Lesson from Aloes, Special Citations to Lena Horne, "The Pirates of Penzance," 1982-The Life and Adventures of Nicholas Nickleby, A Soldier's Play, (no musical honored), 1983-Brighton Beach Memoirs, Plenty, Little Shop of Horrors, 1984-The Real Thing, Glengarry Glen Ross, Sunday in the Park with George

AMERICAN THEATRE WING ANTOINETTE PERRY (TONY) AWARD PRODUCTIONS

1948-Mister Roberts, 1949-Death of a Salesman, Kiss Me, Kate, 1950-The Cocktail Party, South Pacific, 1951-The Rose Tattoo, Guys and Dolls, 1952-The Fourposter, The King and I, 1953-The Crucible, Wonderful Town, 1954-The Teahouse of the August Moon, Kismet, 1955-The Desperate Hours, The Pajama Game, 1956-The Diary of Anne Frank, Damn Yankees, 1957-Long Day's Journey into Night, My Fair Lady, 1958-Sunrise at Campobello, The Music Man, 1959-J. B., Redhead, 1960-The Miracle Worker, Fiorello! tied with The Sound of Music, 1961-Becket, Bye Bye Birdie, 1962-A Man for All Seasons, How to Succeed in Business without Really Trying, 1963-Who's Afraid of Virginia Woolf?, A Funny Thing Happened on the Way to the Forum, 1964-Luther, Hello Dolly!, 1965-The Subject Was Roses, Fiddler on the Roof, 1966-The Persecution and Assassination of Marat as Performed by the

Inmates of the Asylum of Charenton under the Direction of the Marquis de Sade, Man of La Mancha, 1967-The Homecoming, Cabaret, 1968-Rosencrantz and Guildenstern Are Dead, Hallelujah Baby!, 1969-The Great White Hope, 1776, 1970-Borstal Boy, Applause, 1971-Sleuth, Company, 1972-Sticks and Bones, Two Gentlemen of Verona, 1973-That Championship Season, A Little Night Music, 1974-The River Niger, Raisin, 1975-Equus, The Wiz, 1976-Travesties, A Chorus Line, 1977-The Shadow Box, Annie, 1978-Da, Ain't Misbehavin', Dracula, 1979-The Elephant Man, Sweeney Todd, 1980-Children of a Lesser God, Evita, Morning's at Seven, 1981-Amadeus, 42nd Street, The Pirates of Penzance, 1982-The Life and Adventures of Nicholas Nickleby, Nine, Othello, 1983-Torch Song Trilogy, Cats, On Your Toes, 1984-The Real Thing, La Cage aux Folles

1984 THEATRE WORLD AWARD WINNERS

MARTINE ALLARD
of "The Tap Dance Kid"

MARK CAPRI
of "On Approval"

STEPHEN GEOFFREYS
of "The Human Comedy"

JOAN ALLEN
of "And a Nightingale Sang"

TODD GRAFF
of "Baby"

KATHY WHITTON BAKER
of "Fool for Love"

LAURA DEAN
of "Doonesbury"

J. J. JOHNSTON
of "American Buffalo"

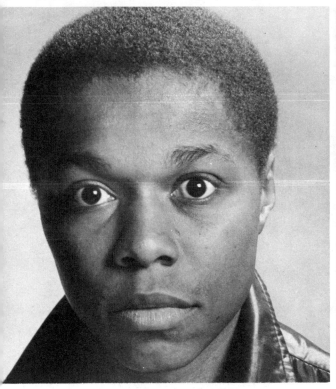

CALVIN LEVELS
of "Open Admissions"

GLENNE HEADLY
of "The Philanthropist"

BONNIE KOLOC
of "The Human Comedy"

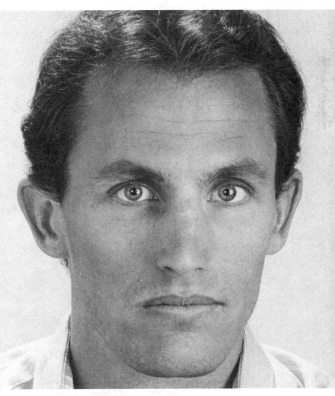

ROBERT WESTENBERG
of "Zorba"

193

THEATRE WORLD AWARDS presentations, Thursday, May 31, 1984. *Top:* Bernadette Peters, Lucie Arnaz, John Malkovich, Joanna Gleason, Gregory Hines, Dorothy Loudon; Juliette Koka; Cliff Robertson, Bonnie Franklin, John Shea, Maureen Stapleton, Peter MacNicol, Daniel Gerroll *Below:* Bernadette Peters, Robert Westenberg; Maureen Stapleton, Sidney Eden (for J. J. Johnston), Cliff Robertson; Lucie Arnaz, Stephen Geoffreys *Bottom:* Bonnie Franklin, Joan Allen; Laura Dean, John Shea; Todd Graff, Dorothy Loudon *Above:* Gregory Hines, Shirley Lauro (for Calvin Levels), Martine Allard, Leonard Harris

Van Williams. J. M. Viade Photos

194

Top: Dorothy Loudon, Mark Capri, Daniel Gerroll; Joanna Ross (for Kathy Whitton Baker); Peter MacNicol; Bonnie Koloc, Cliff Robertson
Below: Russell Nype, Bonnie Franklin, Stephen James, Orrin Reiley; Joanna Gleason; Glenne Headly, John Malkovich, Joan Allen
Bottom: John Shea, Kate Burton, Peter Gallagher; John Cullum, Jacqueline Brookes; Armelia McQueen, Ralph Carter; Lucie Arnaz,
Bernadette Peters, Bonnie Franklin *Above:* Dina Merrill, Cliff Robertson, Stephen Geoffreys, Bonnie Koloc, Mark Capri, Jona Allen, Ron Moody

J. M. Viade, Van Williams Photos

| Harry Belafonte | Jane Fonda | Charlton Heston | Patricia Neal | Jason Robards | Eva Marie Saint |

PREVIOUS THEATRE WORLD AWARD WINNERS

1944-45: Betty Comden, Richard Davis, Richard Hart, Judy Holliday, Charles Lang, Bambi Linn, John Lund, Donald Murphy, Nancy Noland, Margaret Phillips, John Raitt

1945-46: Barbara Bel Geddes, Marlon Brando, Bill Callahan, Wendell Corey, Paul Douglas, Mary James, Burt Lancaster, Patricia Marshall, Beatrice Pearson

1946-47: Keith Andes, Marion Bell, Peter Cookson, Ann Crowley, Ellen Hanley, John Jordan, George Keane, Dorothea MacFarland, James Mitchell, Patricia Neal, David Wayne

1947-48: Valerie Bettis, Edward Bryce, Whitfield Connor, Mark Dawson, June Lockhart, Estelle Loring, Peggy Maley, Ralph Meeker, Meg Mundy, Douglass Watson, James Whitmore, Patrice Wymore

1948-49: Tod Andrews, Doe Avedon, Jean Carson, Carol Channing, Richard Derr, Julie Harris, Mary McCarty, Allyn Ann McLerie, Cameron Mitchell, Gene Nelson, Byron Palmer, Bob Scheerer

1949-50: Nancy Andrews, Phil Arthur, Barbara Brady, Lydia Clarke, Priscilla Gillette, Don Hanmer, Marcia Henderson, Charlton Heston, Rick Jason, Grace Kelly, Charles Nolte, Roger Price

1950-51: Barbara Ashley, Isabel Bigley, Martin Brooks, Richard Burton, Pat Crowley, James Daly, Cloris Leachman, Russell Nype, Jack Palance, William Smothers, Maureen Stapleton, Marcia Van Dyke, Eli Wallach

1951-52: Tony Bavaar, Patricia Benoit, Peter Conlow, Virginia de Luce, Ronny Graham, Audrey Hepburn, Diana Herbert, Conrad Janis, Dick Kallman, Charles Proctor, Eric Sinclair, Kim Stanley, Marian Winters, Helen Wood

1952-53: Edie Adams, Rosemary Harris, Eileen Heckart, Peter Kelley, John Kerr, Richard Kiley, Gloria Marlowe, Penelope Munday, Paul Newman, Sheree North, Geraldine Page, John Stewart, Ray Stricklyn, Gwen Verdon

1953-54: Orsen Bean, Harry Belafonte, James Dean, Joan Diener, Ben Gazzara, Carol Haney, Jonathan Lucas, Kay Medford, Scott Merrill, Elizabeth Montgomery, Leo Penn, Eva Marie Saint

1954-55: Julie Andrews, Jacqueline Brookes, Shirl Conway, Barbara Cook, David Daniels, Mary Fickett, Page Johnson, Loretta Leversee, Jack Lord, Dennis Patrick, Anthony Perkins, Christopher Plummer

1955-56: Diane Cilento, Dick Davalos, Anthony Franciosa, Andy Griffith, Laurence Harvey, David Hedison, Earle Hyman, Susan Johnson, John Michael King, Jayne Mansfield, Sara Marshall, Gaby Rodgers, Susan Strasberg, Fritz Weaver

1956-57: Peggy Cass, Sydney Chaplin, Sylvia Daneel, Bradford Dillman, Peter Donat, George Grizzard, Carol Lynley, Peter Palmer, Jason Robards, Cliff Robertson, Pippa Scott, Inga Swenson

1957-58: Anne Bancroft, Warren Berlinger, Colleen Dewhurst, Richard Easton, Tim Everett, Eddie Hodges, Joan Hovis, Carol Lawrence, Jacqueline McKeever, Wynne Miller, Robert Morse, George C. Scott

1958-59: Lou Antonio, Ina Balin, Richard Cross, Tammy Grimes, Larry Hagman, Dolores Hart, Roger Mollien, France Nuyen, Susan Oliver, Ben Piazza, Paul Roebling, William Shatner, Pat Suzuki, Rip Torn

1959-60: Warren Beatty, Eileen Brennan, Carol Burnett, Patty Duke, Jane Fonda, Anita Gillette, Elisa Loti, Donald Madden, George Maharis, John McMartin, Lauri Peters, Dick Van Dyke

1960-61: Joyce Bulifant, Dennis Cooney, Sandy Dennis, Nancy Dussault, Robert Goulet, Joan Hackett, June Harding, Ron Husmann, James MacArthur, Bruce Yarnell

1961-62: Elizabeth Ashley, Keith Baxter, Peter Fonda, Don Galloway, Sean Garrison, Barbara Harris, James Earl Jones, Janet Margolin, Karen Morrow, Robert Redford, John Stride, Brenda Vaccaro

1962-63: Alan Arkin, Stuart Damon, Melinda Dillon, Robert Drivas, Bob Gentry, Dorothy Loudon, Brandon Maggart, Julienne Marie, Liza Minnelli, Estelle Parsons, Diana Sands, Swen Swenson

1963-64: Alan Alda, Gloria Bleezarde, Imelda De Martin, Claude Giraud, Ketty Lester, Barbara Loden, Lawrence Pressman, Gilbert Price, Philip Proctor, John Tracy, Jennifer West.

1964-65: Carolyn Coates, Joyce Jillson, Linda Lavin, Luba Lisa, Michael O'Sullivan, Joanna Pettet, Beah Richards, Jaime Sanchez, Victor Spinetti, Nicolas Surovy, Robert Walker, Clarence Williams III

1965-66: Zoe Caldwell, David Carradine, John Cullum, John Davidson, Faye Dunaway, Gloria Foster, Robert Hooks, Jerry Lanning, Richard Mulligan, April Shawhan, Sandra Smith, Leslie Ann Warren

1966-67: Bonnie Bedelia, Richard Benjamin, Dustin Hoffman, Terry Kiser, Reva Rose, Robert Salvio, Sheila Smith, Connie Stevens, Pamela Tiffin, Leslie Uggams, Jon Voight, Christopher Walken

1967-68: David Birney, Pamela Burrell, Jordan Christopher, Jack Crowder (Thalmus Rasulala), Sandy Duncan, Julie Gregg, Stephen Joyce, Bernadette Peters, Alice Playten, Michael Rupert, Brenda Smiley, Russ Thacker

1968-69: Jane Alexander, David Cryer, Blythe Danner, Ed Evanko, Ken Howard, Lauren Jones, Ron Leibman, Marian Mercer, Jill O'Hara, Ron O'Neal, Al Pacino, Marlene Warfield

1969-70: Susan Browning, Donny Burks, Catherine Burns, Len Cariou, Bonnie Franklin, David Holliday, Katharine Houghton, Melba Moore, David Rounds, Lewis J. Stadlen, Kristoffer Tabori, Fredricka Weber

1970-71: Clifton Davis, Michael Douglas, Julie Garfield, Martha Henry, James Naughton, Tricia O'Neil, Kipp Osborne, Roger Rathburn, Ayn Ruymen, Jennifer Salt, Joan Van Ark, Walter Willison

1971-72: Jonelle Allen, Maureen Anderman, William Atherton, Richard Backus, Adrienne Barbeau, Cara Duff-MacCormick, Robert Foxworth, Elaine Joyce, Jess Richards, Ben Vereen, Beatrice Winde, James Woods

1972-73: D'Jamin Bartlett, Patricia Elliott, James Farentino, Brian Farrell, Victor Garber, Kelly Garrett, Mari Gorman, Laurence Guittard, Trish Hawkins, Monte Markham, John Rubinstein, Jennifer Warren, Alexander H. Cohen (Special Award)

1973-74: Mark Baker, Maureen Brennan, Ralph Carter, Thom Christopher, John Driver, Conchata Ferrell, Ernestine Jackson, Michael Moriarty, Joe Morton, Ann Reinking, Janie Sell, Mary Woronov, Sammy Cahn (Special Award)

1974-75: Peter Burnell, Zan Charisse, Lola Falana, Peter Firth, Dorian Harewood, Joel Higgins, Marcia McClain, Linda Miller, Marti Rolph, John Sheridan, Scott Stevensen, Donna Theodore, Equity Library Theatre (Special Award)

1975-76: Danny Aiello, Christine Andreas, Dixie Carter, Tovah Feldshuh, Chip Garnett, Richard Kelton, Vivian Reed, Charles Repole, Virginia Seidel, Daniel Seltzer, John V. Shea, Meryl Streep, A Chorus Line (Special Award)

1976-77: Trazana Beverley, Michael Cristofer, Joe Fields, Joanna Gleason, Cecilia Hart, John Heard, Gloria Hodes, Juliette Koka, Andrea McArdle, Ken Page, Jonathan Pryce, Chick Vennera, Eva LeGallienne (Special Award)

1977-78: Vasili Bogazianos, Nell Carter, Carlin Glynn, Christopher Goutman, William Hurt, Judy Kaye, Florence Lacy, Armelia McQueen, Gordana Rashovich, Bo Rucker, Richard Seer, Colin Stinton, Joseph Papp (Special Award)

1978-79: Philip Anglim, Lucie Arnaz, Gregory Hines, Ken Jennings, Michael Jeter, Laurie Kennedy, Christine Lahti, Edward James Olmos, Kathleen Quinlan, Sarah Rice, Max Wright, Marshall W. Mason (Special Award)

1979-80: Maxwell Caulfield, Leslie Denniston, Boyd Gaines, Richard Gere, Harry Groener, Stephen James, Dinah Manoff, Lonnie Price, Marianne Tatum, Anne Twomey, Dianne Wiest, Mickey Rooney (Special Award)

1980-81: Brian Backer, Lisa Banes, Meg Bussert, Michael Allen Davis, Giancarlo Esposito, Daniel Gerroll, Phyllis Hyman, Cynthia Nixon, Amanda Plummer, Adam Redfield, Wanda Richert, Rex Smith, Elizabeth Taylor (Special Award)

1981-82: Karen Akers, Laurie Beechman, Danny Glover, David Alan Grier, Jennifer Holliday, Anthony Heald, Lizbeth Mackay, Peter MacNicol, Elizabeth McGovern, Ann Morrison, Michael O'Keefe, James Widdoes, Manhattan Theatre Club (Special Award)

1982-83: Karen Allen, Suzanne Bertish, Matthew Broderick, Kate Burton, Joanne Camp, Harvey Fierstein, Peter Gallagher, John Malkovich, Anne Pitoniak, James Russo, Brian Tarantina, Linda Thorson

BIOGRAPHICAL DATA ON THIS SEASON'S CASTS

ABRAHAM, F. MURRAY. Born Oct. 24, 1939 in Pittsburgh, PA. Attended UTx. Debut OB 1967 in "The Fantasticks," followed by "An Opening in the Trees," "14th Dictator," "Young Abe Lincoln," "Tonight in Living Color," "Adaptation," "Survival of St. Joan," "The Dog Ran Away," "Fables," "Richard III," "Little Murders," "Scuba Duba," "Where Has Tommy Flowers Gone?," "Miracle Play," "Blessing," "Sexual Perversity in Chicago," "Landscape of the Body," "The Master and Margarita," "Biting the Apple," "The Seagull," "Caretaker," "Antigone," "Uncle Vanya," Bdwy in "Man in the Glass Booth"(1968), "6 Rms Riv Vu," "Bad Habits," "The Ritz," "Legend," "Teibele and Her Demon."

ABUBA, ERNEST. Born Aug. 25, 1947 in Honolulu, HI. Attended Southwestern Col. Bdwy debut 1976 in "Pacific Overtures," followed by "Loose Ends." OB in "Sunrise," "Monkey Music," "Station J.," "Yellow Fever," "Pacific Overtures," "Empress of China."

ACKERMAN, LONI. Born Apr. 10, 1949 in NYC. Attended New School. Bdwy debut 1968 in "George M.!," followed by "No, No Nanette," "So Long 174th Street," "Magic Show," "Evita," OB in "Dames at Sea," "Starting Here Starting Now", "Roberta in Concert," "Brownstone."

ADAMS, BROOKE. Born in NYC in 1949. Attended Dalton School. Debut 1974 OB in "The Petrified Forest," followed by "Split," "Key Exchange," "Linda Her."

ADAMS, MASON. Born Feb. 26, 1919 in NYC. Graduate UWis. Has appeared in "Get Away Old Man," "Public Relations," "Career Angel," "Violet," "Shadow of My Enemy," "Tall Story," "Inquest," "Trial of the Catonsville 9," "Sign in Sidney Brustein's Window," OB in "Meegan's Game," "Shortchanged Review," "Checking Out," "The Soft Touch," "Paradise Lost."

AHEARN, DAN. Born Aug. 7, 1948 in Washington, DC. Attended Carnegie Mellon. Debut OB 1981 in "Woyzek," followed by "Brontosaurus Rex," "Billy Liar," "Second Prize Two Months in Leningrad."

AIDEM, BETSY SUE. Born Oct. 28, 1957 in Eastmeadow, NY. Graduate NYU. Debut 1981 OB in "The Trading Post," followed by "A Different Moon," "Balm in Gilead."

ALBERT, EDDIE. Born Apr. 22, 1908 in Rock Island, IL. Attended UMn. Bdwy debut 1936 in "Brother Rat," followed by "Room Service," "The Boys from Syracuse," "Miss Liberty," "Say, Darling," "Music Man," "No Hard Feelings," "You Can't Take It with You."

ALDREDGE, TOM. Born Feb. 28, 1928 in Dayton, OH. Attended Dayton U., Goodman Theatre. Bdwy bow 1959 in "The Nervous Set," followed by "UTBU," "Slapstick Tragedy," "Everything in the Garden," "Indians," "Engagement Baby," "How the Other Half Loves," "Sticks and Bones," "Where's Charley?," "Leaf People," "Rex," "Vieux Carre," "St. Joan," "Stages," "On Golden Pond," "The Little Foxes," OB in "The Tempest," "Between Two Thieves," "Henry V," "The Premise," "Love's Labour's Lost," "Troilus and Cressida," "Butter and Egg Man," "Ergo," "Boys in the Band," "Twelfth Night," "Colette," "Hamlet," "The Orphan," "King Lear," "The Iceman Cometh," "Black Angel," "Getting Along Famously," "Fool for Love."

ALDRICH, JANET. Born Oct. 16, 1956 in Hinsdale, IL. Graduate UMiami. Debut OB 1979 in "A Funny Thing Happened on the Way to the Forum," followed by "American Princess," "The Men's Group."

ALEXANDER, JASON. Born Sept. 23, 1959 in Irvington, NJ. Attended Boston U. Bdwy bow 1981 in "Merrilly We Roll Along," OB in "Forbidden Broadway."

ALICE, MARY. Born Dec. 3, 1941 in Indianola, MS. Debut OB 1967 in "Trials of Brother Jero," followed by "The Strong Breed," "Duplex," "Thoughts," "Miss Julie," "House Party," "Terraces," "Heaven and Hell's Agreement," "In the Deepest Part of Sleep," "Cockfight," "Julius Caesar," "Nongogo," "Second Thoughts," "Spell #7," "Zooman and The Sign," "Glasshouse," "The Ditch," "Take Me Along," Bdwy 1971 in "No Place to Be Somebody."

ALLARD, MARTINE. Born Aug. 24, 1970 in Brooklyn, NY. Bdwy debut 1983 in "The Tap Dance Kid" for which she received a Theatre World Award.

ALLEN, ELIZABETH. Born Jan. 25, 1934 in Jersey City, NJ. Attended Rutgers U. Bdwy debut 1957 in "Romanoff and Juliet," followed by "The Gay Life," "Do I Hear a Waltz?," "Sherry!," "42nd Street."

ALLEN, JOAN. Born Aug. 20, 1956 in Rochelle, IL. Attended E. Ill. U., W. ILL. U. Debut 1983 OB in "And a Nightingale Sang" for which she received a Theatre World Award.

ALLEN, KAREN. Born Oct. 5, 1951 in Carrollton, IL. Attended Geo. Wash. U., UMD. Bdwy debut 1982 in "Monday After the Miracle" for which she received a Theatre World Award, OB in "Extremities" (1983).

ALLINSON, MICHAEL. Born in London; attended Lausanne U, RADA. Bdwy bow 1960 in "My Fair Lady," (also 1981 revival), followed by "Hostile Witness," "Come Live With Me," "Coco," "Angel Street," "Oliver!," OB in "The Importance of Being Earnest," "Staircase."

AMEEN, KIM. Born Nov. 2 in Charlottesville, VA. Graduate Mt. Holyoke Col. Debut 1978 OB in "K," followed by "Dorothy Parker, A Montage," "Crazy Horse," "Miss Julie," "The Stronger," "Split," "Colette's Music-Hall Sidelights," "Three Sisters," "The Ninth Step," Bdwy in "Othello" (1982).

AMOS, KEITH. Born Oct. 26, 1963 in Annapolis, MD. Attended Howard U. Bdwy debut in "Amen Corner" (1983).

ANDERSON, CHRISTINE. Born Aug. 6 in Utica, NY. Graduate UWi. Bdwy debut in "I Love My Wife" (1980), OB in "I Can't Keep Running in Place," "On the Swing Shift," "Red, Hot and Blue."

ANDERSON, DOUGLAS. Born June 26, 1948 in NYC. Graduate Carnegie-Mellon U. Bdwy debut 1969 in "Malcolm," followed by "Ulysses in Nighttown," OB in "Pinter Review," "Under Milk Wood," "Noye's Fludde," "Moonchildren," "Romeo and Juliet," "A Bold Stroke for a Wife."

ANDERSON, JOEL. Born Nov. 19, 1955 in San Diego, CA. Graduate UUtah. Debut 1980 OB in "A Funny Thing Happened on the Way to the Forum," followed by "Joan of Lorraine," "Last of the Knucklemen."

ANDERSON, SYDNEY. Born Apr. 4 in Tacoma, WA. Graduate UWa. Debut 1978 OB in "Gay Divorce," Bdwy in "A Broadway Musical" (1978), followed by "Charlie and Algernon," "Oklahoma!," "La Cage aux Folles."

ANDERSON, THOMAS. Born Nov. 28, 1906 in Pasadena, CA. Attended Pasadena Jr. Col., AmThWing. Bdwy debut 1934 in "4 Saints in 3 Acts," followed by "Roll Sweet Chariot," "Cabin in the Sky," "Native Son," "Set My People Free," "How Long Till Summer," "A Hole in the Head," "The Great White Hope," "70 Girls 70," OB in "Conquering Thursday," "The Peddler," "The Dodo Bird," "Don't Play Us Cheap," "Anna Lucasta," "Willie."

ANDREAS, CHRISTINE. Born Oct. 1, 1951 in Camden, NJ. Bdwy debut 1975 in "Angel Street," followed by "My Fair Lady" for which she received a Theatre World Award, "Oklahoma (1979), "On Your Toes," OB in "Disgustingly Rich." "Rhapsody in Gershwin," "Alex Wilder: Clues to a Life."

ANDRES, BARBARA. Born Feb. 11, 1939 in NYC. Graduate Catholic U. Bdwy debut 1969 in "Jimmy," followed by "The Boy Friend," "Rodgers and Hart," "Rex," "On Golden Pond," "One Act Play Festival," "Doonesbury," OB in "Threepenny Opera," "Landscape of the Body," "Harold Arlen's Cabaret," "Suzanna Andler."

ANDREYKO, HELENA. Born Feb. 6, 1956 in Philadelphia, PA. Attended Hunter Col. Bdwy debut 1976 in "Music Is," followed by "Zoot Suit," "American Dance Machine," OB in "American Passion."

ANTHONY, FRAN. Born July 18 in Brooklyn, NY. Graduate Queens Col. Debut 1953 OB in "Climate of Eden," followed by "Pappa Is Home," "Summer Brave," "The Warrior's Husband," "Kind Lady," "House Music," "Equinox."

ANTHONY, JAMES. Born Aug. 17, 1947 in St. Louis, MO. Graduate S. Ill.U. Debut 1983 OB in "The Music Man."

ARBEIT, HERMAN O. Born Apr. 19, 1925 in Brooklyn, NY. Attended CCNY, HB Studio, Neighborhood Playhouse. Debut 1939 OB in "The Golem," followed by "Awake and Sing," "A Delicate Balance," "Yentl the Yeshiva Boy," "A Yank in Beverly Hills," "Second Avenue Rag," "Taking Steam, "Christopher Blake," Bdwy in "Yentl" (1975).

ARMISTEAD, DIANE. Born May 26, 1936 in Canton, OH. Attended Wooster Col. Debut OB 1979 in "The Old Maid and the Thief," followed by Light Opera of Manhattan, "Principally Pinter/Slightly Satie," Bdwy 1982 in "A Doll's Life," "Oliver!"

ARMSTRONG, JOHN. Born Oct. 25, 1914 in San Antonio, TX. Graduate Amherst Col. Bdwy debut 1945 in "Dream Girl," followed by "Life with Father," "Life with Mother," "Picnic," "Can Can," "West Side Story," "Diamond Orchid," OB in "Ladies Night in a Turkish Bath," "The Trial," "Yellow Jacket," "Billy Budd," "Point of No Return," "As You Like It," "The King and The Duke," "Time of Vengeance," "Montserrat," "All the Way Home," "A Touch of the Poet."

ARNOLD, BOB. Born Dec. 12, 1948 in Clevland, OH. Graduate Bowling Green State U. Debut 1983 OB in "An Evening of Adult Fairy Tales."

ARNOTT, MARK Born June 15, 1950 in Chicago, IL. Graduate Dartmouth Col. Debut 1981 OB in "Hunchback of Notre Dame," followed by "Buddies," "Love's Labours Lost," "Two Gentlemen of Verona," "The Dining Room," "The Knack," "Marmelade Skies," "The Homecoming."

ARONS, ELLYN. Born Oct. 29, 1956 in Philadelphia, PA. Graduate Temple U. Debut 1979 OB in "Plain and Fancy," Bdwy in "Camelot" (1980), "Mame" (1983).

ARTHUR, HELEN-JEAN. Born Nov. 2, 1933 in Chicago, IL. Graduate Beloit Col. Debut 1957 OB in "Othello," followed by "12 Pound Look," "Streets of New York," "Vera with Kate," "Declasse," "Teach Me How to Cry," "A Touch of the Poet," Bdwy in "Send Me No Flowers" (1960), "Moon Beseiged," "Look Back in Anger."

ASHLEY, ELIZABETH. Born Aug. 30, 1939 in Ocala, FL. Attended Neighborhood Playhouse. Bdwy debut 1959 in "The Highest Tree," followed by "Taker Her, She's Mine" for which she received a Theatre World Award, "Barefoot in the Park," "Ring Round the Bathtub," "Cat on a Hot Tin Roof," "The Skin of Our Teeth," "Legend," "Caesar and Cleopatra," "Hide and Seek," "Agnes of God."

ASTOR, PHILIP. Born Feb. 17 in Park Ridge, NJ. Graduate ILL. WesleyanU. Bdwy debut 1969 in "1776," followed by "All Over Town," "Nuts," "Torch Song Trilogy," OB in "In the Boom Boom Room," "Games," "Troilus and Cressida," "As You Like It."

ASTREDO, HUMBERT ALLEN. Born in San Francisco, CA. Attended SanFranU. Debut 1967 OB in "Arms and the Man," followed by "Fragments," "Murderous Angels," "Beach Children," "End of Summer," "Knuckle," "Grand Magic," "Big and Little," "Jail Diary of Albie Sachs," "Breakfast Conversations in Miami," Bdwy in "Les Blancs" (1970), "An Evening with Richard Nixon . . .," "The Little Foxes."

ATHERTON, WILLIAM. Born July 30, 1947 in Orange, CT. Graduate Carnegie Tech. Debut 1971 OB in "House of Blue Leaves," followed by "The Basic Training of Pavlo Hummel," "Suggs" for which he received a Theatre World Award, "Rich and Famous," "The Passing Game," "Three Acts of Recognition," Bdwy in "The Sign in Sidney Brustein's Window" (1972), "Happy New Year," "The American Clock," "Caine Mutiny Court-Martial."

AUGUST, RON. Born Dec. 25, 1942 in NYC. Attended Brigham Young U. Debut 1983 OB in "Anna Christie," followed by "American Dreams."

AUSTIN, BETH. a.k.a. Elizabeth. Born May 23, 1952 in Philadelphia, PA. Graduate Point Park Col. Pittsburgh Playhouse. Debut 1977 OB in "Wonderful Town," followed by "The Prevalence of Mrs. Seal," "Engaged," "Pastoral," "Head over Heals," "A Kiss Is Just a Kiss," Bdwy in "Sly Fox" (1977), "Whoopee," "Onward Victoria."

AVARI, N. ERICK. Born Apr. 13, 1952 in Calcutta, IN. Graduate Col. of Charleston, SC. Debut 1983 OB in "Bhutan."

BACKER, MELANIE. Born Sept. 4, 1957 in Torrance, CA. Graduate UCLA, USC. Debut OB 1984 in "Pal Joey."

BADILLO, ROBERTO. Born June 12, 1958 in NYC. Attended Goddard Col. Debut 1983 OB in "The House of Ramon Iglesia," followed by "Ariano."

BADOLATO, DEAN. Born June 6, 1952 in Chicago, IL. Attended UIll. Bdwy debut 1978 in "A Chorus Line," followed by "Pirates of Penzance," "On Your Toes."

BAETZ, NORA. Born Apr. 16, 1955 in Hoboken, NJ. Attended Ithaca Col., AADA. Debut OB 1983 in "Day-Dreams."

BAKER, KATHY WHITTON. Born June 8, 1950 in Midland, TX. Graduate UCBerkley. Debut 1983 OB in "Fool for Love" for which she received a Theatre World Award, followed by "Desire under the Elms."

BAKER, RAYMOND. Born July 9, 1948 in Omaha, NE. Graduate UDenver. Debut 1972 OB in "The Proposition," followed by "Are You Now or Have You Ever Been . . .," "Character Lines," "Lunch Hour," "Legends of Arthur," "War Babies," "Bathroom Plays," Bdwy in "Crimes of the Heart," "Division Street," "Is There Life After High School?," "Torch Song Trilogy."

BALL, WARREN. Born Aug. 4, 1939 in Oakland, CA. Graduate LACC. Bdwy debut 1983 in "The Caine Mutiny Court Martial."

BALLARD, KAYE. Born Nov. 20, 1926 in Cleveland, OH. Debut 1954 OB in "The Golden Apple," followed by "Cole Porter Revisited," "Hey, Ma, Kaye Ballard," Bdwy in "The Beast in Me" (1963), "Royal Flush," "Molly," "Pirates of Penzance."

BALLINGER, JUNE. Born Nov. 15, 1949 in Camden, NJ. Attended Briarcliff Col. Debut 1980 OB in "Mr. Wilson's Peace of Mind," followed by "Dona Rosita," "A Man in the House."

BALLOU, KATHRYN. Born June 27, 1956 in Glen Cove, NY. Graduate FlaAtlanticU., Neighborhood Playhouse. Debut 1983 OB in "In the Voodoo Parlor," followed by "He Who Gets Slapped."

BANES, LISA. Born July 9, 1955 in Chagrin Falls, OH. Juilliard grad. Debut OB 1980 in "Elizabeth I," followed by "A Call from the East," "Look Back in Anger" for which she received a Theatre World Award, "My Sister in This House," "Antigone," "Three Sisters," "The Cradle Will Rock," "Isn't It Romantic."

BANNEN, IAN. Born June 29, 1928 in Airdrie, Scot. Attended Ratcliffe Col., Oxford. Bdwy debut 1984 in "Moon for the Misbegotten."

BANTAY, JOHN Born May 10, 1960 in San Francisco, CA. Attended USantaClara. Debut 1984 OB in "Pacific Overtures."

BARANSKI, CHRISTINE. Born May 2, 1952 in Buffalo, NY. Graduate Juilliard Sch. Debut OB 1978 in "One Crack Out," followed by "Says I Says He," "The Trouble with Europe," "Coming Attractions," "Operation Midnight Climax," "Sally and Marsha," "A Midsummer Night's Dream," Bdwy in "Hide and Seek." (1980), "The Real Thing."

BARBER, ELLEN. Born in August, in Brooklyn, NY. Graduate Bard Col. Debut 1970 OB in "The Mod Donna," followed by "Moonchildren," "Apple Pie," "Funeral March for a One Man Band," "Starluster," "Awake and Sing," "Occupations," "Poor Murderer," "Pantagleize," "Modern Ladies of Guanabacoa," "Poisoner of the Wells," "Souvenirs," Bdwy in "The Good Doctor" (1973), "Fame."

BARDEN, PERRY. Born June 5, 1958 in Elmira, NY. Graduate Ithaca Col. Debut 1984 OB in "Flesh, Flash and Frank Harris."

BARKER, CHRISTINE. Born Nov. 26 in Jacksonville, FL. Attended UCLA. Bdwy debut 1979 in "A Chorus Line."

BARKER, JEAN. Born Dec. 20, in Philadelphia PA. Attended UPa., AmThWing. Debut OB 1953 in "The Bald Soprano," followed by "Night Shift," "A Month in the Country," "Portrait of Jenny," "Knucklebones," "About Iris Berman," "Goodnight, Grandpa," "Victory Bonds," Bdwy in "The Innkeepers."

BARKER, MARGARET. Born Oct. 10, 1908 in Baltimore, MD. Attended Bryn Mawr. Bdwy debut 1928 in "Age of Innocence," followed by "Barretts of Wimpole Street," "House of Connelly," "Men in White," "Gold Eagle Guy," "Leading Lady," "Member of the Wedding," "Autumn Garden," "See the Jaguar," "Ladies of the Corridor," "The Master Builder," OB in "Wayside Motor Inn," "The Loves of Cass McGuire," "Three Sisters, "Details without a Map," "The Inheritors."

BARNER, STOCKMAN. Born July 26, 1921 in New London, CT. Graduate UIowa. Bdwy debut 1945 in "Othello," OB in "The Hollow," "Revenger's Tragedy," "The Miser," "Hound of the Baskervilles."

BARNES, FRANCES. Born Feb. 24, 1931 in Windber, PA. Graduate PaStateU, Western Reserve U. Debut OB 1955 in "An Ideal Husband," followed by "Knights Errant," "Tallulah," Bdwy in "Waltz of the Toreadors" (1958).

BARNETT, CRAIG. Born Nov. 1, 1948 in St. Louis, MO. Graduate UMo. Debut 1984 OB in City Theatre Festival's "Midsummer Night's Dream," "Merry Wives of Windsor" and "Lion in Winter."

BARONE, JOHN. Born March 14, 1954 in Staten Island, NY. Graduate Wagner Col. Debut 1982 OB in "Robin Hood," followed by "The Music Man," "Flesh, Flash & Frank Harris."

BARRE, GABRIEL. Born Aug. 26, 1957 in Brattleboro, VT. Graduate AADA. Debut 1977 OB in "Jabberwock," followed by "T.N.T.," "Bodo."

BARRETT, BRENT. Born Feb 28, 1957 in Quinter, KS. Graduate Carnegie-Mellon. Bdwy debut 1980 in "West Side Story," followed by "Dance a Little Closer," OB in "March of the Falsettos," "Portrait of Jenny," "The Death of Von Richthofen," "Sweethearts in Concert."

BARRETT, JOE. Born Nov. 30, 1950 in Webster, NY. Graduate U Rochester. Debut 1975 OB in "Boy Meets Boy," followed by "The Great American Backstage Musical."

BARRETT, JOHN. Born Aug. 3, 1937 in Lebanon, IL. Attended Goodman Theatre. Debut 1967 OB in "Jonah," followed by "Bread," "Victims of Duty," "The Trial," "New Way to Pay Old Debts," Bdwy in "Tricks" (1979)

BARRETT, LAURINDA. Born in 1931 in NYC. Attended Wellesley Col., RADA. Bdwy debut 1956 in "Too Late the Phalarope," followed by "The Girls in 509," "The Milk Train Doesn't Stop Here Anymore," "UTBU," "I Never Sang For My Father," "Equus," OB in "The Misanthrope," "Palm Tree in a Rose Garden," "All Is Bright," "The Carpenters," "Ah, Wilderness!"

BARRIE, BARBARA. Born May 23, 1931 in Chicago, IL. Graduate UTx. Bdwy debut 1955 in "The Wooden Dish," followed by "Happily Never After," "Company," "Selling of the President," "Prisoner of Second Avenue," "California Suite," "Torch Song Trilogy," OB in "The Crucible," "Beaux Stratagem," "Taming of the Shrew," "Twelfth Night," "All's Well That Ends Well," "Horseman, Pass By," "Killdeer," "Big and Little," "Backer's Audition," "Isn't It Romantic."

BARROW, BERNARD E. Born Dec. 30, 1927 in NYC. Graduate Syracuse U, Columbia, Yale. Debut OB 1959 in "Billy Budd," followed by "Poor Murderer," "Scuba Duba," "Uncle Vanya," "Hamlet," "Punchy," "Sympathy."

BARRY, GENE. Born June 14, 1919 in NYC. Bdwy in "New Moon," "Rosalinda," "The Merry Widow," "Catherine Was Great," "The Would-Be Gentleman," "Happy as Larry," "Bless You All," "La Cage aux Folles."

BARTLETT, ALISON. Born in Massachusetts July 14, 1971. Debut 1984 OB in "Landscape of the Body."

BARTLETT, D'JAMIN. Born May 21 in NYC. Attended AADA. Bdwy debut 1973 in "A Little Night Music" for which she received a Theatre World Award, OB in "The Glorious Age," "Boccacio," "2 by 5," "Lulu," "Alex Wilder" Clues to Life," "D'Jamin Sings Lennon & McCartney."

BARTLETT, PETER. Born Aug. 28, 1942 in Chicago, IL. Attended LoyolaU., LAMDA. Bdwy debut 1969 in "A Patriot for Me," followed by "Gloria and Esperanza," OB in "Boom Boom Room," "I Remember the House Where I Was Born," "Crazy Locomotive," "Thurber Carnival."

BARTLETT, ROBIN. Born Apr. 22, 1951 in NYC. Graduate Boston U. Bdwy debut 1975 in "Yentl," followed by "The World of Sholem Aleichem," OB in "Agamemnon," "Fathers and Sons," "No End of Blame," "Living Quarters," "After the Fall," "The Sea Gull," "The Philanthropist," "Fen," "Found a Peanut."

BARTON, FRED. Born Oct. 20, 1958 in Camden, NJ. Graduate Harvard. Debut 1982 OB in "Forbidden Broadway."

BASIL, JOHN. Born Sept. 27, 1950 in Philadelphia, PA. Graduate Temple U. Debut 1978 OB in "Dance on a Country Grave," followed by "The Bacchae," "The Scarecrow," "Innocent Thoughts and Harmless Intentions," "Americans."

BASILE, MARK. Born Feb. 21, 1954 in Baltimore, MD. Graduate Wm. & Mary Col. Debut 1984 OB in "Up in Central Park."

BASSETT, STEVE. Born June 25, 1952 in Escondido, CA. Juilliard graduate. Bdwy debut 1979 in "Deathtrap," OB in "Spring Awakening," "Booth," "Full Hookup."

BATES, KATHY. Born June 18, 1948 in Memphis, TN, Graduate S. Methodist U. Debut 1976 OB in "Vanities," followed by "The Art of Dining," Bdwy in "Goodbye Fidel" (1980), "5th of July," "Come Back to the 5 & Dime, Jimmy Dean," " 'night, Mother."

BATTISTA, LLOYD. Born May 14, 1937 in Cleveland, OH. Graduate Carnegie Tech. Bdwy debut 1966 in "Those That Play the Clowns," followed by "The Homecoming," "The Guys in the Truck," OB in "The Flame and the Rose," "Murder in the Cathedral," "The Miser," "Gorky," "Sexual Perversity in Chicago," "King of Schnorrers," "Francis," "The Keymaker," "The Guys in the Truck."

BATTLE, HINTON. Born Nov. 29, 1956 in Neubraecke, Ger. Joined Dance Theatre of Harlem. Bdwy debut 1975 in "The Wiz," followed by "Dancin'," "Sophisticated Ladies," "Dreamgirls," "The Tap Dance Kid."

BAUERS, DEBORAH. Born July 19, 1953 in Nashville, TN. Graduate UColo., Smith Col. Broadway debut 1982 in "Oh! Calcutta!"

BEACH, GARY. Born Oct. 10, 1947 in Alexandria, VA. Graduate NCSch. of Arts. Bdwy bow 1971 in "1776," followed by "Something's Afoot," "Moony Shapiro Songbook," "Annie," "Doonesbury," OB in "Smile, Smile, Smile," "What's a Nice Country Like You . . .," "Ionescapade," "By Strouse," "A Bundle of Nerves."

BEAN, ORSON. Born July 22, 1928 in Burlington, VT. Bdwy bow 1953 in "Men of Distinction," followed by "John Murray Anderson's Almanac" for which he received a Theatre World Award, "Will Success Spoil Rock Hunter?," "Nature's Way," "Mister Roberts" (CC), "Subways Are for Sleeping," "Say, Darling" (CC), "Never Too Late," "I Was Dancing," "Ilya Darling," OB in "Home Movies," "A Round with Ring," "Make Someone Happy," "I'm Getting My Act Together," "40 Deuce," "A Christmas Carol," "Strange Case of Dr. Jekyll and Mr. Hyde."

BEAN, REATHEL. Born Aug. 24, 1942 in Missouri. Graduate Drake U. OB in "America Hurrah," "San Francisco's Burning," "Love Cure," "Henry IV," "In Circles," "Peace," "Journey of Snow White," "Wanted," "The Faggot," "Lovers," "Not Back with the Elephants," "Art of Coarse Acting," "The Trip Back Down," Bdwy in "Doonesbury" (1983).

BECHER, JOHN C. Born Jan. 13, 1915 in Milwaukee, WI. Graduate UWis. Bdwy bow 1946 with Am. Rep. Theatre, followed by "Skipper Next to God," "Idiot's Delight," "Picnic," "Brigadoon" (CC), "No Time for Sergeants," "Ballad of the Sad Cafe," "Mame" (1966, '83), "Harvey," "Gypsy," OB in "American Dream," "Death of Bessie Smith," "Happy Days," "Dumbwaiter," "Child Buyer," "That Thing at the Cherry Lane."

BECK, JOANNA. Born Feb. 5, 1953 in Asheville, NC. Graduate UNCGreensboro. Debut 1977 OB in "Sound of Music," followed by "Old Fashioned," "Boys from Syracuse," "Music Man," Bdwy 1983 in "Show Boat."

BEECHMAN, LAURIE. Born Apr. 4, 1954 in Philadelphia, Pa. Attended NYU. Bdwy debut 1977 in "Annie," followed by "Pirates of Penzance," "Joseph and the Amazing Technicolor Dreamcoat" for which she received a Theatre World Award. "Some Enchanted Evening" (OB), "Pal Joey in Concert," "Cats."

BEECROFT, GREGORY. Born in Corpus Christi, TX. Attended UNH. Debut 1984 OB in "Just Like the Lions."

BELL, VANESSA. Born Mar. 20, 1957 in Toledo. OH. Graduate OhU. Bdwy debut 1981 in "Bring Back Birdie," followed by "El Bravo!," "Dreamgirls," OB in "Take Me Along."

BENTLEY, GRACE. Born Dec. 1 in NJ. Graduate Hunter Col. Debut 1981 OB in "Suddenly Last Summer," followed by "The Chalk Cross," "Evil Spirit," "Triptych."

BERETTA, JOANNE. Born Nov. 14 in San Francisco, CA. Attended SFState Col. Bdwy Debut in "New Faces of 1962," OB in "The Club" "Colette Collage," "Dementos."

BEREZIN, TANYA. Born Mar. 25, 1941 in Philadelphia, PA. Attended Boston U. Debut OB 1967 in "The Sandcastle," followed by "Three Sisters," "Great Nebula in Orion," "him," "Amazing Activity of Charlie Contrare," "Battle of Angels," "Mound Builders," "Serenading Louie," "My Life," "Brontosaurus," "Glorious Morning," "Mary Stuart," "The Beaver Coat," "Balm in Gilead," Bdwy in "5th of July" (1981), "Angels Fall."

BERGER, STEPHEN. Born May 16, 1954 in Philadelphia, PA. Attended UCinn. Bdwy debut 1982 in "Little Me," OB in "Nite Club Confidential."

BERK, DAVID. Born July 20, 1932 in NYC. Graduate Manhattan Sch. of Music. Debut 1958 OB in "Eloise," followed by "Carnival" (CC), "So Long 174th St.," "Wonderful Town," "Anyone Can Whistle," "The Meehans," "June Moon," "Pal Joey."

BERKSON, SUSAN. Born Apr. 10 in Michigan City, IN. Graduate MacAlester Col., UMn. Debut OB 1982 in "Nymph Errant," "Winds of Change," "Crossroads Cafe."

BERNSTEIN, DOUGLAS. Born May 6, 1958 in NYC. Amherst graduate. Debut 1982 OB in "Upstairs at O'Neals," followed by "Backer's Audition."

BERTRAND, JACQUELINE. Born June 1, 1939 in Quebec, Can. Attended Neighborhood Playhouse, Actors Studio, LAMDA. Debut 1978 OB in "Unfinished Women," followed by "Dancing for the Kaiser," "Lulu," "War and Peace," "Nest of the Wood Grouse."

BIAGINI, SAL. Born Apr. 13, 1952 in Brooklyn, NY. Graduate USFla. Debut 1984 OB in "Sing Me Sunshine."

BILLINGTON, LEE. Born July 15, 1932 in Madison, WI. Bdwy debut 1969 in "But Seriously," OB in "Dance of Death," "3 by O'Neill," "Our Town," "Capt. Brassbound's Conversion," "Henry VIII," "Boy with a Cart," "Epicoene," "The Homecoming," "Paterson," "Windmills," "Within the Year."

BIRNEY, REED. Born Sept. 11, 1954 in Alexandria, VA. Attended Boston U. Bdwy debut 1977 in "Gemini," OB in "The Master and Margarita," "Bella Figura," "Winterplay," "The Flight of the Earls."

BLAINE, VIVIAN. Born Nov. 21, 1923 in Newark, NJ. Bdwy debut 1950 in "Guys and Dolls," followed by "Hatful of Rain," "Say, Darling," "Enter Laughing," "Guys and Dolls" (CC'66), "Company," "Zorba."

BLANKENSHIP, WILL. Born Mar. 7, 1928 in Gatesville, TX. Graduate NTxStateU., Juilliard, Vienna Academy of Music. Bdwy debut 1983 in "My One and Only."

BLAXILL, PETER. Born Sept. 27, 1931 in Cambridge, MA. Graduate Bard Col. Debut 1967 OB in "Scuba Duba," followed by "The Fantasticks," "The Passion of Antigona Perez," "Oh Boy!," "From Brooks With Love," "Who's There," Bdwy in "Marat/Sade," "The Littlest Circus," "The Innocents."

BLAZER, JUDITH. Born Oct. 22, 1956 in Dover, NJ. Graduate Manhattan Sch. of Music. Debut OB 1979 in "Oh, Boy!," followed by "Roberta in Concert."

BLEVINS, MICHAEL. Born Sept. 2, 1960 in Orlando, FL. Attended UNC, NYU. Bdwy debut 1981 in "Bring Back Birdie," followed by "Little Me," "Tap Dance Kid," OB in "Time Pieces," "Bags."

BLISS, JUDITH. Born June 18, 1949 in Evansville, IN. Graduate St. Ambrose. Debut OB 1981 in "The Scarecrow," Bdwy in "Baby" (1983).

BLOCH, PETER. Born Dec. 13, 1955 in Worcester, MA. Debut OB 1984 in "Paradise Lost," followed by "The Hasty Heart."

BLOCK, LARRY. Born Oct. 30, 1942 in NYC. Graduate URI. Bdwy bow 1966 in "Hail Scrawdyke," followed by "La Turista," OB in "Eh?," "Fingernails Blue as Flowers," "Comedy of Errors," "Coming Attractions," "Henry IV Part 2," "Feuhrer Bunker," "Manhattan Love Songs," "Souvenirs."

BOBBIE, WALTER. Born Nov. 18, 1945 in Scranton, PA. Graduate UScranton, Catholic U. Bdwy bow 1971 in "Frank Merriwell," followed by "The Grass Harp," "Grease," "Tricks," "Going Up," "History of the American Film," OB in "Drat!," "She Loves Me," "Up from Paradise."

BODLE, JANE. Born Nov 12 in Lawrence KS. Attended UUtah. Bdwy debut 1983 in "Cats."

BOGGS, ELLEN. Born Mar. 23, 1956 in Palo Alto, CA. Graduate UHi. Debut 1981 OB in "Yellow Is My Favorite Color," followed by "The Barretts of Wimpole Street," "Foreplay," "The Holy Terrors."

BOGOSIAN, ERIC. Born Apr. 24, 1953 in Boston, MA. Graduate Oberlin Col. Debut 1982 OB in "Men Inside/Voices of America," followed by "Funhouse."

BOGYO, PETER. Born Jan. 21, 1955 in Summit, NJ. Yale graduate. Debut 1980 OB in "Hamlet," followed by "Julius Caesar," "The Three Sisters," "After Liverpool."

BOHN, GEORGE A. Born Apr. 26, 1951 in Concord, CA. Graduate St. Mary's Col. Debut 1981 OB in "Your American Girl," followed by "Not So New Faces of '83," "Sing Me Sunshine."

BOJARSKI, STANLEY. Born June 1, 1950 in Fonda, NY. Graduate Marist Col. Debut 1984 OB in "Red, Hot and Blue."

BOOTH, ERIC. Born Oct. 18, 1950 in NYC. Graduate Emerson Col., Stanford U. Bdwy debut 1977 in "Ceasar and Cleopatra," followed by "Golda," "Whose Life Is It Anyway?," OB in "Taming of the Shrew," "The Strange Case of Dr. Jekyll."

BORN, LYNN P. Born Aug. 6, 1956 in Richmond, VA. Attended Northwestern U. Debut 1982 OB in "Catholic School Girls," followed by "Nag and Nell," "Stifled Growls," "Collective Choices."

BOSCO, PHILIP. Born Sept. 26, 1930 in Jersey City, NJ. Graduate Catholic U. Credits" "Auntie Mame," "Rape of the Belt," "Ticket of Leave Man," "Donnybrook," "Man for All Seasons," "Mrs. Warren's Profession," with LCRep in "The Alchemist," "East Wind," "Galileo," "St. Joan," "Tiger at the Gate," "Cyrano," "King Lear," "A Great Career," "In the Matter of J. Robert Oppenheimer," "The Miser," "The Time of Your Life," "Camino Real," "Operation Sidewinder," "Amphitryon," "Enemy of the People," "Playboy of the Western World," "Good Woman of Setzuan," "Antigone," "Mary Stuart," "Narrow Road to the Deep North," "The Crucible," "Twelfth Night," "Enemies," "Plough and the Stars," "Merchant of Venice," and "A Streetcar Named Desire," "Henry V," "Threepenny Opera," "Streamers," "Stages," "St. Joan," "The Biko Inquest," "Man and Superman," "Whose Life Is It Anyway," "Major Barbara," "A Month in the Country," "Bacchae," "Hedda Gabler," "Don Juan in Hell," "Inadmissible Evidence," "Eminent Domain," "Misalliance," "Learned Ladies," "Some Men Need Help," "Ah, Wilderness!," "The Caine Mutiny Court Marital," "Heartbreak House," "Come Back, Little Sheba."

BOUTSIKARIS, DENNIS. Born Dec. 21, 1952 in Newark. NJ. Graduate Hampshire Col. Debut 1975 OB in "Another Language," followed by "Funeral March for a One-Man Band," "All's Well That Ends Well," "A Day in the Life of the Czar, "Nest of the Wood Grouse," Bdwy in "Filumena," "Bent," "Amadeus."

BOVA, JOSEPH. Born May 25 in Cleveland, OH. Graduate Northwestern U. Debut 1959 OB in "On the Town," followed by "Once Upon a Mattress," "House of Blue Leaves," "Comedy," "The Beauty Part," "Taming of the Shrew," "Richard III," "Comedy of Errors," "Invitation to a Beheading," "Merry Wives of Windsor," "Henry V," "Streamers," Bdwy in "Rape of the Belt," "Irma La Douce," "Hot Spot," "The Chinese," "American Millionaire," "St. Joan," "42nd Street."

BOVASSO, JULIE. Born Aug. 1, 1930 in Brooklyn, NY. Attended CCNY. Bdwy in "Monique," "Minor Miracle," "Gloria and Esperanza," OB in "Naked," "The Maids," "The Lesson," "The Typewriter," "Screens," "Henry IV Part I," "What I Did Last Summer," "Angelo's Wedding."

BOZYK, REIZL (ROSE). Born May 13, 1914 in Poland. Star of many Yiddish productions before 1966 Bdwy debut in "Let's Sing Yiddish," followed by "Sing, Israel, Sing." "Mirele Efros," "The Jewish Gypsy," OB in "Light, Lively and Yiddish," "Rebecca, the Rabbi's Daughter," "Wish Me Mazel-Tov," "Roumanian Wedding," "The Showgirl."

BRAUNSTEIN, ALAN. Born Apr. 30, 1947 in Brooklyn, NY. Debut 1962 OB in "Daddy Come Home," followed by "Rhinegold," Bdwy in "Hair," "Jesus Christ Superstar," "Dude," "Oliver" (1984).

BREED, HELEN LLOYD. Born Jan. 27, 1911 in NYC. Debut 1956 OB in "Out of This World," followed by "Winners," "Exiles," "Something Unspoken," "You Never Can Tell," "Liliom," "The Hollow," "Chalk Garden," "Ring Round the Moon," "Richard II," "Kind Lady," "A Little Night Music," "The Holly and the Ivy," "For the Use of the Hall."

BREEN, J. PATRICK. Born Oct. 26, 1960 in Brooklyn, NY. Graduate NYU. Debut 1982 OB in "Epiphany," Bdwy in "Brighton Beach Memoirs" (1983).

BRENNAN, MAUREEN. Born Oct. 11, 1952 in Washington, DC. Attended UCin. Bdwy debut 1974 in "Candide" for which she received a Theatre World Award, followed by "Going Up," "Knickerbocker Holiday," "Little Johnny Jones," OB in "Shakespeare's Cabaret."

BRENNAN, TOM. Born Apr. 16, 1926 in Cleveland, OH. Graduate Oberlin, Western Reserve. Debut 1958 OB in "Synge Trilogy," followed by "Between Two Thieves," "Easter," "All in Love," "Under Milkwood," "An Evening with James Purdy," "Golden Six," "Pullman Car Hiawatha," "Are You Now or Have You . . .," "Diary of Anne Frank," "Milk of Paradise," "Transcendental Love," "The Beaver Coat," "The Overcoat," "Summer," "Asian Shade," "Inheritors," "Paradise Lost," Bdwy in "Play Memory" (1984).

BREWER-MOORE, CATHY. Born Jan 9, 1948 in Brunswick, GA. Attended New School, AADA. Bdwy debut 1973 in "Seesaw," OB in "Wonderful Town," "Pal Joey."

BRIAN, MICHAEL. Born Nov. 14, 1958 in Utica, NY. Attended Boston Conservatory. Debut 1979 OB in "Kennedy's Children," followed by "Street Scene," "Death of Von Richthofen as Witnessed From Earth," "Lenny and the Heartbreakers," Bdwy in "Baby" (1983).

BRILL, FRAN. Born Sept. 30 in PA. Attended Boston U. Bdwy debut 1969 in "Red, White and Maddox," OB in "What Every Woman Knows," "Scribes," "Naked," "Look Back in Anger," "Knuckle," "Skirmishes," "Baby with the Bathwater."

BROADHURST, KENT. Born Feb. 4, 1940 in St. Louis, MO. Graduate UNe. Debut 1968 OB in "The Fourth Wall," followed by "Design for Living," "Marching Song," "Heartbreak House," "Dark of the Moon," Bdwy in "The Caine Mutiny Court-Martial" (1983).

BROCKSMITH, ROY. Born Sept. 15, 1945 in Quincy, IL. Debut 1971 OB in "Whip Lady," followed by "The Workout," "Beggar's Opera," "Polly," "Threepenny Opera," "The Master and Margarita," "Jungle of Cities," "Don Juan," "Dr. Selavy's Magic Theatre," Bdwy in "The Leaf People" (1975), "Stages," "Tartuffe."

BRODERICK, MATTHEW. Born Mar. 21, 1963 in NYC. Debut OB 1981 in "Torch Song Trilogy," Bdwy 1983 in "Brighton Beach Memoirs" for which he received a Theatre World Award.

BROGGER, IVAR. Born Jan. 10, 1947 in St. Paul, Mn. Graduate UMn. Debut 1979 OB in "In the Jungle of Cities," followed by "Collected Words of Billy the Kid," "Magic Time," "Cloud 9," "Richard III," Bdwy in "Macbeth" (1981).

BROOK, PAMELA. Born Jan 21, 1947 in London, Ont. Can. Graduate UToronto, UMn. Debut 1976 OB in "The Philanderer," followed by "The Holly and the Ivy," "Mr. and Mrs.," Bdwy in "Goodbye Fidel" (1980).

BROOKES, JACQUELINE. Born July 24, 1930 in Montclair, NJ. Graduate UIowa, RADA. Bdwy debut 1955 in "Tiger at the Gates," followed by "Watercolor," "Abelard and Heloise," OB in "The Cretan Woman" for which she received a Theatre World Award, "The Clandestine Marriage," "Measure for Measure," "Duchess of Malfi," "Ivanov," "Six Characters in Search of an Author," "An Evening's Frost," "Come Slowly, Eden," "The Increased Difficulty of Concentration," "The Persians," "Sunday Dinner," "House of Blue Leaves," "A Meeting by the River," "Owners," "Hallelujah," "Dream of a Blacklisted Actor," "Knuckle," "Mama Sang the Blues," "Buried Child," "On Mt. Chimorazo," "Winter Dancers," "Hamlet," "Old Flames," "The Diviners," "Richard II," "Vieux Carre," "Full Hookup."

BROOKS, ARTHUR. Born June 27, 1950 in Boston, MA. Graduate UCo, AADA. Debut 1979 OB in "The Show-Off," followed by "Troubleshooters," "Breakfast Conversations in Miami," "Flesh, Flash and Frank Harris."

BROOKS, DOROTHY. Born May 23 in Des Moines, IO. Graduate Buffalo State Col., Fla StateU. Debut 1979 OB in "The Underlings," followed by "Hoffman and Co.," "Pigeons on the Walk."

BROOKS, JEFF. Born Apr. 7, 1950 in Vancouver, Can. Attended Portland State U. Debut 1976 OB in "Titanic," followed by "Fat Chances," "Nature and Purpose of the Universe," "Actor's Nightmare," "Sister Mary Ignatius Explains It All," "Marathon '84," Bdwy in "A History of the American Film" (1978).

BROTHERS, JON. Born Feb. 16, 1957 in Lynn, MA. Graduate Emerson Col. Debut 1980 OB in "The Desert Song," followed by "The Student Prince," "Where's Charley?," "Up in Central Park."

BROWN, GEORGIA. Born Oct. 21, 1933 in London, Eng. NY debut 1957 OB in "Threepenny Opera," followed by "Greek," Bdwy in "Oliver!"(1962), "Side by Side by Sondheim," "Carmelina."

BROWN, ROO. Born July 22, 1932 in Pittsburgh, PA. Graduate Smith Col. Debut 1984 OB in "A . . . My Name Is Alice."

BROWN, SHARON. Born Jan. 11, 1962 in NYC. Bdwy debut 1967 in "Maggie Flynn," followed by "Joseph and the Amazing Technicolor Dream Coat," OB in "Cummings and Goings."

BROWNE, ROSCOE LEE. Born in 1925 in Woodbury, NJ. Attended Lincoln U, Columbia; Debut OB in "Julius Caesar," followed by "Taming of the Shrew," "Titus Andronicus," "Romeo and Juliet," "Othello," "Aria da Capo," "The Blacks," "Brecht on Brecht," "King Lear," "Winter's Tale," "The Empty Room," "Hell Is Other People," "Benito Cereno," "Troilus and Cressida," "Danton's Death," "Volpone," "Dream on Monkey Mountain," "Behind the Broken Words," Bdwy in "General Seeger" (1962), "Tiger, Tiger Burning Bright," "Ballad of the Sad Cafe," "A Hand Is on the Gate," "My One and Only."

BRUMMEL, DAVID. Born Nov. 1, 1942 in Brooklyn, NY. Bdwy debut 1973 in "The Pajama Game," followed by "Music Is," "Oklahoma!," OB in "Cole Porter," "The Fantasticks."

BRUNEAU, RALPH. Born Sept. 22, 1952 in Phoenix, AZ. Graduate UNotre Dame. Debut 1974 OB in "The Fantasticks," followed by "Saints," "Suddenly the Music Starts," "On a Clear Day . . .," "King of the Schnorrers," "The Buddy System," "Chantecler," "Brownstone," Bdwy in "Doonesbury" (1983).

BRUNO, JEAN. Born Dec. 7, 1926 in Brooklyn, NY. Attended Hofstra Col. Bdwy debut 1960 in "Beg, Borrow or Steal," followed by "Midgie Purvis," "Music Man," "Family Affair," "Minnie's Boys," "Lincoln Mask," "Lorelei," OB in "All That Fall," "Hector," "Hotel Paradiso," "Pidgeons in the Park," "Ergo," "Trelawny of the Wells," "Song for the First of May," "The Hairy Ape," "Zoology."

BRYAN, KENNETH. Born July 30, 1953 in New Jersey. Graduate IndU. Bdwy debut 1981 in "Joseph and the Amazing Technicolor Dreamcoat," followed by "The Human Comedy."

BRYANT, DAVID. Born May 26, 1936 in Nashville, TN. Attended TnStateU. Bdwy debut 1972 in "Don't Play Us Cheap," followed by "Bubbling Brown Sugar," "Amadeus," OB in "Up in Central Park," "Elizabeth and Essex."

BRYNE, BARBARA. Born in London, Eng. Attended RADA. NY debut 1981 OB in "Entertaining Mr. Sloane," Bdwy in "Sunday in the Park with George" (1984).
BUCKLEY, BETTY. Born July 3, 1947 in Big Spring, TX. Graduate TCU. Bdwy debut 1969 in "1776," followed by "Pippin," "Cats," OB in "Ballad of Johnny Pot," "What's a Nice Country Like You . . .," "Circle of Sound," "I'm Getting My Act Together . . ."
BUCKLEY, MELINDA. Born Apr. 17, 1954 in Attleboro, MA. Graduate UMa. Bdwy debut 1983 in "A Chorus Line," OB in "Damn Yankees," "Pal Joey."
BUELL, BILL. Born Sept. 21, 1952 in Paipai, Taiwan. Attended Portland State U. Debut 1972 OB in "Crazy Now," followed by "Declassee," "Lorenzaccio," "Promenade," Bdwy in "Once a Catholic," (1979), "The First."
BUFFALOE, KATHARINE. Born Nov. 7, 1953 in Greenville, SC. Graduate NCSch. of Arts. Bdwy debut 1981 in "Copperfield," followed by "Joseph and the Amazing Technicolor Dreamcoat," OB in "Non Pasquale."
BUKA, DONALD. Born Dec. 18, 1921 in Cleveland, OH. Attended Carnegie Tech. Credits include "Twelfth Night," "The Corn is Green" (1950/1983), "Bright Boy," "Helen Goes to Troy," "Sophie," "Live Life Again," "Those That Play the Clowns," "Major Barbara," "Design for Living," OB in "Heritage," "In the Matter of J. Robert Oppenheimer," "Willie."
BURKE, JOHN. Born Feb. 15, 1952 in Hartford, CT. Attended UToledo. Bdwy debut 1983 in "The Ritz."
BURKS, DONNY. Born in Martinsville, VA. Graduate St. John's U. Debut 1964 OB in "Dutchman," followed by "Billy Noname" for which he received a Theatre World Award, "Miracle Play," Bdwy in "Hair" (1968), "The American Clock," "The Tap Dance Kid."
BURKS, STEPHEN. Born July 5, 1956 in Belleville, IL. Graduate Boston U. Debut 1980 on Bdwy in "Division Street," OB in "Steel on Steel," "The Lady's Not for Burning."
BURNS, CATHERINE. Born Sept. 25, 1945 in NYC. Attended AADA. Bdwy 1968 in "The Prime of Miss Jean Brodie," OB in "Dream of a Blacklisted Actor," "The Disintegration of James Cherry," "Operation Sidewinder," "Dear Janet Rosenberg, Dear Mr. Kooning" for which she received a Theatre World Award, "Two Small Bodies," "Voices," "Jungle of Cities," "One Wedding," "Metamorphosis," "Within the Year."
BURNS, JERE. Born Oct. 15, 1954 in Cambridge, MA. Graduate UMa/Amherst, NYU. Debut 1983 OB in "True West."
BURRELL, FRED. Born Sept. 18, 1936. Graduate UNC, RADA. Bdwy debut 1964 in "Never Too Late," followed by "Illya Darling," OB in "The Memorandum," "Throckmorton, Texas."
BURRELL, PAMELA. Born Aug. 4, 1945 in Tacoma, WA. Bdwy debut 1966 in "Funny Girl," followed by "Where's Charley?," "Strider," OB in "Arms and the Man" for which she received a Theatre World Award, "Berkeley Square," "The Boss," "Biography: A Game," "Strider: Story of a Horse," "A Little Madness."
BURRELL, TERRY. Born Feb. 8, 1952 in Trinidad, WI. Attended Pace U. Bdwy debut 1977 in "Eubie!," followed by "Dreamgirls," OB in "That Uptown Feeling."
BURSTYN, ELLEN. Born Dec. 7, 1932 in Detroit, MI. Attended Actors Studio. Bdwy debut 1957 (as Ellen McRae) in "Fair Game," followed by "Same Time Next Year," "84 Charing Cross Road," OB in "The Three Sisters," "Andromeda II," "Park Your Car in Harvard Yard."
BURTON, IRVING. Born Aug. 5, 1923 in NYC. Bdwy debut 1951 in "Peer Gynt," OB in "Three Unnatural Acts," 24 years with the Paper Bag Players, "Pal Joey."
BURTON, KATE. Born Sept. 10, 1957 in Geneva, Switz. Graduate Brown U., Yale. Bdwy debut 1982 in "Present Laughter," followed by "Alice in Wonderland," "Doonesbury," OB in "Winners" for which she received a Theatre World Award, "Romeo and Juliet."
BUSSERT, MEG. Born Oct. 21, 1949 in Chicago, IL. Attended UIll, HB Studio. Bdwy debut 1980 in "The Music Man" for which she received a Theatre World Award, followed by "Brigadoon," "Camelot," "New Moon," "Lola" (OB), "The Firefly."
BUTLER, BRUCE. Born Mar. 11, 1954 in Clanton, NC. Graduate NC Central U. Debut 1982 OB in "Street Scene," followed by "Freedom Days."
BUTTERFIELD, CATHERINE. Born Feb. 5 in NYC. Graduate SMU. Debut 1983 OB in "Marmalade Skies."
BYERS, CATHERINE. Born Oct. 7 in Sioux City, IA. Graduate UIa, LAMDA. Bdwy debut 1971 in "The Philanthropist," followed by "Don't Call Back," "Equus," OB in "Petrified Forest," "All My Sons," "Murder in the Cathedral," "Grace," "The Fuehrer Bunker," "Great Days."
BYRD, LILLIAN M. Born Dec. 15, 1952 in Memphis, TN. Graduate Memphis State U. Debut 1982 OB in "Murder on the Nile," followed by "110 in the Shade," "Lady Windermere's Fan," "Casanova," "Silent Night, Lonely Night."
CAHILL, JAMES. Born May 31, 1940 in Brooklyn, NY. Bdwy debut 1967 in "Marat/deSade," followed by "Break a Leg," OB in "The Hostage," "The Alchemist," "Johnny Johnson," "Peer Gynt," "Timon of Athens," "An Evening for Merlin Finch," "The Disintegration of James Cherry," "Crimes of Passion," "Rain," "Screens," "Total Eclipse," "Entertaining Mr. Sloane," "Hamlet," "Othello," "The Trouble with Europe," "Lydie Breeze," "Don Juan," "Bathroom Plays," "Wild Life," "Uncle Vanya."
CAIN, WILLIAM B. Born May 27, 1931 in Tuscaloosa, AL. Graduate Wash.U., CatholicU. Debut 1962 OB in "Red Roses for Me," followed by "Jericho Jim Crow," "Henry V," "Antigone," "Relatively Speaking," "Bdwy in "Wilson in the Promise Land," "Of the Fields Lately," "You Can't Take It With You."
CALLANDER, BARBARA. Born Mar. 3, 1950 in Washington, D.C. Graduate Oberlin Col. Debut 1980 OB in "The Betrothal," followed by "Period of Adjustment," "Playboy of the Western World," "Spider's Web," "War Games."
CAMERON, HOPE Born Feb 21, 1920 in Hartford, Ct. Attended AADA. Bdwy debut 1947 in "All My Sons," followed by "Death of a Salesman," OB in "The Strindberg Brothers," "The Last Days of Lincoln," "Grace," "Skirmishes," "Big Maggie," "Re-Po."
CAMP, JOANNE. Born Apr. 4, 1951 in Atlanta, GA. Graduate FlAtlanticU, Geo WashU. Debut 1981 OB in "The Dry Martini," followed by "Geniuses," for which she received a Theatre World Award, "June Moon," "Painting Churches."
CANYON, BILL. Born Nov. 17, 1939 in Rochester, NY. Graduate Allegheny Col., Syracuse U. Debut 1983 OB in "The Trial of Adam Clayton Powell, Jr."
CAPRI, MARK. Born July 19, 1951 in Washington, DC. Graduate Stanford U, RADA. Debut 1984 OB in "On Approval" for which he received a Theatre World Award.
CARDEN, WILLIAM. Born Feb. 2, 1947 in NYC. Attended Lawrence U., Brandeis U. Debut 1974 OB in "Short Eyes," followed by Leaving Home," "Back in the Race," "Thin Ice."
CARHART, TIMOTHY. Born Dec. 24, 1953 in Washington, DC. Graduate UIll. Debut 1984 OB in "The Harvesting."
CARIOU, LEN. Born Sept 30 1939 in Winnipeg. Can. Bdwy debut 1968 in "House of Atreus," followed by "Henry V" and "Applause" for which he received a Theatre World Award, "Night Watch," "A Little Night Music," "Cold Storage," "Sweeney Todd," "Dance a Little Closer," OB in "A Sorrow Beyond Dreams," "Up from Paradise."
CARLIN, THOMAS A. Born Dec. 10, 1928 in Chicago, IL. Attended Loyola, Catholic U. Credits include "Time Limit!," "Holiday for Lovers," "Man in the Dog Suit," "A Cook for Mr. General," "Great Day in the Morning," "A Thousand Clowns," "The Deputy," "Players'" OB in "Thieves Carnival," "The Brecht on Brecht," "Summer," "Pigeons on the Walk."
CARLING, P.L. Born March 31. Graduate Stanford, UCLA. Debut 1955 OB in "The Chairs," followed by "In Good King Charles' Golden Days." "Magistrate," "Picture of Dorian Gray," "The Vise," "Lady From the Sea," "Booth Is Back In Town," "Ring Round the Moon," "Philadelphia, Here I Come," "Sorrows of Frederick," "Biography," "Murder on the Nile," "Three Lost Plays of O'Neill," "Verdict," Bdwy in "The Devils" (1965), "Scratch," "Shenandoah."
CARLISLE, KITTY. Born Sept. 3, 1915 in New Orleans, LA. Attended RADA. Bdwy debut 1932 in "Rio Rita," followed by "Champagne, Sec," "White Horse Inn," "Three Waltzes," "Walk With Music," "The Rape of Lucretia," "Anniversary Waltz," "Kiss Me, Kate" (CC'56), "On Your Toes."
CARLO, JOHANN. Born May 21, 1957 in Buffalo, NY. Attended London's Webber-Douglass Academy. Debut 1978 OB in "Grand Magic," followed by "Artichoke," "Don Juan Comes Back From the War," "The Arbor," "Cinders," Bdwy in "Plenty" (1983).
CARLSEN, ALLAN. Born Feb. 7 in Chicago, IL. Bdwy debut 1974 in "Freedom of the City," OB in "The Morning after Optimism," "Iphigenia in Aulis," "Peg o'My Heart," "Star Treatment," "Starry Night," "Accounts."
CARPENTER, CARLTON. Born July 10, 1926 in Bennington, VT. Attended Northwestern U. Bdwy bow 1944 in "Bright Boy," followed by "Career Angel," "Three to Make Ready," "Magic Touch," "John Murray Anderson's Almanac," "Hotel Paradiso," "Box of Watercolors," "Hello, Dolly!," OB in "Stage Affair," "Boys in the Band," "Dylan," "Greatest Fairy Story Ever Told," "Good Old Fashioned Revue," "Miss Stanwyck Is Still in Hiding," "Rocky Road," "Apollo of Bellac."
CARRICART, ROBERTSON Born Dec. 28, 1947 in Norfolk, VA. Graduate UCLA. Debut 1974 OB in "Private Ear/Public Eye," followed by "Cromwell," "Out of the Night," Bdwy in "Oklahoma " (1979), "Design for Living."
CARROLL, DANNY. Born May 30, 1940 in Maspeth, NY. Bdwy bow in 1957 in "The Music Man," followed by "Flora the Red Menace," "Funny Girl," "George M!," "Billy," "Ballroom," "42nd Street," OB in "Boys from Syracuse," "Babes in the Woods."
CARROLL, DAVID-JAMES. Born July 30, 1950 in Rockville, Centre, NY. Graduate Dartmouth Col. Debut 1975 OB in "A Matter of Time," followed by "Joseph and the Amazing Technicolor Dreamcoat," "New Tunes," Bdwy in "Rodgers and Hart" (1975), "Where's Charley?," "Oh, Brother!," "7 Brides for 7 Brothers," "Roberta in Concert."
CARSON, THOMAS. Born May 27, 1939 in Iowa City, IO. Graduate UIo. Debut 1981 OB in "The Feuhrer Bunker," followed by "Breakfast Conversations in Miami."
CARTER, ROSANNA. Born Sept. 20 in Rolle Town, Bahamas. Bdwy debut 1980 in "The American Clock," followed by "Inacent Black," OB in "Lament of Rasta Fari," "Burghers of Callais," "Scottsboro Boys," "Les Femmes Noires," "Killings on the Last Line," "Under Heaven's Eye."
CASEY, EILEEN. Born July 13, 1947 in Boston, MA. Bdwy debut 1963 in "The Unsinkable Molly Brown," followed by "Hello, Dolly!," "Mame," "Promises Promises," "On the Town," "Sugar," "Seesaw," "Pajama Game," "Pippin," "Dancin'," "West Side Story," "Marilyn."
CASHMAN, DAN. Born Feb. 22, 1938 in Minneapolis, MN. Graduate UMn, Carnegie-Mellon U. Debut 1983 OB in "Touch It Where It Hurts," followed by "The Merry Wives of Windsor."
CASON, BARBARA. Born Nov. 15, 1933 in Memphis, TN. Graduate UIo. Bdwy debut 1967 in "Marat/Sade," followed by "Jimmy Shine," "Night Watch," OB in "Firebugs," "Spitting Image," "Enemy of the People," "Oh, Coward!," "The Sea Gull."
CASS, PEGGY. Born May 21, 1926 in Boston, MA. Attended Wyndham Sch. Credits include "Touch and Go," "Live Wire," "Bernardine," "Othello," "Henry V," "Auntie Mame" for which she received a Theatre World Award, "A Thurber Carnival," "Children from Their Games," "Don't Drink the Water," "Front Page" (1969), "Plaza Suite," "Once a Catholic," "42nd Street," OB in "Phoenix '55," "Are You Now or Have You Ever Been," "One Touch of Venus."
CASSESE, ANDREW. Born Feb. 12, 1972 in Patchogue, NY. Bdwy debut 1982 in "Nine," OB in "Christopher Blake."
CASSIDY, TIM. Born March 22, 1952 in Alliance, OH. Attended UCincinnati. Bdwy debut 1974 in "Good News," followed by "A Chorus Line."
CAULFIELD, MAXWELL. Born Nov. 23, 1959 in Glasgow, Scot. Debut 1979 OB in "Class Enemy" for which he received a Theatre World Award, followed by "Crimes and Dreams," "Entertaining Mr. Sloane," "The Inheritors," "Paradise Lost."
CAVANAUGH, ROBERT. Born Oct. 7, 1971 in Sumter, SC. Bdwy debut 1984 in "Oliver!"
CELLARIO, MARIA. Born June 19, 1948 in Buenos Aires, Arg. Graduate Ithaca Col. Bdwy debut 1975 in "The Royal Family," OB in "Fugue in a Nursery," "Declassee," "Equinox."
CERVERIS, MICHAEL. Born Nov. 6, 1960 in Bethesda, MD. Graduate Yale U. Debut 1983 OB in "Moon," followed by "Macbeth."
CHAIKIN, SHAMI. Born Apr. 21, 1931 in NYC. Debut 1966 OB in "America Hurrah," followed by "Serpent," "Terminal," "Mutation Show," "Viet Rock," "Mystery Play," "Electra," "The Dybbuk," "Endgame," "Bag Lady," "The Haggadah," "Antigone," "Loving Reno," "Early Warnings," "Uncle Vanya."
CHALAWSKY, MAX. Born Feb 26, 1956 in Brooklyn, NY. Graduate Bklyn Col. Debut 1980 OB in "D," followed by "I Am a Camera," "Hard to Be a Jew."
CHALFANT, KATHLEEN. Born Jan. 14, 1945 in San Francisco, CA. Graduate Stanford U. Bdwy debut 1975 in "Dance With Me," followed by OB "Jules Feiffer's Hold Me," "Killings on the Last Line," "The Boor," "Blood Relations," "Signs of Life," "Sister Mary Ignatius Explains It All," "Actor's Nightmare," "Faith Healer," "All the Nice People."

Dan Ahearn

Betsy Sue Aidem

Eddie Albert

Mary Alice

Michael Allinson

Kim Ameen

Christine Anderson

Keith Amos

Sydney Anderson

Thomas Anderson

Helena Andreyko

Ron August

Roberto Badillo

Nora Baetz

Raymond Baker

June Ballinger

John Bantay

Jean Barker

Frances Barnes

Gabriel Barre

Deborah Bauers

Gary Beach

Joanna Beck

Gregory Beecroft

Sal Biagini

Sharon Brown

Stephen Burks

Barbara Callander

Thomas A. Carlin

Kathleen Chalfant

201

CHANDLER, DAVID. Born Feb. 3, 1950 in Danbury, CT. Graduate Oberlin Col. Bdwy debut 1980 in "The American Clock," followed by "Death of a Salesman," OB in "Made in Heaven."

CHANNING, STOCKARD. Born in 1944 in NYC. Attended Radcliffe Col. Debut 1970 OB in "Adaptation/Next," followed by "The Lady and the Clarinet," "The Golden Age," Bdwy in "Two Gentlemen of Verona," "They're Playing Our Song," "The Rink."

CHARLES, JIM. Born May 4, 1960 in Albany, NY. Debut 1983 OB in "The Fantasticks."

CHARLES, WALTER. Born Apr. 4, 1945 in East Stroudsburg, PA. Graduate Boston U Bdwy debut 1973 in "Grease," followed by "1600 Pennsylvania Avenue," "Knickerbocker Holiday," "Sweeney Todd," "Cats," "La Cage aux Folles."

CHARNAY, LYNNE. Born Apr. 1 in NYC. Attended UWisc., Columbia, AADA. Debut 1950 OB in "Came the Dawn," followed by "A Ram's Horn," "In a Cold Hotel," "Amata," "Yerma," "Ballad of Winter Soldiers," "Intimate Relations," "Play Me Zoltan," "Grand Magic," "The Time of Your Life," "Nymph Errant," "Nude with Violin," "American Power Play," Bdwy in "Julia, Jake and Uncle Joe" (1961), "A Family Affair," "Broadway," "Inspector General," "Grand Tour."

CHEN, TINA. Born Nov. 2 in Chung King, China. Graduate Brown U. Debut 1972 OB in "A Maid's Tragedy," followed by "Family Devotions," "A Midsummer Night's Dream," "Empress of China," Bdwy in "The King and I," "Rashomon."

CHOATE, TIM. Born Oct. 11, 1954 in Dallas, TX. Graduate UTx. Bdwy debut 1979 in "Da," followed by "Crimes of the Heart," OB in "Young Bucks," "Comedians," "Hackers."

CHOWDHURY, SAMIR. Born Jan. 4, 1972 in Trenton, NJ. Bdwy debut 1984 in "Oliver!"

CHRISTIAN-JONES, LINDA. Born Mar. 19, 1947 in Tonawanda, NY. Graduate Wake Forest U. Debut 1977 OB in "The Bald Soprano," followed by "Partners," "For the Use of the Hall."

CHRISTIANSON, CATHERINE ANN. Born Feb. 10, 1957 in Evanston, IL. Graduate Vassar Col., Goodman School. Debut 1984 OB in "Romance."

CHRISTOPHER, DENNIS. Born Dec. 2, 1954 in Philadelphia, PA. Attended Temple U. Debut 1974 OB in "Yentl, the Yeshiva Boy," Bdwy in "The Little Foxes" (1981), "Brothers."

CHRYST, GARY. Born in 1959 in LaJolla, CA. Joined Joffrey Ballet in 1968. Bdwy debut in "Dancin' " (1979), OB in "One More Song/One More Dance."

CIMINO, PHILIP. Born Jan. 20, 1948 in Brooklyn, NY. Graduate Hunter Col., New Col. of Speech & Drama (London). Debut 1983 OB in "And Things That Go Bump in the Night."

CLARK, BRYAN E. Born Apr. 5, 1929 in Louisville, KY. Graduate Fordham U. Bdwy debut 1978 in "A History of the American Film," followed by "Bent," OB in "Winning Isn't Everything," "Put Them All Together," "Red Rover," "Paradise Lost."

CLARK, CHERYL. Born Dec. 7, 1950 in Boston, MA. Attended Ind. U., NYU. Bdwy debut 1972 in "Pippin," followed by "Chicago," "A Chorus Line."

CLARKE, CAITLIN. Born May 3, 1952 in Pittsburgh, PA. Graduate Mt. Holyoke Col., Yale. Debut 1981 OB in "No End of Blame," followed by "Lorenzaccio," "Summer," "Quartermaine's Terms," "Thin Ice," Bdwy in "Teaneck Tanzi" (1983).

CLARKE, DAVID. Born Aug. 30, 1908 in Chicago, IL. Attended Butler U. Bdwy debut 1930 in "Roadside," followed by "Let Freedom Ring," "Bury the Dead," "Washington Jitters," "200 Were Chosen," "Journey Man," "Abe Lincoln in Illinois," "See the Jaguar," "The Emperor's Clothes," "A View from the Bridge," "Ballad of the Sad Cafe," "Inquest," "Of Mice and Men," OB in "Madam, Will You Walk," "Rose," "Bone Garden," "Flesh, Flash and Frank Harris," "All the Nice People."

CLEAR, PATRICK. Born Apr. 8, 1952 in St. Louis, MO. Graduate Wash.U., PennState U. Bdwy debut 1984 in "Noises Off."

CLEMENT, MARIS. Born July 11, 1950 in Philadelphia, PA. Graduate Rollins Col. Debut 1976 OB in "Noel and Cole," followed by "The Great American Backstage Musical," Bdwy in "On the 20th Century," "Copperfield," "Little Me."

CLEMENTE, RENE. Born July 2, 1950 in El Paso, TX. Graduate WestTxStateU. Bdwy debut 1977 in "A Chorus Line," followed by "Dancin'," "Play Me a Country Song," "Cats."

CLOSE, GLENN. Born May 19, 1947 in Greenwich, CT. Graduate William & Mary Col. Bdwy debut 1974 with Phoenix Co. in "Love for Love," "Member of the Wedding," and "Rules of the Game," followed by "Rex," "Crucifer of Blood," "Barnum," "The Real Thing," OB in "The Crazy Locomotive," "Uncommon Women and Others," "Wine Untouched," "The Winter Dancers," "The Singular Life of Albert Nobbs."

COATS, STEVE. Born Oct. 5, 1954 in Berkeley, CA. Graduate SanFranStateU. Debut 1982 OB in "The World of Ben Caldwell," followed by "Touched," "The Last Danceman."

COATS, WILLIAM ALAN. Born Dec. 3, 1957 in Raleigh, NC. Graduate UCin. Debut 1983 OB in "Tallulah."

COHEN, JULIE. Born June 16, 1964 in NYC. Attended NYU. Debut 1984 OB in "The Nest of the Wood Grouse."

COHEN, NOLE. Born Apr. 5, 1944 in Brooklyn, NY. Graduate Pratt Inst. Debut 1984 OB in "Uncommon Holidays."

COIT, CONNIE. Born Apr. 21, 1947 in Dallas, TX. Graduate SMU. Debut 1980 OB in "A Funny Thing Happened on the Way to the Forum," followed by "Promenade."

COLE, GILBERT. Born July 13, 1955 in Geneva, IL. Graduate Juilliard. Debut 1976 OB in "Henry V," followed by "Midsummer Night's Dream," "Dark at the Top of the Stairs," "Caine Mutiny Court-Martial," "Goodbye Howard," "Souvenirs," Bdwy in "A Meeting by the River" (1979).

COLE, KAY. Born Jan. 13, 1948 in Miami, FL. Bdwy debut 1961 in "Bye Bye Birdie," followed by "Stop the World I Want to Get Off," "Roar of the Greasepaint . . .," "Hair," "Jesus Christ Superstar," "Words and Music," "Chorus Line," OB in "The Cradle Will Rock," "Two If By Sea," "Rainbow," "White Nights," "Sgt. Pepper's Lonely Hearts Club Band," "On the Swing Shift," "Snoopy," "Road to Hollywood."

COLES, CHARLES HONI. Born Apr. 2, 1911 in Philadelphia, PA. Debut 1933 OB in "Humming Sam," Bdwy in "Gentlemen Prefer Blondes" (1949), "Black Broadway," "My One and Only."

COLKER, JERRY. Born Mar. 16, 1955 in Los Angeles, CA. Attended Harvard U. Debut 1975 OB in "Tenderloin," followed by "Pal Joey," Bdwy in "West Side Story," "Pippin," "A Chorus Line."

COLLET, CHRISTOPHER. Born Mar. 13, 1968 in NYC. Attended Strasberg Inst. Bdwy debut in "Torch Song Trilogy" (1983).

COLLINS, PAUL. Born July 25, 1937 in London, Eng. Attended LACC. OB in "Say Nothing," "Cambridge Circus," "The Devils," "Rear Column," "Jail Diary of Albie Sachs," "The Feuhrer Bunker," "Great Days," "Courage," Bdwy in "The Royal Hunt of the Sun" (1965), "A Minor Adjustment," "A Meeting by the River," "Eminent Domain."

COLLINS, RISE. Born Sept. 18, 1952 in Houston, TX. Graduate Carnegie-Mellon U. Bdwy debut in "For Colored Girls Who Have Considered Suicide . . ." (1976), OB in "Pericles," "Blues in the Night," "No," "Incandescent Tones."

COLTON, CHEVI. Born Dec. 21 in NYC. Attended Hunter Col. OB in "Time of Storm," "Insect Comedy," "The Adding Machine," "O Marry Me," "Penny Change," "The Mad Show," "Jacques Brel Is Alive . . .," "Bits and Pieces," "Spelling Bee," "Uncle Money," Bdwy in "Cabaret," "Grand Tour," "Torch Song Trilogy."

COMDEN, BETTY. Born May 3, 1919 in Brooklyn, NY. Graduate NYU. Bdwy debut 1944 in "On the Town," for which she received a Theatre World Award, followed by "A Party with Comden and Green", OB in "A Party with Betty Comden and Adolph Green," "Isn't It Romantic."

CONDOS, DIMO. Born Feb. 29, 1932 in NYC. OB in "The Celebration," "O'Flaherty," "The Cannibals," "Moths," "Pinkville," "Andorra."

CONNELL, GORDON. Born Mar. 19, 1923 in Berkeley, CA. Graduate UCal, NYU. Bdwy debut 1961 in "Subways Are for Sleeping," followed by "Hello, Dolly!," "Lysistrata," "The Human Comedy," OB in "Beggar's Opera," "The Butler Did It," "With Love and Laughter."

CONNELL, JANE. Born Oct. 27, 1925 in Berkeley, CA. Attended UCal. Bdwy debut in "New Faces of 1956," followed by "Drat! The Cat!," "Mame" (1966/'83), "Dear World," "Lysistrata," OB in "Shoestring Revue," "Threepenny Opera," "Pieces of Eight," "Demi-Dozen," "She Stoops to Conquer," "Drat!," "The Real Inspector Hound," "The Rivals," "The Rise and Rise of Daniel Rocket," "Laughing Stock."

CONNOLLY, JOHN P. Born Sept. 1, 1950 in Philadelphia, PA. Graduate Temple U. Debut 1973 OB in "Paradise Lost," followed by "The Wizard of Oz," "Fighting Bob," "For the Use of the Hall."

CONROY, FRANCES. Born in 1953 in Monroe, GA. Attended Dickinson Col., Juilliard, Neighborhood Playhouse. Debut 1978 OB with the Acting Co. in "Mother Courage," "King Lear," "The Other Half," followed by "All's Well That Ends Well," "Othello," "Sorrows of Stephen," "Girls Girls Girls," "Zastrozzi," "Painting Churches," "Uncle Vanya," Bdwy 1980 in "The Lady from Dubuque."

CONVERSE, FRANK. Born May 22, 1938 in St. Louis, MO. Attended Carnegie-Mellon U. Bdwy debut 1966 in "First One Asleep, Whistle," followed by "The Philadelphia Story" (1980/LC), "Brothers," "Design for Living," OB in "House of Blue Leaves."

CONWAY, KEVIN. Born May 29, 1942 in NYC. Debut 1968 OB in "Muzeeka," followed by "Saved," "The Plough and the Stars," "One Flew Over the Cuckoo's Nest," "When You Comin' Back, Red Ryder?," "Long Day's Journey into Night," "Other Places," Bdwy in "Indians" (1969), "Moonchildren," "Of Mice and Men," "The Elephant Man."

COOK, JILL. Born Feb. 25, 1954 in Plainfield, NJ. Bdwy debut 1971 in "On the Town," followed by "So Long, 174th Street," "Dancin'," "Best Little Whorehouse in Texas," "Perfectly Frank," OB in "Carnival," "Potholes," "My One and Only."

COOK, LINDA. Born June 8 in Lubbock, TX. Attended Auburn U. Debut 1974 OB in "The Wager," followed by "Hole in the Wall," "Shadow of a Gunman," "Be My Father," "Ghosts of the Loyal Oaks," "Different People, Different Rooms," "Saigon Rose," "Romantic Arrangements."

COOK, RODERICK. Born 1932 in London. Attended Cambridge U. Bdwy debut 1961 in "Kean," followed by "Roar Like a Dove," "The Girl Who Came to Supper," "Noel Coward's Sweet Potato," "The Man Who Came to Dinner," "Woman of the Year," "Eileen," OB in "A Scent of Flowers," "Oh, Coward!," "Sweethearts in Concert."

COOPER, CHUCK. Born Nov. 8, 1954 in Cleveland, OH. Graduate Ohio U. Debut 1982 OB in "Colored People's Time," followed by "Riff Raff Revue," "Primary English Class," Bdwy in "Amen Corner" (1983).

COOPER, JED. Born Jan. 6, 1955 in NYC. Graduate UMich., Neighborhood Playhouse. Bdwy debut 1977 in "Vieux Carre," OB in "Scenes from La Vie de Boheme," "Second Prize: Two Months in Leningrad."

COPELAND, MAURICE. Born June 13, 1911 in Rector, AR. Graduate Pasadena Playhouse. Bdwy debut 1974 in "The Freedom of the City," followed by "The First Monday in October," "Morning's at 7," OB in "Henry V," "Blood Relations," "Richard III."

COPPLE, MARY. Born Nov. 8, 1950 in Centralia, IL. Graduate IllStateU. Bdwy debut 1982 in "Steaming," OB in "True West" (1983) followed by "Landscape of the Body."

CORNTHWAITE, ROBERT. Born Apr. 18, 1917 in St. Helens, OR. Graduate USCa. Bdwy debut 1978 in "The Devil's Disciple," OB in "And a Nightingale Sang."

CORREIA, DON. Born Aug. 28, 1951 in San Jose, CA. Attended SanJoseStateU. Bdwy debut 1980 in "A Chorus Line," followed by "Perfectly Frank," "Little Me," "Sophisticated Ladies," "5–6–7–8 Dance."

CORREN, DONALD. Born June 5, 1952 in Stockton, CA. Attended Juilliard. Bdwy debut 1980 in "A Day in Hollywood/A Night in the Ukraine," followed by "Tomfoolery" (OB), "Torch Song Trilogy."

CORTEZ, KATHERINE. Born Sept. 28, 1950 in Detroit, MI. Graduate UNC. Debut 1979 OB in "The Dark at the Top of the Stairs," followed by "Corners," "Confluence," "The Great Grandson of Jedediah Kohler," "A Think Piece," "The Sea Gull," Bdwy in "Foxfire" (1982).

CORTLAND, NICHOLAS. Born Oct. 10, 1946 in NYC. Graduate Hofstra U. Debut 1984 OB in "Suzanna Andler."

CORY, KENNETH. Born July 21, 1941 in Hanover, PA. Studied with Stella Adler. Bdwy debut 1971 in "Company," OB in "Out of This World," "Be Kind to People Week," "Flirtations."

COSBY, BILL. Born July 12, 1937 in Philadelphia, PA. Graduate Temple U. Bdwy debut 1983 in "Two Friends."

COSTALLOS, SUZANNE. Born Apr. 3, 1953 in NYC. Attended NYU, Boston Consv., Juilliard. Debut 1977 in "Play and Other Plays by Beckett," followed by "Elizabeth I," "The White Devil," "Hunting Scenes from Lower Bavaria," "Selma," Bdwy in "Zorba" (1983).

COUNTRYMAN, MICHAEL. Born Sept. 15, 1955 in St. Paul, MN. Graduate Trinity Col., AADA. Debut 1983 OB in "Changing Palettes," followed by "June Moon," "Terra Nova."

COWLES, MATTHEW. Born Sept. 28, 1944 in NYC. Attended Neighborhood Playhouse Bdwy bow 1966 in "Malcolm," followed by "Sweet Bird of Youth," OB in "King John," "The Indian Wants the Bronx," "Triple Play," "Stop, You're Killing Me!," "The Time of Your Life," "Foursome," "Kid Champion," "End of the War," "Tennessee," "Bathroom Plays," "Touch Black," "Paradise Lost," "The Hasty Heart," "Ghosts."

COX, CATHERINE. Born Dec. 13, 1950 in Toledo, OH. Wittenberg U. graduate. Bdwy debut 1976 in "Music Is," followed by "Whoopee!" "Oklahoma!," "Shakespeare's Cabaret," "Barnum," "Baby," OB in "By Strouse," "It's Better With a Band."

CRABTREE, DON. Born Aug. 21, 1928 in Borger, TX. Attended Actors Studio. Bdwy bow 1959 in "Destry Rides Again," followed by "Happiest Girl in the World," "Family Affair," "Unsinkable Molly Brown," "Sophie," "110 In the Shade," "Golden Boy," "Pousse Cafe," "Mahagonny" (OB), "The Best Little Whorehouse in Texas," "42nd Street."

CRAIG, BETSY. Born Jan. 5, 1952 in Hopewell, VA. Attended Berry Col. Bdwy debut 1972 in "Ambassador," followed by "Smith," "Brigadoon," "La Cage aux Folles."

CRAIG, JOEL. Born Apr. 26 in NYC. Attended Brandeis U. Bdwy deubt 1961 in "Subways Are for Sleeping," followed by "Nowhere to Go But Up," "Hello, Dolly!," "Follies," "Cyrano," "Very Good Eddie," OB in "Out of This World," "Carnival," "Speakeasy," "Tallulah."

CRAVEN, MATT. Born Nov. 10, 1956 in Port Colborne, Can. Debut 1984 OB in "Blue Windows."

CRISP, QUENTIN. Born Dec. 25, 1908 in Carshalton, Eng. Debut 1978 OB in "An Evening with "Quentin Crisp," followed by "The Importance of Being Earnest," "Lord Alfred's Lover."

CRISWELL, KIM. Born July 19, 1957 in Hampton, VA. Graduate UCin. Bdwy debut 1981 in "The First," followed by "Nine," "Baby."

CROFT, TERRY ASHE. Born May 7 in San Francisco, CA. Graduate SanFranCol. Debut 1959 OB in "Lysistrata," followed by "As You Like It," "Ladies in Retirement," "War Games," "Pericles."

CRONYN, TANDY. Born Nov. 27, 1945 in Los Angeles, CA. Attended London's Central School. Bdwy debut 1969 in "Cabaret," followed by LC's "Playboy of the Western World," "Good Woman of Setzuan," "An Enemy of the People," and "Antigone," OB in "An Evening With the Poet-Senator," "Winners," "The Killing of Sister George."

CROOK, PETER. Born Mar. 17, 1958 in Houston, TX. Graduate Juilliard. Debut 1982 OB in "A Midsummer Night's Dream," followed by "Zones of the Spirit," Bdwy in "Amadeus" (1983).

CROTHERS, JOEL. Born Jan 28, 1941 in Cincinnati, OH. Harvard graduate. Bdwy debut 1953 in "The Remarkable Mr. Pennypacker," followed by "A Case of Libel," "Barefoot in the Park," "The Jockey Club Stakes," OB in "Easter," "The Office Murders," "Torch Song Trilogy."

CROUSE, LINDSAY. Born May 12, 1948 in NYC. Graduate Radcliffe Col. Bdwy debut 1972 in "Much Ado about Nothing," OB in "The Foursome," "Fishing," "Long Day's Journey into Night," "Total Recall," "Father's Day," "Hamlet," "Reunion," "Twelfth Night," "Childe Byron," "Richard II," "Serenading Louie."

CROXTON, DARRYL. Born Apr. 5, 1946 in Baltimore, MD. Attended AADA. Bdwy debut 1969 in "Indians," followed by "Sly Fox," OB in "Volpone," "Murder in the Cathedral," "The Taking of Miss Janie," "Old Glory," "Divine Comedy," "Jack Gelber's New Play," "Cabal of Hypocrites."

CRYER, DAVID. Born Mar. 8, 1936 in Evanston, IL. Attended DePauw U. OB in "The Fantasticks," "Streets of New York," "Now Is the Time for All Good Men," "Whispers On the Wind," "The Making of Americans," "Portfolio Revue, "Paradise Lost," "The Inheritors," "Rain," "Ghosts," Bdwy in "110 In the Shade," "Come Summer" for which he received a Theatre World Award, "1776" "Ari," "Leonard Bernstein's Mass," "Desert Song," "Evita."

CRYER, GRETCHEN. Born Oct. 17, 1935 in Indianapolis, IN. Graduate DePauw U. Bdwy 1962 in "Little Me," followed by "110 in the Shade," OB in "Now Is the Time for All Good Men," "Gallery," "Circle of Sound," "I'm Getting My Act Together . . .," "Blue Plate Special."

CRYER, JON. Born Apr. 16, 1965 in NYC. Attended RADA. Bdwy debut 1983 in "Torch Song Trilogy."

CULLEN, JEANNE. Born Dec. 21, 1951 in Passaic, NY. Graduate UCon. Debut 1982 OB in "Lysistrata," followed by "Punch with Judy," "The Rivals."

CULLEY, JANE. Born Dec. 3, 1943 in Lawrenceburg, TN. Attended Reed Col. Debut 1964 OB in "Of Mice and Men," followed by "Scuba Duba," "Night of the Iguana," "A Phantasmagoria Historia . . .," "Holy Junkie."

CULLITON, JOSEPH. Born Jan 25, 1948 in Boston, MA. Attended CalStateU. Debut 1982 OB in "Francis," followed by "Flirtations."

CUNNINGHAM, JOHN. Born June 22, 1932 in Auburn, NY. Graduate of Yale and Dartmouth. OB in "Love Me Little," "Pimpernel," "The Fantasticks," "Love and Let Love," "The Bone Room," "Dancing in the Dark," "Father's Day," "Snapshot," "Head Over Heels," "Quartermaine's Terms," "Wednesday," "On Approval," Bdwy in "Hot Spot," "Zorba," "Company," "1776," "Rose."

CURLESS, JOHN. Born Sept. 16 in Wigan, Eng. Attended Central Sch. of Speech. NY debut 1982 OB in "The Entertainer," followed by "Sus."

CURRY, CHRISTOPHER. Born Oct. 22, 1948 in Grand Rapids, MI. Graduate UMich. Debut 1974 OB in "When You Comin' Back, Red Ryder?," followed by "The Cherry Orchard," "Spelling Bee," "Ballymurphy," "Isadora Duncan Sleeps with the Russian Navy," "The Promise," "Mecca," "Soul of the White Ant," "Strange Snow," "Love Letters on Blue Paper," "Kennedy at Colonus," Bdwy in "Crucifer of Blood" (1978).

CURTIS, KEENE. Born Feb. 15, 1925 in Salt Lake City, UT. Graduate UUtah. Bdwy bow 1949 in "Shop at Sly Corner," with APA in "School for Scandal," "The Tavern," "Anatole," "Scapin," "Right You Are," "Importance of Being Earnest," "Twelfth Night," "King Lear," "Seagull," "Lower Depths," "Man and Superman," "Judith," "War and Peace," "You Can't Take It With You," "Pantagleize," "Cherry Orchard," "Misanthrope," "Cocktail Party," "Cock-a-Doodle Dandy," and "Hamlet," "A Patriot for Me," "The Rothschilds," "Night Watch," "Via Galactica," "Annie," "Division Street," "La Cage aux Folles," OB in "Colette," "Ride Across Lake Constance."

CWIKOWSKI, BILL. Born Aug. 4, 1945 in Newark, NJ. Graduate Smith and Monmouth Col. Debut 1972 OB in "Charlie the Chicken," followed by "Summer Brave," "Desperate Hours," "Mandrogola," "Two by Noonan," "Soft Touch," "Innocent Pleasures," "3 From the Marathon," "Two Part Harmony," "Bathroom Plays," "Little Victories," "Dolphin Position," "Cabal of Hypocrites," "Split Second."

CYPKIN, DIANE. Born Sept. 10, 1948 in Munich, Ger. Attended Brooklyn Col. Bdwy debut 1966 in "Let's Sing Yiddish," followed by "Papa Get Married," "Light, Lively and Yiddish," "The Jewish Gypsy," OB in "Yoshke Musikant," "Stempenyu," "Big Winner," "A Millionaire in Trouble," "Winner Take All."

DABDOUB, JACK. Born Feb. 5 in New Orleans, LA. Graduate Tulane U. OB in "What's Up," "Time for the Gentle People," "The Peddler," "The Dodo Bird," "Annie Get Your Gun," "Lola," Bdwy in "Paint Your Wagon" (1952), "My Darlin' Aida," "Happy Hunting," "Hot Spot," "Camelot," "Baker St.," "Anya," "Her First Roman," "Coco," "Man of LaMancha," "Brigadoon" ('80), "Moose Murders," "One Touch of Venus."

DANIAS, STARR. Born March 18, 1949 in NYC. Performed with Joffrey Ballet before OB debut 1981 in "El Bravo," followed by "On Your Toes" (Bdwy 1983).

DANIELLE, MARLENE. Born Aug. 16 in NYC. Bdwy debut 1979 in "Sarava," followed by "West Side Story," "Marlowe," "Damn Yankees" (JB), "Cats," OB in "Little Shop of Horrors."

DANO, ELLEN. Born Aug. 21, 1957 in Paterson, NJ. Graduate Paterson Col., AADA. Debut 1970 OB in "Happy Birthday, Wanda June," followed by "Hair," "Brandy Before Breakfast."

DANSON, RANDY. Born Apr. 30, 1950 in Plainfield, NJ. Graduate Carnegie-Mellon. Debut 1978 OB in "Gimme Shelter," followed by "Big and Little," "The Winter Dancers," "Time Steps," "Casualties," "Red and Blue," "The Resurrection of Lady Lester," Jazz Poets at the Grotto," "Plenty," "Macbeth," "Blue Window."

DANTUONO, MICHAEL. Born July 30, 1942 in Providence, RI. Debut 1974 OB in "How to Get Rid of It," followed by "Maggie Flynn," "Charlotte Sweet," "Berlin to Broadway," Bdwy 1977 in "Caesar and Cleopatra," "Can-Can" ('81), "Zorba" (84).

DaPRATO, WILLIAM. Born Sept. 22, 1924 in The Bronx, NY. Attended TSDA. Debut 1963 OB in "The Burning," followed by "Holy Ghosts," "Awake and Sing," "Not Like Him," "Kohlhass," "Angelo's Wedding," "The Life I Gave You," Bdwy in "Mike Downstairs," "Shenandoah."

D'ARCY, MARY. Born in 1956 in Yardville, NJ. Graduate Glassboro State Col. Bdwy debut 1980 in "The Music Man," followed by "Sunday in the Park with George," OB in "Florodora," "Upstairs at O'Neal's," "Backers Audition."

DARKE, REBECCA. Born Dec. 6, 1935 in Brooklyn, NY. Debut 1958 OB in "The Midnight Caller," followed by "Who'll Save the Plowboy," "Undercover Man," "Party for Divorce," "A Piece of Blue Sky," "Hey Rube," "Glory! Hallelujah!," "Orpheus Descending," "Home Again, Kathleen," Bdwy in "The Basic Training of Pavlo Hummel" ('77).

DARLING, CANDY. Born March 6, 1954 in Toronto, Can. Bdwy debut 1976 in "Very Good Eddie," followed by "Censored Scenes from King Kong," "Whoopee," "Dreamgirls."

DARLOW, CYNTHIA. Born June 13, 1949 in Detroit, MI. Attended NCSchool of Arts, PennStateU. Debut 1974 OB in "This Property Is Condemned," followed by "Portrait of a Madonna," "Clytemnestra," "Unexpurgated Memoirs of Bernard Morgandigler," "Actors Nightmare," "Sister Mary Ignatius Explains It All," "Fables for Friends," "That's It Folks!," Bdwy in "Grease" (1976).

DASTEEL, WENDE. Born Apr. 26, 1948 in Los Angeles, CA. Attended Boston U. Debut 1983 OB in "Strange Behavior."

DAVENPORT, COLLEEN. Born Sept. 2, 1958 in Beloit, KS. Graduate LaStateU. Debut 1983 OB in "The Seagull."

DAVID, REGINA. Born in Denver, CO. Graduate UWy. Debut 1963 OB in "Six Characters in Search of an Author," followed by "Beelch," "Istanboul," "Moondreamers," "Subject to Fits," "Wedding Band," "Confetti and Italian Ice," "True West," "Tropical Fever in Key West."

DAVIES, GARY-MICHAEL. Born July 3, 1958 in Queens, NY. Attended Indiana U. Bdwy debut 1980 in "West Side Story," followed by "Marilyn."

DAVIS, SAMMY, JR. Born Oct. 8, 1925 in NYC. Bdwy debut 1956 in "Mr. Wonderful," followed by "Golden Boy," "Stop the World, I Want to Get Off," "Two Friends."

DAVIS, SHEILA KAY. Born May 30, 1956 in Daytona, FL. Graduate Spelman Col. Debut 1982 OB in "Little Shop of Horrors."

DAVIS, SYLVIA. Born Apr. 10, 1910 in Philadelphia, PA. Attended Temple U., AmThWing. Debut 1949 OB in "Blood Wedding," followed by "Tobacco Road," "Orpheus Descending," "Autumn Garden," "Madwoman of Chaillot," "House of Bernarda Alba," "My Old Friends," "Max," "Pahokee Beach," "Mademoiselle," Bdwy in "Nathan Weinstein, Mystic, CT." (1966), "Xmas in Las Vegas."

DAVISON, BRUCE. Born June 28, 1946 in Philadelphia, PA. Graduate PennState, NYU. Debut 1969 OB in "A Home Away From," followed by "Richard III," LCRep's "Tiger at the Gates," "A Cry of Players," and "King Lear," Bdwy in "The Elephant Man" (1980).

DAWSON, SUZANNE. Born Jan 19, 1951 in Montreal, Can. Attended Boston Consv. Debut 1980 OB in "Chase a Rainbow," followed by "New Faces of 1952," "The Great American Backstage Musical."

DEAN, LAURA. Born May 27, 1963 in Smithtown, NY. Debut 1973 OB in "The Secret Life of Walter Mitty," followed by "A Village Romeo and Juliet," "Carousel," "Hey Rube," "Landscape of the Body," "American Passion," Bdwy in "Doonesbury" (1983) for which she received a Theatre World Award.

DeANGELIS, ROSEMARY. Born Apr. 26, 1933 in Brooklyn, NY. Graduate FIT. Debut 1959 OB in "Time of Vengeance," followed by "Between Two Thieves," "To Be Young, Gifted and Black," "In the Summerhouse," "Monsters," "Rocky Road," "Nest of the Wood Grouse."

DEARDORFF, DAVID. Born Apr. 28, 1947 in Bremen, IN. Graduate Manchester Col. Debut 1974 OB in "Oh, Lady! Lady!," followed by "P.S. Your Cat Is Dead," "Oh Approval."

DEERING, NANCY. Born June 1 in Columbus, OH. Graduate OhStateU. Debut 1976 OB in "A Taste of Honey," followed by "Panhokee Beach."

DEGEN, JOHN F. Born Sept. 3, 1946 in Washington, DC. Graduate VaCommonwealthU, George Washington U. Debut 1984 OB in "A Touch of the Poet."

DE LA PENA, GEORGE. Born in NYC in 1956. Performed with American Ballet Theatre before Bdwy debut 1981 in "Woman of the Year," followed by "On Your Toes."

DEMPSEY, JEROME. Born Mar. 1, 1929 in St. Paul, MN. Toledo U graduate. Bdwy bow 1959 in "West Side Story," followed by "The Deputy," "Spofford," "Room Service," "Love Suicide at Schofield Barracks," "Dracula," "Whodunnit," "You Can't Take It With You," OB in "Cry of Players," "Year Boston Won the Pennant," "The Crucible," "Justice Box," "Trelawny of the Wells," "The Old Glory," "Six Characters in Search of an Author," "Threepenny Opera," "Johnny On the Spot," "The Barbarians," "He and She," "Midsummer Night's Dream," "The Recruiting Officer," "Oedipus the King," "The Wild Duck," "The Fuehrer Bunker," "Entertaining Mr. Sloane," "Clownmaker."

DENNIS, RONALD. Born Oct. 2, 1944 in Dayton, OH. Debut 1966 OB in "Show Boat," followed by "Of Thee I Sing," "Moon Walk," "Please Don't Cry," Bdwy in "A Chorus Line" (1975), "My One and Only."

DESAI, SHELLY. Born Dec. 3, 1935 in Bombay, India. Graduate OkStateU. Debut 1968 OB in "The Indian Wants the Bronx," followed by "Babu," "Wonderful Year," "Jungle of Cities," "Gandhi," "Savages," "Cuchulain," "Hamlet," "Merchant of Venice," "Fanshen," "Grunts," "And That's the Way It Is," Bdwy 1981 in "A Talent for Murder."

DeSAL, FRANK. Born Apr. 14, 1943 in White Plains, NY. Attended AmThWing. Credits include "110 in the Shade," "Marco Millions," "Sherry!," "Sweet Charity," "How Now, Dow Jones," "Fig Leaves Are Falling," "Bring Back Birdie," "Zorba" (1983), OB in "Anything Goes."

DeSALVO, ANNE. Born Apr. 3 in Philadelphia, PA. OB in "Iphigenia in Aulis," "Lovers and Other Stangers," "First Warning," "Warringham Roof," "God Bless You, Mr. Rosewater," "Girls Girls Girls," "Thin Ice," Bdwy in "Gemini" (1977).

DeSHIELDS, ANDRE. Born Jan. 12, 1946 in Baltimore, MD. Graduate UWi. Bdwy debut 1973 in "Warp," followed by "Rachel Lily Rosenbloom," "The Wiz," "Ain't Misbehavin'," OB in "2008½," "Jazzbo Brown," "The Soldier's Tale," "The Little Prince," "Haarlem Nocturne."

DEVINE, LORETTA. Born Aug. 21 in Houston, TX. Graduate UHouston, Brandeis U. Bdwy debut 1977 in "Hair," followed by "A Broadway Musical," "Dreamgirls," OB in "Godsong," "Lion and the Jewl," "Karma," "The Blacks," "Mahalia."

DEVLIN, JAY. Born May 8, 1929 in Ft. Dodge, IA. OB in "The Mad Show," "Little Murders," "Unfair to Goliath," "Ballymurphy," "Front Page," "Fasnacht Day," "Bugles at Dawn," "A Good Year for the Roses," Bdwy 1978 in "King of Hearts."

DEWEY, JUDY. Born Oct. 29, 1957 in Detroit, MI. Graduate Central MiU, Cornell U. Debut 1984 OB in "Bodo."

DIANE, THERESA. Born Nov. 19, 1969 in Fresh Meadows, NY. Bdwy debut 1983 in "Brighton Beach Memoirs."

DiFONZO, MICHAEL. Born Sept. 9, 1958 in Richmond, VA. Graduate SUNY/Binghamton. Debut 1984 OB in "Red, Hot and Blue."

DILLON, DENNY. Born May 18, 1951 in Cleveland, OH. Graduate Syracuse U. Bdwy debut 1974 in "Gypsy," followed by "The Skin of Our Teeth," "Harold and Maude," "My One and Only."

DILLION, MIA. Born July 9, 1955 in Colorado Springs, CO. Graduate Penn State U. Bdwy debut 1977 in "Equus," followed by "Da," "Once a Catholic," "Crimes of the Heart," "The Corn Is Green," OB in "The Crucible," "Summer," "Waiting for the Parade," "Crimes of the Heart," "Fables for Friends," "Scenes from La Vie de Boheme," "Three Sisters." "Wednesday," "Roberta in Concert," "Come Back, Little Sheba."

DiNOVI, ANTHONY. Born in NYC. Graduate SanFrancisco State U. Debut 1984 OB in "Flesh, Flash and Frank Harris."

DiPASQUALE, FRANK J. Born July 15, 1955 in Whitestone, NY. Graduate USC. Bdwy debut 1983 in "La Cage aux Folles."

DISQUE, DIANE. Born Apr. 3, 1952 in Wilkes Barre, PA. Attended OhStateU. Debut 1983 OB in "Crossroads Cafe."

DODSON, COLLEEN. Born June 29, 1954 in Chicago, IL. Graduate UIl. Debut 1981 OB in "The Matinee Kids," followed by "Pal Joey," Bdwy 1982 in "Nine."

DOLINER, ROY. Born June 27, 1954 in Boston, MA. Attended Tufts U. Debut 1977 OB in "Don't Cry Child, Your Father's an American," followed by "Zwi Kanar Show," "Big Bad Burlesque," "Lysistrata," "Rats," "Casanova."

DONAHOE, JIM. Born Feb. 13, 1939 in Pittsburgh, PA. Graduate UFla. Debut 1984 OB in "Up in Central Park."

DONHOWE, GWYDA. Born Oct. 20, 1933 in Oak Park, IL. Attended Drake U, Goodman Theatre. Bdwy debut 1957 in "Separate Tables," followed by "Half a Sixpence," "Flip Side," "Paris Is Out," "Applause," "The Show-Off," "War and Peace," "Right You Are," "You Can't Take It With You," "Shadow Box," "A Broadway Musical," OB in "Philosophy in the Boudoir," "Rondelay," "How Far Is It to Babylon?," "Head over Heels," "Rich Girls."

DONNELLY, DONAL. Born July 6, 1931 in Bradford, Eng. Bdwy debut 1966 in "Philadelphia, Here I Come," followed by "A Day in the Death of Joe Egg," "Sleuth," "The Faith Healer," "The Elephant Man," OB in "My Astonishing Self," "The Chalk Garden," "Big Maggie."

DORIAN, JOANNE. Born Nov. 1 in St. Paul, MN. Graduate UCLA. Debut 1978 OB in "Masterpieces," followed by "Hedda Gabler," "Berchtesgaden," "Night Must Fall," "Suddenly Last Summer," "A Touch of the Poet."

DOUGLAS, ERIC. Born June 21, 1960 in Los Angeles, Ca. Graduate Claremont Col., RADA, LAMDA. Debut 1983 OB in "The Man," followed by "Strictly Dishonorable," "The Littlest Clown."

DOUGLASS, PI. Born in Sharon, CT. Attended Boston Consv. Bdwy debut 1969 in "Fig Leaves Are Falling," followed by "Hello, Dolly!," "Georgy," "Purlie," "Ari," "Jesus Christ Superstar," "Selling of the President," "The Wiz," OB in "Of Thee I Sing," "Under Fire," "The Ritz," "Blackberries," "Dementos."

DOW, SUSAN. (formerly Susan Davis) Born Apr. 27, 1960 in Tulsa, OK. Attended AADA. Bdwy debut 1980 in "Barnum," OB in "And Other Songs," "El Bravo," "Preppies," "Something Better," "June Moon."

DRAYER, SALLY. Born Nov. 20, 1951 in Salem, MA. Graduate UVa. Debut 1980 OB in "Images," followed by "Ah, Wilderness!," "Desperate Acts," "The Contrast," "A Midsummer Night's Dream."

DREMAK, W. P. Born Aug. 2 in Akron, OH. Graduate Carnegie Tech. Debut 1967 OB in "Jonah," followed by Bdwy in "Jesus Christ Superstar" (1972),"Eccentricities of a Nightingale," "Oliver!"

DRUM, LEONARD. Born Feb. 21 in Pittsfield, MA. Graduate UNMex, Columbia. OB in "Kaleidoscope" (1957), "The Golden Six," "On the Town," "O Marry Me!," "Giants Dance," "Sing Me Sunshine," "Music Man," Bdwy in "Marat/Sade" (1967), "Whoopee!"

DRUMMOND, ALICE. Born May 21, 1929 in Pawtucket, RI. Attended Pembroke Col. Bdwy debut 1963 in "Ballad of the Sad Cafe," followed by "Malcolm," "The Chinese," "Thieves," "Summer Brave," "Some of My Best Friends," "You Can't Take It With You," OB in "Royal Gambit," "Go Show Me a Dragon," "Sweet of You to Say So," "Gallows Humor," "American Dream," "Giants' Dance," "Carpenters," "Charles Abbot & Son," "God Says There Is No Peter Ott," "Enter a Free Man," "Memory of Two Mondays," "Secret Service," "Boy Meets Girl," "Savages," "Killings On the Last Line," "Knuckle," "Wonderland," "Endgame."

DUDLEY, CRAIG. Born Jan. 22, 1945 in Sheepshead Bay, NY. Graduate AADA, AmThWing. Debut 1970 OB in "Macbeth," followed by "Zou," "Othello," "War and Peace."

DUFF-MacCORMICK, CARA. Born Dec. 12 in Woodstock, Can. Attended AADA. Debut 1969 OB in "Love Your Crooked Neighbor," followed by "The Wager," "Macbeth," "A Musical Merchant of Venice," "Ladyhouse Blues," "The Philanderer," "Bonjour, La, Bonjour," "Journey to Gdansk," "The Dining Room," "All the Nice People," Bdwy in "Moonchildren" (1972) for which she received a Theatre World Award, "Out Cry," "Animals."

DUFOUR, VAL. Born Feb. 5, 1928 in New Orleans, LA. Attended LSU. Credits include "The Grass Harp," "Frankie and Johnny," "Elektra," "Abie's Irish Rose" (1954), OB in "3 by Pirandello," "The Strange Case of Dr. Jekyll."

DUKAKIS, APOLLO. Born Aug. 27, 1937 in Boston, MA. Graduate Boston U. Debut 1969 OB in "The Lower Depths," followed by "Ping-Pong," "The Queen and the Rebels," "Gorky," "Dispatches from Hell."

DUKAKIS, JOHN. Born June 9, 1958 in San Jose, CA. Attended Brown U. Debut 1983 OB in "Ah, Wilderness!," followed by "Flirtations."

DUNCAN, SANDY. Born Feb. 20, 1946 in Henderson, TX. Attended Len Morris Col. Debut 1965 in CC's revivals of "The Music Man," "Carousel," "Finian's Rainbow," "Sound of Music," "Wonderful Town" and "Life with Father," OB in "Ceremony of Innocence" for which she received a Theatre World Award, "Your Own Thing," Bdwy in "Canterbury Tales" (1969), "Love Is a Time of Day," "The Boy Friend" (1970), "Peter Pan" (1979), "5–6–7–8 Dance," "My One and Only."

DUNN, DOREEN. Born Oct. 2, 1946 in Bath, ME. Graduate Northwestern U. Debut 1975 OB in "Celebration," followed by "The Three Musketeers," "Americans."

DUNN, SALLY. Born Dec. 23, 1950 in Detroit, MI. Graduate Stephens Col. Debut 1983 in "The Holly and the Ivy," followed by "How He Lied to Her Husband," "Winners," "As You Like It," "Romeo and Juliet."

EAMES, JOHN. Born Oct. 8, 1924 in Hartford, CT. Graduate Carnegie-Mellon U. Debut 1959 OB in "Leave It to Jane," followed by "The Boss," Bdwy in "1776," (1972), "The Corn Is Green" (1983).

EARLE, EDWARD. Born Dec. 20, 1929 in Santa Barbara, CA. Graduate USC. Bdwy debut 1959 in "Dark at the Top of the Stairs," followed by "Viva Madison Avenue," "Show Me Where the Good Times Are," "Roar of the Greasepaint . . . ," "Musical Chairs," "Charlie and Algernon," OB in "Dispatches from Hell."

EASTLEY, KEELY. Born Feb. 18, 1957 in New Albany, IN. Attended UNev. Debut 1981 OB in "The Lesson," followed by "I Am a Camera," "Flesh, Flash and Frank Harris."

EASTON, SAMUELLE (formerly Eskind) Born Dec. 14 in Tennessee. Graduate SanJoseStateU. Debut 1980 OB in "Towards Zero," followed by "Bravo," "Lysistrata," "Hound of the Baskervilles," "The Land Is Bright."

ECKHOUSE, JAMES. Born Feb. 14, 1955 in Chicago, IL. Graduate Juilliard. Bdwy debut 1982 in "Beyond Therapy," OB in "The Rise and Rise of Daniel Rocker," "Geniuses," "In the Country," "Sister Mary Ignatius Explains It All," "Dubliners."

eda-YOUNG, BARBARA. Born Jan. 30, 1945 in Detroit, MI. Bdwy debut 1968 in "Lovers and Other Strangers," OB in "The Hawk," LCRep's "The Time of Your Life," "Camino Real," "Operation Sidewinder," "Kool Aid" and "A Streetcar Named Desire," "The Gathering," "The Terrorists," "Drinks Before Dinner," "Shout Across the River," "After Stardrive," "Birdbath," "Crossing the Crab Nebula," "Maiden Stakes," "Come Dog Come Night," "Two Character Play," "Mensch Meier," "Glory in the Flower."

EDEIKEN, LOUISE. Born June 23, 1956 in Philadelphia, PA. Graduate GeoWashU. Bdwy debut 1982 in "Nine," OB in "Weekend."

EDELMAN, GREGG. Born Sept. 12, 1958 in Chicago, IL. Graduate Northwestern U. Bdwy debut 1982 in "Evita," followed by "Oliver!" (1983), OB in "Weekend."

EDENFIELD, DENNIS. Born July 23, 1946 in New Orleans, LA. Debut 1970 OB in "The Evil That Men Do," followed by "I Have Always Believed in Ghosts," "Nevertheless They Laugh," Bdwy in "Irene" ('73), "A Chorus Line."

EDMEAD, WENDY. Born July 6, 1956 in NYC. Graduate NYCU. Bdwy debut 1974 in "The Wiz," followed by "Stop the World . . . ," "America," "Dancin'," "Encore," "Cats."

EDMONDS, CHRISTOPHER. Born Jan. 31, 1959 in Tulsa, OK. Attended Tulsa Jr. Col. Bdwy debut 1984 in "The Human Comedy," OB in "Pal Joey."

EDWARDS, ANNIE JOE. Born Sept. 15, 1949 in Birmingham, AL. Graduate Dillard U. Bdwy debut 1975 in "Dr. Jazz," OB in "Be Kind to People Week," "Crossroads Cafe."

EDWARDS, BRANDT. Born Mar. 22, 1947 in Holly Springs, MS. Graduate UMiss. NY debut off and on Bdwy 1975 in "A Chorus Line."

EDWARDS, SUSAN. Born Aug. 14, 1950 in Levittown, NY. Graduate Hofstra U. Bdwy debut 1976 in "Bubbling Brown Sugar," followed by "The Suicide," "Torch Song Trilogy," OB in "Jazz Babies," "Boys from Syracuse," "Scrambled Feet."

EGAN, CALLAN. Born July 4, 1934 in Yonkers, NY. Graduate Cornell U, Columbia. Debut 1983 OB in "The Lady's Not for Burning."

EICHE, JEFFREY D. Born Mar. 28, 1955 in San Diego, CA. Graduate SanDiegoStateU. Debut 1983 OB in "The Taming of the Shrew," followed by "Nude with Violin."

ELLIN, DAVID. Born Jan. 10, 1925 in Montreal, Can. Attended AADA. Bdwy in "Swan Song," "West Side Story," "Education of Hyman Kaplan," "Light, Lively and Yiddish," OB in "Trees Die Standing," "Mirele Efros," "End of All Things Natural," "Yoshe Kalb," "Fiddler on the Roof" (JB), "Rebecca, the Rabbi's Daughter," "Wish Me Mazel-Tov," "Roumanian Wedding," "The Showgirl," "The Jewish Gypsy."

ELLIOTT, PATRICIA. Born July 21,1942 in Gunnison, CO. Graduate U. Colo., London Academy. Debut with LCRep 1968 in "King Lear," and "A Cry of Players," followed OB in "Henry V," "The Persians," "A Doll's House," "Hedda Gabler," "In Case of Accident," "Water Hen," "Polly," "But Not for Me," "By Bernstein," "Prince of Homburg," "Artichokes," "Wine Untouched," "Misalliance," Bdwy bow 1973 in "A Little Night Music" for which she received a Theatre World Award, followed by "The Shadow Box," "Tartuffe," "13 Rue de L'Amour," "The Elephant Man."

ELLIS, FRASER. Born May 1, 1957 in Boulder, CO. Graduate UCo. Bdwy debut 1982 in "A Chorus Line."

ELLIS, SCOTT. Born Apr. 19, 1957 in Washington, DC. Attended Goodman Theatre. Bdwy debut in "Grease," followed by "Musical Chairs," "The Rink," OB in "Mrs. Dally Has a Lover," "Hijinks," "110 In the Shade," "A Midsummer Night's Dream."

ELMORE, STEVE. Born July 12, 1936 in Niangua, MO. Debut 1961 in "Madame Aphrodite," followed by "Golden Apple," "Enclave," Bdwy in "Camelot," "Jenny," "Fade in Fade Out," "Kelly," "Company," "Nash at 9," "Chicago," "42nd St."

EMCH, GEORGE K. Born Oct. 19, 1927 in Poland, OH. Attended New School. Debut 1957 OB in "Macbeth," followed by "Redhead," "How to Succeed in Business . . .," "Up in Central Park," "Ragtime Blues," Bdwy in "Capt. Brassbound's Conversion" (1972).

EMMET, ROBERT. Born Oct. 3, 1952 in Denver, CO. Graduate UWash. Debut 1976 OB in "The Mousetrap," followed by "The Seagull," "Blue Hotel," "Miss Jairus," "Hamlet," "Deathwatch," "Much Ado About Nothing," "Songs and Ceremonies," "Mass Appeal, "Macbeth," "Bell, Book and Candle," "Comes the Happy Hour," "The Gift."

ENGEL, DAVID. Born Oct. 19, 1959 in Orange, CA. Attended UCal/Irvine. Bdwy debut 1983 in "La Cage aux Folles."

ENGLE, DEBRA. Born July 4, 1953 in Baltimore, MD. Graduate IllWesleyanU. Debut 1984 OB in "Balm in Gilead."

ENNIS, FLLOYD. Born June 29, 1926 in Philadelphia, PA. Studied with Stella Adler. Debut 1961 OB in "The Octoroon," followed by "Kid Champion," "Sweet Bird of Youth, "Pigeons on the Walk."

EPSTEIN, ALVIN. Born May 14, 1925 in NYC. Attended Queens Col. Appeared on Bdwy with Marcel Marceau, and in "King Lear," "Waiting for Godot" (1956), "From A to Z," "No Strings," "Passion of Josef D," "Postmark Zero," "A Kurt Weill Cabaret," OB in "Purple Dust," "Pictures in a Hallway," "Clerambard," "Endgame," (1958/1984), "Whores, Wares and Tin Pan Alley," "A Place without Doors," "Crossing Niagara," "Beckett Plays."

ESPOSITO, GIANCARLO. Born Apr. 26, 1958 in Copenhagen, Den. Bdwy debut 1968 in "Maggie Flynn," followed by "The Me Nobody Knows," "Lost In the Stars," "Seesaw," "Merrily We Roll Along," OB in "Zooman and the Sign" for which he received a Theatre World Award, "Keyboard," "Who Loves the Dancer," "House of Ramon Iglesias," "Do Lord Remember Me," "Balm in Gilead."

ESTEY, SUELLEN. Born Nov. 21 in Mason City, IA. Graduate Stephens Col., Northwestern U. Debut 1970 OB in "Some Other Time," followed by "June Moon," "Buy Bonds Buster," "Smile, Smile, Smile," "Carousel," "The Lullaby of Broadway," "I Can't Keep Running," "The Guys in the Truck," Bdwy 1972 in "The Selling of the President," followed by "Barnum," "Sweethearts in Concert."

ETJEN, JEFF. Born June 12, 1953 in Chicago, IL. Graduate Rollins Co. Debut 1983 OB in "Forbidden Broadway," followed by "Romantic Arrangements," "Mandrake."

EVANS, PETER. Born May 27, 1950 in Englewood, NJ. Graduate Yale, London Central School of Speech. Debut OB 1975 in "Life Class," followed by "Streamers," "A Life in the Theatre," "Don Juan Comes Back From the War," "The American Clock," "Geniuses," "Transfiguration of Benno Blimpie," "Endgame," Bdwy in "Night and Day" (1979) "Children of a Lesser God."

EVERS, BRIAN. Born Feb. 14, 1942 in Miami, FL. Graduate Capital U, UMiami. Debut 1979 OB in "How's the House?," followed by "Details of the 16th Frame," "Divine Fire," "Silent Night, Lonely Night," "Uncommon Holidays."

EWING, GEOFFREY C. Born Aug. 10, 1951 in Minneapolis, MN. Graduate UMn. Bdwy debut 1983 in "Guys in the Truck."

EWING, J. TIMOTHY. Born Apr. 3, 1954 in Evansville, IN. Graduate Indiana U. Debut 1983 OB in "Colette Collage," followed by "Promenade," "Pacific Overtures."

FAIRSERVIS, ELF. Born May 19, 1957 in Mt. Kisco, NY. Graduate Bennett Col. Debut 1982 OB in "Independent Study," followed by "Our Town," "A Little More Wine with Lunch," "Dick Deterred," "Shakespeare Marathon."

FANCY, RICHARD. Born Aug. 2, 1943 in Evanston, IL. Attended LAMDA. Debut 1973 OB in "The Creeps," followed by "Kind Lady," "Rites of Passage," "A Limb of Snow," "The Meeting," "Hound of the Baskervilles."

FARR, KIMBERLY. Born Oct. 16, 1948 in Chicago, IL. Graduate UCLA. Bdwy debut 1972 in "Mother Earth," followed by "The Lady from the Sea," "Going Up," "Happy New Year," OB in "More Than You Deserve," "The S. S. Benchley," "At Sea with Benchley," "Suffragett," "Brownstone."

FENNING, STEPHEN. Born Jan. 6 in Washington, DC. Attended AMDA. Bdwy debut 1972 in "Hair," followed by "You're a Good Man, Charlie Brown," OB in "Morality," "Narrow Road to the Deep North," "Godspell," "Snoopy," "Bodo," "The Me Nobody Knows."

FERGUSON, LOU. Born Aug. 8, 1944 in Trinidad, WI. Debut 1970 OB in "A Season in the Congo," followed by "Night World," "La Gente," "Shoe Shine Parlor," "The Defense," "Rum an' Coca Cola," "Remembrance," "Raisin in the Sun."

FICKINGER, STEVEN. Born Apr. 29, 1960 in Chicago, IL. Graduate UCLA. Debut 1982 OB in "Louisiana Summer," followed by "The Robber Bridegroom," "Judy Garland of Songs."

FIELDS, THOR. Born Sept. 19, 1968 in NYC. Bdwy debut in "The King and I" (1978), followed by "Camelot" (80), OB in "Yo Yo," "A Month in the Country," "Mensch Meier."

FIERSTEIN, HARVEY. Born June 6, 1954 in Brooklyn, NY. Graduate Pratt Inst. Debut 1971 OB in "Pork," followed by "International Stud," "Figure In a Nursery," Bdwy 1982 in "Torch Song Trilogy," for which he received a Theatre World Award.

FILIPOV, ALEXANDER. Born Mar. 19, 1947 in Moscow, R. Attended Leningrad Kirov School. With ABT, San Francisco Ballet before Bdwy debut 1983 in "On Your Toes."

FINKEL, FYVUSH. Born Oct. 9, 1922 in Brooklyn, NY. Bdwy debut 1970 in "Fiddler On the Roof" (also 1981 revival), OB in "Gorky," "Little Shop of Horrors."

FIRE, NORMA. Born June 9, 1937 in Brooklyn, NY. Graduate Bklyn Col. Debut 1982 OB in "3 Acts of Recognition," followed by "Merry Wives of Windsor," "Henry V."

FISHER, J. FRANCIS. Born Mar. 27, 1954 in Newark, NJ. Attended UUtah. Debut 1983 OB in "The Music Man."

FITZGERALD, FERN. Born Jan. 7, 1947 in Valley Stream, NY. Bdwy debut 1976 in "Chicago," followed by "A Chorus Line."

FITZPATRICK, JIM. Born Nov. 26, 1950 in Omaha, NE. Attended UNeb. Debut 1977 OB in "Arsenic and Old Lace", followed by "Merton of the Movies", "Oh, Boy!," "Time and the Conways," "Street Scene," "Duchess of Malfi," "Comedy of Errors."

FLAGG, TOM. Born Mar. 30 in Canton, OH. Attended KentStateU, AADA. Debut 1975 OB in "The Fantasticks," followed by "Give Me Liberty," "The Subject Was Roses," "Lola," "Red, Hot and Blue," Bdwy in "Legend" (1976), "Shenandoah," "Players."

FLANAGAN, NEIL. Born May 3, 1934 in Springfield, IL. Debut 1966 OB in "Fortune and Men's Eyes," followed by "Haunted Host," "Madness of Lady Bright," "Dirtiest Show in Town," "The Play's the Thing," "As You Like It," "Hedda Gabler," "Design for Living," "him," "Partnership," "Down by the River," "Lisping Judas," "Elephant in the House," "Exiles," Bdwy in "Sheep on the Runway," "Secret Affairs of Mildred Wild," "Knock Knock," "Beethoven's Tenth."

FLANAGAN, PAULINE. Born June 29, 1925 in Sligo, Ire. Debut 1958 OB in "Ulysses in Nighttown," followed by "Pictures in the Hallway," "Later," "Antigone," "The Crucible," "The Plough and the Stars," "Summer," "Close of Play," "Love Letters on Blue Paper," Bdwy in "God and Kate Murphy," "The Living Room," "The Innocents," "The Father," "Medea," "Steaming."

FLANINGAM, LOUISA. Born May 5, 1945 in Chester, SC. Graduate UMd. Debut 1971 OB in "The Shrinking Bridge," followed by "Pigeons on the Walk," Bdwy in "Magic Show," "Most Happy Fella" (1979), "Play Me a Country Song."

FLEISS, JANE. Born Jan. 28 in NYC. Graduate NYU. Debut 1979 OB in "Say Goodnight, Gracie," followed by "Grace," "The Beaver Coat," "The Harvesting," Bdwy in "5th of July" (1981), "Crimes of the Heart."

FLESS, SCOTT. Born Oct. 13, 1952 in The Bronx, NY. Graduate Queens Col. Bdwy debut 1980 in "Onward Victoria," followed by "Evita," OB in "Road to Hollywood."

FLICKER, TED. (aka as Theodore) Born June 6, 1930 in Freehold, NJ. Graduate RADA. Debut 1954 OB in "Once around the Block," followed by "The Premise," "Getting Along Famously."

FLOREK, DAVE. Born May 19, 1953 in Dearborn, MI. Graduate Eastern MiU. Debut 1976 OB in "The Collection," followed by "Richard III," "Much Ado About Nothing," "Young Bucks," "Big Apple Messenger," "Death of a Miner," "Marvelous Gray," "Journey to Gdansk," "The Last of Hitler," "Thin Ice," Bdwy 1980 in "Nuts."

FORD, BARRY. Born Mar. 27, 1933 in Oakland, CA. Graduate CaStateU. Debut 1972 OB in "Ruddigore," followed by "The Devil's Disciple," "Nymph Errant," "After You've Gone," "The Trial of Adam Clayton Powell, Jr."

FORD, CLEBERT. Born Jan 29, 1932 in Brooklyn, NY. Graduate CCNY, Boston U. Bdwy debut 1960 in "The Cool World," followed by "Les Blancs," "Ain't Supposed to Die a Natural Death," "Via Galactica," "Bubbling Brown Sugar," "The Last Minstrel Show," OB in "Romeo and Juliet," "The Blacks," "Antony and Cleopatra," "Ti-Jean and His Brothers," "Ballad for Bimshire," "Daddy," "Gilbeau," "Coriolanus," "Before the Flood," "The Lion and the Jewel," "Branches from the Same Tree," "Dreams Deferred," "Basin Street," "20 Year Friends."

FORD, DONALD BROOKS. Born Sept. 15, 1960 in Cleveland, OH. Graduate SUNY/Purchase. Debut 1982 OB in "Listen to Me," followed by "French Toast."

FORD, FRANCES. Born Nov. 10, 1939 in Appleton, WI. Graduate UWis. Debut 1964 OB in "A Midsummer Night's Dream," followed by "The Importance of Being Earnest," "She Stoops to Conquer," "The Maids," "Howling in the Night," "The Marquise," Bdwy in "The Stingiest Man in Town" (1971).

FORD, SPENCE. Born Feb. 25, 1954 in Richmond, VA. Attended UVa. Debut 1976 OB in "Follies," followed by "Pal Joey," Bdwy in "King of Hearts," "Carmelina," "Peter Pan," "Copperfield," "Dancin'," "Merlin."

FORD, SUZANNE. Born Sept. 22, 1949 in Auburn, NY. Attended Ithaca Col., Eastman Sch. Debut 1973 OB in "Fashion," followed by "El Grande de Coca-Cola," "Tenderloin," "A Man between Twilights," "Under the Gaslight," "Mandrake."

FORLOW, TED. Born Apr. 29, 1931 in Independence, MO. Attended Baker U. Bdwy debut 1957 in "New Girl in Town," followed by "Juno," "Destry Rides Again," "Subways Are for Sleeping," "Can-Can," "Wonderful Town," "A Funny Thing Happened on the Way to the Forum," "Milk and Honey," "Carnival" (CC), "Man of La Mancha" (1965/1977), OB in "A Night at the Black Pig," "Glory in the Flower," "Perfect Analysis Given by a Parrot," "Cat and the Fiddle," "One Cannot Think of Everything," "Man of Destiny."

FORMAN, CAROLE. Born Mar. 4, 1948 in NYC. Graduate UBuffalo. Bdwy debut 1979 in "Strider," OB in "The Marriage," "Ballad of Raintree Country," "Bad Habits," "Chaturanga."

FORSYTHE, HENDERSON. Born Sept. 11, 1917 in Macon, MO. Attended UIowa. Debut 1956 OB in "The Iceman Cometh," followed by "The Collection," "The Room," "A Slight Ache," "Happiness Cage," "Waiting for Godot," "In Case of Accident," "Not I," "An Evening With the Poet-Senator," "Museum," "How Far Is It to Babylon," "Wild Life," "Other Places," Bdwy in "The Cellar and the Well" (1950), "Miss Lonelyhearts," "Who's Afraid of Virginia Woolf?," "Malcolm," "Right Honourable Gentleman," "Delicate Balance," "Birthday Party," "Harvey," "Engagement Baby," "Freedom of the City," "Texas Trilogy," "Best Little Whorehouse in Texas."

FOSTER, FRANCES. Born June 11 in Yonkers, NY. Bdwy debut 1955 in "The Wisteria Trees," followed by "Nobody Loves an Albatross," "Raisin in the Sun," "The River Niger," "First Breeze of Summer," OB in "Take a Giant Step," "Edge of the City," "Tammy and the Doctor," "The Crucible," "Happy Ending," "Day of Absence," "An Evening of One Acts," "Man Better Man," "Brotherhood," "Akokawe," "Rosalee Pritchett," "Sty of the Blind Pig," "Ballet Behind the Bridge," "Good Woman of Setzuan" (LC), "Behold! Cometh the Vanderkellans," "Origin," "Boesman and Lena," "Do Lord Remember Me."

FOWLER, BETH. Born Nov. 1, 1940 in New Jersey. Graduate Caldwell Col. Bdwy debut 1970 in "Gantry," followed by "A Little Night Music," "Over Here," "1600 Pennsylvania Ave.," "Peter Pan," "Baby," OB in "Preppies."

FOWLER, CLEMENT. Born Dec. 27, 1924 in Detroit, MI. Graduate Wayne State U. Bdwy debut 1951 in "Legend of Lovers," followed by "The Cold Wind and the Warm," "Fragile Fox," "The Sunshine Boys," "Hamlet (1964), OB in "The Eagle Has Two Heads," "House Music," "Transfiguration of Benno Blimpie," "The Inheritors," "Paradise Lost."

FOXWORTH, ROBERT. Born Nov. 1, 1941 in Houston, TX. Graduate Carnegie Tecn. Bdwy debut 1969 in "Henry V," followed by "The Crucible" for which he received a Theatre World Award, OB in "Terra Nova."

FRANCINE, ANNE. Born Aug. 8, 1917 in Philadelphia, PA. Bdwy debut 1945 in "Marriage Is for Single People," followed by "By the Beautiful Sea," "The Great Sebastians," "Tenderloin," "Mame," "A Broadway Musical," "Snow White," "Mame" (1983), OB in "Guitar," "Valmouth," "Asylum," "Are You Now or Have You Ever Been . . ."

FRANCIS-JAMES, PETER. Born Sept. 16, 1956 in Chicago, IL. Graduate RADA. Debut 1979 OB in "Julius Caesar," followed by "Long Day's Journey into Night," "Antigone," "Richard III."

FRANK, ROBERT JOHN. Born May 6 in Montreal, Can. Graduate Purdue, Indiana U, Goodman Sch., RADA. Debut 1984 OB in "The Bone Garden."

FRANKS, LAURIE. Born Aug. 14, 1929 in Lucasville, OR. Bdwy debut 1956 in "Bells Are Ringing," followed by "Copper and Brass," "Pleasures and Palaces," "Something More," "Anya," "Mame," "The Utter Glory of Morrissey Hall," "The Human Comedy," OB in "Leave It to Jane," "Jimmy and Billy," "Around the World in 80 Days."

FRANZ, ELIZABETH. Born June 18, 1941 in Akron, OH. Attended AADA. Debut 1965 OB in "In White America," followed by "One Night Stands of a Noisy Passenger," "The Real Inspector Hound," "Augusta," "Yesterday Is Over," "Actor's Nightmare," "Sister Mary Ignatius Explains It All," Bdwy in "Rosencrantz and Guildenstern Are Dead," "The Cherry Orchard," "Brighton Beach Memoirs."

FRATANTONI, DIANE. Born Mar. 29, 1956 in Wilmington, DE. Bdwy debut 1979 in "A Chorus Line," followed by "Cats."

FRAWLEY, CRAIG. Born July 24, 1959 in Arlington, VA. Attended Carnegie-Mellon U. Debut 1984 OB in "Up in Central Park."

FRAZER, SUSANNA. Born in NYC. Debut 1980 OB in "Kind Lady," followed by "The Enchanted," "A Doll's House," "Scenes from American Life," "Old Friends and Roommates."

FREEMAN, MORGAN. Born June 1, 1937 in Memphis, TN. Attended LACC. Bdwy bow 1967 in "Hello, Dolly!" followed by "The Mighty Gents," OB in "Ostrich Feathers," "Niggerlovers," "Exhibition," "Black Visions," "Cockfight," "White Pelicans," "Julius Caesar," "Coriolanus," "Mother Courage," "The Connection," "The World of Ben Caldwell," "Buck," "The Gospel at Colonus."

FRENCH, ARTHUR. Born in NYC. Attended Brooklyn Col. Debut 1962 OB in "Raisin' Hell in the Sun," followed by "Ballad of Bimshire," "Day of Absence," "Happy Ending," "Jonah," "Black Girl," "Ceremonies in Dark Old Men," "An Evening of One Acts," "Man Better Man," "Brotherhood," "Perry's Mission," "Rosalee Pritchett," "Moonlight Arms," "Dark Tower," "Brownsville Raid," "Nevis Mt. Dew," "Julius Caesar," "Friends," "Court of Miracles," "The Beautiful LaSalles," Bdwy in "Ain't Supposed to Die a Natural Death," "The Iceman Cometh," "All God's Chillun Got Wings," "The Resurrection of Lady Lester," "You Can't Take It With You."

FRIEDLANDER, GINA. Born Mar. 21, 1958 in Sacramento, CA. Graduate Pomona Col. Bdwy debut 1984 in "Beethoven's Tenth."

FRIEDMAN, PETER. Born Apr. 24, 1949 in NYC. Debut 1971 OB in "James Joyce Memorial Liquid Theatre," followed by "Big and Little," "A Soldier's Play," "Mr. and Mrs.," "And a Nightingale Sang," Bdwy in "The Visit," "Chemin de Fer," "Love for Love," "Rules of the Game," "Piaf!"

FRISCH, RICHARD. Born May 9, 1933 in NYC. Graduate Juilliard. Bdwy debut 1964 in "The Passion of Josef D," followed by "Fade Out-Fade In," OB in "Jonah," "Antigone," "The Mother of Us All," "Up from Paradise."

FROOM, MIMI. Born Apr. 18, 1960 in Petaluma, CA. Graduate Brandeis U. Debut 1984 OB in "Up in Central Park."

GABOR, EVA. Born Feb. 11, 1920 in Budapest, Hungary. Bdwy debut 1950 in "The Happy Time," followed by "The Little Glass Clock," "Present Laughter," "You Can't Take It with You."

GAGE, PATRICIA. Born March 3 in Glasgow, Scot. Bdwy debut 1972 in "There's One in Every Marriage," followed by "Whoddunnit," OB in "Thread of Scarlet" (1978), "Sister Mary Ignatious Explains It All."

GALLAGHER, HELEN. Born in 1926 in Brooklyn, NY. Bdwy debut 1947 in "Seven Lively Arts," followed by "Mr. Strauss Goes to Boston," "Billion Dollar Baby," "Brigadoon," "High Button Shoes," "Touch and Go," "Make a Wish," "Pal Joey," "Guys and Dolls," "Finian's Rainbow," "Oklahoma!," "Pajama Game," "Bus Stop," "Portofino," "Sweet Charity," "Mame," "Cry for Us All," "No, No, Nanette," "A Broadway Musical," "Sugar Babies," OB in "Hothouse," "Tickles by Tucholsky," "The Misanthrope," "I Can't Keep Running in Place," "Red Rover," "Tallulah."

GALLAGHER, PETER. Born Aug. 19, 1955 in NYC. Graduate Tufts U. Bdwy debut 1977 in "Hair," followed by "A Doll's Life" for which he received a Theatre World Award, "The Corn Is Green," "The Real Thing."

GALLIONE, GALE. Born Jan. 8, 1958 in NYC. Graduate NYU. Debut 1983 OB in "Crossroads Cafe," followed by "War Babies," "Pal Joey."

GALLOWAY, JANE. Born Feb. 27, 1950 in St. Louis, MO. Attended Webster Col. Debut 1976 OB in "Vanities," followed by "Domino Courts," "Comanche Cafe," "Dementos," Bdwy in "Little Johnny Jones" (1982).

GANAKAS, GREG. Born June 26, 1954 in Lansing, MI. Graduate UMich, NYU. Debut in 1984 OB in "Pal Joey."

GANTRY, DONALD. Born June 11, 1936 in Philadelphia, PA. Attended Temple U. Bdwy debut 1961 in "One More River," followed by "Ah, Wilderness," "The Queen and the Rebels," "Moon for the Misbegotten," OB in "The Iceman Cometh," "Children of Darkness," "Here Come the Clowns," "Seven at Dawn," "Long Day's Journey Into Night," "Enclave," "Bags.

GARBER, VICTOR. Born Mar. 16, 1949 in London, Can. Debut 1973 OB in "Ghosts" for which he received a Theatre World Award, followed by "Joe's Opera," "Cracks," Bdwy in "Tartuffe," "Deathtrap," "Sweeney Todd," "They're Playing Our Song," "Little Me," "Noises Off."

GARFEIN, HERSCHEL. Born Jan. 17, 1958 in NYC. Graduate Yale, New Eng. Consv. Debut 1983 OB in "The Beckett Plays," followed by "Miss Julie."

GARFIELD, JULIE. Born Jan. 10, 1946 in Los Angeles, CA. Attended UWi, Neighborhood Playhouse. Debut 1969 OB in "Honest-to-God Schnozzola," followed by "East Lynne," "The Sea," "Uncle Vanya" for which she received a Theatre World Award, "Me and Molly," "Chekhov Sketchbook," "Rosario and the Gypsies," "Occupations," "Modern Ladies of Guanabacoa," "Broken Eggs," Bdwy in "The Good Doctor," "Death of a Salesman," "The Merchant."

GARNETT, CHIP. Born May 8, 1953 in New Kensington, PA. Attended Ind.U. Debut 1973 OB in "Inner City," followed by "Rhapsody in Gershwin," "Uptown Feeling," Bdwy in "Candide," "Bubbling Brown Sugar" for which he received a Theatre World Award.

GARRETT, BECKY. Born Mar. 18, 1948 in Pendleton, OR. Bdwy debut 1980 in "Blackstone," OB in "Red, Hot and Blue."

GARRISON, DAVID. Born June 30, 1952 in Long Branch, NJ. Graduate Boston U. Debut OB in "Joseph and the Amazing Technicolor Dreamcoat," followed by "Living At Home," "Geniuses," Bdwy in "A History of the American Film," "A Day in Hollywood/A Night in the Ukraine," "Pirates of Penzance," "Snoopy," "Torch Song Trilogy," "One Touch of Venus."

GARSIDE, BRAD. Born June 2, 1958 in Boston, MA. Graduate NorthTexState U. Debut 1983 OB in "Forbidden Broadway."

GASCO, ERNESTO. Born July 10, 1937 in Bagnasco, Italy. Graduate Inst. del Teatro Colon. Bdwy debut 1980 in "Betrayal," OB in "Non Pasquale," "Nest of the Wood Grouse."

GAVON, IGORS. Born Nov. 14, 1937 in Latvia. Bdwy bow 1961 in "Carnival," followed by "Hello Dolly!" "Marat/deSade," "Billy," "Sugar," "Mack and Mabel," "Musical Jubilee," "Strider," "42 St," OB in "Your Own Thing," "Promenade," "Exchange," "Nevertheless They Laugh," "Polly," "The Boss," "Biography: A Game," "Murder in the Cathedral."

GEFFNER, DEBORAH. Born Aug. 26, 1952 in Pittsburgh, PA. Attended Juilliard, HB Studio. Debut 1978 OB in "Tenderloin," Bdwy in "Pal Joey," "A Chorus Line."

GEHMAN, MARTHA. Born May 15, 1955 in NYC. Graduate Sarah Lawrence Co. Debut 1984 OB in "Cinders."

GELFER, STEVEN. Born Feb. 21, 1949 in Brooklyn, NY. Graduate NYU, IndU. Debut 1968 OB and Bdwy in "The Best Little Whorehouse in Texas," followed by "Cats."

GENELLE, JOANNE. Born Nov. 21, 1956 in Brooklyn, NY. Attended Queens Col. Debut 1982 OB in "Get Happy," followed by "The Larry Loeber Show," "Sing Me Sunshine," Bdwy in "Dance a Little Closer" (1983).

GENEST, EDMOND. Born Oct. 27, 1943 in Boston, MA. Attended Suffolk U. Debut 1972 OB in "The Real Inspector Hound," followed by "Second Prize: Two Months in Leningrad," Bdwy in "Dirty Linen/New-Found Land," "Whose Life Is it Anyway?"

GENTRY, ANN. Born Jan. 14, 1954 in Dyersburg, TN. Attended UTn, Goddard Col. Debut 1982 OB in "Night Fishing in Beverly Hills," followed by "Fool for Love."

GEOFFREYS, STEPHEN. Born Nov. 22, 1964 in Cincinnati, OH. Attended NYU. Bdwy debut 1984 in "The Human Comedy" for which he received a Theatre World Award.

GEORGE, DAVID. Born Dec. 5, 1972 in NYC. Debut 1984 OB in "Other Places."

GERARD, WILL. Born July 14, 1943 in Center, TX. Graduate Lamar U, UCLA. Debut 1969 OB in "Your Own Thing," Bdwy in "Mother Earth" (1972), "Marilyn."

GERSHENSON, SUE ANNE Born Feb. 18, 1953 in Chicago, IL. Attended Ind. U. Debut 1976 OB in "Panama Hattie," followed by "Carnival," "Street Scene," Bdwy in "Sunday in The Park with George" (1984).

GERROLL, DANIEL. Born Oct. 16, 1951 in London, Eng. Attended Central Sch. of Speech. Debut 1980 OB in "The Slab Boys," followed by "Knuckle" and "Translations" for which he received a Theatre World Award," "The Caretaker," "Scenes from La Vie de Boheme," "The Knack," "Terra Nova," Bdwy in "Plenty" (1982).

GETTY, ESTELLE. Born July 25, 1923 in NYC. Attended New School. Debut 1971 OB in "The Divorce of Judy and Jane," followed by "Widows and Children First," "Table Settings," "Demolition of Hannah Fay," "Never Too Old," "A Box of Tears," "Hidden Corners," " I Don't Know Why I'm Screaming," "Under the Bridge There's a Lonely Place," "Light Up the Sky," "Pocketful of Posies," "Fits and Starts," Bdwy 1982 in "Torch Song Trilogy."

GIAGNI, D. J. Born Dec. 3, 1950 in NYC. Attended CCNY. Bdwy debut 1983 in "The Tap Dance Kid."

GIANNINI, CHERYL. Born June 15 in Monessen, PA. Bdwy debut 1980 in "The Suicide," followed by "Grownups," OB in "Elm Circle."

GIFFIN, NORMA JEAN. Born Oct. 31, 1956 in Haverhill, MA. Graduate Barat Col., AADA. Debut 1980 OB in "Last Stop Blue Jay Lane."

GILBERT, BARBARA. Born July 20 in Brooklyn, NY. Attended AADA, HB Studio. Bdwy debut 1956 in "Pajama Game," followed by "Fiorello!," "Cop-Out," "Baby," OB in "Threepenny Opera," "Spoon River Anthology," "Archy and Mehitabel."

GILBORN, STEVEN. Born in New Rochelle, NY. Graduate Swarthmore, Col., Stanford U. Bdwy debut 1973 in "Creeps," followed by "Basic Training of Pavlo Hummel," "Tartuffe," OB in "Rosmersholm," "Henry V," "Measure for Measure," "Ashes," "The Dybbuk," "Museum," "Shadow of a Gunman," "It's Hard to Be a Jew," "Isn't It Romantic."

GILPIN, JACK. Born May 31, 1951 in Boyce, VA. Harvard graduate. Debut 1976 OB in "Goodbye and Keep Cold," followed by "Shay," "The Soft Touch," "Beyond Therapy," "The Lady or the Tiger," "The Middle Ages," "The Rise of Daniel Rocket," "No Happy Ending," "Strange Behavior," Bdwy in "Lunch Hour" ('80).

GIOMBETTI, KAREN. Born May 24, 1955 in Scranton, PA. Graduate NYU. Bdwy debut 1978 in "Stop the World, I Want to Get Off," followed by "The Most Happy Fella," "Woman of the Year," "Zorba" (1983).

GIONSON, MEL. Born Feb. 23, 1954 in Honolulu, HI. Graduate UHi. Debut 1979 OB in "Richard II," followed by "Sunrise," "Monkey Music," "Behind Enemy Lines," "Station J," "Teahouse," "A Midsummer Night's Dream," "Empress of China."

GIRARDEAU, FRANK. Born Oct. 19, 1942 in Beaumont, TX. Attended Rider Col, HB Studio. Debut 1972 OB in "22 Years," followed by "The Soldier," "Hughie," "An American Story," "El Hermano," "Dumping Ground," "Daddies," "Accounts," "Shadow Man," "Marathon '84."

GLEASON, JAMES. Born Sept. 30, 1952 in NYC. Graduate Santa Fe Col. Debut 1982 OB in "Guys in the Truck," followed by "Corkscrews!," "Patrick Pearse Motel," Bdwy in "Guys in the Truck" (1983).

GLEASON, JOANNA. Born June 2, 1950 in Toronto, CAN. Graduate UCLA. Bdwy debut 1977 in "I Love My Wife" for which she received a Theatre World Award, OB in "A Hell of a Town."

Jim
Charles

Tina
Chen

Charles "Honi"
Coles

Terry Ashe
Croft

Keene
Curtis

Jane
Culley

Marlene
Danielle

Frank
DeSal

Judy
Dewey

Anthony
DiNovi

Sally
Dunn

Craig
Dudley

John
Eames

Barbara
eda-Young

David
Engel

Wendy
Edmead

Giancarlo
Esposito

Debra
Engle

Elf
Fairservis

Lou
Ferguson

Jane
Fleiss

Barry
Ford

Susanna
Frazer

Richard
Frish

Greg
Ganakas

Becky
Garrett

Edmond
Genest

Cheryl
Giannini

Steven
Gilborn

Joanna
Gleason

207

GLOVER, JOHN. Born Aug. 7, 1944 in Kingston, NY. Attended Towson State Col. Debut 1969 OB in "A Scent of Flowers," followed by "Government Inspector," "Rebel Women," "Treats," "Booth," "Criminal Minds," "The Fairy Garden," Bdwy in "The Selling of the President," "Great God Brown," "Don Juan," "The Visit," "Chemin de Fer," "Holiday," "The Importance of Being Earnest," "Frankenstein," "Whodunnit."

GLUSHAK, JOANNA. Born May 27, 1958 in NYC. Attended NYU. Debut 1983 OB in "Lenny and the Heartbreakers," Bdwy in "Sunday in the Park with George" (1984).

GODFREY, LYNNIE. Born Sept. 11, 1952 in NYC. Graduate Hunter Col. Debut 1976 OB in "I Paid My Dues," followed by "Two Fish in the Sky," "A . . . My Name Is Alice," Bdwy 1978 in "Eubie!"

GOETZ, PETER MICHAEL. Born Dec. 10, 1941 in Buffalo, NY. Graduate SUNY/Fredonia, Southern ILU. Debut 1980 OB in "Jail Diary of Albie Sachs," followed by Bdwy in "Ned and Jack" (1981), "Beyond Therapy," "The Queen and the Rebels," "Brighton Beach Memoirs."

GOLD, ARI. Born Feb. 11, 1974 in NYC. Debut 1983 OB in "The Music Man."

GOLD, DAVID. Born Feb. 2, 1929 in NYC. Attended Antioch Col. Bdwy bow 1955 in "Red Roses for Me," followed by "Copper and Brass," "New Girl in Town," "Redhead," "Greenwillow," "Do Re Mi," "We Take the Town," "Little Me," "Pleasures and Palaces," "Drat! The Cat!," "Sweet Charity," "Education of Hyman Kaplan," "Lorelei," "On Your Toes," OB in "The Trial," "Metamorphosis," "If Five Years Pass," "Carefree Tree," "Dandelion Wine."

GOLDEN, ANNIE. Born Oct. 19, 1951 in Brooklyn, NY. Bdwy debut 1977 in "Hair," OB in "Dementos," "Dr. Selavy's Magic Theatre."

GOLDSMAN, LYNNE. Born May 25, 1962 in Niagra Falls, NY. Debut 1983 OB in "The Music Man."

GONZALEZ, ERNESTO. Born Apr. 8, 1940 in San Juan, PR. Bdwy debut 1953 in "Camino Real," followed by "The Saint of Bleecker St.," "The Innkeepers," "Cut of the Axe," "Ride the Winds," "The Strong Are Lonely," "Oh, Dad, Poor Dad . . .," "The Leaf People," OB in "The Kitchen," "Secret Concubine," "Life Is a Dream," "The Marquise."

GONZALEZ, MARCIAL. Born Mar. 1, 1958 in NYC. Debut 1973 OB in "Hot 1 Baltimore," Bdwy in "Marilyn" (1983).

GOODMAN, DODY. Born Oct. 28, 1915 in Columbus, OH. Bdwy debut 1947 in "High Button Shoes," followed by "Miss Libery," "Call Me Madam," "Wonderful Town," "Fiorello!," "A Rainy Day in Newark," "My Daughter, Your Son," "Front Page," "Lorelei," OB in "Shoestring Revue," "Shoestring '57," "Parade," "New Cole Porter Revue," "Ah, Wilderness!"

GOODMAN, JOHN. Born June 20, 1952 in St. Louis, MO. Graduate Southwerst MoStateU. Debut 1978 OB in "A Midsummer Night's Dream," followed by "The Chisholm Trail," "Henry IV Part II," "Ghosts of the Loyal Oaks," "Half a Lifetime," "Marathon '84."

GOODMAN, LISA. born in Detroit, MI. Attended UMi. Debut 1982 OB in "Talking With," followed by "The First Warning," "The Show-Off," "Escape from Riverdale."

GOODWIN, LYNN. Born Sept. 17, 1958 in Adak, AK. Graduate Yale U. Debut 1982 OB in "The Gnostics," followed by "Baseball Wives," "The Ninth Step."

GORDON, MARK. Born in NYC. Attended AmThWing. OB in "Desire under the Elms," "Man Who Never Died," "The Iceman Cometh," "Deep Are the Roots," "The Caretaker," "The Third Ear," "Conerico Was Here to Stay," "Spookhouse," Bdwy in "Moon Beseiged" (1962), "Compulsion," "The Devils," "Of Mice and Men."

GORMAN, ANDREW. Born May 16, 1951 in Chicago, IL. Graduate KanStateU. Debut 1983 OB in "The Buck Stops Here," followed by "A Touch of the Poet."

GOTLIEB, BEN. Born June 27, 1954 in Kfar Saba, Israel. Attended RADA, CUNY, Bklyn Col. Bdwy debut 1979 in "Dogg's Hamlet and Cahoot's Macbeth," OB in "Kohlhass," "Relatively Speaking," "The Underlings."

GOULD, MURIEL. Born Oct. 12, 1928 in Brooklyn, NY. Graduate Bklyn Col., Columbia U. Debut 1975 OB in "A Little Night Music," followed by "Pelicans Please Mute."

GOULET, CLIFF. Born Oct. 18, 1951 in Lawrence, MA. Attended N.EssexComCol., NewEng. Consv. Debut 1984 OB in "Up in Central Park," followed by "After Today."

GOUTMAN, CHRISTOPHER. Born Dec. 19, 1952 in Bryn Mawr, PA. Graduate Haverford Col., Carnegie-Mellon U. Debut 1978 OB in "The Promise" for which he received a Theatre World Award, followed by "Grand Magic," "The Skirmishers," "Imaginary Lovers," "Balm in Gilead."

GRAAE, JASON. Born May 15, 1958 in Chicago, IL. Graduate Cincinnati Consv. Debut 1981 OB in "Godspell," followed by "Snoopy," "Heaven on Earth," "Promenade," Bdwy 1982 in "Do Black Patent Leather Shoes Really Reflect Up?"

GRADL, CHRISTINE. Born June 29, 1960 in St. Louis, MO. Attended KentStateU. Bdwy debut 1982 in "Do Black Patent Leather Shoes Really Reflect Up?," followed by "Marilyn."

GRAFF, RANDY. Born May 23, 1955 in Brooklyn, NY. Graduate Wagner Col. Debut 1978 OB in "Pins and Needles," followed by "Station Joy," "A . . . My Name Is Alice," Bdwy in "Sarava," "Grease."

GRAFF, TODD. Born Oct. 22, 1959 in NYC. Attended SUNY/Purchase. Debut 1983 OB in "American Passion," Bdwy in "Baby" (1983) for which he received a Theatre World Award.

GRAMMIS, ADAM. Born Dec. 8, 1947 in Allentown, PA. Graduate Kutztown State Col. Bdwy debut 1971 in "Wild and Wonderful," followed by "Shirley MacLaine Show," "A Chorus Line," OB in "Dance Continuum," "Joseph and the Amazing Technicolor Dreamcoat."

GRANT, EVA. Born Nov. 1, 1961 in NYC. Bdwy debut 1970 in "The Grass Harp," OB in "Nymph Errant," "Casanova."

GRAY, KEVIN. Born Feb. 25, 1958 in Westport, CT. Graduate Duke U. Debut 1982 OB in "Lola," followed by "Pacific Overtures," "Family Snapshots."

GRAY, SAM. Born July 18, 1923 in Chicago, IL. Graduate Columbia U. Bdwy debut 1955 in "Deadfall," followed by "Six Fingers in a Five Finger Glove," "Saturday, Sunday, Monday," "Golda," "A View from the Bridge," OB in "Ascent of F-6," "Family Portrait," "One Tiger on a Hill," "Shadow of Heroes," "The Recruiting Officer," "The Wild Duck," "Jungle of Cities," "3 Acts of Recognition," "Returnings," "A Little Madness," "The Danube."

GREEN, DEL. Born July 8, 1938 in Pocatello, ID. Bdwy debut 1967 in "Illya, Darling," followed by "Love-Suicide at Schofield Barracks," "How to Succeed in Business," OB in "Archy and Mehitabel," "Slight Ache," "Bittersuite."

GREENBERG, MITCHELL. Born Sept. 19, 1950 in Brooklyn, NY. Graduate Harpur Col., Neighborhood Playhouse. Debut 1979 OB in "Two Grown Men," followed by "Scrambled Feet," "A Christmas Carol," "A Thurber Carnival," "Isn't It Romantic." Bdwy in "A Day in Hollywood/A Night in the Ukraine" (1980), "Can-Can" (1981), "Marilyn."

GREENE, ELLEN. Born Feb. 22 in NYC. Attended Ryder Col. Debut 1973 in "Rachel Lily Rosenbloom," followed OB by "In the Boom Boom Room," "Threepenny Opera," "Disrobing the Bride," "The Little Shop of Horrors," Bdwy 1981 in "The Little Prince and the Aviator."

GREENE, JAMES. Born Dec. 1, 1926 in Lawrence, MA. Graduate Emerson Col. OB in "The Iceman Cometh," "American Gothic," "The King and the Duke," "The Hostage," "Plays for Bleecker Street," "Moon in the Yellow River," "Misalliance," "Government Inspector," "Baba Goya," LCRep 2 years, "You Can't Take It With You," "School for Scandal," "Wild Duck," "Right You Are," "The Show-Off," "Pantagleize," "Festival of Short Plays," "Nourish the Beast," "One Crack Out," "Artichoke," "Othello," "Salt Lake City Skyline," "Summer," "The Rope Dancers," "Frugal Repast," "Bella Figura," "The Freak," "Park Your Car in the Harvard Yard," "Pigeons on the Walk," "Endgame," "Great Days," Bdwy in "Romeo and Juliet," "Girl on the Via Flaminia," "Compulsion," "Inherit the Wind," "Shadow of a Gunman," "Andersonville Trial," "Night Life," "School for Wives," "Ring Round the Bathtub," "Great God Brown," "Don Juan," "Foxfire," "Play Memory."

GREENE, REUBEN. Born Nov. 24, 1938 in Philadelphia, PA. With APA in "?War and Peace," "You Can't Take It with You," and "Pantagleize," OB in "Jerico-Jim Crow," "Happy Ending," "Boys in the Band," "Twilight Dinner," "Adam," "American Dreams."

GREENE, RICHARD. Born Jan. 8, 1946 in Miami, FL. Graduate FlaAtlanticU. Debut 1971 OB in "Macbeth," followed by "Play Strindberg," "Mary Stuart," "The Crucible," "Family Business," "Richard III," Bdwy in "Romeo and Juliet" (1977), "The Survivor."

GRIER, DAVID ALAN. Born June 30, 1955 in Detroit, MI. Graduate UMich, Yale. Bdwy debut 1981 in "The First" for which he received a Theatre World Award, followed by "Dreamgirls," OB in "A Soldier's Play," "Richard III."

GRIESEMER, JOHN. Born Dec. 5, 1947 in Elizabeth, NJ. Graduate Dickinson Col. URI. Debut 1981 OB in "Turnbuckle," followed by "Death of a Miner," "Little Victories," "Macbeth."

GRIMES, TAMMY. Born Jan. 30, 1934 in Lynn, MA. Attended Stephens Col., Neighborhood Playhouse. Debut 1956 OB in "The Littlest Revue," followed by "Clerambard," "Molly," "Trick," "Are You Now or Have You Ever Been," "Father's Day," "A Month in the Country," "Sunset," Bdwy in "Look After Lulu" (1959) for which she received a Theatre World Award. "The Unsinkable Molly Brown," "Rattle of a Simple Man," "High Spirit," "The Only Game in Town," "Private Lives," "Musical Jubilee," "California Suite," "Tartuffe," "42nd Street," "Pal Joey in Concert."

GROENENDAAL, CRIS. Born Feb. 17, 1948 in Erie, PA. Attended Allegheny Col, Exeter U, HB Studio. Bdwy debut 1979 in "Sweeney Todd," followed by "Sunday in the Park with George," OB in "Francis," "Sweethearts in Concert."

GROENER, HARRY. Born Sept. 10, 1951 in Augsburg, Ger. Graduate UWash. Bdwy debut 1979 in "Oklahoma!," for which he received a Theatre World Award, followed by "Oh, Brother!," "Is There Life after High School," "Cats," OB in "Beside the Seaside."

GROVES, ROBIN. Born Nov. 24, 1951 in Neenah, WI. Graduate Hollins Col. Bdwy debut 1976 in "Lady from the Sea," OB in "Vanities" (1978), "Starluster," "Territorial Rites," "The Carpenters," "Weekend Near Madison."

GRUENEBERG, WILLIAM. Born Mar. 8, 1955 in Santa Monica, CA. Attended CalStateU. Debut 1983 OB in "Twelfth Night."

GUIDALL, GEORGE. Born June 7, 1938 in Plainfield, NJ. Attended UBuffalo, AADA. Bdwy debut 1969 in "Wrong Way Light Bulb," followed by "Cold Storage," OB in "Counsellor-at-Law," "Taming of the Shrew," "All's Well That Ends Well," "The Art of Dining," "Biography," "After All," "Cinders," "Henry V."

GUIDO, MICHAEL. Born Jan 13, 1950 in Woodside, NY. Graduate U South Fl., Brandeis U. Debut 1982 OB in "The Workroom," followed by "Strictly Dishonorable:"

GUNTON, BOB. Born Nov. 15, 1945 in Santa Monica, CA. Attended UCal. Debut 1971 OB in "Who Am I?," followed by "The Kid," "Desperate Hours," "Tip-Toes," "How I Got That Story," "Hamlet," "Death of Von Richthofen," "The Man Who Could See Through Time," Bdwy in "Happy End" (1977), "Working,""King of Hearts," "Evita," "Passion."

GUSKIN, HAROLD. Born May 25, 1941 in Brooklyn, NY. Graduate Rutgers U, Indiana U. Debut 1980 OB in "Second Avenue Rag," followed by "Grand Street," "Crazy for You Revue," "Bold Stroke for a Wife," "Laughing Stock."

GUTIERREZ, GERALD. Born Feb. 3, 1950 in Brooklyn, NY. Graduate SUNY/Stonybrook, Juilliard. Debut 1972 OB in "School for Scandal," followed by "Lower Depths," "U.S.A.," "The Hostage," "The Time of Your Life," "The Cradle Will Rock," "Isn't It Romantic," Bdwy in," "Measure for Measure," (1977), "Beggar's Opera," "Scapin," "Three Sisters.

HACK, STEVEN. Born Apr. 20, 1958 in St. Louis, MO. Attended CalArts, AADA, Debut 1978 OB in "The Coolest Cat in Town," followed by Bdwy in "Cats" (1982).

HACKETT, JEAN. Born Aug. 28, 1956 in York, PA. Graduate NYU, RADA. Debut 1983 OB in "Ah, Wilderness!"

HADARY, JONATHAN. Born Oct. 11, 1948 in Chicago, IL. Attended Tufts U. Debut 1974 OB in "White Nights," followed by "El Grande de Coca-Cola," "Songs from Pins and Needles," "God Bless You, Mr. Rosewater," "Pushing 30," "Scrambled Feet," "Coming Attractions," "Tom-foolery," Bdwy in "Gemini," (1977/also OB), "Torch Song Trilogy.

HAGAN, PETER. Form Oct. 3, 1954 in Alexandria, VA. Graduate UVa. Debut 1980 OB in "Class Enemy," followed by "Scenes from American Life," "Contrast."

HALL, GEORGE. Born Nov. 19, 1916 in Toronto, Can. Attended Neighborhood Playhouse. Bdwy bow 1946 in "Call Me Mister," followed by "Lend an Ear," "Touch and Go," "Live Wire," "The Boy Friend," "There's a Girl in My Soup," "An Evening with Richard Nixon .," "We Interrupt This Program," "Man and Superman," "Bent," OB in "The Balcony," "Ernest in Love," "A Round with Rings," "Family Pieces," "Carousel," "The Case Against Roberta Guardino," "Marry Me!" "Arms and the Man," "The Old Glory," "Dancing for the Kaiser," "Casualties," "The Seagull," "A Stitch in Time," "Mary Stuart," "No End of Blame," "Hamlet," "Colette Collage," "The Homecoming," "And a Nightingale Sang."

HALL, PHILIP BAKER. Born Sept. 10, 1934 in Toledo, OH. Debut 1961 OB in "Donogoo," followed by "The Skin of Our Teeth," "In White America," "World of Gunter Grass," "The Fantasticks," "Gorky," "Secret Honor."

HAMILTON, RICHARD. Born Dec. 31, 1920 in Chicago, IL. Attended Pasadena Jr. Col. Bdwy debut 1952 in "First Lady," (CC), followed by "Cloud 7," "Blood, Sweat and Stanley Poole," "Scratch," "Anna Christie" (77),"A Touch of the Poet," "Morning's at 7," OB in "The Exception and the Rule," "The Bench," "Siamese Connections," "Cream Cheese," "Buried Child," "Fool for Love."

HAMLIN, HARRY. Born Oct. 30, 1951 in Pasadena, CA. Yale graduate. Bdwy debut 1984 in "Awake and Sing."

HAMMER, MARK. Born Apr. 28, 1937 in San Jose, CA. Graduate Stanford, Catholic U. Debut 1966 OB in "Journey of the Fifth Horse," followed by "Witness for the Prosecution," "Cymbeline," "Richard III," Bdwy in "Much Ado about Nothing" (1972).

HANAN, STEPHEN. Born Jan 7, 1947 in Washington, DC. Graduate Harvard, LAMDA. Debut 1978 OB in "All's Well That Ends Well," followed by "Taming of the Shrew," Bdwy in "Pirates of Penzance" (1978), "Cats."

HANDLER, EVAN. Born Jan. 10, 1961 in NYC. Attended Juilliard. Debut 1979 OB in "Biography: A Game," followed by "Strider," "Final Orders," "Marathon '84," "Found a Peanut," Bdwy in "Solomon's Child."

HANDY, JAMES. Born Mar. 19 in NYC. Graduate CCNY. Debut 1983 OB in "Big Maggie," followed by "Kerouac," "Ice Bridge."

HANNUM, KRISTIE. Born June 12, 1955 in Memphis, TN. Graduate Principia Col. Debut 1979 OB in "On a Clear Day You Can See Forever," followed by "Annie Get Your Gun," "Red, Hot and Blue."

HAO, WILLIAM. Born Aug. 10, 1953 in Honolulu, HI. Attended Chaminade Col., Leeward Col. Debut 1981 OB in "The Shining House," followed by "Gaugin in Tahiti," "Teahouse," "A Midsummer Night's Dream," "Rain."

HARA, MARY. Born in Nebraska. Bdwy debut 1968 in "Rosencrantz and Guildenstern Are Dead," followed by "Waltz of the Toreadors," OB in "The Kitchen," "Glorious Ruler," "Dona Rosita," "Americans."

HARLEY, CHARLES W. Born June 29, 1934 in NYC. Graduate Antioch Col. Bdwy debut 1974 in "The Candidate," OB in "The Divine Comedy," "Trial of Adam Clayton Powell, Jr."

HARNEY, BEN. Born Aug. 29, 1952 in Brooklyn, NY. Bdwy debut 1971 in "Purlie," followed by "Pajama Game," "Tree-Monisha," "Pippin," "Dreamgirls," OB in "Don't Bother Me I Can't Cope," "The Derby," "The More You Get."

HARPER, JAMES. Born Oct. 8, 1948 in Bell, CA. Attended Marin Col., Juilliard. Bdwy debut 1973 in "King Lear," followed by "The Robber Bridegroom," "The Time of Your Life," "Mother Courage," "Edward II," OB in "A Midsummer Night's Dream," "Recruiting Officer," "The Wild Duck," "The Jungle of Cities," "The Cradle Will Rock," "All the Nice People."

HARRELSON, HELEN. Born in Missouri; Goodman Theatre graduate. Bdwy debut 1950 in "The Cellar and the Well," followed by "Death of a Salesman," "Days in the Trees," "Romeo and Juliet," OB in "Our Town," "His and Hers," "House of Atreus," "He and She," "Missing Persons," "Laughing Stock."

HARRIS, BAXTER. Born Nov. 18, 1940 in Columbus, KS. Attended UKan. Debut 1967 OB in "America Hurrah," followed by "The Reckoning," "Wicked Women Revue," "More than You Deserve," "Pericles," "him," "Battle of Angels," "Down by the River," "Selma," "Ferocious Kisses," "Three Sisters," "Gradual Clearing," "Dolphin Position," "Paradise Lost," "Ghosts."

HARRIS, ED. Born in 1950 in Tenafly, NJ. Debut 1983 OB in "Fool for Love."

HARRIS, NIKI. Born July 20, 1948 in Pittsburgh, PA. Graduate Duquesne U. Bdwy debut 1980 in "A Day in Hollywood/A Night in the Ukraine," followed by "My One and Only."

HARRIS, RONALD LEW. Born May 29, 1953 in Louisville, KY. Graduate Moorehead State U, AADA. Debut 1976 OB in "Compulsion," followed by "Between Time and Timbuktu," "Going Home," "Midsummer Night's Dream," "Mandrake," "Three Cockolds," "Two Gentlemen of Verona," "Taming of the Shrew," "Julius Caesar," "Henry V."

HARRIS, ROSEMARY. Born Sept. 19, 1930 in Ashby, Eng. Attended RADA. Bdwy debut 1952 in "Climate of Eden" for which she received a Theatre World Award, followed by "Troilus and Cressida," "Interlock," "The Disenchanted," "The Tumbler," "Lion in Winter," "Old Times," "Merchant of Venice," "A Streetcar Named Desire," "The Royal Family," "Heartbreak House," APA's "The Tavern," "School for Scandal," "The Seagull," "Importance of Being Earnest," "War and Peace," "Man and Superman," "Judith" and "You Can't Take It with You," OB in "The New York Idea," "Three Sisters," "The Seagull."

HARRIS, TOMMY. Born May 23, 1972 in Hackensack, NJ. Debut 1983 OB in "Ah, Wilderness!"

HARRIS, VIOLA. Born Sept 14, 1928 in NYC. Graduate Hunter Col., Northwestern U. Debut 1948 on Bdwy in "On the Town," followed by "Zelda," OB in "3 Steps Down," "Berkeley Square," "Ivanov."

HARRISON, REX. Born Mar. 5, 1908 in Huyten, Eng. Attended Liverpool Col. Bdwy debut 1936 in "Sweet Aloes," followed by "Anne of a Thousand Days," "Bell, Book and Candle," "Venus Observed," "Love of Four Colonels," "My Fair Lady" (1956/1981), "Fighting Cock," "Emperor Henry IV," "In Praise of Love," "Caesar and Cleopatra," "The Kingfisher," "Heartbreak House."

HART, KITTY CARLISLE. See Carlisle

HART, ROXANNE. Born in 1952 in Trenton, NJ. Attended Skidmore, Princton U. Bdwy debut 1977 in "Equus," followed by "Loose Ends," "Passion," OB in "A Winter's Tale," "Johnny On a Spot," "The Purging," "Hedda Gabler," "Waiting for the Parade," "La Brea Tarpits," "Marathon '84."

HARTMAN, ELEK. Born Apr. 26, 1922 in Canton, OH. Graduate Carnegie Tech. OB in "Where People Gather," "Loa," "Loyalties," "Matchmaker," "Mirandolina," "Cassett," "Artists and Admirers," "Barber of Seville," "Daydreams," Bdwy in "We Bombed in New Haven" (1968), "Angel."

HARUM, EIVIND. Born May 24, 1944 in Stavanger, Norway. Attended Utah State U. Credits include "Sophie," "Foxy," "Baker Street," "West Side Story" ('68), "A Chorus Line," "Woman of the Year."

HAUSMAN, ELAINE. Born June 8, 1949 in Sacramento, CA. Graduate UCal, Juilliard. Bdwy debut 1975 in "The Robber Bridegroom," followed by "Edward II," "The Time of Your Life," "Three Sisters," "Brigadoon," OB in "Top Girls," "Photographer."

HAWKINS, TRISH. Born Oct. 30, 1945 in Hartford, CT. Attended Radcliffe, Neighborhood Playhouse. Debut OB 1970 in "Oh! Calcutta!" followed by "Iphigenia," "The Hot 1 Baltimore" for which she received a Theatre World Award, "him," "Come Back, Little Sheba," "Battle of Angels," "Mound Builders," "The Farm," "Ulysses in Traction," "Lulu," "Hogan's Folly," "Twelfth Night," "A Tale Told," "Great Grandson of Jedediah Kohler," "Time Framed," "Levitations." Bdwy 1977 in "Some of My Best Friends," "Talley's Folly" (1979).

HAYES, JANET. Born June 11 in Shanghai, China. Graduate NewEngConsv, Hunter Col. Bdwy debut 1954 in "The Golden Apple," followed by "Anyone Can Whistle," "Camelot," "Music Man," "Damn Yankees," OB in "Boys from Syracuse," "A Touch of the Poet," "Plain and Fancy," "Candide," "Rain," "The Subject Was Roses," "Relatively Speaking," "Nude with Violin," "The Buck Stops Here."

HAYNES, TIGER. Born Dec. 13, 1907 in St. Croix, VI. Bdwy bow 1956 in "New Faces," followed by "Finian's Rainbow," "Fade Out-Fade In," "Pajama Game," "The Wiz," "A Broadway Musical," "Comin' Uptown," OB in "Turns," "Bags," "Louis," "Taking My Turn."

HEADLY, GLENNE. Born Mar. 13, 1955 in New London, CT. Graduate AmCol.Switzerland. Debut 1983 OB in "Extremities," followed by "The Philanthropist" for which she received a Theatre World Award, "Balm in Gilead."

HEALD, ANTHONY. Born Aug. 25, 1944 in New Rochelle, NY. Graduate MiStateU. Debut 1980 OB in "The Glass Menagerie," followed by "Misalliance" for which he received a Theatre World Award, "The Caretaker," "The Fox," "Quartermaine's Terms," "The Philanthropist," Bdwy in "The Wake of Jamey Foster" (1982).

HEALY, CHRISTINE. Born June 13 in Buffalo, NY. Graduate UCSanta Barbara. Debut 1984 OB in 'Tierra Nova."

HEARN, GEORGE. Born June 18, 1934 in St. Louis, MO. Graduate Southwestern Col. OB in "Macbeth," "Antony and Cleopatra," "As You Like It," "Richard III," "Merry Wives of Windsor," "Midsummer Night's Dream," "Hamlet," "Horseman, Pass By," Bdwy in "A Time for Singing," The Changing Room," "An Almost Perfect Person," "I Remember Mama," "Watch on the Rhine," "Sweeney Todd," "A Doll's Life," "Whodunnit," "La Cage aux Folles."

HEDGES, MARTA. Born Mar. 30, 1961 in Lansing, MI. Graduate Western Mich. U. Debut 1984 OB in "Sing Me Sunshine."

HEINEMAN, LAURIE. Born Aug. 4 in Chicago, IL. Graduate Radcliffe Col. Debut 1959 in "The Miracle Worker," OB in "The Orphan" (1973), followed by "Close Relations," "The American Clock," "Letters Home," "Goodnight, Grandpa," "Sympathy."

HELLER, ROBERT. Born Dec. 26, 1930 in Brooklyn, NY. Attended Actors Studio. Debut 1955 OB in "Terrible Swift Sword," followed by "The Cradle Will Rock," "My Prince, My King," "Waiting for Lefty," "Upside-Down on the Handlebars," "Briss," "Cabal of Hypocrites," Bdwy in "Marathon '33" (1963).

HENDERSON, JO. Born in Buffalo, NY. Attended WMiU. OB in "Camille," "Little Foxes," "An Evening with Merlin Finch," "20th Century Tar," "A Scent of Flowers," "Revival," "Dandelion Wine," "My Life," "Ladyhouse Blues," "Fallen Angels," "Waiting for the Parade," "Threads," "Bella Figura," "Details without a Map," "The Middle Ages," "Time Framed," "Isn't It Romantic," Bdwy in "Rose" (1981), "84 Charing Cross Road," "Play Memory."

HENIG, ANDI. Born May 6 in Washington, DC. Attended Yale. Debut 1978 OB in "One and One," followed by "Kind Lady," Bdwy in "Oliver!" (1984).

HENNESSEY, NINA. Born July 1, 1957 in Deven, CO. Graduate Barnard Col. Debut 1979 OB in "Sweet Mainstreet," followed by "Odyssey," "Close Enough for Jazz," "Cummings and Goings."

HENRITZE, BETTE. Born May 3 in Betsy Layne, KY. Graduate UTenn. OB in "Lion in Love," "Abe Lincoln in Illinois," "Othello," "Baal," "Long Christmas Dinner," "Queens of France," "Rimers of Eldritch," "Displaced Person," "Acquisition," "Crime of Passion," "Happiness Cage," "Henry VI," "Richard III," "Older People," "Lotta," "Catsplay," "A Month in the Country," Bdwy in "Jenny Kissed Me" (1948), "Pictures in the Hallway," "Giants, Sons of Giants," "Ballad of the Sad Cafe," "The White House," "Dr. Cook's Garden," "Here's Where I Belong," "Much Ado about Nothing," "Over Here," "Angel Street," "Man and Superman," "Macbeth" (1981), "Present Laughter."

HERMAN, DANNY. Born Nov. 2, 1960 in Pittsburgh, PA. Debut 1979 OB in "Big Bad Burlesque," Bdwy in "A Chorus Line" (1981).

HERNDON, JAN LEIGH. Born Apr. 9, 1955 in Raleigh, NC. Graduate VaIntermontCol. Bdwy debut 1982 in "A Chorus Line," followed by "La Cage aux Folles," OB in "Joan and the Devil."

HEWETT, CHRISTOPHER. Born Apr. 5 in England. Bdwy debut 1957 in "My Fair Lady," followed by "First Impressions," "Unsinkable Molly Brown," "Kean," "The Affair," "Hadrian VII," "Music Is," "Peter Pan" (1980), "Sweethearts in Concert," OB in "Tobias and the Angel," "Trelawny of the Wells," "Finian's Rainbow," "New Jerusalem."

HEYMAN, BARTON. Born Jan. 24, 1937. in Washington, DC. Attended UCLA. Bdwy debut 1969 in "Indians," followed by "Trial of the Catonsville 9," "A Talent for Murder," OB in "A Midsummer Night's Drean," "Sleep," "Phantasmagoria Historia," "Enclave," "Henry V," "A Private View."

HICKS, LOIS DIANE. Born Sept. 3, 1940 in Brooklyn, NY. Attended NYCC, AADA. Debut 1979 OB in "On a Clear Day You Can See Forever," followed by "A Yank in Beverly Hills," "Rose Dancers," "Marching to Georga," "The Heiress," "Divine Fire," "The Itch."

HIGGINS, MICHAEL. Born Jan. 20, 1926 in Brooklyn, NY. Attended AmThWing. Bdwy bow 1946 in "Antigone," followed by "Our Lan'," "Romeo and Juliet," "The Crucible," "The Lark," "Equus," "Whose Life Is It Anyway?," OB in "White Devil," "Carefree Tree," "Easter," "The Queen and the Rebels," "Sally, George and Martha," "L'Ete," "Uncle Vanya," "The Iceman Cometh," "Molly," "Artichoke," "Reunion," "Chieftans," "A Tale Told," "Richard II," "The Sea Gull," "Levitations."

HIGLEN, DAVID. Born Aug. 9, 1952 in San Bernardino, CA. Graduate Stephens Col. Debut 1981 on Bdwy in "Heartland," OB in "The Brooklyn Bridge."

HILLARY, ANN. Born Jan 8, 1931 in Jellico, TN. Attended Northwestern U., AADA. Bdwy debut 1953 in "Be Your Age," followed by "Separate Tables," "The Lark," OB in "Dark of the Moon," "Paradise Lost."

HIRSCH, JUDD. Born Mar. 15, 1935 in NYC. Attended AADA. Bdwy debut 1966 in "Barefoot in the Park," followed by "Chapter Two," "Talley's Folly," OB in "On the Necessity of Being Polygamous," "Scuba Duba," "Mystery Play," "Hot 1 Baltimore," "Prodigal," "Knock Knock," "Life and/or Death," "Talley's Folly," "The Sea Gull."

HO, WAI CHING. Born Nov. 16, 1943 in Hong Kong. Graduate UHK, AADA. Debut 1968 OB in "People vs Ranchman," followed by "Moon on a Rainbow Shawl," "Song for Nisei Fisherman."

HODES, GLORIA. Born Aug. 20 in Norwich, CT. Bdwy debut 1969 in "Gantry," OB in "The Club" for which she received a Theatre World Award, "Cycles of Fancy," "The Heroine."

HODES, RYN. Born Dec. 28, 1956 in NYC. Graduate NYU. Debut 1979 OB in "Miradolina," followed by "Boy Meets Swan," " A Collier's Friday Night," "Suicide in B Flat," "Kaspar," "Fanshen," "Holy Terrors."

HOFFMAN, DUSTIN. Born Aug. 8, 1937 in Los Angeles, CA. Attended Santa Monica Col., Pasadena Playhouse. Bdwy debut 1963 in "A Cook for Mr. General," followed by "The Subject Was Roses," "Jimmy Shine," "Death of a Salesman" (1984), OB in "A View from the Bridge," "Harry, Noon and Night," 'Journey of the 5th Horse," "Eh?" for which he received a Theatre World Award.

HOFFMAN, JANE. Born July 24 in Seattle, WA. Graduate UCal. Bdwy debut 1940 in "Tis of Thee," followed by "Crazy with the Heat," "Something for the Boys," "One Touch of Venus," "Calico Wedding," "Mermaids Singing," "Temporary Island," "Story for Strangers," "Two Blind Mice," "The Rose Tattoo," "The Crucible," "Witness for the Prosecution," "Third Best Sport," "Rhinoceros," "Mother Courage and Her Children," "Fair Game for Lovers," "A Murderer Among Us," "Murder Among Friends," OB in "American Dream," "Sandbox," "Picnic on the Battlefield," "Theatre of the Absurd," "Child Buyer," "A Corner of the Bed," "Slow Memories," "Last Analysis," "Dear Oscar," "Hocus-Pocus," "Lessons," "The Art of Dining," "Second Avenue Rag," "One Tiger to a Hill," "Isn't It Romantic," 'Alto Part," "Marathon '84."

HOFFMAN, PHILIP. Born May 12, 1954 in Chicago, IL. Graduate UIl. Bdwy debut 1981 in "The Moony Shapiro Songbook," followed by "Is There Life after High School?" "Baby," OB in "The Fabulous '50's."

HOGAN, JONATHAN. Born June 13, 1951 in Chicago, IL. Graduate Goodman Theatre. Debut OB 1972 in "The Hot l Baltimore," followed by "Mound Builders," "Harry Outside," "Cabin 12," "5th of July," "Glorious Morning," "Innocent Thoughts, Harmless Intentions," "Sunday Runners," "Threads," "Time Framed," "Balm in Gilead," Bdwy in "Comedians" (1976), "Otherwise Engaged," "5th of July," "The Caine Mutiny Court Martial."

HOLBROOK, RUBY. Born Aug. 28, 1930 in St. John's,Nfd. Attended Denison U. Debut 1963 OB in "Abe Lincoln in Illinois," followed by "Hamlet," "James Joyce's Dubliners," "Measure for Measure," "The Farm," "Do You Still Believe the Rumor?," "The Killing of Sister George," Bdwy in "Da" (1979), "5th of July."

HOLMES, GEORGE. Born June 3, 1935 in London, Eng. Graduate ULondon. Debut 1978 OB in "The Changeling," followed by "Love from a Stranger," "The Hollow," "The Story of the Gadsbys," "Learned Ladies," "The Land Is Bright."

HOLMES, HEATHER. Born Sept. 6, 1956 in Worland, Wy. Attended UUtah, NebStateCol. Debut 1979 OB in "Ah, Wilderness!," followed by "June Moon," "Our Hearts Were Young and Gay," "The Grass Harp," "Strictly Dishonorable."

HOLMES, SCOTT. Born May 30, 1952 in West Grove, PA. Graduate Catawba Col Bdwy debut 1979 in "Grease," followed by "Evita," "The Rink."

HONDA, CAROL A. Born Nov. 20 in Kealakekua, HI. Graduate UHi. Debut 1983 OB in "Yellow Fever," followed by "Empress of China."

HOPKINS, BRUCE. Born Jan 4, 1948 in Wilkes-Barre, PA. Graduate Bloomsburg State Col. Debut 1973 OB in "The Faggot," followed by La Gran Scena Opera Co., "Love, Sex and Violence."

HORMANN, NICHOLAS. Born Dec. 22, 1944 in Honolulu, HI. Graduate Oberlin Col., Yale. Bdwy debut 1973 in "The Visit," followed by "Chemin de Fer," "Holiday," "Love for Love," "Rules of the Game," "Member of the Wedding," "St. Joan," "Moose Murders," OB in "Ice Age," "Marco Polo," "Artichoke," "Looking-Glass," "The Dining Room," "A Private View."

HORVATH, JAN. Born Jan. 31, 1958 in Lake Forrest, IL. Graduate Cin.Consv. Bdwy debut 1983 in "Oliver!," OB in "Sing Me Sunshine."

HORWITZ, MURRAY. Born Sept. 28, 1949 in Dayton, OH. Graduate Kenyon Col. Debut 1976 in "An Evening with Sholom Aleichem" (also 1983 revival), "Hard Sell."

HOTY, TONY. Born Sept. 29, 1949 in Lakewood, OH. Attended Ithaca Col., UWVa. Debut 1974 OB in "Godspell" (also Bdwy 1976), followed by "Joseph and the Amazing Technicolor Dreamcoat," "Robin Hood," "Success and Succession."

HOUGHTON, KATHARINE. Born Mar 10, 1945 in Hartford, CT. Graduate Sarah Lawrence Col. Bdwy debut 1965 in "A Very Rich Woman," followed by "The Front Page" (1969), OB in "A Scent of Flowers" for which she received a Theatre World Award, "To Heaven in a Swing."

HOUSEMAN, JOHN. Born Sept. 22, 1902 in Bucharest, Romania. Attended Clifton Col. Made acting debut 1983 in "The Cradle Will Rock."

HOUSTON, JESSICA. Born Apr. 25, 1958 in Warren, PA. Graduate Oberlin Col. Debut 1983 OB in "Promises, Promises," followed by "The Music Man."

HOUTS, ROD. Born Dec. 15, 1906 in Warrensburg, MO. Graduate UMo, NYU, Goodman Theatre. Bdwy debut 1932 in "Lucrece," OB in "Gallery Gods," "The Miracle Worker," "Early Dark," "The Dybbuk," "A Far Country," "Three Sisters," "Exhausting the Possibilities," "The Freak," "Big Apple Messenger."

HOWARD, ARTHUR. Born Jan. 26 in NYC. Graduate Reed Col. Debut 1974 OB in "Decades," followed by "That's It, Folks!," Bdwy in "The Magic Show" (1979).

HOWARD, DAVID. Born Sept. 10, 1928 in Mt. Kisco, NY. Graduate Cornell U. Debut 1964 OB in "Cindy," followed by "Hamp," "Hamlet," "Nude with Violin."

HOXIE, RICHMOND. Born July 21, 1946 in NYC. Graduate Dartmouth Col., LAMDA. Debut 1975 OB in "Shaw for an Evening," followed by "The Family," "Justice," "Landscape with Waitress," "3 from the Marathon," "The Slab Boys," "Vivien," "Operation Midnight Climax," "The Dining Room," "Daddies," "To Gillian on Her 37th Birthday."

HOYT, LON. Born Apr. 6, 1958 in Roslyn, NY. Graduate Cornell U. Bdwy debut 1982 in "Rock 'n' Roll: The First 5000 Years," followed by "Baby."

HUGHES, BARNARD. Born July 16, 1915 in Bedford Hills, NY. Attended Manhattan Col. Credits: OB in "Rosmersholm," "A Doll's House," "Hogan's Ghost," "Lime," "Older People," "Hamlet," "Merry Widows of Windsor," "Pericles," "Three Sisters," "Translations," Bdwy in "The Ivy Green," "Dinosaur Wharf," "The Teahouse of the August Moon," "A Majority of One," "Advise and Consent," "The Advocate," "Hamlet," "I Was Dancing," "Generations," "How Now, Dow Jones?," "Wrong Way Light Bulb," Sheep on the Runway," "Abelard and Heloise," "Much Ado about Nothing," "Uncle Vanya," "The Good Doctor," "All over Town," "Da," "Angels Fall," "End of the World . . ."

HUGHES, LAURA. Born Jan 28, 1959 in NYC. Graduate Neighborhood Playhouse. Debut 1980 OB in "The Diviners," followed by "A Tale Told," "Time Framed," "Fables for Friends."

HUGHES, MICHAELA. Born Mar. 31, 1955 in Morristown, NJ. Debut with Houston Ballet, later with Feld Ballet, and ABT. Bdwy in "On Your Toes" (1983) followed by "Mame."

HULL, BRYAN. Born Sept. 12, 1937 in Amarillo, TX. Attended UNMx, Wayne State U. Bdwy debut 1976 in "Somethin's Afoot," OB in "The Fantasticks."

HUMES, LINDA H. Born Oct. 19, 1955 in NYC. Graduate SUNY/Stonybrook. Debut 1978 OB in "Antigone," followed by "Spirit, Black and Female."

HUNT, LINDA. Born Apr. 2, 1945 in Morristown, NJ. Attended Goodman Th. Debut 1975 OB in "Down by the River . . ." followed by "The Tennis Game," "Metamorphosis in Miniature," "Little Victories," "Top Girls," Bdwy in "Ah, Wilderness!" (1975), "End of the World . . ."

HUNTER, AL NAZARIO. Born Dec. 8, 1954 in NYC. OB in "Testament according to Jean Rousseau," "Leah," "Play Me Zoltan," "Spa," "Cabal of Hypocrites."

HUNTER, HOLLY. Born Mar. 20, 1958 in Atlanta, GA. Graduate Carnegie-Mellon U. Debut 1981 OB in "Battery," "Weekend Near Madison," "The Miss Firecracker Contest," Bdwy in "Crimes of the Heart" (1982), "The Wake of Jamey Foster."

HUNTER, KIM. Born Noc. 12, 1922 in Detroit, MI. Attended Actors Studio. Debut 1947 in "A Streetcar Named Desire," followed by "Darkness at Noon," "The Chase," "The Children's Hour," "The Tender Trap," "Write Me a Murder," "Weekend," "Penny Wars," "The Women," "To Grandmother's House We Go," OB in "Come Slowly, Eden," "All Is Bright," "The Cherry Orchard," "When We Dead Awaken," "Territorial Rites."

HUNTER, PATRICIA. Born Sept. 14, 1954 in Kileen, TX. Graduate Portland State U. OB in "Merry Wives of Windsor," "Victory Bonds," "Phaedra," "Red Peppers," "Asylum."

HURST, LILLIAN. Born Aug. 13, 1949 in San Juan, PR. Attended UPR. Debut 1983 OB in "The Great Confession," followed by "The Cuban Swimmer/Dog Lady," Bdwy in "The Cuban Thing" (1968).

HURST, MELISSA. Born June 8, 1955 in Cleveland, OH. Graduate NYU. Debut 1981 OB in "Dark Ride," followed by "Divine Right," City Theatre Festival.

HURT, MARY BETH. Born in 1948 in Marshalltown, IA. Attended UIa, NYU. Debut 1972 OB in "More Than You Deserve," followed by "As You Like it," "Trelawny of the Wells," "The Cherry Orchard," "Love for Love," "Member of the Wedding," "Boy Meets Girl," "Secret Service," "Father's Day," "Nest of the Wood Grouse." Bdwy in "Crimes of the Heart" (1981), "The Misanthrope."

HURT, WILLIAM. Born Mar. 20, 1950 in Washington, D.C. Graduate Tufts U., Juilliard. Debut 1976 OB in "Henry V," followed by "My Life," "Ulysses in Traction," "Lulu, "5th of July," "The Runner Stumbles." He recieved a 1978 Theatre World Award for his performances with Circle Repertory Theatre, followed by "Hamlet," "Mary Stuart," "Childe Byron," "The Diviners," "Richard II," "The Great Grandson of Jedediah Kohler," "A Midsummer Night's Dream," "Hurlyburly."

IANNUCCI, MICHAEL. Born Feb. 3, 1956 in Philadelphia, PA. Graduate Temple U, RADA. Debut 1983 OB in "Waiting for Lefty."

INGE, MATTHEW. Born May 29, 1950 in Fitchburg, MA. Attended Boston U., Harvard. Bdwy debut 1976 in "Fiddler on the Roof," followed by "A Chorus Line."

INNERARITY, MEMRIE. Born Feb. 11, 1945 in Columbus, MS. Attended USMs. Debut 1976 OB in "The Club," followed by "The Heebie Jeebies," "The Heroine."

INNES, LAURA. Born Aug. 16, 1957 in Pontiac, MI. Graduate Northwestern U. Debut 1982 OB in "Edmond," followed by "My Uncle Sam."

INTROCASO, JOHN C. Born June 3, 1947 in Rutherford, NJ. Graduate St. Peter's Col. Debut 1979 OB in "Sound of Music," followed by "Time and the Conways," "Wild Oates," "Crossroads Cafe."

IRONS, JEREMY. Born Sept. 19, 1948 in Cowes, Eng. Attended Bristol Old Vic School. Bdwy debut 1984 in "The Real Thing."

IRVING, GEORGE S. Born Nov. 1, 1922 in Springfield, MA. Attended Leland Powers Sch. Bdwy bow 1943 in "Oklahoma!," followed by "Call Me Mister," "Along 5th Ave." "Two's Company," "Me and Juliet," "Can-Can," " Shinbone Alley," "Bells Are Ringing," "The Good Soup," "Tovarich," "A Murderer Among Us," "Alfie," "Anya," "Galileo," "4 on a Garden," "An Evening with Richard Nixon," "Irene," "Who's Who in Hell," "All Over Town," "So Long 174th St," "Once in a Lifetime," "I Remember Mama," "Copperfield," "Pirates of Penzance," "On Your Toes," "Rosalie in Concert," "Pal Joey in Concert."

IVEY, DANA. Born Aug. 12, 1941 in Atlanta, GA. Graduate Rollins Col. LAMDA. Bdwy debut 1981 in "Macbeth" (LC), followed by "Present Laughter," "Heartbreak House," "Sunday in the Park with George," OB in "A Call from the East," "Vivien," "Dumping Ground," "Pastorale," "Two Small Bodies," "Candida in Concert," "Major Barbara in Concert," "Quartermaine's Terms," "Baby with the Bathwater."

IVEY, JUDITH. Born Sept. 4, 1951 in El Paso, TX. Bdwy debut 1979 in "Bedroom Farce," followed by "Steaming," "Hurlyburly," OB in "Dulsa, Fish, Stas and Vi," "Sunday Runners," "Second Lady," "Hurlyburly."

JABLONS, KAREN. Born July 19, 1951 in Trenton, NJ. Juilliard graduate. Debut 1969 OB in "The Student Prince," followed by "Sound of Music," "Funny Girl," "Boys from Syracuse," "Sterling Silver," "People in Show Business Make Long Goodbyes," "In Trousers," Bdwy in "Ari," "Two Gentlemen of Verona," "Lorelei," "Where's Charley?," "A Chorus Line."

JACKS, SUSAN J. Born Nov. 5, 1953 in Brooklyn, NY. Graduate SUNY. Debut 1983 OB in "Forbidden Broadway."

JACKSON, ANNE. Born Sept. 3, 1926 in Allegheny, PA. Attended Neighborhood Playhouse. Bdwy debut 1945 in "Signature," followed by "Yellow Jack," "John Gabriel Borkman," "The Last Dance," "Summer and Smoke," "Magnolia Alley," "Love Me Long," "Lady from the Sea," "Never Say Never," "Oh, Men! Oh, Women!," "Rhinoceros," "Luv," "The Exercise," "Inquest," "Promenade All," "Waltz of the Toreadors," "Twice around the Park," OB in "The Tiger," "The Typist," "Marco Polo Sings a Solo," "Diary of Anne Frank," "Nest of the Wood Grouse."

JACKSON, DAVIS. Born Dec. 4, 1948 in Philadelphia, PA. Bdwy debut 1980 in "Eubie!," followed by "My One and Only."

JACOB, STEVEN. Born May 11, 1959 in Lynne, MA. Graduate NYU. Debut 1981 OB in "Florodora," followed by "Bodo," Bdwy in "Merrily We Roll Along" (1981).

JAMES, ELMORE. Born May 3, 1954 in NYC. Graduate SUNY/Purchase. Debut 1970 OB in "Moon on a Rainbow Shawl," followed by "The Ups and Downs of Theopholus Maitland," "Carnival," "Until the Real Thing Comes Along," "A Midsummer Night's Dream," "The Tempest," Bdwy in "But Never Jam Today" (1979), "Your Arms Too Short to Box with God."

JAMES, KRICKER. Born May 17, 1939 in Cleveland, OH. Graduate Denison U. Debut 1966 OB in "Winterset," followed by "Out of Control," "Rainbows for Sale," "The Firebugs," "Darkness at Noon," "Humbug Man," "Babel Circus."

JAMIEL, JOHN. Born Aug. 21, 1952 in Orange, NJ. Graduate Wm. Paterson Col. Debut 1982 OB in "Pinwheel," followed by "Sganarelle," "Chekhov Festival," "Trelawny of the Wells," "Strictly Dishonorable."

JAMROG, JOSEPH. Born Dec. 21, 1932 in Flushing, NY. Graduate CCNY. Debut 1970 OB in "Nobody Hears a Broken Drum," followed by "Tango," "And Whose Little Boy Are You?," "When You Comin' Back, Red Ryder?," "Drums at Yale," "The Boy Friend," "Love, Death Plays," "Too Much Johnson," "A Stitch in Time," "Pantagleize," "Final Hours," "Returnings," "Brass Birds Don't Sing," "And Things That Go Bump in the Night."

JARCHOW, BRUCE A. Born May 19, 1948 in Evanston, IL. Graduate Amherst Col. Debut 1982 OB in "Edmond," followed by "True West."

JAY, MARY. Born Dec. 23, 1939 in Brooklyn, NY. Graduate UMe, AmThWing. Debut 1962 OB in "Little Mary Sunshine," followed by "Toys in the Attic," " Telecast," "Sananda Sez," "Soul of the White Ant," "The Quilling of Prue," Bdwy in "The Student Gypsy," "Candida" (1981), "Beethoven's Tenth."

JENKINS, TIMOTHY. Born Dec. 5, 1949 in Detroit, MI. Graduate Mercy Col., Catholic U. Debut 1980 OB in "Room Service," followed by "The Quilling of Prue," "The Hasty Heart."

JENNER, JAMES. Born Mar. 5, 1953 in Houston, TX. Attended UTx, LAMDA. Debut 1980 OB in "Kind Lady," followed by "Station J.," "Yellow Fever."

JENNINGS, KEN. Born Oct. 10, 1947 in Jersey City, NJ. Graduate St. Peter's Col. Bdwy debut 1975 in "All God's Chillun Got Wings," followed by "Sweeney Todd" for which he received a Theatre World Award, "Present Laughter."

JEROME, TIMOTHY. Born Dec. 29, 1943 in Los Angeles, CA. Graduate Ithaca Col. Bdwy debut 1969 in "Man of La Mancha," followed by "The Rothschilds," "Creation of the World . . . ," "Moony Shapiro Songbook," "Cats," OB in "Beggar's Opera," "Pretzels," "Civilization and Its Discontents," "The Little Prince," "Colette Collage."

JETER, MICHAEL. Born Aug. 26, 1952 in Lawrenceburg, TN. Graduate Memphis State U. Bdwy debut 1978 in "Once in a Lifetime," OB in "The Master and Margarita," "G. R. Point" for which he received a Theatre World Award, "Alice in Concert," "El Bravo," "Cloud 9," "Greater Tuna."

JOHNS, ARIANA. Born Nov. 16, 1960 in California. Attended HB Studio. Debut 1984 OB in "Pigeons on the Walk."

JOHNSON, KNOWL. Born Sept. 16, 1970 in Greenwich, CT. Debut 1982 OB in "A Christmas Carol," followed by "The Itch," Bdwy in "Merlin" (1983).

JOHNSON, KURT. Born Oct. 5, 1952 in Pasadena, CA. Attended LACC, Occidental Col. Debut 1976 OB in "Follies," followed by "Walking Papers," "A Touch of Marble," "A Midsummer Night's Dream," Bdwy in "Rockabye Hamlet" (1976), "A Chorus Line," "A Stitch in Time."

JOHNSON, MEL, JR. Born Apr. 16, 1949 in NYC. Graduate Hofstra U. Debut 1972 OB in "Hamlet," followed by "Love! Love! Love!," "Shakespeare's Cabaret," "The Peanut Man," "The Lottery," "Spell #7," "Do Lord Remenber Me," Bdwy in "On the 20th Century," "Eubie!," "The Rink."

JOHNSON, PAGE. Born Aug. 25, 1930 in Welch, WV. Graduate Ithaca Col. Bdwy bow in 1951 in "Romeo and Juliet," followed by "Electra, "Oedipus," "Camino Real," "In April Once," for which he received a Theatre World Award, "Red Roses for Me," "The Lovers," "Equus," "You Can't Take It With You," OB in "The Enchanted," "Guitar," "4 in 1," "Journey of the Fifth Horse," APA's "School for Scandal," "The Tavern," and "The Seagull," "Odd Couple," "Boys In The Band," "Medea," "Deathtrap," "Best Little Whorehouse in Texas," "Fool for Love."

JOHNSON, TINA. Born Oct. 27, 1951 in Wharton, TX. Graduate NorthTexStateU. Debut 1979 OB in "Festival," followed by "Blue Plate Special," Bdwy in "The Best Little Whorehouse in Texas."

JOHNSTON, J. J. Born Oct. 24, 1933 in Chicago, IL. Debut 1981 in "American Buffalo," and Bdwy 1983 in "American Buffalo" for which he received a Theatre World Award.

JOLLEY, NICK. Born Feb. 17, 1948 in Hindsboro, IL. Graduate S. Ill.U. Bdwy debut 1979 in "Oklahoma!," OB in "Brooklyn Bridge," "Up in Central Park."

JONES, CHARLOTTE. Born Jan. 1 in Chicago, IL. Attended DePaul, Loyola U. Bdwy debut 1953 in "Camino Real," followed by "Buttrio Square," "Mame," "How Now Dow Jones," "Skin of Our Teeth," "A Matter of Gravity," "Johnny Johnson," OB in "False Confessions," "Sign of Jonah," "Girl on the Via Flaminia," "Red Roses for Me," "Night in Black Bottles," "Camino Real," "Plays for Bleecker St.," "Pigeons," "Great Scott!," Sjt. Musgrave's Dance," "Papers," "Beggar's Opera," "200 Years of American Furniture," "Belle Femme," "Heat of Re-entry," "Appointment with Death."

JONES, GORDON G. Born Nov. 1, 1941 in Urania, LA. Graduate LaTech, UAr. Debut 1980 OB in "Room Service," followed by "Front Page," "Caine Mutiny Court-Martial," "Panhandle," "Caveat Emptor," "Progress," "Italian Straw Hat," "The Fantasticks," "June Moon."

JONES, JEFFREY. Born Sept. 28, 1947 in Buffalo, NY. Graduate Lawrence U., LAMDA. Debut 1973 OB in "Lotta," followed by "The Tempest," "Trelawny of the Wells," "Secret Service," "Boy Meets Girl," "Scribes," "Cloud 9," "The Death of Von Richthofen," "Love Letters on Blue Paper."

JONES, LEILANI. Born May 14, in Honolulu, HI. Graduate UHi. Debut 1981 OB in "El Bravo," followed by "The Little Shop of Horrors."

JONES, NEAL. Born Jan. 2, 1960 in Wichita, KS. Attended Webster Col. Debut 1981 OB in "The Dear Love of Comrades," followed by "The Tavern," "Spring's Awakening," "Billy Liar," "Groves of Academe," Bdwy in "Macbeth" (1982), "The Corn Is Green" (1983).

JONES, SABRA. Born Mar. 22, 1951 in California. Debut 1982 OB in "Joan of Lorraine," followed by "Inheritors," "Paradise Lost," "Ghosts."

JONES, SIMON. Born July 27, 1950 in Wiltshire, Eng. Attended Trinity Hall. Debut 1984 OB in "Terra Nova," followed by Bdwy in "The Real Thing" (1984).

JONES, TAD. Born May 5, 1955 in Stuttgart, Ger. Graduate AADA. Debut 1983 OB in "the Inheritors," followed by "Paradise Lost," "Rain," "The Hasty Heart."

JORDAN, RICHARD. Born July 19, 1938 in NYC. Attended Harvard U. Bdwy debut 1961 in "Take Her, She's Mine," followed by "Bicycle Ride to Nevada," "War and Peace," "Generation," "A Patriot for Me," OB in "Judith," "All's Well That Ends Well," "Trial of the Catonsville 9," "Three Acts of Recognition," "A Private View."

JORDAN, SUSAN. Born Apr. 14, 1955 in Norman, OK. Graduate UOk., NYU. Debut 1981 in "We Won't Pay!," followed by "Dusa, Fish, Stas & Vi," "Sweeney Agonistes," "Dear Friends."

JOY, ROBERT. Born Aug. 17, 1951 in Montreal, Can. Graduate Nfd. Memorial U. Oxford U. Debut 1978 OB in "The Diary of Anne Frank," followed by "Fables for Friends," "Lydie Breeze," "Sister Mary Ignatius Explains It All," "Actor's Nightmare," "What I Did Last Summer," "The Death of Von Richthofen," "Lenny and the Heartbreakers," "Found a Peanut."

JOYCE, STEPHEN. Born Mar 7, 1933 in NYC. Attended Fordham U. Bdwy debut 1966 in "Those That Play the Clowns," followed by "The Exercise," "The Runner Stumbles," "Devour the Snow," "The Caine Mutiny Court-Martial," OB in "Three Hand Reel," "Galileo," "St. Joan," "Stephen D" for which he received a Theatre World Award, "Fireworks," "School for Wives," "Savages," "Scribes," "Daisy."

JUDE, PATRICK. Born Feb. 25, 1951 in Jersey City, NJ. Bdwy debut 1972 in "Jesus Christ Superstar," followed by 1977 revival, "Got Tu Go Disco," "Charlie and Algernon," "Marlowe," OB in "The Haggadah," "Dementos."

JULIA, RAUL. Born Mar. 9, 1940 in San Juan, PR. Graduate UPR. OB in "Macbeth," "Titus Andronicus," "Theatre in the Streets," "Life Is a Dream," "Blood Wedding," "Ox Cart," "No Exit," "Memorandum," "Frank Gagliano's City Scene," "Your Own Thing," "Persians," "Castro Complex," "Pinkville," "Hamlet," "King Lear," "As You Like It," "Emperor of Late Night Radio," "Threepenny Opera," "The Cherry Orchard," "Taming of the Shrew," "Othello," "The Tempest," Bdwy in "The Cuban Thing," "Indians," "Two Gentlemen of Verona," "Via Galactica," "Where's Charley?," "Dracula," "Betrayal," "Nine," "Design for Living."

JUSTICE, JIMMY. Born Dec. 31, 1941 in Erie, PA. Graduate Juilliard. Bdwy debut 1968 in "The Cuban Thing," followed by "Indians," OB in "Dementos."

KANSAS, JERI. Born Mar. 10, 1955 in Jersey City, NJ. Debut 1978 OB in "Gay Divorce," Bdwy 1979 in "Sugar Babies," followed by "42nd Street."

KANTOR, KENNETH. Born Apr. 6, 1949 in The Bronx, NY. Graduate SUNY, Boston U. Debut 1974 OB in "Zorba," followed by "Kiss Me, Kate," "A Little Night Music," "Buried Treasure," "Sounds of Rodgers and Hammerstein," Bdwy in "The Grand Tour" (1979), "Brigadoon" (1980), "Mame" (1983).

KAREL, CHARLES "CHUCK". Born Apr. 22, 1935 in Newark, NJ. Attended USCal. Bdwy debut 1962 in "Milk and Honey," followed by "Hello, Dolly!," "Golden Rainbow," "Dear World," "Zorba (1983), OB in "Chase a Rainbow," "Sing Melancholy Baby," "Heather McBride."

KARPEN, PAT. Born Feb. 21, 1951 in Washington, DC. Graduate Catholic U. Debut 1980 OB in "The Marriage," followed by "The Land Is Bright."

KARRAKER, HUGH. Born May 16, 1948 in NYC. Graduate UCt., Guildhall Sch. Debut 1982 OB in "One Night Stand," "Flesh, Flash & Frank Harris."

KAYE, JUDY. Born Oct. 11, 1948 in Phoenix, AZ. Attended UCLA, Ariz. State U. Bdwy debut 1977 in "Grease," followed by "On the 20th Century" for which she received a Theatre World Award, "Moony Shapiro Songbook," "Oh, Brother!," OB in "Eileen in Concert," "Can't Help Singing," "Four to Make Two," "Sweethearts in Concert," "Love."

KEEP, STEPHEN. Born Aug. 24, 1947 in Camden, SC. Attended Columbia, Yale U. Bdwy debut 1972 in "Paul Sills Story Theatre," followed by "Metamorphosis," "Shadow Box," OB in "Clarence," "The Cherry Orchard," "Esther," "A Private View."

KEHR, DON. Born Sept. 18, 1963 in Washington, DC. Bdwy debut 1976 in "Legend," followed by "The Human Comedy," OB in "American Passion," "She Loves Me."

KELLER, JEFF. Born Sept. 8, 1947 in Brooklyn, NY. Graduate Monmouth Col. Bdwy debut 1974 in "Candide," followed by "Fiddler on the Roof," "On the 20th Century," "The 1940's Radio Show," "Dance a Little Closer," OB in "Bird of Paradise," "Charlotte Sweet," "Roberta in Concert."

KELLY, DAVID B. Born Mar. 27, 1954 in Lexington, KY. Graduate Allentown Col. Debut 1983 OB in "Max Cap Comedy Review," followed by "Dancin' on the Third Rail," "Victory Bonds."

KELLY, JULIA. Born July 9, 1954 in Washington, DC. Graduate Webster Col. Debut 1976 OB in "A Taste of Honey," followed by "Still Love," "Cornered," "Revue Sketches," "A Conflict of Fragrances," "Incoming."

KELLY, K. C. Born Nov. 12. 1952 in Baraboo, WI. Attended UWis. Debut 1976 OB in "The Chicken Ranch," "Last of the Knucklemen," "Young Bucks," Bdwy in "Romeo and Juliet" (1977, "The Best Little Whorehouse in Texas."

KELLY-YOUNG, LEONARD. Born Sept. 29, 1948 in Chicago, IL. Attended Loop Jr. Col. Debut 1983 OB in "The Lady's Not for Burning."

KEMLER, ESTELLE. Born March 8 in NYC. Attended Carnegie-Mellon U. Debut 1981 OB in "Amidst the Gladiolas," followed by "Goodnight, Grandpa," "Made in Heaven," "My Three Angels."

KENNEDY, LAURIE. Born Feb. 14, 1948 in Hollywood, CA. Graduate Sarah Lawrence Col. Debut 1974 OB in "End of Summer," followed by "A Day in the Death of Joe Egg," "Ladyhouse Blues," "He and She," "The Recruiting Officer," "Isn't It Romantic," "The Master Builder," Bdwy in "Man and Superman" (1978) for which she received a Theatre World Award, "Major Barbara."

KERSEY, BILLYE. Born Oct. 15, 1955 in Norfolk, VA. Bdwy debut 1981 in "42nd Street."

KERSHAW, WHITNEY. Born Apr. 10, 1962 in Orlando, FL. Attended Harkness Joffrey Ballet Schools. Debut 1981 OB in "Francis," Bdwy in "Cats."

KIESERMAN, DAVID H. Born Jan. 4, 1937 in West Chester, PA. Graduate Ithaca Col., UIll. Debut 1981 OB in "The Fantasticks," followed by "Pontius Pilate," "The Importance of Being Earnest," "Threepenny Opera."

KILLMER, NANCY. Born Dec. 16, 1936 in Homewood, IL. Graduate Northwestern U. Bdwy debut 1969 in "Coco," followed by "Goodtime Charley," "So Long, 174th Street," "A Little Night Music," "Sweeney Todd," "Alice in Wonderland," OB in "Exiles," "Mrs. Murray's Farm," "Pillars of Society," "Threads," "A Tale Told," "The Cherry Orchard," "Sea Gull."

KILTY, JEROME. Born June 24, 1922 in Pala Indian Reservation, CA. Attended London's Guildhall Schl. Bdwy debut 1950 in "The Relapse," followed by "Love's Labour's Lost," "Misalliance," "A Pin to See the Peepshow," "Frogs of Spring," "Quadrille," "Othello," "Henry IV," "Moon for the Misbegotten," OB in "Dear Liar," " A Month in the Country."

KIMBALL, DAVID. Born Feb. 20, 1951 in Memphis, TN. Graduate Carnegie-Mellon U. Debut 1983 OB in "The Last of the Knucklemen."

KIMBROUGH, CHARLES. Born May 23, 1936 in St. Paul. MN. Graduate IndU, Yale. Bdwy bow 1969 in "Cop-Out," followed by "Company," "Love for Love," "Rules of the Game," "Candide," "Mr. Happiness," "Same Time, Next Year," "Sunday in the Park with George," OB in "All in Love," "Struts and Frets," "Troilus and Cressida," "Secret Service," "Boy Meets Girl," "Drinks Before Dinner," "The Dining Room."

KING, GINNY. Born May 22, 1957 in Atlanta, GA. Attended NCSch of Arts. Bdwy debut 1980 in "42nd Street."

KINGSLEY, BEN. Born Jan. 31, 1943 in Scarborough, Yorkshire, Eng. Bdwy debut 1971 in "A Midsummer Night's Dream," followed by "Edmond Kean" (1983).

KIRBY, BRUCE. Born Apr. 28, 1925 in NYC. Debut 1955 OB in "La Ronde." Bdwy 1965 in "Diamond Orchid," followed by "Death of a Salesman" (1984).

KIRCHNER, LISA. Born June 10, 1953 in Los Angeles, CA. Graduate Sarah Lawrence Col. Debut 1974 OB in "Hotel for Criminals," followed by "American Imagination," "Threepenny Opera," "Red Eye," "Plagues for Our Time," Bdwy in "The Human Comedy (1984)

KIRTLAND, LOUISE. Born Aug. 4, 1919 in Lynn, MA. Bdwy debut 1931 in "A Church Mouse," followed by "Rosalinda," "Tunnel of Love," "Gigi," "Tovarich," "Waltz of the Toreadors," "Along 5th Avenue," "Mame" (1983).

KIRWIN, TERRY. Born Oct. 30 in Fort Wayne, IN. Graduate Purdue U. Debut 1982 OB in "Snoopy," followed by "I Can Still Hear Them."

KLAR, GARY. Born Mar. 24, 1947 in Bridgeport, CT. Graduate UAz. Debut 1982 OB in "The Last of the Knucklemen," followed by "Vatzlav," "The Guys in the Trucks" (also Bdwy 1983), Bdwy in "Brothers."

KLATT, DAVID. Born July 15, 1958 in Martins Ferry, OH. Attended West Liberty State Col. Bdwy debut 1984 in "La Cage aux Folles."

KLINE, KEVIN. Born Oct. 24, 1947 in St. Louis, MO. Graduate IndU, Juilliard. Debut 1970 OB in "Wars of Roses," followed by "School for Scandal," "Lower Depths," "The Hostage," "Women Beware Women," "Robber Bridegroom," "Edward II," "The Time of Your Life," "Beware of the Jubjub Bird." "Dance on a Country Grave," "Richard III," "Henry V," Bdwy in "Theee Sisters," "Measure for Measure," "Beggar's Opera," "Scapin," "On the 20th Century," "Loose Ends," "Pirates of Penzance."

KLUNIS, TOM. Born in San Francisco, CA. Bdwy debut 1961 in "Gideon," followed by "The Devils," "Henry V," "Romeo and Juliet," "St. Joan," "Hide and Seek," "Bacchae," "Plenty," OB in "The Immoralist," "Hamlet," "Arms and the Man," "Potting Shed," "Measure for Measure," "Romeo and Juliet," "The Balcony," "Our Town," "Man Who Never Died," "God Is My Ram," "Rise Marlow," "Iphigenia in Aulis," "Still Life," "The Master and Margarita," "As You Like It," "The Winter Dancers," "When We Dead Awaken," "Vieux Carre," "The Master Builder," "Richard III."

KMECK, GEORGE. Born Aug. 4, 1949 in Jersey City, NJ. Attended Glassboro State Col. Bdwy debut 1981 in "Pirates of Penzance," followed by "On Your Toes."

KNIGHT, SHIRLEY. Born July 5 in Goessel, KS. Attended Phillips U., Wichita U. Bdwy debut 1964 in "The Three Sisters," followed by "We Have Always Lived in a Castle," "Watering Place," "Kennedy's Children," OB in "Journey to the Day," "Rooms," "Happy End," "Landscape of the Body," "A Lovely Sunday for Creve Coeur," "Losing Time," "Some Back, Little Sheba."

KNOBELOCH, JIM. Born May 18, 1950 in Belleville, IL. Graduate S.Ill.U. Debut 1983 OB in "Joan of Lorraine," followed by "Paradise Lost."

KNUDSON, KURT. Born Sept. 7, 1936 in Fargo, ND. Attended NDStateU, UMiami. Debut 1976 OB in "The Cherry Orchard," followed by "Geniuses," Bdwy in "Curse of an Aching Heart" (1982), "Sunday in the Park with George."

KOLINSKI, JOSEPH. Born June 26, 1953 in Detroit MI. Attended UDetroit, HB Studio. Bdwy debut 1980 in "Brigadoon," followed by "Dance a Little Closer," OB in "Hijinks!", "The Human Comedy" (off and on Bdwy).

KOLOC, BONNIE. Born in Iowa. Bdwy debut 1984 in "The Human Comedy" for which she received a Theatre World Award.

KONDAZIAN, KAREN. Born Jan. 27, 1941 in Boston, MA. Graduate San Francisco State Col., LAMDA. Debut 1964 OB in "Trojan Woman," followed by "Broken Eggs," "Andorra."

KOPACHE, THOMAS. Born Oct. 17, 1945 in Manchester, NH. Graduate San Diego State, Cal. Inst. of Arts. Debut 1976 OB in "The Architect and the Emperor of Assyria," followed by "Brontosaurus Rex," "Extravagant Triumph," "Caligula," "The Tempest," "Macbeth," "Measure for Measure," "Hunting Scenes from Lower Bavaria," "The Danube," "Friends Too Numerous to Mention."

KOZLOWSKI, LINDA. Born Jan 7 in Bridgeport, CT. Attended Juilliard. Debut 1981 OB in "How It All Began," followed by "Henry IV Part I," "The Ballad of Dexter Creed," Bdwy in "Death of a Salesman" (1984).

KREIZER, DAWN. Born Aug. 25, 1966 in Montclair, NJ. Attended NYU. Debut 1984 OB in "Spookhouse."

KRONENBERG, BRUCE. Born Sept. 1, 1954 in Brooklyn, NY. Graduate Miami Dade Jr. Col. Debut 1981 OB in "Auditions for the Last Round Up," followed by "Baal," "Julius Caesar," "The Relics," "The Rock Stood Still."

LACHOW, STAN. Born Dec. 20, 1931 in Brooklyn, NY. Graduate Roger Williams U. Debut 1977 OB in "Come Back, Little Sheba," followed by "Diary of Anne Frank," "Time of the Cuckoo," "Angelus," "The Middleman," Bdwy in "On Golden Pond."

LACONI, ROBERT. Born Apr. 23, 1954 in Akron, OH. Graduate Kent State U. Debut 1978 OB in "Gulliver's Travels," followed by "A Book of Etiquette," "cummings and goings," "Let's Face It," "Julius Caesar," "Comedy of Errors."

LAGERFELT, CAROLYN. Born Sept. 23 in Paris. Graduate AADA. Bdwy debut 1971 in "The Philanthropist," followed by "4 on a Garden," "Jockey Club Stakes," "The Constant Wife," "Otherwise Engaged," "Betrayal," "The Real Thing," OB in "Look Back in Anger," "Close of Play," "Sea Anchor," "Quartermaine's Terms," "Other Places."

LaGIOIA, JOHN P. Born Nob. 24, 1937 in Philadelphia, PA. Graduate Temple U. OB in "Keyhole," "Lovers in the Metro," "The Cherry Orchard," "Titus Andronicus," "Henry VI," "Richard III," "A Little Madness," Bdwy in "Henry V" (1969).

LAHTI, CHRISTINE. Born Apr. 4, 1950 in Detroit, MI. Graduate UMich, HB Studio. Debut 1979 OB in "The Wood" for which she received a Theatre World Award followed by "Landscape of the Body," Bdwy in "Loose Ends" (1980), followed by "Division Street," "Scenes and Revelations," "Present Laughter."

LAM, DIANE. Born Mar. 6, 1945 in Honolulu, HI. Graduate UHi, SMU. Bdwy debut in "Pacific Overures" (1977), followed by "The King and I" (1977), OB in "Anyone Can Whistle," "Pacific Overtures" (1984).

LAM, JENNIFER. Born Feb. 9, 1967 in Honolulu, HI. Bdwy debut in "The King and I" (1977), OB in "Pacific Overtures" (1984).

LAMPERT, ZOHRA. Born May 13, 1936 in NYC. Attended UChicago. Bdwy debut 1956 in "Major Barbara," followed by "Maybe Tuesday," "Look, We've Come Through," "First Love," "Mother Courage," "Nathan Weinstein, Mystic, Conn.," "Lovers and Other Strangers," "The Sign in Sidney Brustein's Window," "Unexpected Guests," OB in "Venus Observed," "Diary of a Scoundrel," "After the Fall," "Marco Millions," "Drinks before Dinner," "Gifted Children."

LANDON, SOFIA. Born Jan 24, 1949 in Montreal, Can. Attended Northwestern U. Debut 1971 OB in "Red, White and Black," followed by "Gypsy," "Missouri Legend," "Heartbreak House," "Peg o' My Heart," "Scenes and Revelations," "The Hasty Heart."

LANDFIELD, TIMOTHY. Born Aug. 22, 1950 in Palo Alto, CA. Graduate Hampshire Col. Bdwy debut 1977 in "Tartuffe," followed by "Crucifer of Blood," OB in "Actor's Nightmare," "Sister Mary Ignatius Explains It All." "Charlotte Sweet." "Flight of the Earls."

LANE, NANCY. Born June 16, 1951 in Passaic, NJ. Attended Va. CommonwealthU., AADA. Debut 1975 OB and Broadway in "A Chorus Line."

LANE, NATHAN. Born Feb. 3, 1956 in Jersey City, NJ. Debut 1978 OB in "A Midsummer Night's Dream," "Love," Bdwy in "Present Laughter" (1982) followed by "Merlin."

LANG, LISE. Born June 21, 1956 in Bell Bourche, SD. Attended UUtah. Bdwy debut 1983 in "Marilyn, An American Fable."

LANG, STEPHEN. Born July 11, 1952 in NYC. Graduate Swarthmore Col. Debut 1975 OB in "Hamlet," followed by "Henry V," "Shadow of a Gunman," "A Winter's Tale," "Johnny On a Spot," "Barbarians," "Ah, Men," "Clownmaker," "Hannah," Bdwy in "St. Joan" (1977), "Death of a Salesman" (1984).

LANGE, ANN. Born June 24, 1953 in Pipestone, MN. Attended Carnegie-Mellon U. Debut 1979 OB in "Rat's Nest," followed by "Hunting Scenes from Lower Bavaria," "Crossfire," "Linda Her and the Fairy Garden," Bdwy in "The Survivor" (1981).

LANGELLA, FRANK. Born Jan 1, 1940 in Bayonne, NJ. Graduate Syracuse U. Debut 1963 OB in "The Immoralist," followed by "The Old Glory," "Good Day," "White Devil," "Yerma," "Iphigenia in Aulis,," "A Cry of Players," "Prince of Homburg," Bdwy in "Seascape" (1975), "Dracula," "Amadeus," "Passion," "Design for Living."

LANGLAND, LIANE. Born May 11, 1957 in Denver, CO. Juilliard graduate. Debut 1981 OB in "How It All Began," followed by "Ah, Wilderness!," Bdwy in "A Talent for Murder" (1981).

LANNING, JERRY. Born May 17, 1943 in Miami, Fl. Graduate USCal. Bdwy debut 1966 in "Mame" for which he received a Theatre World Award, followed by "1776," "Where's Charley?," "My Fair Lady," OB in "Memphis Store Bought Teeth," "Berlin to Broadway," "Sextet," "Isn't It Romantic."

LANSBURY, ANGELA. Born Oct. 16, 1925 in London, Eng. Bdwy debut 1957 in "Hotel Paradiso," followed by "A Taste of Honey," "Anyone Can Whistle," "Mame" (1966/1983), "Dear World," "Gypsy," "The King & I" (1978), "Sweeney Todd," "A Little Family Business."

LARSON, BRETT. Born June 17, 1955 in Helena, MT. Graduate UUtah. Debut 1983 in "The Music Man."

LARSON, JILL. Born Oct. 7, 1947 in Minneapolis, MN. Graduate Hunter Col. Debut 1980 OB in "These Men," followed by "Peep," "Serious Bizness," "It's Only a Play," "Red Rover," Bdwy in "Romantic Comedy" ('80).

LASKIN, MICHAEL. Born Apr. 3, 1951 in Duluth, MN. Graduate Northwestern U., UMn. Debut 1983 OB in "The Basement Tapes."

LASKY, ZANE. Born Apr. 23, 1953 in NYC. Attended Manhattan Col. HB Studio. Debut 1973 OB in "The Hot 1 Baltimore," followed by "The Prodigal," "Innocent Thoughts, Harmless Intentions," "Time Framed," "Balm in Gilead," Bdwy in "All Over Town" (1974).

LATHAN, BOBBI JO. Born Oct. 5, 1951 in Dallas, TX. Graduate NTexStateU. Bdwy debut 1979 in "The Best Little Whorehouse in Texas," followed by "Guys in the Truck."

LAURANS, LYDIA. Born May 4, in Baltimore, MD. Graduate Towson State U., UMd. Debut 1984 OB in "Pal Joey."

LAURENCE, PAULA. Born Jan. 25 in Brooklyn, NY. Bdwy debut 1936 in "Horse Eats Hat," followed by "Dr. Faustus," "Junior Miss," "Something for the Boys," "One Touch of Venus," "Cyrano de Bergerac," "The Liar," "Season in the Sun," "Tovarich," "The Time of Your Life," "Beggar's Opera," "Hotel Paradiso," "Night of the Iguana," "Have I Got a Girl for You," "Ivanov," "Rosalie in Concert," OB in "7 Days of Mourning," "Roberta in Concert," "One Touch of Venus."

LAURIA, DAN. Born Apr. 12, 1947 in Brooklyn, NY. Graduate SConnState, UConn. Debut 1978 OB in "Game Plan," followed by "All my Sons," "Marlon Brando Sat Here," "Home of the Brave," "Collective Portraits," "Dustoff," "Niagra Falls," "Punchy," "Americans."

LAWRENCE, DELPHI. Born Mar. 23, 1932 in London, Eng. Attended RADA. Debut 1972 OB in "The Divorce of Judy and Jane," followed by "Dylan," 'The Elizabethans," "Souvenirs," Bdwy in "The Constant Wife" (1975).

LAWRENCE, ELIZABETH. Born Sept. 6, 1922 in Huntington, WVa. Graduate UMich, Yeshiva U. Bdwy debut 1954 in "The Rainmaker," followed by "All the Way Home," "Look Homeward Angel," "A Matter of Gravity," "OB in "The Misunderstanding," "Rockaway," "Children."

LAWRENCE, WILLIAM A. Born Sept. 9, 1923 in Brooklyn, NY. Graduate St. Peter's Col., Hofstra U. Debut 1983 OB "June Moon."

LAWSON, ROGER. Born Oct. 11, 1942 in Tarrytown, NY. Attended Fredonia Col. Bdwy debut 1967 in "Hello, Dolly!," OB in "Pins and Needles," "Billy Noname," "Dinner at the Ambassador's," "One Free Smile," "Non-gogo," "Dispatches," "Dementos."

LEACH, JAMES. Born Oct. 2, 1954 in Colon, Panama. Graduate Ithaca Col. Debut 1980 OB in "Romeo and Juliet," followed by "The Lady's Not for Burning."

LEAGUE, JANET. Born Oct. 13, in Chicago, IL. Attended Goodman Theatre. Debut 1969 OB in "To Be Young, Gifted and Black," followed by "Tiger at the Gates," "The Screens," "Mrs. Snow," "Please Don't Cry and Say No," "Banana Box," "The Brothers," "American Dreams," "Suzanna Andler," Bdwy in "First Breeze of Summer" (1975), "For Colored Girls Who Have Considered Suicide . . ."

LEE, BRYARLY. Born May 16, 1935 in Westerly, RI. OB in "Maiden Voyage," "The Seagull," "Soft Shoulders," "My Prince, My King," "Andorra."

LEE, JERRY. Born Jan 23, 1946 in Oak Ridge, TN. Attended E.Mich.U. Debut 1974 OB in "The Gospel According to Mark Twain," followed by "Ruby's Place," "Midsummer," "An Awfully Big Adventure," "The Conversion," "She Loves Me," "The Overcoat," "The Men's Group."

Lynnie
Godfrey

Christopher
Goutman

Randy
Graff

Kevin
Gray

Robin
Groves

Michael
Guido

Peter
Hagan

Mary
Hara

Charles
Harley

Viola
Harris

Elek
Hartman

Elaine
Hausman

Christine
Healy

Danny
Herman

Jan Leigh
Herndon

Christopher
Hewett

Katharine
Houghton

Richmond
Hoxie

Dana
Ivey

Page
Johnson

Leilani
Jones

Hugh
Karraker

Billye
Kersey

Jim
Knobeloch

Robert
Laconi

Jennifer
Lam

Jerry
Lanning

Jill
Larson

Dan
Lauria

Janet
League

213

LEE, PEGGY. Born Norma Deloris Egstrom in Jamestown, ND. Bdwy debut 1983 in her musical autobiography "Peg."

LEIBMAN, RON. Born Oct. 11, 1937 in NYC. Attended Ohio Wesl;eyan, Actors Studio. Bdwy debut 1963 in "Dear Me, the Sky Is Falling," followed by "Bicycle Ride to Nevada," "The Deputy," "We Bombed in New Haven" for which he received a Theatre World Award, "Cop-Out," "I Ought to Be in Pictures," OB in "The Academy," "John Brown's Body," "Scapin," "The Premise," "Legend of Lovers," "Dead End," "Poker Session," "Transfers," "Room Service," "Love Two," "Rich and Famous," "Children of Darkness," "Non Pasquale."

LEMMON, SHIRLEY. Born May 15, 1948 in Salt Lake City, UT. Graduate UtStateU. Bdwy debut 1971 in "Company," followed by "Smith," "Words and Music," "Nine," OB in "2 by 5," "Life Is a Dream."

LENK, VIVIENNE. Born Mar. 8, 1948 in Detroit, MI. Graduate EMiU, UMi. Debut 1979 OB in "The Cavern," followed by "Cuchulain," "Merchant of Venice," "Don Juan," "Leonce and Lena," " After the Fall," "French Toast."

LENZ, THOMAS. Born Jan. 29, 1951 in Madison, WI. Graduate St. Mary's Col. Debut 1975 OB in "Running Deer," followed by "Wild Cats," "Richard II," "Henry IV," "Marquis of Keith," "Madwoman of Chaillot," "Love's Labour's Lost," "The Front Page," "Hamlet," "Big and Little/Scenes," "Faust," "Wild Oats," "Danton's Death."

LEO, MELISSA. Born Sept. 14, 1960 in NYC. Attended SUNY/Purchase. Debut 1984 OB in "Cinders."

LEVELS, CALVIN. Born Sept. 30, 1954 in Cleveland, OH. Graduate CCC. Bdwy debut 1984 in "Open Admissions" for which he received a Theatre World Award.

LEVINE, ANNA. Born Sept. 18, 1957 in NYC. Debut 1975 OB in "Kid Champion," followed by "Uncommon Women and Others," "City Sugar," "A Winter's Tale," "Johnny-On-a-Spot," "The Wedding," "American Days," "The Singular Life of Albert Nobbs," "Cinders."

LEWIS, GENE. Born July 28, 1943 in NYC. Debut 1978 OB in "On the Lock-In," followed by "Nest of the Wood Grouse," Bdwy in "Amen Corner" (1983).

LEWIS, MATTHEW. Born Jan. 12, 1937 in Elizabeth, NJ. Graduate Harvard Col. Debut 1970 OB in "Chicago '70," followed by "Fathers and Sons," "The Freak," "Happy Days Are Here Again," "Levitations," "The Sea Gull," Bdwy in "Angels Fall" (1983).

LIGON, TOM. Born Sept. 10, 1945 in New Orleans, LA. Bdwy debut 1969 in "Angela," followed by "Love Is a Time of Day," OB in "Your Own Thing," "A Place without Mornings," "God Says There Is No Peter Ott," "Geniuses," "Clean Sweep."

LINDO, DELROY. Born Nov. 18, 1952 in London, Eng. Debut 1979 OB in "Spell #7," followed by "Les Blancs," Bdwy in "Master Harold . . . and the boys" (1983).

LINDSAY, PHILLIP. Born July 31, 1924 in Cairo, IL. Attended UChicago, Goodman Theatre. OB in "Clandestine on the Morning Line," "Orpheus Descending," "3 by Wilder," "Mamba's Daughters," "The Blacks," "Crazy Horse," "Willie," Bdwy in "Member of the Wedding," "The Great White Hope," "God's Favorite," "The Skin of Our Teeth," "Sweet Bird of Youth."

LINEHAN, NANCY. Born Dec. 11, 1942 in Washington, DC. Graduate Agnes Scott Col., Wayne State U. Debut 1982 OB in "Baseball Wives," followed by "A Pair of Hearts," "For the Use of the Hall," "A Body in Every Bed."

LINES, SYBIL (aka Marion) Born Feb. 10 in London, Eng. Attended Central School. Debut 1976 OB in "The Philanderer," followed by "Claw," "Penultimate Problem of Sherlock Holmes," "The Team," "The Wit to Woo," "Small Change," "Quartermaine's Terms," Bdwy in "Bedroom Farce" (1979).

LITZSINGER, SARAH E. Born Oct. 22, 1971 in Indianapolis, IN. Bdwy debut 1983 in "Marilyn," followed by "Oliver!"

LOMBARD, MICHAEL. Born Aug. 8, 1934 in Brooklyn, NY. Graduate Bklyn Col, Boston U. OB in "King Lear," "Merchant of Venice," "Cages," "Pinter Plays," "LaTurista," "Elizabeth the Queen," "Room Service," "Mert and Phil," "Side Street Scenes," "Angelo's Wedding," "Awake and Sing," Bdwy in "Poor Bitos" (1964), "The Devils," "Gingerbread Lady," "Bad Habits," "Otherwise Engaged."

LONE, JOHN. Born in 1952 in Hong Kong. Graduate AADA. Debut 1980 in "F.O.B.," followed by "The Dance and the Railroad," "Sound and Beauty."

LONERGAN, LISA. Born July 19, 1959 in West Bend, WI. Graduate Marquette U, Cornell U. Debut 1984 OB in "The Trials of Joan of Arc," followed by "Rich Girls."

LOPEZ, PRISCILLA. Born Feb. 26, 1948 in The Bronx, NY. Bdwy debut 1966 in "Breakfast at Tiffany's," followed by "Henry, Sweet Henry," "Lysistrata," "Company," "Her First Roman," "The Boy Friend," "Pippin," "A Chorus Line," "A Day in Hollywood/A Night in the Ukraine," "Nine," OB in "What's a Nice Country Like you . . . ," "Key Exchange," "Buck," "Extremities," "Non Pasquale."

LOUDON, DOROTHY. Born Sept. 17, 1933 in Boston, MA. Attended Emerson Col., Syracuse U. Debut 1961 in "World of Jules Feiffer," Bdwy 1963 in "Nowhere to Go but Up" for which she received a Theatre World Award followed by "Noel Coward's Sweet Potato," "Fig Leaves Are Falling," "Three Men on a Horse," "The Women," "Annie," "Ballroom," "West Side Waltz," "Noises Off."

LOWERY, MARCELLA. Born Apr. 27, 1945 in Jamaica, NY. Graduate Hunter Col. Debut 1967 OB in "Day of Absence," followed by "American Pastoral," "Ballet Behind the Bridge," "Jamimma," "A Recent Killing," "Miracle Play," "Welcome to Black River," "Anna Lucasta," "Baseball Wives," "Louis," "Bless Mr, Father," Bdwy in "A Member of the Wedding" ('75), "Lolita."

LUCAS, CRAIG. Born Apr. 30, 1951 in Atlanta, GA. Graduate Boston U. Debut 1974 OB in "Carousel," followed by "Marry Me a Little," "Alex Wilder: Clues to Life," "Busbymusic," Bdwy in "Shenandoah" (1975), "Rex," "On the 20th Century," "Sweeney Todd."

LUFT, LORNA. Born in 1953 in Hollywood, CA. Bdwy debut 1971 in "Promises, Promises," OB in "Snoopy," "Extremities."

LUKATHER, SUZANNE. Born Mar. 22, in Sacramento, CA. Graduate UCal. Bdwy debut 1976 in "Rockabye Hamlet," OB in "The Music Man," "Broadway Jukebox."

LUM, ALVIN. Born May 28, 1931 in Honolulu, HI. Attended U Hi. Debut 1969 OB in "In the Bar of a Tokyo Hotel," followed by "Pursuit of Happiness," "Monkey Music," "Flowers and Household Gods," "Station J," "Double Dutch," "Teahouse," "Song for a Nisei Fisherman," "Empress of China," Bdwy in "Lovely Ladies, Kind Gentlemen," "Two Gentlemen of Verona."

LUM, MARY. Born July 26, 1948 in NYC. Graduate Hunter Col. Debut 1982 OB in "Hibakusha: Stories from Hiroshima," followed by "Plaid on Both Sides," "Full-Time Active," "Autumn Dusk," "Afternoon Shower," "Food," "Sister Sister," "Daughters," "Electra Speaks," "Caucasian Chalk Circle," "Julius Casar.".

LuPONE, PATTI. Born Apr. 21, 1949 in Northport, NY. Juilliard graduate. Debut 1972 OB in "School for Scandal," followed by "Women Beware Women," "Next Time I'll Sing to You," "Beggar's Opera, "Scapin," "Robber Bridegroom," "Edward II," "The Woods," "Edmond," "America Kicks Up Its Heels," "The Cradle Will Rock," Bdwy in "The Water Engine" (1978), "Working," "Evita," "Oliver!"

LOUNSBERY, DAN. Born June 23, 1919 in Cincinnati, OH. Graduate Lafayette Col. Bdwy debut 1944 in "The Innocent Voyage," OB in "Travelers Rest," "The Three Sisters," "A Country for Old Men."

LUZ, FRANC. (aka Frank C.) Born Dec. 22 in Cambridge, MA. Attended NMxStateU. Debut 1974 OB in "The Rivals," followed by "Fiorello!," "The Little Shop of Horrors," Bdwy 1979 in "Whoopee!"

LYND, BETTY. Born In Los Angeles, CA. Debut 1968 OB in "Rondelay," followed by "Love Me, Love My Children," Bdwy in "The Skin of Our Teeth" (1975), "A Chorus Line."

LYNG, NORA MAE. Born Jan. 27, 1951 in Jersey City, NJ. Debut 1981 OB in "Anything Goes," followed by "Forbidden Broadway," "Road to Hollywood."

LYNN, JOYCE. Born Nov. 28, 1935 in Norristown, PA. Attended Lamont Sch., AADA. Bdwy debut 1962 in "Milk and Honey," OB in "Jo," "Autumn's Here," "Jane Eyre," "Prisoner of Second Avenue," "Dispatches from Hell."

MACKAY, LIZBETH. Born March 7 in Buffalo, NY. Graduate Adelphi U., Yale. Bdwy debut 1981 in "Crimes of the Heart" for which she received a Theatre World Award.

MACKLIN, ALBERT. Born Nov. 18, 1958 in Los Angeles, CA. Graduate Stanford U. Debut 1981 OB in "Ten Little Indians" followed by "Poor Little Lambs," Bdwy in "Doonesbury" (1983).

MacLAINE, SHIRLEY. Born Apr. 24, 1934 in Richmond, VA. Bdwy debut 1954 in "Pajama Game," followed by "Shirley MacLaine at the Palace," "Shirley MacLaine on Broadway."

MacNICOL, PETER. Born April 10 in Dallas, TX. Attended UMn. Bdwy debut 1981 in "Crimes of the Heart" for which he received a Theatre World Award, OB in "Found a Peanut."

MacVITTIE, BRUCE. Born Oct. 14, 1956 in Providence, RI. Graduate Boston U. Bdwy debut 1983 in "American Buffalo."

MACY, W. H. Born Mar. 13, 1950 in Miami, FL. Graduate Goddard Col. Debut 1980 OB in "The Man in 605," followed by "Twelfth Night," "The Beaver Coat," "A Call from the East," "Sittin'," "Shoeshine," "The Dining Room," "Speakeasy," "Wild Life," "Flirtations," "Baby with the Bathwater."

MAGNUSEN, MICHAEL. Born Jan. 18, 1951 in Oshkosh, WI. Graduate Lawrence U. Debut 1979 OB in "Festival," followed by "Mother."

MAGNUSON, MERILEE. Born June 11, 1951 in Tacoma, WA. Attended UCal/Irvine. Bdwy debut 1973 in "Gigi," followed by "Irene," "The Best Little Whorehouse in Texas," "My One and Only," OB in "Dancing in the Dark."

MAGUIRE, GEORGE. Born Dec. 4, 1946 in Wilmington, DE. Graduate UPa. Debut 1975 OB in "Polly," followed by "Follies," "Antigone," "Primary English Class," "Sound of Music," "Richard III," Bdwy in "Canterbury Tales" (1980).

MAHAFFEY, VALERIE. Born June 16, 1953 in Sumatra, Indonesia. Graduate UTx. Debut 1975 OB in "Father Uxbridge Wants to Marry," followed by "Bus Stop," "Black Tuesday," "Scenes and Revelations," (also Bdwy), "Twelve Dreams," "Translations," "Butter and Egg Man," "Top Girls," Bdwy in "Rex," "Dracula," "Fearless Frank," "Play Memory.

MAKAROVA, NATALIA. Born Nov. 21, 1940 in Leningrad. Joined American Ballet Theatre in 1970. Bdwy debut in "On Your Toes" (1983) for which she received a Special Theatre World Award.

MALAFRONTE, ALBERT. Born Apr. 13, 1954 in Stratford, CT. Graduate American U. Debut 1980 OB in "Tomorrow Morning Lasts All Night," followed by "Cyrano," "Twelfth Night," "Hamlet," "Macbeth," "Three Sisters," "School for Scandal," "The Rivals."

MALKOVICH, JOHN. Born Dec. 9, 1953 in Christopher, IL. Attended EastIllU, IllStateU. Debut 1982 OB in "True West" for which he received a Theatre World Award, Bdwy in "Death of a Salesman" (1984).

MANGANO, NICK. Born Oct. 22, 1958 in Brooklyn, NY. Attended Hofstra U. Debut 1981 in "Oh! Calcutta!"

MANLEY-BLAU, BEATRICE. Born May 23, 1921 in NYC. Attended NYU. Credits include "The Eve of St. Mark," "The Cherry Orchard," "Snafu," "Eastward in Eden," "The Alchemist," "Yerma," "Uncle Vanya."

MANN, JEREMY. Born Aug. 2, 1960 in NYC. Graduate Carnegie-Mellon U. Debut 12984 OB in "Up in Central Park."

MANOFF, DINAH. Born Jan. 25, 1958 in NYC. Attended CalArts. Bdwy debut 1980 in "I Ought to Be in Pictures" for which she received a Theatre World Award, OB in "Gifted Children."

MANTEGNA, JOE. Born Nov. 13, 1947 in Chicago, IL. Attended Goodman Theatre School. Bdwy debut 1978 in "Working," followed by "Glengarry Glen Ross."

MANTEL, MICHAEL ALBERT. Born Dec. 30, 1952 in Cleveland, OH. Graduate Pratt Inst. Debut 1980 OB in "Success Story," followed by "Incident at Vichy," "Awake and Sing," "King John," "The Dolphin Position," "Welcome to the Moon," "Extenuating Circumstances."

MARADEN, FRANK. Born Aug. 9, 1944 in Norfolk, VA. Graduate UMn., MichStateU. Debut 1980 OB with BAM Theatre Co. in "A Winter's Tale," "Johnny on a Spot," "Barbarians," "The Wedding," "Midsummer Night's Dream," "The Recruiting Officer," "The Wild Duck," "Jungle of Cities," "Three Acts of Recognition," "Don Juan," "The Workroom," "Egyptology," "Photographer," "Landscape of the Body."

MARCHAND, NANCY. Born June 19, 1928 in Buffalo, NY. Graduate Carnegie Tech. Debut 1951 in CC's "Taming of the Shrew," followed by "Merchant of Venice," "Much Ado about Nothing," "Three Bags Full," "After the Rain," "The Alchemist," "Yerma," "Cyrano de Bergerac," "Mary Stuart," "Enemies," "The Plough and the Stars," "40 Carats," "And Miss Reardon Drinks a Little," "Veronica's Room," "Awake and Sing," OB in "The Balcony," "Children," "Taken in Marriage," "Morning's at 7," "Sister Mary Ignatius Explains It All."

MARCHETTI, WILL. Born Nov. 11, 1933 in San Francisco, CA. Attended HB Studio. Debut 1983 in "Fool for Love."

MARCUM, KEVIN. Born Nov. 7, 1955 in Danville, IL. Attended UIll. Bdwy debut 1976 in "My Fair Lady," followed by "I Remember Mama," "Cats," "Sunday in the Park with George."

MARCY, HELEN. Born June 3, 1920 in Worcester, MA. Attended Yale U. Bdwy in "Twelfth Night," "In Bed We Cry," "Dream Girl," "Love and Let Love," OB in "Lady Windermere's Fan," "Verdict," "Hound of the Baskervilles," "Appointment with Death."

MARDIROSIAN, TOM. Born Dec. 14, 1947 in Buffalo, NY. Graduate UBuffalo. Debut 1976 OB in "Gemini," followed by "Grand Magic," "Losing Time," "Passione," "Success and Succession," Bdwy in "Happy End," "Magic Show."

MARGOLIS, LAURA. Born Sept. 17, 1951 in Kansas City, MO. Graduate Catholic U. Debut 1978 OB in "Laura," followed by "Getting Ready," "Mantikee."

MARGOLIS, MARK. Born Nov. 26, 1939 in Malta. Attended Temple U. Bdwy debut 1962 in "Infidel Caesar, OB in "Second Avenue Rag," "My Uncle Sam."

MARGULIES, DAVID. Born Feb. 19, 1937 in NYC. Graduate CCNY. Debut 1958 OB in "Golden Six," followed by "Six Characters in Search of an Author." "Tragical Hiustorie of Dr. Faustus," "Tango," "Little Murders," "Seven Days of Mourning," "Last Analysis," "An Evening with the Poet Senator," "Kid Champion," "The Man with the Flower in His Mouth," "Old Tune," "David and Paula," "Cabal of Hypocrites," Bdwy in "The Iceman Cometh" (1973), "Zalmen or the Madness of God," "Comedians," "Break a Leg," "West Side Waltz."

MARINOS, PETER. Born Oct. 2, 1951 in Pontiac, MI. Graduate MiStateU, Bdwy debut 1976 in "Chicago," followed by "Evita," "Zorba."

MARKLIN, PETER. Born Dec. 22, 1939 in Buffalo, NY. Graduate Northwestern U. Appeared OB in "the Brig," "Pigeons on the Walk," Bdwy in "Fiddler on the Roof."

MARR, RICHARD. Born May 12, 1928 in Baltimore, MD. Graduate UPa. Bdwy in "Baker Street," "How to Succeed . . . ,""Here's Where I Belong," "Coco," "The Constant Wife," "So Long, 174th Street.," OB in "Sappho," "Pilgrim's Progress," "Pimpernel," "Witness," "Antiquities," "Two by Tennessee," "King of Hearts," What a life!," "Primal Time," "Christopher Blake."

MARSHALL, E. G. Born June 18, 1910 in Owatonna, MN. Bdwy debut 1938 in "Prelude to Glory," followed by "Jason," "Skin of Our Teeth," "Petrified Forest," "Jacobowsky and the Colonel," "The Iceman Cometh," "Hope's the Thing," "Survivors," "the Crucible," "Red Roses for Me," "Waiting for Godot," "The Gang's All Here," "The Little Foxes," "Plaza Suite," "Nash at 9," "John Gabriel Borkman," OB in "Mass Appeal."

MARTIN, GEORGE. Born Aug. 15, 1929 in NYC. Bdwy debut 1970 in "Wilson in the Promise Land," followed by "The Hothouse," "Plenty," "Total Abandon," OB in "Painting Churches," "Henry V."

MARTIN, JARED. Born Dec. 21, 1943 in NYC. Graduate Columbia. Debut 1967 OB in "Hamlet as a Happening," Bdwy in "Torch Song Trilogy" (1983).

MARTIN, MILLICENT. Born June 8, 1934 in Romford, Eng. Attended Atalia Conti Sch. Bdwy debut 1954 in "The Boy Friend," followed by "Side by Side by Sondheim," "King of Hearts," "42nd Street."

MARTIN, W. T. Born Jan. 17, 1947 in Providence, RI. Attended Lafayette Col. Debut 1972 OB in "Basic Training of Pavlo Hummel," followed by "Ghosts," "The Caretaker," "Are You Now or Have You Ever Been," "Fairy Tales of New York," "We Won't Pay," "Black Elk Lives," "The End of the War," "A Little Madness," "All the Nice People."

MARTYN, GREG. Born Jan 21, 1957 in London, Eng. Attended RADA. Debut 1982 OB in "Barbarians," followed by "Lennon," "Other Places."

MARZORATI, JODI. Born Oct. 10, 1961 in Rockford, IL. Attended Millikin U. Bdwy debut 1983 in "Marilyn: An American Fable."

MASIELL, JOE. Born Oct. 27, 1939 in Brooklyn, NY. Debut 1964 OB in "Cindy," followed by "Jacques Brel Is Alive . . . ," "Sensations," "Leaves of Grass," "How to Ged Rid of It," "A Matter of Time," "Tickles by Tucholsky," "Not at the Palace," "Non Pasquale," Bdwy in "Dear World (1969), "Different Times," "Got Tu Go Disco," "Jacques Brel Is Alice . . . "

MASSA, STEVE. Born July 20, 1955 in Mansfield, OH. Graduate OhU. Debut 1982 on Bdwy in "Alice in Wonderland," OB in "That's It, Folks!"

MASTERS, ANDREA. Born Nov. 16, 1949 in Chicago, IL. Attended Mills Col. Columbia U. Debut 1975 OB in "The Long Valley," followed by "Justice," "Little Eyolf," Bdwy in "The Basic Training of Pavlo Hummel" (1977).

MASTRANTONIO, MARY ELIZABETH. Born Nov. 17, 1958 in Chicago, IL. Attended UIll. Bdwy debut 1980 in "West Side Story," followed by "Copperfield," "Oh, Brother," "The Human Comedy," "Sunday in the Park with George," OB in "The Human Comedy," "Henry V."

MATHERS, JAMES. Born Oct. 31, 1936 in Seattle, WA. Graduate UWA., Beverly Col. Debut 1983 OB in "Happy Birthday, Wanda June," followed by "Uncommon Holidays."

MATHESON, TIM. Born Dec. 31, 1947 in Glendale, CA. Attended CalState. Debut 1984 OB in "True West."

MATHEWS, CARMEN. Born May 8, 1918 in Philadelphia, PA. Graduate RADA. Bdwy debut 1938 in "Henry IV," followed by "Hamlet," "Richard II," "Harriet," "Cherry Orchard," "The Assassin," "Man and Superman," "Ivy Green," "Courtin' Time," "My Three Angels," "Holiday for Lovers," "Night Life," "Lorenzo," "The Yearling," "Delicate Balance," "I'm Solomon," "Dear World," "Ring Round the Bathtub," "Ambassador," "Copperfield," "Morning's at 7," OB in "Sunday in the Park with George."

MATSUSAKA, TOM. Born Aug. 8, in Wahiawa, HI. Graduate MiStateU. Bdwy bow 1968 in "Mame," followed by "Ride the Winds," "Pacific Overtures," OB in "Agamemnon," "Chu Chem," "Jungle of Cities," "Santa Anita '42," "Extenuating Circumstances," "Rohwer," "Teahouse," "Song of a Nisei Fisherman," "Empress of China," "Pacific Overtures" (1984).

MATTHEWS, ANDERSON. Born Oct. 21, 1950 in Springfield, OH. Graduate Carnegie-Mellon U. Bdwy debut 1975 in "The Robber Bridegroom," followed by "Edward II," "The Time of Your Life."

MATZ, JERRY. Born Nov. 15, 1935 in NYC. Graduate Syracuse U. Debut 1965 OB in "The Old Glory," followed by "Hefetz," "A Day Out of Time," "A Mad World, My Masters," "Rise of David Levinsky," "Last Danceman."

MAULDIN, MICHAEL. Born Dec. 17, 1957 in Panama City, FL. Graduate UWestFl. Debut 1983 OB in "The Tempest."

MAY, BEVERLY. Born Aug. 11, 1927 in East Wellington, BC, Can. Graduate Yale U. Debut 1976 OB in "Female Transport," followed by "Bonjour La Bonjour," "My Sister in This House," "Slab Boys," "And a Nightingale Sang." Bdwy 1977 in "Equus," followed by "Once in a Lifetime," "Whose Life Is It Anyway?," "Rose," "Curse of an Aching Heart."

MAY, DAVID. Born Sept. 24, 1953 in Dallas, TX. Graduate Trinity U. Debut 1983 OB in "Paradise Lost," followed by "The Inheritors," "Rain," "The Hasty Heart."

MAYER, JERRY. Born May 12, 1941 in NYC. Graduate NYU. Debut 1968 OB in "Alice in Wonderland," followed by "L'Ete," "Marouf," "Trelawny of the Wells," "King of the Schnorrers," "Mother Courage," "You Know Al," " Goose and Tomtom," "The Rivals," Bdwy in "Much Ado about Nothing" (1972), "Play Memory."

MAZUMDAR, MAXIM. Born Jan. 27, 1953 in Bombay, India. Graduate Loyola Col., McGill U. Debut 1981 OB in "Oscar Rembered," followed by "a/k/a Tennessee," "King Lear."

MAZZA, RICHARD. Born Jan. 15, 1939 in Philadelphia, PA. Graduate Penn State U. Debut 1962 OB in "Tiger Rag," followed by "Hiatus," "All Kinds of Giants," "The Bone Garden."

McADAMS, TED. Born Aug. 19, 1957 in Hartford, CT. Graduate Hampshire Col., LAMDA. Debut 1983 OB in "Mary Barnes."

McCALL, LYNNE. Born Nov. 12, 1955 in Perth Amboy, NJ. Graduate Ithaca Col. OB in "Candida," "A Jubilee," "The Gioconda Smile," "The Bacchae," "A Haunted Place," "At Home," "The Land Is Bright," "Crossroads Cafe."

McCALLUM, DAVID. Born Sept. 19, 1933 in Scotland. Attended Chapman Col. Bdwy debut 1968 in "The Flip Side," followed by "California Suite," OB in "After the Prize," "The Philanthropist."

McCANN, CHRISTOPHER. Born Sept. 29, 1952 in NYC. Graduate NYU. Debut 1975 OB in "The Measures Taken," followed by "Ghosts," "Woyzzeck," "St. Joan of the Stockyards," "Buried Child," "Dwelling in Milk," "Tongues," "3 Acts of Recognition," "Don Juan," "Michi's Blood," "Five of Us," "Richard III."

McCAREN, JOSEPH. Born Sept. 2, 1945 in Los Angeles, CA. Graduate UCLA. Bdwy debut 1980 in "Whose Life Is It Anyway?," OB in "French Toast."

McCARTHY, JEFF. Born Oct. 16, 1954 in Los Angeles, CA. Graduate American Consv. Theatre. Bdwy debut 1982 in "Pirates of Penzance," followed by "Zorba" (1983).

McCARTY, MICHAEL. Born Sept. 7, 1946 in Evansville, IN. Graduate InU., MiStateU. Debut 1976 OB in "Fiorello!," followed by "The Robber Bridegroom," Bdwy in "Dirty Linens," "King of Hearts," "Amadeus," "Oliver!"

McCHESNEY, MART. Born Jan. 27, 1954 in Abilene, TX. Graduate Webster Col Consv. Debut 1979 OB in "Making Pease," followed by "Sometime Soon," "Grunts," "Home Again, Kathleen."

McCLAIN, MARCIA. Born Sept. 30, 1949 in San Antonio, TX. Graduate Trinity U. Debut 1972 OB in "Rainbow," followed by "A Bistro Car on the CNR," "The Derby," "Etiquette," Bdwy in "Where's Charley?" (1974) for which she received a Theatre World Award.

McCLARNON, KEVIN. Born Aug. 25, 1952 in Greenfield, IN. Graduate Butler U., LAMDA. Debut 1977 OB in "The Homecoming," followed by "Heaven's Gate," "A Winter's Tale," "Johnny on a Spot," 'The Wedding," "Between Daylight and Boonville," "Macbeth," "The Clownmaker," "Cinders."

McCRANE, PAUL. Born Jan. 19, 1961 in Philadelphia, PA. Debut 1977 OB in "Landscape of the Body," followed by "Dispatches," "Split," "Hunting Scenes," "Crossing Niagara," "Hooters," "Fables for Friends," Bdwy in "Runaways," "Curse of an Aching Heart."

McCULLOH, BARBARA. Born March 5 in Washington, DC. Graduate Wm. & Mary Col., UMd. Debut 1984 OB in "Up in Central Park."

McDONALD, BETH. Born May 25, 1954 in Chicago, IL. Graduate Juilliard. Debut 1981 OB in "A Midsummer Night's Dream," followed by "The Recruiting Officer," "Jungle of Cities," "Kennedy at Colonus."

McDONALD, TANNY. Born Feb. 13, 1939 in Princeton, IN. Graduate Vassar Col. Debut OB with Am. Savoyards, followed by "All in Love," "To Broadway with Love," "Carricknabauna," "Beggar's Opera," "Brand," "Goodbye Dan Bailey," "Total Eclipse," "Gorky," "Don Juan Comes Back from the War," "Vera with Kate," "Francis," "On Approval," Bdwy in "Fiddler on the Roof," "Come Summer," "The Lincoln Mask," "Clothes for a Summer Hotel."

McDONNELL, MARY. Born in 1952 in Ithaca, NY. Graduate SUNY/Fredonia. Debut OB 1978 in "Buried Child," followed by "Letters Home," "Still Life," "Death of a Miner," "Black Angel," "A Weekend Near Madison," "All Night Long."

McDONOUGH, STEPHEN. Born Oct. 27, 1958 in Brooklyn, NY. Graduate SUNY/Potsdam. Debut 1981 OB in "The Fantasticks," followed by "Teach Me How to Cry."

McFARLAND, ROBERT. Born May 7, 1931 in Omaha, NE. Graduate UMi, Columbia U. Debut 1978 OB in "The Taming of the Shrew," followed by "When the War Was Over," "Divine Fire," "Ten Little Indians," "The Male Animal," "Comedy of Errors," "Appointment with Death."

McGILLIGAN, JUDITH. Born Aug. 22, 1948 in Dublin, IR. Bdwy debut 1966 in "Philadelphia, Here I Come," followed by "Private Lives," OB in "Within Two Shadows," "Hay Fever."

McGOVERN, ELIZABETH. Born July 18, 1961 in Evanston, IL. Attended Juilliard. Debut 1981 OB in "To Be Young, Gifted and Black," followed by "Hotel Play," "My Sister in This House" for which she received a Theatre World Award, "Painting Churches."

McGOVERN, MAUREEN. Born July 27, 1949 in Youngstown, OH. Bdwy debut 1981 in "Pirates of Penzance," followed by "Nine," OB in "Brownstone."

McGREGOR-STEWART, KATE. Born Oct. 4, 1944 in Buffalo, NY. Graduate Beaver Col., Yale U. Bdwy debut 1975 in "Travesties," followed by "A History of the American Film," OB in "Titanic," "Vienna Notes," "Beyond Therapy" (also Bdwy), "Baby with the Bathwater."

McGUIRE, KEVIN. Born Dec. 31, 1958 in Bennington, VT. Attended RADA. Debut 1981 OB in "A Midsummer Night's Dream," followed by "Forbidden Broadway," "Big Maggie," "Waiting for Godot."

McGUIRE, RODNEY ALAN. Born Aug. 2, 1959 in Chicago, IL. Attended Juilliard. Debut 1983 in Bdwy's "The Tap Dance Kid."

McHATTIE, STEPHEN. Born Feb. 3 in Antigonish, NS. Graduate Acadia U., AADA. Bdwy debut 1968 in "The American Dream," followed by "The Misanthrope," "Heartbreak House," OB in "Henry IV," "Richard III," "The Persians," "Pictures in the Hallway," "Now There's Just the Three of Us," "Anna K," "Twelfth Night," "Mourning Becomes Electra," "Alive and Well in Argentina," "The Iceman Cometh," "Winter Dancers," "Casualties," "Three Sisters," "Mensch Meier."

McINTOSH, MARCIA. Born Dec. 30, 1951 in Boston, MA. Graduate WVaU. Debut 1982 OB in "The Bottom Line," followed by "Ball," "Scripts in Comedy."

McINTYRE, MARILYN. Born May 23, 1949 in Erie, PA. Graduate PennState, NCSch. of Arts. Debut 1977 OB in "the Perfect Mollusc," followed by "Measure for Measure," "the Promise," "Action," "Blithe Spirit," "All the Nice People," Bdwy in "Gemini" (1980), "Scenes and Revelations."

McKENNA, CHRISTIANE. Born Mar. 14, 1952 in San Francisco, Ca. Attended Juilliard, Banff, Pacific Consv. Debut 1980 OB in "Merton of the Movies," followed by "Madwoman of Chaillot," "Midsummer Night's Dream," "Sjt Musgrave's Dance," "Boys in the Backroom."

McKEON, DOUG. Born in 1966 in NJ. Bdwy debut 1983 in "Brighton Beach Memoirs."

McMILLAN, LISA. Born May 28, 1955 in Oregon. Graduate Juilliard. Debut 1980 OB in "City Junket," followed by "Snap Shots," "Moose Murders" (Bdwy 1983).

McNAMARA, DERMOT. Born Aug. 24, 1925 in Dublin, IR. Bdwy debut 1959 in "A Touch of the Poet," followed by "Philadelphia, Here I Come," "Donnybrook," "Taming of the Shrew," OB in "The Wise Have Not Spoken," "3 by Synge," "Playboy of the Western World," "Shadow and Substance, "Happy as Larry," "Sharon's Grave," "A Whistle in the Dark," "Red Roses for Me," "The Plough and the Stars," "Shadow of a Gunman," "No Exit," "Stephen D.," "Hothouse," "Home Is the Hero," "Sunday Morning Bright and Early," "The Birthday Party," "All the Nice People."

McNAMARA, ROSEMARY. Born Jan. 7, 1943 in Summit, NJ. Attended Newark Col. OB in "The Master Builder," "Carricknabuana," "Rocket to the Moon," "The Most Happy Fella," "Matchmaker," "Anyone Can Whistle," "Facade," "Marya," "A Good Year for the Roses," Bdwy in "The Student Gypsy" (1963).

McNEELY, ANNA. Born June 23, 1950 in Tower Hill, IL. Graduate McKendree Col. Bdwy debut 1982 in "Little Johnny Jones," followed by "Cats."

McQUEEN, ARMELIA. Born Jan 6, 1952 in North Carolina. Attended HB Studio, Bklyn Consv. Bdwy debut 1978 in "Ain't Misbehavin'" for which she received a Theatre World Award, OB in "Can't Help Singing," "5-6-7-8 Dance."

McRAE, CALVIN. Born Feb. 14, 1955 in Toronto, Can. Attended London Guildhall. Bdwy debut 1971 in "Anne of Green Gables," followed by "Music Man," "A Broadway Musical," "Going Up," "A Chorus Line," "Sophisticated Ladies," OB in "For Ladies Only."

McROBBIE, PETER. Born Jan. 31, 1943 in Hawick, Scot. Graduate Yale U. Debut 1976 OB in "The Wobblies," followed by "The Devil's Disciple," "Cinders," Bdwy in "Whose Life Is It Anyway?" (1979), "Macbeth" (1981).

MEACHAM, PAUL. Born Aug. 5, 1939 in Memphis, TN. Graduate UTn., MiStateU. Debut 1973 OB in "Twelfth Night," followed by "The Homecoming," "The Tempest," "Moby Dick," "The Crucible," "The Passion of Dracula," "Fighting Bob," "Lineman and Sweet Lightnin'."

MEARA, ANNE. Born Sept. 20, 1929 in Brooklyn, NY. Attended HB Studio. OB in "The Silver Tassie," "Dandy Dick," "A Month in the Country," "Spookhouse."

MEEK, JOE. Born Nov. 10, 1944 in Bremerton, WA. Attended UWa. Debut 1981 OB in "Two Gentlemen from Verona," followed by "Edward II," "The Pink Combo," "Taming of the Shrew," "The Tempest," "Julius Caesar."

MEISNER, GUNTER. Born Apr. 18, 1926 in Bremen, Ger. Attended Municipal Drama Sch. Debut 1983 OB in "Report to an Academy."

MELHUSE, PEDER. Born May 5, 1948 in Bethesda, MD. Attended UWis, PennStateU. Debut 1983 OB in "True West."

MELOCHE, KATHERINE. Born June 1, 1952 in Detroit, MI. Bdwy debut 1976 in "Grease," followed by "Dancin'," OB in "Street Scene," "Little Shop of Horrors."

MENDILLO, STEPHEN. Born Oct. 9, 1942 in New Haven, CT. Graduate Colo. Col., Yale. Debut 1973 OB in "Nourish the Beast," followed by "Gorky," "Time Steps," "The Marriage," "Loot," "Subject to Fits," "Wedding Band," "As You Like It," "Fool for Love," Bdwy in "National Health" (1974), "Ah, Wilderness," "A View from the Bridge."

MERCADO, HECTOR JAIME. Born in 1949 in NYC. Attended Harkness Ballet School, HB Studio. Bdwy debut 1960 in "West Side Story," followed by "Mass," "Dr. Jazz," "1600 Pennsylvania Avenue," "Your Arms Too Short to Box with God," "West Side Story" (1980), "Cats," OB in "Sancocho," "People in Show Business Make Long Goodbyes."

MEREDITH, BURGESS. Born Nov. 16, 1908 in Cleveland, OH. Attended Amherst Col. Credits include: "Little Ol' Boy," "She Loves Me Not," "Barretts of Wimpole St," "Flowers of the Forest," "Winterset," "High Tor," "Liliom," "Candida," "Playboy of the Western World," "The Fourposter," "The Remarkable Mr. Pennypacker," "Teahouse of the August Moon," "Major Barbara," "I Was Dancing," OB in "Park Your Car in Harvard Yard."

MERKERSON, S. EPATHA. Born Nov. 28, 1952 in Saginaw, MI. Graduate Wayne State U. Debut 1979 OB in "Spell #7," followed by "Home," "Puppetplay," "Tintypes," "Every Goodbye Ain't Gone," "Hospice," "The Harvesting," Bdwy in "Tintypes" (1982).

MERRELL, RICHARD. Born July 6, 1925 in NJ. Graduate Neighborhood Playhouse. Debut 1953 OB in "Which Way Is Home," followed by "The Investigation," "Feathered Serpent," "Scenes and Revelations," "Busybody," "Family Comedy," "Patrick Pearse Motel," Bdwy in "Viva Madison Avenue" (1960).

MESEROLL, KENNETH. Born Apr. 15, 1952 in NJ. Attended UWisc. Debut 1979 OB in "Funeral Games," followed by "Saved," "Flight of the Earls," Bdwy in "Plenty" (1982).

METCALF, MARK. Born Mar. 11 in Findlay, OH. Attended UMi. Debut 1973 OB in "Creeps," followed by "The Tempest," "Beach Children," "Hamlet," "Patrick Henry Lake Liquors," "Streamers," "Salt Lake City Skyline," "Mr. & Mrs.," "Romeo and Juliet."

METTE, NANCY. Born Jan. 22, 1955 in Pennsylvania. Graduate NCSch. of Arts. Debut 1982 OB in "The Good Parts," followed by "The Alto Part."

MEYER, TARO. Born NYC. Graduate Bklyn. Col. Debut 1972 OB in "Iphigenia," followed by "Circle of Sound," "Astonished Heart," "Snapshots," "Bones," Bdwy in "Two Gentlemen of Verona" (1973), "Zorba" (1983).

MEYERS, KIMBERLY. Born May 6, 1956 in Pittsburgh, PA. Graduate Point Park Col. Debut 1983 OB in "The Music Man."

MICHALSKI, JOHN. Born June 7, 1948 in Hammond, IN. Juilliard graduate. Bdwy debut 1973 in "Beggar's Opera," followed by "Measure for Measure," "Herzl," "Gorey Stories," OB in "Hamlet," "Much Ado about Nothing," "Playing with Fire," "The Rivals."

MICKENS, JAN. Born Feb. 16, 1939 in NYC. Attended Juilliard. Debut 1973 OB in "Thoughts," followed by "My One and Only" (1983).

MILLER, BETTY. Born Mar. 27, 1925 in Boston, MA. Attended UCLA. OB in "Summer and Smoke," "Cradle Song," "La Ronde," "Plays for Bleecker St.," "Desire Under the Elms," "The Balcony," "The Power and the Glory," "Beaux Stratagem," "Gandhi," "Girl on the Via Flaminia," "Hamlet," "Summer," Bdwy in "You Can't Take It With You," "Right You Are," "The Wild Duck," "The Cherry Orchard," "A Touch of the Poet," "Eminent Domain," "The Queen and the Rebels," "Richard III."

MILLER, COURT. Born Jan. 29, 1952 in Norwalk, CT. Debut 1980 OB in "Elizabeth and Essex," followed by "Welded," "Spookhouse," Bdwy in "The First," "Torch Song Trilogy."

MILLER, MARY. Born Apr. 1, 1959 in Atlanta, GA. Graduate Hollins Col. Debut 1980 OB in "Barefoot in the Park," followed by "Incoming," "The Rapids," "Butterflies Are Free."

MILLER, MARY BETH. Born Dec. 18, 1942 in Louisville, KY. Attended Gallaudet Col. Bdwy debut with National Theatre of the Deaf, followed by "The Gin Game."

MILLER, SCOTT GORDON. Born Jan. 21, 1956 in Cleveland, OH. Attended London's Drama Centre. Debut 1983 OB in "Ah, Wilderness!"

MILLIGAN, JOHN. Born in Vancouver, Can. Attended Bristol Old Vic. Credits include: "Matchmaker," "First Gentleman," "Lock Up Your Daughters," "Love and Libel," "Man and Boy," "The Devils," "Portrait of a Queen," OB in "One Way Pendulum," "John Brown's Body," "When You Comin' Back, Red Ryder?," "Esther," "Veronica's Room," "Without Willie," "Souvenirs."

MILLS, STEPHANIE. Born in 1959 in Brooklyn, NY. Bdwy debut 1975 in "The Wiz" followed by 1984 revival.

MINER, JAN. Born Oct. 15, 1917 in Boston, MA. Debut 1958 OB in "Obligato," followed by "Decameron," "Dumbbell People," "Autograph Hound," "A Lovely Sunday for Creve Coeur," "The Music Keeper," Bdwy in "Viva Madison Avenue" (1960), "Lady of the Camelias," "The Freaking Out of Stephanie Blake," "Othello," "The Milk Train Doesn't Stop Here Anymore," "Butterflies Are Free," "The Women," "Pajama Game," "Saturday Sunday Monday," "The Heiress," "Romeo and Juliet," "Watch on the Rhine," "Heartbreak House."

MINNELLI, LIZA. Born Mar 12, 1946 in Los Angeles, CA. Attended UParis, HB Studio. Debut 1963 OB in "Best Foot Forward" for which she received a Theatre World Award, Bdwy in "Flora, the Red Menace" (1965), "Liza," "Chicago," "The Act," "The Rink."

MINNING, STEVEN. Born Jan. 20, 1953 in Washington, MO. Graduate Central Methodist Col., Emporia State U. Bdwy debut 1981 in "Fiddler on the Roof," OB in "Red, Hot and Blue" (1984).

MIRABAL, JEANNETTE. Born Dec. 5, 1958 in Havana, Cuba. Graduate NYU. Debut 1984 OB in "Cuban Swimmer/Dog Lady."

MITCHELL, GREGORY. Born Dec. 9. 1951 in Brooklyn, NY. Graduate Juilliard. Principal with Feld Ballet before Bdwy debut (1983) in "Merlin," OB in "One More Song."

MITZMAN, MARCIA. Born Feb. 28, 1959 in NYC. Attended SUNY/Purchase, Neighborhood Playhouse. Debut 1978 OB in "Promises, Promises," followed by "Taming of the Shrew," "Around the Corner from the White House." Bdwy in "Grease" (1979), "Oliver!" (1984).

MOFFAT, DONALD. Born Dec. 26, 1930 in Plymouth, Eng. Attended RADA. Bdwy bow 1957 in "Under Milk Wood," followed by "Much Ado about Nothing," "The Tumbler," "Duel of Angels," "Passage to India," "The Affair," "Father's Day," "Play Memory," OB in "The Bald Soprano," "Jack," "The Caretaker," "Misalliance," with APA in "You Can't Take It with You," "War and Peace." "Right You Are," "The Wild Duck," "The Cherry Orchard," "Cock-a-doodle Dandy," and "Hamlet," "Painting Churches."

MOFFET, SALLY. Born Apr. 21, 1931 in NYC. Attended Friend's Acad. Bdwy debut 1948 in "The Yound and Fair," OB in "Under Milk Wood," followed by "A Perfect Analysis . . ."

MOHAT, BRUCE. Born Oct. 25, 1948 in Galion, OH. Graduate Miami U. Debut 1984 OB in "Flesh, Flash and Frank Harris."

MOJICA, DAN. Born June 7, 1962 in San Juan, PR. Graduate UMiami. Debut 1983 OB in "The Music Man."

MONFERDINI, CAROLE. Born in Eagle Lake TX. Graduate NorthTexStateU. Debut 1973 OB in "The Foursome," followed by "The Club," "The Alto Part."

MONK, ISABELL. Born Oct. 4, 1952, in Washington, DC. Graduate Towson State U., Yale. Debut 1981 OB in "The Tempest," followed by "The Gospel at Colonus."

MONSON, LEX. Born Mar. 11, 1926 in Grindstone, PA. Attended DePaul U, UDetroit. Debut 1961 OB in "The Blacks," followed by "Pericles," "Macbeth," "See How They Run," "Telemachus Clay," "Keyboard," "Oh My Mother Passed Away," "The Confession Stone," "Linty Lucy," "Burnscape," Bdwy in "Moby Dick," "Trumpets of the Lord," "Watch on the Rhine."

MONTEITH, JOHN. Born Nov. 1, 1948 in Philadelphia, PA. Graduate Boston U. Debut 1973 OB in "The Proposition," followed by "See America First," "Ferocious Kisses," "A Hell of a Town," Bdwy in "Monteith and Rand"(1979).

MONTELLE, CHERYL. Born Aug. 4, 1959 in St. Louis, MO. Attended Ntl. Acad. of Arts. Debut 1983 OB in "The Music Man."

MONTONE, RITA. Born Mar. 7, 1949 in Baltimore, MD. Debut 1979 OB in "The Birds," followed by "Pass with Care," "Sports Czar," "Re-Po."

MOODY, RON. Born Jan. 8. 1924 in London, Eng. Graduate London U. Bdwy debut 1984 in "Oliver!" for which he received a Special Theatre World Award.

MOOR, BILL. Born July 13, 1931 in Toledo, OH. Attended Northwestern, Denison U. Bdwy debut 1964 in "Blues for Mr. Charlie," followed by "Great God Brown," "Don Juan," "The Visit," "Chemin de Fer," "Holiday," "P.S. Your Cat Is Dead," "Night of the Tribades," "Water Engine," "Plenty," "Heartbreak House," OB in "Dandy Dick," "Love Nest," "Days and Nights of Beebee Fenstermaker," "The Collection," "The Owl Answers," "Long Christmas Dinner," "Fortune and Men's Eyes," "King Lear," "Cry of Players," "Boys in the Band," "Alive and Well in Argentina," "Rosmersholm." "The Biko Inquest," "A Winter's Tale," "Johnny on a Spot," "Barbarians," "The Purging," "Potsdam Quartet," "Zones of the Spirit."

MOORE, JUDITH. Born Feb. 12, 1944 in Princeton, WVa. Graduate IndU., Concord Col. Debut 1971 OB in "The Drunkard," followed by "Ten by Six," "Boys from Syracuse," "The Evangelist," Bdwy in "Sunday in the Park with George" (1984).

MOORE, LEE. Born Feb. 19, 1929 in Brooklyn, NY. Debut 1978 OB in "Once More With Feeling," followed by "The Caine Mutiny Court-Martial," "Christopher Blake."

MORALES, MARK. Born Nov. 9, 1954 in NYC. Attended Trenton State, SUNY/Purchase. Debut 1978 OB in "Coolest Cat in Town," followed by "Transposed Heads," Bdwy in "West Side Story" (1980), "America."

MORAN, MARTIN. Born Dec. 29, 1959 in Denver CO. Attended Stanford U., AmConsv Theatre. Debut 1983 OB in "Spring Awakening," Bdwy in "Oliver!" (1984).

MORANZ, BRAD. Born Aug. 29, 1952 in Houston, TX. Bdwy debut in "A Day in Hollywood/A Night in the Ukraine" (1981), OB in "Little Shop of Horrors."

MORANZ, JANET. (formerly Horsley) Born Oct. 13, 1954 in Los Angeles, CA. Attended CaStateU. Bdwy debut 1980 in "A Chorus Line."

MOREY, CHARLES. Born June 23, 1947 in Oakland, CA. Graduate Dartmouth Col., Columbia U. Debut 1970 OB in "Fugue," followed by "Jungle of Cities," "Woyzeck," "Julius Caesar," "In the Shadow of the Glen," "Booth Brothers," "Idle Hands," "Macbeth."

MORGAN, MONIQUE. Born May 4, 1955 in Norfolk, VA. Graduate Stephens Col., Wayne State U. Debut 1980 OB in "Transcendental Love," followed by "A Bold Stroke for a Wife."

MORGENSTERN, SUSAN. Born May 13, 1954 in Glens Falls, NY. Graduate UCal. Debut 1981 OB in "The Killing of Sister George," followed by "Female Transport," "The Sea Horse," "Ball."

MOROZ, BARBARA. Born Feb. 9, 1958 in Dearborn, MI. Bdwy debut 1984 in "Oliver!"

MORRISEY, BOB. Born Aug. 15, 1946 in Somerville, MA. Attended UWi. Debut 1974 OB in "Ionescapade," followed by "Company," "Anything Goes," "Philistines," Bdwy in "The First" (1981), "Cats."

MORRISON, WILLIAM. Born Mar. 24, 1967 in NYC. Bdwy debut 1980 in "One Night Stand," followed by "Macbeth," OB in "American Passion."

MORSE, ROBIN. Born July 8, 1963 in NYC. Bdwy debut 1981 in "Bring Back Birdie," followed by "Brighton Beach Memoirs."

MORTON, JOE. Born Oct. 18, 1947 in NYC. Attended Hofstra U. Debut 1968 OB in "A Month of Sundays," followed by "Salvation," "Charlie Was Here and Now He's Gone," "G. R. Point," "Crazy Horse," "A Winter's Tale" "Johnny on a Spot," "Midsummer Night's Drean," "The Recruiting Office," "Oedipus the King," "The Wild Duck," "Rhinestone," "Souvenirs," Bdwy in "Hair," "Two Gentlemen of Verona," "Tricks," "Raisin" for which he received a Theatre World Award, "Oh, Brother!"

MOSES, MARK. Born Feb. 24, 1960 in NYC. Graduate Northwestern U, NYU. Debut 1983 OB in "The Slab Boys," followed by "Fraternity," "Home Remedies," "The Lady and the Clarinet."

MOSES, STEVEN. Born Oct. 31, 1958 in Brooklyn, NY. Graduate Glassboro State Col. Debut 1984 in Bdwy's "Play Memory."

MUEHL, BRIAN. Born Aug. 24, 1952 in Cannendaugia, NY. Attended UKan. Bdwy debut in "Mummenschanz"(1978), OB in "Elizabeth and Essex," "Boys in the Backroom," "Richard II."

MULLER, FRANK. Born May 5, 1951 in Beverwijk, Netherlands. Attended UMn, NCSch of Arts. Debut 1980 OB in "Salt Lake City Skyline," followed by "Henry V."

MUNDY, MEG. Born in London, Eng. Attended Inst. of Musical Art. Bdwy debut 1936 in "Ten Million Ghosts," followed by "Hoorah for What," "The Fabulous Invalid," "Three to Make Ready," "How I Wonder," "The Respectful Prostitute" for which she received a Theatre World Award, "Detective Story," "Love's Labour's Lost," "Love Me a Little," "Philadelphia Story," "You Can't Take It with You," OB in "Lysistrata," "Rivers Return."

MURPHY, PETER. Born Sept. 13, 1925 in Glenarm, Ire. Attended ULondon, RADA. Debut 1956 OB in "The Comedian," followed by "Macbeth," "Ghosts," "The Fantasticks," "When We Dead Awaken," "Dancing for the Kaiser," "Heartbreak House," "Primal Time," "Strange Case of Dr. Jekyll," "Verdict."

MURRAY, BRIAN. Born Oct. 9, 1939 in Johannesburg, SA. Debut 1964 OB in "The Knack," followed by "King Lear," "Ashes," "The Jail Diary of Albie Sachs," "A Winter's Tale," "Barbarians," "The Purging," "Midsummer Night's Dream," "The Recruiting Officer," "The Arcata Promise," "Candida in Concert" Bdwy in "All in Good Time," "Rosencrantz and Guildenstern Are Dead," "Sleuth," "Da," "Noises Off."

MURRAY, MARY GORDON. Born Nov. 13, 1953 in Ridgewood, NJ. Attended Ramapo Col., Juilliard. Bdwy debut 1976 in "The Robber Bridegroom," followed by "Grease," "I Love My Wife," "Little Me," "Play Me a Country Song," OB in "A . . . My Name is Alice," "Blue Plate Special."

MURRAY, PEG. Born in Denver, CO. Attended Western Reserve U. OB in "Children of Darkness" (1958), "Midsummer Night's Dream," "Oh, Dad, Poor Dad . . . ," "Small Craft Warnings," "Enclave," "Landscape of the Body," "A Lovely Sunday for Creve Couer," "Isn't It Romantic," Bdwy in "The Great Sebastians" (1956), "Gypsy," "Blood, Sweat and Stanley Toole," "She Loves Me," "Anyone Can Whistle," "The Subject Was Roses," "Something More," "Cabaret," "Fiddler on the Roof," "Royal Family."

MYERS, JENNIFER. Born Dec. 21, 1959 in Detroit, MI. Graduate Northwestern U. Debut 1983 OB in "Where's Charley?," followed by "Mighty Fine Music."

NADEL, ARLENE. Born Aug. 15, in Columbus, OH. Graduate Northwestern U. Debut 1967 OB in "You Never Can Tell," followed by "Trelawny of the Wells," "Algonquin Sampler," "She Stoops to Conquer," "Brass Butterfly," "Romeo and Jeanette," "A New Way to Pay Old Debts," Bdwy in "Red, White and Maddox" (1969).

NAKAHARA, RON. Born July 20, 1947 in Honolulu, HI. Attended UHI. Tenri U. Debut 1981 OB in "Danton's Death," followed by "Flowers and Household Gods," "A Few Good Men," "Rohwer," "A Midsummer Night's Dream," "Teahouse," "Song for Nisei Fisherman."

NASTASI, FRANK. Born Jan. 7, 1923 in Detroit MI. Graduate Wayne U., NYU. Bdwy debut 1963 in "Lorenzo," followed by "Avanti," OB in "Bonds of Interest," "One Day More," "Nathan the Wise," "The Chief Things,""Cindy," "Escurial," "The Shrinking Bride," "Macbird," "Cakes with the Wine," "Metropolitan Madness,""Rockaway Boulevard," "Scenes from La Vie de Boheme," "Agamemnon," "Happy Sunset Inc." "3 Last Plays of O'Neill," "Taking Steam."

NEAL, ALBERT. Born Nov. 8, 1953 in South Orange, NJ. Graduate Boston U. Debut 1978 OB in "Family Business" followed by "Julius Caesar."

NEAL, BILLIE. Born Dec. 12, 1955 in Little Rock, AR. Attended NYU, Neighborhood Playhouse. Debut 1984 OB in "Balm in Gilead."

NEASE, BYRON BUD. Born Oct. 22, 1953 in Los Angeles, CA. Debut 1980 OB in "Annie Get Your Gun," followed by "Lola," Bdwy in "Mame" (1983).

NEIL, ROGER. Born Nov. 19, 1948 in Galesburg, IL. Graduate Northwestern U. Debut 1974 OB in "The Boy Friend," followed by "Scrambled Feet," "The Fantasticks."

NELLIGAN, KATE. Born Mar. 16, 1951 in London, Can. Attended York U, Central Sch. of Speech/Drama. Debut 1982 OB in "Plenty," Bdwy in "Plenty" (1983), "Moon for the Misbegotten"(1984).

NELSON, GAIL. Born Mar. 29 in Durham, NC. Graduate Oberlin Col. Bdwy debut 1968 in "Hello, Dolly!," followed by "Applause,""On the Town,""Music!Music!,""Eubie!," "Rockette Spectacular," "The Tap Dance Kid," OB in "Six," "By Strouse," "Broadway Soul," "Songs You Never Heard Before."

NEUBERGER, JAN. Born Jan. 21, 1953 in Amityville, NY. Attended NYU. Bdwy debut 1975 in "Gypsy," OB in "Silk Stockings," "Chase a Rainbow," "Anything Goes," "A Little Madness," "Forbidden Broadway."

NEUMAN, JOAN. Born Oct. 4, 1926 in NYC. Graduate NYU. Debut 1964 OB in "A Woman of No Importance," followed by "Arsenic and Old Lace," "Camino Real," "All the King's Men," "Happy Sunset Inc.," "Triptych."

NEVILLE, KATHERINE. Born Sept. 24, 1954 in Pittsburgh, PA. Graduate Vassar Col. Debut 1978 OB in "The Mikado," followed by "Macbeth," "Incorrect Is Meaning Backwards," "Playboy of the Western World," "Midsummer Night's Dream," "Non-Sequitor," "Angst for the Memories."

NEWMAN, WILLIAM. Born June 15, 1934 in Chicago, IL. Graduate UWVa, Columbia U. Debut 1972 OB in "Beggar's Opera," followed by "Are You Now . . . ," "Conflict of Interest," "Mr. Runaway," "Uncle Vanya," "One Act Play Festival," "Routed," "The Great Divide," "Come Back, Little Sheba," Bdwy in "Over Here" (1974), "Rocky Horror Show," "Strangers."

NICHOLS, ROBERT. Born July 20, 1924 in Oakland, CA. Attended Pacific Col., RADA. Debut 1978 OB in "Are You Now . . . ," followed by "Heartbreak House," "Ah, Wilderness!," Bdwy in "Man and Superman," "The Man Who Came to Dinner," "Einstein and the Polar Bear."

NILES, MARY ANN. Born May 2, in NYC. Attended Miss Finchley's Ballet Acad. Bdwy debut in "Girl from Nantucket," followed by "Dance Me A Song," "Call Me Mister," "Make Mine Manhattan," "La Plume de Ma Tante," "Carnival," "Flora the Red Menace," "Sweet Charity," "George M!," "No, No, Nanette," "Irene," "Ballroom," OB in "The Boys from Syracuse," CC's "Wonderful Town" and "Carnival."

NILES, RICHARD. Born May 19, 1946 in NYC. Graduate, NYU. Debut 1969 OB in "Sourball," followed by "Innocent Thoughts, Harmless Intentions," "Elephants," "The Rivals," Bdwy in "And Miss Reardon Drinks a Little," "Don't Call Back."

NIXON, CYNTHIA. Born Apr. 9, 1966 in NYC. Debut 1980 in "The Philadelphia Story"(LC) for which she received a Theatre World Award, OB in "Lydie Breeze," "Hurlyburly," Bdwy in "The Real Thing" (1983), "Hurlyburly."

NIXON, JAMES E. Born Oct. 12, 1957 in Jersey City, NJ. Attended Kean Col. Debut 1982 OB in "The Six O'Clock Boys," followed by "The Holy Junkie."

NIXON, MARNI. Born Feb. 22, in Altadena, CA. Attended LACC, USCal., Pasadena Playhouse. Bdwy debut 1952 in "The Girl in Pink Tights," followed by "My Fair Lady" (1964), OB in "Thank Heaven for Lerner and Loewe," "Taking My Turn."

NOEL, DANIEL. Born May 1, 1954 in LaCrosse, WI. Attended UWi, UParis,AADA. Debut 1983 OB in "The Human Comedy", also Bdwy 1984.

NOLIN, DENISE. Born Jan. 9, 1959 in Providence, RI. Attended RICol. Debut 1983 OB in "Nite Club Confidential."

NOODT, BRIAN. Born Mar. 13, 1973 in Freehold, NH. Bdwy debut 1984 in "Oliver!"

NOONAN, TOM. Born Apr. 12, 1951 in Greenwich, CT. Yale graduate. Debut 1978 OB in "Buried Child," followed by "The Invitational," "Farmyard," "The Breakers," "Five of Us," "Spookhouse."

NORMAN, DARA. Born Aug. 8 in NYC. Attended UCin, UMiami. Bdwy debut 1975 in "The Magic Show," followed by "Oh! Calcutta!," OB in "Dr. Selavy's Magic Theatre," "Beggar's Opera," "The Boys in the Live Country Band," "Talking Dirty."

NOSTRAND, MICHAEL. Born Mar. 30, 1956 in Hempstead, NY. Graduate Wagner Col., Catholic U. Bdwy debut 1983 in "The Corn Is Green."

NUTE, DON. Born Mar. 13, in Connellsville, PA. Attended Denver U. Debut OB 1965 in "The Trojan Women" followed by "Boys in the Band," "Mad Theatre for Madmen," "The Eleventh Dynasty," "About Time," "The Urban Crisis," "Christmas Rappings," "The Life of a Man," "A Look at the Fifties."

NYGAARD, ROY. Born July 6, 1971 in Syosset, NY. Bdwy debut 1984 in "Oliver!"

NYPE, RUSSELL. Born Apr. 26, 1924 in Zion, IL. Attended Lake Forest Col. Bdwy debut 1949 in "Regina," followed by "Call Me Madam" for which he received a Theatre World Award, "Tender Trap," "Tunnel of Love," "Wake Up, Darling," CC's "Carousel" and "Brigadoon," "The Owl and the Pussycat," "The Girl in the Freudian Slip," "Hello, Dolly!," OB in "Brouhaha," "Private Lives," "Lady Audley's Secret," "Tallulah."

O'BRIEN, DAVID. Born Oct. 1, 1935 in Chicago, IL. Graduate Stanford U., LAMDA. Bdwy in "A Passage to India" (1962), "Arturo Ui," "A Time for Singing," "End of the World . . . ," OB in "Under Milk Wood," "A Month in the Country," "Henry IV," "The Boys in the Band."

O'CONNELL, CHARLIE. Born Apr. 21, 1975 in NYC. Debut 1984 OB in "Dr. Selavy's Magic Theatre."

O'CONNELL, PATRICIA. Born May 17, in NYC. Attended AmThWing. Debut 1958 OB in "The Saintliness of Margery Kemp," followed by "Time Limit," "An Evening's Frost," "Mrs. Snow," "Electric Ice," "Survival of St. Joan," "Rain," "Rapists," "Who Killed Richard Cory?," "Misalliance," "The Singular Life of Albert Nobbs," "Come Back, Little Sheba," Bdwy in "Criss-Crossing," "Summer Brave," "Break a Leg," "The Man Who Came to Dinner."

O'CONNOR, CARROLL. Born Aug. 2, 1925 in the Bronx, NY. Attended Dublin Ntl. U. Debut 1957 OB in "Ulysses in Nighttown," followed by "The Big Knife," Bdwy in "Brothers" (1983).

O'CONNOR, KEVIN. Born May 7, in Honolulu, HI. Attended UHi., Neighborhood Playhouse. Debut 1964 OB in "Up to Thursday," followed by "Six from La Mama," "Rimers of Eldritch," "Tom Paine," "Boy on the Straightback Chair," "Dear Janet Rosenberg," "Eyes of Chalk," "Alive and Well in Argentina," "Duet," "Trio," "The Contractor," "Kool Aid," "The Frequency," "Chucky's Hutch," "Birdbath," "The Breakers," "Crossing the Crab Nebula," "Jane Avril," "Inserts," "3 by Beckett," "The Dicks," "A Kiss Is Just a Kiss," "Last of the Knucklemen," Bdwy in "Gloria and Esperanza," "The Morning after Optimism," "Figures in the Sand," "Devour the Snow," "The Lady from Dubuque."

O'DONNELL, MARY EILEEN. Born May 2, 1948 in Troy, NY. Graduate Catholic U. Debut 1974 OB in "The Measures Taken," followed by "Hamlet," "Mandrake."

O'HARA, PAIGE. Born May 10, 1956 in Ft. Lauderdale, FL. Debut 1975 OB in "The Gift of the Magi," followed by "Company," "The Great American Backstage Musical," Bdwy in "Show Boat" (1983).

O'HARE, MICHAEL. Born May 6, 1952 in Chicago, IL. Debut 1978 OB in "Galileo," followed by "Shades of Brown," Bdwy in "Players" (1978), "Man and Superman."

O'KARMA, ALEXANDRA. Born Sept. 28, 1948 in Cincinnati, OH. Graduate Swarthmore Col. Debut 1976 OB in "A Month in the Country," followed by "Warbeck," "A Flea in Her Ear," "Knitters in the Sun," "The Beethoven," "Clownmaker," "I Am a Camera."

O'KEEFE, MICHAEL. Born Apr. 24, 1955 in Westchester, NY. Attended NYU. Debut 1974 OB in "The Killdeer," followed by "Christmas on Mars," Bdwy in "5th of July," "Mass Appeal" for which he received a Theatre World Award.

O'KELLY, AIDEEN. Born in Dalkey, IR. Member of Dublin's Abbey Theatre. Bdwy debut 1980 in "A Life," follwed by "Othello," OB in "The Killing of Sister George" (1983).

O'MALLEY, ETAIN. Born Aug. 8 in Dublin, Ire. Attended Vassar Col. Debut 1964 OB in "The Trojan Women," followed by "Glad Tidings," "God of Vengeance," "A Difficult Borning," "In the Garden," Bdwy in "The Cherry Orchard" (1968), "The Cocktail Party," "The Misanthrope," "The Elephant Man," "Kingdoms," "The Queen and the Rebels," "84 Charing Cross Road."

ORBACH, JERRY. Born Oct. 20, 1935 in NYC. Attended Northwestern U. Bdwy debut 1961 in "Carnival," followed by "Guys and Dolls," "Carousel," "Annie Get Your Gun," "The Natural Look," "Promises Promises," "6 Rms Riv Vu," "Chicago," "42nd Street," OB in "Threepenny Opera," "The Fantasticks," "The Cradle Will Rock," "Scuba Duba."

O'REILLY, CIARAN. Born Mar. 13, 1959 in Ireland. Attended Carmelite Col., Juilliard. Debut 1978 OB in "Playboy of the Western World," followed by "Summer," "Freedom of the City," "Fannie," "Interrogation of Ambrose Fogarty," "King Lear," "Shadow of a Gunman," Bdwy in "The Corn Is Green" (1983).

OREM, SUSAN. Born June 15, 1949 in Elizabeth, NJ. Graduate NYU. Debut 1979 OB in "Big Bad Burlesque," followed by "Christopher Blake."

ORMAN, ROSCOE. Born June 11, 1944 in NYC. Debut 1962 OB in "If We Grow Up," followed by "Electronic Nigger," "The Great McDaddy," "The Sirens," "Every Night When the Sun Goes Down," "Last Street Play," "Julius Caesar," "Coriolanus," "The 16th Round," "20 Year Friends."

O'ROURKE, KEVIN. Born Jan. 15, 1956 in Portland, OR. Graduate Williams Col. Debut 1981 OB in "Declassee," followed by "Sister Mary Ignatius . . ."

ORR, MARY. Born Dec. 21, 1918 in Brooklyn, NY. Attended Syracuse U, AADA. Bdwy debut 1938 in "Bachelor Born," followed by "Jupiter Laughs," "Wallflower," "Dark Hammock," "Sherlock Holmes," "The Desperate Hours," OB in "Grass Widows," "Appointment with Death."

OWENS, ELIZABETH. Born Feb. 26, 1938 in NYC. Attended New School, Neighborhood Playhouse. Debut 1955 OB in "Dr. Faustus Lights the Lights," followed by "Chit Chat on a Rat," "The Miser," "The Father," "Importance of Being Earnest," "Candida," "Trumpets and Drums," "Oedipus," "Macbeth," "Uncle Vanya," "Misalliance," "Master Builder," "American Gothics," "The Play's the Thing," "The Rivals," "Death Story," "The Rehearsal," "Dance on a Country Grave," "Othello," "Little Eyolf," "The Winslow Boy," "Playing with Fire," "The Chalk Garden," "The Entertainer," "The Killing of Sister George," Bdwy in "The Lovers," "Not Now Darling," "The Play's the Thing.

OWSLEY, STEVE. Born Aug. 2, 1957 in Michigan City, IN. Graduate Western Mich. U. Debut 1984 OB in "Red, Hot and Blue."

OYSTER, JIM. Born May 3, 1930 in Washington, DC. OB in "Coriolanus," "The Cretan Woman," "Man and Superman," "Fallen Angels," "The Underlings," Bdwy in "Cool World" (1960), "Hostile Winners," "The Sound of Music," "The Prime of Miss Jean Brodie," "Who's Who in Hell."

PACE, MICHAEL. Born Aug. 26, 1949 in Kansas City, MO. Graduate Carnegie Tech. Debut 1971 OB in "Shekina," followed by "Marry Me a Little," "Tied by the Leg," "Road to Hollywood," Bdwy in "Rock 'n Roll: The First 5000 Years."

PACINO, AL. Born Apr. 25, 1940 in NYC. Attended Actors Studio. Bdwy bow 1969 in "Does a Tiger Wear a Necktie?" for which he received a Theatre World Award, followed by "The Basic Training of Pavlo Hummel," "Richard III," "American Buffalo," OB in "Why Is a Crooked Letter," "Peace Creeps," "The Indian Wants the Bronx," "Local Stigmatic," "Camino Real," "Jungle of Cities," "American Buffalo."

PAGE, GERALDINE. Born Nov. 22, 1924 in Kirksville, MO. Attended Goodman Theatre. Debut 1945 OB in "Seven Mirrors," followed by "Yerma," "Summer and Smoke," "Macbeth," "Look Away," "The Stronger," "The Human Office," "The Inheritors," "Paradise Lost," "Ghosts," Bdwy in "Midsummer" (1953) for which she received a Theatre World Award. "The Immoralist," "The Rainmaker," "Innkeepers," "Separate Tables," "Sweet Bird of Youth," "Strange Interlude," "Three Sisters," "P.S. I Love You," "The Great Indoors," "White Lies," "Black Comedy," "The Little Foxes," "Angela," "Absurd Person Singular," "Clothes for a Summer Hotel." "Agnes of God."

PAGE, KEN. Born Jan. 20, 1954 in St. Louis, MO. Attended Fontbonne Col. Bdwy debut 1976 in "Guys and Dolls" for which he received a Theatre World Award followed by "Ain't Misbehavin'," "Cats," OB in "Louis," "Can't Help Singing."

PARKER, ROCHELLE. Born Feb. 26, 1940 in Brooklyn, NY. Attended Neighborhood Playhouse. Bdwy debut 1980 in "The Survivor," OB in "Five Points," "Sheepskin," "Side Street Scenes," "Ruby and Pearl," "Within the Year."

PARLATO, DENNIS. Born Mar. 30, 1947 in Los Angeles, CA. Graduate Loyola U. Bdwy debut 1979 in "A Chorus Line," followed by "The First," OB in "Beckett," "Elizabeth and Essex" (1984).

PARRY, WILLIAM. Born Oct. 7, 1947 in Steubenville, OH Graduate Mt. Union Col. Bdwy debut 1971 in "Jesus Christ Superstar," followed by "Rockabye Hamlet," "The Leaf People," "Camelot" (1980/1981), "Sunday in the Park with George," OB in "Sgt. Pepper's Lonely Hearts Club Band," "The Conjurer," "Noah," "The Misanthrope," "Joseph and the Amazing Technicolor Dreamcoat," "Agamemnon," "Coolest Cat in Town," "Dispatches," "The Derby."

PASEKOFF, MARILYN. Born Nov. 7, 1949 in Pittsburgh, PA. Graduate Boston U. Debut 1975 OB in "Godspell," followed by "Words," "Forbidden Broadway."

PASKOW, KAREN. Born Jan. 8, 1954 in Irvington, NJ. Bdwy debut 1978 in "A Broadway Musical," followed by "My Fair Lady" (1982), "The Tap Dance Kid."

PASSELTINER, BERNIE. Born Nov. 21, 1931 in NYC Graduate Catholic U. OB in "Square in the Eye," "Sourball," "As Virtuously Given," "Now Is the Time for All Good Men," "Rain," "Kaddish," "Against the Sun," "End of Summer," "Yentl, the Yeshiva Boy," "Heartbreak House," "Every Place is Newark," "Isn't It Romantic," "Buck," "Pigeons on the Walk," Bdwy in "The Office," "The Jar," "Yentl."

PATINKIN, MANDY. Born in 1953 in Chicago, IL. Attended Juilliard. OB in "Henry IV," "Leave It to Beaver Is Dead," "Rebel Women," "Hamlet," "Trelawny of the Wells," "Savages," "The Split," Bdwy in "Evita" (1979), "Sunday in the Park with George."

PATRICK, DENNIS. Born Mar. 14, 1918 in Philadelphia, PA. Credits include "Harvey," "Cock-a-doodle Doo," "The Liar," "The Wayward Saint" for which he received a Theatre World Award, "St. Joan" (1956), "Marat/Sade" (1967), "The Sea Gull" (1983).

PATTERSON, JAY. Born Aug. 22 in Cincinnati, OH. Attended Ohio U. Bdwy debut 1983 in "K-2."

PATTERSON, KELLY. Feb. 22, 1964 in Midland, TX. Attended Southern Methodist U. Debut 1984 OB in "Up in Central Park."

PATTERSON, RAYMOND. Born Oct. 1, 1955 in Richmond, VA. Graduate UMd. Bdwy debut in "Hair" (1977), followed by "Comin' Uptown," "Rock 'n' Roll: The First 5000 Years," OB in "The Tempest," "The Architect and the Emperor of Assyria," "A Book of Etiquette," "Arturo Ui," "Battle of the Giants," "American Heroes," "Child of the Sun," "Cummings and Goings."

PAYTON-WRIGHT, PAMELA. Born Nov. 1, 1941 in Pittsburgh, PA. Graduate Birmingham Southern Col., RADA. Bdwy debut 1967 in "The Show-Off," followed by "Exit the King," "The Cherry Orchard," "Jimmy Shine," "Mourning Becomes Electra," "The Glass Menagerie," "Romeo and Juliet," OB in "The Effect of Marigolds on . . . ," "The Crucible," "The Seagull," "Don Juan," "In the Garden."

PEARLMAN, STEPHEN. Born Feb. 26, 1935 in NYC. Graduate Dartmouth Col. Bdwy bow 1964 in "Barefoot in the Park," followed by "La Strada," OB in "Threepenny Opera," "Time of the Key," "Pimpernel," "In White America," "Viet Rock," "Chocolates," "Bloomers," "Richie," "Isn't It Romantic."

PEARSON, SCOTT. Born Dec. 13, 1941 in Milwaukee, WI. Attended Valparaiso U, UWisc. Bdwy debut 1966 in "A Joyful Noise," followed by "Promises, Promises," "A Chorus Line."

PELLEGRINO, SUSAN. Born June 3, 1950 in Baltimore, MD. Attended CCSan Francisco, CalStateU. Debut 1982 OB in "The Wisteria Trees," followed by "Steel on Steel," "Master Builder."

PEN, POLLY. Born Mar. 11, 1954 in Chicago, IL. Graduate Ithaca Col. Debut 1978 OB in "The Taming of the Shrew," followed by "The Guilded Cage," "Charlotte Sweet," "A . . . My Name is Alice," Bdwy in "The Utter Glory of Morrissey Hall."

PENA, ELIZABETH. Born Sept. 23, 1959 in NJ. Debut 1969 OB in "Cinderella," followed by "Rice and Beans," "Shattered Image," "La Morena," "Romeo and Juliet," "Night of the Assassins," "Act One and Only," "The Cuban Swimmer."

PENDLETON, DAVID. Born Nov. 5, 1937 in Pittsburgh, PA. Graduate Lincoln U, CCNY. Bdwy debut 1971 in "No Place to Be Somebody," OB in "Screens," "Don't Bother Me, I Can't Cope," "Blueberry Mountain," "Julius Caesar."

PENDLETON, WYMAN. Born Apr. 18, 1916 in Providence, RI. Graduate Brown U. Bdwy in "Tiny Alice" (1964), "Malcolm," "Quotations from Chairman Mao Tse-Tung," "Happy Days," "Henry V," "Othello," "There's One in Every Marriage," "Cat on a Hot Tin Roof," "Scenes and Revelations," OB in "Gallows Humor," "America Dream," "Zoo Story," "Corruption in the Palace of Justice," "Giant's Dance," "Child Buyer," "Happy Days," "Butter and Egg Man," "Othello," "Albee Directs Albee," "Dance for Me, Simeon," "Mary Stuart," "The Collyer Brothers at Home," "Period Piece," "A Bold Stroke for a Wife."

PENN, EDWARD. Born in Washington, DC. Debut 1965 OB in "The Queen and the Rebels," followed by "My Wife and I," "Invitation to a March," "Of Thee I Sing," "The Fantasticks," "Greenwillow," "One for the Money," "Dear Oscar," "Speed Gets the Poppys," "Man with a Load of Mischief," "Company," "The Constant Wife," "Tune the Grand Up!," "Reflected Glory," "Taking My Turn," Bdwy in "Shenandoah" (1975).

PEREZ, LAZARO. Born Dec. 17, 1945 in Havana, Cuba. Bdwy debut 1969 in "Does a Tiger Wear a Necktie?," followed by "Animals," OB in "Romeo and Juliet," "12 Angry Men," "Wonderful Years," "Alive," "G. R. Point," "Primary English Class," "The Man and the Fly," "The Last Latin Lover," "Cabal of Hypocrites," "Balm in Gilead."

PERKEL, JANE. Born Aug. 26, 1964 in New Jersey, Graduate Bard Col. Debut 1983 OB in "Glory in the Flower."

PERKINS, DON. Born Oct. 23, 1928 in Boston, MA. Graduate Emerson Col. OB in "Drums under the Window," "Henry VI," "Richard III," "The Dubliners," "The Rehearsal," "Fallen Angels," "Our Lord of Lynchville," "A Touch of the Poet," Bdwy in "Borstal Boy" (1970).

PERLEY, WILLIAM. Born Nov. 24, 1942 in NYC. Graduate UFL. Debut 1975 OB in "Tenderloin," followed by "Housewives Cantata," "Count of Monte Cristo," "The Marquise," Bdwy in "Vieux Carre" (1977).

PERRY, ELIZABETH. Born Oct. 15, 1937 in Pawtuxet, RI. Attended RISU, AmThWing. Bdwy debut 1956 in "Inherit the Wind," followed by "The Women," with APA in "The Misanthrope," "Hamlet," "Exit the King," "Beckett" and "Macbeth," OB in "Royal Gambit," "Here Be Dragons," "Lady from the Sea," "Heartbreak House," "him," "All the Way Home," "The Frequency," "Fefu and Her Friends," "Out of the Broomcloset," "Ruby Ruby Sam Sam," "Did You See the Elephant?," "Last Stop Blue Jay Lane," "A Difficult Borning," "Presque Isle."

PESATURO, GEORGE. Born July 29, 1949 in Winthrop, MA. Graduate Manhattan Col. Bdwy debut 1976 in "A Chorus Line," OB in "The Music Man" (JB).

PESSANO, JAN. Born Aug. 10, 1944 in San Jose, CA. Graduate Fresno State Col. Debut 1976 OB in "She Loves Me," followed by "The Grass Harp," "Rogues to Riches," "110 in the Shade," "Elizabeth and Essex."

PETERS, BERNADETTE. Born Feb. 28, 1948 in Jamaica, NY. Bdwy debut in "Girl in the Freudian Slip," followed by "Johnny No-Trump," "George M!" for which she received a Theatre World Award, "La Strada," "On the Town," "Mack and Mabel," "Sunday in the Park with George," OB in "Curley McDimple," "Penny Friend," "Most Happy Fella," "Dames at Sea," "Nevertheless They Laugh," "Sally and Marsha."

PETERS, PHIL. Born May 6, 1944 in Worcester, MA. Debut 1978 OB in "Jackson's Dance," followed by "The Chain," "Easy Money," "Cabal of Hypocrites," "Everything in the Garden," "Book of the Dead."

PETERSON, CHRIS. Born Nov. 19, 1962 in Malden, MA. Bdwy debut 1983 in "On Your Toes."

PETERSON, LENKA. Born Oct. 16, 1925 in Omaha, NE. Attended UIowa. Bdwy debut 1946 in "Bathsheba," followed by "Harvest of Years," "Sundown Beach," "Young and Fair," "The Grass Harp," "The Girls of Summer," "The Time of Your Life," "Look Homeward, Angel," "All the Way Home," "Nuts," OB in "Mrs. Minter," "American Night Cry," "Leaving Home," "The Brass Ring," "Father Dreams," "El Bravo," "Levitations."

Shirley
Lemmon

Phillip
Lindsay

Suzanne
Lukather

Alvin
Lum

Merilee
Magnuson

Nick
Mangano

Greg
Martyn

Mary Elizabeth
Mastrantonio

Richard
Mazza

Marcia
McClain

Doug
McKeon

Armelia
McQueen

S. Epatha
Merkerson

John
Milligan

Meg
Mundy

Roger
Neil

Mary Ann
Niles

James
Nixon

Don
Nute

Dara
Norman

Russell
Nype

Patricia
O'Connell

Ciaran
O'Reilly

Steven
Owsley

Rochelle
Parker

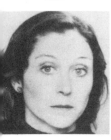

Raymond
Patterson

Pamela
Payton-Wright

Edward
Penn

Jan
Pessano

Chris
Peterson

PETRICOFF, ELAINE. Born in Cincinnati, OH. Graduate Syracuse U. Bdwy debut 1971 in "The Me Nobody Knows," followed by "Grease," "End of the World . . . ," OB in "Hark," "Ride the Winds," "Cole Porter," "Pins and Needles," "Hijinks."

PEW, BRIAN. Born Aug. 7, 1972 in NYC. Debut 1983 OB in "The Buck Stops Here," followed by "Billy Chops Bricks," "The Day Babe Ruth Died."

PEYTON, CAROLINE. Born Oct. 8, 1951 in Brookshaven, MS. Attended Northwestern, UInd. Debut 1983 OB in "Non Pasquale," followed by "The Human Comedy" (off and on Bdwy).

PHELAN, DEBORAH. Born Apr. 15 in New Haven, CT. Graduate Point Park Col. Bdwy debut in "Pippin" (1973), followed by "King of Hearts," "A Chorus Line," "Dancin'," "Encore," "La Cage aux Folles."

PHILLIPS, BARY. Born Nov. 29, 1954 in Indianapolis, IN. Graduate IndU. Debut 1981 OB in "Raisin," followed by "While We're Young," "Cries and Whimpers," "Casanova."

PHILLIPS, LACY DARRYL. Born Feb. 24, 1963 in NYC. Attended Lehman Col. Debut 1981 OB in "Raisin," followed by "Late Great Ladies."

PIDDOCK, JIM. Born Apr. 8, 1956 in Rochester Eng. Graduate London U. Bdwy debut in "Present Laughter" (1982), followed by "Noises Off," OB in "The Boy's Own Story," "The Knack."

PIETROPINTO, ANGELA. Born Feb. 5, in NYC. Graduate NYU. OB credits include "Henry IV," "Alice in Wonderland," "Endgame," "Our Late Night," "The Sea Gull," "Jinx Bridge," "The Mandrake," "Marie and Bruce," "Green Card Blues," "3 by Pirandello," "The Broken Pitcher," "A Midsummer Night's Dream," "The Rivals," Bdwy in "The Suicide" (1980).

PINDER, CRAIG. Born Aug. 15, 1952 in Nassau, Bahamas. Graduate Reading U., RADA. Debut 1982 OB in "Hard Times," "The Dwarfs," "Find Your Way Home," "Love at the Raccoon Lodge."

PITONIAK, ANNE. Born Mar. 30, 1922 in Westfield, MA. Attended UNC Women's Col. Debut 1982 OB in "Talking With," followed by Bdwy in "'night, Mother" (1983) for which she received a Theatre World Award.

PLACE, DALE. Born Feb. 27, 1950 in Hastings, MI. Graduate Oakland U. Debut 1983 OB in "Starstruck," followed by "Happy Birthday, Wanda Jane," "Lady Windermere's Fan."

PLANK, SCOTT. Born Nov. 11, 1958 in Washington, DC. Attended NCSch of Arts. Bdwy debut 1981 in "Dreamgirls," followed by "A Chorus Line."

PLAYTEN, ALICE. Born Aug. 28, 1947 in NYC. Attended NYU. Bdwy debut 1960 in "Gypsy" followed by "Oliver," "Hello, Dolly!," "Henry Sweet Henry," for which she received a Theatre World Award, "George M!," OB in "Promenade," "The Last Sweet Days of Isaac," "National Lampoon's Lemmings," "Valentine's Day," "Pirates of Penzance," "Up from Paradise," "A Visit," "Sister Mary Ignatius Explains It All," "An Actor's Nightmare," "That's It, Folks."

PLUMMER, AMANDA. Born Mar. 23, 1957 in NYC. Attended Middlebury Col., Neighborhood Playhouse. Debut 1978 OB in "Artichoke," followed by "A Month in the Country," "A Taste of Honey" for which she received a Theatre World Award, "Alice in Concert," "A Stitch in Time," Bdwy in "A Taste of Honey," "Agnes of God," "The Glass Menagerie."

POLITO, JON. Born Dec. 29, 1950 in Philadelphia, PA. Graduate Villanova U. Debut 1976 OB in "The Transfiguration of Benno Blimpie," followed by "Gemini," "New Jerusalem," "Emigres," "A Winter's Tale," "Johnny on a Spot," "Barbarians," "The Wedding," Bdwy in "American Buffalo" (1977), "Curse of an Aching Heart," "Death of a Salesman" (1984).

POLLACK, DANIEL. Born July 25, 1927 in NYC. Graduate CCNY, Adelphi U., NYU. Debut 1949 OB in "An American Tragedy," followed by "Goodnight, Grandpa," "Victory Bonds," Bdwy in "The Price" (1979).

PONAZECKI, JOE. Born Jan. 7, 1934 in Rochester, NY. Attended Rochester U, Columbia U. Bdwy debut 1959 in "Much Ado About Nothing," followed by "Send Me No Flowers," "A Call on Kuprin," "Take Her, She's Mine," "Fiddler on the Roof," "Xmas in Las Vegas," "3 Bags Full," "Love in E-Flat," "90 Day Mistress," "Harvey," "Trial of the Catonsville 9," "The Country Girl," "Freedom of the City," "Summer Brave," "Music Is," "The Little Foxes," OB in "The Dragon," "Muzeeka," "Witness," "All Is Bright," "The Dog Ran Away," "Dream of a Blacklisted Actor," "Innocent Pleasures," "Dark at the Top of the Stairs," "36," "After the Revolution," "The Raspberry Picker," "Raisin in the Sun."

POOLE, ROY. Born Mar. 31, 1924 in San Bernardino, CA. Graduate Stanford U. Bdwy debut 1950 in "Now I Lay Me Down to Sleep," followed by "St. Joan," "The Bad Seed," "I Knock at the Door," "Long Day's Journey into Night," "Face of a Hero," "Moby Dick," "Poor Bitos," "1776," "Scratch," "Once a Catholic," OB in "27 Wagons Full of Cotton," "A Memory of Two Mondays," "Secret Service," "Boy Meets Girl," "Villager," "Quartermaine's Terms."

PORTER, BRETT. Born Dec. 31, 1956 in Geulph, Ont. Can. Graduate UTn. Debut 1982 OB in "Hamlet," followed by "Macbeth."

PORTER, HOWARD. Born Oct. 31, 1946 in Gary, WVa. Attended WVaU, AMDA. Bdwy debut 1970 in "Hello, Dolly!," followed by "Purlie," "Two Gentlemen of Verona," "The Wiz" (1984), OB in "The Great McDaddy."

POTTER, MICHAEL. Born Oct. 23, 1943 in San Diego, CA. Graduate UNCol. Debut 1983 OB in "Basin Street."

PRESCOTT, KEN. Born Dec. 28, 1945 in Omaha, NE. Attended Omaha U. UUtah, Bdwy debut 1971 in "No, No, Nanette," followed by "That's Entertainment," "Follies," "Lorelei," "42nd Street," "The Tap Dance Kid."

PRICE, LONNY. Born Mar. 9, 1959 in NYC. Attended Juilliard. Debut 1979 OB in "Class Enemy" for which he received a Theatre World Award, followed by "Up from Paradise," Bdwy 1980 in "The Survivor," followed by "Merrily We Roll Along," "Master Harold and the boys."

PRINCE, WILLIAM. Born Jan. 26, 1913 in Nicholas, NY. Attended Cornell U. Bdwy debut 1937 in "The Eternal Road," followed by "Richard II," "Hamlet," "Ah, Wilderness," "Guest in the House," "Across the Board on Tomorrow Morning," "Eve of St. Mark," "John Loves Mary," "Forward the Heart," "As You Like It," "I Am a Camera," "Affair of Honor," "Third Best Sport," "Highest Tree," "Venus at Large," "Strange Interlude," "Ballad of the Sad Cafe." "Little Foxes," "Man with Three Arms," "Heartbreak House," OB in "Stephen D," "Mercy Street," "The Caretaker," "Tausk."

PRINCI, ELAINE. Born Dec. 14 in Chambersburg, PA. Attended UCal/Northridge. Debut 1983 OB in "13."

PRITCHETT, JAMES. Born Oct. 27 in Lenoir, NC. Graduate UNC, UChicago., AADA. Debut 1955 OB in "An Ideal Husband," "Report to the Stockholders," "Electra," "Home of the Brave," "New Girl in Town," "Embers," "The Killer," "Death of Bessie Smith," "A Round with Ring," "An Evening's Frost," "Phaedre," "The Inheritors," Bdwy in "Two for the Seesaw" (1959), "Sail Away," "Lord Pengo."

PROVENZA, SAL. Born Sept. 21, 1946 in Brooklyn, NY. Debut 1980 OB in "The Fantasticks," Bdwy in "Oh, Brother!" (1981).

PUDENZ, STEVE. Born Sept. 25, 1947 in Carroll, IA. Graduate UIa. Debut 1980 OB in "Dona Rosita," followed by "Dick Deterred."

PUGH, RICHARD WARREN. Born Oct. 20, 1950 in NYC. Graduate Tarkio Col. Bdwy debut 1979 in "Sweeney Todd," followed by "The Music Man," "The Five O'Clock Girl," "Copperfield," "Zorba" (1983), OB in "Chase a Rainbow."

PURDHAM, DAVID. Born June 3, 1951 in San Antonio, TX. Graduate UMd., UWa. Debut 1980 OB in "Journey's End," followed by "Souvenirs," Bdwy in "Piaf" (1981).

QUAID, DENNIS. Born in 1955 in Samoa. Debut 1983 OB in "Last of the Knucklemen," followed by "True West."

QUIGLEY, BERNADETTE. Born Nov. 10, 1960 in Coldspring, NY. Debut 1983 OB in "Ah, Wilderness!"

QUIMBY, GERALD J. Born May 29, 1941 in Fond du Lac, WI. Graduate UWis. Debut 1981 OB in "The Investigation," followed by "Blood Relations," "Rock Island," "A Touch of the Poet."

QUINLAN, MICHAEL. Born Oct. 9, 1953 in NYC. Graduate Fairfield U. Debut 1984 on Bdwy in "Death of A Salesman."

QUINN, AIDAN. Born March 8, 1959 in Chicago, IL. Debut 1984 OB in "Fool for Love."

QUINN, ANTHONY. Born Apr. 21, 1915 in Chihuahua, Mex. Bdwy debut 1947 in "The Gentleman from Athens," followed by "Borned in Texas," "A Streetcar Named Desire," "Becket," "Chin Chin," "Born Yesterday," "Zorba" (1983).

QUINN, HENRY J. Born Aug. 6, 1928 in Boston, MA. Graduate Catholic U. Debut 1979 OB in "The Sound of Music," followed by "Mrs. Warren's Profession," "Towards Zero."

QUINN, PATRICK. Born Feb. 12, 1950 in Philadelphia, PA. Graduate Temple U. Bdwy debut 1976 in "Fiddler on the Roof," followed by "A Day in Hollywood/A Night in the Ukraine," OB in "It's Better with a Band," "By Strouse," "Forbidden Broadway."

RACKLEFF, OWEN S. Born July 16, 1934 in NYC. Graduate Columbia U, London U. Bdwy debut 1977 in "Piaf," OB in "The Lesson" (1978), "Catsplay," "Arms and the Man," "Escoffier: King of Chefs," "New Way to Pay Old Debts."

RAINES, ROGER. Born Nov. 25, 1965 in New York City; Attended NYU. Bdwy debut 1983 in "Brighton Beach Memoirs."

RAKOV, THERESA. Born Sept. 6, 1952 in Clarkson, NY. Graduate SUNY/Fredonia. Bdwy debut 1978 in "Hello, Dolly!," followed by "The Grand Tour," OB in "Florodora," "Romance Is," "Bittersuite."

RANDALL, CHARLES. Born Mar. 15, 1923 in Chicago, IL. Attended Columbia U. Bdwy debut 1953 in "Anastasia," followed by "Enter Laughing," "Trial of Lee Harvey Oswald," OB in "The Adding Machine," "The Cherry Orchard," "Brothers Karamazov," "Susan Slept Here," "Two for Fun," "Timon of Athens," "Endgame," "Yank in Beverly Hills," "The Homecoming."

RANDEL, MELISSA. Born June 16, 1955 in Portland, ME. Graduate UCal/Irvine. Bdwy debut 1980 in "A Chorus Line."

RANDELL, RON. Born Oct. 8. 1920 in Sydney, Aust. Attended St. Mary's Col. Bdwy debut 1949 in "The Browning Version," followed by "Harlequinade," "Candida," "World of Suzie Wong," "Sherlock Holmes," "Mrs. Warren's Profession," "Measure for Measure," "Bent," OB in "Holy Places," "After You've Gone," "Patrick Pearse Motel."

RAPHAEL, GERRIANNE. Born Feb. 23, 1935 in NYC. Attended New Sch., Columbia U. Bdwy debut 1941 in "Solitaire," followed by "A Guest in the House," "Violet," "Goodbye, My Fancy," "Seventh Heaven," "Li'l Abner," "Saratoga," "Man of LaMancha," "King of Hearts," OB in "Threepenny Opera," "The Boy Friend," "Ernest in Love," "Say When," "Prime of Miss Jean Brodie," "The Butler Did It," "The Ninth Step."

RASCHE, DAVID. Born Aug. 7, 1944 in St. Louis, MO. Graduate Elmhurst Col. U. Chicago. Debut 1976 OB in "John," followed by "Snow White," "Isadora Duncan Sleeps with the Russain Navy," "End of the War," "A Sermon," "Routed," "Geniuses," "Dolphin Position," "To Gillian on Her 37th Birthday," Bdwy in "Shadow Box" (1977), "Loose Ends," "Lunch Hour."

RASHOVICH, GORDANA. Born Sept. 18 in Chicago IL. Graduate Roosevelt U, RADA. Debut 1977 OB in "Fefu and Her Friends" for which she received a Theatre World Award, followed by "Selma."

RAUSCH, MARY A. Born July 26, 1933 in Elgin, IL. Graduate UIl. Debut 1962 OB in "Little Mary Sunshine," followed by "The Music Man," "The Best of Everything," "Willie," Bdwy in "The Paisley Convertible" (1968).

RAVELO, HENRY. Born Aug. 14, 1958 in Manila, Phil. Attended UWis. Debut 1984 OB in "Pacific Overtures."

RAWLS, EUGENIA. Born Sept. 11 1916 in Macon, GA. Attended UNC. Bdwy debut 1934 in "The Children's Hour," followed by "To Quito and Back," "Journeyman," "The Little Foxes," "A Guest in the House," "The Man Who Had All the Luck," "Strange Fruit," "The Shrike," "The Great Sebastians," "First Love," "A Case of Libel," "Sweet Bird of Youth," OB in "Poker Session," "Just the Immediate Family," "Tallulah, A Memory."

RAWLS, HARDY. Born Nov. 18, 1952 in Jacksonville, FL. Graduate FlaAtlanticU, UCLA. Debut 1982 OB in "Who'll Save the Plowboy?" followed by "A Thurber Carnival."

REAMS, LEE ROY. Born Aug. 23, 1942 in Covington, KY. Graduate U. Cinn. Cons. Bdwy debut 1966 in "Sweet Charity," followed by "Oklahoma!" (LC), "Applause," "Lorelei" "Show Boat" (JB), "Hello, Dolly!" (1978), "42nd Street," OB in "Sterling Silver," "Potholes," "The Firefly in Concert."

REAVES-PHILLIPS, SANDRA. Born Dec. 23 in Mullins, SC. Bdwy debut 1973 in "Raisin," OB in "Li'l Bit," "Ragtime Blues," "Blues in the Night," "Basin Street," "Karma," "Sparrow in Flight," "Take Care," "American Dreams," "Late Great Ladies."

REBHORN, JAMES. Born Sept. 1, 1948 in Philadelphia, PA. Graduate Wittenberg U, Columbia U. Debut 1972 OB in "Blue Boys," "Are You Now Or Have You Ever Been," "Trouble with Europe," "Othello," "Hunchback of Notre Dame," "Period of Adjustment," "The Freak," "Half a Lifetime," "Touch Black," "To Gillian on Her 37th Birthday," "Rain," "The Hasty Heart."

REBICH, CISSY. Born May 20, 1952 in Aliquippa, PA. Graduate Duquesne, U. Debut 1980 OB in "Annie Get Your Gun," followed by "Mame" (Bdwy 1983).

REDFIELD, ADAM. Born Nov. 4, 1959 in NYC. Attended NYU. Debut 1977 OB in "Hamlet," followed by "Androcles and the Lion," "Twelfth Night," "Reflected Glory," "Movin' Up," "The Unicorn," Bdwy 1980 in "A Life" for which he received a Theatre World Award, followed by "Beethoven's Tenth."

REDGRAVE, LYNN. Born Mar. 8, 1943 in London, Eng. Attended Central Sch. of Speech. Bdwy debut 1967 in "Black Comedy," followed by "My Fat Friend," "Mrs. Warren's Profession," "Knock, Knock," "St. Joan," OB in "Sister Mary Ignatius . . ."

REDWOOD, JOHN HENRY. Born Sept 10, 1942 in Brooklyn, NY. Attended UKs. Debut 1970 OB in "Cartouche," followed by "One Flew over the Cuckoo's Nest," "Black Visions," "Success and Succession."

REED, ALAINA. Born Nov. 10, 1946 in Springfield, OH. Attended Kent State U. Bdwy debut in "Hair" (1967/1977), followed by "Eubie!," OB in "Sgt. Pepper's Lonely Hearts Club Band," "In Trousers," "A . . . My Name is Alice."

REED, MARGARET. Born Nov. 15, 1956 in Calinas, CA. Graduate UCal/Santa Barbara, Cornell U. Debut 1983 OB in "Pericles," followed by "Tartuffe," "Play and Other Plays," "Catastrophe."

REED, PAMELA. Born Apr. 2, 1949 in Tacoma, WA. Graduate UWa. Bdwy debut 1978 in "November People," OB in "The Curse of the Starving Class," "All's Well That Ends Well," "Seduced," "Getting Out," "The Sorrows of Stephen," Standing on My Knees," "Criminal Minds," "Fen."

REGAN, CHARLES. Born Sept. 21, 1934 in New Haven, CT. Debut 1969 OB in "Make Me Disappear," followed by "The Killer Thing," "The Frankenstein Affair," "Joan of Lorraine," "Paradise Lost," "The Wig Lady."

REID, KATE. Born Nov. 4, 1930 in London, Eng. Attended Toronto U. Bdwy debut 1962 in "Who's Afraid of Virginia Woolf?," followed by "Dylan," "Slapstick Tragedy," "The Price," "Freedom of the City," "Cat on a Hot Tin Roof," "Bosoms and Neglect," "Morning's at 7," "Death of a Salesman."

REINKING, ANN. Born Nov. 10, 1949 in Seattle, WA. Attended Joffrey School, HB Studio. Bdwy debut 1969 in "Cabaret," followed by "Coco," "Pippin," "Over Here" for which she received a Theatre World Award, "Goodtime Charley," "A Chorus Line," "Chicago," "Dancin'," OB in "One More Song/One More Dance."

RENDERER, SCOTT. Born in Palo Alto, CA. Graduate Whitman Col. Bdwy debut in "Teaneck Tanzi" (1983), OB in "And Things That Go Bump in the Night," "Crossfire," "Just Like the Lions."

RICE, SARAH. Born Mar. 5, 1955 in Okinawa. Attended AzStateU. Debut 1974 OB in "The Fantasticks," followed by "The Enchantress," "The Music Man," Bdwy 1979 in "Sweeney Todd" for which she received a Theatre World Award.

RICH, JAMES. Born Apr. 29, 1955 in Boston, MA. Attended Boston U. Debut 1975 OB in "Let My People Come," followed by "Livin' Dolls," "Non Pasquale," Bdwy in "Hair" (1977), "The Best Little Whorehouse in Texas," "Joseph and the Amazing Technicolor Dreamcoat."

RICH, JOSEPH. Born June 2, 1958 in Pittsfield, MA. Attended UMa, Juilliard. Bdwy debut 1982 in "A Chorus Line," followed by "Mame," OB in "The Music Man," "The Roumanian Wedding."

RICH, SYLVESTER. Born May 24, 1950 in Geneva, NY. Attended UHouston, Debut 1983 OB in "Dick Deterred."

RICHARDS, CAROL. Born Dec. 26 in Aurora, IL. Graduate Northwestern U, Columbia U. Bdwy debut 1965 in "Half a Sixpence," followed by "Mame," "Last of the Red Hot Lovers," "Company," "Cats."

RICHARDS, JESS. Born Jan. 23, 1943 in Seattle, WA. Attended UWash. Bdwy debut 1966 in "Walking Happy," followed by "South Pacific" (LC) "Two by Two," "On the Town" for which he received a Theatre World Award, "Mack and Mabel," "Musical Chairs," "A Reel American Hero," "Barnum," OB in "One for the Money," "Lovesong," "A Musical Evening with Josh Logan," "The Lullaby of Broadway," "All Night Strut!,""Station Joy."

RICHARDS, PAUL-DAVID. Born Aug. 31, 1935 in Bedford, IN. Graduate IndU. Bdwy debut 1959 in "Once Upon a Mattress," followed by "Camelot," "It's Superman!," "A Joyful Noise," "1776," "Devour the Snow," "My One and Only," OB in "Black Picture Show," "Devour the Snow," "Elizabeth and Essex."

RICHARDSON, DON R. Born Mar. 3, 1953 in Jacksonville, FL. Attended Lehman Col. Debut 1983 OB in "The Duchess of Malfi."

RICHERT, WANDA. Born Apr. 18, 1958 in Chicago, IL. Bdwy debut 1980 in "42nd Street" for which she received a Theatre World Award, followed by "Nine," "A Chorus Line."

RIEBLING, TIA. Born July 21, 1964 in Pittsburgh, PA. Attended NYU. Debut 1983 OB in "American Passion," followed by "Preppies."

RIEGELMAN, RUSTY. Born Sept. 9, 1948 in Kansas City, MO. Attended UCincinnati. Bdwy debut in "This Was Burlesque" (1981), followed by OB in "Not Now Darling," "Pal Joey."

RIEGERT, PETER. Born Apr. 11, 1947 in NYC. Graduate UBuffalo, Debut 1975 OB in "Dance with Me," followed by "Sexual Perversity in Chicago," "Sunday Runners," "Isn't It Romantic," "La Brea Tarpits," "A Hell of a Town," Bdwy in "Censored Scenes from King Kong" (1980).

RIGAN, MICHELE. Born May 15, 1975 in Bridgeport, CT. Bdwy debut 1984 in "Sunday in the Park with George."

RILEY, LARRY. Born June 21, 1952 in Memphis, TN. Graduate Memphis State U. Bdwy debut 1978 in "A Broadway Musical," followed by "I Love My Wife," "Night and Day," "Shakespeare's Cabaret," OB in "Street Songs," "Amerika," "Plane Down," "Sidewalkin'," "Frimbo," "A Soldier's Play," "Maybe I'm Doing It Wrong."

RINEY, MICHAEL. Born July 7 in Michigan City, IN. Graduate Goodman Theatre. Bdwy debut 1977 in "Grease," OB in "Mrs. Dally Has a Lover," "El Bravo!," "All Night Long."

RINGHAM, NANCY. Born Nov. 16, 1954 in Minneapolis, MN Graduate St. Olaf Col. Oxford U. Bdwy debut 1954 in "My Fair Lady" (also 1981), OB in "That Jones Boy," "Bugles at Dawn," "Not-so-New Faces of '82," "Trouble in Tahiti," "Lenny and the Heartbreakers."

RITCHIE, MARGARET. Born May 31 in Madison, WI. Graduate UWis., NYU. Debut 1981 OB in "Last Summer at Bluefish Cove," followed by "Who's There," "Telling Tales."

RIVERA, CHITA. Born Jan. 23, 1933 in Washington, DC. Bdwy debut 1950 in "Guys and Dolls," followed by "Call Me Madam," "Can-Can," "Seventh Heaven," "Mr. Wonderful," "West Side Story," "Bye Bye Birdie," "Bajour," "Chicago," "Bring Back Birdie," "Merlin," "The Rink," OB in "Shoestring Revue."

RIVERA, MANUEL. Born Jan. 27, 1959 in NYC. Debut 1984 OB in "Cuban Swimmer/Dog Lady."

RIVERA, MICHAEL. Born Jan. 21, 1949 in NYC. Attended Richmond Col. Bdwy debut 1979 in "Carmelina," followed by "West Side Story," "Marilyn, An American Fable."

RIZZOLI, TONY. Born Aug. 1, 1952 in Newark, NJ. Graduate Catholic U. Debut 1983 OB in "The Last of the Knucklemen."

ROBARDS, JASON. Born July 26, 1922 in Chicago, IL. Attended AADA. Bdwy debut 1947 with D'Oyly Carte, followed by "Stalag 17," "The Chase," "Long Day's Journey into Night," for which he received a Theatre World Award, "The Disenchanted," "Toys in the Attic," "Big Fish, Little Fish," "A Thousand Clowns," "Hughie," "The Devils," "We Bombed in New Haven," "The Country Girl," "Moon for the Misbegotten," "A Touch of the Poet," "You Can't Take It with You," OB in "American Gothic," "The Iceman Cometh," "After the Fall," "But for Whom Charlie," "Long Day's Journey into Night."

ROBARDS, JASON III. Born Mar. 28, 1949 in NYC. Graduate UVt. Bdwy debut 1983 in "You Can't Take It with You."

ROBARE, MARY C. Born May 23, 1959 in Havelock, NC. Bdwy debut 1982 in "Little Me," followed by "On Your Toes," OB in "Emperor of My Baby's Heart."

ROBB, R. D. Born Mar. 31, 1972 in Philadelphia, PA. Bdwy debut 1980 in "Charlie and Algernon," followed by "Oliver!"

ROBBINS, REX. Born in Pierre, SD. Bdwy debut 1964 in "One Flew over the Cuckoo's Nest," followed by "Scratch," "The Changing Room," "Gypsy," "Comedians," "An Almost Perfect Person," "Richard III," "You Can't Take It with You," "Play Memory," OB in "Servant of Two Masters," "The Alchemist," "Arms and the Man," "Boys in the Band," "A Memory of Two Mondays," "They Knew What They Wanted," "Secret Service," "Boy Meets Girl," "Three Sistes," "The Play's the Thing," "Julius Caesar," "Henry IV Parts 1 and 2," "The Dining Room."

ROBERTS, GRACE. Born Nov. 9, 1935 in NYC. Debut 1956 OB in "Out of This World," followed by "Affairs of Anatol," "Beethoven/Karl," "Friends Too Numerous to Mention," "Applesauce," "A . . . My Name is Alice," "Briss."

ROBERTSON, SCOTT. Born Jan. 4, 1954 in Stamford, CT. Bdwy debut 1976 in "Grease," followed OB by "Scrambled Feet," "Applause," "A Lady Needs a Change," "A Backer's Audition," "She Loves Me."

ROBINSON, HAL. Born in Bedford, IN. Graduate IndU. Debut 1971 OB in "Memphis Store-Bought Teeth," followed by "From Berlin to Broadway," "The Fantasticks," "Promenade."

ROBINSON, LISA. Born Feb. 11, 1954 in Woodland, CA. Graduate Occidental Col. Bdwy debut 1983 in "Baby."

ROBINSON, MARTIN P. Born Mar. 9, 1954 in Dearborn, MI. Graduate WiStateU, AADA. Debut 1980 OB in "The Haggadah," followed by "Yellow Wallpaper," "The Lady's Not for Burning," "Little Shop of Horrors."

ROBINSON, ROGER. Born May 2, 1941 in Seattle, WA. Attended USCal. Bdwy debut 1969 in "Does a Tiger Wear a Necktie?," followed by "Amen Corner," OB in "Walk in Darkness," "Jerico-Jim Crow," "Who's Got His Own," "Trials of Brother Jero," "The Miser," "Interrogation of Havana," "Lady Day," "Do Lord Remember Me."

ROCHE, TUDI. Born July 19, 1955 in Lubbock, TX. Attended TxChristianU. Bdwy debut 1980 in "A Day in Hollywood/A Night in the Ukraine," followed OB in "Preppies" (1983).

ROCKAFELLOW, MARILYN. Born Jan. 22, 1939 in Middletown, NJ. Graduate Rutgers U. Debut 1976 OB in "La Ronde," followed by "The Art of Dining," "One Act Play Festival," "Open Admissions," "Bathroom Plays," Bdwy in "Clothes for A Summer Hotel" (1980), "Open Admissions," "Play Memory."

ROCKEFELLER, LAURA. Born Oct. 13, 1959 in NYC. Graduate Syracuse U. Debut 1983 OB in "Mighty Fine Music."

RODGERS, JERRY. Born Aug. 20, 1941 in Stockton, CA. Graduate UPortland. Debut 1971 OB in "Miss Lizzie," followed by "Shakuntala," "Life in Bed," "Rainbow Rape Trick," "The Contrast," "Lady Windermere's Fan."

RODOLITZ, LYNDA. Born Nov. 6, 1943 in Brooklyn, NY. Graduate Boston U, NYU. Debut 1978 OB in "Becca," followed by "Ubu Rides Again," "Hooray for What," "A Sensation Novel," "Bound to Rise."

ROFFMAN, ROSE. Has appeared OB in "La Madre," "Harold Pinter Plays," "Arthur Miller Double Bill," " Happy Hypocrite," "Under Gaslight," "Beaux Stratagem," "Tea Party," "The Boy Friend," "Marlon Brando Sat Here," "Sing Me Sunshine."

ROGAN, PETER. Born May 11, 1939 in County Leitrim, Ire. Bdwy debut 1966 in "Philadelphia, Here I Come," OB in "The Kitchen," "Nobody Hears a Broken Drum," "Picture of Dorian Gray," "Macbeth," "Sjt. Musgrave's Dance," "Stephen D," "People Are Living There," "The Plough and the Stars," "Look Back in Anger," "Sea Anchor," "The Arbor," "All the Nice People."

ROGERS, ANNE. Born July 29, 1933 in Liverpool, Eng. Attended St. John's Col. Bdwy debut 1957 in "My Fair Lady," followed by "Zenda," "Half a Sixpence," "42nd Street."

ROGERS, GIL. Born Feb. 4, 1934 in Lexington, KY. Attended Harvard U. OB in "The Ivory Branch," "Vanity of Nothing," "Warrior's Husband," "Hell Bent fer Heaven," "Gods of Lightning," "Pictures in a Hallway," "Rose," "Memory Bank," "A Recent Killing," "Birth," "Come Back, Little Sheba," "Life of Galileo," "Remembrance," Bdwy in "The Great White Hope," "The Best Little Whorehouse in Texas," "The Corn Is Green" (1983).

ROGERS, KEN LEIGH. Born Aug. 2, 1951 in NYC. Attended Southern Ill. U., RADA. Bdwy debut in "Hello, Dolly!" (1975), followed by "A Chorus Line," "My One and Only."

ROOS, CASPER. Born Mar. 21, 1925 in The Bronx, NY. Attended Manhattan School of Music. Bdwy debut 1959 in "First Impressions," followed by "How to Succeed in Business . . . ," "Mame," "Brigadoon," "Shenandoah," "My One and Only," OB in "Street Scene."

ROSE, CRISTINE. Born Jan. 31, 1951 in Lynwood, CA. Graduate Stanford U. Debut 1979 OB in "The Miracle Worker," followed by "Don Juan Comes Back from the War," "Hunting Scenes from Bavaria," "Three Acts of Recognition," "Winterplay," "Isn't It Romantic."

ROSE, GEORGE. Born Feb. 19, 1920 in Bicester, Eng. Bdwy debut with Old Vic 1946 in "Henry IV," followed by "Much Ado About Nothing," "A Man for All Seasons," "Hamlet," "Royal Hunt of the Sun," "Walking Happy," "Loot," "My Fair Lady," (CC'68), "Canterbury Tales," "Coco," "Wise Child," "Sleuth," "My Fat Friend," "My Fair Lady," "She Loves Me," "Peter Pan," BAM's "The Play's the Thing," "The Devil's Disciple," and "Julius Caesar," "The Kingfisher," "Pirates of Penzance," "Dance a Little Closer," "You Can't Take It with You," "Beethoven's Tenth."

ROSENBLATT, SELMA. Born Jan. 21, 1926 in NYC. Graduate Hunter Col. Debut 1982 OB in "Primal Time," followed by "The Coarse Acting Show," "Gertie's Gone," "Bless Me, Father," "Question Marks and Periods."

ROSENGARD, ALICE. Born Mar. 15 in Chicago, IL. Graduate IndU., Brandeis U. Debut 1975 OB in "Mr. Runaway," followed by "House of Blue Leaves," "I Never Saw Another Butterfly," "The Male Animal," "Comedy of Errors," "Louis Quinze."

ROSENSTOCK, SUSAN. Born Mar. 5, 1952 in Greensboro, NC. Attended UMd. Debut 1983 OB in "America Kicks Up Its Heels," followed by "The Cradle Will Rock."

ROSNER, FRANK. Born May 19, 1956 in Budapest, Hungary. Graduate St. Peter's Col. Debut 1983 OB in "Crossroads Cafe."

ROSS, BERTRAM. Born Nov. 14, 1920 in Brooklyn, NY. Attended Oberlin Col. With Martha Graham Company before debut 1983 OB in "The Tempest."

ROSS, JAMIE. Born May 4, 1939 in Markinch, Scot. Attended RADA. Bdwy debut 1962 in "Little Moon of Alban," followed by "Moon Beseiged," "Ari," "Different Times," "Woman of the Year," "La Cage aux Folles," OB in "Penny Friend," "Oh, Coward!"

ROSS, JUSTIN. Born Dec. 15, 1954 in Brooklyn, NY. Debut 1974 OB in "More Than You Deserve," followed by "Fourtune," "Ready for More?," "Weekend," Bdwy in "Pippin" (1975), "A Chorus Line," "Got To Go Disco."

ROSS, LARRY. Born Oct. 18, 1945 in Brooklyn, NY. Attended AADA. Bdwy debut 1963 in "How to Succeed . . . ," followed by "Fiddler on the Roof," "Frank Merriwell," "Annie," OB in "Burnscape."

ROSSETTER, KATHY. Born July 31 in Abington, PA. Gradaute Gettsburg Col. debut 1982 OB in "After the Fall," Bdwy in "Death of a Salesman" (1984).

ROTHHAAR, MICHAEL. Born June 22, 1953 in Pittsburgh, PA. Graduate Catholic U, Wayne State U. Debut 1982 OB in "Who'll Save the Plowboy," followed by "Dispatches from Hell," Bdwy in "The Corn Is Green" (1983).

ROTHMAN, JOHN. Born June 3, 1949 in Baltimore, MD. Graduate Wesleyan U, Yale. Debut 1978 OB in "Rats Nest," followed by "The Impossible H. L. Mencken," "The Buddy System," "Rosario and the Gypsies," "Italian Straw Hat," "Modern Ladies of Guanabacoa," Bdwy in "End of the World . . ." (1984).

RUBINSTEIN, JOHN. Born Dec. 8, 1946 in Los Angeles, CA. Attended UCLA. Bdwy debut 1972 in "Pippin" for which he received a Theatre World Award, followed by "Children of a Lesser God," "Fools," "The Soldier's Tale." "The Caine Mutiny Court-Martial."

RUCKER, BO. Born Aug. 17, 1948 in Tampa, FL. Debut 1978 OB in "Native Son" for which he received a Theatre World Award, followed by "Blues for Mr. Charlie," "Streamers," "Forty Deuce," "Dustoff."

RUDD, PAUL. Born May 15, 1940 in Boston, MA. OB in "Henry IV," followed by "King Lear," "A Cry of Players," "A Midsummer Night's Dream," "An Evening with Merlin Finch," "In the Matter of J. Robert Oppenheimer," "Elagabalus," "Streamers," "Henry V," "Boys in the Band," "Da," "The Show-Off," "The Lady and the Clarinet," Bdwy in "The Changing Room" (1973), "The National Health," "The Glass Menagerie," "Ah, Wilderness!," "Romeo and Juliet," "Bosoms and Neglect."

RUSKIN, JEANNE. Born Nov. 6 in Saginaw, MI. Graduate NYU. Bdwy debut 1975 in "Equus," OB in "Says I, Says He," "Cassatt," "Inadmissible Evidence," "Hedda Gabler," "Misalliance," "Winners," "Great Days," "Desire under the Elms."

RUSSELL, CATHY. Born Aug. 6, 1955 in New Canaan, CT. Graduate Cornell U. Debut 1980 OB in "City Sugar," followed by "Miss Schuman's Quartet," "A Resounding Tinkle," "Right to Life," "Collective Choices."

RUSSOM, LEON. Born Dec. 6, 1941 in Little Rock, AR. Attended Southwestern U. Debut 1968 OB in "Futz," followed by "Cyrano de Bergerac," "Boys in the Band," "Oh! Calcutta!," "Trial of the Catonsville 9," "Henry VI," "Richard III," "Shadow of a Gunman," "The New York Idea," "Three Sisters," "Old Flames," "Loving Reno," "Ruffian on the Stair," "Royal Bob," "Our Lord of Lynchville," "Laughing Stock."

RYER, ALEXANA. Born Nov. 17, 1953 in Denver, CO. Attended Loretta Heights Col., UCol. Debut 1983 OB in "Basin Street," followed by "The Buck Stops Here."

RYLAND, JACK. Born July 2, 1935 in Lancaster, PA. Attended AADA. Bdwy debut 1958 in "The World of Suzie Wong," followed by "A Very Rich Woman," "Henry V," OB in "A Palm Tree in a Rose Garden," "Lysistrata," "The White Rose and the Red," "Old Glory," "Cyrano de Bergerac," "Mourning Become Electra," "Beside the Seaside," "Quartermaine's Terms."

SABIN, DAVID. Born Apr. 24, 1937 in Washington, DC. Graduate Catholic U. Debut 1965 OB in "The Fantasticks," followed by "Now Is the Time for All Good Men," "Threepenny Opera," "You Never Can Tell," "Master and Margarita," "Preppies," Bdwy in "The Yearling," "Slapstick Tragedy," "Jimmy Shine," "Gantry," "Ambassador," "Celebration," Music Is," "The Water Engine," "The Suicide," "Othello," "Dance a Little Closer."

SADUSK, MAUREEN. Born Sept. 8, 1948 in Brooklyn, NY. Attended AADA. Debut 1969 OB in "We'd Rather Switch," followed by "O Glorious Tintinnabulation," "New Girl in Town," "McKean Street," "Making of Americans," "Canterbury Tales," "Wings," "Non Pasquale," Bdwy in "Fiddler on the Roof" (1976), "Canterbury Tales," "Ladies at the Alamo."

SAINT, DAVID. Born June 20, 1957 in Boston, MA. Graduate Holy Cross Col. Debut 1979 OB in "South across the River," followed by "The Loves of Cass McGuire," "Escape from Riverdale."

ST. JOHN, MARCO. Born May 7, 1939 in New Orleans, LA. Graduate Fordham U. Bdwy bow 1964 in "Poor Bitos," followed by "And Things That Go Bump in the Night," "The Unknown Soldier and His Wife," "Weekend," "40 Carats," "We Comrades Three," "War and Peace," OB in "Angels of Anadarko," "Man of Destiny," "Timon of Athens," "Richard III," "Awake and Sing," "Desire under the Elms."

SALATA, GREGORY. Born July 21, 1949 in NYC. Graduate Queens Col. Bdwy debut 1975 in "Dance with Me," followed by "Equus," "Bent," OB in "Piaf, A Remembrance," "Desire under the Elms."

SALE, RICHARD. Born Apr. 27, 1954 in TX. Graduate UMi., Neighborhood Playhouse. Debut 1977 OB in "The Wayside Motor Inn," followed by "The Danube."

SAMUEL, D. PETER. Born Aug. 15, 1958 in Pana, IL. Graduate East Ill.U. Bdwy debut 1981 in "The First," OB in "Little Eyolf," "The Road to Hollywood," "Elizabeth and Essex."

SANDLER, SUSAN. Born Mar. 21, 1948 in NYC. Graduate VaCommonwealthU. Debut 1974 OB in "Hedda Gabler," followed by "Under Milkwood," "Miss Julie," "Out of Our Father's House," "Birthday Party," "Second Prize: 2 Months in Leningrad."

SANTELL, MARIE. Born July 8 in Brooklyn, NY. Bdwy debut 1957 in "Music Man," followed by "A Funny Thing Happened on the Way . . . ," "Flora, the Red Menace," "Pajama Game," "Mack and Mabel," "La Cage aux Folles," OB in "Hi, Paisano!," "Boys from Syracuse," "Peace," "Promenade," "The Drunkard," "Sensations," "The Castaways," "Fathers and Sons."

SAPUTO, PETER J. Born Feb. 2, 1939 in Detroit, MI. Graduate EMiU, Purdue U. Debut 1977 OB in "King Oedipus," followed by "Twelfth Night," "Bon Voyage," "Happy Haven," "Sleep-walkers," "Humulus the Mute," "The Freak," "Promises, Promises," "The Last of Hitler," "A Touch of the Poet," Bdwy in "Once in a Lifetime."

SARNO, JANET. Born Nov. 18, 1933 in Bridgeport, CT. Graduate SCTC, Yale U. Bdwy debut 1963 in "Dylan," followed by "Equus," "Knockout," OB in "6 Characters in Search of an Author," "Who's Happy Now," "Closing Green," "Fisher," "Survival of St. Joan," "The Orphan," "Mama's Little Angels," "Knuckle Sandwich," "Marlon Brando Sat Here," "Last Summer at Bluefish Cove," "Brass Birds Don't SIng."

SAUNDERS, NICHOLAS. Born June 2, 1914 in Kiev, Russia. Bdwy debut 1942 in "Lady in the Dark" followed by "A New Life," "Highland Fling," "Happily Ever After," "The Magnificent Yankee," "Anastasia," "Take Her, She's Mine," "A Call on Kuprin," "Passion of Josef D.," OB in "An Enemy of the People," "End of All Things Natural," "The Unicorn in Captivity," "After the Rise," "All My Sons," "My Great Dead Sister," "The Investigation," "Past Tense," "Scenes and Revelations," "Zeks," "Blood Moon," "Family Comedy," "American Power Play."

SAVIN, RON LEE. Born July 20, 1947 in Norfolk, VA. Graduate Wm. & Mary Col. Debut 1981 OB in "Francis," followed by "Greater Tuna," "Road to Hollywood."

SAVIOLA, CAMILLE. Born July 16, 1950 in The Bronx, NY. Debut 1970 OB in "Touch," followed by "Rainbow," "Godspell," "Starmites," "Battle of the Giants," "Dementos," "Spook-house," "A Vaudeville," "Road to Hollywood," Bdwy in "Nine" (1982).

SAYRE, CLARK. Born Mar. 23, 1960 in Santa Barbara, CA. Attended UCLA. Bdwy debut 1981 in "Merrily We Roll Along," followed by "Oliver!" (1984).

SCALISE, THOMAS DAVID. Born Mar. 12, 1953 in Conneaut, OH. Attended Kent State U. Bdwy debut 1981 in "Fiddler on the Roof," followed by "Zorba" (1983).

SCANLON, BARBARA. Born Jan. 17, 1956 in Detroit, MI. Graduate MiStateU. Debut 1984 OB in "Elizabeth and Essex."

SCHACT, SAM. Born Apr. 19, 1936 in The Bronx, NY. Graduate CCNY. OB in "Fortune and Men's Eyes," "Cannibals," "I Met a Man," "The Increased Difficulty of Concentration," "One Night Stands of a Noisy Passenger," "Owners," "Jack Gelber's New Play," "The Master and Margarita," "Was It Good for You?," "True West," Bdwy in "The Magic Show," "Golda."

SCHAUT, ANN LOUISE. Born Nov. 21, 1956 in Minneapolis, MN. Attended UMn. Bdwy debut 1981 in "A Chorus Line."

SHEINE, RAYNOR. Born Nov. 10 in Emporia, VA. Graduate VaCommonwealthU. Debut 1978 OB in "Curse of the Starving Class," followed by "Blues for Mr. Charlie," "Salt Lake City Skyline," "Mother Courage," "The Lady or the Tiger," "Bathroom Plays," "Wild Life," "Re-Po."

SCHENKKAN, ROBERT. Born Mar. 19, 1953 in Chapel Hill, NC. Graduate UTex, Cornell U. Debut 1978 OB in "The Taming of the Shrew," followed by "Last Days at the Dixie Girl Cafe," "New Jerusalem," "G. R. Point," "Midnight Visitor," "Key Exchange," "The Knack."

SCHERER, JOHN. Born May 16, 1961 in Buffalo, NY. Graduate Carnegie-Melon U. Debut 1983 OB in "Preppies," followed by "Jass."

SCHIFF, ERIC. Born Aug. 10, 1958 in Huntington, WVa. Attended Amherst Col. Debut 1980 OB in "Details of the 16th Frame," followed by "Levitation."

SCHLARTH, SHARON. Born Jan. 19 in Buffalo, NY. Graduate SUNY/Fredonia. Debut 1983 OB in "Full Hookup," followed by "Fool for Love."

SCHLAMME, MARTHA. Born Sept. 25 in Vienna, Aust. Debut 1963 OB in "The World of Kurt Weill," followed by "A Month of Sundays," "Mata Hari," "Beethoven and Karl," "Aspirations," "God of Vengeance," "Twilight Cantata," "Mrs. Warren's Profession," Bdwy in "Fiddler on the Roof," "Threepenny Opera," "Solitaire/Double Solitaire," "A Kurt Weill Cabaret."

SCHNEIDER, DOUG. Born Apr. 25, 1953 in Tulsa, OK. Graduate UCLA. Debut 1983 OB in "Nite Club Confidential."

SCHNEIDER, JANA. Born Oct. 24, 1951 in McFarland, WI. Graduate UWis. Debut 1976 OB in "Women Behind Bars," followed by "Telecast," "Just Like the Lions," Bdwy in "The Robber Bridegroom."

SCHNEIDER, JAY. Born May 8, 1951 in Brooklyn, NY. Graduate Brandeis U. Debut 1979 OB in "On a Clear Day You Can See Forever," followed by "Pal Joey."

SCHOB, HANK. Born Sept. 18 in Philadelphia, PA. Attended AADA. Debut 1969 OB in "Your Own Thing," followed by "Pirates of Penzance," "The Mikado," "Dark of the Moon," "An Evening of Adult Fairy Tales."

SCHOPPERT, BILL. Born Apr. 25, 1948 in Iowa. Graduate UMin. Debut 1983 OB in "Base-ment Tapes."

SCHRAMM, DAVID. Born Aug. 14, 1946 in Louisville, KY. Attended Western KyU, Juilliard. Debut 1972 OB in "School for Scandal," followed by "Lower Depths," "Women Beware Women," "Mother Courage," "King Lear," "Duck Variations," "The Cradle Will Rock," Bdwy in "Three Sisters," "Next Time I'll Sing to You," "Edward II," "Measure for Measure," "The Robber Bridegroom," "Bedroom Farce," "Goodbye, Fidel," "The Misanthrope."

SCHREINER, WARNER. Born Sept. 24, 1923 in Washington, DC. Graduate Geo.Wash.U. Debut 1960 OB in "Paths of Glory," followed by "Hooray for Paul," "Crawling Arnold," "Daydreams," Bdwy in "The Skin of Our Teeth" (1961), "Can Can" (CC'62).

SCHULL, REBECCA. Born Feb. 22 in NYC. Graduate NYU. Bdwy debut 1976 in "Herzl," followed by "Golda," OB in "Mother's Day," "Fefu and Her Friends," "On Mt Chimborazo," "Mary Stuart," "Balzamov's Wedding," "Before She Is Ever Born," "Exiles," "Nest of the Wood Grouse."

SCHUMACHER, TOM. Born June 15, 1956 in Chicago, IL. Graduate Yale U. Debut OB 1984 in "Red, Hot and Blue."

SCHUSSLER, ERIC. Born May 11, 1951 in Ashland, OH. Graduate Ashland Col. Debut 1983 OB in "The Music Man," followed by "Love in the Country."

SCHWEID, CAROLE. Born Oct. 5, 1946 in Newark, NJ. Graduate Boston U, Juilliard. Bdwy debut 1970 in "Minnie's Boys," followed by "A Chorus Line," "Street Scene," OB in "Love Me, Love My Children," "How to Succeed in Business . . . ," "Silk Stockings," "Children of Adam," "Upstairs at O'Neal's," "Not-So-New Faces of '82," "Unreasonable Expectations."

SCOTLAND, CHARLES. Born May 18, 1934 in Hartford, CT. Graduate UToronto. Debut 1982 OB in "Requiescent in Pace," followed by "Henry IV Part I," "Hooray for Paul," "Richard II."

SCOTT, HAROLD. Born Sept. 6, 1935 in Morristown, NJ. Graduate Harvard U. OB in "Land Beyond the River," "I, Too, Have Lived in Arcadia," "The Egg and I," "Deathwatch," "God's Trombones," "Jackass," "Program One," "Death of Bessie Smith," "The Blacks," "Trials of Brother Jero," "The Strong Breed," "Boys in the Band," "After the FAll," "Marco Millions," "But for Whom Charlie," "The Changeling," "Incident at Vichy," "Julius Caesar," Bdwy in "Cool World" (1960), "The Cuban Thing," "Les Blancs."

SCOTT, SUSAN ELIZABETH. Born Aug. 9 in Detroit, MI. Graduate UDenver. Debut 1971 OB in "The Drunkard," followed by "Mother," Bdwy in "Music Is" (1976), "On the 20th Century," "Fearless Frank," "1940's Radio Hour."

SEAL, ELIZABETH. Born Aug. 28, 1934 in Genoa, Italy. Graduate RADA. Bdwy debut 1960 in "Irma La Douce," followed by "A Shot in the Dark," "The Corn is Green" (1983).

SEALE, DOUGLAS. Born Oct. 28, 1913 in London, Eng. Graduate Washington Col., RADA. Bdwy debut 1974 in "Emperor Henry IV," followed by "Frankenstein," "The Dresser," "Noises Off."

SEAMON, EDWARD. Born Apr. 15, 1937 in San Diego, CA. Attended San Diego State Col. Debut 1971 OB in "The Life and Times of J. Walter Smintheous," followed by "The Contractor," "The Family," "Fishing," "Feedlot," "Cabin 12," "Rear Column," "Devour the Snow," "Buried Child," "Friends," "Extenuating Circumstances," "Confluence," "Richard II," "Great Grandson of Jedediah Kohler," "Marvelous Gray," "Rime Framed," "The Master Builder," "Full Hookup," "Fool for Love," "The Harvesting," Bdwy in "The Trip Back Down," "Devour the Snow," "The American Clock."

SECREST, JAMES. Born Nov. 17 in Thomasville, NC. Graduate UNC. Bdwy debut 1967 in "The Girl in the Freudian Slip," OB in "John Brown's Body," "Trial of the Catonsville 9, " "Private Ear/Public Eye," "The Adding Machine."

SECUNDA, SUSAN. Born May 11, 1955 in Pittsfield, MA. Graduate Eastman School of Music. Debut 1983 OB in "The Music Man."

SEDERHOLM, KAREN. Born July 18, 1954 in Pittsburgh, PA. Graduate PaStateU. Debut 1980 OB in "The Diviners," followed by "Last Summer at Bluefish Cove," "Young Playwrights Festival," "Time and the Conways," "Balm in Gilead."

SEFF, RICHARD. Born Sept. 23, 1927 in NYC. Attended NYU. Bdwy debut 1951 in "Darkness at Noon," followed by "Herzl," OB in "Big Fish, Little Fish," "Modigliani," "Childe Byron," "Richard II," "Time Framed," "The Sea Gull."

SELDES, MARIAN. Born Aug. 23, 1928 in NYC. Attended Neighborhood Playhouse. Bdwy debut 1947 in "Medea," followed by "Crime and Punishment," "That Lady," "Tower Beyond Tragedy," "Ondine," "On High Ground," "Come of Age," "Chalk Garden," "The Milk Train Doesn't Stop Here Anymore," "The Wall," "A Gift of Time," "A Delicate Balance," "Before You Go," "Father's Day," "Equus," "The Merchant," "Deathtrap," OB in "Different," "Ginger Man," "Mercy Street," "Isadora Duncan Sleeps With the Russian Navy," "Painting Churches," "Richard III."

SERRANO, CHARLIE. Born Dec. 4, 1952 in Rio Piedras, PR. Attended Brooklyn Col. Debut 1978 OB in "Allegro," followed by "Mama, I Want to Sing," "El Bravo," "Non Pasquale," Bdwy in "Got Tu Go Disco," "Joseph and the Amazing Technicolor Dreamcoat."

SERRECCHIA, MICHAEL. Born Mar. 26, 1951 in Brooklyn, NY. Attended Brockport State U. Teachers Col. Bdwy debut 1972 in "The Selling of the President," followed by "Heathen!," "Seesaw," "A Chorus Line," OB in "Lady Audley's Secret."

SESMA, THOM. Born June 1, 1955 in Sasebo, Japan. Graduate UCal. Bdwy debut 1983 in "La Cage aux Folles."

SEVIER, JACK. Born Apr. 1, 1925 in Chattanooga, TN. Graduate, UChatt., UNC. Bdwy debut 1959 in "Destry Rides Again," followed by "My Fair Lady" (1981), OB in "Brooklyn Bridge."

SEVRA, ROBERT. Born Apr. 15, 1945 in Kansas City, MO. Graduate Stanford U., UMi. Debut 1972 OB in "Servant of Two Masters," followed by "Lovers," Bdwy in "Charlie and Algernon" (1980), "Torch Song Trilogy."

SHACKELFORD, SANDI. Born Nov. 5, 1950 in Ft. Bragg, NC. Graduate SMU, USCal. Debut 1984 OB in "Henry V."

SHAKAR, MARTIN. Born Jan. 1, 1940 in Detroit, MI. Attended Wayne State U. Bdwy bow 1969 in "Our Town," OB in "Lorenzaccio," "Macbeth," "The Infantry," "Americana Pastoral," "No Place to Be Somebody," "World of Mrs. Solomon," "And Whose Little Boy Are You," "Investigation of Havana," "Night Watch," "Owners," "Actors," "Richard III," "Transfiguration of Benno Blimpie," "Jack Gelber's New Play," "Biko Inquest," "Second Story Sunlight," "Secret Thighs of New England Women," "After the Fall," "Faith Healer."

SHALLO, KAREN. Born Sept. 28, 1946 in Philadelphia, PA. Graduate PaStateU. Debut 1973 OB in "Children of Darkness," followed by "Moliere in spite of Himself," "We Won't Pay!," "The Overcoat," "Angelus," "Question Marks and Periods," Bdwy 1980 in "Passione."

SHAPIRO, DEBBIE. Born Sept. 29, 1954 in Los Angeles, CA. Graduate LACC. Bdwy debut 1979 in "They're Playing Our Song," followed by "Perfectly Frank," "Blues in the Night," "Zorba" (1983), OB in "They Say It's Wonderful," "New Moon in Concert."

SHAW, MARCIE. Born June 19, 1954 in Franklin Square, NY. Attended UIl. Bdwy debut 1980 in "Pirates of Penzance," OB in "A Midsummer Night's Dream," "Non Pasquale," "Promenade."

SHEA, JOHN V. Born Apr. 14 in North Conway, NH. Graduate Bates Col., Yale. Debut OB 1974 in "Yentl, the Yeshiva Boy," followed by "Gorky," "Battering Ram," "Safe House," "The Master and Margarita," "Sorrows of Stephen," "American Days," "The Dining Room," Bdwy in "Yentl" (1975) for which he received a Theatre World Award. "Romeo and Juliet," "A Soldier's Tale," "End of the World . . ."

SHELTON, SLOANE. Born Mar. 17, 1934 in Asheville, NC. Attended Berea Col. RADA. Bdwy debut 1967 in "The Imaginary Invalid," followed by "A Touch of the Poet," "Tonight at 8:30," "I Never Sang for My Father," "Sticks and Bones," "The Runner Stumbles," "Shadow Box," "Passione," "Open Admissions," OB in "Androcles and the Lion," "The Maids," "Basic Training of Pavlo Hummel," "Play and Other Plays," "Julius Caesar," "Chieftans," "Passione," "The Chinese Viewing Pavilion," "Blood Relations," "The Great Divide."

SHEPART, JOAN. Born Jan. 7 in NYC. Graduate RADA. Bdwy debut 1940 in "Romeo and Juliet," followed by "Sunny River," "The Strings, My Lord, Are False," "This Rock," "Foolish Notion," "A Young Man's Fancy," "My Romance," "Member of the Wedding," OB in "Othello," "Plot Against the Chase Manhattan Bank," "Philosophy in the Boudoir," "Knitters in the Sun," "School for Wives," "Importance of Being Earnest," "Enter Laughing," "World War Won."

SHEPARD, JOHN. Born Dec. 9, 1932 in Huntington Park, CA. Graduate UCal/Irvine. Debut 1982 OB in "Scenes from La Vie de Boheme," Bdwy in "A View From the Bridge" (1983), followed by "American Buffalo."

SHEPHERD, LEE. Born July 20 in Kansas City, MO. Graduate UMo. Debut 1983 OB in "Waiting for Lefty," followed by "Till The Day I Die," "Sympathy."

SHERWOOD, MADELEINE. Born Nov. 13, 1926 in Montreal, Can. Attended Yale U. OB in "Brecht on Brecht," "Medea," "Hey, You, Light Man," "Friends and Relations," "Older People," "O Glorious Tintinnabulation," "Getting Out," "Secret Thighs of New England Women," "Rain," "Ghosts," Bdwy in "The Chase" (1952), "The Crucible," "Cat on a Hot Tin Roof," "Invitation to a March," "Camelot," "Arturo Ui," "Do I Hear a Waltz?," "Inadmissible Evidence," "All Over!"

SHIMONO, SAB. Born in Sacramento, Cal. Gradute UCal. Bdwy bow 1965 in "South Pacific," followed by "Mame," "Lovely Ladies, Kind Gentlemen," "Pacific Overtures," "Ride the Winds," "Mame" (1983), OB in "Santa Anita."

SHORE, HARRIS. Born Sept. 22, 1946 in Phoenixville, PA. Graduate Franklin-Marshall Col. Debut 1971 OB in "A Christmas Carol," followed by "Earthlings," "The Seducers," "Montpelier Pazazz," "Unlikely Heroes," "The Buck Stops Here," Bdwy in "Rainbow Jones" (1974).

SHORT, JOHN. Born July 3, 1956 in Christopher, IL. Graduate Hanover Col. Debut 1981 OB in "Unfettered Letters," followed by "Sister Mary Ignatius . . ."

SHROPSHIRE, NOBLE. Born Mar. 2, 1946 in Cartersville, GA. Graduate LaGrange Col., RADA. Debut 1976 OB in "Hound of the Baskervilles," followed by "The Misanthrope," "The Guardsman," "Oedipus Cycle," "Gilles de Rais," "Leonce and Lena," "King Lear," "Danton's Death," "Tartuffe," "The Maids," "Midsummer Night's Dream," "Henry IV," "Richard II," "Marquis of Keith," "Wozzeck," "Peter Gynt," "The Cherry Orchard," "Ghost Sonata," "Faust," "Hamlet," "Big and Little."

SHULTZ, PHILIP. Born July 24, 1953 in NYC. Graduate NYU. Debut 1974 OB in "Patience," followed by "Rehearsal," "The Coolest Cat in Town," "Basement Skylight," "Guys and Dolls," "Bugles at Dawn," "The Coarse Acting Show," "Red, Hot and Blue."

SIEBERT, RON. Born Feb. 26, in Kenosha, I. Graduate UWis., Brandeis U. Bdwy debut 1973 in "The Changing Room" followed by "The Iceman Cometh," OB in "A Little Madness."

SIEGLER, BEN. Born Apr. 9, 1958 in Queens, NY. Attended HB Studio. Debut 1980 OB in "Innocent Thoughts, Harmless Intentions," followed by "Threads," "Many Happy Returns," "Snow Orchid," "The Diviners," "What I Did Last Summer," "Time Framed," "Gifted Children," "Levitations," "Elm Circle," Bdwy 1981 in "5th of July."

SIFF, IRA. Born Feb. 15, 1946 in NYC. Graduate Cooper Union. Debut 1972 OB in "Joan," followed by "Faggot," "The Haggadah," "Love, Sex and Violence."

SIGNORELLI, TOM. Born Oct. 19, 1939 in Brooklyn, NY. Attended UCLA. Debut 1960 OB in "Look Back in Anger," followed by "Bury the Dead," "Scapin," "Pretenders," Bdwy in "General Seeger" (1958), "Borstal Boy," "Death of a Salesman" (1984).

SILLIMAN, MAUREEN. Born Dec. 3 in NYC. Attended Hofstra U. Bdwy debut 1975 in "Shenandoah," followed by "I Remember Mama," "Is There Life after High School?," OB in "Umbrellas of Cherbourg," "Two Rooms," "Macbeth," "Blue Window."

SILVER, JOE. Born Sept. 28, 1922 in Chicago, IL. Attended UIl., AmThWing. Bdwy bow 1942 in "Tobacco Road," followed by "Doughgirls," "Heads or Tails," "Nature's Way," "Gypsy," "Heroine," "Zulu and the Zayda," "You Know I Can't Hear You . . . ," "Lenny," "The Roast," "World of Sholom Aleichem," OB in "Blood Wedding," "Lamp at Midnight," "Joseph and His Brethern," "Victors," "Shrinking Bride," "Family Pieces," "Cakes with Wine," "The Homecoming."

SILVER, RON. Born July 2, 1946 in NYC. Graduate SUNY, St. John's U. Debut OB in "El Grande de Coca Cola," followed by "Lotta," "Kaspar," "More Than You Deserve," "Emperor of Late Night Radio," "Friends."

SIMON, ROGER HENDRICKS. Born Oct. 21, 1942 in NYC. Graduate Middlebury Col, Yale U. Debut 1967 OB in "Volpone," followed by "Shadow of a Gunman," "Benya the King," "Uncle Money," "Cabal of Hypocrites."

SIMONS, LESLIE A. Born Aug. 8, 1957 in Hatboro, PA. Graduate Beaver Col. Bdwy debut 1983 in "La Cage aux Folles."

SLATER, CHRISTIAN. Born Aug. 18, 1969 in NYC. Bdwy debut 1980 in "The Music Man," followed by "Copperfield," "Macbeth," "Merlin," OB in "Between Daylight and Boonville," "Landscape of the Body."

SLEETH, TOM. Born Sept. 26, 1927 in Dayton, OH. Graduate UNMex. Debut 1981 OB in "Italian Straw Hat," followed by "The Cherry Orchard."

SLEZAK, VICTOR. Born July 7, 1957 in Youngstown, OH. Debut 1979 OB in "The Electra Myth," followed by "The Hasty Heart," "Ghosts."

SLOAN, GARY. Born July 6, 1952 in New Castle, IN. Graduate Wheaton Col., SMU. Debut 1982 OB in "Faust," followed by "Wild Oats," "Balloon," "Danton's Death," "Hamlet," "Big and Little."

SLUTSKER, PETER. Born Apr. 17, 1958 in NYC. Graduate UMi. Bdwy debut 1983 in "On Your Toes."

SMALL, LARRY. Born Oct. 6, 1947 in Kansas City, MO. Attended Manhattan School of Music. Bdwy debut 1971 in "1776," followed by "La Strada," "Wild and Wonderful," "A Doll's Life," OB in "Plain and Fancy," "Forbidden Broadway."

SMITH, FRED G. Born Aug. 19, 1945 in Jersey City, NJ. Graduate UMich. Debut 1983 OB in "The Inheritors."

SMITH, JENNIFER. Born Mar. 9, 1956 in Lubbock, TX. Graduate TxTechU. Debut 1981 OB in "Seesaw," followed by "Suffragette," Bdwy in "La Cage aux Folles" (1983).

SMITH, LARALU. Born Oct. 21, 1950 in Chicago, IL. Graduate OhStateU, Northwestern U. Debut OB in "Separate Tables," followed by "The Chinese," "Green Fields," "Carolyn," "Little Eyolf."

SMITH, LIONEL MARK. Born Feb. 5, 1946 in Chicago, IL. Attended Goodman ThSchool. Debut 1982 OB in "Edmond," followed by "The Harvesting."

SMITH, MICHAEL O. Born Aug. 27, 1941 in Tupelo, MS. Graduate InterAmericanU. Bdwy debut 1979 in "Dracula," OB in "Paradise Lost," "Ghosts."

SMITH, NICK. Born Jan. 13, 1932 in Philadelphia, PA. Attended Boston U. Debut 1963 OB in "The Blacks," followed by "Man Is Man," "The Connection," "Blood Knot," "No Place to Be Somebody," "Androcles and the Lion," "So Nice They Named It Twice," "In the Recovery Lounge," "Liberty Call," "Raisin in the Sun."

SMITH, PAUL P. Born Aug. 21, 1959 in Hackensack, NJ. Graduate Syracuse U. Debut 1983 OB in "Mighty Fine Music."

SMITH, REX. Born Sept. 19, 1955 in Jacksonville, FL. Bdwy debut 1978 in "Grease," followed by "The Pirates of Penzance" for which he received a Theatre World Award, "The Human Comedy."

SMITH, SHEILA. Born Apr. 3, 1933 in Coneaut, OH. Attended Kent State U., Cleveland Play House. Bdwy debut 1963 in "Hot Spot," followed by "Mame" for which she received a Theatre World Award, "Follies," "Company," "Sugar," "Five O'Clock Girl," "42nd Street," OB in "Taboo Revue," "Anything Goes," "Best Foot Forward," "Sweet Miami," "Florello," "Taking My Turn."

SMITH, YEARDLEY. Born July 3, 1965 in Paris, France. Bdwy debut 1984 in "The Real Thing."

SMITH-CAMERON, J. Born Sept. 7 in Louisville, KY. Attended FlaStateU. Bdwy debut 1982 in "Crimes of the Heart," OB in "Asian Shade," followed by "The Knack," "Second Prize: 2 Weeks in Leningrad," "The Great Divide."

SMITS, JIMMY. Born July 9, 1955 in NYC. Graduate Brooklyn, Col, Cornell U. Debut 1982 OB in "Hamlet," followed by "Little Victories," "Buck," "Ariano."

SMYTHE, MARCUS. Born Mar. 26, 1950 in Berea, OH. Graduate Otterbein Col. Debut 1975 OB in "Tenderloin," followed by "Ten Little Indians," "Bhutan," Bdwy in "The Suicide" (1980).

SOD, TED. Born May 12, 1951 in Wilkes-Barre, PA. Graduate King's Col. Debut 1976 OB in "Henry V," followed by "Savages," "City Junket," "A Midsummer Night's Dream," "Recruiting Officer," "Jungle of Cities," "The Wild Duck," "Buck," "Landscape of the Body."

SOMMER, JOSEF. Born June 26, 1934 in Griefswald, Ger. Graduate Carnegie Tech. Bdwy bow 1970 in "Othello," followed by "Children, Children," "Trial of the Catonsville 9," "Full Circle," "Who's Who in Hell," "Shadow Box," "Spokesong," "The 1940s Radio Show," "Whose Life Is It Anyway?," OB in "Enemies," "Merchant of Venice," "The Dog Ran Away," "Drinks Before Dinner," "Lydie Breeze," "Black Angel," "The Lady and the Clarinet," "Love Letters on Blue Paper."

SPACKMAN, TOM. Born Oct. 4, 1950 in Binghamton, NY. Graduate WayneStateU. Debut 1981 OB in "Peer Gynt," followed by "King Lear," "Ghost Sonata," "Faust," "Wild Oats," "I Am a Camera," "Dance of Death," "Flirtations."

SPANO, NEALLA. Born Sept. 26, 1958 in NYC. Graduate Northwestern U. Debut 1981 OB in "Lady Windermere's Fan," followed by "The Night is Young," "The Coarse Acting Show," "Serious Bizness," "Found a Peanut."

SPARER, KATHRYN C. Born Jan. 5, 1956 in NYC. Graduate UChicago. Debut 1982 OB in "Beside the Seaside," followed by "About Iris Berman," "The Rise of Daniel Rocket."

SPEART, JESSIE. Born Feb. 1 in Washington, DC. Graduate New School. Debut 1984 OB in "The Land Is Bright."

SPENCER, VERNON. Born Dec. 1, 1955 in Brooklyn, NY. Attended Queens Col. Debut 1976 OB in "Panama Hattie," followed by "Happy with the Blues," "Street Jesus," Bdwy in "The Human Comedy" (1984).

SPILLMAN, HARRY. Born Oct. 20, 1935 in Buffalo, NY. Graduate UBuffalo. Debut 1966 OB in "The Rape of Bunny Stuntz," followed by "Trial of the Catonsville 9," "Rocket to the Moon," "Ghosts," "The Seagull," "Troilus and Cressida," "Knights Errant," "The Bone Garden."

SPOLAN, JEFFREY. Born July 14, 1947 in NYC. Graduate Adelphi U. Debut 1982 OB in "Yellow Fever."

STADLEN, LEWIS J. Born Mar. 7, 1947 in Brooklyn, NY. Attended Stella Adler Studio. Bdwy debut 1970 in "Minnie's Boys" for which he received a Theatre World Award, followed by "The Sunshine Boys," "Candide," OB in "The Happiness Cage," "Heaven on Earth," "Barb-A-Que," "Don Juan and Non Don Juan."

STANLEY, GORDON. Born Dec. 20, 1951 in Boston, MA. Graduate Brown U., Temple U. Debut 1977 OB in "Lyrical and Satirical," followed by "Allegro," "Elizabeth and Essex," "Red, Hot and Blue," "Two on the Isles," Bdwy in "Onward Victoria" (1980), "Joseph and the Amazing Technicolor Dreamcoat."

STANNARD, NICK. Born Dec. 2, 1948 in Cohasset, MA. Attended Carnegie-Mellon U. Debut 1975 OB in "Wings," followed by "Beyond Therapy," "I Am Who I Am," "Verdict," Bdwy in "Dracula" (1979).

STATTEL, ROBERT. Born Nov. 20, 1937 in Floral Park, NY. Graduate Manhattan Col. Debut 1958 OB in "Heloise," followed by "When I Was a Child," "Man and Superman," "The Storm," "Don Carlos," "Taming of the Shrew," "Titus Adronicus," "Henry IV," "Peer Gynt," "Hamlet," LCRep's "Danton's Death," "Country Wife," "Caucasian Chalk Circle," and "King Lear," "Iphigenia in Aulis," "Ergo," "The Persians," "Blue Boys," "The Minister's Black Veil," "Four Friends," "Two Character Play," "The Merchant of Venice," "Cuchulain," "Oedipus Cycle," "Gilles de Rais," "Woyzeck," "King Lear," "The Fuehrer Bunker," "Learned Ladies," "Domestic Issues," "Great Days."

STEFFY, DON. Born Sept. 30, 1950 in Canton, OH. Graduate KentStateU. Bdwy debut 1982 in "Seven Brides for Seven Brothers," followed by "On Your Toes."

STEIN, JUNE. Born June 13, 1950 in NYC. Debut 1979 OB in "The Runner Stumbles," followed by "Confluence," "Am I Blue," "Balm in Gilead," "Danny and the Deep Blue Sea."

STENBORG, HELEN. Born Jan. 24, 1925 in Minneapolis, MN. Attended Unter Col. OB in "A Doll's House," "A Month in the Country," "Say Nothing," "Rosmersholm," "Rimers of Eldrich," "Trial of the Catonsville 9," "The Hot l Baltimore," "Pericles," "Elephant in the House," "A Tribute to Lili Lamont," "Museum," "5th of July," "In the Recovery Lounge," "The Chisolm Trail," "Time Framed," "Levitations," Bdwy in "Sheep on the Runway" (1970), "Da," "A Life."

STENDER, DOUGLAS. Born Sept 14, 1942 in Nanticoke, PA. Graduate Princeton U, RADA. Bdwy debut 1973 in "The Changing Room," OB in "New England Eclectic," "Hamlet," "Second Man," "How He Lied to Her Husband," "Bhutan."

STERLING, CLARK. Born Dec. 13, 1956 in San Diego, CA. Graduate Stanford U. Bdwy debut 1982 in "Seven Brides for Seven Brothers," followed by OB in "Tallulah."

STERLING, DOROTHY. Born July 23, 1955 in Englewood, NJ. Graduate NYU. Debut 1983 OB in "Daydreams."

STERN, CHERYL. Born July 1, 1956 in Buffalo, NY. Graduate Northwestern U. Debut 1984 OB in "Up in Central Park."

STERN, DANIEL. Born in 1957 in Bethesda, MD. OB in "Frankie and Annie," "Lost and Found," "Almost Men," "Pastorale," "The Undefeated Rumba Champs," "How I Got That Story," "True West."

STERNER, STEVE. Born May 5, 1951 in NYC. Attended CCNY. Bdwy debut 1980 in "Clothes for a Summer Hotel" followed by "Oh, Brother!," OB in "Lovesong," "Vagabond Stars," "Fabulous '50's," "My Heart Is in the East," "Mandrake."

STERNHAGEN, FRANCES. Born Jan. 13, 1932 in Washington, DC. Vassar graduate. OB in "Admirable Bashful," "Thieves' Carnival," "Country Wife," "Ulysses in Nighttown," "Saintliness of Margery Kemp," "The Room," "A Slight Ache," "Displaced Person," "Playboy of the Western World," "The Prevalence of Mrs. Seal," "Summer," "Laughing Stock," Bdwy in "Great Day in the Morning," "Right Honorable Gentleman," with APA in "Cocktail Party," and "Cock-a-Doodle Dandy," "The Sign in Sidney Brustein's Window," "Enemies," (LC), "The Good Doctor," "Equus," "Angel," "On Golden Pond," "The Father," "Grownups," "You Can't Take It with You."

STEVENS, FISHER. Born Nov. 27, 1963 in Chicago, IL. Attended NYU. Bdwy debut 1982 in "Torch Song Trilogy," followed by "Brighton Beach Memoirs."

STEVENS, FRAN. Born Mar. 8 in Washington, DC. Attended Notre Dame, Cleveland Playhouse. Bdwy in "Pousse Cafe," "Most Happy Fella," "A Funny Thing Happened on the Way to the Forum," "How Now Dow Jones," "Her First Roman," "Cry for Us All," "On the Town," "Mame" (1983), OB in "Frank Gagiano's City Scene," "Debris," "Polly."

STEVENS, SUSAN. Born in 1942 in Louisville, KY. Attended Jackson Col., AMDA. Debut 1978 OB in "The Price of Genius," followed by "Dream Play," "Zeks," "Philistines," "The Last of Hitler," "Brass Birds Don't Sing."

STEVENS, WESLEY. Born Apr. 6, 1948 in Evansville, IN. Graduate UVa, OhStateU. Debut 1978 in "Othello," followed by "The Importance of Being Earnest," "Candida," "Platonov," "King Lear."

STEWART, SCOT. Born June 3, 1941 in Tylerstown, MS. Graduate UMis. Debut 1975 OB in "New Girl in Town," Bdwy in "Sugar Babies" (1979), "Mame" (1983).

STILLER, JERRY. Born June 8, 1931 in NYC. Graduate USyracuse. Debut 1953 in "Coriolanus," followed by "The Power and the Glory," "Golden Apple," "Measure for Measure," "Taming of the Shrew," "Carefree Tree," "Diary of a Scoundrel," "Romeo and Juliet," "As You Like It," "Two Gentlemen of Verona," "Passione," "Hurlyburly," Bdwy in "The Ritz," "Unexpected Guests," "Passione."

STOTTS, SALLY. Born Mar. 12, 1961 in Tampa, FL. Attended NCSch.ofArts. Debut 1983 OB in "Lenny and the Heartbreakers."

STOUT, MARY. Born Apr. 8, 1952 in Huntington, WVa. Graduate Marshall U. Debut 1980 OB in "Plain and Fancy," followed by "Sound of Music," "Crisp," "A Christmas Carol," Bdwy in "Copperfield" (1981).

STOVALL, COUNT. Born Jan. 15, 1946 in Los Angeles, CA. Graduate UCal. Debut 1973 OB in "He's Got a Jones," followed by "In White America," "Rashomon," "Sidnee Poet Heroical," "A Photo," "Julius Caesar," "Coriolanus," "Spell #7," "The Jail Diary of Albie Sachs," "To Make a Poet Black," "Transcendental Blues," "Edward II," "Children of the Sun," "Shades of Brown," "American Dreams," Bdwy in "Inacent Black" (1981), "The Philadelphia Story."

STRAUSS, JANE. Born in Philadelphia, PA. Graduate USoFla. Bdwy debut 1984 in "Oliver!"

STRIKER, DANIELLE R. Born Feb. 22, 1961 in Queens, NY. Debut 1983 OB in "Skyline," Bdwy in "Zorba" (1983).

STRYKER, CHRISTOPHER. Born Jan. 3, 1963 in NYC. Attended Actors Inst. Bdwy debut in "Torch Song Trilogy" (1982).

STUBBS, JIM. Born Mar. 19, 1949 in Charlotte, NC. Graduate NCSchool of Arts. Bdwy debut 1975 in "Dance with Me," OB in "The Passion of Dracula," "Willie."

SULLIVAN, JEREMIAH. Born Sept. 22, 1937 in NYC. Graduate Harvard. Bdwy debut 1957 in "Compulsion," followed by "The Astrakhan Coat," "Philadelphia, Here I Come!," "A Lion in Winter," "Hamlet," OB in "Ardele," "A Scent of Flowers," "House of Blue Leaves," "Gogol," "The Master and Margarita," "Breakfast Conversations in Miami."

SULLIVAN, KIM. Born July 21, 1952 in Philadelphia, PA. Graduate NYU. Debut 1972 OB in "The Black Terror," followed by "Legend of the West," "Deadwood Dick," "Big Apple Messenger," "Dreams Deferred," "Raisin in the Sun."

SUNG, ELIZABETH. Born Oct. 14, 1954 in Hong Kong. Graduate Juilliard. Debut 1982 OB in "Station J," followed by "A Midsummer Night's Dream," "Sound and Beauty."

SUROVY, NICOLAS. Born June 30, 1944 in Los Angeles, CA. Attended Northwestern U., Neighborhood Playhouse. Debut 1964 in "Helen" for which he received a Theatre World Award, followed by "Sisters of Mercy," "Cloud 9," Bdwy in "Merchant," "Crucifer of Blood," "Major Barbara," "You Can't Take It with You."

SWANSEN, LARRY. Born Nov. 10, 1930 in Roosevelt, OK. Graduate UOk. Bdwy debut 1966 in "Those That Play the Clowns," followed by "The Great White Hope," "The King and I," OB in "Dr. Faustus Lights the Lights," "Thistle in My Bed," "A Darker Flower," "Vincent," "MacBird," "Unknown Soldier and His Wife," "Sound of Music," "Conditioning of Charlie One," "Ice Age," "Prince of Homburg," "Who's There."

SWARBRICK, CAROL. Born Mar. 20, 1948 in Inglewood CA. Graduate UCLA, NYU. Debut 1971 OB in "Drat!," followed by "The Glorious Age," Bdwy in "Side by Side by Sondheim," "Whoopee!," "42nd Street."

SYKES, ROSEMARY. Born Jan. 12 in Manchester CT. Graduate State U/Albany, Neighborhood Playhouse. Debut 1981 OB in "The Diviners," followed by "Three Lost Plays of O'Neill," "A New Way to Pay Old Debts."

SZARABAJKA, KEITH. Born Dec. 2, 1952 in Oak Park, IL. Attended Trinity U, UChicago. Bdwy debut 1973 in "Warp!," followed by "Doonesbury," OB in "Bleacher Bums," "Class Enemy."

TALMAN, ANN. Born Sept. 13, 1957 in Welch, WVa. Graduate PaStateU. Debut 1980 OB in "What's So Beautiful about a Sunset over Prairie Avenue?," followed by "Louisiana Summer," "Winterplay," "Prairie Avenue," "Broken Eggs," "Octoberfest," Bdwy in "The Little Foxes" (1981).

TANDY, JESSICA. Born June 7, 1909 in London, Eng. Attended Greet Acad. Bdwy debut 1930 in "The Matriarch," followed by "Last Enemy," "Time and the Conways," "White Steed," "Geneva," "Jupiter Laughs," "Anne of England," "Yesterday's Magic," "A Streetcar Named Desire," "Hilda Crane," "The Fourposter," "The Honeys," "A Day by the Sea," "Man in the Dog Suit," "Triple Play," "Five Finger Exercise," "The Physicists," "A Delicate Balance," "Home," "All Over," "Camino Real," "Not I," "Happy Days," "Noel Coward in Two Keys," "The Gin Game," "Rose," "Foxfire," "The Glass Menagerie."

TARADASH, LAURI. Born June 4, 1959 in NYC. Graduate NYU. Debut 1984 OB in "The Emperor of My Baby's Heart."

TARANTINA, BRIAN. Born Mar. 27, 1959 in NYC. Debut 1980 OB in "Innocent Thoughts and Harmless Intentions," followed by "Time Framed," "Fables for Friends," "Balm in Gilead," Bdwy 1983 in "Angels Fall" for which he received a Theatre World Award.

TARLETON, DIANE. Born Oct. 25, in Baltimore, MD. Graduate UMd. Bdwy debut 1965 in "Anya," followed by "A Joyful Noise," "Elmer Gantry," "Yentl," "Torch Song Trilogy," OB in "A Time for the Gentle People," "Spoon River Anthology," "International Stud," "Too Much Johnson," "To Bury a Cousin," "A Dream Play."

TARLOW, FLORENCE. Born Jan. 19, 1929 in Philadelphia, PA. Bdwy debut 1968 in "Man in the Glass Booth," followed by "Good Woman of Setzuan," "Inner City," "Medea," OB in "Beautiful Day," "Istanbul," "Gorilla, Queen," "America Hurrah," "Red Cross," "Promenade," "A Visit," "Blonde Leading the Blonde," "Flo and Max."

TASK, MAGGIE. Born July 4 in Marion, OH. Attended Wright Col. Bdwy debut 1960 in "Greenwillow," followed by "A Family Affair," "Tovarich," "Most Happy Fella," "Carousel," "Funny Girl," "Kelly," "Anya," "A Time for Singing," "Darling of the Day," "Education of Hyman Kaplan," "Sound of Music," "Coco," "Sweeney Todd," OB in "Sing Melancholy Baby," "Road to Hollywood."

TATUM, MARIANNE. Born Feb. 18, 1951 in Houston, TX. Attended Manhattan School of Music. Debut 1971 OB in "Ruddigore," followed by "The Sound of Music," "The Gilded Cage," Bdwy 1980 in "Barnum" for which she received a Theatre World Award.

TAYLOR-DUNN, CORLISS. Born Dec. 1, 1945 in Cleveland, OH. Graduate Central State U., UMi. Bdwy debut 1977 in "Bubbling Brown Sugar," OB in "Pins and Needles" (1978), followed by "Late Great Ladies."

TAYLOR-YOUNG, LEIGH. Born Jan. 25, 1945 in Washington, DC. Attended NorthwesternU. Debut 1983 OB in "Catastrophe."

TEAL, DANNY. Born May 3, 1952 in Bennettsvile, SC. Graduate NCSU. Debut 1983 OB in "Boo: An Evening of Ghost Stories." followed by "Dispatches from Hell."

TEETER, LARA. Born in 1955 in Tulsa, OK. Graduate OkCityU. Bdwy debut in "The Best Little Whorehouse in Texas," followed by "Pirates of Penzance," "7 Brides for 7 Brothers," "On Your Toes."

TEITEL, CAROL. Born Aug. 1, 1929 in NYC. Attended AmTh Wing. Bdwy debut 1957 in "The Country Wife," followed by "The Entertainer," "Hamlet," "Marat/deSade," "A Flea in Her Ear," "Crown Matrimonial," "All Over Town," OB in "Way of the World," "Juana La Loca," "An Evening with Ring Lardner," "Misanthrope," "Shaw Festival," "Country Scandal," "The Bench," "Colombe," "Under Milk Wood," "7 Days of Mourning," "Long Day's Journey into Night," "The Old Ones," "Figures in the Sand," "World of Sholom Aleichem," "Big and Little," "Duet," "Trio," "Every Good Boy Deserves Favor" (LC), "Fallen Angels," "A Stitch in Time," "Faces of Love," "Keymaker," "Learned Ladies," "Major Barbara in Concert," "Baseball Wives," "Flight of the Earls."

TESTA, MARY. Born June 4, 1955 in Philadelphia, PA. Attended URI. Debut 1979 OB in "In Trousers," followed by "Company," "Life Is Not a Doris Day Movie," "Not-so-New Faces of '82," "American Princess," "Mandrake," Bdwy 1980 in "Barnum," "Marilyn" (1983), "The Rink."

THOMAS, RICHARD. Born June 13, 1951 in NYC. Bdwy debut 1958 in "Sunrise at Campobello," followed by "A Member of the Wedding," "Strange Interlude," "The Playroom," "Richard III," "Everything in the Garden," "Fifth of July," OB in "The Seagull."

THOMAS, WILLIAM, JR. Born Nov. 8 in Columbus, OH. Graduate OhStateU. Debut 1972 OB in "Touch," followed by "Natural," "Godspell," "Poor Little Lambs," "Loose Joints," "Not-So-New Faces of '81," Bdwy in "Your Arms Too Short to Box with God" (1976), "La Cage aux Folles."

THOME, DAVID. Born July 24, 1951 in Salt Lake City, UT. Bdwy debut 1971 in "No, No, Nanette," followed by "Different Times," "Good News," "Rodgers and Hart," "A Chorus Line," "Dancin'," "Dreamgirls."

THOMPSON, EVAN. Born Sept. 3, 1931 in NYC. Graduate UCal. Bdwy bow 1969 in "Jimmy," OB in "Mahagonny," "Treasure Island," "Knitters in the Sun," "Half-Life," "Fasnacht Dau," "Importance of Being Earnest," "Under the Gaslight," "Henry V."

THOMPSON, JEFFREY V. Born Mar. 21, 1952 in Cleveland, OH. Graduate OhU. Debut 1976 OB in "Homeboy," followed by "Macbeth," "Season's Reasons," "Helen," "Louis," "Edward II," "Take Me Along," Bdwy in "Eubie!" (1978), "Amen Corner."

THOMSPON, MARTIN. Born Apr. 22, 1953 in Charlottesville, VA. Graduate EastCarolinaU. Debut 1984 OB in "Flesh, Flash and Frank Harris," followed by "Lady from the Sea," "Summer People."

THOMPSON, OWEN. Born Sept. 16, 1962 in Los Angeles, CA. Debut 1974 OB in "The Trojan Women," followed by "The Importance of Being Earnest," "She Loves Me," "The Browning Version," "King John," "Richard III," "Enter Laughing."

THOMPSON, SADA. Born Sept. 27, 1929 in Des Moines, IO. Graduate Carnegie Tech. Debut 1953 OB in "Under Milk Wood," followed by "Clandestine Marriage," "Murder in the Cathedral," "White Devil," "Carefree Tree," "The Misanthrope," "U.S.A.," "River Line," "Ivanov," "The Last Minstrel," "An Evening for Merlin Finch," "Effect of Gamma Rays on Man-in-the-moon Marigolds," "Wednesday," Bdwy in Festival," "Juno," "Johnny No-Trump," "American Dream," "Happy Days," "Twigs," "Saturday Sunday Monday."

THOMPSON, WEYMAN. Born Dec. 11, 1950 in Detroit, MI. Graduate Wayne State U, UDetroit. Bdwy debut 1980 in "Clothes for a Summer Hotel," followed by "Dreamgirls."

THORSON, LINDA. Born June 18, 1947 in Toronto, Can. Graduate RADA. Bdwy debut 1982 in "Steaming" for which she received a Theatre World Award, followed by "Noises Off."

THURSTON, TED. Born Jan. 9, 1920 in St. Paul, MN. Attended Drake U. Bdwy debut 1951 in "Paint Your Wagon," followed by "Girl in Pink Tights," "Kismet," "Buttrio Square," "Seventh Heaven," "Most Happy Fella," "Li'l Abner," "13 Daughters," "Happiest Girl in Town," "Celebration," "Gantry," "Wild and Wonderful," "Onward Victoria," OB in "Bible Salesman," "Smith," "Fiddler on the Roof," "Celebration," "Turns," "Taking My Turn."

TIGHE, KEVIN. Born Aug. 13, 1944 in Los Angeles, CA. Graduate USCal. Bdwy debut 1983 in "Open Admissions."

TILLMAN, JUDITH. Born Apr. 25, 1934 in Cleveland, OH. Graduate Case Western Reserve U. Debut 1963 OB in "The Darker Flower," followed by "Do I Hear a Waltz?" "Ten Little Indians," "Patrick Pearse Motel."

TOLAYDO, MICHAEL. Born July 23, 1946 in Kenya, Nairobi. Attended Oakland U. Bdwy debut 1970 in "The Cherry Orchard," followed by "The TIme of Your Life," "The Robber Bridegroom," "Dirty Linen," "Kingdoms," "Moon for the Misbegotten," OB in "Hamlet," "White Liars."

TOM, LAUREN. Born Aug. 4, 1959 in Highland Park, IL. Graduate NYU. Debut 1980 OB in "The Music Lesson," followed by "Family Devotions," "Non Pasquale," Bdwy in "A Chorus Line (1980), "Doonesbury."

TOMEI, CONCETTA. Born Dec. 30, 1945 in Kenosha, WI. Graduate UWisc, Goodman School. Debut 1979 OB in "Little Eyolf," followed by "Cloud 9," "Lumiere," "Richard III," "A Private View," "Fen," Bdwy 1979 in "The Elephant Man."

TORAN, PETER. Born July 16, 1955 in McLean, VA. Graduate Tufts U. Debut 1980 OB in "Romeo and Juliet," followed by "It's Wilde," "The Marquis."

TOREN, SUZANNE. Born Mar. 15, 1947 in NYC. Graduate CCNY, UWis. Bdwy debut 1980 in "Goodbye Fidel," OB in "Who'll Save the Plowboy?," "The Further Inquiry," "French Toast."

TORRES, DONALD. Born June 14, 1935 in Ft. Knox, KY. Graduate IndU. Debut 1958 OB in "The Balcony," followed by "The Wall," "The Boy Friend," "King Lear," "Orpheus Descending," Bdwy 1983 in "Mame."

TORRES, MARK. Born May 7, 1955 in Brownsville, TX. Graduate InU, Temple U. Bdwy debut 1980 in "Amadeus," OB in "King Lear."

TOTO, KAREN. Born Mar. 30, 1956 in Philadelphia, PA. Graduate Temple U. Bdwy debut in "My Fair Lady" (1981), OB in "Red, Hot and Blue."

TOWBIN, BERYL. Born June 14, 1938 in NYC. Bdwy debut 1951 in "The King and I," followed by "Hazel Flagg," "Girl in Pink Tights," "Ziegfeld Follies," "Plain and Fancy," "A to Z," "Bells Are Ringing," "Family Affair," "Hallelujah Baby," "Education of Hyman Kaplan," "Beggar on Horseback," OB in "The Sea Gull."

TOWLER, LAURINE. Born Oct. 19, 1952 in Oberlin, OH. Graduate Stanford U., UCal. Debut 1981 OB in "Godspell," followed by "The Tempest."

TRAMON, DAN. Born Mar. 15, 1965 in Passaic, NJ. Attended Columbia U, Juilliard. Debut 1978 OB in "The American Imagination," Bdwy 1984 in "The Human Comedy."

TREAT, MARTIN. Born May 9, 1945 in Yreka, CA. Graduate UOr. Debut 1977 OB in "Heartbreak House," followed by "The Balcony," "Cuchulian Cycle," "Dr. Faustus," "A Dream Play," "The Danube," "Further Inquiry," "The Last of Hitler."

TREVISANI, PAMELA. Born Nov. 3, 1960 in NYC. Graduate Syracuse U. Bdwy debut 1983 in "Zorba."

TRIGGER, IAN. Born Sept. 30, 1942 in England. Graduate RADA. Debut 1973 OB in "The Taming of the Shrew," followed by "Scapino," "True History of Squire Jonathan," "Slab Boys," "Cloud 9," "Terra Nova," Bdwy in "Scapino," "Habeas Corpus," "13 Rue de l'Amour."

TROY, LOUISE. Born Nov. 9 in NYC. Attended AADA. Debut 1955 OB in "The Infernal Machine," followed by "Merchant of Venice," "Conversation Piece," "Salad Days," "O, Oysters!," "A Doll's House," "Last Analysis," "Judy and Jane," "Heartbreak House," "Rich Girls," Bdwy in "Pipe Dream" (1955), "A Shot in the Dark," "Tovarich," "High Spirits," "Walking Happy," "Equus," "Woman of the Year."

TRUMBULL, ROBERT. Born Feb. 8, 1938 in San Rafael, CA. Graduate UCal/Berkeley. Debut 1983 in "Guys in the Truck" (Off and on Bdwy.)

TUCKER-WHITE, PAMELA. Born Mar. 6, 1955 in Peoria, IL. Graduate UWis., Juilliard. Debut 1981 OB in "How It All Began," followed by "The Dubliners," "The Country Wife," "Home Again Kathleen."

TUNE, TOMMY. Born Feb. 28, 1939 in Wichita Falls, TX. Graduate UTs. Bdwy debut 1965 in "Baker Street," followed by "A Joyful Noise," "How Now Dow Jones," "Seesaw," "My One and Only," OB in "Ichabod."

TURKEN, GRETA. Born Nov. 23, 1959 in NYC. Graduate Sarah Lawrence Col. Debut OB in "Cinders."

TWIGGY. Born Lesley Hornby Sept. 19, 1949 in London, Eng. Bdwy debut 1983 in "My One and Only."

TWOMEY, ANNE. Born June 7, 1951 in Boston, MA. Graduate Temple U. Debut 1975 OB in "Overruled," followed by "The Passion of Dracula," "When We Dead Awaken," "Vieux Carre," "Vampires," Bdwy 1980 in "Nuts" for which she received a Theatre World Award, "To Grandmother's House We Go."

TYSON, CICELY. Born Dec. 19 in NYC. OB in "Dark of the Moon," "The Blacks," "Moon on Rainbow Shawl," "Blue Boy in Black," "To Be Young, Gifted and Black," Bdwy in "A Hand Is on the Gate" (1966), "Carry Me Back to Morningside Heights," "Trumpets of the Lord," "The Corn Is Green" (1983).

USTINOV, PETER. Born Apr. 16, 1921 in London, Eng. Attended London Theatre School. Bdwy debut 1957 in "Romanoff and Juliet," followed by "Photo Finish," "Who's Who in Hell," "Beethoven's Tenth."

VALE, MICHAEL. Born June 28, 1922 in Brooklyn, NY. Attended New School. Bdwy debut 1961 in "The Egg" followed by "Cafe Crown," "Last Analysis," "The Impossible Years," "Saturday Sunday Monday," "Unexpected Guests," "California Suite," OB in "Autograph Hound," "Moths," "Now There's the Three of Us," "Tall and Rex," "Kaddish," "42 Seconds from Broadway," "Sunset," "Little Shop of Horrors."

VAN BENSCHOTEN, STEPHEN. Born Aug. 27, 1943 in Washington, DC. Graduate LaSalle Col, Yale U. Debut 1967 OB in "King John," followed by "The Tempest," Bdwy in "Unlikely Heroes" (1971), "Grease."

VANCE, DANA. Born June 23, 1952 in Steubenville, OH. Graduate WVaU. Debut 1981 OB in "An Evening with Sheffman and Vance," "Backers Audition," Bdwy in "Teaneck Tanzi" (1983).

VAN GRIETHUYSEN, TED. Born Nov. 7, 1934 in Ponca City, OK. Graduate UTx, RADA. Bdwy debut 1962 in "Romulus," followed by "Moon Beseiged," "Inadmissible Evidence," OB in "Failures," "Lute Song," "O Marry Me," "Red Roses for Me," "Basement," "Hedda Gabler," "Othello," "First Time Anywhere!"

VAN ZYL, MEG. Born Apr. 8, 1958 in Portland, OR. Attended Mt. Hood Col. Debut 1982 OB in "Magic Time," followed by "Behind a Mask," "Presque Isle."

VARRONE, GENE. Born Oct. 30, 1929 in Brooklyn, NY. Graduate LIU. Bdwy in "Damn Yankees," "Take Me Along," "Ziegfeld Follies," "Goldilocks," "Wildcat," "Tovarich," "Subways Are for Sleeping," "Bravo Giovanni," "Drat! The Cat," "Fade Out-Fade In," "Don't Drink the Water," "Dear World," "Coco," "A Little Night Music," "So Long 174th St.," "Knickerbocker Holiday," "The Grand Tour," "The Most Happy Fella" (1979), OB in "Promenade," "Kuni Leml."

VEAZEY, JEFF. Born Dec. 6, in New Orleans, LA. Bdwy debut 1975 in "Dr. Jazz," followed by "The Grand Tour," "Sugar Babies," OB in "Speakeasy," "Trading Places."

VENORA, DIANE. Born in 1952 in Hartford, CT. Graduate Juilliard. Debut 1981 OB in "Penguin Touquet," followed by "A Midsummer Night's Dream," "Hamlet," "Uncle Vanya."

VENTRISS, JENNIE. Born Aug. 7, 1935 in Chicago, IL. Graduate DePaul U. Debut 1964 OB in "Ludlow Fair," followed by "I Can't Keep Running in Place," "The Ninth Step," Bdwy in "Luv" (1966), "Prisoner of Second Avenue," "Gemini."

VERNON, RICHARD. Born Jan. 19, 1946 in Washington, DC. Graduate Catholic U. Bdwy debut 1976 in "Poor Murderer," OB in "Lady Windermere's Fan."

VICKERS, LARRY. Born June 8, 1947 in Harrisonburg, VA. Attended Howard U. Bdwy debut 1970 in "Purlie," followed by "Shirley MacLaine at the Palace," "Shirley MacLaine on Broadway."

VICKERY, JOHN. Born in 1951 in Alameda, CA. Graduate UCaBerkeley, UCaDavis. Debut 1981 in "Macbeth" (LC), followed by "Ned and Jack," "Eminent Domain," "The Real Thing," OB in "American Days," "A Call from the East," "Henry IV Part I," "Looking-Glass," "The Death of Von Richtofen," "Vampires."

VIDNOVIC, MARTIN. Born Jan. 4, 1948 in Falls Church, VA. Attended Cincinnati Consv. Debut 1972 OB in "The Fantasticks," followed by "Some Enchanted Evening," Bdwy in "Home Sweet Homer," "The King and I" (1977), "Oklahoma!" (1979), "Brigadoon" (1980), "Baby."

VINCENT, LAWRENCE. Born June 2, 1920 in Detroit, MI. Graduate UMich., Western Reserve U. Debut 1983 OB in "Champeen," followed by "Basin Street."

VINOVICH, STEVE. Born Jan. 22, 1945 in Peoria, IL. Graduate UIl, UCLA, Juilliard. Debut 1974 OB in "The Robber Bridegroom," follwed by "King John," "Father Uxbridge Wants to Marry," "Hard Sell," "Ross," "Double Feature," "Tender Places," "A Private View," "Love," Bdwy in "Robber Bridegroom" (1976), "The Magic Show," "The Grand Tour," "Loose Ends," "A Midsumme Night's Dream."

VIRTUE, CHRISTIE. Born Aug. 23 in Berkeley, CA. Graduate San Diego State U. Debut 1971 OB in "The House of Blue Leaves," followed by "Wonderful Lives," "Lessons," "The Trip Back Down," "Children."

VITA, MICHAEL. Born in NYC. Studied at HB Studio. Bdwy debut 1967 in "Sweet Charity," followed by "Golden Rainbow," "Promises, Promises," "Cyrano," "Chicago," "Ballroom," "Charlie and Algernon," "A Doll's Life," "On Your Toes," OB in "Sensatons," "That's Entertainment," "Rocket to the Moon," "Nymph Errant."

VOET, DOUG. Born Mar. 1, 1951 in Los Angeles, CA. Graduate BYU. Bdwy debut in "Joseph and the Amazing Technicolor Dreamcoat" (1982), OB in "Forbidden Broadway."

VOIGTS, RICHARD. Born Nov. 25, 1934 in Streator, IL. Graduate InU, Columbia U. Debut 1979 OB in "The Constant Wife," followed by "Company," "The Investigation," "Dune Road," "The Collection," "Miracle Man," "As Time Goes By," "Silence," "Station J," "Frozen Assets," "Happy Birthday, Wanda June," "My Three Angels."

VON DOHLEN, LENNY. Born Dec. 22, 1958 in Augusta, GA. Graduate Loretto Heights Col. Debut 1982 OB in "Cloud 9," followed by "Twister," "Asian Shade," "Desire under the Elms."

WAITE, JOHN THOMAS. Born Apr. 19, 1948 in Syracuse NY. Attended Syracuse U. Debut 1976 OB in "The Fantasticks," Bdwy in "Amadeus" (1982).

WALDECK, NONA. Born Feb. 2, 1956 in Cincinnati, OH. Graduate Edgecliff Col., OhioU. Debut 1982 OB in "The Coarse Acting Show," followed by "Dickens Reflection on the Carol," "Romantic Arrangements."

WALDREN, PETER. Born Sept. 7, 1933 in Manila, PI. Graduate Colgate U. Debut 1962 OB in "Bell, Book and Candle," followed by "When the War Was Over," "Napoleon's Dinner," "Open Meeting," "Cabin Fever," "Zin Boogie," "Father Uxbridge Wants to Marry."

WALDRON, MICHAEL. Born Nov. 19, 1949 in West Orange, NJ. Graduate Columbia U. Debut 1979 OB in "Mary," followed by "Dulcy," "Romance Is," "New Faces of '52," Bdwy in "Baby" (1983).

WALDROP, MARK. Born July 30, 1954 in Washington, DC. Graduate Cincinnati Consv. Debut 1977 OB in "Movie Buff," Bdwy in "Hello, Dolly!" (1978), "The Grand Tour," "Evita," "La Cage aux Folles."

WALKEN, CHRISTOPHER. Born Mar. 31, 1943 in Astoria, NY. Attended Hofstra U. Bdwy debut 1958 in "J.B.," followed by "High Spirits," "Baker Street," "The Lion in Winter," "Measure for Measure," "The Rose Tattoo" for which he received a Theatre World Award, "The Unknown Soldier and His Wife," "Rosencrantz and Guildenstern Are Dead," "Scenes from American Life," "Cymbeline," "Enemies," "The Plough and the Stars," "Merchant of Venice," "The Tempest," "Troilus and Cressida," "Macbeth," "Sweet Bird of Youth," OB in "Best Foot Forward" (1963), "Iphigenia in Aulis," "Lemon Sky," "Kid Champion," "The Seagull," "Cinders," "Hurlyburly."

WALKER, JENNIFER. Born May 13, 1955 in Knoxville, TN. Graduate UAkron, Cornell U. Debut 1983 OB in "Cubistique," followed by "Episode under the Southern Cross," "The Alto Part."

WALLACH, ELI. Born Dec. 7, 1915 in Brooklyn, NY. Graduate UTx, CCNY. Bdwy debut 1945 in "Skydrift," followed by "Henry VIII," "Androcles and the Lion," "Alice in Wonderland," "Yellow Jack," "What Every Woman Knows," "Antony and Cleopatra," "Mr. Roberts," "Lady from the Sea," "The Rose Tattoo" for which he received a Theatre World Award, "Mlle. Colombe," "Teahouse of the August Moon," "Major Barbara," "The Cold Wind and the Warm," "Rhinoceros," "Luv," "Staircase," "Promenade All," "Waltz of the Toreadors," "Saturday, Sunday, Monday," "Every Good Boy Deserves Favor," "Twice Around the Park," OB in "The Diary of Anne Frank," "Nest of the Wood Grouse."

WALSH, DEBORAH. Born Jan. 24, 1952 in NYC. Attended Hollins Col., Stanford U, Trinity Col. Debut 1984 OB in "Catchpenny Twist."

WALSH, ROBERT. Born Oct. 8, 1953 in Mt. Kisco, NY. Graduate Ohio U. Debut 1981 OB in "Half-Life," followed by "Penelope," "Big Maggie," "Julius Caesar."

WARFIELD, JOE. Born Nov. 6, 1937 in Baltimore, MD. Graduate UMD. Debut 1959 OB in "Little Mary Sunshine," followed by "O Say Can You See," Bdwy in "110 in the Shade" (1964), "Jimmy Shine," "Baby."

WARING, TODD. Born Apr. 28, 1955 in Saratoga Springs, NY. Graduate Skidmore Col. Debut 1980 OB in "Journey's End," followed by "Mary Stuart," "Henry IV Part II," "Paradise Lost," Bdwy in "The Real Thing" (1984).

WARNER, AMY. Born June 29, 1951 in Minneapolis, MN. Graduate Principia Col. Debut 1982 OB in "Faust," followed by "Ghost Sonata," "Wild Oats," "Big Little/Scenes," "Hamlet."

WARNERS, ROBERT. Born Aug. 11, 1956 in Oakland, CA. Bdwy debut 1979 in "Dancin'," followed by "Woman of the Year," "Merlin," OB in "One More Song/One More Dance."

WARNING, DENNIS. Born June 18, 1951 in East St. Louis, IL. Graduate Southwest Mo. State U. Bdwy debut 1976 in "The Robber Bridegroom," followed by "The Most Happy Fella" (1979), "Baby," OB in "Jimmy and Billy."

WARREN, JENNIFER LEIGH. Born Aug. 29 in Dallas TX. Graduate Dartmouth Col. Debut 1982 OB in "Little Shop of Horrors."

WASHINGTON, DENZEL. Born Dec. 28, 1954 in Mt. Vernon, NY. Graduate Fordham U. Debut 1975 OB in "The Emperor Jones," followed by "Othello," "Coriolanus," "Mighty Gents," "Becket," "Spell #7," "Ceremonies in Dark Old Men," "One Tiger To a Hill," "A Soldier's Play," "Every Goodbye Ain't Gone."

WASHINGTON, MELVIN. Born Dec. 19 in Brooklyn, NY. Attended CCNY, HB Studio. Debut 1980 OB in "Streamers," followed by "Something to Live For," Bdwy in "My One and Only" (1983).

WATERMAN, WILLARD. Born Aug. 29, 1914 in Madison, WI. Bdwy debut 1966 in "Mame," followed by "The Pajama Game," "Mame" (1983).

WEARY, A. C. Born June 7, 1951 in Chicago, IL. Graduate Ohio U. Debut 1978 OB in "Moliere in spite of Himself," followed by "Tooth of Crime," "A Christmas Carol," "Red, Hot and Blue."

WEAVER, FRITZ. Born Jan. 19, 1926 in Pittsburgh, PA. Graduate UChicago. Bdwy debut 1955 in "Chalk Garden," for which he received a Theatre World Award, followed by "Protective Custody," "Miss Lonelyhearts," "All American," "Lorenzo," "The White House," "Baker Street," "Child's Play," "Absurd Person Singular," "Angels Fall," OB in "The Way of the World," "White Devil," "Doctor's Dilemma," "Family Reunion," "The Power and the Glory," "The Great God Brown," "Peer Gynt," "Henry IV," "My Fair Lady" (CC), "Lincoln," "The Biko Inquest," "The Price," "Dialogue for Lovers," "A Tale Told," "Time Framed."

WEAVER, LYNN. Born May 17, in Paris, TN. Graduate UTn, Neighborhood Playhouse. Debut 1981 OB in "The Italian Straw Hat," followed by "Tiger at the Gates," "The Cherry Orchard."

WEAVER, SIGOURNEY. Born in 1949 in NYC. Attended Yale, Stanford U. Debut 1976 in "Titanic," followed by "Das Lusitania Songspiel," "Beyond Therapy," "Hurlyburly."

WEBB, ALYCE. Born June 1, 1934 in NYC. Graduate NYU. Bdwy debut 1946 in "Street Scene," followed by "Lost in the Stars," "Finian's Rainbow," "Porgy and Bess," "Show Boat," "Guys and Dolls," "Kiss Me, Kate," "Wonderful Town," "Hello, Dolly!," "Purlie," "You Can't Take It with You," OB in "Simply Heavenly," "Ballad of Bimshire," "Trumpets of the Lord," "Streetcar Named Desire."

WEBER, STEVEN. Born Mar. 4, 1961 in NYC. Attended SUNY/Purchase. Debut 1983 OB in "The Inheritors," followed by "Rain," "Paradise Lost," "Ghosts," "Come Back, Little Sheba."

WEEKS, JAMES RAY. Born Mar 21, 1942 in Seattle, WA. Graduate UOre., AADA. Debut 1972 in LCR's "Enemies," "Merchant of Venice," and "A Streetcar Named Desire," followed by OB's "49 West 87th," "Feedlot," "The Runner Stumbles," "Glorious Morning," "Just the Immediate Family," "The Deserter," "Life and/or Death," "Devour the Snow," "Innocent Thoughts, Harmless Intentions," "The Diviners," "A Tale Told," "Confluence," "Richard II," "Great Grandson of Jedediah Kohler," "Black Angel," "Serenading Louie," "The Harvesting," Bdwy in "My Fat Friend," "We Interrupt This Program," "Devour the Snow."

WEIMAN, KATE. Born Sept. 16, 1948 in Rockville Center, NY. Attended NYU, AADA. Debut 1981 OB in "Engaged," followed by "A Thurber Carnival."

WEIL, ROBERT E. Born Nov. 18, 1914 in NYC. Attended NYU. Bdwy bow in "New Faces of 1941," followed by "Burlesque," "Becket," "Once upon a Mattress," "Blood, Sweat and Stanley Poole," "Night Life," "Arturo Ui," "Beggar on Horseback," "Lenny," "Happy End," OB in "Love Your Crooked Neighbor," "Felix," "My Old Friends," "Linda Her and the Fairy Garden" "The Golem."

WEINER, JOHN. Born Dec. 17, 1954 in Newark, NJ. Graduate Wm. & Mary Col. Bdwy debut 1983 in "La Cage aux Folles."

WELAND, MADI. Born Dec. 9, 1958 in Fukoka, Japan. Graduate UCol. Debut 1983 OB in "Sister Mary Ignatius Explains It All."

WELDON, CHARLES. Born June 1, 1940 in Wetumka, OK. Bdwy debut 1969 in "Big Time Buck White," followed by "River Niger," OB in "Ride a Black Horse," "Long Time Coming," "Jamimma," "In the Deepest Part of Sleep," "Brownsville Raid," "The Great MacDaddy," "The Offering," "Colored People's Time," "Raisin in the Sun."

WELLER, PETER. Born June 24, 1947 in Stevens Point, WI. Graduate AADA. Bdwy bow 1972 in "Sticks and Bones," followed by "Full Circle," "Summer Brave," OB in "Children," "Merchant of Venice," "Macbeth," "Rebel Women" "Streamers," "Woolgatherer," "Serenading Louie."

WELLS, CHRISTOPHER. Born June 18, 1955 in Norwalk, CT. Graduate Amherst Col. Debut 1981 OB in "Big Apple Country," followed by "Broadway Jukebox," "Savage Amusement," "Overruled," "Heart of Darkness."

WEST, MATT. Born Oct. 2, 1958 in Downey, CA. Attended Pfiffer-Smith School. Bdwy debut in "A Chorus Line" (1980).

WESTENBERG, ROBERT W. Born Oct. 26, 1953 in Miami Beach, FL. Graduate UCal/Fresno. Debut 1981 OB in "Henry IV Part I," followed by "Hamlet," "The Death of von Richtofen," Bdwy in "Zorba" (1983) for which he received a Theatre World Award, "Sunday in the Park with George."

WESTPHAL, ROBIN. Born Nov. 24, 1953 in Salt Lake City, UT. Graduate UUtah. Debut 1983 OB in "June Moon."

WHITE, ALICE. Born Jan. 6, 1945 in Washington, DC. Graduate Oberlin Col. Debut 1977 OB in "The Passion of Dracula," followed by "La Belle au Bois," "Zoology."

Elaine Princi	Richard Warren Pugh	Bernadette Quigley	Aidan Quinn	Melissa Randel	John Henry Redwood

James Rich	Tudi Roche	Leon Russom	Camille Saviola	Paul P. Smith	Nealla Spano

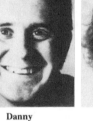

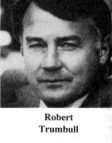

Danielle Striker	Kim Sullivan	Lauri Taradash	Danny Teal	Karen Toto	Robert Trumbull

Michael Vale	Meg Van Zyl	Michael Vita	Jennifer Walker	Matt West	June White

Hattie Winston	Time Winters	Mary Catherine Wright	Ray Xifo	Jo Ann Yeoman	Mark Ziebell

WHITE, JUNE. Born June 10, 1947 in Richmond, KY. Graduate UDayton, NYU. Debut 1982 OB in "Village Wooing," followed by "Flesh, Flash and Frank Harris."

WHITEHEAD, PAXTON. Born in Kent, Eng. Attended Webber-Douglas Acad. Bdwy debut 1962 in "The Affair," followed by "Beyond the Fringe," "Candida," "Habeas Corpus," "Crucifer of Blood," "Camelot" (1980), "Noises Off," OB in "Gallow's Humor," "One Way Pendulum," "A Doll's House," "Rondelay."

WHITELAW, BILLIE. Born June 6, 1932 in Coventry, Eng. NY debut 1984 OB in "Rockaby."

WHITFIELD, DEBRA. Born July 1, 1957 in Charlotte, NC. Graduate OhStateU, KentStateU. Debut 1983 OB in "Brandy Before Breakfast," followed by "Dr. Jekyll and Mr. Hyde," "Bravo," "Appointment with Death," "Hound of the Baskervilles," "The Land Is Bright."

WHITTON, MARGARET. (formerly Peggy). Born Nov. 30 in Philadelphia, PA. Debut 1973 OB in "Baba Goya," followed by "Arthur," "The Wager," "Nourish the Beast," "Another Language," "Chinchilla," "Othello," "The Art of Dining," "One Tiger to a Hill," "Henry IV, Parts 1 & 2," "Don Juan," "My Uncle Sam," Bdwy in "Steaming" (1982).

WIDDOES, JAMES. Born Nov. 15, 1953 in Pittsburgh, PA. Attended NYU. Debut 1977 OB in "Wonderful Town," Bdwy 1982 in "Is There Life after High School?" for which he received a Theatre World Award, followed by "Caine Mutiny Court-Martial."

WIDDOES, KATHLEEN. Born Mar. 21, 1939 in Wilmington, DE. Attended Paris Theatre des Nations. Bdwy debut 1958 in "The Firstborn," followed by "World of Suzie Wong," "Much Ado about Nothing," "The Importance of Being Earnest," "Brighton Beach Memoirs," OB in "Three Sisters," "The Maids," "You Can't Take It with You," "To Clothe the Naked," "World War 2½," "Beggar's Opera," "As You Like It," "A Midsummer Night's Dream," "One Act Play Festival," "Hamlet."

WIEST, DIANE. Born Mar. 28, 1948 in Kansas City, MO. Attended UMd. Debut 1976 OB in "Ashes," followed by "Leave It to Beaver Is Dead," "The Art of Dining" for which she received a Theatre World Award, "Bonjour La Bonjour," "Three Sisters," "Serenading Louie," "Other Places," Bdwy in "Frankenstein" (1980), "Othello," "Beyond Therapy."

WILDE, ZACHARY. Born Feb. 24 in NYC. Attended UCal. Debut 1981 OB in "Damn Yankees," followed by "Heartfelt Odds."

WILKOF, LEE. Born June 25, 1957 in Canton, OH. Graduate UCincinnati. Debut 1977 OB in "Present Tense," followed by "Little Shop of Horrors."

WILLIAMS, CARL. Born July 27, 1938 in Charlotte, NC. Graduate UNC. Debut 1959 OB in "Julius Caesar," followed by "Hadrian VII," "Hermit," "Murder in the Cathedral," "Portrait of an Unknown Woman," "Blood Wedding," "Dark of the Moon," "The Infernal Machine," "Heartbreak House," "Dick Deterred."

WILLIAMS, CURT. Born Nov. 17, 1935 in Mt. Holly, NJ. Graduate Oberlin Col. UMiami. Debut 1964 OB in "The Fantasticks," followed by "Pinafore," "Mikado," "Night Must Fall," "The Hostage," "Macbeth," "Ice Age," "Colored People's Time," "About Heaven and Earth," "Appointment with Death," Bdwy in "Purlie" (1970), "Play Memory."

WILLIAMS, JENNIFER. Born in Houston, TX. Debut 1969 OB in "Geese," followed by "Look Where I'm At," "Here Comes a Chopper," "Who's There," Bdwy in "Frank Merriwell" (1971).

WILLIAMS, KEITH. Born Oct. 2, 1954 in Scranton, PA. Graduate Mansfield Col., Catholic U. Debut 1983 OB in "Lady Windermere's Fan," followed by "Verdict," "My Three Angels."

WILLIAMS, L. B. Born May 7, 1949 in Richmond, VA. Graduate Albion Col. Bdwy debut 1976 in "Equus," OB in "Spa," "Voices," "5 on the Blackhand Side," "Chameleon," "Forbidden Copy."

WILLIAMSON, RUTH. Born Jan. 25, 1954 in Baltimore, MD. Graduate UMd. Bdwy debut 1981 in "Annie," OB in "Preppies" (1983), "Bodo."

WILLIS, SCOTT. Born Nov. 9, 1956 in Eldorado, IL. Graduate Murray State U. Debut 1981 OB in "Something for the Boys," followed by "Damn Yankees," "Encore," "Sing Me Sunshine."

WILLIS, SUSAN. Born in Tiffin, OH. Attended Carnegie Tech, Cleveland Play House. Debut 1953 OB in "The Little Clay Cart," followed by "Love and Let Love," "Glorious Age," "The Guardsman," "Dangerous Corners," Bdwy in "Take Me Along" (1959), "Gypsy," "Dylan," "Come Live with Me," "Cabaret," "Oliver!"

WILSON, MARY LOUISE. Born Nov. 12, 1936 in New Haven, CT. Graduate Northwestern U. Bdwy debut 1963 in "Hot Spot," followed by "Flora the Red Menace," "Criss-Crossing," "Promises, Promises," "The Women," "The Gypsy," "The Royal Family," "Importance of Being Earnest," "Philadelphia Story," "Fools," "Alice in Wonderland," OB in "Our Town," "Upstairs at the Downstairs," "Threepenny Opera," "A Great Career," "Whispers on the Wind," "Beggar's Opera," "Buried Child," "Sister Mary Ignatius Explains It All," "Actor's Nightmare," "Baby with the Bathwater."

WILSON, THICK. Born Born Feb. 13, 1929 in Hamilton, Ont., Can. Debut 1983 OB in "Last of the Knucklemen."

WILSON, TUG. Born Feb. 16, 1959 in Lansdowne, PA. Attended UHouston. Debut 1982 OB in "Louisiana Summer," followed by "Blackberries."

WINDE, BEATRICE. Born Jan. 6 in Chicago, IL. Debut 1966 OB in "In White America," followed by "June Bug Graduates Tonight," "Strike Heaven on the Face," "Divine Comedy," "Crazy Horse," "My Mother, My Father and Me," "Steal Away," Bdwy 1971 in "Ain't Supposed to Die a Natural Death" for which she received a Theatre World Award.

WINKLER, KEVIN. Born Feb. 9, 1954 in Nowata, OK. Graduate San Diego State U. Debut 1978 OB in "A Midsummer Night's Dream," followed by "Pal Joey," Bdwy in "Little Me" (1981).

WINSETT, JERRY. Born July 19, 1950 in Clarksville, TN. Graduate Austin Peay State U. Debut 1980 OB in "Smiling Assassins," followed by "Lorenzaccio," "The Rivals."

WINSTON, HATTIE. Born Mar. 3, 1945 in Greenville, MS. Attended Howard U. OB in "Prodigal Son," "Day of Absence," "Pins and Needles," "Weary Blues," "Man Better Man," "Billy Noname," "Sambo," "The Great MacDaddy," "A Photo," "Oklahoma!," "The Michigan," Bdwy in "The Me Nobody Knows," "Two Gentlemen of Verona," "I Love My Wife," "The Tap Dance Kid."

WINTERS, TIME. Born Feb. 3, 1956 in Lebanon, OR. Graduate Lane Com. Col., Stephens Col. Debut 1981 OB in "Nathan the Wise," followed by "Round and Round the Garden," "Fanshen," "Henry V," Bdwy in "Amadeus" (1983).

WIRTH, DANIEL. Born Oct. 3, 1955 in Bay City, MI. Graduate Central MiU, UCal. Debut 1982 OB in "Twelfth Night," followed by "The Country Wife," "Dubliners," "Hamlet," "Beckett Plays."

WISE, WILLIAM. Born May 11 in Chicago, IL. Attended Bradley U, Northwestern Ill. U. Debut 1970 OB in "Adaptation/Next," followed by "Him," "The Hot l Baltimore," "Just the Immediate Family," "36," "For the Use of the Hall."

WOLPE, LENNY. Born Mar. 25, 1951 in Newburgh, NY. Graduate Geo. Wash. U, UMn. Debut 1978 OB in "Company," followed by "Brownstone," Bdwy in "Onward Victoria" (1980), "Copperfield."

WOODALL, OLIVER. Born Aug. 28, 1953 n Clarksdale, MS. Attended NCSchool of Arts. Bdwy debut 1983 in "The Tap Dance Kid."

WOODARD, CHARLAINE. Born Dec. 29 in Albany, NY. Graduate Goodman Sch., SUNY. Debut 1975 OB in "Don't Bother Me, I Can't Cope," followed by "Dementos," "Under Fire," "A . . . My Name Is Alice," Bdwy in "Hair" (1977), "Ain't Misbehavin'."

WOODESON, NICHOLAS. Born in England and graduate of USussex, RADA. Debut 1978 OB in "Strawberry Fields," followed by "The Taming of the Shrew," "Backers Audition," Bdwy in "Man and Superman" (1978), "Piaf," "Good."

WOODS, RICHARD. Born May 9, 1923 in Buffalo, NY. Graduate Ithaca Col. Bdwy in "Beg, Borrow or Steal," "Capt. Brassbound's Conversion," "Sail Away," "Coco," "Last of Mrs. Lincoln," "Gigi," "Sherlock Holmes," "Murder among Friends," "The Royal Family," "Deathtrap," "Man and Superman," "The Man Who Came to Dinner," "The Father," "Present Laughter," "Alice in Wonderland," "You Can't Take It with You," "Design for Living," OB in "The Crucible," "Summer and Smoke," "American Gothic," "Four-in-one," "My Heart's in the Highlands," "Eastward in Eden," "The Long Gallery," "The Year Boston Won the Pennant," "In the Matter of J. Robert Oppenheimer" (LC), with APA in "You Can't Take It with You," "War and Peace," "School for Scandal," "Right You Are," "The Wild Duck," "Pantagleize," "Exit the King," "The Cherry Orchard," "Cock-a-doodle Dandy," and "Hamlet," "Crimes and Dreams," "Marathon 84."

WORTH, IRENE. Born June 23, 1916 in Nebraska. Graduate UCLA. Bdwy debut 1943 in "The Two Mrs. Carrolls," followed by "The Cocktail Party," "Mary Stuart," "Toys in the Attic," "King Lear," "Tiny Alice," "Sweet Bird of Youth," "The Cherry Orchard," "Lady from Dubuque," "John Gabriel Borkman," OB in "Happy Days," "Letters of Love and Affection," "The Chalk Garden," "The Golden Age."

WRIGHT, AMY. Born Apr. 15, 1950 in Chicago, IL. Graduate Beloit Col. Debut 1977 OB in "The Stronger," followed by "Nightshift," "Hamlet," "Miss Julie," "Slacks and Tops," "Terrible Jim Fitch," "Village Wooing," "The Stronger," "Time Framed," Bdwy in "5th of July" (1980), "Noises Off."

WRIGHT, MARY CATHERINE. Born Mar. 19, 1948 in San Francisco, CA. Attended CCSF, SFState Col. Bdwy debut 1970 in "Othello," followed by "A History of the American Film," "Tintypes," OB in "East Lynne," "Mimi Lights the Candle," "Marvin's Gardens," "The Tempest," "The Doctor in Spite of Himself," "Love's Labour's Lost," "Pushcart Peddlers," "Sister Mary Ignatius Explains It All," "Actor's Nightmare," "Marathon 84."

WRIGHT, REBECCA. Born Dec. 5, in Springfield, OH. With Joffrey Ballet, ABT before Bdwy debut 1983 in "Merlin," followed by "On Your Toes."

WYATT, JOE S. Born Feb. 5, 1958 in Kansas City, MO. Graduate Stephens Col. Debut 1984 OB in "Up in Central Park."

XIFO, RAY. Born Sept. 3, 1942 in Newark, NJ. Graduate Don Bosco Col. Debut OB 1974 in "The Tempest," followed by "Frogs," "My Uncle Sam."

YAMAMOTO, RONALD. Born Mar. 13, 1953 in Seattle, WA. Graduate Queens Col. Debut 1983 OB in "A Song for a Nisei Fisherman," followed by "Pacific Overtures."

YANCEY, KIM. Born Sept. 25, 1959 in NYC. Graduate CCNY. Debut 1978 OB in "Why Lillie Won't Spin," followed by "Escape to Freedom," "Dacha," "Blues for Mr. Charlie," "American Dreams."

YEOMAN, JOANN. Born Mar. 19, 1948 in Phoenix, AZ. Graduate AzStateU, Purdue U. Debut 1974 OB in "The Boy Friend," followed by "Texas Starlight," "Ba Ta Clan," "A Christmas Carol."

YORK, SUSANNAH. Born Jan. 9, 1941 in London, Eng. Attended RADA. Debut 1981 OB in "Hedda Gabler," followed by "The Human Voice."

YORKE, SALLY. Born Dec. 8, 1953 in Williamsport, PA. Graduate PennStateU. Debut 1982 OB in "Oh, Johnny!," followed by "Class Act," "Elizabeth and Essex."

ZACHARY, ALAINA. Born Oct. 6, 1946 in Cleveland, OH. Graduate Boston U. Debut 1971 OB in "The Proposition," followed by "Secrets," "El Bravo!," Bdwy in "Grease" (1972), "Nine," "Baby."

ZAGNIT, STUART. Born Mar. 28, 1952 in New Brunswick, NJ. Graduate Montclair State Col. Debut 1978 OB in "The Wager," followed by "Manhattan Transference," "Women in Tune," "Enter Laughing," "Kuni Leml."

ZAPP, PETER. Born Oct. 2, 1951 in Cleveland, OH. Graduate Baldwin Wallace Col. Debut 1983 OB in "Half a Lifetime," followed by "Strange Behavior," "Plainsong," "Brass Bell Superette," Bdwy in "End of the World . . ." (1984).

ZELLER, MARK. Born Apr. 20, 1932 in NYC. Attended NYU. Bdwy debut 1956 in "Shangri-La," followed by "Happy Hunting," "Wonderful Town" (CC), "Saratoga," "Ari," OB in "Candle in the Wind," "Margaret's Bed," "Freud," "Kuni Leml."

ZETTLER, STEPHEN. Born Dec. 21, 1947 in New Jersey. Debut 1981 OB in "The Amazin' Casey Stengel," followed by "A Soldier's Play."

ZIEBELL, MARK. Born May 16, 1959 in Milwaukee, WI. Attended UWis. Bdwy debut 1983 in "Marilyn, An American Fable."

ZIEMBA, KAREN. Born Nov. 12, 1957 in St. Joseph, MO. Graduate UAkron. Debut 1981 OB in "Seesaw," Bdwy in "A Chorus Line" (1982), "42nd Street."

ZIEN, CHIP. Born in 1947 in Milwaukee, WI. Attended UPa. OB in "You're a Good Man, Charlie Brown," followed by "Kadish," "How to Succeed . . . ," "Dear Mr. G," "Tuscaloosa's Calling," "Hot l Baltimore," "El Grande de Coca Cola," "Split," "Real Life Funnies," "March of the Falsettos," "Isn't It Romantic," Bdwy in "All Over Town" (1974), "The Suicide."

ZORICH, LOUIS. Born Feb. 12, 1924 in Chicago, IL. Attended Roosevelt U. OB in "Six Characters in Search of an Author," "Crimes and Crimes," "Henry V," "Thracian Horses," "All Women Are One," "Good Soldier Schweik," "Shadow of Heroes," "To Clothe the Naked," "Sunset," "A Memory of Two Mondays," "They Knew What They Wanted," "The Gathering," "True West," "The Tempest," "Come Dog, Come Night," Bdwy in "Becket," "Moby Dick," "The Odd Couple," "Hadrian VII," "Moonchildren," "Fun City," "Goodtime Charley," "Herzl," "Death of a Salesman" (1984).

OBITUARIES

OSCEOLA ARCHER, 93, Georgia-born actress and teacher, died Nov. 20, 1983 in NYC. After her Bdwy debut (1934) in "Between Two Worlds," she appeared in "Panic," "The Cat Screams," "Hippolytus," "Romeo and Juliet," "Ring Round the Moon," "The Crucible," "The Seagull," "The Guide," "The Screens." She was the widow of Dr. Numa P. G. Adams, and their son survives.

BROOKS ATKINSON, 89, born Justin Brooks Atkinson in Melrose, MA., was the drama critic for the NY Times for 31 years and a winner of the Pulitzer Prize in 1947 for foreign correspondence. He died of pneumonia in Huntsville, AL., on Jan. 13, 1984. He retired in 1965. In 1960 the Mansfield Theatre was re-named the Brooks Atkinson in his honor. He is survived by his wife and a step-son.

KATHARINE BARD, 66, Illinois-born actress and wife of producer Martin Manulis, died July 28, 1983 in Los Angeles, CA. After her Bdwy debut (1939) in "Life with Father," she appeared in "Ring Around Elizabeth," "Lily of the Valley," "Three's a Family," "Made in Heaven," "The Hallams," "I Know My Love," "Pride's Crossing," "The Long Days." She is survived by her husband, a son, and two daughters.

MICHAEL BEIRNE, 46, actor, born in Endicott, NY, died June 20, 1983 in Johnson, City, NY. After graduating from NYU, Harvard and Neighborhood Playhouse, he made his Bdwy debut in "Hallelujah, Baby"(1968), followed by "Cactus Flower," "The Anvil," "Score" and "The Ritz." He also appeared in numerous tv productions, and serials. His mother survives.

LUCILLE BENSON, 69, character actress, died of cancer Feb. 17, 1984 in Scottsboro, AL. Her Bdwy roles were in "Good Night, Ladies," "The Day Before Spring," "Hotel Paradiso," "Orpheus Descending," "Seven Scenes for Yeni," "Billygoat Eddie," "Walking Happy," "The Music Man," "Huckleberry Finn," and "Period of Adjustment." She had also been active on tv and in films. No reported survivors.

BEN BONUS, 63, Poland-born Yiddish actor-producer, died of a heart attack Apr. 6, 1984 in Miami, FL. He acted in and produced more than a hundred plays and musicals, some of which are "From Rome to Jerusalem," "Let There Be Joy," "The Joyous Town," "Rich and Honorable," "Father and Son," "Life Begins with Love," "Rich Paupers," "Hooray for Reno," "A Gift for Mother," "Flaming Love," "Let's Sing Yiddish," "Sing, Israel, Sing," "Light, Lively and Yiddish," "Let There Be Joy." He took his company of actors throughout the U. S. and Latin America. Surviving are his widow, actress Mina Bern, a daughter and two sons.

MARY BOYLAN, 70, character actress and playwright, died Feb. 18, 1984 in NYC. A native of Plattsburgh, NY., she made her Bdwy debut in "Dance Night" (1938), followed by "Susannah and the Elders," "The Walrus and the Carpenter," "Our Town," "Live Life Again," "To Bury a Cousin," "Curley McDimple" which she co-authored, "Blood," "Middle of the Night," "Girls Most Likely to Succeed," "Biography of a Woman" and "Women Behind Bars." She also appeared in films and on tv. Two brothers survive.

PETER BRANDON, 57, stage and tv actor, was found dead in Rochester, MI, where he was appearing at the Meadowbrook Theatre. Born in Germany, he made his Bdwy debut in "Cry of the Peacock" (1950), followed by "Come of Age," "Tovarich," "Cyrano de Bergerac," "Ondine," "The Young and Beautiful," "Hidden River," "The Infernal Machine," "Man for All Season," "The Investigation," "An Evening with the Poet-Senator," and "Medea" (1982). Surviving are his widow, a daughter and a son.

HAZEL BRYANT, 44, producer and founder of the Richard Allen Center for Culture and Arts, died of a heart disease Nov. 7, 1983 in her home in NYC, after having spoken earlier in the day at the United Nations. She had produced over 200 musicals and plays, including "Black Nativity" and "Long Day's Journey into Night" with an all-black cast, and was an organizer of the Black Theatre Alliance. She is survived by her parents, a brother and two sisters.

PETER BULL, 72, actor on stage, tv and films, died May 20, 1984 of a heart attack in his native London, Eng. He came to Bdwy in 1935 with the London cast of "Escape Me Never," subsequently appearing in "The Lady's Not for Burning," "Luther," "Pickwick," "Black Comedy" and "An Evening of Bull." Two brothers survive.

JUDY CANOVA, 66, Florida-born stage, film, tv, radio and nightclub comedienne, died of cancer Aug. 5, 1983 in Hollywood, CA. After her Bdwy debut (1934) in "Calling All Stars," she appeared in "Ziegfeld Follies of 1935," "Ziegfeld Follies of 1936," and "Yokel Boy." She frequently appeared in country garb with hair in braids and played the guitar. Two daughters survive, Julieta and actress Diana Canova.

CHAZ CHASE, 81, comedian, died Aug. 4, 1983 in Hollywood, CA. He is best remembered for his act of eating anything in sight, including cigarettes, matches, cardboard and other indigestibles. He was a popular nightclub entertainer, and most recently was in the long-running "Sugar Babies." His other credits include "Follies of 1925," "Ballyhoo," "Saluta," "Laughter over Broadway" and "High Kickers." A daughter survives.

JAN CLAYTON, 66, New Mexico-born singer-actress, died of cancer Aug. 28, 1983 at her home in West Hollywood, CA. After her 1945 Bdwy debut as Julie in "Carousel," she appeared in "Show Boat," "South Pacific," "Guys and Dolls," "Kiss Me, Kate," "The King and I" and "Follies." She had also acted in films and on tv was the mother in the popular series "Lassie." Surviving are a son and two daughters.

PETER COFFIELD, 38, actor on stage, film and tv, died Nov. 19, 1983 after a long illness. Born in Wilmette, IL, and a graduate of Northwestern U., he appeared in NYC in "The Misanthrope," "Cock-a-Doodle Dandy," "Hamlet," "Abelard and Heloise," "Vivat! Vivat Regina!," "Merchant of Venice," "Tartuffe," "The Man Who Came to Dinner" and "Misalliance." He is survived by his mother, two brothers and two sisters.

ROBERT COLSON, age unreported, Ohio-born actor, and stage manager, died July 19, 1983 in Englewood, NJ. After his 1963 debut in "The Importance of Being Earnest," he appeared in "Awakening of Spring," and "Vieux Carre." A sister survives.

EDWIN COOPER, 89, character actor on stage, film and tv, died Feb. 2, 1984 in Danbury, CT. He made his NY debut in "Twelfth Night"(1926), followed by "A Ship Comes In," "Let Freedom Ring," "Bury the Dead," "Prelude," "It Can't Happen Here," "Miss Quis," "Stop-Over," "Washington Jitters," "Dame Nature," "Life with Father," "Big Blow," "Time Out for Ginger," "Ring Around Elizabeth," "War and Peace," "The Eve of St. Mark," "Snafu," "The Gang's All Here," "Deep Are the Roots," "Best Foot Forward," "Displaced Person," "To Bury a Cousin," "Kiss and Tell." His widow survives.

ANTHONY COSTELLO, 42, artist, novelist, and actor on stage, film and tv, died Aug. 15, 1983 after a long illness. After his 1963 debut in "The Riot Act," he appeared in "Brecht on Brecht," and several off Bdwy productions. No reported survivors.

ROLAND CULVER, 83, British stage and film actor, died Feb. 29, 1984 of a heart ailment in his native London. He had appeared on Bdwy in "The Deep Blue Sea," "The Little Hut," "Five Finger Exercise" and "Ivanov." He is survived by his widow, and two sons.

LEORA DANA, 60, stage, film and tv actress, died of cancer Dec. 13, 1983 in her native NYC. After her Bdwy debut (1947) in "Madwoman of Chaillot," she appeared in "Happy Time," "Point of No Return," "Sabrina Fair," "Best Man," "Beekman Place," "The Last of Mrs. Lincoln" (for which she won a Tony Award), "The Women," "Mourning Pictures," "In the Summer House," "Wilder's Triple Bill," "Collision Course," "Bird of Dawning," "The Increased Difficulty of Concentration," "Place without Mornings," "Rebel Women," "The Tennis Game," "The Loves of Cass McGuire" and "Time Steps." A sister survives.

RONALD DAWSON, 81, South Africa-born stage, radio and tv actor, died of pneumonia Jan. 24, 1984 in Silver Spring, MD. His Bdwy credits include "Witness for the Prosecution," "The Sleeping Prince," "Penny Change," and "Traveller without Luggage." He wrote and performed in the radio series "Inner Sanctum," and had a sustaining role in the tv series "Edge of Night." A daughter survives.

ALAN DEXTER, 65, stage, film and tv actor, died of a heart attack Dec. 19, 1983 in Oxnard, CA. On Bdwy he had appeared in "This Is the Army," "The Stovepipe Hat," "Dark Hammock," "Hamlet," "The Assassin," "Call Me Mister," "Julius Caesar," "The Man Who Corrupted Hadleyburg" and a revival of "The Music Man." His widow survives.

WILLIAM DaPRATO, 59, NY-born actor, died Nov. 30, 1983. After his 1963 debut in "The Burning," he appeared in "Holy Ghosts," "Awake and Sing," "Not Like Him," "Kohlhass," "Mike Downstairs," and "Shenandoah." No reported survivors.

HOWARD DIETZ, 86, lyricist, died of Parkinson's disease July 30, 1983 in his native NYC. He had collaborated with such composers as Jerome Kern, George Gershwin and Vernon Duke, but after 1929 he wrote most of his songs with Arthur Schwartz, including the musicals "The Little Show," "The Band Wagon," "Dear Sir," "Three's a Crowd," "Sadie Thompson" and "The Gay Life." Surviving are his widow, a daughter, and two step-children.

RAY DOOLEY, 93, Scotland-born comedienne, died Jan. 28, 1984 at her home in East Hampton, NY. After appearing as a child with her family's act, she made her debut in a Philadelphia minstrel show. Her Bdwy debut was in "Hitchy-Koo"(1919), followed by eight editions of "Ziegfeld Follies" (1920–28), "Sidewalks of New York," "Thumbs Up," and "Hope's the Thing," "Earl Carroll's Vanities," "No Foolin'," "Bunch and Judy," "The Comic Supplement," Widow of actor-director-producer Eddie Dowling, she is survived by a daughter.

LYNN FONTANNE, 95, one of America's most celebrated actresses, died of pneumonia July 30, 1983 in her home in Genesee Depot, WI. After her marriage to Alfred Lunt in 1922, they became one of the theatre's greatest husband-and-wife acting teams, appearing together in 27 plays from 1923 to 1960. In 1958, the Globe, a Broadway theatre, was re-named the Lunt-Fontanne, and they opened it with their last vehicle, "The Visit." London-born (Lillie Louise Fontanne), she made her NY debut in 1910 in "Mr. Preedy and the Countess," followed by "Dulcy," "The Guardsman," "Goat Song," "At Mrs. Beam's," "The Second Man," "Strange Interlude," "Sweet Nell of Old Drury," "In Love with Love," "Arms and the Man," "Pygmalion," "Brothers Karamazov," "The Doctor's Dilemma," "Caprice," "Meteor," "Elizabeth the Queen," "Reunion in Vienna," "Design for Living," "Point Valaine," "Taming of the Shrew," "Idiot's Delight," "Amphitryon 38," "The Sea Gull," "There Shall Be No Night," "The Pirate," "O Mistress Mine," "I Know My Love," "Quadrille," "The Great Sebastians." She had appeared in three films, "Second Youth," "The Guardsman" with Mr. Lunt," and "Stage Door Canteen." She and her husband received Emmys for their tv performances in "The Magnificent Yankee." Mr. Lunt died in 1977. They had no children.

DAVID CONANT FORD, 58, California-born stage and tv character actor, died in his sleep in his NYC home on Aug. 7, 1983. After making his debut in "Billy Budd," he appeared in "Tea Party," "Mary Stuart," "The Vagrant," "Abe Lincoln in Illinois," "The White Rose and the Red," "A Majority of One," "Middle of the Night," "A Man for All Seasons," "1776," "The Physicists." For two years he was Sam Evans on the tv series "Dark Shadows." Two sisters survive.

DANIEL FORTUS, 31, Brooklyn-born actor-singer on stage and tv, died May 19, 1984 in NYC after a long illness. His stage career began at 9 in "Oliver!," followed by "Everybody Out, the Castle Is Sinking," "A Day in the Life of Just about Everyone," "Molly," "Minnie's Boys," "Friends and Enemies," "Antony and Cleopatra," "Two by Five," "Paintin' the Town," and "Pins and Needles." He is survived by his mother.

EDDIE FOY, JR. 78, comedian of stage, vaudeville, film and tv, died of cancer July 15, 1983 in Woodland Hills, CA. His career began at the age of 5 with his father and family in a vaudeville act called "Eddie Foy and the 7 Little Foys," and he was the only one to remain in show business throughout his life. His Bdwy credits include "Smiles," "Show Girl," "Ripples," "The Cat and the Fiddle," "Humpty Dumpty," "At Home Abroad," "Orchids Preferred," "The Red Mill," "The Pajama Game," "High Button Shoes," and "Donnybrook." Surviving are a son, two sisters and two brothers.

ROGER FURMAN, 59, founder and director of New Heritage Repertory Theatre in Harlem, died in his NYC home of a heart and kidney disease on Nov. 27, 1983. He had also been an actor on stage and film before establishing the company, and was a teacher and founder of the Black Theatre Alliance. Surviving is his mother.

HAROLD GARY, 77, character actor in more than 40 plays and 200 tv episodes, died of a stroke Jan. 21, 1984 in his native NYC. After his Bdwy bow in "Diamond Lil" (1928), he appeared in such productions as "Crazy with the Heat," "A Flag Is Born," "Guys and Dolls," "Oklahoma!," "Arsenic and Old Lace," "Billion Dollar Baby," "Fiesta," "The World We Make," "Born Yesterday," "Will Success Spoil Rock Hunter?," "Let It Ride," "Counting House," "Arturo Ui," "A Thousand Clowns," "Enter Laughing," "Illya, Darling," "The Price," "The Sunshine Boys," "Pal Joey" and "Family Business." He had the lead in the tv series "Captured." No reported survivors.

IRA GERSHWIN, 86, Manhattan-born lyricist and brother of George Gershwin, with whom he worked, died Aug. 17, 1983 in his sleep at his home in Beverly Hills, CA. His career began in 1918 with his brother on the musical "Ladies First," followed by "Half-Past Eight," "A Dangerous Maid," "Two Little Girls in Blue," for which he used the name of Arthur Francis. By 1924 he was using his own name and subsequently wrote lyrics for "Primrose," "Lady Be Good," "Tell Me More," "Tip-Toes," "Americana," "Oh, Kay!," "Funny Face," "Show Girl," "Strike Up the Band," "Rosalie," "Treasure Girl," "9:15 Revue," "Garrick Gaieties," "Girl Crazy," "Of Thee I Sing" for which he and George won a Pulitzer Prize, "Pardon My English," "Let 'Em Eat Cake," "Life Begins at 8:40," "Porgy and Bess," "Ziegfeld Follies of 1936," "The Show Is On," "Lady in the Dark," "Firebrand of Florence," "Park Avenue," "The Goldwyn Follies," and several films, including the original "A Star Is Born." He is survived by his wife of 56 years, and a sister.

FRANCES GOODRICH, 93, New Jersey-born Pulitzer-Prize-winning playwright, died of lung cancer Jan. 29, 1984 in her NYC home. With her husband, Albert Hackett, she wrote "Up Pops the Devil," "Bridal Wise," "The Great Big Doorstep," and "The Diary of Anne Frank" which won the Pulitzer. She began her career as an actress in 1916 in "Come Out of the Kitchen," followed by "Fashions for Men," "Queen Victoria," "Skin Deep" and "Excess Baggage." Surviving are her husband, a brother and a sister.

GILBERT GREEN, 68, actor on stage, film and tv, and a teacher, died Apr. 15, 1984 in Tarzana, CA., following an extended illness. He appeared in "First American Dictator," "Hall of Healing," "The World of Sholom Aleichem," "Tevya and His Daughters," "Look Homeward, Angel," "Murderous Angels," and "The Diary of Anne Frank." A daughter survives.

JOAN HACKETT, 49, NYC-born actress on stage, film and tv, died of cancer Oct. 8, 1983 in Encino, CA. She made her debut on the NY stage OB in 1960 in "A Clearing in the Woods," followed by "Call Me by My Rightful Name" for which she received a Theatre World Award, Bdwy in "Peterpat," "Much Ado about Nothing," "Park," and "Night Watch." She was nominated for an "Oscar" for her role in the film "Only When I Laugh." Her marriage to actor Richard Mulligan ended in divorce. She is survived by a brother and a sister.

JAMES HAYDEN, 29, Brooklyn-born actor on stage and film, died from a heroin overdose on Nov. 8, 1983 in his NYC apartment shortly after his Bdwy opening in "American Buffalo." Previously he had made his Bdwy debut in the 1983 revival of "A View from the Bridge." He had served with the army in Vietnam, and after his discharge, attended AADA and Actors Studio. He is survived by his estranged wife and his parents.

SAM JAFFE, 93, NYC-born character actor on stage, tv and screen, died of cancer Mar. 24, 1984 in his home in Beverly Hills, CA. After his Bdwy debut (1915) in "The Clod," he had roles in "Samson and Delilah," "The Idle Inn," "God of Vengeance," "Main Line," "Izzy," "The Jazz Singer," "Grand Hotel," "Bride of Torozko," "The Eternal Road," "Divine Drudge," "A Doll's House," "The Gentle People," "King Lear," "Cafe Crown," "Thank You, Svoboda," "This Time Tomorrow," "Mlle. Colombe," "The Sea Gull," "St. Joan," "The Adding Machine," "Idiot's Delight," "An Enemy of the People" and "A Meeting by the River." He is survived by his second wife, Bettye Ackerman, who appeared with him in the tv series "Ben Casey." In 1943 he was a co-founder and for 6 years was chairman of the Equity Library Theatre.

DOLLY JONAH, 53, Baltimore-born singer and actress, died of cancer July 14, 1983 in Bridgton, ME. After her debut in "The Iceman Cometh," she appeared in "Jackknife," "Signs along the Scenic Route," and "That 5 A.M. Jazz." She also appeared in films and night clubs. She is survived by her husband, composer-lyricist Will Holt, and a son.

ANDY KAUFMAN, 35, NY-born comedian, died of cancer May 16, 1984 in Los Angeles, CA. Best known for his tv appearances as Latka Gravas on "Taxi," and on "Saturday Night Live," he made his Bdwy debut in 1983 in "Teaneck Tanzi: The Venus Flytrap." Surviving are his parents, a brother and a sister.

MIKE KELLIN, 61, Connecticut-born character actor on stage, screen and tv, and whose career spanned 35 years, died of lung cancer Aug. 26, 1983 in Nyack, NY. He had appeared in over 50 plays, 75 films, and 200 tv programs. After his Bdwy debut (1949) in "At War with the Army," his credits include "The Bird Cage," "The Emperor's Clothes," "Time of Storm," "The Time of Your Life," "Ankles Aweigh," "Pipe Dream," "The Taming of the Shrew," "Diary of a Scoundrel," "Purple Dust," "Tevya and His Daughters," "Winkelberg," "God and Kate Murphy," "Rhinoceros," "Mother Courage and Her Children," "King Lear," "Winterset," "Joan of Lorraine," "Bread," "Stalag 17," "American Buffalo," "Who Was That Lady . . . ," "The Odd Couple," "Duck

Variations," "Are You Now . . . ,"Q.E.D.," "The Ritz." He is survived by his wife, actress Sally Moffet, a daughter, and three step-sons.

SUSAN KINGSLEY, 37, Kentucky-born actress, died in surgery Feb. 6, 1984 of injuries received in a two-car accident on an icy road in Athens, GA. After studying at the UKy and LAMDA, she became the premiere actress at the Actors Theatre of Louisville. Her NY debut was in 1978 OB in "Getting Out" for which she received a Theatre World Award. She made her Bdwy debut in 1982 in "The Wake of Jamey Foster." She is survived by her husband, actor David Hurt, and two daughters.

WALTER KLAVUN, 77, stage and film actor, died in his native NYC on Apr. 13, 1984. The many productions in which he appeared include "Say When," "No More Ladies," "Arms for Venus," "Annie Get Your Gun," "Twelfth Night," "Dream Girl," "Auntie Mame," "Say, Darling," "Desert Incident," "How to Succeed in Business . . . ," "What Makes Sammy Run," "Twigs," "Morning's at 7," "Dandy Dick," "The Dubliners," "Ballad of the Sad Cafe." Surviving are a son and two daughters.

SEYMOUR KRAWITZ, 59, theatre and film press agent, died of cancer Sept. 20, 1983 in his native NYC. Before becoming a press agent, he co-founded the University Playhouse in Mashpee, MA, and the Falmouth (MA) Playhouse. He is survived by his widow, Patricia McLean Krawitz, a son and a daughter.

EDWARD KOGAN, 72, NYC-born actor-producer-director, died May 4, 1984 in his home in Weston, CT. His career began with the Eva LeGallienne repertory company, and subsequently included such productions as "Keep Covered," "Weep for the Virgins," "Counselor-at-Law," "This Is the Army," "Having a Wonderful Time," "Lysistrata," "Auntie Mame," "Say Darling," "Desert Incident," "What Makes Sammy Run?" He had also appeared on tv and film. He leaves his widow and a daughter.

JOHN KUHNER, 41, ne Ponyman in Cleveland, OH, actor-musician-singer, died Feb. 4, 1984 in San Francisco, CA., of pneumasistic pneumonia. After his NY debut in "Your Own Thing"(1968), his credits include "House of Leather," "Tarot," "Wanted," "We Bombed in New Haven," "Babes in Arms," "Spring Rites," "Kitchen Duty," "Listen to Me," and "The Future." He also had appeared on tv and film. He is survived by his parents, a brother and a sister.

AVON LONG, 73, Baltimore-born actor-singer, died Feb. 15, 1984 of cancer in NYC. His career began in 1936 in "Black Rhythm," followed by "La Belle Helene," "Porgy and Bess" (his most acclaimed role as Sportin' Life), "Memphis Bound," "Carib Song," "Beggar's Holiday," "Green Pastures," "Shuffle Along," "Mrs. Patterson," "Ballad of Jazz Street," "Fly Blackbird," "Don't Play Us Cheap," "Bubbling Brown Sugar," "The Wisteria Trees"(OB 1982). He had also performed in clubs, films and tv. Surviving are his widow and two daughters.

GERTRUDE MACY, 79, California-born producer-writer-manager, died of cancer Oct. 18, 1983 in NYC. Began her career as assistant stage manager of "The Age of Innocence" in 1928, later becoming stage manager, company manager, and finally general manager for the late actress Katharine Cornell. As a producer her credits include "One for the Money," "Two for the Show," "Forever Is Now," "The Happiest Years," "I Am a Camera." A niece and a nephew survive.

MERLE MADDERN, 96, former prominent actress, died Jan. 15, 1984 in Denver, CO. She had roles in "Nice People," "In the Next Room," "Expressing Willie," "Enchanted April," "Sinner," "Trial of Mary Dugan," "The Sea Gull," "Women Have Their Way," "Five Star Final," "The Left Bank," "O Evening Star," "The Fields Beyond," "Around the Corner," "Mme. Capet," "Susanna, Don't You Cry," "The Distant City," "Apology," "A New Life," "Decision," "Down to Miami," "Antigone," "Land's End," "The Druid Circle," "Romeo and Juliet," and "Hedda Gabler." She was the niece of novelist Jack London. No reported survivors.

JOHN MARLEY, 77, NYC-born stage, film and tv actor, died after open-heart surgery May 22, 1984 in Los Angeles, CA. He appeared on Bdwy in "Johnny Doodle," "Stop the Press," "Dinosaur Wharf," "Gramercy Ghost," "An Enemy of the People," "The Strong Are Lonely," "Sing Me No Lullaby," "Compulsion," "The Investigation," "Skipper Next to God," "Sing Till Tomorrow," "Hope Is the Thing with Feathers." He was nominated for an Academy Award for his role in the film "Love Story." Surviving are his widow, two daughters, and two sons.

RAYMOND MASSEY, 86, Canada-born actor in all media, died of pneumonia July 29, 1983 in Los Angeles, CA. He had worked as an actor, director and producer on both Broadway and London stages. After a successful career in London, he made his Bdwy bow as "Hamlet" in 1931, followed by "Never Come Back," "The Rats of Norway," "The Ace," "Acropolis," "The Shining Hour," "Ethan Frome," "Night of January 16," "Idiot's Delight," "Abe Lincoln in Illinois" (his most celebrated role), "The Doctor's Dilemma," "Candida," "Lovers and Friends," "Pygmalion," "How I Wonder," "The Father," "ANTA Album," "John Brown's Body," "Julius Caesar," "The Tempest," "J.B." For 5 years he was co-star of the popular tv series "Dr. Kildare." He was married 3 times. Surviving are two sons, Geoffrey and actor Daniel, and a daughter, actress Anna.

ETHEL MERMAN, 76, one of Broadway's greatest musical stars, died in her sleep Feb. 15, 1984 in her NYC apartment. She had been hospitalized for several months previous with a brain tumor. Born Ethel Zimmerman in Astoria, NY, she worked as a secretary before making her successful Bdwy debut in 1930 in "Girl Crazy," followed by such hits as "Anything Goes," "Red, Hot and Blue," "DuBarry Was a Lady," "Panama Hattie," "Annie Get Your Gun," "Call Me Madam," "Gypsy" and "Hello, Dolly!" Other credits include "George White's Scandals," "Humpty Dumpty," "Take a Chance," "Stars in Your Eyes," "Happy Hunting." She made 14 movies and had her own radio show, and had appeared on tv. Her four marriages ended in divorce. A son, Robert Levitt, survives.

MAX METH, 83, Austria-born musical director of more than 25 Bdwy shows, died Jan. 3, 1984 in Wyckoff, NJ. His Bdwy credits include, "Pal Joey," "Finian's Rainbow," "Artists and Models," "As the Girls Go," "Revenge with Music," "Roberta," "Band Wagon," "Gentlemen Prefer Blondes," and "The Unsinkable Molly Brown." No reported survivors.

Osceola
Archer

Katherine
Bard

Michael
Beirne

Mary
Boylan

Peter
Brandon

Peter
Bull

Judy
Canova

Jan
Clayton

Peter
Coffield

Robert
Colson

Anthony
Costello

Roland
Culver

Leora
Dana

William
DaPrato

Lynne
Fontanne

David
Ford

Daniel
Fortus

Eddie
Foy

Harold
Gary

Joan
Hackett

Sam
Jaffe

Dolly
Jonah

Mike
Kellin

Susan
Kingsley

Walter
Klavun

John
Kuhner

Avon
Long

John
Marley

Raymond
Massey

Ethel
Merman

231

RAY MIDDLETON, 77, Chicago-born actor-singer, died of a heart attack Apr. 10, 1984 at his home in Panorama City, CA. He began his career as an opera singer, but made his Bdwy debut in 1933 in "Roberta," followed by "Knickerbocker Holiday," "Scandals of 1939," "American Jubilee," "Winged Victory," "Annie Get Your Gun," "Love Life," "ANTA Album," "Too True to Be Good," "South Pacific," "Man of La Mancha," "1776." He also appeared in films and tv. He was married and divorced three times. No reported survivors.

ROBERT MOORE, 56, actor-director, died of pneumonia May 10, 1984 in NYC. Born in Washington, DC, he began his career as an actor in 1942 in "This Is the Army," followed by "Jenny Kissed Me," "The Owl and the Pussycat," "Cactus Flower," and "Everything in the Garden." His directorial chores included Bdwy, films and tv. Bdwy credits include "Promises Promises," "Boys in the Band," "Last of the Red Hot Lovers," "The Gingerbread Lady," "They're Playing Our Song," "Lorelei," "My Fat Friend," "Woman of the Year" and "Deathtrap." Surviving are his mother and a brother.

BRAM NOSSEN, 87, San Francisco-born actor-singer, died Dec. 25, 1983 in Philadelphia, PA. His many credits include "The Dark Hours," "Love Kills," "Twelfth Night," "Henrietta the Eighth," "Othello," "Macbeth," "Bright Honor," "Richard II," "Kind Lady," "Censored," "Mme. Capet," "Family Portrait," "Medicine Show," "Johnny Belinda," "Days of Our Youth," "Pie in the Sky," "Nathan the Wise," "Magic," "Star Spangled Family," "The Tempest," "Oedipus Rex," "Buoyant Billions," "Getting Married," "The Gang's All Here." No reported survivors.

SIMON OAKLAND, 61, Brooklyn-born stage, film and tv actor, died Aug. 29, 1983 at his home in Cathedral City, CA. After his Bdwy debut (1948) in "Skipper Next to God," his credits include "Light Up the Sky," "Inherit the Wind," "Caesar and Cleopatra," "Harvey," "Sands of the Negev," "The Shrike," "Men in White," "The Great Sebastians," "Trial of Dmitri Karamazov," "Five Evenings," "Have I Got a Girl for You!," "Angela," "Twigs," "The Shadow Box." He had performed in more than 550 tv episodes, including leads in the series "Baa Baa Black Sheep," "Toma" and "Kolchak." His widow and a daughter survive.

ESTELLE OMENS, 55, Chicago-born actress on stage, film and tv, died Dec. 4, 1983 in North Hollywood, CA. After her NY debut (1952) in "Summer and Smoke," she appeared in "The Grass Harp," "Legend of Lovers," "Plays for Bleecker Street," "Pullman Car Hiawatha," "The Brownstone Urge," "Gandhi," "Shadow of a Gunman," "Bright and Golden Land," "The Watering Place." She is survived by her husband, writer Frank Gregory.

SAMSON RAPHAELSON, 87, playwright, and screen writer, died in his sleep July 16, 1983 in his native NYC. His first play was "The Jazz Singer" (1925) that later became the basis for the first talking picture. Other plays are "Young Love," "The Magnificent Heel," "The Wooden Slipper," "Accent on Youth," "Jason," "White Man," "Skylark," "The Perfect Marriage," "Hilda Crane," "The Heel." He had been a professor at Columbia U. for the last ten years. Surviving are his widow, a son and a daughter.

RALPH RICHARDSON, 80, one of England's most celebrated stage and film actors, died Oct. 10, 1983 in a London hospital after being admitted with digestive problems. He made his Bdwy debut in 1935 in "Romeo and Juliet," followed by "Henry IV Parts I & II," "Uncle Vanya," "Oedipus," "The Critic," "Waltz of the Toreadors," "School for Scandal," "Home," "No Man's Land." After the death of his first wife, he married actress Meriel Forbes-Robertson who survives, as does their son.

WILLIAM RITMAN, 56, Chicago-born scenic, costume and lighting designer, died of cancer May 6, 1984 in NYC. Among the sets he designed in a career of almost 25 years are "On the Town"(1959), "Zoo Story," "Krapp's Last Tape," "The American Dream," "Death of Bessie Smith," "Gallows Humor," "Happy Days," "Endgame," "Mrs. Dally Has a Lover," "Who's Afraid of Virginia Woolf?," "The Dumbwaiter," "The Collection," "The Riot Act," "Play," "Funnyhouse of a Negro," "Dutchman," "A Midsummer Night's Dream," "Absence of a Cello," "The Giant's Dance," "Entertaining Mr. Sloane," "Malcolm," "A Delicate Balance," "Come Live with Me," "Birthday Party," "The Promise," "Everything in the Garden," "Box-Mao-Box," "Loot," "Play It Again, Sam," "Gingham Dog," "Three Sisters," "Hello and Goodbye," "What the Butler Saw," "Morning's at 7," "Tiny Alice," "The Devil's Disciple," "6 Rms Riv Vu," "Moonchildren," "Same Time Next Year," "Noel Coward in Two Keys," "Chapter Two." He is survived by a sister and a brother.

DAVID ROUNDS, 53, Bronxville-born actor, died of cancer Dec. 9, 1983 in his home in Lamontville, NY. After his Bdwy debut (1965) in "Foxy," he appeared in "Child's Play" for which he received a Theatre World Award, "The Rothschilds," "The Last of Mrs. Lincoln," "Chicago," "Romeo and Juliet," "Morning's at 7" for which he received a "Tony," OB in "You Never Can Tell," "Money," "The Real Inspector Hound," "Epic of Buster Friend," "Enter a Free Man," "Metamorphosis in Miniature," "Herringbone" his last (a one-man performance). He also appeared in films, and for 3 years on the tv series "Love of Life." A brother survives.

ALFRED SANDOR, 64, Hungary-born actor, died of cancer Sept. 22, 1983 in Sydney, Australia. In 1952 he made his Bdwy debut in "Wish You Were Here," followed by "No Time for Sergeants," "Time Limit," "Third Best Sport," "Gypsy," "On an Open Roof," "My Mother, My Father and Me," "Tchin-Tchin," "Luther," "The Odd Couple," "Plaza Suite," "Zelda." After appearing in Australia in "Plaza Suite," he decided to remain, and built a career on stage, screen and tv. No reported survivors.

ALAN SCHNEIDER, 66, Russia-born director, ne Abram Leopoldovich, died May 3, 1984 of injuries after being struck by a motorcyclist in London, Eng., where he was directing a play. He had become the primary director in America of plays by Beckett, Brecht, Pinter, Albee and Shaw. In addition he had directed "The Remarkable Mr. Pennypacker," "All Summer Long," "Anastasia," "The Skin of our Teeth," "A View from the Bridge," "Summer of the 17th Doll," "Clandestine on

the Morning Line," "Caucasian Chalk Circle," "Ballad of the Sad Cafe," "Play," "Entertaining Mr. Sloane," "Gnadges Fraulein," "You Know I Can't Hear You When the Water's Running," "I Never Sang for My Father," "The Gingham Dog," "Inquest," "The Lady from Dubuque." He had been a teacher at Juilliard, and Artistic Director of the Acting Company. He is survived by his wife of 31 years, a daughter and a son.

DANNY SCHOLL, 61, singer-actor, died June 21, 1983 in his native Cincinnati, OH. He had appeared on Bdwy in "Winged Victory," "Call Me Mister," "Texas Li'l Darlin'," and "Top Banana." No reported survivors.

IRWIN SHAW, 71, Brooklyn-born prolific writer of plays, short stories, screenplays and novels died of a heart attack May 16, 1984 in Davos, Switzerland. His plays include "Bury the Dead," "Siege," "The Gentle People," "Retreat to Pleasure," "Sons and Soldiers," "The Assassin," "The Survivors," "Children from Their Games." His widow and a son survive.

BETTY SINCLAIR, 76, England-born actress, died Sept. 20, 1983 in Tenafly, NJ. After her Bdwy debut (1947) in "The Winslow Boy," she appeared in "The Deep Blue Sea," "The Doctor's Dilemma," "The Sleeping Prince," "The Apple Cart," "Auntie Mame," "Port-Royal," "Lord Pengo," "Ivanov," "The Seagull," "The Crucible," "The Incomparable Max." She had also appeared in tv series. No reported survivors.

MICHAEL SKLAR, 39, California-born actor-writer, died of lymphoma Mar. 5, 1984 in NYC. He had appeared in "June Moon," "Scapino," and on the tv series "The Laugh-In" and "Sha-Na-Na." He is survived by his mother, a sister and a brother.

JACK SOMACK, 64, Chicago-born stage, film and tv actor, died of a heart attack Aug. 24, 1983 in Los Angeles, CA. After his debut Off Bdwy in 1966 in "A View from the Bridge," his credits include "The Kitchen," "The Country Girl," "Cannibals," "The Shrinking Bride," "Born Yesterday," and "Prisoner of Second Avenue." On tv he had roles in "Barney," "Kojak," "Rockford Files," "All in the Family," "Sanford and Son." Surviving are his widow, a son and a daughter.

HANS SPIALEK, 89, Vienna-born orchestrator, died of cancer Nov. 20, 1983 in NYC. He had orchestrated 147 musicals, including "On Your Toes," "I Married an Angel," "Babes in Arms," "Boys from Syracuse," "Pal Joey," "Anything Goes," "Gay Divorce," "DuBarry Was a Lady" and "Strike Up the Band." A daughter survives.

ROBERT THOMSEN, 70, actor, stage manager, playwright and novelist, died of cancer Oct. 28, 1983 in NYC. On Bdwy he appeared in "They Shall Not Die," "Valley Forge," "It's You I Want," "Let Freedom Ring," "Bury the Dead," "Prelude," "Stage Door," "Excursion," "Western Waters," "Stop-Over," "Washington Jitters," "Jeremiah," and "Mamba's Daughters." He is survived by two brothers.

SHEPARD TRAUBE, 76, retired producer, director, and teacher, died of cancer July 23, 1983 in NYC. He produced and directed one of Bdwy's longest running plays, "Angel Street." His other credits include "No More Frontier," "A Thousand Summers," "The Sophisticates," "Sailor Beware!," "But Not for Love," "Winter Soldiers," "The Patriots," "The Stranger," "The Gioconda Smile," "The Green Bay Tree," "Time Out for Ginger," "The Girl in Pink Tights," "The Grand Prize," "Goodbye Again," "Holiday for Lovers," "Carnival." He was elected first president of the Society of Stage Directors and Choreographers, and was managing director of Equity Library Theatre. He leaves his widow, and two daughters.

DEE VICTOR, 57, actress, died of a heart attack Dec. 18, 1983 in her NYC apartment. After her 1954 debut in "The Way of the World," she appeared in "The White Devil," "The Carefree Tree," "Dandy Dick," "Diary of a Scoundrel," "Right You Are If You Think You Are," "Fashion," "The Child Buyer," "Judith," "You Can't Take It with You," "School for Scandal," "War and Peace." A brother survives.

STUART WHITE, 33, director and choreographer, died July 5, 1983 in New London, CT. He was a founder and artistic director of Off-Bdwy's WPA Theatre, and a director for two years of the Circle Repertory Theatre Lab. Among the Off-Bdwy productions he staged were "Ballad of the Sad Cafe," "Days to Come," "The Trading Post," "What Would Jeanne Moreau Do?," "Lone Star," and "Early Dark." He spent the 1981–82 season as a directing fellow at the Yale School of Drama. No reported survivors.

Robert Moore   **Ralph Richardson**   **David Rounds**

INDEX

235

244

248

255